REA

Russian and West European Women, 1860–1939

Russian and West European Women, 1860–1939

Dreams, Struggles, and Nightmares

MARCELLINE J. HUTTON

ROWMAN & LITTLEFIELD PUBLISHERS, INC.
Lanham • Boulder • New York • Oxford

ROWMAN & LITTLEFIELD PUBLISHERS, INC.

Published in the United States of America
by Rowman & Littlefield Publishers, Inc.
4720 Boston Way, Lanham, Maryland 20706
www.rowmanlittlefield.com

12 Hid's Copse Road, Cumnor Hill, Oxford OX2 9JJ, England

Copyright © 2001 by Rowman & Littlefield Publishers, Inc.

British Library Cataloging in Publication Information Available

Library of Congress Cataloging-in-Publication Data

Hutton, Marcelline J., 1939–
    Russian and West European women, 1860–1939 : dreams, struggles, and
    nightmares / Marcelline J. Hutton.
        p. cm.
    Includes bibliographical references and index.
    ISBN 0-7425-1043-3 (alk. paper) — ISBN 0-7425-1044-1 (paper : alk. paper)
        1. Women—Russia—History—19th century. 2. Women—Russia—History—20th
    century. 3. Women—Soviet Union—History. 4. Women—Europe—History—19th
    century. 5. Women—Europe—History—20th century. I. Title.

HQ1662 .H88 2001
305.4'094—dc21

                                                        2001018061

Printed in the United States of America

♾™ The paper used in this publication meets the minimum requirements of American
National Standard for Information Sciences—Permanence of Paper for Printed Library
Materials, ANSI/NISO Z39.48-1992.

Contents

List of Tables   vii

Acknowledgments   ix

Abbreviations Used in the Endnotes   xi

Introduction: Russian and West European Women, 1860–1939   1

  1. Society in the Late Nineteenth Century   11

  2. Education in the Late Nineteenth Century   47

  3. Employment before World War I   73

  4. Political Activity, 1860–1914   109

  5. Society in the 1920s   139

  6. Education in the 1920s   177

  7. Employment in the 1920s   197

  8. Political Dreams in the 1920s   233

  9. Society in the 1930s   263

  10. Education in the 1930s   297

  11. Employment in the 1930s   323

  12. Political Participation in the 1930s   365

Conclusion   399

Bibliography   409

Index   449

About the Author   468

List of Tables

1.1. Women's Aggregate Marriage Rates, 1890s   13
1.2. Marital Status of Textile Workers, 1890s   19

3.1. Women in Paid Agricultural Work, 1890s   75
3.2. Women in Paid Domestic Service, 1890s   76
3.3. Women in Manufacturing, 1890s   80
3.4. Women in Commerce, Transport, and Service, 1890s   85
3.5. Professional Female Workers, 1890s   90
3.6. Changes in Professional Employment, 1891–1911   92

5.1. Marital Status of Occupied Women, Mid 1920s   146
5.2. Divorce, 1880s and 1920s   148
5.3. Married Women Working in Agriculture, 1920s   149
5.4. Marital Status of Domestic Servants, 1920s   159
5.5. Marital Status of Women in Commerce, 1920s   160
5.6. Marital Status of Career Women, 1920s   161

6.1. Students in Universities, 1920s   185
6.2. Distribution of Women in the Professions, 1920s   187

7.1. Distribution of Women in the Economy, 1920s   200
7.2. Russian Population Changes, 1897–1926   201
7.3. Women in Agricultural Work   202
7.4. Married Women Working in Agriculture   202
7.5. Women in Manufacturing, 1890s and 1920s   206
7.6. Women in Manufacturing by Area, 1920s   206
7.7. Marital Status of Women in Manufacturing, 1920s   209
7.8. Marital Status of Domestic Servants, Mid 1920s   216
7.9. Select Low-Level Service Positions, 1897–1926   218

7.10. Employees in Commerce, Service, and Transport   219
7.11. Distribution of Women in Professions, 1920s   222
7.12. Russian and Soviet Career Women   223

8.1. Female Party Members   236
8.2. Peasant Women's Political Participation, 1929   245

10.1. Female University Students, 1920s   307
10.2. Female Students in Higher Education   308

11.1. Women Engaged in Agriculture, 1920s and 1930s   326
11.2. Women's Employment and Unemployment, 1930s   335
11.3. Women in Manufacturing, 1930s   336
11.4. Women in Domestic Service, 1920s and 1930s   340
11.5. Women in Commerce and Banking, 1920s and 1930s   344
11.6. Women in Select Professions, 1930s   347
11.7. Soviet Women in Select Professions, 1926–1939   351

12.1. Paid Female Officials, 1920s and 1930s   388
12.2. Women as Presidents of Village Soviets, 1939   391

Acknowledgments

Encouragement for this project has come from many sources. The Kennan Institute provided a grant that enabled me to consult many nineteenth- and twentieth-century women's diaries, memoirs, and biographies at the Library of Congress in 1993. The Center for Post-Soviet Studies at the University of Texas, Austin, provided a grant in 1996 to review census materials at the Research Population Library. A National Endowment for the Humanities grant for the study of Russian nationalism at Columbia University in 1996 gave me new persective on my book, and countless Summer seminars at the University of Illinois in the 1980s deepened my knowledge of Slavic women. Librarians Rosemary Fry (Library of Congress), Marianna Tax Choldin, Bob Burger, Helen Sullivan, Richard Seits (University of Illinois Slavic Library), Juan Sandovol and Carolyn Kahl (University of Texas, El Paso), and Donna Schwisher (Linda Hall Library) have enormously aided my research.

Mentors who have inspired me include Sarah Hanley, Linda Kerber, and Jaroslav Pelenski, and colleagues who have encouraged me include Mary Conroy, Birgitta Ingamanson, Elaine Kruse, David Hackett, Carole Levin, Cheryl Martin, Veronica Shapovalov, and Valery Shekter. Friends who have supplied German materials and helped with translations include Helmi Mays, the late Frank Oppenheimer, Helmtrud Schaaf, and Fred Schmidt.

Others who have helped me along the way include my son Martin Stack and my sister Kathryn Hutton; students: Nancy Blasch, Phyllis Crowell, and Lauri Tice; finally, friends: Laura Julier, John Dechon, John Fahey, Nancy and Fred Griffen, Kay Jordan, Ol'ia Krainovich, Diana Olsen, Gracie Pinon, Molly Shapiro, the late John Stack, and the late Betty Wetlaufer.

Editors Susan McEachern, Sharon Wolchik, and Mary Holliman have shepherded this manuscript through its various versions to final publication.

Abbreviations Used in the Endnotes
(see Bibliography for full citation)

An. Stat.	Statistique Générale de la France, *Annuaire Statistique*
An. Stat. Russie, 1915	*Annuaire Statistique de la Russie, 1915*
Autobiography	Alexandra Kollontai: *Autobiography of a Sexually Emancipated Communist Woman*, ed. I. Fescher
Chislennost' Rossii 1897 g.	*Chislennost' i sostav' rabochikh' Rossii 1897 g.*
Dic. Stat.	*Dictionary of Statistics*
Dnevnik N.K. and *Diary of N.K*	*The Diary of Nina Kosterina*
ILR	*International Labor Review*
Itogi perepisi 1959 g.	TsSU, *Chislennost', Sostav, i Razmeshchenie Naseleniia SSSR: Kratkie Itogi Vsesoiuznoi perepisi naseleniia 1959 goda*
JRSS	*Journal of the Royal Statistical Society*
Kom.	*Kommunistka*
KPTad, 1924–74 and *KPTurk, 1924–77*	Istittut istorii partii pri TsK KP Turkmenistana, *Kom. Partiia Turkkmenistana v tsifrakh*
LPR	*The Labour Party Report of 38th Annual Conference, May 29–June 2nd, 1939*
MLR	*Monthly Labor Review*
NYT	*New York Times*

Perepis' 1939g	Upravlenie Statistiki Naseleniia Goskomstata, *Vsesoiuznaia Perepis' Naseleniia 1939 goda, Osnovnye Itogi*
PKh.	*Planovoe Khoziaistvo*
RDDM	*Revue des Deux Mondes*
RSDRP	France, *Resultats Statistiques de denombrement de 1896*
SDDR	*Statistik des Deutschen Reichs*
S.O.	*Stenograficheskii otchet*
SYB League of Nations	*Statistical Yearbook of the League of Nations*
Svod Perepisi 1897 g	*Obshchii svod po imperii rezultatov razrabotki dannykh pervoi vseobshchei perepisi naseleniia Rossiiskoi imperii 1897 g.*
Who's Who of Parliament	*Who's Who of British Members of Parliament*

Introduction

Russian and West European Women, 1860–1939

Two central themes in history are continuity and change. It is especially fascinating to reflect on women's history over the past 100 years to see what has changed and what has remained similar. Although this book compares Russian and European women from 1860 to 1939, contemporary Western readers may see aspects of themselves reflected in women's social, educational, economic, and political situations. Class, then as now, affected women, as did nationality, ethnicity, and religion.

Although scholars have produced many excellent monographs about Russian and European women in recent years, this study moves beyond to provide a gender and class analysis within a broad chronological framework. It weaves together statistical data, belles lettres, contemporary materials, and current research to illustrate patterns in women's lives showing what was unique and what was common to women of particular classes and nationalities. Statistical data provide information about those who left no memory texts. This book shows women of different epochs, classes, and nationalities defining and redefining themselves, realizing some of their dreams, struggling with ordinary life, and confronting disaster with incredible courage and resourcefulness. Although they did not achieve all their hopes in this century, many gained a greater sense of dignity in the family, opportunity in education and in employment, and participation in politics: important steps forward.

Major Themes and Leitmotifs

Central to women's lives were class, nationality, and religion. Prior to World War I, class and occupation often defined identity more than did nationality.

1

Women resembled their class counterparts in Russia, England, France, and Germany far more than they did their countrywomen. However, the blurring of class differences in World War I, the shared fate during the war, and different political settlements in the 1920s and 1930s made nationality as well as class a significant factor. Religion also affected women's lives, as more Protestant than Catholic women in Europe sought secular education and careers in the late nineteenth century. Although religion positively influenced women's educational attainment in the nineteenth-century Russian Empire, it was a detriment to their mobility in the Soviet period. The fate of German and Russian Jewish women was also strongly affected by their religion in both the nineteenth and twentieth centuries.

A leitmotif running through this history of Russian and European women is the discussion of the dreams, struggles, and nightmares that women of the same or different classes shared in various epochs. In both centuries, most women of all classes dreamed of marrying, yet marriage often brought unexpected difficulties. In the nineteenth century, it was mainly middle- and upper-class women who dreamed of higher education, careers, and political participation. Yet they often encountered struggles and nightmares in obtaining university education, employment, and suffrage. In contrast to middle- and upper-class women, working-class and peasant women often settled for survival as an end in itself. Although they shared some of the same employment nightmares of career women—low wages, sexual harassment, and low rates of unionization—their work was often for their family's survival rather than for the self-fulfillment that many middle-class women sought.

Women's Social Situation

Just as many Westerners today dream of romance and marriage, so most Russian and European women hoped for happy family life and expected to marry. However, gender imbalances in the late nineteenth century and following World War I meant that many women could not find a spouse and that many married women became widowed. Some thought marriage would fulfill their romantic desires; others believed it would provide economic sustenance. Some sought status, respectability, or psychological and sexual fulfillment in marriage. Many middle- and upper-class women strove to be better wives, mothers, and household managers by reading child-rearing and housekeeping manuals. Then, as now, the institution of marriage did not always live up to women's dreams. In all periods, wives in all classes struggled against poverty and to keep up appearances. Some experienced spouse abuse. Some became dour and wintry and in turn abused their children physically and/or emotionally. Some desperate ones resorted to infanticide.

Then, as now, a minority of women chose not to marry. Some strongminded and talented artists, intellectuals, suffragists, and revolutionaries sought fulfillment in their work and portrayed marriage not as bliss but as moral suicide for women of talent and ambition. Some combined marriage and career. For a variety of reasons French and Russian women were more likely to choose this option than were English and German women. In Russia, the professions were not overcrowded as in England and Germany, and in France both Republican politicians and churchmen bade career women marry and increase the birth rate. Although the rejection of conventional gender roles empowered some women in the nineteenth century, it produced self-doubt, neurasthenic illness, and depression among others. Some feared becoming unsexed, mannish, or unwomanly.

In the 1920s, feminist, liberal, and conservative ideologies collided. Some women pursued independent feminist lifestyles or the hedonistic flappergirl life, but most still yearned for marriage and family life. However, millions were unable to fulfill this dream after the devastating male losses in World War I. Although millions bobbed their hair, wore short skirts, and affected the look of liberated women, European society generally adhered to traditional gender roles. When Victor Margueritte portrayed disillusioned women in *La Garçonne* (*The Bachelor Girl*, 1922), conservatives condemned it as obscene because his heroine blurred sexual distinctions and threatened middle-class morality. Similarly, many Germans resented liberated women, Bubikopf haircuts, and masculinized women in Weimar society.

In the 1930s, European marriage rates rose and Soviet ones remained high, so many women achieved their dream of respectable family life. However, this decade also produced intense social struggles as pronatalists glorified motherhood, made childbearing a patriotic duty, banned birth control and abortion, dismissed married working women, and increased stress in poor women's lives. In the Soviet Union, International Women's Day became more like the capitalist celebration of Mother's Day with flowers and children and less like a serious remembrance of women workers.

Women's Educational Situation

From the perspective of the late twentieth century it is astounding to see how class, nationality, religion, and gender restricted women's education 100 years ago. Generally, girls had less access to education than did boys of their class, and parents expressed low educational expectations for their daughters. The quest for higher education occupied mainly middle- and upper-class women. Given the gendered nature of nineteenth-century society, it is remarkable that so many women journeyed hundreds, even thousands, of miles to pursue higher education. Personality and religion also affected women's educational choices. Protestants in France and Protestants and Jews in Germany were proportionally better represented in secondary and higher education than Catholics. In Russia, Protestant women had the highest literacy rates. The deficit of English and German men in the upper and middle classes and the difficult economic situation of many Russian gentry-class families intensified these women's need for education and careers. Obtaining higher education in the late nineteenth century usually involved dedication and expense, limiting it to a select few. Few peasant or working-class girls dreamed of secondary education, and those who did had to sacrifice to achieve their goals.

In the 1920s, gender, class, and nationality still influenced women's educational opportunities. Women struggled against internalized class and gender inferiority particularly in the English and German academic worlds. The 1930s produced both banes and blessings. In England, access to higher education remained an upper-class, male prerogative, as Parliament reduced the number of teacher training positions available and restricted the number of secondary school scholarships for working-class children during the Depression. Believing that intellectual development and motherhood were mutually exclusive, the Nazis restricted women's access to university study and steered girls into domestic science courses. In contrast, the Soviets increased availability of education for women so lower-class girls could fulfill their dreams of becoming teachers and doctors. Yet alongside Soviet women's triumphs came restrictions against the children of gentry, clerical families, purge victims, and kulaks. Still, resourceful women in those groups managed to evade government restrictions and obtain higher education. In France, socialists tried to democratize education by reducing school fees, yet few peasant or working-class girls obtained secondary or higher education. However, higher education remained open to middle- and upper-class French women. Contrary to the situation of the 1890s, when foreign university scholars outnumbered French ones, by 1936 French women predominated.

Women's Economic Situation

Women's economic situation shows an amazing continuity from the nineteenth to the twentieth centuries. Then, as now, women earned lower wages than men, held few positions of power, suffered from sexual harassment, and lacked child care and unionization. Female agricultural workers earned lower wages than did men, and when agriculture became mechanized in the Soviet Union in the 1930s, men became tractor and combine operators on the kolkhoz, earning more than women. Moreover, peasants' dreams of owning their own land lasted only a decade—from 1918 to 1929, when the Soviet government decided to collectivize agriculture and draw all the peasants and their land into large kolkhozy (collective farms). Collectivization resulted in famine, death, and the exile of countless kulaks, and the general disorganization yielded smaller than expected harvests. While peasant women only worked eight hours on the kolkhoz, they still had their private plot, animals, families, and households to tend to. So, their actual workday was not eight hours, but the same old fifteen- to eighteen-hour day during the summer. Nor did the life of French or German peasant women improve in the 1930s. They still washed their clothes in streams, cared for the garden plot and animals, cooked and washed for their families, and never had a day off.

The occupation that contemporary readers may find most difficult to fathom is domestic service. In the late nineteenth century, thousands of girls left the country for life in the city. Some dreamed of earning a dowry and returning to their village to marry. Many probably succeeded. Some servants in France saved their wages, opened shops, and experienced upward mobility. However, hundreds of thousands of others found life in service a terrible struggle. Most Russian and European families employed only one servant, who had an astounding amount of work to do. So, many servants changed jobs frequently to escape demanding employers. In the late nineteenth century, the worst nightmare for a servant was being seduced and abandoned. Pregnant and jobless, some became destitute and desperate, descending into unemployment, unwed motherhood, and occasionally infanticide and crime.

Contemporary readers may easily relate to the situation of clerks and shopgirls whose jobs resemble those of sales clerks and secretaries today.

From 1880 to 1939, young women often preferred white-collar work as clerks to factory work. Such jobs did not pay much and the conditions were terrible—ten- to twelve-hour days during the late nineteenth century. Worst of all, employers expected shop assistants to dress like ladies, which was impossible to do on their wages; so they often had to prostitute themselves to their bosses and wealthy customers to keep their jobs. Then, as now, employers hired only the youngest, prettiest girls. Seduced and abandoned clerks might also experience downward mobility. With the unionization of clerks around 1900, some gained shorter working hours, although their wages remained low. Economically and psychologically vulnerable in the 1920s and 1930s, they sought relief in romantic movies, in which secretaries married their bosses and lived happily ever after.

Readers may also see a great deal of continuity in the economic situation of factory workers. Their work was hard, dirty, unhygienic, and low paid. However, it offered a day off, and some peasants regarded factory work as a relief from the never-ending drudgery of farm life. Indeed, some factory workers found camaraderie in their work and independence in wage earning that were lacking in domestic service or farm work. Their high spirits and economic independence usually evaporated after marriage. As married women, they seldom had money for a new dress and often ate the poorest food, saving the best for their husband and children. In most cities, workers lived in crowded, dingy, unhealthy housing. Hauling and heating water to wash clothes made laundry an all-day affair. In the 1920s and 1930s, more workers enjoyed quarters with running water and heat. Better-paid European workers moved to suburbs where housing was less crowded. Just when life was becoming easier, economic depression hit Germany and England, throwing millions out of work. In the Soviet Union, the conditions of industrialization in the 1930s were about as cruel as those in nineteenth-century Europe—low wages, harsh working conditions, and crowded living conditions. Yet Soviet women workers benefited from the free elementary, secondary, and even technical education that many plants provided, and some became engineers, experiencing upward mobility.

Contemporary readers can sympathize with the situation of career women. In the late nineteenth century, the professions were crowded in Germany and England, and men did not want women competing with them. (Social attitudes were similar to those in the United States in the 1950s when counselors and teachers discouraged young women from studying law and medicine, encouraging them instead to become teachers and nurses.) In France and Russia different conditions prevailed. Russia had a huge population and a very small intelligentsia, so career women did not pose a threat, but were welcomed to provide educational and medical services to the lower classes. Then, as now, government agencies considered women more docile and cheaper than men. French society created a slightly different pattern. Their low birth rate allowed for female workers in all categories, including the professions.

Some women achieved their dream of becoming a teacher, doctor, pharmacist, artist, writer, journalist, social worker, suffragist, revolutionary, and so forth. Yet they faced serious obstacles. English female university professors seldom obtained the highest posts and found research money less available to them than to men. While Russian and European societies sanctioned women's work as elementary teachers, it balked at hiring them as superintendents, principals, or school inspectors. Positions offering high status and wages were usually reserved for men. In the nineteenth century, educated European women often had to take low-paying positions as governesses and even had to travel to foreign countries to obtain employment.

Political Situations

In looking at women's political situation, we see them risking imprisonment for challenging the establishment, yet attaining some of their dreams after long struggles. In the mid-nineteenth century, increasing numbers of middle- and upper-class women sought change in their personal lives and in their societies. Many rejected their subordinate social position and sought a life of their own. In existentialist language, they sought to be Subjects, not (sex) Objects. In the 1860s, they developed rhetoric to justify self-development, higher education, employment, and political participation. With the exception of working-class women's involvement in trade unionism, political activity was confined to middle- and upper-class women prior to World War I. Writers in Russia employed the phrase "woman question"—and in France the term "feminism"—to describe changes in women's attitudes, behavior, and position. English writers employed the words *feminist*, *suffragist*, and *suffragette* to describe radical women. German and French women organized suffrage groups and participated in organized political parties to a limited extent. Women generally participated in philanthropic, suffragist, and revolutionary movements. The Tsarist government alienated people so profoundly that some privileged women eschewed their pampered gentry-class life in favor of revolutionary work to improve the lot of peasants, workers, and women. Some European women also participated in socialist movements to change their societies. However, most European middle-class women did not find revolutionary politics "in good taste" and preferred reformist methods. Regardless of system, it took English, German, and Russian women sixty years to gain suffrage (1860–1917/18).

After their long struggle to gain the vote, English women were dumbfounded when conservative women, not feminists, were elected in the 1920s. They were dismayed that male M.P.s laughed at their issues. So, some middle-class English feminists saw their dreams turn to ashes. Middle-class Russian feminists experienced similar disenchantment. After struggling for decades for suffrage, and after being enfranchised by the liberal Provisional Government in the spring of 1917, many lost their voting rights under the Bolsheviks, who disenfranchised the well-to-do in 1918. Both the Weimar Constitution in the 1920s and the 1936 Soviet Constitution proclaimed women's equality, thereby rejecting any need to improve their real status. Stenographic records of the Communist Party in the Soviet Union, the Labour Party in England, and the German Reichstag Handbuchs show a small female elite, composed mainly of middle- and upper-class women, with little circulation into it by working-class or peasant women during the 1920s and 1930s.

Although socialist women thought their dream had come true when the Bolsheviks came to power, some faced demotion, exile, even imprisonment if they criticized party leaders. German feminists felt dismayed that political parties did not take women's issues seriously. In France, senators refused to grant women the franchise. In the 1920s and 1930s, pacifism eclipsed feminism in France and England. In Germany and the Soviet Union, women suffered arrest, torture, and imprisonment for opposing their regimes. In prison and labor camps, some Soviet and German political prisoners formed surrogate families, which helped them survive and live to write about their experiences.

Chronology and Terminology

This book covers the years 1860 to 1939. It begins in 1860 because it was then that feminism, or the woman question, began to be widely discussed in Russia, England, France, and Germany. Throughout the rest of the century, writers strove to define women's social, legal, educational, economic, and political rights and duties. This work skirts World War I, partly because a great deal has been written on this topic and partly because it is organized around the censuses of the 1890s, 1920s, and 1930s. It analyzes the adjustments that war, revolution, and women's enfranchisement produced in the new Soviet Union and postwar Europe. In the 1930s the depression, collectivization, and industrialization in the Soviet Union; Hitlerism and Stalinism; and the reassertion of patriarchal attitudes undermined some of the gains that women made in the 1920s. This work ends in 1939 on the eve of World War II, another watershed in European women's lives. For convenience, the terms "European" and "Europe" are used to refer to France, Germany, and England.

Sources

A variety of sources provide insight into women's situation during the years 1860 to 1939. Statistical handbooks and the Russian, German, English, and French censuses of the 1890s, 1920s, and 1930s provide quantitative evidence about the majority of women who left no written records. Such data show patterns in women's marital status, literacy, and employment. While census data is not exact, it provides a broad picture of women's social, educational, and economic situation.

Novels and plays reveal the texture of women's lives, as do cookbooks, child-care manuals, and housekeeping guides; all indicate that most upper- and middle-class women in the nineteenth and early twentieth centuries strove to fulfill the social expectations placed upon them. In his play *Poor Bride* (1851), Alexander Ostrovsky portrays a character who asks her friend not to disillusion her about marriage because she needs her dreams to get through life. Most women dreamed of marriage and found it socially respectable, economically necessary, and sometimes emotionally and sexually gratifying. Yet George Eliot writes in *The Mill on the Floss* (1860): "The happiest women, like the happiest nations, have no history." My book both supports and refutes Eliot's words, as memory texts by "happy" women are harder to find than those by disgruntled ones. Eliot's quote seems particularly apt for the nineteenth century, when memoirs and autobiographies of critically minded women reveal dissatisfaction with their social, educational, economic, and political lots, yet also express self-realization in their professional lives as writers, painters, teachers, nurses, doctors, union organizers, suffragettes, and revolutionaries. In the 1920s and 1930s, feminists and dissidents again expressed their unhappiness in memoirs and belles lettres. Weaving together information from statistical data, belles lettres, newspapers, journals, and contemporary histories of the eras provides a fascinating portrait of Russian and European women throughout the period from 1860 to 1939.

Because social history is not just about the great, this book focuses on the lives of ordinary as well as extraordinary women. While belles lettres provide useful information about upper- and middle-class women's lives, they neglect lower-class women. Folk songs, folk tales, and proverbs bring to light the peasant mentality in the late nineteenth and early twentieth centuries, and some peasant women recorded their own memoirs in the twentieth century. Accounts about working-class women are also richer in this later period. English working-class women's autobiographies reveal traditional attitudes toward women and their place in society in the 1920s. In contrast, Soviet sources describe sexually liberated political activists in the 1920s, but more subdued, family-oriented women workers in the 1930s.

Party documents capture part of women's political experience. The Annual Conference of the Labour Party contains speeches by women and describes the Women's Section in the 1920s and 1930s. Reichstag Handbuchs list women members according to party affiliation and provide short biographies of them. Communist Party stenographic reports list women delegates and indicate the spheres in which they clustered.

The chapters that follow show in greater detail the similarities and differences in Russian and European women's lives during the years 1860 to 1939. As you read these chapters, I hope you will enjoy becoming acquainted with the Russian and European women of these epochs. I also hope you will appreciate which issues have been settled—e.g., the vote and access to higher education—and which problems, such as contraception, abortion, egalitarian marriage, spouse abuse, unequal pay, low status, child care, housework, and marginal political power, still haunt women today.

Chapter 1

Society in the Late Nineteenth Century

One is not born a woman, one becomes one.
—Simone de Beauvoir, *The Second Sex*

Simone de Beauvoir's words well describe women's social situation in the nineteenth century. Although women in different classes and countries received a variety of messages about womanliness, they were generally expected to marry and devote themselves to their families. Society usually sanctioned only peasant and working-class women's work outside the home. It lamented middle-class women's work and firmly believed that "ladies do not work for pay." Nonconformists often experienced ridicule and psychological conflict. Middle-class women living in genteel poverty often worked surreptitiously to earn money and to keep up class appearances. Professional men looked upon women of their class as "fragile flowers," regarding their proper profession as ladies of leisure, bearing and educating children and cultivating decorum. The following verse captures the situation of English women in 1875:

> 'Tis a marvelous thing, a woman's sphere!
> She may starve at her needle, with fast-falling tear;
> She may hammer nails, or sell gin and beer;
> But she shan't be a lawyer or clerk at most,
> Or take any nice little government post,
> For the Law and Society'd give up the ghost,
> If she stepped so far out of her sphere.[1]

Societal Attitudes toward Women

Social attitudes toward women changed in the late nineteenth century due to population imbalance between the genders, lack of dowries, and new

11

attitudes toward women's abilities. It became easier for women to attend elementary and secondary school, to become schoolteachers, and for persevering ones to pursue university study and careers in the helping professions. An exceptional few—the mathematician Sofia Kovalevskaia, the physicist Marie Curie, and the historian Eileen Power—became university professors.

In the 1860s, John Stuart Mill thought educated women had the right to enter the professions but that most would choose marriage as their career. Yet English women who eschewed marriage often feared that professional work would undermine their femininity and make them "mannish." Still, gender imbalance meant that thousands could not marry. Many sought higher education as the first step to independence. At mid-century, society sanctioned unmarried middle-class women's work as governesses and by 1900 regarded public school teaching as a respectable position for them.[2]

Russia and France were more tolerant of career women than were England and Germany. With twice the population of Germany and thrice that of England or France, Russia had a small educated class. Russian local and provincial governments hired women in the helping professions, partly because such positions were not "overcrowded" as in England and Germany, partly because they could pay women less, and partly because the intelligentsia condoned the work of educated women as "ministering angels" and did not perceive them as a threat to traditional values. Russian and European liberals believed women should be good wives and mothers, even philanthropists; and some Russians thought women also had the right to medical and legal careers so they could extend their ministering functions to society.[3] Low population rates meant that French women worked at all levels of employment.

English women disguised their desire for freedom and adventure in various ways. Mary Kingsley wanted to explore Africa but claimed she wanted to further her father's anthropological research. Many felt severe conflicts in rejecting the values of their class. In Russia, Praskovia Tatlina thought marriage did not make women happy and perceived self-sacrifice and humility as old-fashioned.[4] Gentry-class Russian women often found marriage and career compatible. Indeed, the emancipation of the serfs in 1861 meant that many families could no longer support dependent relatives, and countless gentry-class Russian women survived by writing and translating. Russian career women encountered both support and ridicule among their colleagues, but met less hostility than European women. In 1912, H. P. Kennard noticed Russian women managing businesses, factories, and estates; practicing dentistry and medicine;

working in telegraphy and the railway; and taking a more independent position than English or European women.[5] Professional work did not necessarily undermine marriage and the family. While some Russian revolutionaries abstained from marriage in principle, many combined marriage and political life. In France, physicians and politicians encouraged career women to marry and have children to prevent further depopulation. In England and Germany, married career women were less common.

Marriage and Social Status

Marriage was crucial to most women's lives, and most made the best of it. In Russia and Europe, well-to-do women bought household and child-rearing manuals in order to raise their children and run their households well.[6] Still, women's preponderance meant that not all could marry. The imbalance was greatest in England, where women outnumbered men 1,047 to 1,000 in the 1890s. The ratio was lower in Germany (1,037 females to 1,000 males), lower yet in Russia (1,011 females to 1,000 males), and the lowest in France (1,004 females to 1,000 males). Marriage rates varied according to class, nationality, and geography. Gender imbalance affected the middle and upper classes most, but it also plagued certain geographical areas. Several French rural areas lacked women.[7]

In the Russian Empire, nationality, class, and geography affected marriage rates. Among women twenty-three to twenty-eight years old, 60% in the Baltic provinces were married in 1897, while 63% of those in European Russia, 71% in the Caucasus, 66% in Siberia, and 77% of those in Central Asia were married.[8] Their aggregate marriage rate exceeded European women's because Russia was agricultural and peasants had very high marriage rates (table 1.1).

The 1897 Imperial Russian census was unique in listing its population by estate: nobility, clergy, bourgeois, peasant, or indigenous people. In the

Table 1.1. Women's Aggregate Marriage Rates, 1890s*

Russia	62.5
France	54.8
Germany	52.0
England	49.6

*In percent. Calculated from *Svod Perepisi 1897 g.*, 1: xii; Table XI: "Femmes mariées de plus de 15 ans," *Annuaire Statistique*, 52: 252.

hereditary nobility, females outnumbered males 1,090 to 1,000; in the personal nobility (nobility for one's lifetime), 1,075 to 1,000. In the clerical estate, women exceeded men 1,135 to 1,000. (Like Protestants, Orthodox clergy could and did marry.) The ratio of women to men in the *meshchane* (petty bourgeois) was 1,048 to 1,000. By the 1890s, gender imbalance, distaste for marriage, and divorce among women in the upper ranks produced writers, critics, career women, feminists, and revolutionaries.

Population disparity in the Russian Empire was lower among peasants (1,020 females to 1,000 males). In the *grazhdane* estate (honored citizens or haute bourgeoisie), men outnumbered women 1,000 to 951. Men also predominated in the Central Asian indigenous population by a margin of 1,000 to 875. Gender balance was equal until their teens when a sizable discrepancy arose, possibly due to child marriage, maternal mortality, and economic exploitation.[9]

Peasant Women

Peasants enjoyed high marriage rates. In Russia, marriage was nearly universal. Whether peasant women held romantic, realistic, fatalistic, or mixed views is unknown because they left few records. Arranged marriages might or might not include love and affection.[10] Until more social histories become available, it is impossible to know whether these women achieved their hopes and dreams in marriage, or whether they rejected some of the pain of married life by seeking employment as domestic servants and workers in cities. Court records, statistical data, ethnographic reports, and belles lettres reveal more about their difficulties than their dreams.

Descriptions of peasants were usually made by biased outsiders. Gentry-class Tatyana Kuzminskaya described her servants as slovenly and simple. Ethnographer Olga Semyonova Tian-Shanskaia spoke condescendingly of peasants to counteract idealizations of them. Ethnographer Aleksandr Engelgardt portrayed peasant women as independent and greedy, yet hardworking and sacrificial. Leo Tolstoy and Anton Chekhov depicted them as scheming matriarchs, or victims—physically and mentally crippled.[11] Gender and class filtering also occurred in the 1897 Imperial Russian Census, which counted only 2 million of 28 million adult peasant women as "employed," because government census takers did not consider women's household and field work to be labor. French and German censuses of the 1890s also undercounted peasant women.

Marriage was the norm in the Russian Empire, where 20 million adult peasant women were married, 4 million widowed, but only 27,000 divorced and 4 million single in 1897. Marriage was based on economic considerations and involved parental and village sanction. It denoted social status, respectability, economic security, and at times affection or brutality. In France, Meme Santerre's father was gentle and kind, yet he limited her suitors and crushed an inappropriate romance.[12]

Russian folk songs expressed parental power in choosing a spouse. One song says: "Nothing can be done, poor sister. The match has been made. Father promised you. Mother has agreed. Now you go to the home of a stranger." Wedding songs fell into two groups: laments in which the bride bid farewell to her family and friends prior to the wedding, and happy ones celebrating the wedding. Sometimes it is difficult to distinguish the bride's real anguish from the rituals marking her movement from her home to her in-laws'. In Tula province, girls showed their approaching marriage by wearing mourning garments of dark blue.[13]

Wedding laments were also sung in Germany. As late as the 1930s, they sang: "So fare thee well, thou quiet home. Grieving I leave thee, grieving and sad I go forth, not yet knowing whither."[14]

Russian peasants fulfilled their dreams as well as the norms of their communities by marrying, yet some experienced sexual and economic exploitation. *Snokhachestvo* (rape of a bride by her father-in-law) and heavy workloads imposed by mothers-in-law often shattered ideas of "wedded bliss." Peasant girls may have adopted realistic views of marriage, dreaming of the day when they too would be able to lord it over others in an extended family. Yet desire for one's own house increasingly broke up extended families prior to 1900, and after the 1917 revolution 10 million new households emerged.[15]

The proverb "A hen is not a bird and a woman is not a human being," is often quoted to show peasant women's victimization. Yet others indicate appreciation: "With a good wife grief is only half grief, and joy is double," and "The peasant's wife is his best friend." Still, a visiting American heard one woman remark: "No beating, no jealousy; no jealousy, no love."[16]

The English saying "A wife, a dog, and a walnut tree, the more you beat them the better they'll be" suggests that wife beating flourished there too. French literature and court cases also depict spouse abuse among the peasantry. Guy de Maupassant's "A Matter of Business" describes a Norman peasant selling his wife to another man. Emilie Carles had seen so many abusive peasant marriages that she initially rejected wedded life.[17]

Patriarchy and matriarchy were prominent features in peasant life, yet superstition and tradition mitigated some abuse. Some Russians believed that whoever first stepped on the altar carpet during the wedding ceremony would "rule the roost." In Smolensk province, Engelgardt noticed that village women sometimes ruled. When they became the mistresses in one or two families in a village their behavior spread to other households. These women were splendid, strong, and healthy; but where men ruled, women were beaten, unattractive, and worn out.[18]

In Russia and Western Europe, peasant women took a dowry into marriage, a practice that may have strengthened their position. Their dowry was usually untouchable. Those who felt cheated out of their dowry, property, or inheritance sometimes took their cases to court. In several Russian provinces, women were involved in half the inheritance claims coming before the local courts. Women's contribution to the household could also improve their situation. They sold garden produce, berries, mushrooms, chickens, and eggs. Many prepared flax, carded wool, and helped in the domestic production of linen, wooden spoons, felt hats, rope, yarn, gloves, buttons, pins, lace, and other commodities. In France and Russia, some served as wet nurses for babies from big cities. The Russian government even paid peasant women to nurse babies from state orphanages.[19] While women's contributions to the family economy may have enhanced their status, it is unclear if their earnings protected them from beatings.

Slavic peasant women's social, sexual, and psychological status was ambiguous. Embroideries sewn for their dowries often portrayed strong images of fertile goddesses. Viewing fertility positively, the Russian Orthodox church venerated Mary as the Mother of God, not as Virgin. Still, people had ambivalent views about sex. To be on the safe side, they covered their household icons when making love. Villages controlled young women's sexuality by encouraging early marriage and allowing them to attend dances, engage in kissing games, and participate in innocent bundling. Ritual shaming was used to enforce morality: cutting off the braid of unwed mothers and tarring the clothes of women caught in adultery.[20] By 1900, sexual standards had relaxed in some areas, and prenuptial pregnancy became more common. Nor were peasant women always victims. According to Engelgardt, women sometimes took a lover when their husbands were unfaithful. Some expressed a cavalier attitude, arguing that sex was not like soap: it would not be used up, and something would be left over for the husband. In the meantime, they might receive a shawl or several rubles from a gentry-class man for their services.[21]

While marriage was most peasants' dream, frequent pregnancy created difficulties. Many bore eight to twelve children, half of whom died in infancy. Destitute and unwed mothers sometimes smothered their babies. Russian soldiers' wives who gave birth in their husbands' absence might resort to infanticide. Yet they were seldom punished for these crimes. Youthful, almost universal marriage kept Russian illegitimacy rates low—less than 2%. In France, an illegitimate child created shame, but among Bavarian farm servants illegitimacy rates were as high as 15%. Because illegitimacy was a common phenomenon, they were not punished.[22]

Despite the difficulties of married life, being unmarried was the worst possible disaster. Crippled, single, and widowed women were shunned and could barely eke out an existence as matchmakers, funeral mourners, lacemakers, seamstresses, or handicraft workers. As wards of their villages or families, unmarried women were resented as economic burdens. In Russia, they were allowed the use of the plot around their house but were seldom entitled to a land allotment or a voice in the village assembly. Customs varied, and some villages allowed widows to become heads of household, vote and hold office in the commune, or become preachers in dissenting religions.[23]

Most peasant women in the Russian Empire had few alternatives to marriage and traditional life. While the poet Nikolai Nekrasov's description of peasant women as "married, mated, and subjugated to a slave" seems exaggerated, life was hard. Both Russian and European peasant women's chores included cooking, cleaning the house, tending the family garden, weaving, sewing, knitting, washing clothes in a nearby pond or river, raising the children, caring for livestock, helping in the fields from sunup to sundown in the summer, and participating in handicraft production in the winter. Despite all their labor, few households lived well, as most were burdened with heavy taxes and mortgages. In the 1890s, 6.5 million peasants in the Russian Empire had no horses for farming, 30% had no machinery for farming, and roughly 15% had no land under cultivation. About 65% of peasant households were poor, 20% were middling, and only 15% wealthy. They produced eleven bushels of rye per acre, whereas European farmers produced seventeen to twenty-four bushels.[24]

The high cost of weddings, need for a dowry, oppressive family relations, and the lack of available husbands pushed more than 2 million peasant women in the Russian Empire into the cities, where they sought employment as domestic servants, laundresses, bath attendants, or garment workers. It is uncertain if migration represented a strategy for acquiring a dowry, expressed hopes and dreams of a new and better life, or was a necessity for single, widowed, or unmarriageable women.[25] Without personal records, it is impossible to judge whether work in the cities fulfilled hopes for higher wages and adventure or represented a survival strategy. Although many fulfilled their dream of acquiring a dowry, others struggled in their work with demanding employers, while some encountered sexual harassment, seduction, rape, even downward mobility into prostitution. Compared to their peasant sisters, only 17% of urban domestics in the Russian Empire married, 15% of French, and less than 10% of English and German female servants.[26]

Significant differences in Russian and European marriage rates existed among female agricultural workers. The 1897 Russian census listed 1,982,000 females as "gainfully employed" in agricultural labor. In the Russian and Ukrainian provinces, two-thirds of female agricultural workers were married. German census data for 1895 found 20% of them married, and French data for 1896 showed roughly a third.[27]

While most rural women in the Russian Empire engaged in agricultural work, half a million also engaged in paid handicraft work. Most were daughters living at home; only 30% were married. Large numbers of French and German rural women also engaged in handicraft production. As mechanization of textile production advanced, they had to work longer hours to earn enough to survive. In Normandy, some handicraft workers worked from four A.M. until ten P.M. Large families were the norm, and children left school at age eleven to work on family looms. They had no holidays. When someone married, siblings did not attend the wedding because they had to continue weaving. One bride even borrowed her mother's wedding ring for her wedding. In the summer, families worked on large sugar beet or wheat farms, where they earned good wages to help them survive the winter.[28]

Working-Class Women

> I was very poor but no one outside my door knew how often I was hungry or how I had to scheme to get my husband nourishment.   —Mrs. Layton, "Memories of Seventy Years"

Like peasant women, working-class women also desired the respectability that marriage conferred. Yet among them prenuptial pregnancy was not so disgraceful. Germans said, "You marry not to have a child but because you already have one." Few women workers could support themselves and

Table 1.2. Marital Status of Textile Workers, 1890s*

Country	% Single	% Married	% Widowed/Divorced
Russia	50	45	5
France	50	36	8
Germany	69	17	15
England	68	32	0

*Calculated from Chislenost' Rossii 1897g. 1: x, xi, 2–3; *Annuaire Statistique*, 20: 28–37; *Jarhbuch*, 1914, 35: 16–17; P.P. 97; *Gt. Br. Census 1891*, p. 180; B. L. Hutchins, "A Note on the Distribution of Women in Occupations," *JRSS*, Sept. 1904, 488.

preferred concubinage to destitution. Many European women lived in consensual unions because they could not afford weddings. Some cohabited because they were waiting for a divorce or because they could not afford a divorce but had separated from an abusive husband and needed a man to provide for them.[29]

Russian and French women workers formed different marriage patterns than did German and English women. In Russia and France more women worked as domestics than in factory production, and those in manufacturing were more likely to be older and married than were the English or German women, who usually left work at the time of marriage (table 1.2).[30]

Differences in age and marital status affected government regulations. European factories employed female factory inspectors to supervise working conditions, while Russian plants provided midwives. Although the proportion of married German women factory workers was low, these workers were not always free of family duties. German marriage laws required financial proof of ability to maintain a household, and many German women cohabited with a man and had illegitimate children until they could accrue a dowry to marry.[31]

Lenin thought women factory workers possessed greater dignity and equality than rural women had, because urban migration loosened the patriarchal power of parents over children and of husbands over wives. Oppressive as marriage was for many working women, it was preferable to the starvation wages a single woman earned. Moreover, marriage provided respectability and status that spinsterhood lacked.[32]

Workingmen thought factory work degraded women and preferred that their wives not work outside the home. German and French delegates to a worker's meeting in 1864 declared that a wife and mother should stand for coziness, be an ennobling influence, and instill their children with moral principles. English workingmen thought their wage should suffice for the family, their home was their castle, and their wives their servants. Since many men suffered from unemployment and underemployment, their wives sometimes had to work in factories, do housework, take in laundry, pawn the family's clothes, or even lay out the dead for the family to survive.[33]

Working-class women were subject to the exploitation of capitalist employers, patriarchal husbands, and government reformers. Employers paid them low wages and sometimes humiliated them by requiring them to perform personal chores. English charitable institutions often distributed food in a condescending manner, and wives resented begging Poor Law guardians for aid.[34] French protective legislation also reinforced the patriarchal order. According to Mary Lynn Stewart, French industrial hygienists noticed working women's low energy but attributed it to their menstrual periods, not to heavy household duties, which were defined as women's sacred duty, not as unpaid work. Despite the rhetoric of reproduction, few French reformers suggested a family wage or wages for housework to sustain full-time housewives.[35]

Socialist feminists saw capitalism and family life oppressing women. In their own writings, working-class women poignantly depict the self-sacrifice, hazards, and hardships that accompanied marriage and motherhood. One woman indicated that she had six children and performed her sexual duty to keep her husband faithful. Yet she resented being a sex object.[36]

Other wives describe not sentimental motherhood but the perils of too-frequent pregnancy, overwork, and depression. They sacrificed food, clothing, even their health so their husbands and children could go to work and school decently fed and clothed. They enjoyed new clothes only while young and single. Inadequate diet and health care produced sickly babies, high numbers of miscarriages, and high infant mortality. It was not uncommon for a working-class wife to have ten to sixteen pregnancies, several stillbirths and miscarriages, and only a few children who grew to adulthood. Lack of birth control sometimes led to abortion, infanticide, even child abandonment. Too-frequent pregnancies and ill health rendered many women incapable of properly caring for their families. Poverty and drudgery made mothers short-tempered. One woman described the mental illness she suffered trying to keep a growing family together on her husband's inadequate wages. The strain of keeping up a decent standard of living unbalanced some mothers, who turned their anger and frustration against their children, telling them that they were a burden and should never have been born.

Home life could be wintry when mothers had no love or affection to give their children. Sex and motherhood sometimes turned daughters against marriage.[37]

Lack of running water plus high standards of cleanliness turned some mothers into shrews. Rickets, fever, and consumption decimated poor families. Fathers were often unemployed, so families lived in poverty and hunger. Without the financial contribution of older siblings, families could not survive. After 1900, school breakfasts provided some nourishment. Yet many working-class families had to pawn their "best clothes" each week after doing the laundry. Mothers often found solace in song and alcohol and in donning their best clothes for a Saturday night drink at the local pub. Many ignored the church except when it dispensed blankets to them.[38]

Crowded housing, poverty, and high infant mortality also plagued French working-class households. French industrial hygienists saw a connection between infant mortality and women's work, but they did not understand the roles played by poor nutrition and inadequate medical care. Until 1913, French workers lacked paid maternity leave and often returned to work to help their families survive. When they stopped breastfeeding within the baby's first month, the child often died. English infants also died during their first year when mothers stopped breastfeeding in order to return to work. English health experts saw the correlation between poverty and infant mortality and knew infant mortality was 50% higher in households where the father was unemployed or earned less than a pound per week. When the National Health Insurance Act of 1911 provided maternity benefits for wives of employed men, infant mortality declined further.[39] Preferring not to engage in infanticide, some English workers took their babies to "angel makers," who allowed them to die, since the mothers could not afford to care for them.

In Russia, many working women could not keep their children with them because of their low wages and crowded yet expensive housing. Some Russian and French workers sent their children to village relations to raise, while others paid rural wet nurses to care for their infants. Some abandoned their babies to foundling homes, where they usually died. Forty percent of babies of German working mothers also died during their first year, and German birth rates dropped from 33 per 1,000 in 1905 to 29.8 in 1910. Falling birth rates due to stillbirths, premature deliveries, and infant and maternal mortality created a "natality crisis" in Europe prior to World War I.[40]

Yet another hardship working-class women endured was spouse abuse. In the 1860s, John Stuart Mill drew attention to wife beating, cautioning that English law permitted men to behave as tyrants and many did. Several thousand cases of aggravated assaults on English women and children appeared in the judicial statistics each year. Some working women had their earnings confiscated by their husbands, and they had no recourse as their property belonged to their husbands prior to the Married Women's Property Act of 1870. In one case, a Lancashire man beat his wife so badly she lost an eye. In the trial that followed, male magistrates fined him ten shillings and court costs because his wife had provoked him. In Germany, police also discounted women's complaints. Some sought relief in divorce, which rose dramatically prior to 1914. French provincial court records also document wife beating among artisans.[41]

In the early twentieth century, wives of British miners appreciated their husbands' improved working conditions, which eased their lives. They had long complained about the dirt their husbands brought into the home and the impossibility of heating water for the menfolks' baths while preparing supper on the same fire. With the installation of bath facilities at the mines, their lives became easier.[42] Since trade unionism was more advanced in Europe than Russia, benefits such as unemployment insurance, accident insurance, and baths at the workplace improved the lot of European housewives more than that of Russian ones.

Middle-Class Women

Wife abuse occurred in the middle classes but was not discussed in polite society. A new divorce law was passed in England in the 1850s but proved unhelpful to women trying to leave bad marriages. In 1862, Frances Power Cobbe compared the personal unhappiness, physical abuse, and frequent illnesses experienced by married women to the rewarding life single women led through female friendship and philanthropic work. Aghast at the brutality revealed in divorce cases, she saw selfishness as a sacred male privilege, negating companionate marriage. Given the genteel poverty marriage created for many English middle-class couples, she advocated celibacy.[43]

German middle-class men valued cozy family life and expended large sums on elaborate houses for public display, yet they also displayed frugality, severity, and harshness in disciplining their children. German housekeeping manuals suggested ways to economize, veil housework, and keep up the appearance of being a lady of leisure. De Maupassant showed the hypocrisy and dishonesty of French tradesmen in many stories, depicting them as liars, rogues, and deceivers.[44]

The Russian petit bourgeois outlook resembled that described by de Maupassant. Authoritarian German and Russian men believed in their right to rule the household as lords and masters, while their wives served as comforters and servants. Many German men wanted pretty, submissive, hardworking, obedient wives and endorsed Goethe's adage: "Let women learn early to serve as is their destiny." Harsh family life among the German and Russian bourgeoisie remained common. In Germany, Toni Sender remembered her Jewish father's authoritarian attitude and her parents' demand for absolute obedience, which she rejected.[45]

In Russia, the middle class was composed of several elements. Those closest to European liberals were probably the *grazhdane* and the *raznochintsy* (those of various ranks including the intelligentsia). These two groups probably comprised less than 1 million people, whereas the *meshchanstvo* totaled 13.5 million. Family life in these ranks could be patriarchal, paternal, or egalitarian. Good examples of paternalism are seen in the families of Anna Ostroumova and Liubov Popova, who allowed their daughters to study art in Moscow and Paris and to marry the men they loved. Examples of egalitarian marriages among the intelligentsia are those of the Chernyshevskys and Kovalevskys.

While abusive family life was common in the meshchanstvo, not all women were victimized. According to Catriona Kelly, women in the *kupechskie* estate (merchant estate) could inherit and dispose of family property and could even vote in the elections of merchant representative bodies. They had small families and businesses. Men in this estate valued their wives' financial acumen and industriousness and conducted endogamous marriage.[46]

Among the petit bourgeois, however, a daughter seldom married the man she loved, but the one selected by her parents. Wedding negotiations resembled sales transactions in which the size of the dowry was most important. Endogamy remained the norm, and dowries often enabled a husband to establish or expand his business. Petty bourgeois families often felt the incongruence of the middle-class doctrine of separate spheres (where the man worked and the wife remained at home) and their need for the wife to work in the family enterprise. In French bakeries, the man often baked the bread and his wife sold it and kept the books. By 1900, the core relationship among many small English and French shopkeepers and artisans was the married couple rather than the father and son.[47]

Russian merchant high-handedness stemmed from rigid Old Believer religion and serf origins. Some Russian businessmen gained their freedom prior to the emancipation of 1861. Having paid dearly for their liberation, they often lorded it over others. *Samodur* (the desire to dominate others) pervaded this estate, and merchants forced family members, employees, and others to submit to their will. Success seldom softened them, and they ruled their family and workers with an iron hand. Unlike European middle-class life, which was influenced by liberal values, in Russia the petty bourgeois spirit dominated. In 1897, the meshchanstvo (peit bourgeois) numbered 13,500,000, while the kupechestvo (middle class) totaled 281,000, and the grazhdane (high middle class) comprised 343,000 members.[48]

Meshchanstvo Marital Relations

The meshchanstvo was the largest social group in Russian cities, and writers and critics portrayed its domestic life as despotic, cunning, and cruel. Whereas Ivan Turgenev entitled his play about the nobility *Nest of Gentlefolk* (1858), Nikolai Ostrovsky called his play about the merchant class *The Storm* (1859). Analyzing Ostrovsky's plays in 1860, literary critic Nikolai Dobroliubov described merchant family life as a "Kingdom of Darkness" where women lived lives of softly sighing grief. Those who did not conform might be beaten, locked up, or starved into submission. No one trusted anyone else, friends boasted of robbing each other, fathers-in-law tricked sons-in-law out of dowries, bridegrooms cheated matchmakers, and brides deceived their husbands. Nothing was sacred or pure, and everyone was dragged down into the quagmire.[49]

In the 1870s, Maxim Gorky depicted his petty-bourgeois grandfather cheating his best workers and beating his family. His grandmother acquiesced, saying: "All the same, beatings today don't compare with those we used to get." Gorky was bewildered at his grandmother's submission, since she was bigger than her husband. Dostoevsky also described behavior in that estate. Disturbed by rising numbers of female suicides, he investigated women's condition and wrote "A Gentle Creature" in 1876. It depicted a pawnbroker humiliating his wife and driving her to suicide.[50]

Wives, mothers, and mothers-in-law also engaged in despotic behavior. Unlike Coventry Patmore's "Angel in the House," some French and Russian writers portray women as cruel matriarchs. In *The Storm,* Ostrovsky depicts a widow driving her son to alcoholism and bullying her daughter-in-law into suicide. The seclusion in which merchant families lived fostered dominating behavior, and few were able to break away from this pattern.

Around 1900, the conscience-stricken industrialist Savva Morozov tried to improve the situation of his textile workers, but his mean- spirited mother removed him from the board of directors, and he committed suicide.[51]

Rarely do Russian literary characters rebel against family tyranny. An exception is Nikolai Leskov's story "Lady Macbeth of the Mtsensk District," in which the heroine Katerina Izmailova murders her tormenting husband and father-in-law, takes control of the family business, and lives openly with her lover. When her deeds are discovered, she is sent to Siberia. Although she drowns on her way to exile, she represents an avenging woman who overcomes maltreatment and inflicts it upon others.

Family life could be oppressive anywhere. The French socialist Flora Tristan described middle-class English women treated as property and offered for sale to anyone willing to pay the price. She thought their lack of rights created their taste for materialism, hardened their hearts, and numbed their souls. She hated the tyranny of fathers and husbands, the pride of the high, and the obsequiousness of the low. She was amazed that novelist Jane Austen described family life so differently. Tristan found a wife's fate sadder than an old maid's, since the English husband was the lord and master of the home, while a spinster could go out into the world or travel with relatives or friends. While middle-class girls often married to escape parental authority, men sought a wife's dowry, which they could use to pay their debts, squander in clubs, or spend with their mistresses. She thought the marriage bond heavier for women than for men.[52]

Some agreed with Tristan's critique. In 1868, the journalist Eliza Lynn Linton denounced pleasure-loving young women who were indifferent to duty. She thought they placed money before love or happiness.[53] Others lamented English girls raised for the marriage market but not trained for the wedded estate.

Changes in Middle-Class Family Life

In the late nineteenth century, change occurred in many bourgeois families. Some fathers recognized the lack of suitors and dowries for their daughters and urged them to seek education and careers. Some Russian merchants rejected their Old Believer faith, educated their children, and displayed a more cultured outlook. Some families allowed their daughters to study art in Paris.[54]

Russian novelist Mikhail A. Il'in depicts some changes in middle-class life. In *My Sister's Story*, the sisters lead very different lives than those depicted by Ostrovsky. Lisa is a good housewife, and her husband is kind-hearted and cheerful. She has a cozy home and does not chafe under her husband's paternal rule. The student Il'in prefers his sister Lisa's family, where the food is tasty and attractively served. Yet he does not respect her because she is too conventional. For companionship, he prefers his sister Katia. Unhappily married to a prosperous businessman, she remains married to please her mother, keep her children, and avoid scandal. (A divorced woman had no right to her children because they were the husband's property.) Being a bourgeois wife bores her, so she studies architecture and graduates as a fine architect. She does not practice this profession, because she feels like a sex object when her professor gazes at her as though she were naked.[55] Poorly prepared for marriage and professional life, she never becomes the person she longs to be but settles for the role of "martyred mother."

European middle-class men prided themselves on their education, civic mindedness, liberalism, and egalitarianism. Still, they believed that women were to provide order, intimacy, and felicity in the home—a haven from the heartless world of capitalist competition in which they worked. They believed Rousseau's injunction that women should please, flatter, and serve men.[56] Strong-minded French women sometimes resisted these injunctions. Yet poet Judith Gautier (1845–1917) discovered that romantic love could be expensive and destructive. Marrying against her father's advice, she endured a degrading eight-year marriage (1866–1874) to the philanderer Catulle Mendes. She supported Mendes and herself by writing, and divorced him only after her father's death. More damning critiques of marriage were made by Madeleine Pelletier and Sidonie Colette. Pelletier declared marriage moral suicide for an intelligent woman, while Colette described a marriageable man as the enemy, stealing her from herself. Simone de Beauvoir observed her mother's unhappy marriage and criticized the toll the double standard took on women. That her father had a variety of mistresses undermined his wife's sexual and social life. Her mother had been taught to serve her husband and children and not to take her own needs seriously. A spirited woman, she became deformed and mutilated. De Beauvoir concluded that bourgeois marriage was an unnatural institution.[57]

Not all middle-class men were the same. A few were feminists who suffered financially and politically for their views. Marriage to such a man made life happy. In England, Emmeline Pankhurst and Emmeline Pethick Lawrence enjoyed such marriages. Their model husbands made wedded life as ideal as was possible in an imperfect world. As a young woman,

Emmeline Pethick felt the restrictions of her middle-class upbringing and chafed at the notion of depending on a man, marriage, and small-town life. In London, she worked in a Methodist mission for working-class girls, where she found camaraderie with other social workers and a sense of well-being in helping the less fortunate. After a decade of this work, she married Fred Lawrence, who joined her name to his. Pacifists and feminists, they opposed the Boer War and supported women's suffrage. Together they edited the paper *Votes for Women* (1907–1914).[58]

Some middle-class husbands and fathers loved and cared for their families in paternal, not patriarchal, ways. Carl Woldemar Becker had lost his post in the German civil service and was unable to provide adequate dowries for his daughters, so he encouraged them to obtain an education so they could take care of themselves. When their artist daughter Paula became engaged, Becker and his wife insisted she attend cooking school and learn to be a good housewife. Paula begrudged the time spent on domestic chores and balked at further training. Sympathetic to her situation, her father advised her to put up with her husband's shortcomings, since it was the wife's task to practice consideration. Paula observed that it was women who were tested in marriage. Men were permitted to remain the way they were. After her wedding, life felt tender. Later, family life became repressive, and she escaped to pursue her artistic career in Paris. She died at age thirty from childbirth complications, just when she was becoming the painter she longed to be.[59]

Coventry Patmore's poem "The Angel in the House" reflected the ideal English middle-class spouse. Such "angels in the house" were expected to care for all family relations. Even gifted women—Harriet Martineau, Florence Nightingale, and Beatrice Potter Webb—could not escape family duties and second-class status. Fathers required daughters to be at their disposal. Beatrice Potter, the only unmarried daughter in a wealthy family, nursed her father until the end of his life. When Vera Brittain's father called her home during the war to care for her mother, she complied, but resented the double standard that defined her nursing as less important than her brother's army service. Unlike others in her class, Brittain wanted more out of life than marriage, and she declined her first proposal because it would tie her to provincial life. Neighbors cruelly dismissed her interest in university study as "unnatural." They assured her mother that she should abandon all hope of finding Brittain a husband if she went to Oxford. Rebelling against the notion that women could obtain power only by acquiring a brilliant husband, Brittain adopted feminist views, believing that personal freedom and dignity were incompatible with economic dependence and social conformity.[60]

While it is tempting to focus on the felicity of middle-class couples such as the Pankhursts and Pethick Lawrences, many men felt entitled to women's social and sexual submissiveness. English society accepted an elegant bank balance as compensation for sexual brutality and venereal disease in marriage. Efforts to keep middle-class women sexually innocent meant that doctors did not inform wives of their husbands' venereal diseases, and this shadowy side of marriage ruined many women. French doctors routinely undertreated the wives of male syphilitic patients because it was inappropriate to disclose their husbands' syphilis. The "myth of male protectiveness" meant French wives were "protected" from the knowledge and treatment of syphilis, but not from its ravages.[61] Fearful of the health hazards in marriage, some radical feminists launched a moral crusade urging "Votes for Women and Chastity for Men" and cautioned women not to enter marriage blindfolded, stating that it was dangerous because men were not as chaste and clean-living as women.[62] Marriage might include venereal infection without any treatment for it.

Marriage and the Clerical Estate

Russian Orthodox and Anglican clerical families in the nineteenth century seemed less tyrannical than meshchanstvo ones, but less cozy than gentry-class ones. Dobroliubov found similarities between his clerical family life and the meshchanstvo "Kingdom of Darkness." Many Russian priestly families lived in poverty. The Tsarist budget allocated 10.5 million rubles for the Holy Synod, which was divided unequally among 90,000 priestly families with 589,000 members. Some families received 300 rubles a year, others nothing. Village clergy often lived in poverty, supporting themselves from fees charged for the sacraments of baptism, matrimony, and burial. Yet their fees created bad feelings between them and the peasantry. With increasing family size and a limited number of clerical appointments, the economic plight of this estate intensified in the second half of the century. Many clerical families experienced a severe status incongruity, defining themselves as personal nobility while their incomes reduced them to peasant status. Their precarious economic situation stemmed partly from endogamous marriages that provided no opportunity to improve family fortunes through marriage to wealthy merchants or peasants. Daughters were often pawns in a system whereby their father's parish was offered as a dowry. Praskovaia Ivanovskaia remembered her childhood in a poor priestly household as one of neglect and indigence, orphaned by her mother's death and ignored by her father. A family friend funded her education at the Tula church school, where she developed a taste for the radical literature that circulated in the provinces in the 1860s.[63]

In Vitebsk, Sofia Kovalevskaia knew clerical families torn apart by children's demands for higher education and new life. Local seminary students were often influenced by the radical ideas of the 1860s. The preponderance of adult women (134,000) to men (120,000) in impoverished priestly families meant many daughters could not hope to marry. Some attended diocesan schools and became elementary-school teachers in rural areas. Some became feldshers or doctors.[64] Some, such as Praskovaia Ivanovskaia and Konkordia Gromova, became revolutionaries.

Many English clerical families also lived in genteel poverty similar to that of Russian priests. Daughters often sought higher education and professional employment because their fathers could not afford dowries for them and because of the scarcity of eligible husbands in their circle. Daughters in Russian and English priestly families were often sensitive to social injustice and active in reform movements. Margaret Llewelyn Davies (1861–1944) exemplified this kind of English woman. Born into an Anglican and Unitarian family, she studied at Queens College, London, and Girton College, Cambridge. She devoted her life to working-class women and the cooperative movement. In 1899, she became general secretary of the Women's Cooperative Guild and directed its social, political, and educational activities. In 1915 she published *Maternity: Letters from Working Women* to pressure the government to provide maternity coverage as part of the national health service. She also advocated suffrage and divorce reform.[65]

Upper-Class Women

The economic position of many Russian gentry-class families declined following the emancipation of the serfs in 1861, and women outnumbered men in that estate. Despite these problems, most noblewomen married and led fairly traditional lives. The 1897 census reveals that 318,214 or 56% of noblewomen over the age of twenty were married, 134,664 or 22% were widowed, and less than 1% were divorced. That left 110,000 single women with a need to provide for themselves. Since the English, French, and German censuses were not class-based, the civil status of upper-class women in those countries is unknown. Russian and English women generally had lower divorce rates than French or German women. For 10,000 marriages in the 1880s there were 19 divorces in England, 22 in Russia, but 152 in Germany and 127 in France.[66] Divorce was usually expensive and troublesome. Men could divorce on the basis of adultery alone, but women had to prove additional causes such as desertion, cruelty, sodomy, incest, or bigamy. Fathers had legal guardianship of minor children, and mothers feared losing their children if they divorced.

Novels sometimes illustrated the problems of marriage and divorce. Tolstoy's heroine in *Anna Karenina* would have lost her beloved son Seryozha if she had divorced her husband Karenin and married her lover Vronsky, yet she faced social ostracism for leaving her family to live openly with Vronsky. The English aristocracy accepted infidelity, as long as people were discreet. In *The Edwardians*, Vita Sackville-West describes Lord T., who wants to divorce his wife for infidelity but who is told that only the vulgar divorce. He later threatens his wife with divorce if she does not renounce her lover and court life. Bound by convention, she sacrifices the young man she loves because the scandal of divorce is worse than a broken heart.[67]

Tolstoy suggests that unhappily married women put up with philandering husbands. In *Anna Karenina*, Dolly Oblonskaia is humiliated by her husband's liaisons with household servants, but she does not think of divorcing him. Grudgingly she accepts the double standard, lamenting: "I do not respect him. He is necessary to me . . . I put up with him."[68] Likewise, Caleb Garth in George Eliot's *Middlemarch* warns his daughter that a woman has to "put up" with the life her husband makes for her. Women often served as pawns of the male relatives who married them off for family benefit. Having endured an unhappy arranged marriage, the French writer George Sand (pen name of Aurore Dudevant, 1803–1876) cautioned husbands against mistreating their wives and called for the right to divorce. She did not think people should divorce lightly, but she preferred spending the rest of her life in jail to remarriage.[69]

While most gentry-class families practiced endogamous marriage based on economic arrangements, romantic notions of marriage also flourished. While young people thought marriage brought happiness, Praskovia Tatlina felt marriage had destroyed her. She had heard of passionate love, but she had never experienced it. She educated her daughter so she would not have to marry, but her daughter embraced George Sand's notions of romantic love and married against her mother's advice.[70] The position of many married Russian gentry-class women resembled that of their European sisters. Marriage bound them to obey and cohabit with their husbands. Still, primogeniture was not the rule in Russia as in Europe, and daughters could inherit land as well as movable property. In upper-class families, land was normally divided among all children, although daughters usually received smaller portions than sons did. Russian women had de jure, if not de facto, control of their property after marriage, whereas European women seldom did.

Aristocratic English women sometimes managed to preserve an allowance for themselves in prenuptial marriage agreements. Yet, until the Married Women's Property Acts of the 1870s and 1880s, most English women, like their European sisters, lost control of their property and earnings upon marriage. French and German laws provided for communal property in marriage but allowed the husband to administer it, effectively nullifying the wife's rights. Profligate husbands often squandered their wives' property. Although Russian gentry-class women possessed legal protection and power within marriage, when they sought redress against unscrupulous husbands, society often condemned them.

Russian women experienced a special form of legal subjection, through the government's internal passport system, that European women experienced only through custom. The Tsarist government required a male guardian to authorize the passports of minors, women, and peasants whenever they moved from one place to another, entered a university, or took a job. The endorsement of passports could exacerbate power struggles as young people broke away from parental control in the 1860s.

The norm in Russian and European societies was for upper-class women to marry, and most did. The popularity of household and child-rearing manuals indicates women's desire to be good wives and mothers. Prior to the 1890s, women often had large families and sometimes lost children in infancy, but then they began using birth control and having smaller families. Like women in other classes, some encountered a gap between their romantic dreams and the struggles of married life. Tatyana Kuzminskaya observed the morbid jealousy of her sister Sonia and brother-in-law Leo Tolstoy. Sonia did not go to balls because Tolstoy did not approve of married women wearing low-cut gowns. Indeed, Sonia Tolstaya (1844–1919) was pregnant for sixteen consecutive years. After her first child was born, Tolstoy refused to allow her to use a wet nurse to feed the baby despite her childbirth illness. Thus, aristocratic women were not free of struggles and nightmares. Like their middle-class sisters, upper-class women were expected to perform their household duties effortlessly. In her youth, it appeared to Kuzminskaya that everything was being done inconspicuously and easily.[71] In retrospect, she noticed how much trouble and care a hostess expended to feed and accommodate everyone, and how much extra work the maids had to do.

Russia

In the early nineteenth century, Russian writers Evdokiia Rostopchina (1811–1858), Nadezhda Durova (1783–1866), and Karolina Pavlova (1807–1893) condemned arranged marriages and complained about the shallowness of life. During the reign of Alexander I (1801–1825), Nadezhda Durova expressed her disdain for gentry-class married life by fleeing her family and living as a cavalry officer. Serving with distinction during the Napoleonic Wars, she left military life only at the insistence of her invalid father. Her memoirs (1837) never discuss her roles as wife and mother, but concentrate on how military life allowed her to lead a free, adventurous, and satisfying life—one normally reserved for men. Her rejection of sexual stereotypes showed other women how exciting life could be. In one passage she addresses young women, saying: "You, who must account for every step, can comprehend the joyous sensations I feel at the sight of vast forests, fields, and streams and at the thought that I can roam them with no fear of prohibition."[72]

The poet Iuliia Zhadovskaia (1824–1883) complained of the boredom, pettiness, and gossip of high society. She abhorred surface beauty and empty minds.[73] In a similar vein, Evdokia Rostopchina criticized Russian society for crushing true love and valuing gold instead. Her marriage into an aristocratic family provided her access to high society, but not personal happiness. In the 1840s, she attributed women's alienation, isolation, and disillusionment to arranged marriages, which she condemned. Her disenchantment deepened when she returned from Europe to discover she was no longer the darling of the literary circles. Her poem "Song of Return" asked: "Who greets my arrival with a blessing? Who needs me? Whose melancholy glance seeks me with desire and longing?. . . Two years have passed without me, and what of it?"[74]

Around the same time, Karolina Pavlova attacked women's subordinate position in *A Double Life* (1844–1847). A dream spirit tells her heroine that marriage will destroy her creativity and warns:

> Get used to a different path
> and learn the strength of the weak. . . .
> Learn as a wife, the suffering of a wife,

Know that, submissive, she
Should not seek the path
To her own dreams, her own desires . . .
That her duty is implacable,
That all her soul is in his power,
That even her thoughts are fettered.[75]

In her own marriage, Pavlova discovered that her husband had squandered her dowry on his gambling debts. When she asked the Third Section (secret police of Tsar Nicholas I) to investigate the misuse of her money, Moscow society shunned her. Consequently, as soon as her son was old enough to attend Moscow University, she left Russia to work as a translator in Dresden, Germany. There, fate smiled on her in middle age, when she fell in love with a young law student who inspired some of her best poetry.[76]

Avdotia Panaeva (1819–1893) also laments women's lot in *Women's Fate* (1852). She argues that women need better education to prevent oppression, degradation, abandonment, and exploitation by unscrupulous men. She dedicates her book to young people, who she hopes will change society.[77]

After the 1860s, some enterprising gentry-class women made interesting lives for themselves outside marriage. Both single and married women rejected provincial life and went to St. Petersburg to study and prepare for careers in teaching, medicine, music, and writing. Some contracted "fictitious marriages" (ones in name only) with an obliging "spouse" who endorsed their passports so they could pursue higher education or obtain employment. Marriages of convenience were often egalitarian, modeled on Nikolai Chernyshevsky's heroine Vera Pavlova, who strives for self-development and social usefulness in *What Is to Be Done?* (1861).[78]

Europe

While most English women accepted the values of their society, some felt alienated. In 1852, Florence Nightingale (1820–1910) penned a bitter critique of English social life, arguing that "a man gains everything by marriage: he gains a 'helpmeet,' but a woman does not." Lamenting the midday "Sacred Sacrament of Dinner," which interrupted her work, she found her time was not her own. A "lady" had to continually make herself available to others, losing sight of her own vision in caring for others. She found high society indifferent to women's minds and hearts, interested only in their bodies. Her writing was so bitter that friends persuaded her not to publish it.[79]

At times, the social investigator Beatrice Potter Webb (1858–1943) agreed with the French radical Madeleine Pelletier's view of marriage as moral suicide. At other times, she desired the "restfulness of an abiding love," longed to be a mother, and yearned for the status of a well-married woman. Infatuated with the politician Joseph Chamberlain in the 1880s, she speculated about whether marriage to a great man would give her a bigger role to play in world affairs than would life as a spinster. After discussing marriage with Chamberlain in 1884, she realized that he desired servility in a woman and that, if she let her passion control her life, she would be absorbed in the life of a man whose aims were not hers.[80]

Yet life without love produced years of depression, and Webb wailed: "God knows celibacy is as painful to a woman . . . as it is to a man. It could not be more painful than it is to a woman." Fighting her sexual impulses and weakness, she implored: "God preserve me from a lover between thirty-five and forty-five. No woman can resist a man . . . during the last years of an unrealized womanhood."[81] Yet marriage proposals did not tempt her to destroy her "self" for the mere possibility of happiness. Susceptible to the charm of being loved, she did not think herself capable of loving. Despite two years of courtship, her work remained more attractive than Sidney Webb. Eventually, she decided that work and marriage were not mutually exclusive. Since marrying Sidney meant downward social mobility, she married after her father's death. Yet she had a long marriage, devoting herself to Fabian Socialism, eugenics, and pronatalism.[82]

After 1900, countless strong-minded English women married according to their convictions, not those of their parents. The beautiful, talented heiress Vita Sackville-West (1892–1962) married the penniless Harold Nicolson in 1912 over her parents' objections. When they suggested she marry a suitor possessing status and money, she ignored their pleas. Despite lesbian and homosexual liaisons, they had a happy fifty-year marriage.[83]

Career Women

Given women's subordination within marriage, many independent women chose careers instead. The journalist Harriet Martineau (1802–1876) believed herself psychologically unfit for marriage, saw disadvantages in it, and observed rare cases of conjugal love. She thought her business was to think, learn, and speak out with absolute freedom, which was incompatible with domestic duties. She found the single life the very best for her and considered herself the happiest woman in England.[84] Others experienced mixed emotions pursuing a career instead of marriage. Eliza Lynn Linton, a journalist, and Mary Kingsley (1862–1900), an explorer and ethnologist, masked their love of learning and desire for professional work from their families and themselves. They even urged other women to be domestic, while they pursued adventure. Combining marriage and career proved difficult, and few had both.[85] Small numbers of English career women married because the high emigration of middle-class men to the colonies destroyed their hopes for family life. Yet some unconventional ones combined marriage and career. Politically active women sometimes found marriage and professional work compatible. Emmeline Pethick Lawrence played an active role in the suffrage movement while married to a lawyer. Devoting herself to social causes, she had no children. Elizabeth Garrett Anderson (1836–1917) became a physician and developed her own ideas and causes. Moreover, she refused to resign her place on the London school board after her marriage in 1871. Another school board member, Florence Fenwich Miller, kept her own name when she married in 1877.[86] These, of course, were unusual career women.

The German government hired few women teachers and required celibacy of those it did. Only in France and Russia did appreciable numbers combine work and marriage. Forty percent of secular French female schoolteachers married, due to the value of motherhood in bourgeois society and the Catholic church. The declining birth rate made French politicians favor marriage and motherhood for all women, even teachers. Before World War I, it was disgraceful for a French woman not to marry; after the war it was merely a misfortune.[87]

French secondary-school teachers hated being neither *jeune fille* nor *femme*. While some became teachers because they lacked a dowry, many eventually married fellow educators. Conjugal life was hard because household responsibilities fell entirely upon the woman's shoulders. A third of French primary-school teachers married. Yet, if they hired a maid and wet nurse, their household economy became strained, and married life devolved into conflicts. Some preferred the status and coziness of married life apart from low-paid elementary-school positions.[88]

Both Russian and French village schoolmistresses faced obstacles in marrying. They did not want to experience downward mobility by marrying a peasant, nor could they marry tradesmen since they lacked a dowry. Yet marriage to an impoverished schoolteacher meant a life of struggle, so many shunned marriage altogether. Some found teaching so nurturing they felt no need to marry or have a family.[89]

Many educated women wanted romance and marriage but loved their work so much that they devoted themselves to full-time careers. The youthful, well-to-do Mariia Bashkirtseva (1860–1884) created a stir in Europe by adopting the unconventional life of an artist. She abhorred arranged marriages and wryly observed: "Commerce, traffic, speculation are honorable words properly applied, but sordid applied to marriage; yet they are the only words that justly describe French marriages."[90] Her Russian contemporaries Zinaida A. Vengerova and Anna Verbitskaia also rebelled against social conventions by becoming writers. Vengerova believed that Russian women already took an active part in social, intellectual, and professional life, so they did not need a feminist movement. Focusing on personal development, Vengerova and Bashkirtseva devoted themselves to the service of art and self-realization, free of women's roles within the family, society, or political movements.[91]

Unlike Bashkirtseva and Vengerova, the Russian mathematician Sofia Kovalevskaia felt depressed outside marriage and sought a romantic soulmate after the death of her husband. Yearning for love, she was convinced that men married beautiful singers and actresses, but not successful intellectuals like herself, because they found educated women threatening.[92] Settling for scholarship and friendship, she died young.

The French writer Sidonie Colette (1873–1954) also found marriage and career difficult to combine. Her first marriage (1893–1906) resulted in sexual, intellectual, and financial exploitation by her husband, Henri Gauthier Villars. He published her writings under his name and retained the copyright and income from them even after their divorce. She describes his infidelities and the service he required in *The Vagabond* (1910). She hated conjugal domesticity, which turned wives into nurses—e.g., tying her husband's tie, packing his suitcase, and cutting his toenails. Shattered by her first experience, she decided that while marriage might be the dream of a young girl ignorant of life, it was not for her. She refused to be dwarfed by a monogamous, bourgeois, home-loving paterfamilias.[93]

Colette wanted to have a life of her own, earn her own living, and handle her own money. While she had what it took to please and dazzle a man, she feared growing older and being rejected. At one point she weighed the benefits of lesbian love compared to married love. She appreciated women's delicate motherliness and skill in looking after people.[94] In 1910, she married again, but her husband's demands curbed her independence. A child kept them together for a while, but she was unwilling to subordinate her artistic self and divorced a second time.[95]

Dissatisfaction with marriage and noblesse oblige toward the peasants were two of the reasons that some gentry-class Russian women abandoned the role of angel in the house. Some became ministering angels as teachers and doctors, while others became avenging angels in revolutionary movements. They often invoked the "rhetoric of service" to make their employment and revolutionary activity respectable. Gentry-class women Ekaterina Breshko-Breshkovskaia (1844–1934) and Aleksandra Kollontai (1872–1952) forsook marriage, motherhood, and philanthropy in favor of revolutionary work to ameliorate the condition of the lower classes. In the mid- 1860s, Breshkovskaia realized that marriage and motherhood could not cure her ennui. Unhappy with her husband's liberalism, she left their estate and devoted the rest of her life to agrarian socialism. She endured repeated arrest, imprisonment, and exile to Siberia as a political prisoner.[96]

Decades later, Kollontai experienced similar crises in her married life, rejected her husband's liberalism, and became a socialist. She left her husband, entrusted her infant son to the care of her parents and servants, and traveled to Europe to study economics and politics. Upon completion of her studies, she returned to Russia, reclaimed her son, and served society by publishing critical articles and books from a socialist-feminist viewpoint. After 1900, Kollontai worked for the Social Democratic Party as a speaker, lecturer, and writer. In 1908, she accepted arrest, imprisonment, and exile in Western Europe until it was safe for her to return to her family, friends, and work in Russia in 1917.[97]

Socialists such as Nadezhda Krupskaia (1869–1939), Maria Golubeva (1861–1936), Konkordia Samoilova (1876–1921), Maria Kostelovskaia, and Tatiana Liudvinskaia combined marriage and party activity, but found it hard to reconcile motherhood and revolutionary work. So, while some gentry-class women criticized and rejected marriage, others did not necessarily find it incompatible with higher education, careers, or political activity.

Notes

1. Eva Figes, *Patriarchal Attitudes*, 20; James Albisetti, *Schooling German Girls and Women*, 188; Joanne Schneider, "Volksschullehrerinnen: Bavarian Women Defining Themselves through Their Profession," *The German Family*, 85; poem in *Englishwoman's Review*, Sept. 6, 1875, 429–30.

2. For conflicts English career women experienced, see Phyllis Crowell, "Studies in Contradictions: The Effects of Gender Ideology on Middle Class Women in Late Nineteenth Century England," M.A. thesis, University of Texas, El Paso, July 1996.

3. *Russia through Women's Eyes: Autobiographies from Tsarist Russia*, 24, 41.

4. *Russia through Women's Eyes*, 243, 255.

5. A. E. Ivanov, "Facty, Sobytiia, Liudi," *Voprosy Istorii* 1: 208-10; Christine Johanson, "Autocratic Politics, Public Opinion, and Women's Medical Education during the Reign of Aleksandr II, 1855-1881," *Slavic Review* 38: 426-43; H. P. Kennard, *The Russian Year Book, 1912*, 89-97; Varvara Kashevarova-Rudneva, *Russia through Women's Eyes*, 159, 171. Vernadskaia is quoted in Richard Stites, "Mikhailov and the Emergence of the 'Woman Question' in Russia," *Canadian Slavic Studies* 3 (2): 181, and in Carolina de Maegd-Soep, *The Emancipation of Women in Russian Literature and Society*, 49.

6. The most popular English manual, *Mrs. Beeton's Cookery and Household Management*, sold more than 2 million copies by 1870. In Germany Frau Davidis's *The Housewife: A Present for Future Housewives* went through sixteen editions by 1897. In France, Cora-Elisabeth Millet-Robinet's *La Maison rustique des dames* (*The Lady's Rustic Household*) went through twenty-one editions between 1844 and 1920. Ekaterina A. Avdeeva's Russian manuals *Guidance for Household Managers; Housewives, Housekeepers, and Cooks;* and *Pocket Cookbook* (nine editions by 1874) were also influential. In 1882, Catholic employers printed 150,000 copies of *Das Hausliche Gluck* (*Domestic Happiness*) for their workers; see Kathleen Canning, *Languages of Labor and Gender, Female Factory Work in Germany, 1850-1914*, 122.

7. Michael G. Mulhall, *Dictionary of Statistics*, 443; TsSK. *Obshchii svod po imperii rezultatov razrabotki dannykh pervoi vseobshchei perepisi naseleniia Rossiiskoi imperii 1897 g.* 2: 4 (hereafter cited as *Svod Perepisi 1897 g.*); France, *Resultats Statistiques de denombrement de 1896*, 56; *1906*, 16 (hereafter cited as *RSDRP*). The number of women for 1,000 men was 1,096 for Seine, 1,092 for Nord, and 1,082 for Gironde, but 874 for Meuse and 888 for Basses-Alpes.

8. "Introduction," *Svod Perepisi 1897 g.* 2: xii.

9. *Svod Perepisi 1897 g.* 2: iii; R. E. Johnson, "Mothers and Daughters in Urban Russia: A Research Note," *Canadian Slavonic Papers*, Sept. 1988, 374-77. In Central Asia, men predominated from age ten on. In 1897 there were 685,992 male Turko-Tatar speakers, but only 600,952 females. This 85,000 difference remained in all the older age cohorts. *Svod Perepisi 1897 g.* 1: 134-39; 2: 170-74. In 1926, men also predominated among Central Asian groups, and the Soviet census reported more men than women. So this was not an undercounting of women, but a structural aspect of society that eliminated women. *Perepisi 1926*, Kirgiz, 25: 208; Turkman, 33: 10; Uzbek, 32: 20; Kazakh, 25: 14.

10. M. V. Dovnar-Zapol'skii, *Issledovanie i stat'i*, 8-9 as cited in V. T. Kolokol'nikov," Marriage and Family Relations Among the Collective Farm Peasantry," *Soviet Sociology* 16 (3): 20-22; Christine Worobec, *Peasant Russia, Family and Community in the Post Emancipation Period*, 151–74; Mary Matossian, "The Peasant Way of Life," *Russian Peasant Women*, ed. Beatrice Farnsworth and Lynne Viola, 11-40; Elaine Elnett, *Historic Origin and Social Development of*

Family Life in Russia, 90-143; Geroid T. Robinson, *Rural Russia under the Old Regime*, 160-255; Henri Troyat, *Daily Life in Russia under the Last Tsar*, 215-25.

11. Olga Semyonova Tian-Shanskaia, *Village Life in Late Tsarist Russia*, xxviii; Tatyana A. Kuzminskaya, *Tolstoy as I Knew Him, My Life at Home and at Yasnaya Polyana*, 19; Anton Chekhov, "Peasants" (1897), Lev Tolstoy, "The Power of Darkness" (1886); Toby Clyman, "Women in Chekhov's Prose Works," Ph.D. diss., New York University, 1971.

12. Table X, *Svod Perepisi 1897 g.* 220; Dovnar-Zapol'skii, *Issledovanie i stati'*, 8–9, as quoted in Kolokol'nikov, "Marital and Family Relations among the Collective Farm Peasantry," 20–21; *Meme Santerre, A French Woman of the People*, told to Serge Grafteaux, 5, 7,41.

13. Peter Czap, "Marriage and the Peasant Joint Family in the Era of Serfdom," *The Family in Imperial Russia*, 104–5; Troyat, *Daily Life in Russia*, 204–5; Stephen M. Wolownik's notes for the record "'How the Mistress Met Ivan,' and Other Favorites," produced by Westminster Gold, ABC Records; Tian-Shanskaia, *Village Life*, 79–83; Isabel Hapgood, *Russian Rambles*, 188–89. Regarding ritualized grief, the author is indebted to lectures by Natalie Moyle on Slavic women at the Summer Slavic Laboratory, University of Illinois, 1989.

14. Collected and translated by Nora Waln in *Reaching for the Stars*, 177–89.

15. Cathy A. Frierson, "Razdel: The Peasant Family Divided," *Russian Peasant Women*, 75; William T. Shinn, Jr., "The Law of the Russian Peasant Household," *Slavic Review* 20: 612; Mark Harrison, "Resource Allocation and Agrarian Class Formation, The Problem of Social Mobility Among Russian Peasant Households, 1880–1930," *The Journal of Peasant Studies* 4 (1976–1977): 150.

16. Elnett, *Family Life in Russia*, 116–20; Hapgood, *Russian Rambles*, 188–89.

17. Cynthia Story Bisson, "Entre lui et sa femme: Domestic Violence in Nineteenth Century Provincial France," paper given at the 110th Annual Meeting of the American Historical Association, Atlanta, Georgia, January 7, 1996; Guy de Maupassant, "A Matter of Business," *Selected Tales*, 70–72; Carles, *A Life of Her Own*, 149.

18. Troyat, *Daily Life in Russia*, 204–5; Mikhail A. Il'in, *My Sister's Story*, 61; Aleksandr N. Engelgardt, Letter VII, *Letters from the Country, 1872–1887*, 167.

19. Worobec, "Customary Law and Property Devolution," *Canadian Slavonic Papers* 26: 232–33; Beatrice Farnsworth, "The Litigious Daughter-in-Law: Family Relations in Rural Russia in the Second Half of the Nineteenth Century," *Russian Peasant Women*, 95; Englegardt, *Letters from the Country,* 119; V. I. Lenin, *Razvitie Kapitalisma v Rossii*, 221–308; David L. Ransel, *Mothers of Misery*; Troyat, *Daily Life in Russia*, 101–7; Engelgardt, *Letters from the Country*, 113.

20. Mary Kelly, "Goddess Embroideries of Russia and the Ukraine," *Women's Art Journal*, Fall/Winter 1983, 10–13; "Goddess Embroideries Women's Heritage Rediscovered," Anthony Netting, "Images and Ideas in Russian Peasant Art," *The World of the Russian Peasant*, 169–91; Julie Vail Brown, "Female Sexuality and Madness in Russian Culture: Traditional Values and Psychiatric Theory," *Social Research*, 53: 369–85; Christine Worobec, "Temptress or Virgin? The Precarious Sexual Position of Women in Postemancipation Ukrainian Peasant Society," *Slavic Review*, Summer 1990, 227–28; Worobec, *Peasant Russia*, 122–49.

21. Damon Orlow, *Red Wedding*; Engelgardt, *Letters from the Country*, 119, 168.

22. Regarding infanticide and illegitimacy, see Worobec, *Peasant Russia*, 122–49; Ransel, *Mothers of Misery*, 99, 166–67; Tian-Shanskaia, *Village Life in Late Tsarist Russia*, 98–99; Orlow, *Red Wedding*; Tolstoy's "The Power of Darkness"; Guy de Maupassant, "The Story of a Farm-Girl," 73–84; Regina Schulte, "Peasants and Farmer's Maids, Female Farm Servants in Bavaria at the End of the Nineteenth Century," *The German Peasantry*, 158–71.

23. Worobec, "Customary Law and Property Devolution"; Robinson, *Rural Russia*, 163, 286; Hermann Schoenfeld, *Woman* 8: 384–86. Regarding their talent in composing and improvising songs as funeral mourners, see Schoenfeld, 384.

24. Lenin, *Razvitie Kapitalizma v Rossii*, 88-89; Hapgood, *Russian Rambles*, 191, 257-58; Webb, *New Dic. of Stat.*, 10; *The Russian Almanac*, 82-3; "Sotsialisticheskoe sel'skoe khoziaistvo Soiuza SSR," *Planovoe Khoziaistvo* 7: 163 (hereafter cited as *PKh.*).

25. The 1897 Russian census recorded 200,000 women who were blind, deaf, mute, or physically handicapped and presumably unmarriageable. See *Svod Perepisi 1897 g.* 2: 206–10. According to Johnson, many young peasant women migrated to the city and returned to the countryside with a dowry. High numbers of older women, especially childless widows, moved to and remained in the cities. See Johnson, "Mothers and Daughters." In a visit to Tula in the 1890s, the American Isabel Hapgood heard peasants complaining about priests who charged seven rubles for baptisms and weddings (Hapgood, *Russian Rambles*, 160).

26. Martha Bohachevsky-Chomiak, *Feminists Despite Themselves: Women in Ukrainian Community Life, 1884–1939*, 162; *Chislennost' i sostav' rabochikh' Rossii 1897 g.* 1: xvii, xviii, 8–13 (hereafter cited as *Chislennost' Rossii 1897 g.*); *Svod Perepisi 1897 g.* 1: 206–7; 2: 288; *RSDRP*, Tome IV, 418–19; Table XVII, *Annuaire Statistique* 20 (1900): 30–31 (hereafter cited as *An. Stat.*); *Stat. Jarbuch*, 35: 16–17; *P.P. vol. 97 Gt. Br. Census 1891*, 180; Clara Collet, "Statistics of Employment of Women and Girls," *Journal of the Royal Statistical Society*, Sept. 1895, 522–25 (hereafter cited as *JRSS*).

27. *Svod Perepisi 1897 g.* 1: xlvi; 2: xlvi–xlvii, 264–65; *An. Stat.* 30 (1910): 14; *Stat Jarbuch*, vol. 35.

28. *Chislennost' i sostav' rabochikh' v Rossii 1897 g.* 1: 10; *Meme Santerre*, 5-55.

29. Canning, *Languages of Labor*, 196–98, 314; Heilwig Schomerus, "The Family Life-Cycle," 183–86, *The German Family*; Lynn Abrams, "Concubinage, Cohabitation and the Law: Class and Gender Relations in Nineteenth-Century Germany," *Gender and History* 5 (Spring 1993): 89–100. Schomerus indicates that 65% of textile workers' children were born or conceived before marriage.

30. Table calculated from the following sources: *Chislennost' Rossii 1897 g.* 1: x, xi, 2-3; *An. Stat.* 20: 28–37; *Stat. Jarbuch* 35 (1914): 16–17; *P.P., vol. 97, Gt. Br. Census 1891*, 180.; B. L. Hutchins, "A Note on the Distribution of Women in Occupations," *JRSS*, Sept. 1904, 488.

31. Schomerus, "The Family Life-Cycle," 183–86; Abrams, "Concubinage, Cohabitation and the Law," 89–100; Canning, *Languages of Labor and Gender*, 263.

32. Lenin, *Razvitie Kapitalizma v Rossii*, 239, 283, 302-3, 394–95. The 1897

occupational census found 49% of women factory workers lived alone and 40% of female day laborers lived alone or outside a family. *Chislennost' i sostav' rabochikh v Rossii 1897 g.* 1: 3–11.

33. Werner Thonnessen, *The Emancipation of Women: The Rise and Decline of the Women's Movement in German Social Democracy 1863–1933*, 20–22; Eric Richards, "Women in the British Economy Since about 1700: An Interpretation," *History* 59 (October 1974): 343; H. J. Perkin, "Social Causes of the British Industrial Revolution," *Transactions of the Royal Historical Society* 5th Series, 123–44; Kathleen Woodward, *Jipping Street*, 16, 43; Rose Gamble, *Chelsea Child*; Dorothy Scannell, *Mother Knew Best*; Catherine Cookson, *Our Kate, An Autobiography*; Carl Chinn, *They Worked All Their Lives*, 29.

34. Woodward, *Jipping Street*, 16–17; Gamble, *Chelsea Child*, 47–48.

35. Mary Lynn Stewart, *Women, Work, and the French State*, vii, 50, 67, 199.

36. Madeleine Pelletier thought the church, the state, and men oppressed women, while Leonine Rouzade argued that motherhood more than capitalism doomed women to subordination. Marilyn Boxer, "French Socialism, Feminism, and the Family," *Troisième République* 1977 (3–4): 132, 137, 167; Boxer, "The Extraordinary Failure of Madeleine Pelletier," *European Women on the Left*, 51–74; Mrs. Layton, "Memories of Seventy Years," *Life As We Have Known It*, 32, 50; Letter 41 in *Maternity: Letters from Working Women*, 67–68.

37. Canning, *Languages of Labor*, 177, 196–98, 314; *Maternity: Letters from Working Women*, Letter 20: 45–46, 64, 85; Mrs. Layton, "Memories of Seventy Years," *Life As We Have Known It*, 32, 50, 238; *The German Worker: Working Class Autobiographies from the Age of Industrialization*, 23, 73, 366; Woodward, *Jipping Street*, xiv–xv, 17–19, 94–95.

38. Kathleen Dayus, *Her People*, 2, 4, 25, 54ff.

39. Stewart, *Women, Work, and the French State*, 50–52, 171–72; Mary Lynn McDougall, "Protecting Infants: The French Campaign for Maternity Leaves, 1890s–1913," *French Historical Studies* 13: 93–95; Dayus, *Her People*, xv–xx; *English Historical Documents, 1874–1914*, 607–8; Anna Davin, "Imperialism and Motherhood," *History Workshop* 5: 32. In Birmingham, 45% of the households in the central districts had incomes of less than a pound per week, and high rates of infant mortality only declined from 163/1,000 in 1898-99 to 105/1,000 in 1910.

40. Johnson, "Mothers and Daughters," 372–73; Ransel, *Mothers of Misery*, 167–71; Canning, *Languages of Labor*, 196–98; McDougall, "Protecting Infants: The French Campaign for Maternity Leaves, 1890s-1913," 104.

41. Harriet Taylor and John S. Mill, "The Enfranchisement of Women," *The Westminster and Foreign Quarterly Review* 55: 299; Frances Power Cobbe, "Wife-Torture in England," *Contemporary Review* 32: 55–87; Cobbe, "Criminals, Idiots, Women, and Minors: Is the Classification Sound?", 14–15; "Assault and Battery," *The Life and Writings of Ada Nield Chew*, 181–83; Woodward, *Jipping Street*, 4, 41; Vera Brittain, *Lady into Woman*, 24; Lynn Abrams, "Concubinage, Cohabitation, and the Law," 90–91; Cynthia Story Bisson, "Entre Lui et sa femme: Domestic Violence in Nineteenth-Century Provincial France"; Maxim Gorky, *My Childhood*.

42. For comments about the benefits of having baths installed at the pitheads, see *Life As We Have Lived It*, 136–40.

43. Harriet Martineau, "Brutality to Women," *London Daily News*, 8 September 1853, 4, reprinted in *Harriet Martineau on Women*, 221–24; Frances Cobbe, "Celibacy vs. Marriage," *Fraser's Magazine* 65 (Feb. 1862): 228–35; Barbara Caine, "Beatrice Webb and the 'Woman Question'," *History Workshop Journal*, Autumn 1982, 13: 29.

44. De Maupassant, "Was It a Dream?," *Selected Tales*, 104; Sibyl Meyer, "The Tiresome World of Conspicuous Leisure: On the Domestic Duties of the Wives of Civil Servants in the German Empire, 1871–1918," *Connecting Spheres*.

45. Alice Miller, *For Your Own Good: Hidden Cruelty in Child Rearing and the Roots of Violence*, 3–91; Ralf Dahrendorf, *Germany*, 54, 61–62; Gordon A. Craig, *Germany*, 207 ff.; Sagara, *A Social History of Germany*, 379, 408, 413; Toni Sender, *The Autobiography of a German Rebel*, 10–13; Dolores L. Augustine, "Arriving in the Upper Class: The Wealthy Business Elite of Wilhelmine Germany," *The German Bourgeoisie*, 46–75; Meyer, "The Tiresome Work of Conspicuous Leisure," 156–64. For Russian use of shame and guilt, see Jessica Tovrov, "Mother-Child Relationships among the Russian Nobility," *The Family in Imperial Russia*, 25–43.

46. See Catriona Kelly, "Teacups and Coffins: The Culture of Russian Merchant Women," 64–67, 71, in *Women in Russia and Ukraine*.

47. V. V. Pukirev's painting, "Neravnyi brak" (Unequal Marriage), 1862; Valentine Bill, *The Forgotten Class*, 189; A. Ostrovsky's plays, *The Storm* and *Poor Bride*; Karin Kaudelka-Hanisch, "The Titled Businessman: Prussian Commercial Councillors in the Rhineland and Westphalia during the Nineteenth Century," *The German Bourgeoisie*, 89, 98; Jo Burr Margadant, *Madame le Professeur: Women Educators in the Third Republic*, 138–49; Geoffrey Crossick and Heinz-Gerhard Haupt, *The Petite Bourgeoisie in Europe 1780–1914*, 87–90.

48. W. Bruce Lincoln, *In War's Dark Shadows*, 79; Dobroliubov, "Temnoe tsarstvo," *Sochinenii, Tom III*, 244–47; T.S., "Contemporary Life and Thought in Russia," 621; Bill, *The Forgotten Class*, 146–53; Jo Ann Ruchman, *The Moscow Business Elite, A Social and Cultural Portrait of Two Generations, 1840–1905*, 15–49; Elnett, *Family Life in Russia*, 29–36, 139; *Svod Perepisi 1897 g.* 1: 3; table VIII, 160-61; 2: 64-67; *Annuaire Statistique de la Russie, 1915*, 88 (hereafter cited as *An. Stat. Russie, 1915*); D. R. Brower, "Urban Revolution in the Late Russian Empire," *The City in Late Imperial Russia*, 325.

49. Dobroliubov, "Temnoe tsartsvo" (Kingdom of Darkness), 1859, and "Luch sveta v temnom tsarstve" (Ray of Light in the Kingdom of Darkness), 1860; *Sochinenii*, Tom III, 244–47, 495–520.

50. Gorky, *My Childhood*, 63-64; Fedor Dostoevsky, "A Gentle Creature," *The Best Short Stories of Dostoevsky*, 278 ff; Dostoevsky, *The Diary of a Writer*, 2: 690, 913–35.

51. Ostrovsky, *The Storm*; B. I. Pak, "Savva Timofeevich Morozov," *Soviet Studies in History* 20: 74–95; Bill, *The Forgotten Class*, 31–32; de Maupassant, "A Family Affair" and "Toine," *Selected Tales*, 119–33, 292–98.

52. Flora Tristan, *Promenades Dans Londres*, 262-70. Tristan was shocked that Englishwomen could not inherit if they had a brother or other close male relative.

53. Eliza Lynn Linton, "The Girl of the Period," *Saturday Review*, 14 March 1868, as quoted in Janet Murray, *Strong Minded Women*, 42–44.

54. Old Believers rejected the reforms of Patriarch Nikon in the seventeenth century. For nineteenth century, see T. S., "Contemporary Life and Thought in Russia," 599–624; Dobroliubov, "Temnoe tsartsvo," *Sochenenii* 3: 28; D. V. Sarabianov and N. L. Adashkina, *Popova*, 12–13, 41; Anna P. Ostroumova-Lebedeva, *Avtobiograficheskii Zapiski*, 48–86.

55. See Il'in, *My Sister's Story,* 77–79, 198–99.

56. Georges Dupaux, *La Societé Française 1789-1970*, 97; Theodore Zeldin, *Conflicts in French Society,* 14–15; Jean Flandrin, *Families in Former Times*, 118–73.

57. Joanna Richardson, *Judith Gautier, A Biography*, 110. During her marriage, her husband had five children with his mistress but none with her. See also Pelletier, *Le Célibat état supérieur*; Colette, *The Vagabond*, 431; Simone de Beauvoir, *A Very Easy Death*, 34, 36, 43. Simone's mother stopped seeing her own friends, whose husbands her spouse found boring. Many evenings M. de Beauvoir wined and dined elsewhere, depriving the family of money and his wife of companionship.

58. Emmeline Pankhurst, *My Own Story, The Suffragettes*, 12; Emmeline Pethick Lawrence, *My Part in a Changing World*, 61, 65, 345–46. It is surprising that Pankhurst's "happy marriage" occupied only two paragraphs of her 400-page autobiography.

59. Paula Modersohn Becker, *The Letters and Journals*, 216, 242, 249, 254, 255.

60. Vera Brittain, *Lady into Woman*, 27–28; Brittain, *Testament of Youth*, 33–35, 72–73, 181–82, 261.

61. Brittain, *Testament of Youth*, 182, 405; Jill Harshin, "Syphilis, Wives, and Physicians: Medical Ethics and the Family in Late Nineteenth Century France," *French Historical Studies*, 16: 73, 75.

62. Quoted by Andrew Rosen in *Rise Up, Women!*, 207.

63. *Statesman's Year Book*, 1885; Theophile Gautier, "Russia;" *Russia*, 182–83; *Svod Perepisi 1897 g.*, 2: 191; Praskovaia Ivanovskaia, in Barbara Alpern Engel and Clifford N. Rosenthal, *Five Sisters: Women Against the Tsar*, 95–101; Gregory Freeze, "Caste and Emancipation: The Changing Status of Clerical Families in the Great Reforms" in *The Family in Imperial Russia*, 124–50.

64. Sofia Kovalevskaia, *Vospominaniia detstva*, 81–83; *Svod Perepisi 1897 g.* 2: 236–37; Ben Eklof, "The Adequacy of Basic Schooling in Rural Russia: Teachers and Their Craft, 1880–1914," *History of Education Quarterly* 26: 201–4.

65. "Margaret L. Davies," *Dictionary of Labour Biography* 2: 96–99.

66. *Svod Perepisi 1897 g.* 1: 217; 2: 3, 190, 200; Mulhall, *Dictionary of Statistics*, 217.

67. Vita Sackville-West, *The Edwardians*, 111, 152–95.

68. Tolstoy, *Anna Karenina*, 661.

69. Georges Sand, "Letter to Hippolyte Chatiron, February, 1843" and "Letter to Abbe Lamennais," February 28, 1837, as quoted and translated by Joseph Barry in *George Sand In Her Own Words*, 419, 407; also, Sand, *Indiana*.

70. For the importance of love in gentry-class marriages, see Jessica Tovrov, "Mother-Child Relationships Among the Russian Nobility," *The Family in Imperial Russia*, 15–43. For descriptions of gentry-class entertainments where endogamous marriages were often contracted, see Kuzminskaya, *Tolstoy as I Knew Him*,

336. For accounts of strong-minded women, see *Russia Through Women's Eyes*, especially Praskovia Tatlina, 255–73.

71. Kuzminskaya noted that her mother had thirteen children and lost five in infancy. Her sister Sonia had sixteen children and lost nine. Kuzminskaya, *Tolstoy as I Knew Him*, 27, 234–36, 360, 374–75; Isabel Hapgood, *Russian Rambles*, 199. Gentry-class radicals Breshkovskaia and Kollontai had only one child each before leaving their husbands and becoming full-time revolutionaries.

72. See Nadezhda Durova, *The Cavalry Maiden, Journals of a Russian Officer in the Napoleonic Wars*, ix–xxxiii, 32.

73. As quoted in V. I. Belinsky, *Vzgliad na russkuiu literaturu 1846 g.* 36, and as translated in "A View on Russian Literature in 1846," *Selected Philosophical Works*, 378.

74. Evdokiia Rostopchina, "Chiny i Dengi" (Rank and Money), *Sochineniia*, Tom vtorai, 1–38; her poem "Pesnia Vozvrata" (Song of Return) in V. F. Khodasevich, *Stati o Russkoi poezii*, 37 (my translation). See "Rank and Money" in Helena Goscilo, *Russian and Polish Women's Fiction*, 44–84.

75. Karolina Pavlova, "'Dvoinaia Zhizn'," in *Polnoe Sobranie Stikhotvorenii*, 276, and as translated by Barbara H. Monter in *A Double Life*, 65–66.

76. Munir Sendich, "Karolina Pavlova: A Survey of Her Poetry, *Russian Literature Triquarterly* 3: 229–47; "Twelve Unpublished Letters of Karolina Pavlova to Alexey Tolstoy," *RLT* 9: 546–47. See also Diana Greene, "Karolina Pavlova's 'At the Tea Table' and the Politics of Class and Gender," *The Russian Review* 53: 281–82.

77. Antonia Glasse, "The Formidable Woman: Portrait and Original," *Russian Literature Triquarterly* 9: 423–32; Jehanne Gheith, "Evgeniia Tur and Avdot'ia Panaeva—The Precursors?" a paper presented at the AAASS, November 1992; Marina Ledkovsky, "Avdotya Panaeva: Her Salon and Her Life," *RLT* 9: 423–31.

78. "Varvara Kashevarova-Rudneva, M.D.," "Emiliia Pimenova," and "Anastasiia Verbitskaia," in Clyman, *Russia Through Women's Eyes*, 158–85, 311–34, 335–80; Eklof, "Basic Schooling in Rural Russia," *History of Education Quarterly* 26 (2): 201–4.

79. Florence Nightingale, *Cassandra*, as printed in Ray Strachey, *The Cause: A Short History of the Women's Movement in Great Britain*, 395, 399–408.

80. *Diary of Beatrice Webb, Vol. I, 1873–1892*: 2 October 1890, 342; 25 May 1889, 84, 115, 117; 12 January 1884, 102; 16 March 1884, 111–12; 9 May 1884, 118. Several years after writing these emotional entries, Beatrice Potter married Sidney Webb in 1892.

81. See *Diary of Beatrice Webb, Vol. I*, 7 March 1889, 275; 5 May 1889, 284; 30 September 1899, 300; 1 December 1890, 346.

82. *Diary of Beatrice Webb*, 1 December 1890, 345; 19 August 1891, 362; 28 August 1888, 260; Anna Davin, "Imperialism and Motherhood," *History Workshop* 5: 10, 18.

83. Nigel Nicolson, *Portrait of a Marriage*, 88–89. Vita's mother remarks in her diary: "It is not at present a good marriage . . . . there is no money . . . ."

84. Harriet Martineau, "The Single Life," *Harriet Martineau on Women*, 78–80.

85. For an excellent discussion of women's need to mask their love of education and professional work, see Crowell, "Studies in Contradictions."

86. Annmarie Turnbull, "So extremely like Parliament': The Work of the Women Members of the London School Board, 1870–1904," *The Sexual Dynamics of History*, 125, 129.

87. Joanne Schneider, "Volksschullehrerinnen: Bavarian Women Defining Themselves Through Their Profession," 93–94; Margadant, *Madame le Professeur*, 138–45; Steven Hause and Anne Kenny, *Women's Suffrage and Social Politics in the French Third Republic*, 202.

88. Margadant, *Madame le Professeur*, 138–45; Leslie Page Moch, "Government Policy and Women's Experience: The Case of Teachers in France," *Feminist Studies* 14: 301–21.

89. Christine Ruane, "The Vestal Virgins of St. Petersburg: Schoolteachers and the 1897 Marriage Ban," *The Russian Review* 50: 163–82.

90. *Journal de Marie Bashkirtseff*, Tome Second, entry for Thursday, October 30, 1879, 153; *The Journal of a Young Artist 1860–1884*, 213.

91. Zinaida Vengerova, "La Femme Russe," *Revue des Revues*, 15 September 1897, 489–99, reprinted as "Feminizm i zhenskaia svoboda," *Obrazovaniye* 5-6: 73–90; Charlotte Rosenthal, "Zinaida Vengerova: Modernism and Women's Liberation," *Irish Slavonic Studies* 8: 100–3.

92. Anna Carlotta Leffler, Duchess of Cajanello, *Biography of Sofia Kovalevskaia*, 266–68.

93. Sidonie Colette, *The Vagabond* in *The Colette Omnibus*, 376–77, 382.

94. Colette, *The Vagabond*, 403, 413.

95. Margaret Davies, "Colette," *Dictionary of Literary Biography*, 65: 45–51.

96. Katherine Breshkovskaia, *Hidden Springs of the Russian Revolution*, 8-30; *The Little Grandmother of the Russian Revolution, Reminiscences and Letters of Catherine Breshkovsky*, 19–26, 30–31.

97. Kollontai, *Iz Moei Zhizni i Raboty*, 64-126; *Slavnye Bolshevichki*, 75–77, 193–97, 213–15.

Chapter 2

Education in the Late Nineteenth Century

Gender, class, nationality, and religion affected education in the late nineteenth century. Few peasant or working-class women aspired to higher education, as many bourgeois women did. More Russian than European women obtained higher education prior to World War I, perhaps because of the support they received from liberal and radical Russian men who generally sanctioned their education and their work in the helping professions among the lower classes. Yet they encountered obstacles to entering the civil service. Indeed, their pursuit of higher education often involved long journeys to foreign countries. Beginning in the 1870s, scores of Russian women traveled to Europe to study medicine and art. While European women struggled to obtain higher education and careers, some English women feared that higher education would make them mannish. Still, their greatest problem remained the double standard, since their societies valued and invested more in men's education than in women's.

The educational desires of middle- and upper-class women in the nineteenth century are fascinating and fairly well known. However, those of peasant and working-class women also merit study in order to have a fuller picture of women's educational situation. Just as societies constructed social roles for women in the nineteenth century, they also inculcated feelings of class and gender inferiority. Yet Russian and French middle- and upper-class women seemed to suffer less from this than did English and German women. A Royal Schools Inquiry Commission of 1864 study of English middle-class education concluded that parents generally believed girls "less capable of mental cultivation" than boys; since daughters would marry, they need not be as well educated as sons. English and German middle-class society believed that intellectual training made women unfeminine. Some English parish schools excluded girls because educators thought they lowered the tone. Growing up in patriarchal families, many middle-class English girls internalized their subordinate status. Many famous English women writers remained convinced in adulthood that they could never be the intellectual equals of men.[1]

Social and familial educational expectations were extremely low for most peasant and working-class girls. Their formal schooling was limited, but they received informal instruction at home. Mothers trained daughters to cook, clean, sew, knit, and care for other siblings. European social reformers often thought working-class girls lacked proper housekeeping skills, and a domestic science movement arose to improve them. In France, primary-school inspectors reprimanded teachers for not emphasizing domesticity for the nation's future wives and mothers, and science lessons in girls' schools devolved into homemaking.[2]

The French feminist Madeleine Pelletier was unique in advocating a virile education for girls. She suggested girls be raised like their brothers, be given cold baths, simple food, physical exercise, and pantaloons to wear under their dresses for freedom of motion. She thought girls would become stronger if they played the same games as boys and more vigorous if given masculine-sounding names like Renée and Andrée. She also advised reading about heroines like Joan of Arc. She warned against raising girls as coquettes or inculcating them with notions of female inferiority.[3]

European governments provided vocational schools for boys in the nineteenth century, but not for girls. Considering education a requirement for citizenship and greater industrial prosperity, European governments made primary schooling for children compulsory in the 1870s. Most children attended school and learned to read and write. England and France had 5 million elementary-school children by 1900, while Germany had 8 million, and Russia, which had a much greater population, had only 4 million. While 90% of adults in England, France, and Germany were literate by 1900, less than 30% of Russians were.[4]

Civic leaders did not link education and upward social mobility. Secondary education remained a preserve of middle- and upper-class children, and university education a perquisite of upper-class men. Only teacher-training schools reflected little gender and class bias. In France, ninety of these schools existed for men in 1887 and eighty-one for women.[5] In England there were several hundred teacher-training colleges sponsored by the universities, local education authorities, the Church of England, and other churches. By 1900, women predominated in these colleges. Unlike European governments, the Tsarist regime was autocratic and did not think elementary education appropriate for the lower orders. Consequently, gentry- and middle-class children received elementary and secondary education, but only a small proportion of peasant children attended school. The policy of Russification (instruction in Russian, not children's native language) stymied the education of minorities in the Empire until 1905, when native languages were permitted.

While compulsory education tended to equalize the literacy rates of European men and women, significant differences persisted in Tsarist Russia. According to the 1897 Imperial Russian Census, 18 million men but only 8 million women were literate. Class, nationality, religion, and geography also affected education. Thus, 70% of gentry-class women were literate, 67% of those in the clerical estate, 31% in the city estates, but only 9% of peasant women. Women in European Russia were only 13.7% literate (due to the high proportion of peasant women), whereas in the Germanized Baltic and Westernized Polish provinces it was 27%. The lowest literacy rates were among those in the Caucasus (6%), Siberia (5%), and Central Asia (2%). In terms of religion, over 60% of Lutheran women were literate, a proportion very close to that of Lutheran men. Jewish women had aggregate literacy rates of 28%, Polish Catholic women 29%, Russian Orthodox women 9%, and Muslim women 5%.[6]

Peasant Women

Most peasant women in the Russian Empire received training from their mothers in performing household tasks. Few received formal schooling, and most were illiterate. Yet this was not necessarily a terrible misfortune. Since the Orthodox Church focused on the liturgy, not Bible reading, literacy was not crucial for peasant religious life. Peasants generally utilized their children's labor in the family economy and took a functional attitude toward education. They valued the ability to read and calculate but shunned efforts by liberal educators to alter their way of life.[7] Since male heads of household read important documents, literacy was more important for men than women.

Unlike Slavic girls, rural German girls normally attended village schools. Yet neither they nor their families thought of upward social mobility. A turn-of-the-century German domestic servant's autobiography reflected her desire for more humane treatment by her employer, not aspirations for higher education.[8] The 1906 French census indicates lower literacy rates among agricultural women workers (83%) than among urban women. Although the new educational law of 1880 abolished tuition fees, many peasant families lacked money for books and other school supplies. Inadequate clothing and poor roads kept many from attending school. Some lived in isolated or mountainous regions far from village schools.[9] Language could also impede education. Some spoke not French but Breton, Basque, Gascon, Flemish, or even German. This hindered their learning, since textbooks and instruction were in French. Some English children also encountered language problems at school. In the midlands, Yorkshire might be spoken at home and on the school grounds, while pupils had to speak, read, and write standard English in the classroom. Russification policies made learning problematic for most ethnic groups in the Russian Empire. Another similarity to the situation in France was the great distance between school and home in rural areas in the Russian Empire. Over half the women aged twenty to twenty-nine in the city of Kiev could read and write in 1897, but only 6% of young women in the rural Kiev district were literate.[10]

Few Russian peasant women dreamed of higher education, but 103 had obtained it by 1897. Most of them lived in cities, an indication that they had really shed their peasant status. While the Tsarist government tried to train peasant women as midwives to reduce maternal and infant mortality in the countryside, middle- and upper-class women predominated in midwifery schools. Peasants constituted only 25% of midwife trainees in 1910. Yet Nadezhda Suslova, the daughter of well-to-do peasants, became a doctor. She traveled to St. Petersburg, where she studied medicine until 1863. Then she studied at the University of Zurich, from which she graduated in 1865, not only as a medical doctor but also with a Ph.D. in medicine. Whether higher education represented a dream and a way out of humdrum, harsh peasant life is uncertain, but census figures indicate that few in that estate obtained higher education and still remained in the countryside. Like their European sisters, most peasants in the Russian Empire knew that their labor in the family economy took priority over school.[11]

Likewise, few European farm girls dreamed of higher education. Most became housewives or traveled to urban areas to work as domestic servants to support themselves and contribute to their family's economy. Occasionally, bright French girls pursued higher education, despite their parents' low educational expectations. Such an exception was Emilie Carles, whose village teacher and district school inspector encouraged her to become a primary-school teacher. Initially, her father refused, saying she had to earn her keep. School officials arranged a scholarship for Carles in the nearby town of Briançon, but she had to complete her share of household and farm chores to placate her envious siblings. Although she was offered additional scholarship aid, she had to stop with the brevet license for elementary teaching in 1916 because her father insisted she take over the household duties.[12]

Working-Class Girls

Girls in urban households had greater access to education than did those in rural areas. In 1897, 35% of working-class girls in the Russian Empire were literate. While they lagged behind their more literate European cohorts, they surpassed their peasant sisters. Working-class parents often regarded girls' education as less important than boys'. Like peasant households, working-class families required daughters' participation in the family economy. Russian and European school investigators found that urban families were much more likely to keep daughters than sons at home to help in household work and production. Moscow school questionnaires returned by parents in 1910 revealed that they desired further education for their daughters only if it was affordable or free.[13] Provision of elementary education in the Russian Empire varied according to the willingness of city governments to tax themselves. At the turn of the century, civic-minded local authorities in provincial cities supported more elementary schools than the capital did. St. Petersburg had 1,805 elementary schools, but Kharkov, Kiev, Odessa, Kazan, Warsaw, and Riga all had a thousand more, and Moscow three times as many. Still, half of Moscow's school-age children and large proportions of those in other cities in the empire remained unschooled prior to World War I.[14]

Low educational and employment expectations for working-class girls were not unique to Russia. A questionnaire filled out by 2,000 Parisian schoolgirls in 1877 revealed that the overwhelming majority wanted to augment their families' incomes by working as seamstresses. By the age of thirteen or fourteen, two-thirds of school-age girls were already working and no longer attending school. Most pupils expected to become *ouvrières* (unskilled workers). Only the daughters of better-off families could afford to remain in school after the age of thirteen.[15]

A similar mentality existed among English and German children, who also left school at young ages in order to contribute to household income. In 1880, the school-leaving age in England was ten, rising to twelve by 1899.

Schoolteachers often encouraged working-class children to attend grammar school, but family needs and peer pressure often undermined such plans. Yet several thousand working-class girls and boys were able to become pupil teachers. This apprenticeship began at the age of thirteen, and many were able to earn some money for their families and pursue higher education at the same time. When the age level for pupil teachers rose to seventeen, however, fewer working-class girls were able to stay in school until that age before contributing to the family income. By the time of the First World War, even fewer working-class girls were able to obtain secondary or teacher-training scholarships. It was then that the daughters of skilled workers and the lower middle classes, whose families could afford to keep their children in school for longer periods, accepted scholarships for secondary education and teacher training. As they aged, many English women became functionally illiterate and unable to calculate simple arithmetic.[16]

The German socialist Lily Braun observed that poverty and class limited working-class children to primary school. Fourteen-year-olds supported themselves and contributed to their family's maintenance regardless of their intellectual ambition. For example, Ottilie Baader had to quit school and work as a seamstress to help her family survive in Berlin. Girls reflected the norms of their societies in placing the needs of the household above their own. Internalizing their low class and gender status, they often gave up school for a job, when their family required their wages. English girls often began working at age twelve to help support their families.[17]

The educational pattern that emerged was that Russian society sacrificed working-class girls' elementary education, and European societies their secondary schooling. Although French secondary education became more available to girls after 1881, few peasant or working-class girls took advantage of that opportunity due to family obligations and low expectations. Few took advantage of scholarships to study at normal schools in their *département*. Since schools reproduced social inequality, some socialists subordinated educational issues to the revolution, thinking that only after the socialist revolution would a new form of education become available to working-class children.[18]

Middle- and Upper-Class Girls

Low family educational expectations produced a sizable gender gap for middle- and upper-class girls, compared with boys. German and English families often believed girls' mental development and marriageability were incompatible. According to Harriet Martineau, English society feared that educating women would make them mannish and forced women to hide their intellectual work. She heard that novelist Jane Austen kept a piece of needlework nearby so that she could cover up her manuscripts whenever visitors arrived. In Martineau's generation, young ladies could not study openly. They were expected to sew in the parlor to be available for callers. The double standard sanctioned men's studies and intellectual pursuits but not women's. Indeed, families often used even the most brilliant daughter as a domestic servant, nurse, or hostess if the need arose for their services.[19] Prior to World War I, rich families invested more money and thought in their sons' than their daughters' education. As a result, girls' educational dreams, opportunities, and attainments fell far short of those of their brothers, since they often internalized society's low expectations for them.

Russian and European families sometimes sheltered their daughters by employing governesses for them long after they sent their sons to private boarding schools or gymnasia. However, this ploy sometimes backfired. Aleksandra Kollontai's, Marina and Anastasiia Tsvetaeva's, and Virginia Woolf's governesses all turned out to be radicals who imbued their students with revolutionary and feminist ideas. While deficient in some areas, governesses often provided excellent language instruction. Russian families adopted different strategies for language acquisition. Some spoke French to each other three days of the week, English three days of the week, and Russian on Sundays. Some spoke French or German to their governess, English to their parents, and Russian to everyone else. Precocious children learned to read and write German and French at the age of six. In 1912, Liubov Popova's father even sent her governess with her when she went to study art in Paris when she was twenty-two. By the 1890s, well-to-do Russian families allowed their daughters to attend gymnasia (advanced secondary schools) and art academies.[20]

Systemic gender imbalance and educational investment in secondary education existed in all European countries. The French government spent 26 million francs on boys' secondary education but only 3.5 million on girls' in 1908. In 1900, almost 200,000 boys attended lycées, colleges, or seminaries, while only 13,000 girls received secondary education. This disparity persisted despite the secularization of French education and establishment of teacher-training schools in each département in the 1880s. The situation of young French women improved but lagged behind that of French men during the Third Republic. In 1881, there was only one lycée for girls and three public colleges with a total of 342 pupils, whereas more than 100 such establishments with 33,000 female secondary students had evolved by 1913.[21]

In addition to the gender gap, class affected higher education. Girls who attended lycées and colleges in the 1880s nearly all belonged to well-to-do families. Their bearing, manners, and language were impeccable, and they had no "pernicious contacts" with girls from the lower classes. Protecting the daughters of good families, school principals sometimes turned down working-class applicants and refused scholarships and fee waivers to poor female students. Only a few working-class girls made their way through the secondary school system, and they were exceptional. In Germany, considerable gender and class imbalances existed, yet there too change occurred. Only 100 secondary schools for Prussian girls existed in 1860, but by 1900 there were almost 900.[22] Still, at the turn of the century, 160,000 boys but only 22,000 girls were enrolled in gymnasia.

In England and Russia, class more than gender influenced access to secondary education. Roughly 100,000 boys and girls attended Russian gymnasia and English grammar schools in the 1890s. In Moscow, middle-class girls attended courses in pedagogy, medicine, business, and agriculture. While English and Russian statistics suggest that secondary education was separate and equal, financial inequalities existed for women in both countries. In England, girls' grammar schools had smaller endowments and fewer scholarships than boys' schools did. Only the teacher-training colleges offered girls scholarships on the same basis as boys. In Tsarist Russia, the government offered stipends for male but not female gymnasium students. Consequently, education required more money, dedication, and commitment on the part of young women. Moreover, since women had to pay up to 200 rubles per year for gymnasium education, it was mainly women from wealthy families or with rich benefactors who obtained it. Indeed, impoverished gentry-class girls in the Russian Empire often attended boarding schools due to philanthropists in major cities such as Riga.[23]

Of course, many gentry and aristocratic young women were still educated at home by governesses in the mid and late nineteenth century. While their scientific education may have been weak, their instruction in the humanities was usually good. Russification also hindered women's education, since students from different ethnic backgrounds had to master Russian as well as overcome family opposition in order to pursue higher education. Since Russian secondary schools were mainly boarding schools, women had to be rather adventurous to leave their families to pursue their dream of gymnasium education in the provincial or national capitals. It was difficult for provincial women to obtain university education. When Aniuta Korvin-Krukovskaia begged her father (a general) for permission to study in St. Petersburg in the early 1860s, he vehemently refused, reminding her that ladies lived at home until marriage. However, she outmaneuvered him, arranging travel and study with her married sister in Germany.[24]

In the 1860s, the Grand Duchess Elena encouraged her nephew Tsar Alexander II to found additional provincial secondary schools for young women. According to Vera Figner, her gentry-class family had expected her to study at the exclusive Smolny Institute in St. Petersburg until a boarding school for noblewomen opened in Kazan. However, such schooling remained inferior to that available to boys. Six years at a girls' school gave her a cultivated manner, a sense of camaraderie, and a habit of discipline, but nothing as far as scientific knowledge or intellectual training. This was a common experience. Praskovia Tatlina perceived traditional education as "grooming a girl for slavery" and turning her into an object. She resolved to provide her daughter a good education, despite the advice of relatives who thought girls should be taught at home, trained as housewives, and occupied with needlework. Prior to 1914, many English middle-class families also regarded education as a finishing school to refine their daughters' manners. Thus, girls' boarding schools remained academically inferior to public elementary education until the 1880s, and working-class girls who graduated from elementary school could pass the scholarship exams for teachers' college, while many middle-class girls from private schools failed them. Yet some, such as Emmeline Pethick (1870s) and Vera Brittain (1910s), loved academics and set themselves apart from their peers who had no interest in learning. Girls' education remained intellectually inferior to boys' until the end of the century, when reformers pushed for more rigorous education to prepare young women for careers other than marriage.[25]

England and Germany provided opportunities for women's secondary education, and middle-class girls could attend day schools in the cities where they lived. Yet expectations for daughters remained low. As a youngster in the 1870s, Emmeline Pankhurst was puzzled that her brothers' education was a much more serious matter than hers.[26]

Young English women's education tended toward genteel dilettantism. The brothers and nephews of famous women attended university, while their sisters received tutoring at home. One wonders what kind of writers Beatrice Potter Webb and Virginia Woolf might have been had they re-

ceived university education. Would Potter Webb have become an economist instead of a social investigator? Would Woolf have become a philosopher instead of slipping her feminist ideas into her novels and essays? Would
Emily Davies and Mary Kingsley have made greater educational and anthropological contributions if they had not internalized their intellectual inferiority?

Besides gender and class, public opinion and curriculum also shaped
women's education. Many segments of middle-class French and German
society espoused traditional views regarding women's education. German
men thought girls should become healthy mothers and men's sympathetic
companions, not their professional competitors. Likewise, French politicians in the 1880s expected girls to become good housewives and mothers,
to converse intelligently with their husbands, to raise their children well,
and to be good citizens, not independent career women. Likewise, English
families thought education fostered manly qualities of rationality and independence, which they feared would "unsex" women and foster an "unfeminine" spirit of competition. It was only toward the end of the nineteenth century that segments of English and European society realized that
women were capable of serious intellectual effort and shifted the emphasis
of girls' education from cultivating good manners to training minds. By
1900, feminists, liberals, and young middle-class women were pressuring
their governments to provide more rigorous secondary education so that
they could support themselves through respectable work.[27]

Religion also affected women's education. In Germany, 72% of the
girls who passed the *abitur* (university entrance exam) were Protestant,
18% Jewish, and 7% Catholic, whereas the general population was 62%
Protestant, 36% Catholic, and 1% Jewish.[28] Since public secondary schools
in Germany often attracted daughters from bourgeois Jewish families, upper-class German families forbade their daughters to attend them. In France,
public secondary schools likewise attracted daughters of the Protestant
bourgeoisie, not girls from wealthy Catholic families. French Catholic families sent their daughters to convent schools. Geneviève Tabouis attended a
Catholic convent school prior to the war, but her education resembled that
of an English finishing school and she did not learn much there. So in both
France and Germany it was Protestant and Jewish women who were proportionately better represented in higher secular education. In some instances, girls chose commercial rather than academic higher education.
The German Jew Toni Sender found school boring, hated her bourgeois
parents' control, and secretly desired to make her own living as soon as

possible. At thirteen, she attended a commercial high school about forty miles from her hometown and lived in a boardinghouse with friends of her parents.[29]

Traditionally, the Catholic Church in France and Germany provided secondary education for middle-class women and educated many female teachers and nuns. When the French government closed convent schools in 1904, some French Catholic women sent their daughters into exile with convent personnel, and one bought a convent to use on a private basis before it could be taken over by the municipality. Some Catholic women did not think that secular education prepared women for life's sorrows and troubles, as convent schools did.[30]

In Russia, Protestant women enjoyed much higher rates of literacy (60%) than did Orthodox women (9%). Most Protestants lived in cities and presumably were middle class, whereas most Orthodox were peasants and lived in the country. Of course, upper-class Orthodox women possessed very high rates of literacy, and state institutions for secondary education were reserved mainly for them. Although Alexander II eased class and religious educational restrictions from 1855 to 1863, the underfunding of provincial education for young girls meant that many had to travel to Moscow and St. Petersburg to study. While the Tsarist government tolerated special courses in higher education for women in the capitals in the 1860s and 1870s, it obstructed such courses in Ukraine until 1879. Moreover, the closing of Ukrainian women's courses in the mid-1880s forced Ukrainian women to travel to St. Petersburg or abroad.[31]

In 1897, Tsar Nicholas II enforced quotas against Jewish female students, compelling many to travel abroad to study. Some eluded the quotas in medical study by opting for a career as *feldsher* (physician's assistant) instead of physician. In 1910, 20% of feldsher students were Jewish, and the majority were female. Apparently, Jewish women chose this lower-ranking and lower-paying career because the position provided them a passport out of the Pale of Settlement along the western border of the Empire to Russia proper. According to Bella Rosenfeld Chagall, restrictions against Jews' studying in Moscow and St. Petersburg eased prior to World War I. Graduating from the Vitebsk Gymnasium for Girls in 1912, she then studied in Moscow. More than 1,000 Russian Jewish women studied in Swiss universities prior to the war, but only 300 in German universities, since they did not grant women degrees prior to 1908. A few also enrolled in German higher technical schools. When German institutions increased matriculation, laboratory, and certification fees for foreign students, it became harder for Russian Jews to complete their medical education in Germany.[32]

Some gentry-class women in Russia and Europe fulfilled their dream of acquiring secondary and higher education. Others struggled with the same problems of those in lower estates: low family expectations for them, a sense of intellectual inferiority, and second-rate schools. In her slightly autobiographical novel *The Edwardians*, Vita Sackville-West depicts a heroine whose mother prevents her from attending Cambridge University.[33]

Generally, Russian radicals encouraged women to enter the helping professions in order to serve the people. However, they were less supportive of women's personal, intellectual, and artistic development. Still, the memoirs of Marie Bashkirtseva, an artist; Sophia Kovalevskaia, a mathematician; and revolutionaries Katherine Breshko-Breshkovskaia, Vera Figner, and Aleksandra Kollontai do not show the feelings of intellectual inferiority that many English women expressed in theirs. In Russia from 1863 to 1897 and in Germany from 1879 to 1908, women were excluded from university study. French authorities allowed women to attend university but did not provide them the rigorous secondary education to pass the baccalaureate exam (the prerequisite for university study). As a result, more foreign than French women matriculated at French universities until the 1890s. Likewise, German secondary education did not prepare young women for the abitur exam, effectively barring them from university study. In 1881, only 277 girls passed the abitur exam in Prussia, the largest state in Germany.[34] In the late nineteenth century, English women were admitted to university study and degrees at city universities in London, Manchester, Liverpool, and Leeds, while the most prestigious ones—Oxford and Cambridge—allowed women to study but excluded them from degrees and discounted their achievements when they won university prizes.

Achievements

The story of middle- and gentry-class women's education includes notable achievements as well as hardship. From the time of Catherine II, who founded Smolny Institute for daughters of high-ranking families in 1764, some Russian noblewomen obtained secondary education. Prior to 1914, they had greater access to higher education than did women in the other estates. For both economic and personal reasons, many gentry-class Russian women pursued higher education and professional work in the late nineteenth century. Loss of land and free labor after the emancipation of the serfs in 1861 impoverished some noble families, who were no longer able to provide for unmarried relations. At the same time, radicals encouraged gentry-class people to atone for their earlier exploitation of the serfs by becoming educated and serving the peasantry in the helping professions. As a result, 4,300 noblewomen had obtained university and higher education by 1897, whereas only 227 women in the clerical estate and 1,500 in the merchant estates did so. In addition, 400 noblewomen gained special and technical training, 5,000 special secondary education, and 225,000 general secondary education.[35]

Most educated noblewomen lived in European Russia and were Russian, Ukrainian, or Jewish. They often displayed a remarkable sense of adventure in journeying long distances for education. Whereas European girls usually attended secondary schools in their own city, those in the Russian Empire often had to travel vast distances to study at a gymnasium. After Russian universities were closed to them in 1863, scores journeyed to Swiss, French, and German universities.

Dreams

In the late nineteenth century, significant changes occurred in Russian and European attitudes toward women's education. During the period 1855 to 1863, Russian liberals such as Dr. N. I. Pirogov, Minister of War D. A. Miliutin, and Professor K. D. Ushinsky supported improvements in women's education. Like their European cohorts, Russian liberals thought women deserved better education so that they could become better wives and mothers. Radicals such as M. A. Mikhailov, N. G. Chernyshevsky, N. A. Dobroliubov, and D. I. Pisarev also championed women's educational and professional rights and duties. Although radicals thought educated women should serve the people in the scientific intelligentsia, some women sought knowledge for its own sake and their own self-fulfillment.

Women writers—Pavlova, Panaeva, and Vernadskaia—urged women to become educated to avoid men's deception, to compete with them in the marketplace, and to provide for themselves. In the throes of reform, the Grand Duchess Elena endorsed women's access to education. Liberal and radical reforming elites in Ukraine and the secular Muslim intelligentsia also championed women's educational rights. Yet despite gains made after the Russian Revolution of 1905, secondary-school instruction remained Russified. Muslim girls' education remained problematic because of conservative social mores, but increasing numbers of Muslim families in Baku sought secondary education for their daughters prior to 1914.[36]

A variety of factors stimulated Russian noblewomen's educational pursuits. Liberal and radical public opinion sanctioned their access to higher education and careers in the arts and helping professions. Their estate's declining economic situation in the second half of the century as well as the gender imbalance lowered their chances of marrying and increased their need for careers as alternatives to marriage. Discontent with institutionalized marriage also increased the attraction of careers. Finally, an increasing sense of self enabled some Russian noblewomen to assume careers as writers, translators, editors, painters, teachers, and doctors. Statistics indicate that 16,800 women engaged in university-level education in 1914; 2,000 studied in pedagogical institutes, 2,000 in medical institutes, and 1,500 in schools for the beaux arts. Roughly 300,000 studied at gymnasia and other secondary-level schools; 9,000 in teacher training for primary school, 25,000 in ecclesiastical seminaries, 5,600 in medical schools for physician assistants; 10,000 in commerce, 7,000 in technical and handicraft courses, and 3,500 in the fine arts. Gymnasium graduates obtained civil service rank upon graduation but lacked the status of the free professions that university education conferred. As early as 1870, the Stroganov Art School in Moscow had 35 women students in one class. Anna Ostroumova, who studied at the Russian Academy of Art in St. Petersburg in the 1890s, reported no harsh words from male colleagues or professors.[37]

Similar factors transformed Russian and English women's higher education. The larger number of women than men in the middle and upper classes meant that not all English women could marry. Therefore, English feminists, parents, and educators advocated reforming girls' education so that it focused not on manners and dependence but on intellect, independence, achievement, self-reliance, and reason.[38] By 1900, teaching had become an acceptable profession for women, and increasing numbers of middle-class women attended teacher-training colleges to become secondary-school teachers.

In the 1860s and 1870s, some French, German, and Russian universities and professors permitted women to attend courses as auditors. While traditional gentry-class Russian parents bade their daughters marry and accept their subordinate role, some daughters had other dreams and ideas. Sofia Kovalevskaia wanted to study mathematics in St. Petersburg in the late 1860s, but her father refused.[39] According to Prince Peter Kropotkin, Count and Countess Z. also rejected the pleas of their daughters to attend lectures in Moscow. It was only after the elder daughter poisoned herself that the parents allowed their younger daughter to follow her own inclinations.[40] Yet access to university study lasted only a short time. The Tsarist Minister of Education used student demonstrations in 1863 as a pretext to exclude women, lower-class men, and Jews from the universities. The Minister of War also closed the Army Surgical Academy to women in the 1870s. Until the 1890s, the Russian government adopted ambiguous policies on women's higher education. Fortunately for women in the Russian Empire, liberal and radical public opinion supported their right to higher education. Indeed, some professors offered their services to them in "Special Courses." While women obtained teaching degrees by staying at the gymnasium an additional year, those desiring medical or scientific courses had to attend the special evening classes or complete their studies in foreign countries.

Social and Personal Struggles

In the late nineteenth century, it was particularly difficult for women to obtain scientific education, and so it was then that the tradition arose of Russian, German, and English women traveling abroad to undertake medical and scientific training. In 1870, Elizabeth Garrett obtained her medical degree in France. In Russia, Chernyshevsky's famous novel *What Is to Be Done?* (1862) popularized the roles of physician and revolutionary for women. Gentry-class scientists—Sofia Kovalevskaia and Iuliia Lermontova—as well as revolutionaries—Ekaterina Breshkovskaia, the Figner sisters, and Aleksandra Kollontai—were all deeply influenced by Chernyshevsky's solution to "the woman question." So, education and revolutionary work became intertwined for many Russian women.

While many women in the Russian Empire sought higher education so they could "serve the people" in the helping professions, others wanted to develop their own intellectual and artistic talents. Sofia Kovalevskaia craved intellectual development and engaged in a "fictitious" marriage in order to go to St. Petersburg to study mathematics. Since university education in mathematics was not available to her in Russia, her husband in-name-only endorsed her passport, enabling her to travel and study at Heidelberg (1869), Berlin (1870), and Gottingen, where she received her doctorate in 1874. Her friend Iuliia Lermontova studied and traveled with her, earning her doctorate in chemistry before German universities closed their doors to women in 1879.[41]

Like Europeans, Russian merchants believed that higher education was more important for their sons than their daughters. The literacy rate for meshchanstvo men was over 50%, but only 30% for women, and only 1,500 women in that estate had completed some form of higher education by 1897. Nationality and geography also influenced women's educational attainment. Those obtaining higher education tended to live in European Russia (1,331), with only a few score in the Polish provinces, Kazan, and Siberia.[42]

Prior to 1900, Russian and European women's access to university education remained a controversial issue. Some professors argued that women were physically and intellectually weaker than men and were incapable of serious academic study. Others argued that education would "unsex" women, making them mannish. So patronizing were the attitudes of English academics that the ratio of female to male students was limited to 1 to 6 at Oxford and 1 to 10 at Cambridge.[43]

While many Russian and European liberals believed that women deserved education to be good wives and mothers, some regarded women as intellectually inferior and incapable of professional work. Viewing women as spiritually pure and sexually undefiled, they considered women to be naturally submissive to patriarchal authority and economically dependent. Some thought intense studying would damage women's reproductive systems and undermine their natural calling as wives and mothers. They feared that allowing women to become physicians would lead to overcrowding of the profession. Opposition to German women's access to higher education and careers came from men in the professions and civil service who felt threatened by their competition. Many French men were also loath to admit women to the professions and discounted women's intellectual attainment. French girls therefore did not receive the same preparation for the baccalaureate that boys did.[44]

In Russia, the professions were not "overcrowded," and progressive public opinion supported women's training as cultural and scientific personnel. Thus, enterprising women trained abroad for scientific careers. However, they underestimated the economic double standard that city and provincial governments would apply in paying them less than men were paid to work in the helping professions.

Not all scientists believed in women's intellectual inferiority. Some suspended judgment to see if women could succeed in university study. In 1897, German professors Klein and Meyer indicated that many female students were adept at science and math. They especially praised Sofia

Kovalevskaia for solving difficult mathematical problems. Indeed, some scientists were more open-minded about women's abilities than their colleagues in the humanities. German historians Treitschke and Busolt refused to admit women as students. In a famous incident, Treitschke ejected women from his class. Busolt argued that only men possessed strictness of method, exactness in conducting research, discernment in interpreting evidence, sure judgment, and a proper general view. Agreeing with conservative German academics, the Cambridge historian Canon Creighton thought women lacked the discipline to do good work and that their mission was to charm, not instruct.[45]

Women struggled against the double standard in university education throughout the century. Conservative attitudes in Europe meant that fewer French and German than Russian and English women obtained university degrees in the 1870s and 1880s. Only in 1899 did more French (559) than foreign women (258) attend French universities. Prejudice against female university students remained strong, and an incredible gender imbalance existed: only 1,000 women but more than 26,000 men enrolled at French universities in 1900. In Russia, a similar gap appeared: 6,000 women but more than 98,000 men had higher education. In England, 26,000 men but only 4,000 women attended university in 1900. German women suffered when the universities excluded them from 1879 until 1908. Still, by World War I, increasing numbers of women were obtaining higher education.[46]

English women's struggle for university education revolved around family expectations and social constraints more than government restrictions. The duties of family life hindered many women from pursuing sustained intellectual work. Parents' educational double standard persisted well into the twentieth century. They often interrupted their daughters' education, keeping them home to help with domestic duties, whereas they considered their sons' education necessary for their careers. Boys' schools and colleges were also better endowed than girls'. In *Three Guineas*, Virginia Woolf observed that, while English families carefully set aside money for "Arthur's Educational Fund"—which included holidays abroad, good clothes, and an allowance while he learned his trade or profession—daughters seldom received such benefits. In Woolf's case, her brother was sent to grammar school and Cambridge University, while she received an informal education at home from her father and a tutor, and attended some classes at the University of London. Emily Davies and Mary Kingsley also resented the expensive training their parents provided their brothers but not them.

Kingsley's father spent 2,000 pounds on her brother's education, while providing only a German tutor for her.[47]

Prior to 1914, Vera Brittain's father planned for her brother to take over the family business even though he had no aptitude for commerce, while his daughter did. Despite her brother's limited educational achievements, the family destined him for university, while her flattering school reports never aroused comment. Luckily, a family lawyer, who endorsed women's higher education, made her father revise his opinion regarding Vera's desire for university study.[48]

While higher education remained off-limits to most English women, some notable achievements occurred. Elizabeth Garrett became an important role model for other women after she completed her medical studies in Paris in 1870 and practiced medicine in England. Eileen Power graduated from Girton College, Cambridge, in 1909, studied medieval economic history at the University of Paris from 1910 to 1911, and worked as a research student at the London School of Economics and Political Science. From 1913 to 1921 she directed studies in history at her alma mater. Another role model, the chemist Ida Smedley, took a fellowship at the Lister Institute in London. Despite the seriousness with which most English women pursued their studies, some displayed the same high spirits and frivolous attitudes that male students did. The famous biographer Cecil Woodham-Smith was dismissed from the Royal School for Officers' Daughters at Bath for taking "French leave" to visit the National Gallery. At St. Hilda's College, Oxford, she was suspended a term for joining an Irish demonstration.[49]

The Tsarist government refused to confer prestigious degrees on women, since higher degrees entailed rank and privilege in the civil service. When Varvara Rudneva, a physician and Doctor of Medicine (Ph.D.), requested a post at the Women's Medical Courses in the Army Surgical Academy, Tsarist officials refused her request, since she would command higher rank and salary as a professor than she did as a physician. Nor was she allowed to serve in the Russo-Turkish War, since her Ph.D. would have given her civil service rights, perquisites, and promotion. However, the regime allowed ordinary female physicians to serve in the war because their education confined them to the lower ranks.[50]

Revolution

Nothing stemmed the tide of dedicated women pursuing higher education. From as far away as Tula and Irkutsk, Siberia, Praskovaia Ivanovskaia and Konkordia Gromova journeyed to St. Petersburg to study at the

Alarachinsky and Bestuzhev courses in the late nineteenth century. Like many others from the clerical estate, they found higher education a radicalizing experience. Dispirited by the peasant's plight, Ivanovskaia joined the People's Will (1880), and Gromova joined the Social Democrats (1890). Arrested and imprisoned in 1901, Gromova emigrated to Paris, where she studied at Lenin's school. After 1872, many women went abroad to pursue medical and scientific careers. There, some became attracted to the revolutionary ideas of Bakunin, Lavrov, and Tkachev, who were living in exile in the 1870s. While most Russian women medical students remained revolutionary sympathizers, some such as Vera Figner gave up their studies to become full-time revolutionaries. Fearing the taint of "revolution," German women stayed away from Swiss universities until the Russian government recalled its female students.

Since the revolutionary Vera Figner had been a medical student prior to planning the assassination of Tsar Alexander II in 1881, his successor Alexander III closed medical training to women. Despite Figner's imprisonment and other women's participation in revolutionary causes, Russian public opinion still supported their access to higher education. So, in the mid-1890s, Tsar Nicholas II allowed a privately funded Women's Medical Institute to open in St. Petersburg.[51]

The journeys of so many Russian women for higher education resulted from a variety of factors: (1) the open educational policies during Alexander II's early reign; (2) liberal and radical public support for their study; (3) disenchantment with arranged marriage; (4) inability to marry due to gender imbalance; (5) the declining fortunes of the nobility following the emancipation of the serfs; (6) the influence of Chernyshevsky's novel *What Is to Be Done?*; and (7) the quota system in Russian educational institutions, which forced many Jewish women to travel to Europe to obtain higher education. European women sought higher education and access to professional positions for similar reasons: the preponderance of middle- and upper-class English and German women in relation to men in the late nineteenth century and the lack of dowries to wed. Social support for women's higher education in Russia meant that by 1914 there were 16,800 women in the Empire enrolled in university-level institutions, representing 23% of the total number of students, while German and French women constituted only 6% and 10% of their respective university bodies. Although English women comprised 20% of university students in 1910, they were mainly enrolled in teacher-training programs.[52]

Rhetoric

In the late nineteenth century, women used various rhetorical phrases to rationalize access to higher education and the professions. Bourgeois French women justified their teaching careers as a "sacerdotal mission." Their society considered teaching a natural profession for women because it utilized their maternal qualities. Russian radical writers spoke of gentry-class women's obligation "to serve the people" in the helping professions. German society presented teaching as an opportunity for spinsters to exercise "spiritual motherhood." English women spoke of their right to support themselves and their duty "to minister as reformers, philanthropists, teachers, and nurses."[53]

Yet the "service ethic" did not give them access to the medical profession. Appealing to the ideal of "ministering angel" relegated them to nursing instead of the practice of medicine as physicians. In trend-setting German bourgeois circles, the idea of men and women studying medicine together was regarded as gravely damaging to femininity. It was feminine for nurses to care for the sick of both sexes, but joint medical education was inappropriate.[54] Thus, European women claimed that "ladies" required the services of female physicians. In Russia, Muslim women's modesty and religion necessitated female doctors, and there were not enough male doctors to treat the lower orders. Different social needs and attitudes led to a great discrepancy between the number of European and Russian women obtaining medical and teacher education before 1914.

Nightmares of Educated Women

By the late nineteenth century, several hundred thousand women had obtained teaching certificates and found employment as low-paid elementary-school teachers. Fewer became well-paid secondary-school teachers or school inspectors. Many obtained education for a particular profession, but were prevented from entering it. Few English women gained appointments as professors but were employed as assistant lecturers, on temporary contracts. Some experienced discrimination. When Mary Bentinck Smith inquired about a language post at the University of Edinburgh, she was informed that they did not contemplate the appointments of women to such posts. Even when they obtained university positions, women encountered difficulties getting money for research projects and being promoted to high academic positions. Particularly galling were the appointments of men to senior posts in women's colleges and to positions that women had previously filled in the London School of Medicine for Women. Instead of occupying the position of professor, they were more likely found in posts as wardens of women residence halls. When Christabel Pankhurst received her law degree in 1903, she had no hope of employment as a lawyer. Until the Sex Disqualification (Removal) Act of 1919, English women were unable to practice law, and the first woman was not called to the bar until 1922. In France, Jeanne Chauvin was admitted to the bar in 1900, but only eleven others followed her example prior to 1914. German women experienced similar struggles in becoming lawyers.[55]

Despite changing attitudes regarding English women's education, some were still ridiculed for developing their minds. Beatrice Potter's sisters scoffed at her studies as a waste of time and considered them a way of showing off in front of philosophers. They questioned the value of mental training for a pretty girl whose job was to make a good marriage. Likewise, the journalist Eliza Linton was ridiculed for her attainments, and Mary Kingsley was humiliated by a famous chemist for her outdated knowledge. Educated English women discovered that their intellectual development sometimes brought ostracism and self-doubt instead of satisfaction. The undaunted managed to carve out careers for themselves when and where they could.[56]

Notes

1. For an excellent discussion of English women's family life and educational problems, see Virginia Woolf, *Three Guineas*, 24–117; Crowell, "Studies in Contradictions…", 92–106.

2. Linda Clark, "A Battle of the Sexes in a Professional Setting: The Introduction of Inspectrices Primaires, 1899–1914," *French Historical Studies* 16 (Spring 1989): 116.

3. Madeleine Pelletier, *L'education feministe des filles*, 67–85.

4. See *Statesman's Year Book, 1900*, "United Kingdom," 33–39; "France," 517–20; "Germany," 591–93; "Russia," 933–37; Ts.SK, *Ezhegonik' Rossii, 1915 g.* (*An. Stat. Russie, 1915*), 144; *Russian Year Book 1916*, 99; Mary Jo Maynes, *Schooling in Western Europe, A Social History*, 143–45; Mulhall, *Dic. of Stat.*, 693. In 1896, Mulhall found Germany 99% literate, France 95%, England 94%, and Russia 22%. The Russian census defined literacy as the ability to both read and write, while Mulhall used signature at marriage as an indication of literacy.

5. Eugene Weber, *Peasants into Frenchmen*, 547.

6. *Pervaia perepisi 1897 g.* 1: xvi, xix; *Svod Perepisi 1897 g,,* Table IX-a, 1: 188–209; 2: xxxvi, xxxvii, 4.

7. Ben Eklof, "Peasants and Schools," *The World of the Russian Peasant: Post-Emancipation Culture and Society*, 117–18; for Europe, see Maynes, *Schooling in Western Europe*, 85–86.

8. "Doris Viersbeck, Cook and Housemaid," *The German Worker*, 135-59.

9. Regarding literacy and non-French speakers, see *An. Stat.* 30: 14; Weber, *Peasants into Frenchmen*, 319, 325.

10. Michael F. Hamm, "Kiev, Continuity and Change in Late Imperial Kiev," *The City in Late Imperial Russia*, 109; *Svod Perepisi 1897*, 2: 44, which records the female literacy rate for Kiev province as 8.9%.

11. Lipinska, *Les Femmes et le Progrès des Sciences Médicales*; *Svod Perepisi 1897 g.* 1: 200–7; Samuel C. Ramer, "Childbirth and Culture," *Russian Peasant Women*, 111. Ramer found 90% of "trained village midwives" passed examinations entitling them to an urban practice and a higher standard of living. Regarding the subordination of French and German peasant children's education to work in the family economy, see Maynes, *Schooling in Western Europe*, 85–86.

12. Carles, *A Life of Her Own*, 44–45, 60.

13. Filippova, "Iz Istorii zhenskogo obrazovaniia," *Voprosy Istorii* 38 (1963): 211–12; Joseph Bradley, "Moscow, From Big Village to Metropolis," *The City in Late Imperial Russia*, 33; Maynes, *Schooling in Western Europe*, 135.

14. For educational statistics, see *Statesman's Year Book* (1900), "Russia," 937; Mulhall, *Dic. of Stat.*, 235; Webb, *Dic. of Stat.*, 219; *Statesman's Year Book* (1892), 36, 477, 540, 866; Robert Thurston, "Developing Education in Late Imperial Russia: The Concerns of State, 'Society,' and People in Moscow, 1906–1914," *Russian History* 2 (Spring 1984): 64; Hamm, *The City in Late Imperial Russia*.

15. John Shaffer, "Occupational Expectations of Young Women in Nineteenth Century Paris," *Journal of Family History* 3 (1): 2–77; Laura Strumingher, *Women and the Making of the Working Class*, 57–64, who found low employment expectations for young girls among teachers in religious orders.

16. Mrs. Scott, "A Felt Hat Worker," in *Life as We Have Known It*, 85; Widdowson, *Going Up into the Next Class: Women and Elementary Teacher Training, 1840–1914*, 15–17, 68–79; Joanna Bornat, "Home and Work: A New Context for Trade Union History," *Radical America* 12 (5): 53–69; Clara Collet, "Statistics of Employment of Women and Girls," *JRSS*, Sept. 1895, 522; Maynes, *Schooling in Western Europe*, 108-09; Willmott, *Growing Up in a London Village*, 38; Dayus, *Her People*, 123, 132.

17. Lily Braun, "Children's Liberation," *Selected Writings on Feminism and Socialism*, 224, 226; "Ottilie Baader, Seamstress" and "Adelaid Popp, Factory Worker," *The German Worker*, 66–67, 131.

18. Maynes, *Schooling in Western Europe*, 109–12, 121.

19. Harriet Martineau, "What Women Are Educated For," originally published 1861, reprinted in *Harriet Martineau on Women*, 98–99; Brittain, *Lady into Woman*, 20, 92.

20. Kollontai, *Iz Moei Zhizni i Raboty Gody i Liudi*; Anastasiia Tsvetaeva, *Vospominaniia*, 84; *Memories of Revolution: Russian Women Remember*, 39, 99; "Natalia Grot," in *Russia Through Women's Eyes: Autobiographies from Tsarist Russia*, 223; Elena Skrjabina, *Coming of Age in the Russian Revolution*, 7, 11, 16–24; V. Saralianov and N. Adashina, *Popova*, 12, 41; Camile Gray, *The Russian Experiment in Art, 1863–1922*, 97; Ostroumova-Lebedova, *Avtobio-graficheskii zapiski*, 37–86.

21. For figures regarding women's secondary education in the nineteenth century, see *An. Stat* 52: 274*; Maynes, *Schooling in Western Europe*, 64, 99.

22. Maynes, *Schooling in Western Europe*, 100–2.

23. *Jahr. Amt. Stat. Preuss. Staates*, 576–77; *Album Graphique, RSDRP 1901*, 236; Margadant, *Madame le Professeur*, 204–5; *Statesman's Year Book* (1900), 33–39, 517–20, 591–93, 935–37; *Statesman's Year Book* (1908), 927; *Statesman's Year Book* (1914), 30–31, 816–17, 894–97, 1236–38; Mulhall, *Dic. of Stat.*, 231–35; Webb, *New Dic. of Stat.*, 219–26; J. Bradley, "Moscow," *The City in Late Imperial Russia*, 33; Satina, *Education of Women in Pre-Revolutionary Russia*, "Zhenskoe Obrazovanie," *BSE* 25: 266; Brittain, *Lady into Woman*, 125; Rita McWilliams-Tullberg, "Women and Degrees at Cambridge University, 1862–1897," *A Widening Sphere*, 134.

24. Bohachevsky-Chomiak, *Feminists Despite Themselves*, 14–16; Kovalevskaia, *Vospominaniia detstva*, 86.

25. Vera Figner, *Memoirs of a Revolutionist*, 23; "Praskovia Tatlina," Clyman, *Russia Through Women's Eyes*, 260; Pethick Lawrence, *My Part in a Changing World*, 58–59; Brittain, *Testament of Youth*, 34, 40; Widdowson, *Going Up into the Next Class*, 68–79.

26. See Albisetti, *Schooling German Girls and Women*, 23–57; Emmeline Pankhurst, *My Own Story* in *The Suffragettes*, 5–6.

27. Albisetti, *Schooling German Girls and Women*, 268; Edmee Charrier, *L'Evolution Intellectuelle Feminine*, 294–98; Tabouis, "Newspaper Woman: French Style," *The Living Age*, August 1939, 564; Jacques Leonard, *La France Medicale*, 266; Weber, *Peasants into Frenchmen*, 175; Margadant, *Madame Le Professeur*, 3, 14–22; John Talbot, *The Politics of Educational Reform in France, 1918–1940*, 10–11; Karen Offen, "The Second Sex and the Baccalaureat in Republican France, 1880–1924," *French Historical Studies* 13 (Fall 1983): 252–86; Crowell, "Studies in Contradictions," 92–106; Joyce Senders Pedersen, "The Reform of Women's Secondary and Higher Education: Institutional Change and Social Values in Mid and Late Victorian England," *History of Education Quarterly*, Spring 1979, 61–86.

28. In 1911, 40% of German women university students came from families where fathers had a university degree, whereas only 20% of male students came from such families. See Albisetti, *Schooling German Girls and Women*, 271.

29. Sender, *The Autobiography of a German Rebel*, 15–16.

30. Regarding secondary education, see Bonnie G. Smith, *Ladies of the Leisure Class*, 184–86; Margadant, *Madame Le Professeur*, 81, 140, 178, 316; Albisetti, *Schooling German Girls and Women*, 216, 290; *Jahr. Amt. Stat. Preuss. Staates*, 576–77.

31. Bohachevsky-Chomiak, "Women in Kiev and Kharkiv: Community Organizations in the Russian Empire," 164–65 in *Imperial Russia 1700–1917 State, Society, Opposition, Essays in Honor of Marc Raeff*; Bohachevsky-Chomiak, *Feminists Despite Themselves*, 14–16, 33.

32. Samuel Ramer, "The Transformation of the Russian Feldsher, 1864–1914," in *Imperial Russia 1700–1917*, 149–54; Claudia Weil, "Gli Studenti Russi in Germania, 1900–1914: Un Saggio Prosopografico," in C. Weil and C. Lupi, *Movimento Operaio e Socialista*, 302; Jack Wertheimer, "The Auslanderfrage at

Institutions of Higher Learning: A Controversy over Russian-Jewish Students in Imperial Germany," *Leo Baeck Institute Year Book*, 27: 188, 196; Wertheimer, "Between Tsar and Kaiser: The Radicalization of Russian Jewish University Students in Germany," *Leo Baeck Institute* 28: 338–39; Bella Chagall, *Burning Lights*.

33. Vita Sackville-West, *The Edwardians*, 312.

34. *Jahr. Amt. Stat. Preuss. Staates*, 576–77.

35. *Svod Perepisi 1897 g.*, Table IX-a, 1: 200–7.

36. Johanson, *Women's Struggle for Higher Education in Russia, 1855–1900*; Satina, *Education of Women in Pre-Revolutionary Russia*; *The Englishwoman's Review*, 1870–1900; *Selected Philosophical Writings* of Belinsky, Chernyshevsky, and Dobroliubov; Bohchevsky-Chomiak, *Feminists Despite Themselves*, 13–19; Azade-Ayse Rorlich, "The 'Ali Bayromov' Club, the Journal Charg Gadini and the Socialization of Azeri Women: 1920–1930," *Central Asian Survey* 5 (3/4): 221–22; Audrey Altstadt-Mirhadi, "Baku, Transformation of a Muslim Town," 296, 303, *The City in Late Imperial Russia*; Audrey L. Altstadt, *The Azerbaijani Turks*, 54–56.

37. *An. Stat. Russe* (1915), 118–19, 132–35; interview with Valery Shekhter, Russian language professor, UTEP, 27 March 1997; J. Beavington Atkinson, *An Art Tour to Russia*, 252; Ostroumova-Lebedeva, *Avtobiograficheskie zapiski*, t. 1–2: 76.

38. Pedersen, "The Reform of Women's Secondary and Higher Education," 61–86.

39. Kovalevskaia, *Vospominaniia detstva*, 86.

40. Peter Kropotkin, *Memoirs of a Revolutionist*, 266. In exile, Kropotkin wrote his memoirs in English. Later they were translated into Russian as *Zapiski Revoliutsionera*.

41. Albisetti, *Schooling German Girls and Women*, 122–25; G. Valbert, "Ce que pensent Les Professeurs Allemands de l'admission des femmes dans les universités," *Revue des Deux Mondes*, tome 140, Ap. 1897, 675–77 (hereafter cited as *RDDM*).

42. *Svod Perepisi 1897 g.* 2: 204; Filippova, "Iz istorii zhenskogo obrazovanii v Rossii," 211–12.

43. Brittain, *Lady into Woman*, 87. Brittain contends that this quota remained in place until the 1950s.

44. Regarding English attitudes, see Jill Conway, "Stereotypes of Femininity in a Theory of Sexual Evolution," in Martha Vicinus, *Suffer and Be Still: Women in the Victorian Age*, 140–54. Regarding Germans, see G. Valbert, "Ce que pensent Les Professeurs Allemands," *RDDM*, 675–77; Albisetti, *Schooling German Girls and Women*, 126–35, 179.

45. Ann Hibner Koblitz, *A Convergence of Lives: Sofia Kovalevskaia, Scientist, Writer, Revolutionary*, xv, 4; diary entry 15 August 1888, *Diary of Beatrice Webb* 1: 254–55.

46. *Album Graphique, RSDRP 1901*, 236; *Ezhegodnik' Rossii 1915*, 118–19; *Svod Perepisi 1897 g.*, 1: 188; *Statesman's Year Book* (1900), "France," 521, "United Kingdom," 34–35; Charrier, *L'Evolution Intellectuelle Feminine*, 294–98; Albisetti, *Schooling German Girls and Women*, 130–35; Carol Dyhouse, "The British Federation of University Women and the Status of Women in Universities, 1907–

1939," *Women's History Review* 4 (1995): 469. Of the 4,000 women university students, a high proportion were preparing for teaching. Prior to 1914, London, Manchester, Liverpool, and Leeds universities granted women degrees equal to men's, while Oxford and Cambridge granted women degrees but did not allow them to matriculate.

47. Florence Nightingale, *Cassandra*: *Diary of Beatrice Webb, vol. I, 1873–92*, 67–227; Pedersen, "The Reform of Women's Secondary and Higher Education," 67–68; Woolf, *Three Guineas*, 4–6, 77; Lyndall Gordon, *Virginia Woolf: A Writer's Life*, 17, 67–91; Crowell, "Studies in Contradictions" 92-106.

48. Brittain, *Testament of Youth*, 57–60.

49. *The Englishwoman's Review*, "Record of Events," 1870: 225; R. H. Tawney, "Eileen Edna le Poer Postan," *DNB*, 1931–40, 718; Dyhouse, "The British Federation of University Women," 472; "Cecil Woodham-Smith," *DNB*, 1971–80, 925.

50. Regarding women's inability to obtain titles and rank in the civil service, I am indebted to Toby Clyman's translation of A. Kashevarova-Rudneva, *Vospominanie*, 9; Dek, 1868; Lipinska, *Les Femmes et le Progrès des Sciences Médicales*; Jeannette Tuve, *The First Russian Women Physicians*.

51. Lipinska, *Les Femmes et le Progrès des Sciences Médicales*, 147–55; Barbara Engle, *Five Sisters: Women Against the Tsar*, 100ff; Figner, *Memoirs of a Revolutionist*, 39–42; Stites, *The Women's Liberation Movement in Russia*, 177–78; Barbara Alpern Engel, "Women Medical Students in Russia, 1872–82: Reformers or Rebels?" *Journal of Social History*, Spring 1979, 12 (3): 394–406; Engel, *Mothers and Daughters*; Albisetti, *Schooling German Girls and Women*, 135.

52. *Album Graphique, RSDRP* (1901), 236; *Ezhegodnik' Rossii* (1915), 118–19; Dyhouse, "The British Federation of University Women," 469; Albisetti, *Schooling German Girls and Women*, 299; *Russian Year Book* (1915), "Peacock," 95. Peacock found 5,177 women students at the higher courses in Petrograd; 5,318 in Moscow; and 1,360 at the Petrograd Medical Institute for Women in 1911.

53. Margadant, *Madame le Professeur*; Linda Clark, "A Battle of the Sexes in a Professional Setting: The Introduction of Inspectrices Primaires, 1899–1914," *French Historical Studies* 16 (1): 99; Elizabeth K. Helsinger et al., *The Woman Question, Social Issues, 1837–1883*, 2: 110–41.

54. Braun, "Femininity" (1902) in *Selected Writings on Feminism and Socialism*, 136.

55. Women predominated in elementary teaching in England and France, but there were more German male than female teachers. *Jahr. Amt. Stat. Preuss. Staates*, 576–79; Albisetti, *Schooling German Girls and Women*, 301. In France, male secondary-school teachers outnumbered females 84,000 to 7,043, *Statesman's Year Book* (1900), "France," 477. Regarding English women, see Dyhouse, "The British Federation of University Women," 471–78; Rosen, *Rise Up, Women!*; John Stevenson, *British Society, 1914–45*, 169.

56. Crowell, "Studies in Contradictions," 96–102.

Chapter 3
Employment before World War I

For demographic and other reasons, millions of women did not marry and devote themselves solely to household work in the nineteenth century. Peasant, working-class, and lower middle-class married women often worked for their families to survive. They usually received lower status and wages than did male workers and sometimes experienced sexual harassment and ridicule. Servants and factory workers at times experienced downward mobility into unemployment, prostitution, and crime. Paid work could mean the attainment of some dreams, as well as struggles and nightmares.

Some women sought higher education as the first step to careers. Upper-class women were censured for taking money for their work. While society sanctioned lower-class women's right to work for money, it fostered the myth that "ladies do not work for pay." Florence Nightingale's gentry-class father provided her with an annuity, so that she would not have to take money for her nursing. Likewise, Sophia Jex-Blake (1840–1912) had to refuse a tutorship in mathematics because her father believed payment would debase her. The Russian general Korvin-Krukovsky criticized his daughter Anna for accepting 300 rubles for stories she had published, saying: "If you take money for writing now, perhaps in the future you will sell yourself!"[1]

Middle-class households also rejected women's taking pay for their work, and some women internalized this ethic. In the 1880s, Emmeline Pethick thought she would be taking money from someone less fortunate than herself if she took a job. In the 1910s, the Russian artist Anna Ostroumova-Lebedeva's parents objected to her selling her engravings. The few vocations open to educated women offered poor conditions and pay. The most proper profession remained that of wife and mother. Middle-class men often considered themselves egalitarian, but when it came to women's public employment they reverted to patriarchal behavior. Women composed only 2% of the contributors to the *Encyclopaedia Britannica*, but the editors heralded this as a sign of women's ability to enter intellectual fields even though the office hierarchy reinforced traditional gender roles.[2]

Agricultural Workers

Peasant women constituted the largest unpaid labor force in Europe and Russia in the 1890s. Few alternatives to marriage and work on the family plot existed for them, and most bore the double burden of household and field work. Their chores were daunting. Laundry was done in village streams regardless of season, and daughters assisted in the daily chores of house, garden, and fields from the age of four or five. Farm work was arduous during harvest time, and Russian peasants called it *strada* (suffering). Still, in the winter, village youth spent the evenings singing, dancing, and courting.[3]

The 1897 Imperial Russian census listed 1.9 million adult peasant women paid workers, but 23 million unpaid ones working on family plots. Taxes and tradition bound most to their native villages. Yet 5.5 million peasant women migrated significant distances—to Siberia or other land-rich areas—to continue traditional peasant life. Another 2 million went to cities to work as domestics, laundresses, bath attendants, or textile workers. Similar movement occurred in France, where 340,000 domestic servants were born in one province but worked in another.[4] English and German girls also migrated long distances to work as servants or in factories.

The number of women listed in agricultural work is incredibly low because the censuses of the 1890s listed as "occupied" only those who received wages for their work. Most adult farm women worked as unpaid members of family enterprises, and this skewed the censuses. While 950,000 Russian women were employed as paid agricultural workers, 19.8 million helped on family farms. A similar ratio occurred among Ukrainian, Belorussian, and Polish women. Since Jews were usually prevented from owning land, only 4,000 Jewish women were listed as paid agricultural workers, and 78,000 as engaged on family farms. Women in paid agricultural work earned lower wages than men but higher ones than domestics. In 1900, women farm workers in Riazan province earned twenty-four to thirty-six rubles a year, or ten to forty kopeks per day. In Smolensk gubernia, they earned fifteen kopeks a day gathering berries or mushrooms, four kopeks for carding wool, and seventy kopeks for breaking flax.[5] The peasantry constituted 86% of the population of the Russian Empire, 40% of Germany's, and 60% of France's.

Poverty also distinguished the Russian peasantry from the European: over half were exceedingly poor, lacking horses, farm machinery, even land to cultivate. They were more backward, illiterate, and patriarchal than peasants in Europe. Both Russian and European peasant women worked to help their families survive. They sold garden produce, eggs, and berries; participated in handicraft production; and worked as lacemakers and wet nurses. Vast geographical distances and ignorance allowed middlemen in these enterprises to siphon off parts of their wages in Russia, so only wet nurses who went to Moscow to nurse infants in state orphanages received all their pay.[6]

The 1895 German census also undercounted women working on family farms, recording 2.7 million, while the 1907 census listed 5 million. The 1895 census found 1.5 million Protestant farm women, 1.2 million Catholic women, but only 1,200 Jewish women. The 1896 French census recorded 2.7 million women agricultural workers, while the 1906 census found several million more. Land enclosures had almost eradicated English yeoman farmers, and English dairy maids worked very hard milking the cows twice daily, churning butter, and making cheese. Some women worked in agricultural gangs organized by contractors for specific seasonal crops. Contractors preferred hiring women and children because they could pay them lower wages than men, six pence or a shilling a day. Prior to World War I, English women picking hops earned only two shillings a day and had to buy their food from their wages.[7] Table 3.1 shows the patterns of gainfully employed agricultural workers.

Table 3.1. Women in Paid Agricultural Work, 1890s*

Country	# of women occupied	% of female labor force	% of agricultural labor force
England (1891)	52,000	1	4
Germany (1895)	2,753,000	43	33
France (1896)	2,760,000	43	32
Russia (1897)	2,100,000	39	11

*Sources: *An. Stat.*, 20: 21-22; *Stat. Jarbuch fur das Deutsche Reich,* 35: 16-17; *P.P. Vol. 97 Gt. Br., Accounts & Papers* [cmd. 2411] Census 1891, 180; *Svod Perepisi 1897 g.,* 2: 240-44. "Occupied," according to the Russian Census, meant "gainfully" employed, which excluded the 23 million women working on family farms.

Being crippled, unmarried, or widowed was a terrible misfortune, and such women may have migrated to work as domestic servants, laundresses, or factory workers in the city. Emigration may have represented hope for a new life or a way to earn a dowry for marriage. It is difficult to sort out the reasons for migration, since few left records.

Domestic Servants

In the 1890s, domestic servants were the largest group of gainfully employed women outside agriculture. The 1897 Russian census reported 1.8 million female domestics. Half were Russian, about one-third were Ukrainian and Polish, and the rest distributed among the other nationalities. They were usually young, single migrants who traveled considerable distances to work. Only 25% were literate and 80% were single. Half of all occupied women in St. Petersburg were servants. In England and Germany, 90% of domestic servants were literate and single, while 80% of French domestics were literate and 68% single. Among German servants, 1.5 million were Protestant, 900,000 Catholic, and 3,100 Jewish.[8] Table 3.2 shows the number and proportion of female servants.

While domestic service provided security, a way to acquire a dowry, and acculturation to urban life, it was not easy work. Most urban households in Russia and Europe had only one servant. In the Russian Empire, roughly 1 million households had one servant; 400,000 had two or three; and only 100,000 had four or more. For their labor, these women usually received room and board, cast-off clothing, and low wages. In urban households, they received three to five rubles per month, while those working for landlords in the countryside earned only fourteen rubles per year. Some gentry wept over Turgenev's stories about peasants, yet their servants re-

Table 3.2. Women in Paid Domestic Service, 1890s*

Country	# of women domestics	% of female labor force	% of total domestics
Russia (1897)	1,800,000	33	80
England (1891)	1,760,000	45	93
Germany (1895)	1,600,000	24	87
France (1896)	790,000	11	76

*Calculated from *Svod Perepisi 1897 g.*, 2: 288; *Census of Eng. and Wales, 1891*, 3: vii; *SDDR*, Neue Folge, Band 102, Tabelle 9, 372; *An. Stat.*, 20: 22.

mained poor, wore shawls instead of coats in the winter, and went barefoot in the summer because shoes cost too much. Few had beds of their own, and most slept wherever they could. While old nannies received shelter, their food was poor. Servants usually gained household skills and contributed some of their wages to their parents' household economy. French domestic servants sometimes saved their wages and achieved upward social mobility. Servants in the Russian Empire were more literate (25%) than their peasant sisters (9%) and perhaps achieved some pleasure, status, and independence in urban acculturation.[9]

European servants also emigrated from the country to work in urban households. They often went into service to spare their parents the cost of their upkeep and sent their meager salaries home to help their families. Young English girls earned five pounds per year in wages, whereas adult maids received thirteen to twenty-four pounds per year, and cooks earned thirty pounds.[10]

In Europe and Russia, sexually exploited servants often bore illegitimate children and fell into unemployment, prostitution, and crime. The Riazan Foundling Home reported that domestic servants made up 85% of abandoning mothers in the 1860s, and the London Foundling Hospital found that domestic servants constituted 65% to 70% of those admitted. Naive and lonesome, they were sometimes seduced by their masters, sometimes by men of their own class who promised marriage but abandoned them during pregnancy. Although the reported number of illegitimate babies in Russia reached 130,000 in 1899, the illegitimacy rate remained low due to strict peasant mores and youthful marriage. In rural areas the rate was 2%, and in Moscow and St. Petersburg 4%. In contrast, France had 80,000 illegitimate births per annum and an illegitimacy rate of 8%. English illegitimacy peaked at 7% at mid-century. German illegitimate births numbered 185,000 in 1896, and the illegitimacy rate among Bavarian farm servants was 15%. Paying their parents to care for their offspring, they had to work a long time to accrue a dowry for marriage.[11]

Demoralized servants often became prostitutes. In her study of prostitution (1899), Russian doctor Maria Pokrovskaia found that most were young, illiterate domestic servants and orphans. In interviews with 103 of them, Pokrovskaia discovered that they turned to prostitution as an alternative to their long hours of menial work, lack of free time, demanding mistresses, and rapacious masters. Seduced and abandoned, as "fallen women" they were unable to find other employment. The 1897 Russian census was unique in recording prostitutes as employed. Of the 15,000 prostitutes listed,

9,600 were Russian, about 1,000 Polish and Jewish, and a few hundred Ukrainian, German, Belorussian, and Latvian. Few from the Caucasus or Central Asia appeared in this category. Restricted to the borderlands of the empire, Jewish women sometimes took the prostitute's yellow ticket without becoming prostitutes because it allowed them to live and study in St. Petersburg.[12]

German prostitutes also carried an identity card, and about 30% of Berlin and Munich streetwalkers were former servants. About 16,000 prostitutes worked in Berlin in 1870, but there were 40,000 by 1909. Literature shows how vulnerable domestic servants were to seduction and abandonment by their masters. Once registered as *Kontrollmadchen*, they often felt too stigmatized for normal life.[13]

English servants were also prey to illegitimacy, unemployment, prostitution, infanticide, and imprisonment. A high proportion of women convicted of drunkenness were actually prostitutes who had lost their jobs. While the connections between domestic servitude, poverty, and crime are tenuous, there was a high correlation between impoverished domestic servants, paupers in workhouses, infanticide, and imprisonment. The 1901 and 1911 English censuses listed 230 and 349 domestic servants among the 2,500 female inmates in local and convict prisons. Two-thirds were unwed, indicating that they may have committed crimes after being seduced and abandoned. The number of unwed servants in workhouses rose from 15,000 in 1901 to 19,000 in 1911. They also constituted a large proportion of those in lunatic asylums. Lack of sleep, overwork, and demanding mistresses and masters could induce mental illness. French reformers saw a direct relationship between prostitution and unemployment. In 1878, a committee in Nice provided a home where unemployed servants could find board and lodging for one franc per day.[14]

More women experienced the stigmas of illegitimacy and prostitution than prison: 75,000 illegitimate births were listed in France in 1898, but only 4,400 women were in prison; in England there were 38,000 illegitimate births but 2,500 imprisoned women; 130,000 illegitimate births but 9,500 women prisoners and exiles were counted by the 1897 Russian census; and 184,000 illegitimate births but 32,000 women imprisoned, sentenced to hard labor, or detained by the police in the Prussian states. Infanticide accounted for a high proportion of all reported homicides in Berlin and London, and the higher incarceration rate of German women suggests severe treatment there. English, French, and Russian judicial personnel saw little purpose in prosecuting women whose lives were already desperate. Russian juries often excused women guilty of infanticide on the basis of mental incapacity. They sometimes sentenced married women guilty of infanticide to hard labor for life but merely exiled unmarried mothers guilty of a first offense of infanticide. Servants accounted for many of the 1,000 infanticides that occurred in European Russia in the late nineteenth century. French juries also refused to convict domestic servants and unmarried women for infanticide or abortion. In contrast, Prussian courts convicted 82 women of *Kindermord* (infanticide) in 1881, sentencing 18 to hard labor and 55 to prison. Few escaped with a fine or other light punishment, as in other countries.[15]

Domestic servants fulfilled some of their dreams by obtaining employment, acculturation to urban life, increased literacy, and sometimes upward social mobility. Yet their work entailed daily struggles with dirt, disorder, and demanding employers.[16] At times they had to contend with sexual exploitation, illegitimate children, prostitution, and crime. To avoid financial and sexual exploitation they frequently changed employment, causing their mistresses to lament the high turnover rate of servants!

Women in Manufacturing

We earn too much to die but not enough to live.
                              —French flowermakers, 1870s

The third-largest employer of women in the nineteenth century was the manufacturing sector. Despite its huge population, the Russian Empire had a smaller number of women working in manufacturing than did European countries. Russia's low rate was due to the country's lack of industrial development; more women were employed in domestic production (600,000) than in factories (300,000). Both European and Russian women predominated in textile and clothing production. Almost 500,000 Russian women were engaged in these activities, while Jewish women ranked second (65,000), Polish third (53,000), and Ukrainians fourth (38,000). Far fewer Tatars, Uzbeks, Belorussians, Lithuanians, Georgians, and Armenians were so occupied. The high proportion of Jewish and Polish women engaged in dressmaking shows their urbanization, while the low level of the other nationalities shows their rural origins. Uzbek and Tatar women produced cotton and rugs. The low number of Russian women in factory production was partly due to migration patterns. Whereas European workers migrated from rural areas to towns and cities, over half of Russian migration re-

Table 3.3. Women in Manufacturing, 1890s*

	# of women in manufacturing	% of female labor force	% of total manufacturing labor force
Russia	1,000,000	18	14
Germany	1,521,000	24	20
France	1,900,000	30	34
England	1,640,000	42	26

*Calculated from *Svod Perepisi 1897 g.*, 2: 242-52; *Stat. Jarbuch,* 35: 16-17; *An. Stat.,* 20: 22; *P.P. vol. 97 Gt. Br. Census 1891,* 180.

mained rural. Most peasants moved to Siberia and Kazakhstan, where they could continue an agrarian way of life, obtain large land allotments, and command higher agricultural wages than in the heartland. Fewer went to large cities. Migration patterns also show that 2 million more men than women migrated, and more men migrated to cities.[17]

One reason fewer women migrated to large cities was that their wages fell below the subsistence level of seventeen rubles per month. They generally earned six to fifteen rubles per month, which was more than domestic servants earned but less than male factory workers, who received twenty-five rubles per month. Women also faced housing shortages, since factories provided barracks only for male workers. Housing was scarce, expensive, and unhygienic. Labor historians, factory inspectors, geographers, statisticians, and novelists Dostoevsky and Gorky depict grim housing situations in Russian cities. Women factory workers often lived in a corner of a room or even shared a bed.[18] Table 3.3 compares women in manufacturing.

In both Germany and France, large numbers worked at home in sweated trades as well as in factories. English women's high participation was due to the rationalization of production where women with machines replaced skilled male workers, to their factory work prior to marriage, and to late age of marriage. Differences in age and marital status of factory workers meant European governments hired female factory inspectors to supervise the needs of young working women, while Russian plants employed midwives for their older, married women workers. Both Russian and European workers suffered from expensive, unhygienic, crowded housing. Between 1860 and 1880, Berlin's population doubled and housing conditions deteriorated. Social observers also documented the terrible housing conditions in English towns, where it was common for ten people to sleep in one room and for many workers to live in poorly lit, unventilated cellars.[19]

Many workers also had to cope with inadequate child care. Few factories provided child care. In Germany, half of married women textile workers used family members to care for their childen; a third used baby-sitters, and a sixth left their children unattended. Although Imperial Germany provided maternity leave, women received only one-half of their wages while on leave. Since most needed all their wages for family survival, they often returned to work early, a practice that led to high rates of infant mortality. French and English women also stopped breastfeeding their babies in order to return to work, helping to produce a high infant mortality rates in those countries.[20]

Domestic Production

> They don't go on strikes, they don't make demands. They die
> of hunger, or consumption.[21]

This quote applied to European and Russian women working in sweated or domestic production in the late nineteenth century. In France, Germany, and Russia, a sizable proportion of married women worked in domestic production, where they earned low wages and had to cope with expensive housing and transportation. Only one-third of the 600,000 Russian women in textile production worked in factories. Almost all of the 300,000 engaged in clothing manufacture were occupied in the "putting out" system. Half of those employed in manufacturing in St. Petersburg and Moscow worked in sewing, and a third in textile sweatshops.[22]

One advantage of domestic production was that women did not have to leave their children and households. Disadvantages included low wages, long hours, unhygienic conditions, oppressive masters, and family control. French investigators found 60% of workshops unsanitary, many homeworkers suffering from lead poisoning used in dyes, and many having little time to care for their family, since they spent long hours sewing for low wages. Their children often helped as well, instead of going to school or taking an apprenticeship. In Russia, Lenin also observed dirty, unhygienic domestic production, and stocking makers earning only eight kopeks per day, while those in factories earned fourteen to twenty-four kopeks per day. Women in Olonets Gubernia earned only two to three rubles per month for sewing squirrel skins, while those working in Moscow province earned twenty to forty rubles per year; those making stockings and gloves fifteen to thirty rubles; and those sewing kid gloves and gluing cigarette tubes thirty-two to forty-five rubles. Among rural workers, church vestment embroiderers netted the highest wages: forty to sixty rubles per annum. Yet they earned less than Moscow garment workers, who made up to 200 rubles per year. While domestic production was physically and psychologically unhealthy for women, low agricultural productivity meant that peasants had to augment their incomes through the production of lace, silk, caps, and hemp.[23]

Slightly more than a million French women engaged in garment making, mostly in the home. This differed from textile production, where two-thirds worked in factories or establishments. In 1885, Parisian dressmakers received nineteen pence per day, but provincial ones seventeen pence. In Lille, women sewing at home had to work twelve to fourteen hours per day to earn what a factory worker received for an eight- to ten-hour day.[24]

Flower making was one occupation in which women earned relatively high wages. Skilled ones earned three to ten francs per day, whereas women factory workers earned only two francs per day in the 1870s. Unskilled flower makers complained, "We earn too much to die but not enough to live." Still, many preferred working at home because they felt freer than in factories and could save on clothes and food and control the rhythm of their work and housework, and because their work enhanced their status within the family.[25]

In the 1890s, 1.5 million English and German women also worked in manufacturing, 700,000 in clothing alone. Like their French and Russian sisters, Berlin seamstresses and ironers earned only twelve marks per week, while young girls under sixteen received six to seven marks. Widows and married women working at home earned even less, five to ten marks per week.[26] Women did as much overtime as possible during the peak season, and during slack times they lived on savings and credit. Other forms of light industry included paper bag and box making, food and beverages, buttons, even chain making. Many engaged in domestic production because their spouses did not earn enough to support the family. Both married and single women worked when and where they could for their families' survival.[27]

Factory Production

Only 300,000 women worked in large-scale factory production in the Russian Empire in 1897, yet they were important because their workplace association sometimes increased their political consciousness and action. During the 1905 and 1917 revolutions, some participated in strikes and in political marches such as Bloody Sunday (1905). Textile workers even elected female delegates to the Soviets (worker councils) during the revolutions of 1905 and 1917. Government prohibitions against women's trade union activity in Russia and Germany, male dominance in trade unions, and a lack of time and energy undermined their political activity. Desire for upward mobility among French entrepreneuses hindered the *syndicat* (trade union) movement there.

Nor did governments provide protective legislation. Only in 1890 did England and Germany prohibit women from night and Sunday work, exclude them from unhealthy and dangerous industries, limit their workday to eleven hours, and entitle them to four weeks off after confinement. The French and Russians agreed to most of these regulations except the one regarding confinement. Moreover, not all workers welcomed government interference. Some French workers resented regulation of their hours because they counted on overtime pay to survive the off-seasons. Pieceworkers often resented wages lost during factory inspections. All feared that safety infractions would create temporary unemployment while a plant was renovated. They disliked government regulations making a shorter, more intense workday, loss of control of the workplace, workplace sociability, and overtime pay.[28]

In the 1890s, 75% of Russian women workers were occupied in clothing and textile production and 25% in food processing, tobacco, printing, paper, or chemical industries. Few worked in wood, leather, mining, or metals. While 72,000 English women worked in metal and mineral manufacturing, far fewer German, French, or Russian women did so.[29] Rationalization of heavy industry occurred prior to World War I in England but later elsewhere. It is difficult to assess how many women in light industry worked at home, in small workshops, or in factories. One-half to two-thirds of the those in food, tobacco, printing, chemicals, wood, leather, or metals worked in factories or small shops. The Russian census listed few in those categories, while the French census found that 60% of women in those fields were employees in small establishments.[30]

Wages

They earned not a living wage, but a lingering, dying wage.
—English saying, 1880s

In the late nineteenth century, women earned less than men. Young English girls earned seven to eight shillings per week and worked eleven to twelve hour days in the 1880s. English adult women earned more (ten to nineteen shillings per week), French and German slightly less (twelve to eighteen francs and 10.4 marks per week), but Russian women the least (four rubles or eight shillings per week). Female textile workers earned less than those in heavy industry, yet low as their wages were, they exceeded domestic servants'. One English factory worker indicated they received not a living wage, but a lingering, dying one. When hours were limited, many took work home to earn extra money. This could take up to four hours per night, thus lengthening the work day from nine to thirteen or fourteen hours.[31]

Although factory work was arduous, low-paid, and injurious to their health, many young German factory girls made the most of their lot by singing and decorating their machines with ribbons and saints' pictures. Freed from family control, many enjoyed the independence that their earnings gave them. Single ones sometimes earned enough to buy new clothing or jewelry. Once married, they seldom bought anything new and often had to pawn their clothes and linens to survive.[32]

Nightmares of Factory Workers

Since England, France, and Russia lacked insurance against sickness and unemployment in the 1890s, working women feared those afflictions. They also suffered from fines for absenteeism, late arrival, shoddy production, laughter, even nursing their babies. A St. Petersburg calendar factory sometimes fined them 0.50 rubles per day while paying them 0.45 rubles. Likewise, weavers earned 1.25 rubles per day but after fines received only 0.25 rubles. English workers were subject to wage deductions for breakage of machinery. They also complained of fines, bullying foremen, irregular lunch hours, and inadequate washrooms. One English worker refused to pay a fine for laughing and was dismissed.[33] Textile workers suffered from brown lung and tuberculosis caused by dirt and dust, pottery workers succumbed to lead poisoning, matchworkers died from necrosis, and many were plagued by miscarriages due to poisonous substances. Inadequate toilet facilities fouled the air in most workplaces.

Workers also dreaded rape and sexual harassment. They often had to exchange sexual favors with employers and mechanics to obtain or keep their jobs. During unemployment, they sometimes resorted to prostitution in order to augment family income. One of their worst problems was lack of child care. Even when children were sick, mothers often had to leave them unattended to earn money for food and rent.[34]

Women in Commerce, Trade, and Low-Level Service

Women worked as medical orderlies, bath house attendants, laundresses, barmaids, shop assistants, clerks, telephone operators, typists, telegraphers, hawkers, and transport workers. They suffered from many of the same conditions as factory workers: low pay, long hours, poor light and ventilation, inadequate sanitary facilities, tuberculosis, tedious work, fines, sudden firing, sexual harassment, and lack of trade union organization.[35] Moreover, employers demanded that clerks dress and act like "ladies," on meager salaries. While sizable numbers worked in this sector, only a small proportion of the total female labor force did so, as table 3.4 indicates.

Female Clerks and Shopkeepers

The number of women employed in low-level service positions had skyrocketed by 1910. In Russia, there were 210,000 female shop assistants and, like their European sisters, they earned low wages (200 rubles per year), were expected to dress fashionably, and experienced sexual harassment in obtaining and keeping their jobs. Bosses generally hired only pretty, young, docile women as clerks. Women over thirty seldom obtained sales positions in smart shops. To dress well, some prostituted themselves with lecherous supervisors or customers. In Germany, 42% of prostitutes came from the combined ranks of saleswomen and domestic employees. Destitution, if not prostitution, awaited scores of female English shopkeepers, hawkers, and street sellers who ended up in workhouses (1,254) or prison (326) in 1901.[36]

Russian sales clerks often worked in a despotic atmosphere and had to have "the knack" of both attracting and fleecing customers. Shop assistants in Odessa often lived in basements or attics, seldom had dinner breaks

Table 3.4. Women in Commerce, Transport, and Service, 1890s*

Country	# of women in commerce, transport, and service positions	% of female labor force
Russia	500,000	8
Germany	600,000	9
France	700,000	11
England	235,000	7

*Calculated from *Svod Perepisi 1897 g.*, 2: 250-55; *Stat. Jarbuch*, 35: 16-17; *An. Stat.*, 20: 22-37; *P.P. Vol. 97 Gt. Br. Census 1891*, 180.

or hot food, and earned low wages—ten to thirty rubles per month. Although French female clerks had better housing conditions than did Russians, their employers might lock them in dining rooms during lunch, pay a concierge to watch them, or pressure them to marry their beaux. Their long workday (ten to twelve hours in France and England and fifteen to nineteen hours in Russia) usually passed without a break and undermined their health. Often they had to clean the shop or do alterations for customers until 11 at night. The dream of owning their own shop kept many alive. Economic exploitation pushed some like Margaret Bondfield into trade union activity to improve their situation. Roughly 3,000 belonged to the English Shop Assistants' Union in 1898, but 125,000 by 1919. In France, only 160 women belonged to the clerks' union in 1900.[37]

In the Russian Empire, most women worked in small scale commerce. Russian women predominated (150,000), Jewish women ranked second (64,000), Ukrainians third (14,000), and Poles fourth (9,000). The 1895 German census reported 600,000 women employed in commerce. Half were under thirty years of age, 90% were single, 6% married, and 4% widowed or divorced. Half were Protestant, a third Catholic; only 3% were Jewish. Although more Jewish women worked in this sector than in any other, few were gainfully employed because most worked in family businesses. The French census reported many married female employees, and one wonders if census takers in other countries omitted married women working in family enterprises since they were unpaid. European grocers, bakers, and cafe owners seldom succeeded without their wives' bookkeeping and retail talents.[38]

The 1891 English census showed a high proportion of single, young shopgirls and clerks, yet their inadequate education prevented them from competing with men for high-level civil service posts. Moreover, they had to resign civil service jobs upon marriage. In 1909, female post office clerks earned sixty-five pounds per year, but shorthand typists a mere fifty-two.[39]

Service Occupations

English barmaids also worked long hours for low wages. They often lived together above the bar, working from 5:30 in the morning until midnight. They were supposed to receive two hours of rest per day, but seldom did. During their breaks, they were not allowed to go outside for fresh air, and had to breathe smoke, gas, and the foul breath of their customers for long periods. In 1913 their workday was limited to sixty-three hours per week. Hairdressers also worked long hours for only fifteen shillings per week.[40]

An unknown number of English women engaged in service occupations such as laundry and ironing, which married women often did at home, earning eight to ten shillings per week. Russian (66,000), Polish (12,000), and Ukrainian (11,000) women also worked as laundresses, bath attendants, and beauticians. Russian cleaning ladies tended to be older, married workers. They earned very low wages, worked long hours, and lacked trade union protection. Maria Botchkareva earned nine rubles per month as a dishwasher, and worked from five A.M. to eight P.M. as a laundress. (She escaped exploitative working and marital conditions by joining the Tsar's army during World War I.) Before 1914, Russian laundresses earned about a pound per month, those in England two pounds, and French laundresses one and a half pounds. The lowest-paid occupation everywhere was child care. Poor women in England and Russia also laid out the dead.[41]

Women in the Professions

'Tis *on* our sex, not *for* our sex,
That men now break their lances!
—*Englishwoman's Review*, March 18, 1878

Career women found it socially, financially, and emotionally difficult to support themselves in the nineteenth century. French writer Judith Gautier found herself intellectually alone and earning little for her journal articles.[42] Separate girls' schools allowed a small number of women to support themselves as secondary teachers. They earned less than their male cohorts, but more than primary-school teachers. Prior to 1880, a French teacher earned fifty-six francs per month, while later as a professeur (teacher) at a girl's lycée she earned 3,000. Yet only a handful of French women trained as professeurs at the Ecole Normale Supérieure at Sèvres and became well paid for their work.[43]

English women faced strong opposition in attempting to enter the professions. During the Crimean War, Florence Nightingale battled British officers and surgeons in carrying out her nursing work and reforms. Academics often disapproved of career women. Cambridge don Alfred Marshall thought masculine ability in women should be firmly trampled and that men would not marry competitors as wives.[44] The journal *Punch* declared: "The women who want women's rights, Want mostly, Women's charms." Some

Frenchmen also ridiculed career women, saying *"Une femme médecin repugne, une femme notaire fait rire, une femme avocat effraye."* Yet some male French principals and school inspectors encouraged young girls to become teachers. Persevering French women found university study open to them. Exceptional women such as Madame Curie even became university professors.[45]

European liberals believed that most middle-class women would choose marriage as their career. At mid-century, they sanctioned a spinster's work as governess, since it took place in the private sphere of the household. Only slowly did teaching in the public sphere become respectable for middle- and lower-middle-class women. Women from poorer families had a relatively easy time convincing their parents that it was honorable to earn their own living. Before World War I, English working-class girls dominated elementary-school teaching, serving as pupil teachers (assistants) in their mid-teens. However, their numbers declined when the training lengthened.[46]

Russian society accepted career women because it condoned their work as "ministering angels" in the helping professions and because such work was low paid and uncrowded. Indeed, the army allowed women to serve as doctors during the Russo-Turkish War of 1877 and during World War I. During the Great Reforms in Russia (1856–1870), the Liberal Minister of War Dmitri Miliutin strongly supported women's medical education. In the 1860s, Mariia Vernadskaia thought married and single gentry-class women had a right and duty to work and become independent.[47]

Married but separated gentry-class women such as Karolina Pavlova and Avdotia Panaeva supported themselves through writing and translating. Having servants, most married women were not restricted by household or child care duties. Nor did their careers threaten their marriage or the family. Even socialists such as Nadezhda Krupskaia, Konkordia Samoilova, and Maria Kostelovskaia found marriage and full-time revolutionary work compatible. While these women met with some ridicule, foreigners observed their presence in intellectual, cultural, and economic life.[48]

Russian authorities slowly adopted benevolent attitudes toward women's higher education and employment, and by 1905 there existed seventeen male, sixteen female, and eleven mixed feldsher schools. Although women predominated in education and medicine by 1916, they faced certain restrictions. They could treat only women and children, and they could not use the title Ph.D. in medicine because of the high pay, rank, and prestige it carried.[49]

In contrast to Russia, the professions were crowded in Europe. While German women were excluded from university study from 1879 till 1908, discrimination against women was more discreet in France and England. English matrons argued that no man would marry a woman who attended university. French women were not legally excluded from university study, but their schooling did not prepare them for it. Still, demographic imbalance and economic necessity increased the number of middle- and upper-class women seeking higher education and careers. Some have stressed women's sacrificial nature in their choice of the helping professions, but their work also provided independence, a means of earning a living, and a satisfying life outside marriage and motherhood. Indeed, careers became a way of creating a "self" and a "life" of one's own. In retrospect, Emmeline Pethick wondered if she were truly moved to serve the poor as a social worker or if she only wanted the independence it offered.[50] Teachers, writers, painters, and political activists saw their work as serving art, truth, feminism, and socialism as well as a means of self-realization.

By the 1890s, scores also worked as public school teachers, translators, journalists, social investigators, trade union leaders, doctors, midwives, writers, and artists. Few held the rank of university professor. While the Russian mathematician Sofia Kovalevskaia won international acclaim for her mathematical genius in 1874, she found employment only at the University of Stockholm (1883). Eileen Power taught history at Girton College, Cambridge, but few others seem to have been kissed by Clio (the muse of history).

Liberal myths of "male protectiveness" and male entitlement accepted women as low-paid governesses, elementary-school teachers, nurses, and midwives, but not as professors or doctors. During the Franco-Prussian War (1870–1871), French women served as nurses but not as doctors. In World War I the British government excluded female doctors from the front and rejected women's offers to organize a military hospital. The English attitude is well expressed in the 1875 poem:

> 'Tis a beautiful thing, a woman's sphere!
> She may nurse a sick bed thro' the small hours drear;
> Brave ghastly infection, untouched by fear,
> But she mustn't receive a doctor's fee,
> And she mustn't (oh shocking!) be called an M.D.,
> For if woman were suffered to take a degree,
> She'd be lifted quite out of her sphere.[51]

Generally, Russian and French country physicians were poorly paid, so women were not perceived as an economic threat. The Russian Senate condoned women's right to practice law in criminal cases in 1895, and the French in 1900, but the English and Germans only in the 1920s. Although a small proportion of the female labor force was occupied in professional work, historians know their legacy because they were the most literate and influential. Table 3.5 reveals their professional representation.

Distribution in Professional Ranks

By the 1890s, Russian and European women dominated primary-school teaching and lower church and medical ranks. There were so many English governesses and schoolmistresses that the census listed 249,000 women and 265,000 men in professional occupations in 1881. In terms of careers, however, 256,000 men served in the civil service, but only 15,000 women. Most women were teachers. In France, male civil servants outnumbered female ones 542,000 to 90,000.[52] In Russia and Germany, women lacked access to high- and mid-level civil service positions. Given the patriarchal nature of Russian and European society, it is remarkable that they gained the footholds they did. Certainly class, education, service ethic, desire for self-realization, public opinion, and economic necessity affected their access to careers. Most career women came from the upper and middle classes. The preponderance of upper-class women to men in Russia, England, and Germany increased their need to work. Gender disparity did not arise in France until after World War I, when the number and proportion of French career women increased dramatically.[53]

Table 3.5. Professional Female Workers, 1890s*

	# of women professionals	% of female labor force	% of total professional labor force
Russia	210,000	4	21
Germany	176,000	3	22
France	240,000	4	23
England	260,000	6	48

*Calculated from *Svod Perepisi 1897 g.*, 2: 236–55; *An. Stat.*, 20: 22-38; *P.P. Vol. 97 Gt. Br. Census 1891*, 2: 180–90.

Education for Professional Work

The expansion of public education in late nineteenth-century Europe demanded large cadres of teachers, and teaching became a respectable career for women. Still, large numbers remained governesses, traveling long distances to obtain jobs. In 1897, the artist Paula Becker realized she was unlikely to become a governess in Germany, but perhaps she might in England, Austria, or Russia. European governesses were common in Russian gentry-class households.[54]

By 1900, women dominated elementary education, except in Germany, and had made inroads into secondary teaching. During the Belle Epoque, French women transferred their role as nurturer to the school setting, making secondary teaching respectable. They spoke of their work as a "sacerdotal mission." In the 1860s, radical Russian writers used sacrificial rhetoric to define the gentry's obligation to serve society in the helping professions. Germans stressed teaching as an extension of women's natural maternal functions and their need to fulfill themselves as "spiritual mothers." In medicine, appeals to nurturing roles restricted them to nursing, so they argued that modesty made women physicians necessary.[55]

Women had to be tenacious to acquire higher education and serve their society in the face of social and family opposition. Thus, higher education was both a cause and a product of their emancipation. At the turn of the century, women still remained outside most schools and universities. Higher education generally remained a male preserve. Oxford and Cambridge had a combined student body of 13,000 males but only 286 females. Although segments of Russian society sanctioned women's right to higher education and careers in low-ranking positions, some opposed their advancement. No Russian university hired women professors, and Tsarist officials rejected the applications of both Mariia Bokova and Varvara A. Kashevarova-Rudneva (1842–1898) for the degree and title Doctor of Medicine, since that degree entitled them to status and rank in the bureaucracy.[56] Yet despite official discrimination, they enjoyed more public support for their professional work than many European women did.

In Germany and England, a surplus of educated men retarded women's entrance into higher education and the professions. Interviews with 100 German academics in 1897 revealed entrenched sexist attitudes. Like their English colleagues, some argued that women could not undertake university study because rigorous intellectual work would sicken and weaken them. Still others thought that women lacked the intelligence for study and that their role was to marry and have children. Some admitted that the professions were overcrowded and they did not want women's competition. While some Jewish women obtained higher education, few were listed as cultural workers in the 1907 German census because most German Jews approved of educating their daughters but preferred their wives not to work outside the home.[57] After 1900, women entered most professions except high civil service posts, law, and religion, as table 3.6 shows.

In England, elementary education became feminized, with 172,000 English female but only 59,000 male teachers in 1901. Primary-school teaching in England also changed from an avenue of upward mobility for working-class pupil teachers to a path of economic independence for lower-middle-class women. Before the war, pupil-teacher apprenticeship was replaced by a scholarship system that kept girls in school longer and then trained them as teachers from the ages of seventeen to twenty. Working-class families needed their children's wages and could not postpone their wage earning to age twenty when they finished teacher-training college. Lower-middle-class families were less dependent upon their children's contributions, so their daughters could pursue teaching careers. Census statistics support these claims; the 1891 census records 6,000 teachers ten to fourteen years old and 35,000 fifteen to nineteen years old, while the 1911

Table 3.6. Changes in Professional Employment, 1891–1911*

Occupation	Russia	England	France	Germany
	(1897)	(1891)	(1896)	(1895)
Teachers	71,500	144,400	91,000	39,000
Religious	80,000	10,000	130,000	18,000
Doctors	600	100	122	100+
Dentists	590	345	284	—
	(1911)	(1911)	(1906)	(1907)
Teachers	100,000	183,000	122,000	99,000
Religious	60,000	13,500	29,000	21,000
Doctors	1,750	477	533	195
Dentists	2,000	250	326	165

*Calculated from *Svod Perepisi 1897 g.* 2: 236-55; *Russian Year Book, 1912, 1915, 1916,* 89, 493, 464; *Statesman's Year-Book 1914*, 815-19, 898-95, 922, 1235-36; *P.P. Vols. 97 and 10 Census for Eng. and Wales, 1891, 1911,* 180-90, 75 respectively; *RSDRP 1896,* Tome IV, 254; *An. Stat.,* 30: 152; 52: 35*; *SDDR,* 1907 Band 203: 269-79; *Statesman's Year-Book 1908,* 1420. Albisetti found 233 female German doctors in 1915 and 1,500 in 1926 (Albisetti, "Female Physicians," 121).

census found 353 in the younger cohort and 16,600 in the older group. The decline from 41,000 to 17,000 youthful teachers shows the replacement of the pupil-teacher method with the scholarship approach. Middle-class women preferred secondary to elementary teaching because they believed elementary-school students were rough and uncouth.[58]

In England, men dominated high civil service posts, the church, and medicine. There were 50,000 men in church professions, but only 14,000 women; 22,486 male physicians, surgeons, and general practitioners, but only 212 women; 5,000 male dentists, but 140 female ones. This pattern also prevailed in France. By 1886, female primary-school teachers exceeded male teachers 72,000 to 63,000. While nuns initially predominated among female teachers, the secularization of education reduced their number. Although rural posts often made teachers feel isolated, teaching remained an attractive occupation for French women, and they continued to dominate the profession.[59]

Unlike England and France, teaching remained a male preserve in Germany. In 1900, women accounted for only 25% of primary-school teachers and 30% of all education personnel. Although Germany had a substantial Catholic population, Bismark's *Kulturkampf* (struggle with the Catholic church over education and other issues) resulted in the expulsion of the Jesuits, the restriction of teaching orders, and the relegation of women to nursing and contemplative orders. Consequently, the 1907 census found only 18,000 Catholic nuns, 4,000 Protestant women, and 35 Jewish women in religious occupations. German women comprised less than 1% of the doctors and 5% of the dentists. Neither English nor German women matched the Russian proportion of 10% of the medical profession prior to World War I. Women generally made up 100% of the midwives and most of the nurses and hospital personnel.[60]

Russia lacked compulsory education, and the 1897 census found fewer teachers than priests: 170,000 men in church occupations and 129,000 in education; 81,000 nuns and 71,000 women teachers. There were 70,000 Orthodox women religious, 244 Catholic women, and 25 Jewish women listed in religious vocations.[61] Men dominated the medical profession: 13,000 male doctors to 600 female. Still, several paths were open to Russian women doctors: the liberal path of serving the poor in urban and rural medical clinics, the patriotic path of serving the wounded during the Russo-Turkish War of 1877–1878, or the radical way of combining medical and revolutionary work. The excellent service of women doctors in the war gained them public support among both physicians and journalists, who became their champions.

Marriage and Professional Employment

Unlike English and German society, Russia and France society regarded marriage and careers as compatible. Educated women in the Russian Empire often came from families with servants, so they thought combining marriage and career agreeable. In France, the Catholic Church, politicians of the Third Republic, and bourgeois culture encouraged even career women to marry and procreate. Indeed, the proportion of French career women who were married increased from 14% in 1896 to 23% in 1906, and about 40% of female schoolteachers were married. In contrast, only 10% of English and German women teachers and 25% of female doctors and dentists were married. A common pattern among London teachers was late marriage, so that married women often held high positions as headmistresses. When expediency demanded it, the marriage bar was lifted. During the war, a teacher shortage arose in England, and young teachers who married did not lose their jobs. The professions in which large numbers of Teutonic women married were nursing and midwifery.[62]

It was not easy for career women to combine work and marriage, yet some married English teachers continued working because they preferred teaching to keeping house. Some wanted the better quality of life for their family that their income provided. Few women left their husbands and children for their work, but some did. Some upper-class Russian women—Ekaterina Breshkovskaia, Aleksandra Kollontai, and Inessa Armand—left their husbands and children for revolutionary work. German artist Paula Modersohn Becker also fled social and household duties. In 1906, she wrote: "Now I have left Otto Modersohn and am standing between my old life and my new life. I wonder what the new one will be like." She wondered how to sign her name since she was neither Modersohn nor Becker anymore.[63]

Wage Discrimination

Career women faced many of the same obstacles other working women did. They received lower wages and a lower rank than their male colleagues, and sometimes endured ridicule and sexual harassment in the workplace. Women teachers generally occupied the lowest ranks and held the lowest-paid positions. Many female teachers worked for privately funded educational institutions that paid low salaries. Both governesses and primary-school teachers earned lower salaries than did secondary instructors. While Russian governesses received 200 rubles per year, female elementary-school teachers earned 200 to 400 rubles (20 to 40 pounds). Higher-ranking male teachers in the gymnasia, which the Ministry of Education funded, earned up to 900 rubles per year.[64] In the 1890s, positions for governess in per London were advertised for 25 pounds a year — the same salary as a parlormaid. Elementary teachers earned 90 pounds and secondary teachers 100 pounds. In 1909, salaries of uncertificated female teachers were 54 pounds per year, compared to men's 66 pounds. To save money, many local school boards hired trained teachers at the uncertificated rate! In London, many elementary-school teachers could barely survive on their salaries. Schoolmistresses and superintendents earned 150 to 300 pounds per year, while their male counterparts received 400 to 1,000 pounds.[65]

The school reforms of 1881 narrowed the gap between French men's and women's secondary-school salaries: male *professeurs* earned 2,400 to 3,400 francs, females slightly less. Yet male normal-school directors received higher salaries than did females, and men generally retired with better pensions than women. In Germany, wage differentials were also great because only men obtained university diplomas entitling them to civil service salaries. In the 1870s, German male elementary teachers earned 1,650 to 2,100 marks, while women received 900 to 1,350. When French and German primary-school teachers unionized at the turn of the century, women's salaries began to approximate those of men. Yet German teachers who endorsed socialism risked dismissal.[66]

Wage discrimination in medicine meant Russian women doctors generally earned half the salaries men did. Although there were 2,000 female doctors in Russia by 1900, more clustered in the lower ranks as feldshers (5,000) and midwives (14,000). They endured harsh working conditions in the provinces, where medical care was underfunded and patients could not afford medications. Consequently, doctors such as A. I. Veretennikova used their salaries to buy medicine for their patients. Female pharmacists earned modest salaries, about 600 to 800 rubles per year in rural areas. Pharmacy assistants earned half that.[67]

Oppressive working conditions and wage discrimination were not confined to Russia. English female university graduates sometimes earned forty pounds per year, less than elementary- or secondary-school teachers. English staff nurses received twenty to thirty pounds per year, worked ten to twelve hours per day, and had only one-half day off each week, while higher-ranking nursing sisters received thirty-five to sixty pounds per year, and matrons 100 to 350 pounds in 1890. The double standard in pay was pervasive; female factory inspectors earned 200 pounds per year, one-third of what male inspectors made. Women civil-service employees occupied low-level positions and earned forty to eighty pounds per year. Male postal employees received twenty to sixty-five shillings per week, whereas women received fourteen to thirty. Advantages of civil service employment were short periods of training, job security, and pensions. Yet the marriage bar for women was absolute. Once married, a woman lost her post. While the Russian government denied women civil servants the pensions and perquisites men received, the German *Beamten* (civil service) absolutely refused to employ them.[68]

Sexual Harassment and Other Difficulties

Career women also suffered from sexual harassment and unsafe working conditions. Russian women doctors who served in the Russo-Turkish War encountered sexual overtures from military officers, while those in private practice experienced sexual harassment by some male patients.[69] A good account of sexual harassment is found in Mikhail Il'in's novel *My Sister's Story,* in which his sister, who has trained as an architect, complains about her employer touching her with his eyes. She feels as though she has no clothes on.[70] Although many segments of Russian society tolerated women's study and professional work, some women were unable to bear the harassment of the male-dominated workplace and retreated to the private sphere of the home. Well-to-do married women had this option, but single ones did not. They sometimes had to endure harassment, sexual exploitation, and ridicule in their work. Well-educated, gentry-class gymnasium graduates who went to teach in the Russian countryside experienced incredible culture shock and isolation. Daughters of rural clerical families adjusted better.[71]

As a social investigator, Beatrice Potter Webb was surprised at the response of her male trade union and socialist colleagues, who considered her attractive. She asked herself: "Are all women nailed to their sex?" The French writer Judith Gautier hated the part that physical attraction played in her male admirers' response to her and wanted appreciation for her intellect.[72]

Harassment sometimes took the form of condescending remarks. Cambridge historian Canon Creighton told Beatrice Webb that it was women's mission to charm, not instruct. School inspectors sometimes humiliated female teachers and ruined their careers by writing bad reports. Some teachers committed suicide, while others literally worked themselves to death trying to please their inspectors. While sexual harassment, humiliation, and isolation in rural areas made the workplace psychologically unpleasant for many career women, some conditions actually threatened their lives. Large classes physically exhausted teachers, making them susceptible to diseases such as scarlet fever that pupils brought to school. Still, dying in childbirth was not uncommon, and motherhood was more lethal than teaching.[73]

Radicalization of Career Women

Unfair treatment pushed some career women into union and political activity. To reduce socialism's allure, the German government granted female elementary teachers civil service status in 1885 and pension rights in 1887. In 1888, German women organized a Women's Reform Association to help spinsters find suitable employment; it grew from 99 members to 900, while the German Women's Teachers' Association grew from 9,000 in 1895 to 16,000 by 1900. Bourgeois German and French women shunned militant tactics as "not in good taste," so women's suffrage movements were smaller and less visible there than in England.

In 1870, English teachers founded a national union, which negotiated pensions and secured jobs for certificated teachers by 1898. Women comprised 53% of union membership in 1891, but union leadership remained male dominated until 1912. During the war, they persuaded their union to endorse equal pay for teachers. Afterwards, male supremacy reasserted itself, and nothing came of their demands for equal pay. Since male union leaders seldom advanced suffrage and equal pay, radicalized women teachers formed two other groups to press their causes: the National Federation of Women Teachers and the Women Teachers' Franchise Union. Like working-class women, female teachers often lacked the time, effort, and money to pursue trade union causes and the confidence to participate in executive committees or money for membership dues and travel to meetings. The marriage bar radicalized some teachers to help married women teachers keep their jobs. While established married women often retained their posts, young teachers who married often lost theirs. So mothers sometimes told their daughters that a woman would be a fool to give up a well-paid job and a pension for marriage. French female primary teachers, who were often better educated but less well paid than male ones, also joined feminist organizations such as the Fédération Feministes Universitaire and Conseil National des Femmes Françaises, which endorsed equal pay for equal work, whereas male-dominated socialist groups did not.[74]

While some women were welcomed into cultural circles, many received a mixed response. Russian writer and painter Maria Bashkirtseva won a general competition at her Parisian school and a gold medal, but she was allowed to exhibit only one of her pictures at the Salon in 1880 and another in 1884. Upon her death, the society of French women artists exhibited all her pictures and sculptures. In 1881, the sculptor and educator Madame Bertaux (1825–1909) founded the Union des Femmes Peintres et Sculpteurs. By 1890, it published its own *Journal des Femmes Artistes,* and by 1897 it had 900 exhibitors. However, these became Pyrrhic victories as avant-garde exhibitions moved away from state institutions to private dealers who discriminated against women. The double standard still stymied women's work, and the sculptor Camille Claudel (1864–1943) lost her mind because French society refused to recognize her talent. Artist Paula Modersohn Becker discovered that family duties and attitudes interfered with her career. Her dedication was regarded as egotistic and hurtful to the family. She contemplated divorce and left her husband and stepchild in order to concentrate on her painting in Paris.[75] Married Russian artists such as Anna Ostruomova-Lebedeva (1871–1944), Natalia Goncharova (1881–1962), and Liubov Popova (1889–1924) encountered less discrimination in their artistic careers because their society was more tolerant.

Liberal Russian doctors Maria Pokrovskaia and Anna Shabanova founded suffrage organizations in efforts to improve their situation. Other career women sometimes became disenchanted with educational and medical work among the poor and became full-time revolutionaries to improve life for the masses. It is misleading to focus exclusively on women who gave up professional work to become revolutionaries. There were 70,000 women teachers and several thousand medical personnel in the late nineteenth century, but only a few thousand revolutionaries. By 1914, Russian and European professional women had come a long way. Careers that Russian radicals only wrote about in 1860 had become more common, and middle- and upper-class women who could not or would not marry had many more career and life options than were available fifty years earlier.

Notes

1. Cecil Woodham Smith's biography of Florence Nightingale; Nellie Alden Franz, *English Women Enter the Professions*, 104–5; Silver, "Salon, Foyer, Bureau Women and the Professions in France," *Journal of Sociology* 78: 848. Silver indicates that the higher the class in France, the less compatible women's working outside the home was.

2. Ostroumova-Lebedeva, *Avtobiograficheskie zapiski*, 249–50; Pethick-Lawrence, *My Part in a Changing World*, 65; Barbara Corrado Pope, "Cherchez la Femme: New Books on Women and Gender in France," *Journal of Women's His-*

tory 9 (Summer 1977): 179; Kate Perry, review of Gillian Thomas, "A Position to Command Respect: Women and the Eleventh Britannica," *Gender and History*, 1996: 21.

3. Frevert, *Women in German History*, 83–85; Carles, *A Life of Her Own*, 5–126; de Maupassant, "A Family Affair," in *Selected Tales*, 124; Tian-Shanskaia, *Village Life*; Orlaw, *Red Wedding*; Hapgood, *Russian Rambles*, 188–258. An evening gathering in Russia was called *posidelka* and, in France, *veillée*.

4. The 1897 Russian census found that 3.1 million peasant women had been born in one *guberniia* (province) but were living in another, and about 2.2 million had been born in one *uezd* (district) but lived in another. *Svod Perepisi 1897 g.* 1: 85; *An. Stat.* 1910, 30: 14.

5. *Svod Perepisi 1897 g.* 2: 3, 264–67, 326–27, 335; Antonia Valentin, "The Employment of Women Since the War," *International Labor Review* 25 (April 1932): 483 (hereafter cited as *ILR*); Tian-Shanskaia, *Village Life*, 48–49; Hapgood, *Russian Rambles*, 258; *RSDRP* (1896), 29; *Statesman's Year Book* (1888), 251; (1899), 49; (1910), 16–17; *Stat. Jarbuch* (1935), 10; (1939), 19; Wolfgang Kollman, "The Process of Urbanization in Germany at the Height of the Industrialization Period," *Journal of Contemporary History* 4 (1969): 61. The disparity among Ukrainian women was 383,000 to 9.3 million, among Belorussians 94,000 to 2.6 million, and Poles 184,000 to 2.3 million. A ruble contained 100 kopeks and was worth about 50 American cents, 25 pence, 2.6 francs, or 2.1 marks.

6. "Sotsialisticheskoe sel'skoe khoziaistvo Soiuza SSR," *PKh*, 7 (1939): 163; Worobec, *Peasant Russia*, 151–74; Barbara Alpern Engel, "The Woman's Side: Male Out-Migration and the Family Economy in Kostroma Province," *Slavic Review*, Summer 1986, 257–71; Farnsworth, "The Litigious Daughter-In-Law," *Slavic Review*, Spring 1986, 49–64; Rose Glickman, "Peasant Women and Their Work," *The World of the Russian Peasant*, 45–64; Cathy Frierson, *Peasant Icons*, 161–80; Lenin, *Razvitie kapitalizma v Rossii*, chapter V, part VI, 244–49; Troyat, *Daily Life in Russia*, 105; Ransel, "Abandonment and Fosterage of Unwanted Children," *The Family in Imperial Russia*, 189–217; Engelgardt, *Letters from the Country, 1872–1887*, 113.

7. *Statistik des Deutschen Reichs, Band 102*, table 9, "Religion. und Beruf . . . des Reichs am 14 Juni 1895," 372 (hereafter cited as *SDDR*); Bernard A. Cook, "Agricultural Laborers,"*Victorian Britain, An Encyclopedia*, 11; Dayus, *Her People*, 132.

8. In 1897, there were 100,000 domestics in Moscow province, 119,000 in St. Petersburg province, 58,000 in Siberia, 18,000 in Central Asia, 237,000 in the Polish provinces, 60,000 in Caucasia, 736,000 in Central Russia, 327,000 in Ukraine, and 211,000 in Belorussia. *Svod Perepisi 1897 g.* 1: 206–07; 2: 10–12, 206–7, 288, 326–86; *Pervaia Perepisi 1897 goda*, 24 (tom 2, Moscow): 182–83; 37 (tom 2, St. Petersburg): 158–205. For marital and literacy status, see *SDDR*, Band 102, Table 9, 372; *Stat. Jarbuch* 35: 16–17; Clara Collet, "Statistics of Employment of Women and Girls," *JRSS*, September 1895, 522-25; *An. Stat.*, table XVII, 20 (1910): 30–31; *Chislennost' Rossii 1897 g.*, 1: xvii, xviii, 8–13; Joan Scott and Louise Tilly, *Women, Work, and Family*, 108.

9. *Svod Perepisi 1897 g.* 1: vii; Clara Collet, "The Social Status of Women Occupiers," *JRSS*, September 1908, 513. Collet found only 10% of the English population had servants. Theresa McBride found that one out of six French house-

holds had a servant. McBride, "Social Mobility for the Lower Class Domestic Service in France," *Journal of Social History*, Fall 1974, 64. For wages and treatment of Russian and Ukrainian servants, see Kollontai, *Iz Moei Zhizni i Raboty*, 18–19; Troyat, *Daily Life in Russia*, 30; Orlow, *Red Wedding*, 129; Kuzminskaya, *Tolstoy As I Knew Him*, 19.

10. W. T. Layton, "Changes in Wages of Domestic Servants during Fifty Years," *JRSS*, September 1908, 518–19; *The London Times*, 4 May 1895, 6; 7 May 1895, 15; Clark, *Position of Women in France*, 34. German servants earned 150 to 200 reichmarks per year according to Frewert, *Women in German History*, 86. McBride found that some deposited their wages in savings accounts, and about one-third achieved upward social mobility by setting themselves up in shops or marrying above their original social status (McBride, "Social Mobility for the Lower Class," 64, 74).

11. McBride found that servants could experience downward mobility, falling into prostitution, alcoholism, theft, and suicide ("Social Mobility for the Lower Class," 74–75). Russian domestics were also prone to downward mobility, as Kollontai notes in "Working Woman and Mother" (1914), *Alexandra Kollontai: Selected Writings*, 128-29. Regarding illegitimacy, see *RSDRP* (1896), 21; *Statesman's Year Book* (1892, 1900): "United Kingdom," 26; "France," 474, 514; "Germany," 537, 589; Worobec, *Peasant Russia*, 143; Ransel, *Mothers of Misery*, 99, 163, 166–67; Ransel, "Abandonment and Fosterage of Unwanted Children," *The Family in Imperial Russia*, 196–99; John R. Gillis, *For Better, For Worse: British Marriages, 1600 to the Present*, 322; Regina Schulte, "Peasants and Farmers' Maids, Female Farm Servants in Bavaria at the End of the Nineteenth Century," *The German Peasantry*, 158–71.

12. Two-thirds of prostitutes had been servants, according to V. Bronner, *La Lute Contre la Prostitution*. See also Famina Halle, *Women in Soviet Russia* 1: 206–7, 221; Barbara Alpern Engel, "St. Petersburg Prostitutes in the Late Nineteenth Century: A Personal and Social Profile," *Russian Review*, January 1989, 21–44. For Pokrovskaia's studies, see Jeanette Tuve, *The First Women Physicians*, 95–96. The 1897 census found 14,000 declared prostitutes, about 3,700 seventeen to nineteen years old, and 9,000 twenty to thirty-nine years. *Svod Perepisi 1897 g.* 2: 254–55, 326–48. For Jewish women, see Richard Stites, "Prostitute and Society in Pre-Revolutionary Society," *Jarbucher fur Geschichte Ost europas*, Band 31, 1983, Heft 3: 348–65.

13. Regarding Germany, see "Prostitiutsiia," *BSE* 47, 332–33; E. Milovidova, *Zhenskii Vopros i Zhenskoe Dvizhenie*, 183; Frevert, *Women in German History*, 87–88. In Tolstoy's novel *Resurrection*, Prince Nekhliudov seduces his servant Katiusha Maslova, who becomes a prostitute. This novel was based on a true story that a lawyer told Tolstoy. See introduction by Michael Schammell, *Resurrection*, viii–ix.

14. Philip Priestley, *Victorian Prison Lives: English Prison Biography, 1830–1914*, 72–73; Wanda Neff, *Victorian Working Women*, 54; Ann R. Higginbotham, "'Sins of the Age': Infanticide and Illegitimacy in Victorian London," *Victorian Studies*, Spring 1989, 320–37; *Census for Eng. and Wales, 1901*, tables XLII, XLIII, 242–45; *Census for Eng. and Wales, 1911*, Part I, tables 18 and 19, 475–76; Murray,

Strong Minded Women, 330; "Foreign Notes and News, France," *Englishwoman's Review*, 15 March 1878, 139.

15. *Jahr. Amt. Stat. Preuss. Staates, Heraugegeben vom Koniglichen Statistichen Bureau*, V. Jahrgang, 710–25; *Census of Eng. and Wales, 1891*, General Report, 4: 81; *Statesman's Year Book* (1900), "British Empire," 26, 41; "France," 514, 523; "Germany," 589, 594; "Russia," 938; *Svod Perepisi 1897 g*. 2: 240–41, 292–93; Eric A. Johnson, "The Roots of Crime in Imperial Germany," *Central European History* 15 (4): 362; Higginbotham, "Infanticide and Illegitimacy in Victorian London," 323–37; Ransel, *Mothers of Misery*, 19, 134, 166; Laura Engelstein, "Gender and the Juridical Subject Prostitution and Rape in Nineteenth-Century Russian Criminal Codes," *Journal of Modern History* 60 (September 1988): 493; Rachel G. Fuchs, *Poor and Pregnant in Paris*, 184–98, 203–16; James M. Donovan, "Abortion, the Law, and the Juries in France, 1825–1920," *Proceedings of Western Society for French History*, 15 (November 1987): 217. By 1900, punishment for minor offenses in England had diminished, but average sentences became longer, resulting in the incarceration of fewer women but for longer periods.

16. Regarding demanding employers, see Doris Viersbeck, who served as a cook in Hamburg in 1888, *The German Worker*, 135–59. For England, see Mrs. Layton, "Memories of Seventy Years," *Life as We Have Known It*, 22–28.

17. *Svod Perepisi 1897 g*. 1, 2, 3: 325–49. About 6.6 million men and 4.7 million women were born in one *guberniia* but living in another at the time of the census; about 3 million women and 3 million men were born in one *uezd* but lived in another in 1897. Moscow and St. Petersburg had a preponderance of men to women. There were 453,500 peasant men but only 294,000 peasant women in St. Petersburg. In Moscow, there were 413,427 peasant men and 249,236 women. *Pervaia Perepisi 1897 g*. 37 (St. Petersburg): 48–49, 24 (Moscow): 50–55; Alexander Gershenkron, "The Rate of Industrial Growth in Russia," *Journal of Economic History* 7 (1947): 144–57.

18. *The Russian Year Book*, 475–76; Mulhall, *Dic. of Stat.*, 476; K. A. Pazhitnov in Milovidova, *Zhenskii Vopros...*, 186; Rose Glickman, *The Russian Factory: Women, Workplace and Society*, 39, 44, 65; Halle, *Woman in Soviet Russia*, 220. Halle indicates many Russian women earned less than ten rubles per month, and cigarette makers earned only one to two rubles per month in 1900. Gudvan found that 48% of Odessa shop assistants lived in cellars, 29% on third and fourth floors, and only 13% on the first or second floor of a house. Gudvan, *Prikazchiki v Odessa*, 42–43. See also Reginald Zelnik, *Labor and Society in Tsarist Russia*, 242–43. Dostoevsky and Gorky also depict crowded housing in *Crime and Punishment* (1869) and *The Lower Depths*. James Bater decries the inadequate public transportation system in St. Petersburg, which forced workers to live in the central district of the city where the rents were high and the facilities poor. Bater, *St. Petersburg Industrialization and Change*, 271–74.

19. Ann-Louise Shapiro, "Housing Reform in Paris: Social Space and Social Control," *French Historical Studies* 12 (Fall 1982): 486–507; J. J. Lee, "Aspects of Urbanization in Germany, 1815–1914," *Towns and Societies*, 291. Lee found that 370,000 Berliners lived in cellars or upper stories of houses during the late nineteenth century. For England, see Neff, *Victorian Working Women*, 44–46; Elizabeth Gaskell, *Mary Barton*; Webb, *Dic. of Stat.*, 312. Webb found housing density

the highest in Germany and Russia, with 8 persons per house; lower in England with 5.4; and lowest in France with 4.2.

20. See Canning, *Languages of Labor*, 176, 211.

21. Cited by Judith Coffin in "Social Science Meets Sweated Labor: Reinterpreting Women's Work in Late Nineteenth Century France," *Journal of Modern History* 63 (June 1991): 252.

22. Robert A. Lewis and Richard H. Rowland, "Urbanization in Russia and the USSR, 1897–1966," *Annals of the Association of American Geographers*, 59 (December 1969): 791; P. A. Orlov found 875,764 factory workers in 1881, Lenin, *P.S.S. Vol. 3 Razvitie Kapitalisma v Rossi*, 463; *The Statesman's Year Book* (1899), 951, found only 1 million men and about 300,000 women occupied in large scale factory production and approximately 100,000 working in small factories in 1891. In 1897, 92,133 women were involved in the home production of cotton, 85,031 were occupied in linen and flax, 9,202 in wool, 10,504 in silk, 44,418 in embroidery, and 1,050 in dyeing. About 242,338 (47%) of women textile workers were engaged in some form of domestic or artisan production. *Svod Perepisi 1897 g.* table XX-a, 2: 272; *Chislennost' Rossii 1897 g.* 1: 2–11; *Pervaia perepisi 1897 g.* 24 (Moscow): 152–53, 160–61; 37 (St. Petersburg): 164–65, 172–73; *Russian Year Book* (1912), 2, 711

23. Coffin, "Social Science Meets Sweated Labor," 254; Stewart, *Women, Work, and the French State*, 69; Lenin, *PSS. vol. 3*, 386–408, 548; Glickman, *The Russian Factory*, 39, 44, 65; Kelly, *The German Worker*, 68–69; Neff, *Victorian Working Women*, 47; Ivy Pinchbeck, *Women Workers and the Industrial Revolution, 1750–1850*, 235–37; Lucy Middleton, *Women in the Labour Movement*, 99–100. In *My Childhood*, Gorky shows family members and hired workers living in one household, working together in domestic production.

24. *An. Stat.* 20 (1900): 22, Tableau XV "Population active par groups, 1896"; Mulhall, *Dictionary of Statistics*, "Wages," 582; Stewart, *Women, Work, and the French State*, 68–69.

25. Marilyn J. Boxer, "Women in Industrial Homework: The Flowermakers of Paris in the Belle Epoque," *French Historical Studies*, 406, 416–17.

26. *P.P. Vol. 97 Gt. Br. Census 1891*, 180; *Stat. Jarbuch*, 35: 216–17; Robyn Dasey, "Women's Work and the Family: Women Garment Workers in Berlin and Hamburg Before the First World War," 221–55 in *The German Family*; autobiography of Ottilie Baader, Seamstress, in *The German Worker*, 68–69.

27. J. H. Treble, "The Seasonal Demand for Adult Labor in Glasgow, 1890–1914," *Social History* 3 (1): 54–60; Clara Collet, "Statistics of Employment of Women and Girls," *JRSS*, September 1895, 522–25; Sally Alexander, Anna Davin, and Eric Hostettler, "Laboring Women: A Reply to Eric Hobsbawn," *History Workshop* 7–8 (1979): 174–82; Scott and Tilly, *Women, Work, and Family*; Neff, *Victorian Working Women*; Pinchbeck, *Women Workers and the Industrial Revolution*, 235–37.

28. "Reports and Correspondence on Factory Hours and Regulations, Industrial Health Hazards and the Berlin Labour Conference, 1872–1891," in *British Parliamentary Papers*, Industrial Revolution, Factories, 28 (Shannon, Ireland): 70–71; Stewart, *Women, Work, and the French State*, 201.

29. *P.P. Vol. 97 Gt. Br. Census 1891*, 180; *An. Stat.* 20 (1900): 22; *Stat. Jarbuch*, 26: 11; *Svod Perepisi 1897 g.* 2: 244–50; B. L. Hutchins, "IV–A Note on the Distribution of Women in Occupations," *JRSS*, September 1904, 480.

30. *Svod Perepisi 1897 g.* 2: 244–50; *An. Stat.* 20 (1900): 22.

31. *Russian Year Book* (1915), 503; *Russian Year Book* (1912), 703; "Wages of the Working Classes in Berlin," *JRSS*, December 1888, 825–26; Webb, *New Dic. of Stat.*, 620–22; Madeleine Gilbert, *Les Fonctions des Femmes*, 46–47; Mulhall, *Dic. of Stat.*, Part II, 85, 153, 186, 582; Mary Agnes Hamilton, *Margaret Bondfield*, 103–4; Pethick-Lawrence, *My Part in a Changing World*, 777–78; Appendix N. in Irene O. Andrews and Margaret A. Hobbs, *Economic Effects of the World War upon Women and Children in Great Britain*; Kaethe Schirmacher, *The Modern Women's Rights Movement*, 84, 226. A franc and a mark were each worth about one shilling, and a ruble about two shillings; twenty shillings made one pound. *Statesman's Year Book* (1900), 546, 617, 984; "A Living Wage for Factory Girls at Crewe," 5 May 1894 and 19 May 1984, Letters to Crewe newspaper in *The Life and Writings of Ada Nield Chew*, 76–81.

32. *Russian Year Book* (1912), 703; Schomerus, "The Family Life-Cycle: A Study of Factory Workers in Nineteenth Century Wurttemberg," 189ff., in *The German Family*; Mrs. Layton, "Memories of Seventy Years," *Life as We Have Known It*, 26; "Working Conditions of a Female Textile Worker in Germany, 1880s and 1890s," *Discovering the Western Past,* 2: 130–31.

33. Pokrovskaia's report on women factory workers in *European Women: A Documentary History*, 15–16; Rose Glickman, "The Russian Factory Woman," in *Women in Russia*, 69; Glickman, *The Russian Factory,* 122; *Russian Year Book* (1915), 501; Gorky's novel *(Mother)*; "Life in a Crewe Factory," 23 June 1894, *The Life and Writings of Ada Nield Chew*, 89; Norbet C. Soldon, *Women in the British Trade Unions 1874–1976*, 30–32.

34. Regarding women workers, see *Life as We Have Known It*, xxxvii–xxxix; Pokrovskaia, "A Woman Doctor's Report," 17; Rose Glickman, *Russian Factory Women*, 141–45; Judith and Daniel Walkowitz, "We Are Not Beasts of the Field: Prostitution and the Poor in Plymouth and Southampton under the Contagious Diseases Acts," *F.S.* 1 (3): 73–106. Duma doctor Ekaterina Slanskaia describes her discovery of abandoned sick children during their mother's work hours in her memoirs translated in Clyman, *Russia Through Women's Eyes*, 210.

35. For conditions in low-level service jobs, see Theresa McBride, "A Woman's World: Department Stores and the Evolution of Women's Employment, 1870–1920," *French Historical Studies* 10 (Fall 1978): 664–83; Gudvan, "Essays on the History of the Movement of Sales-Clerical Workers in Russia," in Victoria Bonnell, *The Russian Worker*, 192–206; Maria Botchkareva, *Yahska, My Life as Peasant, Officer, and Exile*, 27, 30ff; Rose Glickman, *Russian Factory Worker*, 66–68.

36. English women in government increased from 15,000 in 1891 to 26,400 in 1901; in commerce from 20,800 to 58,000; in food and lodging from 199,000 to 292,500: *P.P. Vol. 97 Gt. Br. Census* (1891), 180; *P.P. Vol. 108 Census for Eng. and Wales* (1901), 243–45, 256–69; Hutchins, "A Note on the Distribution of Women in Occupations," *JRSS*, 480. Regarding Russian shopgirls, see Rose Glickman, *Russian Factory Women*, 66–68; Gudvan, "Essays on the History of the Movement of Sales-Clerical Workers in Russia," 195–97; McBride, "A Woman's World," 668, 679. Well-paying jobs in banks were rarely available unless one first granted favors to the director or manager. Some shop managers asked prospective female employees if they were "ticklish." If one batted one's eyes or nodded one's head

suggestively, one got the job. Bosses courted cooperative sales girls, paid them on time, and gave them presents — until they grew "heavy around the waist." Then they might fire them.

37. Gail A. Savage, "Civil Service," and P. D. Edwards, "Clerks and Clerical Work," in *Victorian Britain*, 165, 170–71; Soldon, *Women in the British Trade Unions*, 51-52; Gudvan, *Prikazchiki v Odessa*, 22–24, 37–43; McBride, "A Woman's World," 664–83; Stewart, *Women, Work, and the French State*, 72–75.

38. *Svod Perepisi 1897 g.* 2: 325–35; *An. Stat.* 30 (1910): 16; *Stat. Jarbuch* 35: 16–17; Crossick and Haupt, *The Petite Bourgeoisie in Europe, 1780–1914*, 87–98.

39. Dora M. Jones, "The Cheapness of Women" (1909) in *Strong Minded Women*, 322–25; Widdowson, *Going Up into the Next Class*, 63–64.

40. "A Bar Maid's Work," *Victoria*, June 1876, *Strong Minded Women*, 362; Jones, "The Cheapness of Women," *Strong Minded Women*, 322–25.

41. Clementina Black, *Married Women's Work*, 7–9; Cadbury, *Women's Work and Wages*, 106, 326–30; *Svod Perepisi 1897 g.* 2: xlviii–xlix; table XX: 254–55; *Chislennost' Rossii 1897 g.* 1: 10; Laura Engelstein, *Moscow, 1905 Working-Class Organization and Political Conflict*, 20, 237; Mulhall, *Dic. of Stat.*, 852; Maria Botchkareva, *Yashka My Life*, 27; "Ekaterina Slanskaia," in Clyman, *Russia Through Women's Eyes*, 195.

42. Richardson, *Judith Gautier, A Biography*, 60, 168.

43. Margadant, *Madame le Professeur*, 46–47; Clark, "A Battle of the Sexes in a Professional Setting: The Introduction of Inspectrices Primaires, 1899–1914," 97, 100–01; Pope, "Cherchez la Femme," 180.

44. *The Diary of Beatrice Webb, Vol. I*, 28 February 1899, 274; 7 June 1889, 286.

45. See *Punch*, quoted by Figes in *Patriarchal Attitudes*, 20. French quotation from Charrier, *L'Evolution Intellectuelle Feminine*, 1 (trans: A woman doctor is repugnant, a woman notary makes one laugh, a woman lawyer is frightening.). Also Carles, *A Life of Her Own*, 56–63; Clark, *The Position of Women*, 48ff.

46. Albisetti, *Schooling German Girls and Women*, 59, 100; Widdowson, *Going Up into the Next Class*, 21–28, 68–73; Dina M. Copelman, *London's Women Teachers, Gender, Class and Feminism 1870–1930*, 10ff.

47. Satina, *Education of Women in Pre-Revolutionary Russia*; A. E. Ivanov, "Facty, Sobytiia, Liudi," *Voprosy Istorii* (1973), 1: 208–10; Johanson, "Autocratic Politics, Public Opinion, and Women's Medical Education During the Reign of Aleksandr II, 1855–1881," 426–43. Quotes from Vernadskaia are found in Richard Stites, "Mikhailov and the Emergence of the 'Woman Question' in Russia," 181; Carolina de Maegd-Soep, *The Emancipation of Women in Russian Literature and Society*, 49.

48. Kennard, *The Russian Year Book, 1912*, 89–97. Kennard thought women dominated dentistry, and women doctors abounded. Professor Hermann Schoenfield thought Russian career women experienced greater tolerance than in other societies. They had the right to practice law, participate in the local dumas, and conduct businesses. Hermann Schoenfield, *Women*, 8: 383–84. Russian art, such as Dmitriev-Orenburgsky's sketch of Korzukhin's birthday at the Artel (1865), Makovsky's "An Evening Gathering," and Yaroshenko's portrait of Anna Chertkova in "Kursistka" (Girl Student, 1883), depict women in cultural, intellectual, political,

and artistic situations. Elizabeth Valkenier, *Russian Realist Art: The State and Society*, 49, 94, 114.

49. See Mary Schaeffer Conroy, "Pharmacy in Pre-Soviet Russia," *Pharmacy in History* 27 (1985): 124; Ts.SK, *Ezhegodnik' Rossii, 1907g*. (St. Petersburg, 1908): 374–77; TsSK, *Ezhegodnik' 1915 (Petrograd, 1916)*, 118; Toby Clyman, "Women Physicians' Autobiography in the Nineteenth Century," in *Women Writers in Russian Literature*, 111–26.

50. Pethick Lawrence, *My Part in a Changing World*, 66–67.

51. Brittain, *Testament of Youth*, 304; Pethick Lawrence, *My Part in a Changing World*, 306–7; quote from *Englishwoman's Review*, 6 September 1875, 429–30.

52. *Svod Perepisi 1897 g.* 2: 257; *Statesman's Year Book* (1914), "Russia," 1235–36; "Summary of 1891 Census," *P.P. Vol. 97 Gt. Br. Census*, 180–81; *An. Stat.* 20 (1900): 22.

53. Mulhall, *Dic. of Stat.*, 142; Webb, *New Dic. of Stat.*, 476; *Perepisi 1897 g.* 2: xi–xii.

54. Becker, *Letters and Journals*, 87; Kollontai, *Iz Moei Zhizni i raboty*; Kuzminskaya, *Tolstoy as I Knew Him*; Helene Scriabina, *Coming of Age in the Russian Revolution*, 7–18.

55. *The Diary of Beatrice Webb, Vol. I*, 28 August 1888, 260; Margadant, *Madame Le Professeur*; Ruth Dudgeon, "The Forgotten Minority: Women Students in Imperial Russia, 1872–1917," *Russian History* 9, Pt. l (1982): 26; Albisetti, *Schooling German Girls and Women*, 59; Albisetti, "Female Physicians in Imperial Germany," 107–8.

56. *Statesman's Year-Book* (1900), 35–36; Kovelevskaia, *Memoirs*; Kashevarova-Rudneva, *Vospominanie*, 9; Dekabria (1868), in "Women Physicians' Autobiography in the Nineteenth Century," *Women Writers in Russian Literature*, 111–26; Lipinska, *Les Femmes et le Progrès des Sciences Médicales;* Tuve, *The First Russian Women Physicians*.

57. Valbert, "Ce que pensent Les Professeurs Allemands de l'admission des femmes dans les universites," 675–85; Schneider, "Volksschullehrerinnen: Bavarian Women Defining Themselves Through Their Profession," 89; Margadant, *Madame le Professeur*. For religion, see *SDDR*, Band 222, Table 4, 75.

58. *P.P. Census for Eng. and Wales*, table 5, 3 (1891): xi; 10, part I (1911): 75; Widdowson, *Going Up into the Next Class*, 21–29, 68–79.

59. In 1897–1898, 245 certificates were presented to French midwives, according to *Statesman's Year Book* (1900). The 1906 French census found 28,700 women religious, whereas there had been 130,000 in the 1890s. *An. Stat.* 30 (1910): 152; *Statesman's Year Book* (1914), "France," 815–16. For the number of male and female primary-school teachers in France, see Mulhall, *Dictionary of Statistics*, 234. According to a law of 1901, religious communities had to be authorized by the state; 753 associations were not recognized, 305 dissolved themselves, and 448 were refused authorization. Prior to 1900, 30,136 men and 129,492 women were in monasteries and convents.

60. *SDDR*, Band 203, 12 June 1907 (Berlin, 1910), 269–79 and Band 222, 75; *Statesman's Year Book* (1914), "Germany," 894–95; *P. P. Vol. 97 Gt. Br. Census*, 180–81. In 1907, there were 70,000 Germans listed in religious vocations, but only 19,000 were women. There were 45,00 female elementary teachers and 99,000 fe-

male educational personnel out of a total of 299,000. Regarding France and Russia, see *RSDRP* (1896), Tome IV, 254; A. Kraval, *Zhenshchina v SSSR Statisticheskii Sbornik*, 110.

61. *Svod Perepisi 1897 g.* 2: 235–39, and table XXII, 326–35.

62. Ben Eklof, "The Village and the Outsider, the Rural Schoolteacher in Russia, 1864–1914," *Slavic and European Educational Review* 1979 (1): 8; Ruane, "The Vestal Virgins of St. Petersburg: Schoolteachers and the 1897 Marriage Ban," 168ff; *An. Stat.* 20 (1900): 29–35; 30 (1910): 14–16; Margadant, *Madame le Professeur,* 139; August Bebel, *Women and Socialism,* 212; Engel, "Women Medical Students, Reformers or Revolutionaries?" 394–414; *SDDR* (1907), 269–79; Frederick W. Tickner, *Women in English Economic History,* 184; A. H. Halsey, *Trends in British Society Since 1900,* 166; Alison M. Oram, "Serving two masters? The introduction of a marriage bar in teaching in the 1920s," in *The Sexual Dynamics of History,* 146; Copelman, *London's Women Teachers,* 176–78. Copelman finds 26% of women teachers in state schools married in 1908 and 45% of nurses married in 1901.

63. Becker, *Letters and Journals,* 384.

64. For salaries of *zemstvo* teachers, see Patrick Alston, *Education and the State in Tsarist Russia,* 222-28; Dmitry M. Odinetz, *Russian Schools and Universities in the World War,* 10-18; P. A. Zaionchkovskii, "Officialdom," *Soviet Studies in History,* Fall 1979, 80-81; Engel, *Mothers and Daughters,* 213, footnote 27.

65. For teachers' salaries, see *Times* (London), 4 May 1895, 6; Jones, "The Cheapness of Women" (1909) in *Strong Minded Women,* 322–25; Kathe Schirmacker, *The Modern Woman's Rights Movement,* 144; Copelman, *London's Women Teachers,* 11.

66. For France, see Margadant, *Madame le Professeur,* 46-47, 98-99; Linda Clark, "A Battle of the Sexes," 100; Persis Hunt, "Revolutionary Syndicalism and Feminism among Teachers in France, 1900–1921," 82, 88, 101, 191, 215. For Germany, see Albisetti, *Schooling German Girls and Women,* 82; Marjorie Lamberti, "State, Church, and the Politics of School Reform during the Kulturkampf," *Central European History* 19 (1): 79-80; Lamberti, "Elementary School Teachers and the Struggle against Social Democracy in Wilhelmine Germany, *History of Education Quarterly* 32 (Spring 1992): 79. German men resented women teaching in urban girls' schools because it forced them into lower-paying rural schools. In the 1870s, urban teachers earned 1,470 marks per year, while rural ones earned only 1,064 marks.

67. For medical personnel, see *Russian Year-Book 1915,* 493; Zaionchkovskii, "Officialdom," 64; "Ekaterina Slanskaia," in *Russia Through Women's Eyes,* 215; Engel, *Mothers and Daughters,* 170-71; Conroy, "Pharmacy in Pre-Soviet Russia," 119-20, 135. Veretennikova, a cousin of Lenin's, worked among the Bashkirs in Ufa and Perm. She apparently died at an early age from overwork.

68. Cadbury, *Women's Work and Wages,* 110-11; Schirmacker, *The Modern Woman's Rights Movement,* 79, 185; Jones, "The Cheapness of Women," in Murray, *Strong Minded Women,* 322-25; Widdowson, *Going Up into the Next Class,* 61, 63; Dina Copelman, *London's Women Teachers,* 15, 76.

69. Engel, *Mothers and Daughters,* 169.

70. Il'in, *My Sister's Story,* 198-99.

71. Ben Eklof, "The Adequacy of Basic Schooling in Rural Russia: Teachers and Their Craft, 1880–1914," *History of Education Quarterly* 26 (Summer 1986): 203–4, 212. Eklof found graduates of diocesan and urban schools were more comfortable with rural life than were gentry-class gymnasium graduates.

72. *Diary of Beatrice Webb,* 1: 346, entry for December 1, 1890; Richardson, *Judith Gautier, A Biography*, 193.

73. *Diary of Beatrice Webb*, 1: 255–56, August 15, 1888; Copelman, *London's Women Teachers*, 12, 27, 109, 157.

74. Widdowson, *Going Up into the Next Class*, 57–66; Copelman, *London's Women Teachers*, 80–81, 200–2, 229–30; Albisetti, *Schooling German Girls and Women*, 159, 161; Hunt, "Revolutionary Syndicalism and Feminism, 1900–1921," 82–101, 191–215; Margadant, *Madame le Professeur*, 255–63.

75. Hermann Schoenfeld, *Woman* 8: 381; Anne Higonnet, "Images — Appearances, Leisure, Subsistence," in *A History of Women in the West IV. Feminism from Revolution to World War*, 255; Richardson, *Judith Gautier, A Biography*, 24–25, 35, 60, 165; Becker, *Letters and Journals*, 253, 390–411.

Chapter 4

Political Activity, 1860–1914

By the 1860s, political consciousness was stirring among some women. In Russia, the discussion centered on the woman question, in France on feminism, in England on suffrage, and in Germany on women's education and employment. By 1905, many English and Russian women were pursuing the vote. Women behaved patriotically during World War I, thinking their efforts would earn them the franchise. During the February 1917 revolution in Russia and the November 1918 revolution in Germany, women gained suffrage and became more politically conscious and active. Fearing upheaval in 1918, English politicians enfranchised women over the age of twenty-nine and all men who still lacked the franchise. In France, woman did not gain the vote.

German socialist Clara Zetkin (1857–1933) observed that the women's movement meant different things to women in various classes.[1] Her analysis was a sound one but did not take nationality into account. The woman question for Slavic women was slightly different than for European women. This chapter analyzes how women came to participate in suffrage and suffragette campaigns in England, in the Russian revolutionary movement from 1870–1917, in the German revolution of 1918, and in French politics. While class and ideology influenced women's political consciousness and activity, deteriorating economic conditions in Russia during the war pushed many housewives, working-class women, peasant women, and soldiers' wives into political activity.

Peasant Women

In the late nineteenth century, most peasant women probably had never heard about the "woman question." However, the quest for social justice and human dignity were common to women in all classes. While middle- and upper-class women sought access to higher education, employment, and participation in public arenas, peasant women often sought greater fairness in the family and more land for their family to farm. In France, peasant women did not participate in established political parties, but some vineyard workers participated in strikes in the early 1900s. In Russia, many peasant women encouraged their husbands to leave the extended family, where wives sometimes experienced sexual and household exploitation. Since family divisions resulted in smaller land allotments, they needed more land to make their nuclear families economically viable.

The majority of peasant women lacked a public voice in the village assembly and remained outside political parties and movements prior to 1905. In the 1870s, peasants often distrusted populist propagandists who encouraged the overthrow of the Tsar and reported them to the police. By 1907–1908, however, their political views had changed, and a survey by the Socialist Revolutionary (SR) Party revealed that women showed significant political differences, with the richest and poorest peasants supporting the reactionary Black Hundreds, and the middle and poor ones backing the agrarian SR Party.[2] Land hunger and difficulties on the home front during the Russo-Japanese War of 1904–1905 and World War I propelled many into rural uprisings following those wars.

Certainly, Russian peasant women possessed little political consciousness in the traditional sense of the word. However, a combination of factors galvanized them into political activity in the early twentieth century. Poverty and land hunger radicalized many. High birth rates, rural overpopulation, and lack of land impoverished huge segments of the population. While population growth skyrocketed at the turn of the century, land holdings barely increased from 112 million *desiatiny* (a *desiatina* was 2.7 acres) in 1877 to 123 million in 1905. Constituting 85% of the population at the turn of the century, peasants owned only one-third of the land, while the crown and nobility, comprising less than 1% of the population, held two-thirds.[3] Until 1906, peasants had to pay redemption payments for their land and taxes to their communes. It was difficult to escape these responsibilities by migrating from their village to "land-rich" Siberia or to the cities in search of jobs. Prior to the revolution of 1917, 65% of the peasantry was poor, 20% were middling, and 15% were wealthy. Backward agricultural technology contributed to their low grain yields and dire economic straits. Tsarist taxation policy also impoverished them. By 1900, households in Riazan province paid twenty-three rubles per year in national, county, township, village, and *zemstvo* taxes and something more in the form of indirect taxation in their purchases of kerosene, sugar, tea, and vodka.[4] Anton Chekhov's short story "The Peasants" describes a village elder requisitioning the samovars of poor peasants in payment for back taxes. Recognizing their economic plight makes their expropriation of gentry-class land and goods during the revolutions of 1905–1907 and 1917–1918 more understandable.

Worsening their grinding poverty was their moral indignation over the land situation. Unlike the gentry class, which believed in the sanctity of private property, many peasants thought the land belonged to those who tilled it and felt cheated by the Emancipation settlements (1861–1881). In 1905, the Peasant Union declared: "Land was created by the Holy Spirit, and therefore should not be bought and sold . . . it is not necessary to pay compensation to anyone." It did not matter how the Tsar and landlords had obtained the land; it was their right to have it and to take it. In the revolutions of 1905–1907 and 1917–1918, some peasants seized the estates, forests, and pastures of the gentry under the slogan "Land to those who work it."[5]

After the rural upheavals of 1905–1907, the Imperial Free Economic Society conducted an inquiry into peasant political behavior. Questionnaires showed that women were generally more passive than men in the revolutionary movement but shared their husbands' attitudes. However, women's revolutionary political activity during 1905–1907 and 1917 sometimes foreshadowed men's. Women sometimes served as a vanguard. If they safely pillaged gentry-class orchards and forests, the men followed their example. Russian and Ukrainian gentry-class memoirs indicate that women were often in the front ranks seizing food, wood, and clothing. Just as European women often participated in urban bread riots and rural disturbances in the eighteenth and early nineteenth centuries, so Russian and Ukrainian peasant women pillaged gentry-class property in 1905 and 1917.[6]

In addition to economic and moral factors, there were also personal reasons for women's participation in the revolutions of 1905 and 1917. They often lived in extended families where fathers- and mothers-in-law oppressed them. Russian literature is replete with examples of sexual and economic exploitation of daughters-in-law by their in-laws. In extremely antagonistic circumstances, some peasant women took abusive in-laws to *volost* courts. More commonly, they complained to their husbands, encouraging them to leave the extended family and to set up their own nuclear family within the commune. Although government officials and the intelligentsia viewed the increasing number of divisions with dismay, some historians think that daughters-in-laws were seeking better situations for themselves in promoting family division. Russian and Ukrainian women's revolutionary activity in 1905–1907 and 1917–1918 becomes understandable in view of their personal desires to escape oppressive family relations and create their own nuclear families. One of the immediate results of the land distribution of 1917 was the establishment of 10 million new nuclear families during the years 1917 to 1924, with the average number of people per household dropping from 6.1 in 1917 to 4.5 in 1929.[7]

Another action agitating peasant women in 1905 was the enfranchisement of men in their estate but not themselves. Some women addressed a petition to Duma delegates lamenting this situation. Until the men gained suffrage, men and women had decided their affairs together. However, after the men were enfranchised, they looked down on their wives, and women resented being treated as inferior. They distrusted men's representing their needs and appealed to the Tver Duma delegates to enfranchise them so they too could have a hand in political decisions.[8] Thus poverty, abusive in-laws, need for one's own household, desire to represent their own political agenda, and demand for equality with men all propelled peasant women's participation in the revolutions of 1905 and 1917. They exemplified the slogan that "the personal is political."

Working-Class Women

The political and trade union participation of Russian and European working-class women shows similarities and differences. Differences in union organization resulted from the size, distribution, and marital status of the working classes. Only one million women in the Russian Empire engaged in manufacturing at the turn of the century, whereas 1 million to 2 million did so in Germany, France, and England.[9] Since the Russian population was two to three times as large as that of the other countries, the proportion of Russian women engaged in factory work was significantly smaller. Moreover, most manufacturing in Russia occurred in handicraft production, where no unions existed. In France, clothing construction also took place at home outside of the syndicats. It was mainly in factory settings that unionization occurred.

Age was also a factor in union activity. In England and Germany, most women factory workers were young and unmarried. Since they did not intend to remain factory workers, they often displayed little interest in joining a union. In contrast, Russian and French women workers were often older, married women who had no time for trade union or political activity.[10] Illiteracy also undercut Russian organization. Trade unions, strikes, or political parties remained illegal for men and women in the Russian Empire until 1905 and for German women until 1908. In England and France, it was not illegal for women to join trade unions or political parties, but patriarchal customs and lack of time undermined their participation. Also, the harsh treatment of working-class women who participated in the uprising of the Paris Commune of 1870 probably repressed French women's political activity. The only legal organization that Russian workers could establish was a mutual aid fund, and government approval of them could take years. Only highly paid workers could afford the fees, so most women remained outside.[11]

Trade union membership among English women workers increased from 10,000 in 1876 to 358,000 in 1914. Prior to World War I, 100,000 women in the North of England Weavers' Association signed a manifesto urging the government to enfranchise women. In France 57,000 women union members constituted 9% of syndicat membership. Prior to 1906, German and Russian women composed only a tiny percentage of union members.[12] Illegality and illiteracy hurt propaganda work among Russian women. Union members and organizers in all countries sometimes lost their jobs. In most countries, male trade unionists saw little need to organize women workers since they often left work upon marrying.

In France, male workers and trade unionists believed that women were depressing their wages and neglecting the family, belonged at home, and were "not ready" for trade union organization. Generally, they regarded female workers as women and did not take their unionization seriously. Some syndicalists rejected female-controlled syndicats like the flower makers, complaining that they might have succeeded among the women if feminists had not interfered. But some women spurned trade union organization because they hoped to move out of the working class and become entrepreneuses. Flower makers earning high wages often aspired to employ unskilled workers to perform the less creative and less artistic work. Indeed, few working-class women joined a producer's cooperative that opened in Paris in 1908.[13]

Prior to the war, both Russian and European trade unions remained male preserves, with male-dominated leadership and language. Controlling the female-dominated textile unions, men often treated women workers and organizers with condescension. English male trade unionists used female trade union funds to pay election expenses and salaries of Members of Parliament (M.P.s) for whom women could not vote. Socialist activists such as Esther Roper, Eva Gore-Both, and Christabel Pankhurst were outraged that Socialist candidates and M.P.s took women's money, but did not always support female suffrage. In 1900, Roper and Gore-Both obtained 29,000 signatures from women cotton operatives in Lancashire asking their M.P.s to work for women's enfranchisement.

Of course, there were some exceptional women in union work. Margaret Bondfield (1873–1953), daughter of a factory worker, was drawn into the National Union for Shop Assistants and Clerks in the 1890s. She moved from Brighton to London to make a better life for herself, but was surprised that working conditions and wages were not any better in London. She worked sixty-five hours per week for fifteen to twenty-five pounds a year, and this exploitation radicalized her. She joined the Union for Shop Assistants, wrote articles for its paper, was elected to the district council of the union, and attended national meetings. She had no vocation for wifehood or motherhood, only the urge to serve the union. Her interest in public causes rather than domesticity shows how unusual she was. Most of the shop assistants she roomed with wanted to marry to escape their work and achieve economic security. In 1898, she became the first woman elected assistant secretary of an English trade union. However, male dominance in the trade unions prevented her election to the Executive Council of the Trade Union Congress until 1921. Similar conditions existed in Germany, where Helene Grunfeld was the first woman to occupy a paid position in the workers' secretariat in Nurenburg in 1905. During the Third Republic, French women could belong to trade unions and pay dues, but they could not hold office or vote on union decisions.[14]

Factory work sometimes radicalized women, imbuing them with dreams of a better life. Kathleen Woodward experienced the hardships of working-class life and work, and she vowed not to accept the endless suffering that came to most. She joined trade union, suffrage, and socialist groups. At times it seemed to her "that the women in the factory were too tired for the revolt urged upon them." Ada Nield Chew also became politicized by her factory work and tried to organize women workers to demand higher pay, but she was fired before she could do much. However, her writings in a local newspaper attracted the attention of a socialist group, and she began working for the Independent Labour Party (ILP) in the 1890s. Indeed, many of her ideas resembled those of socialist feminists like Aleksandra Kollontai and Clara Zetkin. Chew believed that married women had a right and duty to work and support themselves. This set her apart from workers who believed that the man was the head of the household and should support it. She also believed that women needed the vote if they were to change their downtrodden situation. They could not rely upon male trade unionists, male socialists, or even middle-class suffragists to improve their lot. She thought most feminists were content to work for the vote. They were well-meaning but lacked an understanding of working-class life and conditions. And most working-class women were too deadened by the hardships of life to respond to political or economic organization. She had hoped to arouse a sense of resentment against their unjust situation and attract them to feminist and trade union activity. But she realized that young working-class women would not contribute their meager wages to organizations promising improvement. So she worked for the feminist and socialist transformation of English society.[15]

Regardless of nationality, working-class women often faced familial and social ostracism if they became politically active. German working-class women who read August Bebel's *Woman and Socialism* often found themselves rejecting family ties and traditional values. Although some husbands helped their wives cultivate a knowledge of socialist ideas, this was not the norm. Luise Zeitz's husband recognized and supported her oratorical and organizational ability, but such support was uncommon. Although she served as the German Social Democratic (SPD) Party's women's representative in Hamburg from 1900 to 1908, the male-dominated Executive Committee eventually squeezed her out. The common pattern in prewar Germany was for wives of SPD members to join the party and work in the women's sphere on social welfare issues, not on political questions.[16]

Traditional German working-class social life excluded young, single women from trade union politicking, because without male escorts they were not allowed into cafes where members retired to discuss business. English unions also remained male preserves because meetings were also conducted at public houses, which unmarried women were reluctant to patronize. In France, unions also remained male dominated despite the large number of female factory workers and the significant number of female unions. Socialist unions regarded women workers as females, while the syndicalists patronized them as helpless victims, despite their decades of strike activity. Thus, French women workers felt unheard and ignored by their male colleagues. French government officials also related to them in a sexist manner. When making inquiries regarding their working conditions, they sent questionnaires to male unions, not female ones.[17]

By 1900, socialist parties generally supported equal rights for women, without taking them seriously. The influence of the misogynist Pierre Proudhon limited French women to silent participation in the socialist unions. After the turn of the century both the Bolshevik and Menshevik wings of the Russian Social Democratic Labor Party (SD) advocated equal rights and endorsed labor protection for women, including prohibition of night work, employment of female factory inspectors, work breaks for nursing mothers, and childcare facilities at factories that employed large numbers of women. Yet many SDs resented the time and effort spent recruiting women, since it yielded little return. Nadezhda Krupskaia (Lenin's wife) explained that party leaflets were usually addressed to working men, because the class consciousness of workers was low, and women were the most backward element.[18]

The SPD also treated women as politically backward, regarding their loyalty to the conservative Catholic Church as a hindrance to union or party recruitment. Clara Zetkin believed the party needed a different kind of propaganda for women—entertainment, not enlightenment. She thought the party needed booklets with simple phrases and large type to appeal to the wives and daughters of workers. While European socialists directed written propaganda to female workers, Russian women's illiteracy precluded such contacts. Exceptions such as Klavdiia Nikolaeva and Alexandra Artiukina learned to read, worked from an early age, and joined the Social Democrats.[19]

Socialists subordinated gender to the class struggle, thinking that the triumph of the working class presupposed women's liberation. August Bebel and Frederick Engels believed that socialism would eradicate private property and wage and sex slavery, and free women from men's control by allowing them to work and achieve economic independence. Krupskaia in her brochure *Woman Worker* (1901) also asserted the pre-eminence of class over gender, arguing that only the victory of the working class under socialism would assure the liberation of women. Likewise, Eleanor Marx advised English women to identify themselves with the working class and not to think in terms of gender. In France, Marie Vidal urged women to organize themselves as workers, so their political problems would fall into place. In Germany, the SPD supported women's rights but without undermining patriarchal family life. The cleavage between SPD theory and practice made Lily Braun embrace bourgeois feminism, while Clara Zetkin believed that only the overthrow of capitalist property relations could free women.[20] Socialists in all countries feared feminism's divisive effect on working-class women.

The "woman question" created dissension among socialists prior to the war. Zetkin put the SPD ahead of feminism, believing that the socialist revolution would usher in women's equality, while trade unionists Gertrude Hanna and Marie Juchacz advocated higher wages, shorter hours, maternity leave, and insurance. In France, politicians urged a shorter workday for men so they would have more time for education and become better citizens, but a shorter workday for women so they could perform their sacred household chores.[21]

In Russia, Kollontai had a difficult time persuading Social Democrats to take women's issues seriously. Party leaders opposed her participation in a feminist conference in 1908, arguing that such agitation among workers would prove divisive and useless. After she rallied fifty working women to attend the congress, party leaders spitefully appointed Vera Slutskaia and Praskovia Kudelli heads of the delegation, not Kollontai.

Although Russian socialists regarded working-class women as a "backward element," and the government forbade them to join labor unions or political parties, some became politically active during the 1905 revolution. In the textile centers of Moscow, St. Petersburg, and Ivanovo-Voznesensk they participated in strikes and the formation of workers' soviets (councils). In May 1905, workers at Ivanovo-Voznesensk textile factories elected twenty-eight female deputies to the local soviet. They demanded the eight-hour day, a minimum wage, better working conditions, freedom of speech, and the right to strike. Textile, tobacco, and service workers participated in the St. Petersburg Workers' Soviet in 1905, but they might have eschewed revolutionary organizations if unions and political parties had been legal. Indeed, it was middle- and upper-class women who dominated the female membership of the underground socialist parties in Russia and legal ones in prewar France, Germany, and England. It was only after 1908, when German women could legally join the SPD, that their membership soared from 4,000 in 1905 to 174,000 in 1914. Most of the SPD female membership were wives and relatives of male party members. Few young, single women belonged.[22]

After unions and parties were repressed again in 1907, Russian women workers' political activity was restricted to factory insurance boards. In 1912, the Russian Duma established a social insurance system that included workers' compensation and maternity coverage for women factory workers. It was modeled on research that Kollontai had conducted during her exile in Europe from 1908 to 1912. In textile and tobacco factories, women were elected to the boards. Since they were legal institutions, Social Democrats infiltrated them to conduct political propaganda. During the war, the regime became aware of their infiltration, and the secret police kept them under observation.[23]

Prior to 1914, some English women also sat on factory insurance boards. However, they more likely belonged to suffrage groups and the quasi-political Women's Cooperative Guild than to socialist parties such as the ILP. Thousands found new hope when they joined the guild. They began to read, study socialist tracts, and speak in public meetings. These activities gave some the confidence to seek election as Poor Law guardians, aldermen, and county and municipal councilors. Although politically active working-class women might be criticized and urged to "stay at home and cook their husbands' dinners," some became empowered and invigorated. Commenting on the women she met at a Women's Cooperative Guild meeting in 1913, Virginia Woolf admitted that she had expected to meet poor, downtrodden, exhausted women, but instead found humorous, vigorous, and independent ones.[24] Though not necessarily representative of their class, they expressed hope and belief in political reform.

Russian women workers seemed more prone to mass action and spontaneous political activity than Bolshevik leaders desired. In 1915, women at Ivanovo-Voznesensk demonstrated against the war, and forty people were killed and wounded by the police. In February 1917, Bolshevik Party leaders provided them with propaganda for celebrating International Women's Day (February 25), but declared that the time was not ripe for revolution. Contrary to these directives, women textile workers and disgruntled soldiers' wives organized massive demonstrations, protesting food shortages, the war, and the Tsarist regime in general. Drawing metal workers into their march, they cajoled the garrisoned soldiers and local police to tolerate their demonstration. Soon students, government employees, and soldiers joined the protests against the regime. Thus, the women proved more revolutionary than party leaders. Later, the Menshevik Nikolai Sukhanov remarked: "No one led the February Revolution, the people made it themselves."[25] Much to the professional revolutionaries' surprise, especially exiled ones including Lenin, Kollontai, and Trotsky, the Tsar abdicated one week after the demonstrations. The First Provisional Government, formed in February 1917, enfranchised women, freed political and religious prisoners, and generally adopted a liberal program. Its downfall lay in staying in the war, which had become unpopular.

In May 1917, striking women workers again became the vanguard, protesting the foreign policy of the Provisional Government. When large numbers of male workers joined them, their demonstration toppled the Provisional Government. Their political actions had a political but not necessarily a party basis. Shortly after the February Revolution, the Moscow Workers' Soviet announced that it would operate without factions, party organizations, or strife. Moscow trade unionists had their own legislative, economic, and political agendas and did not want their unity undermined by infighting of SDs and SRs.[26]

According to Diane Koenker, party consciousness among workers was very low during the spring and summer of 1917, and many were unable to distinguish between parties. One woman worker reportedly scolded a friend for joining the Bolsheviks because she thought the term "Bolshevik" meant "well-to-do." Since the Mensheviks had drafted special social insurance legislation for women factory workers in 1912, they earned the support of many female workers in the municipal elections of June and September 1917. Women voters in Moscow tended to support Menshevik and Kadet candidates, not Bolsheviks or SRs.[27] Having participated in the elections of September 1917, some women also took part in the October Revolution. Millions were indirectly and directly involved in the Civil War (1918–1923).

Middle-Class Women

Russia

One of the striking similarities between Russian and European middle-class women in the nineteenth century was their degree of political consciousness and activity. After 1860, increasing numbers of them joined suffrage organizations to protest their unfair legal situation. When the Tsar enfranchised illiterate peasant men in October 1905, without granting suffrage to educated women, increasing numbers became politically active. Moreover, the reforms of 1905 made political activity legal, so more middle-class women could become politically active without severe consequences.

By 1900, significant numbers of middle-class women in the Russian Empire had obtained higher education, pursued careers, and become politically involved. Some joined the SRs, some became SDs, and others supported liberal suffrage organizations. Prior to World War I, 15,000 women in the empire belonged to suffrage organizations. Like their European sisters, they split into various factions. One group was called the All Russian Union of Women's Equality, another the Women's Progressive Party. Most were shocked when the October Manifesto (1905) granted suffrage to illiterate peasant men but not to them, and they were indignant that male politicians balked at enfranchising them. Like their European cohorts, Russian liberals believed that granting women the vote would result in the election of more conservatives, so they withheld the franchise.[28] However, when the First Provisional Government formed in February 1917, women demanded and got the vote.

Not all women thought suffrage was the answer to Russia's problems. Some shunned philanthropic work and the pursuit of suffrage to become revolutionaries. Some, such as Rozalia Zalkind (Zemliachka, 1876–1947), grew up in families sympathetic to revolutionary struggle. Her brother introduced her to revolutionary literature, and at fifteen she was arrested. In prison, she began doubting whether populism was the right path. In Kiev, she saw workers more prone to revolt than peasants. She read Marx and joined the RSDLP in 1896. Like many other Bolshevichki (female members of the Party), she found relatively egalitarian conditions in underground party work and held several important offices. She worked as an Iskra agent in Odessa in 1901, served as secretary of the Moscow Party Committee in 1905, and headed the Bolshevik Moscow district Central Committee during World War I. Like many others, she was arrested and imprisoned several times. Toughened by her underground work and imprisonments, she became firm and unsentimental.[29]

England

Constitutional methods are impossible for those who do not possess the constitutional weapon of the franchise.
—Christabel Pankhurst, 1908

In nineteenth-century England, women's politics remained a middle-class affair. Unmarried English women who met property qualifications had been able to vote in borough elections since 1869, but married women of property could not vote or be elected until 1900. By 1900, several hundred women had been elected to school boards, to urban and county district councils, and as Poor Law guardians. From the 1860s on, many middle-class men and women worked for women's suffrage. In liberal households, daughters sometimes became radicalized at early ages. In 1872, at the age of fourteen, Emmeline Pankhurst attended her first suffrage meeting with her mother. A decade later, she became further agitated by her work as Poor Law guardian. She got "sympathy" from M.P.s, but no change in the laws. Therefore, she endorsed women's parliamentary suffrage so they could change laws that affected the poor. Social workers such as Emmeline Pethick Lawrence also thought female suffrage would remedy human suffering. In the 1890s, Millicent Garret Fawcett founded the National Union of Women's Suffrage Societies to secure it in a constitutional manner.[30] Eventually, Pankhurst and Pethick Lawrence became militant suffragettes to ameliorate the plight of poor women.

Middle-class women elected to the London school board during the period 1870 to 1904 encountered difficulties working within the male-dominated system. Elizabeth Garrett, a doctor, and Emily Davies, a school reformer, were asked to run in the first school board elections in 1870, and did so. Having won, they encountered a hostile atmosphere in which single and widowed women were more easily accepted than married ones. When Garret married in 1871, the *Times* suggested she resign, fearing a conflict of interest between her husband's rights and her duties. Apparently, married men suffered no such conflict. Another woman, Honnor Morton, was forced to resign her seat when she was observed smoking on the street! As a group, the women tended to be progressive feminists. Emma Maitland, a school board member for nine years, observed that women looked first to what was right and then to what was expedient, whereas men were more concerned with what was expedient than what was right. Generally, women board members tried to obtain parity for female teachers, clerks, and cleaners. While liberal women fared well on the London school board, it was more difficult for radicals. In 1882, the socialist Helen Taylor complained about women's problems in election campaigns. Annie Besant, who advocated birth control and socialism, and Florence Fenwick Miller, an avowed feminist, were other radical members of the London school board in the late nineteenth century.[31]

Liberal Eleanor Rathbone also sought parliamentary suffrage for women and participated in local Liverpool politics around 1900. As a philanthropist, Eleanor served in the Victoria Women's Settlement in Liverpool. She also ran for the City Council and was elected in 1909. Four years later, she cofounded the Liverpool Women Citizens Association to educate women as citizens and electors. During the war, Rathbone sought the help of her cousin Herbert Rathbone, Lord Mayor of Liverpool, to make relief funds available to wives, dependents, and "unofficial wives." In seeking help from well-connected male politicians, Eleanor resembled other liberals such as Pankhurst, Pethick Lawrence, and the Russian physician, philanthropist, and politician Anna Shabanova.

By 1915, the liberal National Union of Women's Suffrage Societies (NUWSS) had attracted 2 million members, more than one thousand women were serving as Poor Law guardians, and several hundred participated on school boards. Despite their contribution to English political life, Liberals refused to grant women the parliamentary franchise.[32] Fed up with equivocating Liberals and Socialists, Emmeline Pankhurst, her daughter Christabel, and Emmeline Pethick Lawrence formed a militant suffrage society called the Women's Social and Political Union (WSPU) in 1906. It demanded complete dedication to women's suffrage and renunciation of other social reform work. Breaking with the ILP, Christabel complained that socialists were silent on the position of women. If they were not actually antagonistic to the issue of women's status, they held themselves aloof from it. She thought perhaps some day, when they were in power and had nothing else to do, the ILP would give women the vote as a finishing touch to their arrangements. She wondered why women should have confidence in the Labour Party when working-class men were as unjust to women as were those in other classes. Pethick Lawrence was also disillusioned with male socialists. In the 1890s, she had been convinced that all injustice and wrong would come to an end if socialism replaced capitalism. But she realized that male socialists did not care much about votes for women.[33]

In 1906, the English press refused to publish speeches or articles on women's suffrage, considering it a dead issue. Liberal Prime Minister Asquith refused to grant or discuss woman's suffrage, and M.P.s in the House of Commons joked and laughed about female suffrage. Indignant, Emmeline and Christabel Pankhurst decided to adopt militant tactics to gain the vote, and their demonstrations attracted a large middle-class following. The Pethick Lawrences took care of organizational and financial matters and published the paper *Votes for Women* (1907). To gain public attention, WSPU members began interrupting Liberal candidates' campaigns, and they were subsequently arrested and imprisoned. Devotion to women's suffrage created camaraderie and helped many discover their real selves hidden behind bourgeois social masks. Many WSPU speakers were young, smart speakers who found adventure, excitement, and humor as well as sacrifice in their service to the cause. Militant behavior gained them more attention and respect in the press and the country than forty years of petitioning had garnered the NUWSS. Mrs. Fawcett admitted that suffragette prisoners had touched the imagination of the country in a manner that quieter, constitutional methods did not. Yet demonstrations with hundreds of thousands of marchers, and the imprisonment and force-feeding of hundreds of women and men, did not make the government yield on the issue of female suffrage. So, in 1912, Emmeline and Christabel Pankhurst decided to engage in violent attacks on public and private property.

The Pethick Lawrences disagreed with these tactics and left the WSPU. They thought force-feeding had embarrassed the government and that the suffragettes had the country on their side. They were right. For while the Pankhursts gained notoriety during the years 1912 to 1914, they lost public support. Indeed, the Pankhursts discovered how far the double standard went. When men broke windows, it was considered an expression of political opinion. When women did so, it was a crime. Once World War I began, the WSPU abandoned militant tactics and supported the war effort, hoping to be rewarded with the vote, which they gained in 1918.[34] Some suffragettes refused to support the war, working for peace instead.

Attending an international suffrage meeting in London prior to the war, the Russian socialist feminist Aleksandra Kollontai criticized the WSPU for focusing exclusively on the vote. She saw the flower of European and English feminism seated on the stage of Albert Hall, but was disappointed that no workers were on stage. Even leftists spoke only on suffrage issues. She was irritated that English feminists focused on the struggle between the sexes and ignored the class struggle. Some working-class women belonged to the WSPU, and Kollontai thought they would soon realize that their true interests lay with those of their class, not their gender. Like Kollontai, Ada Chew thought it a mistake for suffragists to devote all their energy to gaining the vote. She thought working women needed a social revolution as well as the vote in order to improve their situation.[35]

France

In France, bourgeois and upper-class women founded a variety of suffrage groups. There were several conservative Catholic feminist organizations; a moderate Protestant organization, Ligue Française pour les Droits des Femmes; a moderate Republican group, Union Française Pour le Suffrage des Femmes, under the leadership of Jane Misme, Jeanne Schmahl, and Cecile Brunschwicg; and a militant group, Suffrage des Femmes (1893), under the leadership of Hubertine Auclert. Auclert published a feminist paper called *The Citizen* from 1881 to 1891, but French society considered her tactics "not in good taste." Nelly Roussel advocated birth control and emerged as a powerful speaker for Ligue pour la Régénération Humaine. She denounced *masculinisme* (male supremacy) and opposed French socialists for putting class issues above gender. Prior to 1900, French suffrage organizations had only a few hundred members, but by 1914 their membership had grown to 100,000.[36] Like their English sisters, they eschewed political confrontation during the war and devoted themselves to war work, expecting to gain the vote after the war. Unlike their English sisters, they were rudely disappointed.

Steven Hause suggests that the war undermined French feminism in a variety of ways: it truncated the political movement that had just taken off by 1914, diverted women's energies into charitable works, made suffragists less militant, and made feminists overconfident. After the war, Bolshevism diverted energy away from feminism, and women split over asking for the municipal or parliamentary vote. Finally, senators delayed voting on the issue, thus allowing people to forget women's contribution to the war effort.[37]

Germany

Prior to World War I, there were four main factions in the nonsocialist suffrage movement: the conservative Protestant Women's Association, the conservative Alliance for Women's Suffrage, the moderate Organization of German Women, and the somewhat radical German Women's Suffrage League. Many feminists thought education, employment, and social welfare more important than suffrage. Like French bourgeois women, German *hausfrauen* thought public demonstrations inappropriate. European suffragists wanted legal and economic rights as well as the vote. While liberal women did not perceive their work as radical, society did. Conservatives rejected their demand for suffrage as a threat to the patriarchal family, and liberals found their desire for the vote "inopportune."

Upper-Class Women

From the 1860s on, women became more aware of how few their rights were. Until the Married Women's Property Acts of the 1870s and 1880s, English women lost control of their property, children, and earnings upon marriage. English women of property received the right to vote in school board and municipal elections in the 1870s, but it was not easy for them to exercise these rights. In France and Germany, civil law mandated communal property in marriage, allowing the husband to administer the property, thereby diminishing a wife's control. French women obtained a Married

Women's Property Act in 1907, allowing them to dispose of their wages and property. Unlike Europe, primogeniture was not the rule in Russia, and daughters could inherit land and movable property. Moreover, property-owning women could vote by proxy through a male relative in provincial *zemstva* and city duma elections in the late 1870s. Like their European sisters, married gentry-class Russian women had little recourse when unscrupulous husbands squandered their dowries. Although inheritance and property rights offered them more protection and power within marriage than their European sisters had, they were circumscribed by internal passports that a male guardian had to endorse so they could move from one place to another, enter the university, or take a job. European women were not subject to this control, but their lives were limited by custom and tradition.

England

English married women of property found their de jure and de facto legal situations quite different. In 1898, one woman complained that when she tried to pay local taxes so that she could qualify to vote in local elections, the water and gas collectors would not receive her money. One said: "We never take a woman's name on our books. If we had known you were a woman, we should not have connected the gas." She had to give her husband's name for the rate receipt—unless she could prove that she was divorced or legally separated. Without receipts in her name, she was ineligible to vote.[38]

English women became politicized in a variety of ways. Josephine Butler became outraged at the unfair treatment of women arrested under the Contagious Diseases Acts (1862–1870). These acts allowed local authorities to threaten innocent women who lived near military bases with charges of prostitution, forced medical inspection, and even prison. Butler thought the acts an affront to women's civil rights since women were prosecuted and persecuted, but men patronizing prostitutes were not arrested, medically inspected, or sent to prison. While the acts were a threat to women's civil liberties, they had not diminished disease during their period of enforcement, and she saw no reason to keep them. Like female Poor Law guardians, Butler and members of her cause found it took incredible time (sixteen years) and patience to persuade Parliament to rescind the hurtful laws.[39] Although she gave up her suffrage work to crusade against the acts, her work galvanized others to obtain the vote in order to change patriarchal legislation.

Russia

Russian and European gentry-class women lacked the freedom of English women to form philanthropic, educational, or political groups. The Tsarist regime opposed the formation of private philanthropic organizations, and those who tried to create them encountered bureaucratic obstruction. By the 1860s, some influential Russian gentry-class women began to chafe from their lack of civil and political rights, and the period 1860 to 1917 is one in which their political consciousness and activity increased.

The revolutions of 1905 and 1917 tended to focus on the revolutionary heritage of Russian society, but this is not an accurate picture of most Russian gentry-class women. Most married and led fairly traditional lives, since the role of perfect wife and mother was as popular there as in Europe. However, those dissatisfied with married life sometimes sought fulfillment in philanthropic, professional, artistic, or revolutionary work.

While critical discussion had been difficult during the reign of Nicholas I (1825–1855), female writers Zhadovskaia, Rostopchina, and Pavlova had attacked the worst aspects of arranged marriages. Avdotia Panaeva took a different tack in nurturing radical writers who championed women in the 1850s and 1860s. She interceded with high-ranking government officials to aid Alexander Herzen in 1857 and Chernyshevsky when he was arrested and imprisoned from 1861 to 1862. She also intervened on behalf of young radical women who ran afoul of the authorities. She encouraged women's education, so they would not be so easily duped by men. She embodied the socially concerned, emancipated woman of the 1860s.[40]

Unlike alienated urban writers who lamented women's oppressive social situation, rural gentry-class writers often concentrated on the plight of the peasants. From childhood, Ekaterina Breshko-Breshkovskaia (1844–1919) had worried about the serfs on her father's estates. Growing up in a liberal household, she read Voltaire, Rousseau, and Diderot and developed a heightened sense of social justice. She established a free school for peasants, and she worked with her father and her husband to enable peasants to gain their rightful share of land after emancipation. She and her husband set up an agricultural school and bank for peasants, but reactionary nobles denounced them to the Third Section, which threatened them with exile. Her husband refused to challenge the government and risk exile to Siberia, but not Ekaterina. She sacrificed not only her marriage but also her child for the peasant cause. She could not be a mother and a revolutionist. Although it broke her heart to entrust her child to relatives to raise, she preferred being a fighter for justice to being the mother of a victim of tyranny.

Like other women of her estate and generation, she was more in love with the revolution and serving the people than with family happiness. Participating in the "To the People Movement" in the early 1870s, she was arrested in 1874 for preaching the overthrow of the government. Along with 300 others, she was kept in severe solitary confinement from 1874 to 1878 and then was sentenced to penal servitude in Siberia. Of 300 young people arrested, 18% were women.

Breshkovskaia served her eighteen-year sentence in Siberia from 1878 to 1896, returning to work once again for the agrarian socialist SR Party. Arrested again during the revolution of 1905, she was exiled to Siberia from 1907 until 1917, when the Provisional Government amnestied all political prisoners.[41] She worked in the SR Party until she left Russia in 1918.

Breshkovskaia was not alone in wanting to help impoverished peasants, nor in finding gentry-class life shallow. Other gentry-class women, including the sister of P. D. Ouspensky, gave their lives for the revolutionary cause. Russian men also discussed the plight of the peasantry, and their writings helped shape their country's political consciousness. Radicals such as Chernyshevsky, Dobroliubov, Mikhailov, and Pisarev advocated women's right to higher education and professional employment so they could help poor peasants and workers. Mikhailov denied upper-class women's physical and intellectual inferiority.[42]

Dobroliubov stressed women's moral strength, finding remarkable strength in Russian heroines. While Russian literature depicted men as indecisive, superfluous heroes, it portrayed female protagonists as having revolutionary potential. He believed their love of the oppressed, desire to do good, and noblesse oblige would help usher in the new social order.[43]

Chernyshevsky's novel *What Is to Be Done?* influenced generations of Russian youth because it criticized parental domination and arranged marriages, idealized women's education and employment, and espoused the life of a professional revolutionary. His heroine, Vera Pavlovna, represented the new socialist woman. She escaped her family's control by contracting a "fictitious marriage." Learning utopian socialist ideas from her "husband," she sponsored a cooperative sewing establishment to help unemployed women. Eventually she became a doctor to be more useful to society.[44]

The Personal Is Political

While many young people embraced radical and liberal ideas in the 1860s, many parents bade their daughters marry and accept their subordinate but respected role as wife and mother. The famous mathematician

Sofia Kovalevskaia (1850–1891) remembered her sister Anna begging their father, General Krukovsky, for permission to study in St. Petersburg. Refusing her request, he reminded her that "it was the duty of every respectable girl to live with her parents until she marries."[45] Anna tried to escape parental control by arranging a fictitious marriage, but her scheme failed. Later, such a marriage worked for Sofia, and Anna accompanied her younger sister to St. Petersburg and then to Paris, where she founded the Society for Struggle for the Rights of Women and the newspaper *Women's Rights*. During the Paris Commune, Anna married Frenchman Victor Jaclard and participated with him in the uprising of 1871. When her husband was arrested, her father intervened with a French general to rescue them both. Other Russian women, including Elizaveta Dmitrieva and E. Bardeneeva, also participated in the Paris Commune.[46]

In the late nineteenth century, some emulated the character Vera Pavlovna by contracting "fictitious marriages," pursuing higher education, or engaging in professional and revolutionary work. Chafing at the government's ambivalent educational and employment policies, some Russian, Ukrainian, and Jewish women demanded access to higher education and professional work. Several groups of frustrated upper-class women existed: one circle consisted of philanthropists who pursued social justice for others, especially peasants, poor working women, prostitutes, and women students. A second affiliation included feminists seeking higher education, access to professional work, and the vote. A third group was made up of revolutionaries who believed that only a political and social revolution would improve the lot of the downtrodden. The first two groups may be termed "ministering angels" or liberal feminists, since they wanted to improve sociey but not overthrow it. Nadezhda Stasova, Maria Trubnikova, Anna Filosofova, and Drs. Anna Shabanova and Mariia Pokrovskaia belonged to this reformist category. Initially, Shabanova had been quite radical, but after being arrested and imprisoned in the 1860s, she became more moderate. In the late nineteenth century, some gentry-class parents underwrote their daughters' pursuit of higher education and professional, philanthropic, even revolutionary activity. Kollontai's parents gave her money to study Marxism in Europe and cared for her son in her absence.

Unlike the ministering angels, revolutionaries and radical feminists can be called "avenging angels" since they aimed to overthrow the status quo. These included terrorists Vera Zasulich, Elizaveta Kovalskaia, and the Figner sisters; Populists Ekaterina Breshko-Breshkovskaia and Maria Spiridonova; and Marxists Nadezhda Krupskaia, Inessa Armand, Elena Stasova, and

Aleksandra Kollontai. Some women became so outraged at the plight of the poor that they moved from liberal to radical groups. Breshkovskaia, Armand, and Kollontai changed from idealistic philanthropists to romantic revolutionaries. As a young woman, Elena Stasova rejected her family's philanthropic approach, decided she wanted to engage in socially useful work, and took up teaching. As a Sunday school teacher in St. Petersburg in the 1890s, she came in contact with wretchedly poor workers. She also met other teachers, including Krupskaia. By 1895, she had joined the Marxists and was smuggling underground literature to workers.

Some disaffected teachers and medical personnel decided that only revolutionary agitation could improve the lot of downtrodden peasants. Perovskaia began as a village teacher and medical worker administering smallpox inoculations in 1872. Two years later, she was arrested for her efforts on behalf of political prisoners in the Peter and Paul Fortress in St. Petersburg. Bailed out of prison by her father, she began to study medicine. A Populist, she pursued propaganda and terror simultaneously. As a member of the Executive Committee of the People's Will, she helped assassinate Tsar Alexander II in 1881. Depressed by her act, she refused to flee abroad and was arrested and hanged. Iasneva Golubeva began as a village teacher, then became a Populist in the 1870s and a Marxist in the 1890s. Exiled to Samara, she came in contact with Lenin in 1889 and met her future husband, V. S. Golubev. Convinced of the need to work among the proletariat, she became a Social Democrat and secretary of the Bolshevik wing of the Samara party.[47]

Unable to ameliorate the situation of the poor in England, Emmeline Pankhurst, Emmeline Pethick Lawrence, Annie Besant, and Beatrice Potter Webb moved from philanthropy to political agitation. German teacher Clara Zetkin and liberal feminist Lily Braun also gave up reform work for socialism. French feminists Marie Deraismes, Hélène Brion, Hubertine Auclert, Paula Minck, and Madeleine Pelletier also renounced philanthropic enterprises for feminist politics.

Organized feminism did not attract all educated women. Many found self-fulfillment in art, religion, or social work. Some gentry-class Russian women found self-realization in their writing, painting, religion, mathematics, and medical work and felt little need for a women's movement. In 1897, Zinaida Vengerova thought it unnecessary to espouse feminism because Russian women already took active parts in social, intellectual, and professional life and were the most liberated in Europe. They were human beings, equal to men. As useful members of society, she thought they did not need feminist or suffrage movements.[48]

In her poetry, Mirra Lokhvitskaia took a different feminist stance, describing women as powerful queens: Queen of Flowers, Queen of Dreams, Queen of the Nether World, and "priestess of secret revelations." Like many other symbolists, Lokhvitskaia preferred the transcendental to the revolutionary world. She and the poet Zinaida Gippius lived in an artistic milieu that glorified Sofia as the feminine element of the Godhead and flirted with androgyny.[49]

In the late nineteenth century, Beatrice Potter disdained the suffrage movement and even signed an antisuffrage petition. She did not think that she needed the vote in order to carry out her work for the Charity Organization Society. After her marriage, she financially supported the Fabian Socialist Women's Group, but did not attend their meetings or identify herself with women's causes.[50] Nor did Florence Nightingale support suffragists. Annie Besant worked tirelessly for feminist and socialist causes during the 1870s and 1880s, but in 1899 she became a disciple of the Theosophist Madame Blavatsky. Then she dedicated her life to reform work in India. Others—Ekaterina Kuskova, Elena Stasova, Angelika Balabanova, and Rosa Luxemburg—devoted themselves to socialism instead of feminism.

Some philanthropic women transferred their role of "angel in the house" into the philanthropic sphere in which they taught poor peasants and workers in Sunday schools. Josephine Butler in England and Inessa Armand in Russia sought to rescue and rehabilitate prostitutes. Still others established cooperatives in which women could earn their living by translating, writing, bookbinding, or sewing. With the exception of the Women's Cooperative Guild in England, few of these organizations reached significant numbers of women.

Some gentry-class Russian women became disgruntled with philanthropic and professional work and became suffragists or revolutionaries. Inessa Armand became so disenchanted with philanthropy that she left her pampered life to became a professional revolutionary. Like other reformers, upper-class women held different views about improving their societies. Many believed the vote would empower them to reform society. Some founded and joined liberal, bourgeois suffrage societies. Russian physicians Maria Pokrovskaia and Anna Shabanova organized suffrage groups to improve educated women's situation. Shabanova organized the Mutual Philanthropic Society in the late nineteenth century, and Pokrovskaia founded the Women's Progressive Party after the October Manifesto failed to enfranchise women in 1905.

Many upper-class women were disappointed that liberals and socialists dragged their feet on the suffrage issue. The Emancipation of Labor Party (Marxist) did not adopt planks advocating women's suffrage in the late nineteenth century, although the Social Democrats (RSDLP) did so in 1903. In France, Hubertine Auclert realized that liberals and socialists discounted women's suffrage. In Germany, Lily Braun believed that socialist feminist and bourgeois reformist ideas were converging, and she urged reform, not revolution. However, she encountered hostility in bridging the differences between them. When Braun wanted to attend an international women's congress held in Berlin in 1896, her SPD colleague Clara Zetkin cautioned her not to do so and accused her of putting feminism ahead of the class struggle.[51] Socialists Elena Stasova, Angelika Balabanova, and Rosa Luxemburg felt personally liberated, saw no need for feminism, and refused to work in the "women's sphere" of the party. Male socialists paid scant attention to women's issues or to the socialist feminists—Kollontai in Russia, Pelletier in France, Christabel Pankhurst in England, or Lily Braun in Germany.

In England, the Independent Labour Party (ILP) equivocated on enfranchising women, so in 1906 the Pankhursts left it to devote themselves exclusively to women's suffrage, in the Women's Social and Political Union. While the ILP had 30,000 women members in 1907, the WSPU attracted more than 200,000. During their struggle for the vote, more than 1,000 English women went to jail for the sake of suffrage. Despite imprisonment, hunger strikes, forced feeding, and sexual harassment by police, WSPU members persevered in their quest for the parliamentary franchise.[52]

Like their English sisters, hundreds of politically active Russians also suffered for their causes. It is unclear from the 1897 Russian census how many of the 8,000 women in prison and 1,200 in exile were political prisoners, but certainly several hundred were. After the 1905 revolution, thousands of radicals were rounded up and imprisoned, and Breshko-Breshkovskaia spent another ten years in prison and exile. Traditionally, Russian socialist female party members came from the upper ranks of society, possessed high occupational status, and attained higher education than did male party members. European socialist parties also attracted women from the educated and upper classes. Prior to World War I, Russian women constituted 15% of the Social Revolutionaries and 2% to 6% of the Social Democrats, while French, German, and English women comprised about 2% of their respective socialist parties.[53] Although the SPD had supported women's suffrage since 1875, it still subordinated the "woman question" to class struggle and revolution.

The 1848 revolutions and the Paris Commune of 1871 initially attracted French and German women to radical circles, but as the century wore on their numbers shrank. Prior to World War I, few upper-class French or German women considered political activity "in good taste." From the 1870s to 1900, more upper- and middle-class English women became radicalized and politically active. Yet Russia was unique in linking the woman question to the situation of downtrodden peasants and workers. In the 1870s, scores of "repentant" Russian nobles participated in revolutionary groups. In the 1870s, they participated in the Populist "to the people" movement, and in the 1880s they were active in the terrorist actions of the People's Will. In the 1890s, they participated in both the SR and SD parties, constituting 60% of female revolutionaries. After 1905, the proportion of middle-class women increased.[54]

Most career women in the Russian Empire struggled long and hard to obtain their positions, and few gave up their humanitarian work to become full-time revolutionaries. Yet some did. From 1870 to 1875, Vera Figner struggled with the decision of whether to pursue a medical career so that she would be able to serve the peasants as a physician, or to become a full-time revolutionary. When she was very close to finishing her medical studies, she decided to return to Russia to work for the People's Will. Possessing sufficient medical training to pass the feldsher exam, she returned home. Disenchanted with her inability to improve the lot of the peasants through medical treatment, and considering such work a mere palliative, she joined a terrorist organization to bring down the existing order. As a member of the Central Executive Committee of the People's Will, she plotted the assassination of Alexander II in 1881. Yet she did not believe in the indiscriminate use of terror and condemned the assassination of an American president, since other tactics were available in the United States.[55]

A variety of events radicalized women. The schoolteacher Ludmilla Gromozova became a Marxist in 1904, because Marxism offered a method of struggle, compared to Populism's hazy romanticism.[56] Vera Zasulich became so outraged by General Trepov's cruel treatment of political prisoners that she shot and wounded him in 1878. Hundreds of gentry-class women gave up family life and philanthropic and professional work to become full-time revolutionaries. They regarded their political work in a very positive light. The worst disaster for them was not arrest, exile, or confinement, but their inability to change society while imprisoned. Many gentry-class women participated in the revolutions of 1905 and February 1917 and demanded a more democratic state. Many were not wed to the idea of constitutional monarchy. Indeed, the All Russian Union for Women's Equality called for the overthrow of the autocracy and the election of a Constituent Assembly on the basis of equal, direct, secret, and universal suffrage.[57] Many gentry-class Russian women became radicalized in 1905 when they were not enfranchised but millions of uneducated peasant men were.

As the Bolsheviks established their regime in 1917–1918, they adopted most of the planks of the suffragists. However, the new Soviet government devised a suffrage that excluded members of the clergy, the bourgeoisie, former servants of the Tsarist regime, and their families. So the political dreams of some middle and upper-class Russian women, who had been enfranchised by the Provisional Government, died after the Bolsheviks came to power. Suffragists Anna Miliukova, Countess Sofia Panina, and Ariadna Tyrkova-Williams and the revolutionary Breshkovskaia left Russia totally disillusioned with the Bolsheviks. Other gentry-class revolutionaries—Kollontai, Armand, Krupskaia, and Stasova—welcomed the October Revolution as a dream come true. In England, suffragists and suffragettes, who were initially delighted at their enfranchisement in 1918, slowly realized that suffrage was not the panacea they had expected. Suffragettes Emmeline and Christabel Pankhurst stood for election in 1918, but neither they nor moderate suffragists were elected. Instead, conservative—Lady Astor and the Duchess of Atholl—and moderate—Susan Lawrence and Margaret Bondfield (1873–1953)—Labour Party members were elected M.P.s in the 1920s. Only ten women were elected to the House of Commons prior to 1928. On the continent, the socialist revolution of November 1918 enfranchised German women, and it was primarily the Socialist and Communist parties that elected women delegates to the Reichstag in the 1920s. French senators refused to enfranchise women in the 1920s, so French women's dream of changing their society remained stillborn.

Notes

1. Clara Zetkin, *Selected Writings*, 73–74.

2. Laura L. Frader, "Women's Work and Family Labor in the Vineyards of Lower Languedoc: Coursan 1860–1913," *Proceedings of Western Society for French History* 7 (1979): 97; Perrie, "The Russian Peasantry in 1907–1908," *History Workshop* (Autumn 1977), 3–4: 171–91. The Black Hundreds were a right-wing political group that engaged in violent attacks on Jews and leftists prior to World War I.

3. Robinson, *Rural Russia under the Old Regime*, 162, 268. Robinson indicates that the peasants held 146 million desiatiny of land while the gentry and crown held 224 million desiatiny. Some middle-class industrialists such as Pavel M. Tretiakov refused to buy landed property because they believed that land should be owned by those who cultivated it. See the memoirs of Tretiakov's daughter as quoted by Bill in *The Forgotten Class*, 153.

4. For land distribution in 1877 and 1905, see Robinson, *Rural Russia*, 268. Regarding the classification of peasants prior to the revolution of 1917, see "Sotsialisticheskoe sel'skoe khoziaistvo Soiuza SSR," *PKh*, no. 7, 1939, 163. For taxes, see Tian-Shanskaia, *Village Life in Late Tsarist Russia*, 130.

5. For a good discussion of the participation of the peasantry in the revolutions of 1905 and 1917, see Teddy Uldricks, "The 'Crowd' in the Russian Revolution: Towards Reassessing the Nature of Revolutionary Leadership," *Politics and Society*, 1974, 405–7; Maureen Perrie, "The Russian Peasant Movement of 1905–1907: Its Social Composition and Revolutionary Significance," *Past and Present* 57: 123–55; Kollontai, "Women Fighters in the Days of the Great October Revolution," in *Selected Articles and Speeches*, 126; Barbara Evans Clements, "Working Class and Peasant Women in the Russian Revolution, 1919–1923," *Signs* 8 (21): 216–17.

6. For gentry-class accounts of peasant land seizures, see Olga E. Tchernoff, *New Horizons: Reminiscences of the Russian Revolution*, 67–68, 88; Sophia Kossak, *The Blaze: Reminiscences of Volynia 1917–1919*, 24–28, 42–47; Elena Skrjabina, *Coming of Age in the Russian Revolution*, 33–34. See also Maureen Perrie, "The Russian Peasant Movement of 1905–1907," *Past and Present* 57: 145.

7. Frierson, "Razdel: The Peasant Family Divided," 73–75; Farnsworth, "The Litigious Daughter-in-Law," 98, in *Russian Peasant Women*; Shinn, "The Law of the Russian Peasant Household," 20 (1961): 612; Benet, *The Village of Viriatino*, 243.

8. Peasant women's petition to the Duma trans. in Gail Lapidus, *Women in Soviet Society*, 33.

9. For women in manufacturing around 1900, see *Svod Perepisi 1897 g.* 2: 242–52; *An. Stat.* 20: 22; *Stat. Jarbuch* 35: 16–17; *P.P. Vol. 97 Gt. Br.Census 1891*, 180.

10. *Chislennost i sostav rabochikh perepisi 1897 g.* 1: x, xi, 2–3; *Stat. Jarbuch* 35 (1914): 16–17; *An. Stat.* 20: 28–37; *P.P. Vol. 97 Gt.Br. Census 1891*, 180; Hutchins, "A Note on the Distribution of Women in Occupations," *JRSS*, September 1904, 488.

11. Regarding mutual aid funds, see Johnson, *Peasant and Proletarian*, 88ff.

12. Glickman, *Russian Factory Women*, 196; *An. Stat.* 23: 167; Thonnessen, *The Emancipation of Women*, 57; Gertrude Hanna, "Women in the German Trade Union Movement," *ILR* 8: 24–25; Zetkin, "Women's Work and the Trade Unions" (1893), in *Selected Writings*, 51–59; Soldon, *Women in the British Trade Unions, 1874–1976*, 49; Barbara Drake, *Women in Trade Unions*, 238 Table I, 99; Mitchell, *Abstract of British Historical Statistics*, 68; Pankhurst, *My Own Story*, reprinted in *The Suffragettes*, 53.

13. *Life as We Have Known It*, 90, 103; Bornat, "Home and Work, A New Context for Trade Union History," *Radical America* 12 (5): 53–69; Patricia J. Hilsen, "Women and the Labour Movement in France, 1869–1914," *The Historical Jour-*

nal 29 (1986): 812–17; Thonnessen, *The Emancipation of Women*, 23–24; Sheila Rowbatham, *Hidden from History*, 34; Boxer, "Women in Industrial Homework: The Flowermakers of Paris," *French Historical Studies* 12 (Spring 1982): 420–21.

14. Rosen, *Rise Up, Women!*, 26–27; Lucy Middleton, *Women in the Labour Movement*, 96–98, 206; Margaret Bondfield, "A Life's Work," in *Strong Minded Women* (1982), 357–59; Hamilton, *Margaret Bondfield*, 71; Hilsen, "Women and the Labour Movement in France, 1869–1914," 819.

15. Woodward, *Jipping Street*, 97–121; *The Life and Writings of Ada Nield Chew*, 75–131, 209–47.

16. Jean Quataert, *Reluctant Feminists*, 59–60; Richard Evans, "Politics and the Family," *The German Family*, 266–67, 275.

17. Quataert, *Reluctant Feminists*, 75, 80–82; Mrs. Yearn, "A Public Spirited Rebel," in *Life as We Have Known It*, 96; *The Life and Writings of Ada Nield Chew*, 75–134, 209–47; Hilden, "Women and the Labour Movement in France, 1869–1914," *The Historical Journal* 29 (1986): 809–32; Stewart, *Women, Work, and the French State*, 42–48.

18. Regarding programs for women in the Social Democratic party, see N. Krupskaia, *Biografiia*, 38–39; G. Plekhanov, "Programme of the Social Democratic Emancipation of Labour Group," in *Selected Philosophical Works* 1: 356, 361. Showing that the 1884 and 1888 platforms did not advocate women's suffrage: "The Draft Programme of the RSDLP" in V. I. Lenin, *The Emancipation of Women*, 17–19; N. Krupskaia, preface to V. I. Lenin, *The Emancipation of Women*, 5; Anne Bobroff, "The Bolsheviks and Working Women, 1905–1920," *Soviet Studies* 26 (1974): 545–67.

19. Clara Zetkin, "Only in Conjunction with the Proletarian Woman Will Socialism Be Victorious" (Speech at Gotha, 1896), *Selected Writings*, 82–83; Clements, *Bolshevik Women*, 28–29, 45–46.

20. Krupskaia, *Biografii*, 38–39; Eleanor Marx as quoted in Barbara Taylor, "Lords of Creation," *New Statesman*, March 1980, 362; Persis Hunt, "Revolutionary Syndicalism and Feminism among Teachers in France, 1900–1921," 96; Zetkin, "For the Liberation of Women, Speech at the International Workers' Congress, Paris, July 19, 1889," *Selected Speeches*, 45–50.

21. Stewart, *Women, Work, and the French State*, 201.

22. Alfred Levin, *The Second Duma*, Appendix D "Strikes," 366–67; David Lane, *The Roots of Russian Communism*, 143; "Zhenskoe dvizhenie," *BSE*, 25: 230; Evans, "Politics and the Family," 264–67, 281.

23. Sandra Milligan in "The Petrograd Bolsheviks and Social Insurance, 1914–17," *Soviet Studies* 20: 373.

24. See *Life as We Have Known It*, xii, xxvii, 103, 131–34.

25. Leon Trotsky, *History of the Russian Revolution*, 1: 101 ff; Temma Kaplan, "Women's Activities in Launching the February 1917 Revolution in Russia, 432–38 in *Becoming Visible*; Uldricks, "The 'Crowd' in the Russian Revolution," 405–7.

26. Diane Koenker, "The Evolution of Party Consciousness in 1917: The Case of the Moscow Workers," *Soviet Studies* 30 (1): 39–41.

27. Koenker, "The Evolution of Party Consciousness in 1917," 41, 49–50.

28. Linda H. Edmondson, *Feminism in Russia, 1900–1917*; Robert McNeal, "Women in the Russian Radical Movement," 150–59.

29. "Rozaliia Samoilovna Zemliachka," by A. Razumova i S. Arina in *Slavnye Bolshevichki*, 135–47; Clements, *Bolshevik Women*, 19, 23–24.

30. R. S. Neale, *Class and Ideology in the Nineteenth Century*, 163; E. Pankhurst, "Sympathy—Not Deeds" and Dora Downright, "Why I Am a Guardian," in *European Woman, A Documentary History*, 67–71, 78–79; Pankhurst, *My Own Story*, in *The Suffragettes*, 9–12.

31. Annmarie Turnbull, "So Extremely like Parliament: The Work of the Women Members of the London School Board, 1870–1904," in *The Sexual Dynamics of History*, 120–32; Copelman, *London's Women Teachers*, 61–62.

32. Regarding women elected to Poor Law and school boards, see *The Englishwoman's Review*, 15 July 1907, 192. For membership numbers of NUWSS, see Bonnie Smith, *Changing Lives*, 348–49.

33. Emmeline Pankhurst, *My Own Story*, in *The Suffragettes*, 57; Christabel Pankhurst in Rosen, *Rise Up, Women!*, 28–29; Pethick Lawrence, *My Part in a Changing World*, 146.

34. Rosen, *Rise Up, Women!*; Pethick Lawrence, *My Part in a Changing World*, 153–292, esp. 162, 171, 181, 184–85, 215; Pankhurst, *My Own Story*, in *The Suffragettes*, 119.

35. Kollontai, "Sufrazhetki za rabotoi," in *Po Rabochei Evrope, Siluety i Eskizy*, 112–16; Ada Nield Chew, "Men, Women and the Vote, 2 September 1913," *The Life and Writings of a Working Woman*, 213–16.

36. Bonnie Smith, *Changing Lives*, 349; *Chronology of Women Worldwide*, 239–40.

37. Steven Hause, "Women Who Rallied to the Tricolor: The Effects of World War I on the French Women's Suffrage Movement," *Proceedings of the Western Society for French History* 6 (1978): 371–76.

38. Correspondence, "Experiences of a Wife as a Ratepayer," *Englishwoman's Review*, 15 October 1898.

39. Josephine Butler, "The Ladies Appeal and Protest Against the Contagious Diseases Acts," *The Shield*, 14 March 1870, in Murray, *Strong Minded Women*, 430–32.

40. Jehanne Gheith, "Evgeniia Tur and Avdot'ia Panaeva — The Precursors?" *AAASS*, Nov. 1992; Marina Ledkovsky, "Avdotya Panaeva: Her Salon and Her Life," *RLT* 9: 423–31.

41. Ekaterina Breshko-Breshkovskaia, *Iz vospominanii*; *Babushka o samoi sebe*, 1–16; *Hidden Springs of the Russian Revolution*, 8–30; *Little Grandmother of the Russian Revolution*, 1–31; P. D. Ouspensky, *Letters from Russia 1919*, 56–57.

42. Stites, "A. M. Mikhailov and the Emergence of the Woman Question in Russia," *Canadian Slavic Studies* (1969), 189–91; Armand Coquart, *D. I. Pisarev et l'idéologie du nihilism Russe,* 12, 50.

43. Dobroliubov, "Chto takoe Oblomovshchina?" (What is Oblomovshchina?, 1859) and "Kogda zhe pridet' nastoiashchii den'?" (When Will the Day Come?, 1860) in *Sochnenii*, Tom II: 569–71 and Tom III: 279ff, 320–23; Dobroliubov, *Selected Philosophical Essays*, 215–17, 391, 403–19.

44. N. G. Chernyshevsky, *What Is to Be Done?*; *Chto delat? iz rasskazov o*

novykh liudiakh. The impact of his novel in the 1860s and 1870s is found in the memoirs of Kropotkin, Figner, and Breshkovskaia.

45. Kovalevskaia describes severe family discord in Vitebsk regarding children's rights to higher education and nontraditional lives in the 1860s and 1870s. See *Vospominaniia detsva*, 86; also Kropotkin, *Memoirs of a Revolutionist*, 266.

46. Engel, *Mothers and Daughters*, 66–67, 216.

47. Engel, "Sof'ia L'vovna Perovskaia," in *Modern Encyclopedia of Russian and Soviet History* 27: 197–200; Clements, *Bolshevik Women*, 22–23; *Slavnye Bolsheviki*, 125–27ff.

48. Zinaida Vengerova, "La Femme Russe," *Revue des Revues*, 15 September 1897, 489–99, reprinted 1898; "Feminizm i zhenskaia svoboda," *Obrazovaniye*, 5-6 (1898): 73–90. Thanks to Charlotte Rosenthal for discussing Vengerova at a workshop on Slavic Women at the University of Illinois, and to her article "Zinaida Vengerova, Modernism and Women's Liberation," *Irish Slavonic Studies* 8 (1987): 97–105.

49. Sam Cioran, "The Russian Sappho: Mirra Lokhvitskaya," *RLT* 9 (1974): 317–35; M. A. Lokhvitskaia, *Stikhotvoreniia*, Tom I–IV; Sam Cioran, *Vladimir Solov'ev and the Knighthood of the Divine Sophia*; Sergius Bulgakov, *The Wisdom of God, A Brief Summary of Sophiology*; Temira Pachmus, *Between Paris and St. Petersburg: Selected Diaries of Zinaida Hippius*.

50. Barbara Caine, "Beatrice Webb and the 'Woman Question,'" *History Workshop Journal* 13 (1982): 43.

51. For dissension among socialist feminists, see Jean Quataert, "Diversity within Unity," in *Reluctant Feminists*, 55–83, 105–27.

52. Lucy Middleton, *Women in the Labour Movement*, 194; *Report of the 21st Annual Conference of the Labour Party*, Brighton (1921), 32; Ross McKibbin, *The Evolution of the Labour Party, 1910–1924*, 141; Rosen, *Rise Up, Women!*, 123–28, 271.

53. *Svod Perepisi 1897 g.* 2: 240–41; Robert McNeal, "Women in the Russian Radical Movement," *Journal of Social History* 5: 143–63; Norman M. Naimark, *The History of the "Proletariat*," 202–5; Perrie, "The Social Composition and Structure of the Social Revolutionary Party Before 1917," *Soviet Studies* 24 (2): 235–39; Stites, *The Women's Liberation Movement in Russia*, 129, 139, 149; F. Roitov, "Zhenskie Dvizhenie," *Bol'shaia Sovetskaia Entskilopediia* 25:194, 245; Werner Thonessen, *The Emancipation of Women*, 116; *The 27th Annual Conference of the Labour Party*, 24; Sowerine, "The Organization of French Socialist Women," *Historical Reflections* 3 (2): 3–24; Boxer, "Foyer or Factory: Working Class Women in Nineteenth Century France," *Proceedings of the Western Society of French History* (1978), 194–203; Persis Hunt, "Revolutionary Syndicalism and Feminism among Teachers in France, 1900–1921," 91, 190.

54. Stites, *The Liberation Movement in Russia*, 129, 139, 149; McNeal, "Women in the Radical Movement," 143–63.

55. Figner, *Memoirs of a Revolutionist*, 39-45.

56. Stites, *The Women's Liberation Movement in Russia*, 276.

57. Ruth Goldberg, "The Russian Women's Movement, 1859–1917," Ph.D. diss., Rutgers Univerity, 1975, 283–93.

Chapter 5
Society in the 1920s

> The position of women is one thing in theory, another in legal
> position, yet another in everyday life....the true position of
> women was a blend of all three.
> —Eileen Power, *Medieval Women*

Eileen Power's observations about medieval women are applicable to European and Soviet women in the 1920s. Their theoretical, legal, and real positions overlapped but did not always coincide. Patriarchal, legal egalitarian, and radical feminist views competed for women's allegiance. While traditional society constructed women's role around marriage and family life, the destruction of millions of men in World War I ruined many women's chances for family happiness. Yet the war also produced economic and educational opportunities for women and loosened social conventions. While women's legal situation improved slightly in the 1920s, their real social, psychological, and marital situations remained complex.

In Theory

Despite changes wrought by the war, patriarchal social views remained entrenched in Europe and Russia. The English view was that women's work ended with marriage, and the husband's wage should provide for the family. Working-class women did not require vocational education because their work was temporary. Higher education and careers for middle-class women were tolerated because many could not hope to marry due to the loss of men in the war and to the lack of dowries. Governments and politicians were more concerned about restoring their nation's economies than in liberating women. Only in Soviet Russia did avant-garde strategies and theories for women's liberation develop, yet even there socialists were preoccupied with economic recovery and spent little time on women's issues.

In the 1920s, the German Social Democratic Party expelled Wilhelm Reich for writing about the sexual misery of the working class, and the Bolsheviks attacked Kollontai for advocating sexual liberation. While Aleksandra Kollontai wanted women to take romance and sex seriously, she did not want them to dominate women's lives. Still, she thought it a mistake to consider sexual problems "private matters" or to think they did not affect all classes. When political and economic revolutions were changing class relations, sexual and family relations also needed redefinition. Kollontai believed that capitalism exploited women, yet thought paid work wrested them away from the home, transforming them from obedient slaves of their husbands into self-respecting persons.[1]

Still, Kollontai misunderstood women's emotional lives. Few women saw their work as equal to their husbands'. The famous poet Anna Akhmatova could not support herself in the 1920s and subordinated her writing to that of her lovers by transcribing notes and translating academic books for them.[2] Like most party members, Kollontai undervalued women's social and reproductive work, asking them to become like men, valuing paid employment more than household work. By involving women in the public sphere, yet not engaging men in housework, Bolsheviks did not establish a just society. Soviet society was too poor to provide communalization programs to liberate women from household responsibilities. Yet Bolshevik ideas and policies remained more advanced than European ones.

In the 1920s, socialists Kollontai, Reich, and Clara Zetkin focused on sexual liberation. Zetkin did not think women could obtain equality with men in capitalist, patriarchal society. She believed motherhood matured women and helped them develop ethical values that contributed to their roles as workers and citizens. Reich believed that sexual oppression was an integral part of capitalism and that a satisfactory sex life was necessary for good work. For him the proletarian mass movement included birth control, marriage, and sexuality.[3] Although German sexologists played a role in working-class culture, their English cohorts were more marginal. Young girls in all countries participated in hedonistic flapper culture, which often represented rebellion more than liberation. Even liberated women desired marriage.

Under the Law

In 1918, the Soviet government introduced emancipatory legislation, and the Weimar Republic and the British Parliament passed egalitarian laws. Worried about low birth rates and high infant mortality (100 in 1,000), French politicians restricted access to birth control and abortion in the 1920s. Since juries were loath to convict women for abortion, such cases were referred to the more severe magistrates' courts. Still, new laws allowed French married women to join labor unions without the consent of their husbands, permitted them to retain their nationality upon marriage to a foreigner, and decreed equality in civil service employment—even equal wages in some professions.[4]

The Weimar Constitution (1919) granted women greater equality than German society endorsed. Articles 22, 109, and 128 granted women the franchise, civic rights, and access to most civil service posts. Yet in 1923, inflation moved Reichstag politicians to dismiss married women civil servants if their economic future seemed secure. The prevailing notion in the government and society was that a woman's place was in the home. Women's issues such as divorce reform were often divisive, and the Center Party (Catholic) withdrew from the Reichstag until the chancellor promised to postpone it. While maternity benefits and access to higher education for women improved, the Civil Code basically left patriarchal power intact. Married women had to assume their husband's name, residence, and lifestyle. Their wages and property remained under their husband's control; the father retained authority over the children; married women were obliged to work without payment in their husband's business; and abortion remained a misdemeanor punishable by a fine and jail sentence for both woman and doctor. Thousands died from unhygienic abortions each year.[5]

Apprehensive of the revolutionary upheavals in Germany and Russia, the British government improved soldiers' and women's legal situations. The Representation of the People Act (1918) granted all men and women thirty years of age and older the right to vote and be elected to Parliament. Fearful of being swamped by the female vote, the government did not extend full civic equality to women twenty-one to thirty until 1928. The Sex Disqualification (Removal) Act (1919) suggested gender equity but did not open positions in the higher civil service, the Church of England, or the House of Lords. Women still had to resign from civil service appointments upon marriage, and female teachers lacked pay equity. As Power observes, women's situation was one thing in law, another in real life. The Matrimonial Causes Act (1923) provided greater equality in cases of judicial separation and divorce, and the Guardianship Act of 1925 made mothers as well as fathers guardians of their children in case of separation. Yet patriarchal power in ordinary family life remained untouched.[6]

Building upon the Provisional Government's progressive legislation, including female suffrage, the Soviets in 1918 provided equal access to employment, protective labor legislation, maternity coverage for working women, and formal equality in marriage and divorce. Unlike Tsarist and European laws, Soviet law allowed wives to keep their own name, take their husband's, or use a new joint name. Women revolutionaries kept their own names, and Nadezhda Krupskaia was never referred to as "Mrs. Lenin." They retained their citizenship if marrying a foreigner and did not have to promise to obey their husbands.[7]

Soviet family legislation of 1918 required spouses to support each other and, in the event of divorce, to provide for each other for six months to one year. It bound both spouses to provide for children and granted mothers custody of children. Then, as now, collecting child support payments proved difficult, and many divorced mothers became impoverished heads of household. Divorce was registered at a civil record office, making lawyers and trials obsolete. Spouses were required to notify each other, and some did so by placing a notice in a newspaper, others by sending a letter or postcard, making it known as "postcard divorce." Unscrupulous peasant men sometimes took a "summer bride," using her unpaid labor during the harvest, and then divorced her in the fall. In the wake of such abuse, a Revised Family Law of 1926 considered all children legitimate and upheld women's right to child support in both de jure and de facto marriages. Since the Central Asian areas had come under Soviet control in 1925, the 1926 legislation forbade Muslim practices of selling girls into marriage (*kalym*), abducting girls and marrying them against their will, marrying women less than eighteen years old, or allowing men to have more than one wife. These stipulations antagonized many Muslim men, just as provisions for alimony and division of property angered Slavic men. So the regime found it easier to draft laws than to enforce them, and Soviet courts were crowded with women seeking child support. Returning from her ambassadorial post to attend the debate over the new marriage law, Kollontai suggested that the state support mothers and children instead of making women dependent on alimony. Party members ridiculed her ideas, saying that men would not pay a tax to support other men's wives and children. Thus, the legislation of 1926 helped women escape abusive marriages but failed to guarantee child support or make women economically and psychologically independent.[8]

In England, Eleanor Rathbone proposed family allowances to help mothers and widows, but male members of Parliament refused to support her idea.

Alarmed at unhygienic abortion deaths, the Soviet government decriminalized abortion in 1921, providing free, hygienic abortion. The harsh economic times produced skyrocketing rates of divorce and abortion in both Moscow and Berlin. Moscow's abortion rate jumped from 10 per 100 live births in 1911 to 55 per 100 in 1928. In Saratov, the proportion of abortions in gynecological hospitalizations rose from 33% in 1921 to 60% in 1923. One million German women had abortions each year, 100,000 suffered ill effects from unhygienic abortion, and 10,000 died from illegal ones. While the number of German women convicted of infanticide declined, almost 5,000 women per year were incarcerated for breaking the abortion law. Approximately 100,000 women per year had abortions in France.[9] In England, abortion also remained common, since the working classes were only beginning to practice birth control. European policies remained contradictory: they provided condoms to fight venereal disease but shied away from dispensing contraceptive devices for birth control. Instead of making condoms cheap and available, governments doomed working-class women to illegal abortion and sterilization.

In the 1920s, the Soviets decriminalized prostitution, treating it as an economic, social, and medical problem, not a criminal or moral one as Europeans did. Initially, they had outlawed prostitution, closed bordellos, and arrested pimps and prostitutes. During the Civil War (1918–1921), prostitution almost disappeared from the major cities, and the party journal *Kommunistka* (*Woman Communist*) reported that of 6,577 women arrested and imprisoned in Petrograd in 1919, only 338 (5%) were prostitutes.[10] With the adoption of the New Economic Policy (NEP) in 1921, unemployment and prostitution increased, so the government softened its stance, instructing the police to arrest bordello operators and pimps but to take prostitutes to venereal disease clinics instead of imprisoning them. The Commissariat of Health established prophylactoria (rehabilitation centers) where prostitutes could receive shelter, job training, education, and medical care. By 1927, Moscow had eight prophylactoria, each housing nearly 200 residents who stayed from six to eighteen months for medical care, job training, and rehabilitation. Venereologist V. M. Bronner estimated that these centers provided treatment and housing for half the known prostitutes.[11]

Returning veterans in all countries displaced employed women, creating a great deal of female unemployment, hardship, and even prostitution.

Governments seldom provided unemployment payments to married women workers. Unlike the Soviets', English and German shelters for homeless women and prostitutes lacked education and job training features.

Generally, it proved easier for the Soviets to enact legislation than to change society. They deregulated prostitution, but they could not eradicate unemployment or create compassionate public attitudes. Whereas nineteenth-century Russian writers—Dostoevsky, Tolstoy, and Chekhov—depicted prostitutes as martyred victims, Soviet writers, with the exceptions of Mikhail Bulgakov in "Zoya's Apartment" (1926) and Kollontai in "Sisters" (1923), were less sympathetic.

In Reality

Social attitudes made it difficult for governments to legislate women's liberation. Patriarchal views held sway, and feminists expected more change than laws could provide. In the Soviet Union, which passed avant-garde laws for women, sexist behavior persisted. On one occasion, Valery Bryusov insulted women poets by categorizing them as poets of love and passion who could only write using "I". In response, Marina Tsvetaeva refused to read her lyric works at the poetry readings. In England, Arnold Bennett and H. G. Wells also spoke of women as second-rate writers. Wells believed that women were able to support, but not share, the serious work of men. Though his mistress Rebecca West established a literary reputation in the 1920s, Wells refused to acknowledge her talent. While the Supreme Soviet issued decrees urging political leaders in Central Asia to free women from the old ways, laws remained unenforced. Zhenotdel leaders (members of the women's department of the Party) found no legal protection there, and 800 perished for participating in unveiling ceremonies between 1927 and 1929.[12] Yet, despite patriarchy, some women in all classes and nationalities improved their situations. Many Soviet women responded to new opportunities.

The furor that Victor Margueritte's novel *La Garçonne* (*The Bachelor Girl*) created shows French society's rejection of equality. Women might discreetly engage in sexual experimentation, but public expressions of their social and sexual liberation were unacceptable. Bourgeois men still considered women sex objects, or the "second sex," as Simone de Beauvoir later put it.[13] German papers also condemned women for adopting masculine hairstyles and the "boy" look. They were criticized for cutting and dyeing their hair, having operations to reduce their bosoms to achieve the boyish look, and indulging in adultery, cocaine, nicotine, psychoanalysis, and fad diets.[14] Less outcry over boyish fashions occurred in Russia because women's emancipation, civil war, and poverty diminished the importance of high fashion. In the early 1920s, the flapper culture embraced the trappings of women's emancipation, but not its substance. It attracted youth of all classes and nationalities. Even working-class and rural women bobbed their hair, wore short skirts, and accepted the outward appearance of the liberated woman. In their hearts and minds, however, they retained traditional values, dreaming of marriage and children as a way to escape family control.

The 1920s were a time of mixed progress for European and Soviet women. Society honored married women more than single ones, and most women still dreamed of marriage. In an era when most women lacked political and economic power, most chose to exert power through family life. Historian Carl Chinn speaks of a covert matriarchy that became overt in the English working class after the war. While this seems an overstatement, wives and mothers did exert considerable control over family members. Simone de Beauvoir's friend Zaza Mabille literally died of a broken heart because her mother would not let her marry the man she loved.

In the 1920s, German middle-class housewives still took the honorary titles of their husbands, such as Frau Professor, Frau Doktor, and Frau Lehrer. Some preferred the title Haus Frau to Doktor. Maternal roles were lavishly praised, and Mother's Day became a national holiday. According to Marian Kaplan, German Jewish women served as keepers of tradition and nurtured Jewish customs in the home. As secularism increased, national holidays began to replace religious ones. Yet patriarchal authority was less formidable in Jewish than in German households.[15] Factory workers only had money for new clothes prior to marriage, and the flapper craze may have represented their attempt to have a good time before marriage and motherhood directed their energy away from themselves and into their families. Like German bourgeois women, working-class girls preferred the role of hausfrau to low-paid, unpleasant jobs.

As in earlier periods, the overwhelming majority of married women worked on family farms. Despite war losses and the creation of millions of widows, aggregate marriage rates in the 1920s were higher than those of the 1890s, and the number of employed married women was high, as table 5.1 shows.

Table 5.1. Marital Status of Occupied Women, Mid 1920s*

Country	# Single	# Married	# Widowed/Divorced
Soviet Union	9,000,000	20,000,000	5,000,000 / 470,000
Germany	6,800,000	3,600,000	1,000,000
France	2,700,000	3,900,000	1,000,000
England	3,000,000	700,000	425,000

*Calculated from *Perepisi 1926 g.*, 34: iii, 8; 51: iii, 27; *RSDRP 1926*, Tome I, 4eme partie, 38; Gt. Britain, *1921 Census of Eng. and Wales*, Table 4, 54; *SDDR 1925*, Band 402, Teil III, 438.

World War I eased some social and sexual restrictions, and public discussion of sexuality became a feature of progressive society. Some leftists promoted a more liberal sexual code, and sexual reformers insisted that women had a right to sexual satisfaction. In Germany, public lectures on sex education and family planning were popular, and writings on these topics sold quickly. Even the Federation for the Protection of Mothers stressed the right of women to self-determined motherhood and free sexual relations.[16]

Although working-class women embraced flapper culture, some career women took emancipation more seriously. Feminists—Vera Brittain, Winifred Holtby, and Virginia Woolf in England; Simone de Beauvoir in France; Lilo Linke and Toni Sender in Germany; and Aleksandra Kollontai, Vera Popova, and others in the Soviet Union—all embodied and described the New Woman. They expressed their power in their own work and careers, not through marriage to powerful men or through wifely flattery. They repudiated sexist social constructions, spurned the idealization of the lady, and like Virginia Woolf struggled to kill "the Angel in the House." Most found fulfillment in their work. They considered work and economic independence essential for the New Woman. The employment of young, middle-class women during the war made it more acceptable afterwards. Inflation eliminated the dowries of many well-to-do families, and many women in those classes had to obtain higher education and employment to support themselves. While university study became more open to women in the 1920s, cultural norms encouraged them to pursue low-paying jobs as teachers or social workers. Few entered high-paying fields such as engineering.

In England and Germany, it remained difficult for married women to have a career and a home, since governments dismissed married teachers and civil servants. It was socially acceptable, but not easy, for French and Russian women to have marriage, career, and family. Some combined marriage and a career, but found it difficult to include children as well. Childcare facilities were inadequate, and leftists did not require men to participate in household work or child rearing. The solution for some career women was the use of low-paid servants and nannies—the continued economic exploitation of one group of women by another. Those who successfully combined marriage, career, and children were usually rich women— such as Vita Sackville-West, Vanessa Bell (Virginia Woolf's sister), and Vera Brittain—who could employ help to free themselves for writing and painting. In the late 1920s, Colette Yver observed that many French career women renounced their work in favor of domesticity because their husbands desired their perpetual presence at home. She hoped women's higher education would redefine gender relations within marriage, but thought career women's marriages fragile.[17]

Marriage often became a liability for strong-minded women. Politicians—Aleksandra Kollontai, Ellen Wilkinson, Lilo Linke, and Toni Sender, as well as writers—Simone de Beauvoir and Winifred Holtby—found marriage and work incompatible. While European society sanctioned men's marrying and having a family and a career, it did not support women's right to do likewise.

Married life did not always live up to women's dreams. While the war freed many middle-class women from chaperons and allowed them more voice in their selection of a spouse, struggles within marriage remained. Married women remained economically dependent and subordinate to their husbands. When husbands suffered from underemployment and unemployment, their anger was often directed at their wives. The lack of cheap contraceptives adversely affected poor women in all countries, and too-frequent pregnancy led to ill health among working-class women. Fear of becoming pregnant led some women to ignore their husbands' conjugal demands, which sometimes resulted in adultery and family violence. Wives put up with abuse and adultery because of their economic dependence and the expense of separation or divorce.[18]

Wife beating remained common, even though new divorce laws technically enabled women to escape abusive marriages. Poverty contributed to the discrepancy between women's liberation and their actual subordinate situations. Still, easy divorce changed the dynamics of marriage in the

Table 5.2. Divorce, 1880s and 1920s*

Country	# of Div. 1882–86	Divorces/1,000 March, 1880s	# of Div. 1925	Divorces/1,000 March 1925
Russia	6,563	2.3	110,935	20
England	1,891	3.1	4,000	N/A
France	22,750	12.1	20,002	17
Germany	29,140	16.2	35,451	62

*Calculated from Mulhall, *The Dictionary of Statistics*, 218–22; *Statesman's Year Book, 1926*, "France," 846; *Statesman's Year Book, 1929*, "Germany," 925; Albrecht Classen, "Germany: Weimar Republic," in *Women's Studies Encyclopedia, vol. III*, ed. Helen Tierney, 181; Anne-Marie Sohn, "Between the Wars in France and England," 113.

Soviet Union. Indeed, the number of divorced women rose dramatically, as table 5.2 reveals.

In the first half of 1927, there were 530,000 marriages and 130,000 divorces in Russia. In Moscow, the divorce rate was 10,000 divorces to 13,000 marriages. The 1926 Soviet census reported 530,000 divorced women, but only 12,000 were receiving alimony. Divorce, lack of alimony, poverty, and high unemployment plagued several hundred thousand Soviet women in the mid 1920s.[19]

Divorce remained rare in peasant households, but it occurred more often in the 1920s. Sometimes the threat of it produced better behavior. In 1924, there were twenty-eight divorces for every 10,000 inhabitants in district towns, twelve in smaller towns, and eight in the smallest villages. By 1926, half of all divorced women lived in rural areas.[20] As part of the revolution from below, a peasant woman in Kalinin Oblast decided that if her husband beat her or treated her in a derogatory way by calling her *baba* (old hag), she would divorce him. This was new! Never in old Russia would she have threatened to divorce her abusive husband. Some husbands learned to respect their wives because they were afraid of being divorced. In Orel province, peasant women organized a boycott in 1926 to protest their husbands' abusive treatment. They vowed not to return home until their spouses agreed to treat them better. In banding together to collectively demand better treatment, they displayed a new sense of dignity.[21]

In Central Asia, the divorce rate remained low, yet slightly higher among *delegatki* (politically active women). Their higher divorce rate may indicate that Muslim men divorced wives who became politically active, or that divorced women were political. In 1924, the German socialist Clara Zetkin visited a women's club in Transcaucasia, where she met Muslim women who had divorced cruel husbands. They told her that before the revolution, their fathers sold them into marriage when they were ten or twelve years old. Their husbands beat them with clubs or whips, made them serve like slaves, rented them out as mistresses to their friends, and sold their daughters. No mullah (Muslim cleric) helped them, and no judge provided legal aid. Only the Zhenotdel offered them lawyers. So their club in Tiflis grew from 40 members in 1923 to 200 in 1924.[22]

Peasant Women

Census data reveal a high number and proportion of married women in agriculture. In Russia and Europe, marriage rates varied according to type of household. Those living on family farms had the highest rates of marriage, as table 5.3 indicates.

In contrast to the 1890s, Soviet, French, and German censuses of the 1920s defined paid and unpaid agricultural workers as "occupied." The 1926 Soviet census listed 32 million Soviet peasant women working on family farms, of whom 28 million were fifteen years old and over. The second-largest category of married women included heads of household working with members of the family. A huge proportion of women in this

Table 5.3. Married Women Working in Agriculture, 1920s
(in numbers and percent)*

Married Women	Soviet Union		France		Germany	
Family farms	19,400,000	63	2,221,000	94	3,600,000	59
Alone**	223,000	27	92,000	26	325,000	10
Employers***	45,000	23	200	21	12,000	9
Employees****	-------	---	100,000	15	1,054,000	21

*Calculated from *Perepisi 1926 g.*, 51: 18–38; 34: 10–11; *RSDRP 1926*, Tome I, 4ème partie, 38–39; *Gt. Britain Census of 1921 for Eng. and Wales*, 54–56; *SDDR 1925*, Band 402, III (Berlin, 1929): 446–47.

** Female heads of household.

*** Women in this category tended to be widowed or divorced. Among Soviet peasant women who worked alone, 380,000, or 47%, were widows; among French women 51%, and among German women 79%. The proportion of widows among employers was 64% for the Soviets but only 8% for the French.

**** Among employees and workers, the proportion of single women was exceptionally high: 77% in France, 72% in Germany. Relatively few English women engaged in agriculture, so they are not included in this table.

category were widows. Another category included widows with paid helpers. A third group was those working alone, including widows and single or
divorced women. In the mid 1920s, most French female heads of establishment were married, while most paid agricultural workers were single. The
status of German women resembled both the Russian and the French patterns. The vast majority of German women worked on family farms, but
20% were employed as agricultural workers, and a few were independent
owners or civil service employees.[23]

The lives of rural women were especially arduous. Few rural households had running water, and doing laundry was an all-day affair. Farm
wives often rose at four A.M. and were busy with household and farmyard
tasks until ten at night in the summer. Unlike factory workers, they had no
days off. They had to milk the cows, feed the animals, and do their household chores seven days a week. In Russia, farm women were the most
illiterate and seemingly the most traditional. Yet during the land distribu-
tions of 1917–1918, 10 million peasant women freed themselves from the
control of their in-laws and established their own households. Influenced
by revolutionary rhetoric, many opted for a more egalitarian family life.
However, many peasant men professed different values. They believed
that man was created to be the master, and "you had to beat a woman to
make her obey."[24]

In the 1920s, some young peasant women joined the Komsomol and
rejected traditional marriage, opting for civil ceremonies, which were cheaper
than church weddings but offered less stability and protection. Isabel Tirado
indicates that peasant girls' songs (*chastushki*) reveal their *mentalité* (attitudes). While the chastushki centered on themes of love and courtship,
they also recorded views about fashion, technology (radios, sewing machines, motor bikes), anticlericalism, spouse abuse, divorce, and politics.
One song proclaimed: "Don't threaten me, I'm not afraid; tomorrow I'll
register with some one else." Some showed a preference for suitors who
offered shoes, watches, and cosmetics, symbolizing affluence and the flapper mentality.[25]

Like their predecessors, they socialized in *posidelki* (gatherings). Girls
could not go out unchaperoned, but the posidelka, supervised by an adult
woman, provided opportunities for singing, dancing, kissing, and some ca-
ressing. All the young people were supposed to pair off, and girls without a
partner left the festivities early. During courtship, girls could accept or reject suitors. One song exclaimed: "Girlfriend of mine, let's make an exchange. You take mine and I take yours; let's organize a gathering." Once

young people were established as a couple, they generally had a betrothal and wedding. The engagement took place before the family icon and included a parental blessing. Few risked parental disapproval and forgoing the dowry that was essential for establishing a new household. While girls often modified courtship songs and lullabies, they left wedding laments intact. These dirges described their sadness in leaving their carefree life, friends, and family and moving in with in-laws where they would be expected to show humility and subservience. Some young brides wept about drunken and abusive husbands. After 1917, parents considered the wishes of their children in arranging marriages, but parents remained decisive, and unhappy arranged marriages were common among poor peasants.[26]

Zhenotdel established daycare centers, reading rooms, legal-aid centers, as well as handicraft and agricultural cooperatives. Its journal *Krest'ianka (Woman Peasant)* promoted cleanliness in peasant households and encouraged village Soviets to provide maternity and well-baby clinics to reduce infant mortality. The reduction in infant mortality from 273 per 1,000 in 1913 to 187 per 1,000 in 1926 seems to have been due to improved hygiene and diet, since households kept more of the grain they produced.[27]

Working-Class Women

> Poverty could not defeat them, men could not command them
> and society could not subdue them. Hard work remained their
> lot . . . and women of the urban poor worked all their lives.
> —Carl Chinn, *They Worked All Their Lives*

Like peasant women, working-class women usually engaged in traditional courtship practices, married young, and had large families. Few working-class women earned enough to support themselves and had to marry to survive. An English adage advised: "Better a bad husband than no husband at all." In both Europe and the Russian Republic, most working-class women married and became economically dependent on their husbands. There were 2.7 million Soviet working-class housewives, but only half that number employed in manufacturing. In Germany, 70% of all married women depended on their husband and children for wages. In the Soviet Union, 42% of female factory workers were married, 39% of French, but only 20% of English and German. High numbers of widows also worked in manufacturing: 20% in the Soviet Union and 13% in France. Roughly 39% of French craft workers were married, while 66% of the heads of handicraft workshops were married.[28]

Age also set Soviet and French workers apart from Teutonic ones. English and German industrial women workers were young, single, literate, and employed mainly in light industry, whereas in France and the Soviet Union older, married women were employed in domestic and industrial production. Soviet workers were also less literate than their European sisters. The majority of women industrial workers were unskilled, earned lower wages than male workers, lacked adequate child care, and had less free time than working men. Moreover, unemployment hit them hard when returning veterans took their jobs. In the Soviet Union, NEP (1921–1929) increased unemployment among women, and half the 58,000 unemployed female factory workers were married. Half the 88,000 French female unemployed were also married.[29]

According to Carl Chinn, working-class English women did the foulest, dirtiest work, begged food and clothes from charities, and sent their children out to work in order for the family to survive. Many poor English people were never baptized, lacked "best clothes" to attend church, and stayed indoors on Sundays. It was the aristocracy of the laboring classes who could afford proper clothes. In the slums, neighbors helped each other by contributing to a bundle of clothing to be pawned weekly. Even families with regular wages sometimes had to pawn their goods, including their wedding rings. Destitute wives shopped at night so no one could see their shabby clothing and slippers. Poverty-stricken women developed strategies for their families' survival. They worked intermittently when their husbands were out of work or underemployed. Some laid out the dead to earn money. Unlike the free divorce Soviet women enjoyed, few English women could afford a divorce or separation. Their culture expected them to stay in abusive situations. While a family could survive without a father, it could not do without a mother, and Chinn thought a powerful matriarchy provided women devotion and economic support from their children. While overt power lay in the hands of men, covert power resided in women, who were the souls of their families. He thought World War I shattered the myth of male dominance and enabled the hidden matriarchy to emerge. Yet autobiographies suggest that unemployed husbands and fathers remained powerful and abusive in the 1920s.[30]

Like Chinn, Robert Roberts indicates that women's lives changed in the 1920s. After the war, wives no longer referred to their husbands as "my boss" or "my master." During the war, they left their homes and neighborhoods more often and had extra money to spend. Some received higher pensions when their husbands served in the army than when they worked. Roberts saw working-class people and the unemployed faring better during wartime employment. He thought British working-class families became better fed and dressed due to the extension of unemployment benefit from 3 million prior to the war to 11 million afterwards.[31]

Writings of the 1920s suggest some generational differences. Whereas working-class mothers schemed to provide food and shelter for their families, their daughters sometimes struggled with different issues. While working-class mothers were content to stay in their "place," helping their husbands provide for the family, daughters had different expectations and opportunities. Factory girls displayed a sense of independence and imitated their betters by wearing fashionable clothes. Their lack of deference created anxiety among social critics striving to maintain class differences.[32]

Young factory workers often engaged in romantic escapism by going to the cinema. They enjoyed this freedom for a brief period before marriage. They usually contributed to the family income and perhaps spent money for their own pleasure if their families were not destitute. Young people continued traditional courtship practices and wed in conventional ways. Once married, they spent the family income on food and clothing for the male breadwinner and children. Sex was often steeped in secrecy and ignorance, and birth control little practiced. Fear of sexual looseness and disease during the war led to increased use of condoms by soldiers and working-class couples. They also practiced coitus interruptus and abstinence. Birth rates declined during the war and rose slightly in the 1920s, but never matched those of the late nineteenth century. Although birth control had become more accessible to the well-to-do in the nineteenth century, it was mainly in the 1920s that working-class couples began limiting the size of their families.[33]

Single factory workers differed from rural and married working-class women because they had access to more education, earned wages, went to movies and dances, spent their wages on stylish clothing, used cosmetics, and developed romantic attitudes toward life. In Germany, high wages, shorter working hours, and inflation made people want to spend their money before it lost value. The shorter workday meant that young people had more time for fun and frolic. In England, some young people "jigged" six times a week. Like their Soviet sisters, young English women often worked in textile factories, belonged to trade unions, and experienced some independence until marriage.[34]

England

The notion that a man's wages should support his family spread among workers in the late nineteenth and early twentieth centuries. Housewives were expected to leave employment upon marriage. After the war, the government supported a boom in public housing to provide "Homes Fit for Heroes" returning from the front. Inner-city dwellers dreamed of a house with spacious rooms, piped water, electricity, and a garden. For workers, a home represented comfort, status, dignity, pride, and a sense of belonging. Having shared toilets, wash houses, and hallways in crowded inner-city tenements, those living in the suburbs appreciated the privacy and respectability a home provided.[35]

Yet inadequate and irregular incomes kept many in extreme poverty. Working-class mothers often fed their children and husbands but skimped on food for themselves. Marriage could be disillusioning, as the song indicates:

> Love, it is teasing,
> Love, it is pleasing,
> Love is a pleasure
> When it is new;
> But as it grows older
> And days grow colder
> It fades away like the
> Morning dew.[36]

Birth rates fell late among the poor. In 1900 the birth rate was 18 per 1,000 in middle-class areas in Birmingham, 24 per 1,000 among better-off workers, and 40 per 1,000 in poorer working-class families. Although fertility declined in the 1920s, the rate of decline did not approximate that of the middle classes. Rose Naylor Gamble's mother had fourteen pregnancies, and Dorothy Scannell's mother ten. On her honeymoon, Scannell discovered that her husband was as ignorant about sex, birth control, and condoms as she was. In poor areas of Birmingham, infant mortality was 207 per 1,000 compared to 131 per 1,000 in better parts of city. The English urban poor had little access to trained midwives or doctors, although medical care and public clinics become more available after the war. Still, childbirth remained more life-threatening than mining was.[37]

While illegitimacy in Great Britain fell from 17 per 1,000 in 1870 to 3.6 per 1,000 in the 1920s, it still provoked great shame. Katherine Cookson, an illegitimate child, experienced the cruelty of the bigoted poor. She felt rejected when her playmates excluded her from their birthday parties, and she saw her grandparents make her mother pay for her sin her entire life. Neighbors and kin never forgave or forgot a "fallen woman." An unmarried, pregnant woman whose parents could not help her was sent to the workhouse (welfare institution) for fourteen years. Her child was given to a Cottage Home, but the mother was not free to leave the workhouse until her child was old enough to work.[38]

Sexual abuse and harassment affected children as well as wives. As a child, Dorothy Scannell was molested by a soldier, and Katherine Cookson was fondled by her mother's suitor. Katherine's mother was harassed by her stepbrother and stepfather, but she couldn't complain because everyone would blame her, as an unmarried mother, rather than them.[39]

Some English working-class girls felt class antagonism at school. If older siblings contributed to household finances, younger ones could take advantage of grammar school scholarships. Yet they might experience animosity in the middle-class atmosphere of grammar school. Attending a birthday party, Rose Gamble realized how out of place her old-fashioned clothes and shoes were, so she decided not to attend social affairs where she would feel like an outsider. Her sisters also dealt with class issues when applying for jobs.[40]

Cookson describes the estrangement her own illegitimacy and her mother's alcoholism created for her, and she wondered where her education and striving would get her. Leaving school at fourteen, she obtained a position in a hospital laundry and parlayed that job into managing a large laundry. Displeased with the men she attracted, she decided to buy her own house instead of waiting for a man to provide it. Decades later, her isolation led to psychiatric treatment for depression. Her autobiography shows that while her mother waged financial battles, she fought psychological ones.[41]

Wartime prosperity led to a decline in crime in Great Britain, but postwar business slumps and inflation led to increased rates of theft, robbery, embezzlement, bigamy, rape, incest, and abortion. During the war, workers had gotten used to earning "big money" and having luxuries that they could no longer afford in the 1920s. Some stole to retain their standard of living. Some English men squandered their money without settling their weekly grocery bills. In the early 1920s grocers had to take creditors to court to get payment. During and after the war, German women pilfered food for their families. They accounted for 20% of those convicted of theft, 100% convicted of infanticide, and 70% convicted of abortion.[42]

Germany and France

Young French workers enjoyed social evenings of dancing and flirting, but they maintained traditional family mores. The construction of 2.6 million new homes in postwar Germany made family life possible for many workers and rural migrants. Yet in poor areas of Berlin, working-class households remained crowded, with five people sharing one room. Inflation and low wages made birth control necessary. Douching and coitus interruptus were common, because condoms and diaphragms were too expensive. The German government restricted the public display and sale of contraceptives, but private clinics and pharmacies provided birth control information and condoms, and the birth rate fell from 30 per 1,000 in 1910 to 21.1 in 1924. Many poor German working-class housewives were unable to use contraceptive methods effectively due to a lack of privacy and information. They swamped birth control clinics, begging for abortions and sterilization. Some doctors considered these women irresponsible, but others realized how ignorant they were and that crowded housing contributed to poor health and sexual disturbances. Many German working-class women aged prematurely from countless pregnancies. French couples had practiced birth control for decades and resisted the government's pro-natal policy to increase the birth rate.[43]

In response to rising rates of illegal abortion, some German physicians used sterilization as a safer measure. Aggregate statistics do not indicate the proportion of working-class German women having abortions, but some accounts suggest they had higher abortion rates and incarceration rates for abortion than did women in other countries. In municipal clinics, physicians treated working-class women during pregnancy and childbirth, provided birth control information, and treated them for drug addiction, alcoholism, rape, attempted suicide, and infertility. Yet, when the Marxist psychologist Wilhelm Reich drew attention to workers' sexual misery, he was drummed out of the SPD.[44]

Oppressed women often found more consolation in their families and friends than in organized religion. Many poor German families resented church taxes and refused to pay them. Some felt estranged from the church and refused to support a nationalist, conservative clergy. Many found more comfort in socialism than in the established church.[45]

The Soviet Union

Soviet working-class women distinguished themselves from peasant women by spending more time on education and politics.[46] Trade unions established reading rooms, worker schools, and nurseries. By the end of the decade, unions and the Commissariat of Welfare provided 739 factory nurseries, 585 well-baby clinics, 281 prenatal clinics, and 140 legal consultations. The Soviets established birth control centers and abortion clinics for urban women.

Young Soviet factory workers, like those in Europe, often spent their salaries on dancing, movies, and fashionable clothes. One factory worker earned sixty-five rubles per month but spent two-thirds of it on manicures, cosmetics, silk stockings, and dances. Some deprived themselves of food to buy luxuries. Many sought the sophistication of flapper culture to make their drab lives more bearable. Some distanced themselves from proletarian culture by adopting bourgeois fashion; others associated with the children of NEP men (capitalists). Many puritanical Party leaders condemned free love, jazz, and flapper culture. Komsomol leaders frowned upon young people who based their attachments on the physical attraction of dancing, but their voices were drowned out by the music of the foxtrot. Considering dance halls to be counter-revolutionary, Party and state institutions tried to woo youth with theater and concert tickets.[47]

In patriarchal culture, it was hard for working-class women to develop political consciousness, and family life remained more attractive to them than politics. Soviet literature portrayed many characters who preferred security to change. One character in Gladkov's novel *Cement* observes: "To be born again is as terrible as to die." Another taunts a liberated woman: "You've got one of the best men in the world, and yet you don't want to sleep with him. I'd like to slap you in the face."[48]

In Glebov's play *Inga*, Nastia is beaten by her husband. Unable to cope any longer, she asks a Zhenotdel leader in her factory to help her. She admits that living with him is worse than a sentence of hard labor. But where would she go, alone, with the kids?[49] She lacks the resources to make a new life.

In the same play, the character Glafira attempts suicide when she discovers her husband's adultery. As she recovers, she gives up some of her romantic notions and learns to respect herself and her work. By the end of the play, she becomes a liberated woman, telling her husband: "What do you think I am, a complete fool? A river doesn't flow backwards, and I won't ever be the same as I used to be. I won't allow anyone, even you, to stand in my way."[50] She represents working-class women who believe in love, marriage, and the family but reject the old, male-dominated institution. It is difficult to know how representative Glafira is, but she does symbolize a politically active worker.

In *Cement*, the character Dasha Chumalova approaches life differently from Nastia and Glafira. She takes her Party work more seriously than her family life. She realizes the old ways have broken up and remarks to her husband: "You've been quite free with regard to women. Now, women have equal rights."[51] As a sexually emancipated Communist, she tries to prevent her husband and child from defining her. Yet, after Nurka's death, she realizes that her daughter needed affection as well as food, and that she has sacrificed Nurka for the revolution. Yet she works effectively for the Party. Although Party chief Badin rapes the intellectual Zhenotdel leader Polia Mekhova, he cannot take Dasha against her will. She is stronger than Polia, who succumbs to doubts. Dasha tells Polia that she should be ashamed of her tears and nervous attacks. As a Communist, she must be strong. Party-minded, not critically minded, Dasha represents "comrade absolute" and presages the obedient Party member of the 1930s.

Kollontai creates a worker heroine named Vasia who also parts from her unfaithful husband with great difficulty. The threads that bind her to him are artfully tied, and it is his unscrupulous NEP-man mentality, not his adultery, that makes her leave him. She struggles to reconcile romantic ideas about love and marriage while seeking equality. Glafira and Vasia discover that emancipation creates tensions in their personal lives. Glafira resolves her problem by rejecting the role of subordinate wife and creating a more equitable monogamous marriage. Vasia cannot have a monogamous marriage, so she renounces it and immerses herself in Party work. When she discovers she is pregnant, she does not have an abortion, but decides to establish a factory nursery to raise her baby in the collective.

These heroines do not find marriage satisfying, but seek fulfillment in the public spheres of paid work and Party membership. Glafira no longer defines herself solely as a wife and mother but also values her Party work. Dasha reveres her Party work, viewing her roles of wife and mother as secondary ones. Vasia reluctantly rejects marriage but accepts motherhood, work, and Party membership as important. These characters spend their time in social work: Dasha in Zhenotdel, organizing groups of Cossack women and establishing a child care center; Vasia in a communal nursery and housing project; and Glafira in collecting Party dues at her factory. None holds a high-ranking Party position, which are male dominated.

Domestic Servants

The status of domestic servants changed little from the 1890s to the 1920s. Most remained young, single, rural migrants. While low unemploy-

Table 5.4. Marital Status of Domestic Servants, 1920s*

Country	Number	% Single	% Married	%Widowed/Divorced
Germany	1,016,022	95	1	3
England	1,149,000	87	6	3
France	661,000	58	23	18
Soviet Union	448,000	75	6	17/5

*Calculated from *SDDR 1925*, Band 402, 34: 446–7; *RSDRP 1926*, Tome I 4ème partie, 38–39; P.P. *Census for Eng. and Wales 1921*, Table 4, 104; *Perepisi 1926 g.*, Table III, 34: 74.

ment was a benefit of the work, prostitution remained a pitfall. Peasant migrants were vulnerable and sometimes prostituted themselves for emotional and financial support. In the Soviet Union and Germany, the overwhelming majority of known prostitutes were peasant migrants.[52]

While their work remained almost the same, attitudes changed. In the nineteenth century, servants perceived their work as hard but bearable. In the 1920s, many resented the work because they had experienced more freedom and better-paying factory jobs during the war. In Europe and Russia, returning veterans forced women out of well-paid jobs in manufacturing and back into low-paid service positions. Many English girls considered domestic service degrading and resisted such jobs if they could. Yet young girls who left school at age fourteen did not have many options. Katherine Cookson realized she had two possibilities: writing or doing housework. She didn't think she could earn her living from writing but she knew she lacked the obedient personality domestic service required. After two unpleasant stints as a servant, she got a job in a laundry. Another English girl, Lu Gamble, begged her mother to get her a job in a shop so she wouldn't have to become a charwoman. But she was so small that shopkeepers would not hire her. At fourteen, Lu became a charwoman, but later her sister Dodie got her a job assisting in the gallery where she worked.[53]

Servant marital status changed considerably from the 1890s to the 1920s. France had significant numbers of married, widowed, and divorced domestics. In the Soviet Union, high numbers were also widowed or divorced, but many left service to take factory jobs or upon marriage.

Women in Commerce

Young European women generally preferred jobs in commerce to factory work because they offered status, fashionable dress, and a clean work environment. Yet shop assistants, typists, and bank tellers did not earn high wages, and they struggled to dress well on their incomes. After the war, most worked an eight-hour day instead of the ten- to fourteen-hour day of the 1890s. Having more time, many participated in the dancing and chic dress of flapper culture.

Soviet census figures reveal a largely married work population and a small bureaucracy. Aggregate French statistics are complicated because 71% of women employees in commerce were single, but 82% of *chefs d'établisements* were married. Table 5.5 reveals the large number of Teutonic single women in commerce.

In Germany, cinemas, dance halls, and cafes mushroomed after the war. By 1925, 1.5 million German women worked in white-collar positions and regarded themselves as a cut above factory workers. The German cinema fed their fantasy that a wealthy boss or elegant customers would whisk a salesgirl off to a life of happiness and luxury. While all classes attended films and read pulp novels, white collar workers were the greatest consumers. Therefore, filmmakers and novelists portrayed the typist or shop assistant as young, sexy, and elegant—one who could climb the social ladder by marrying the right man. Living at home, most longed to escape parental control and low-paid work through marriage or extra-marital affairs. Since their wages were too small to allow fashionable dress, they sometimes resorted to casual prostitution to augment their meager incomes. Some engaged in extra-marital affairs because women outnumbered men in Germany: 1,116 to 1,000.[54]

Table 5.5. Marital Status of Women in Commerce, 1920s*

Country	Number	% Single	% Married	%Widowed/Divorced
Germany	1,575,000	62	27	11
England	989,000	83	11	6
France	1,008,000	37	45	18
Soviet Union	114,000	40	34	25

*Calculated from *SDDR 1925*, Band 402, III, *Berufszahlung*, 446; *RSDRP 1926*, Tome I 4ème partie, 38–39; P.P., Gt. Britain, *1921 Census of Eng. and Wales*, Table 4, 92–97, 105–6; and *Perepisi 1926 g.*, Table III, 34: 66.

Table 5.6. Marital Status of Career Women, 1920s*

Country	Number	% Single	% Married	% Widowed/Divorced
Soviet Union	488,000	44	41	14
England	432,000	85	9	6
France	421,000	71	28	1
Germany	290,000	81	9	10

*Calculated from *Perepisi 1926 g.*, 34: 3: 68–92; *1921 Census of Eng. and Wales*, Table 4, 99–103; *RSDRP 1926*, Tome I 4ème partie, 38–39; *SDDR 1925* Band 402, 3: 446.

Educated Women

> . . . love and marriage are not mere investments, but a woman's whole life!
> —Monique in *The Bachelor Girl* (Victor Margueritte)

The situation of educated women resembled that of other employed women. In England and Germany, most career women were single, in France and the Soviet Union more were married, and in the Soviet Union and Germany a significant proportion were widowed, as table 5.6 shows.

The high marriage rates of Soviet and French career women resulted from tolerant nineteenth-century traditions as well as France's pronatal policies. Patriarchal English and German societies demanded that female civil servants resign their posts upon marriage. English school boards often dismissed married teachers, and the crowded German civil service rejected career women. Germany had only half as many female teachers as England or Russia. Negative attitudes toward career women remained strong in Teutonic countries, and women often internalized the attitude. Margarethe Bockholt Haussleiter forsook her Ph.D. degree and career in social work to marry an economist and take the more "respectable title" Frau (wife). At thirty-three, she hated being a spinster and was delighted to marry. English writer Rebecca West seemed a liberated woman as H.G. Wells's mistress in the 1920s, but deep down she too longed for marriage.[55]

The Soviet Intelligentsia

Soviet writings concentrate on women's professional work, providing little information about their personal lives. Party members Nadezhda Krupskaia, Elena Stasova, Paulina Vinogradskaia, and Anna and Elizaveta Ulianova (Lenin's sisters) devoted their memoirs to others and shunned discussion of their personal lives. Collective biographies tend to glorify women as heroic revolutionaries without telling how they balanced their personal and political lives. Most memoirs contain little information describing women's personal, emotional, or sexual relationships. Kollontai's *Autobiography of a Sexually Emancipated Communist Woman* (1926) barely mentions her two marriages and divorces. Although she repeatedly fell in love, and longed to be understood by a man, when she felt treated as a sex object, she freed herself from the relationship.[56]

Her writings demystify the role of erotic love in women's lives and urge women to dislodge romance from the center of their lives. Yet she found this hard to do. She subordinated romance to Party work, but in the midst of political activity took time for the "joys and pangs of love." She believed that a New Woman invested in her own work, refused to live vicariously through her beloved, and rejected the punishing behavior of lovers or husbands. She thought life created New Women, and literature reflected them. In her novella *Love of Three Generations* (1927), she depicts a young Party worker named Zhenia who lacks the time to fall in love. No sooner does she get to like someone than he is called to the front or assigned to some other town.[57] She even has an affair with her mother's lover, thinking that her busy mother would not mind! Kollontai's writings reflect discord and divorce among married, politically active career women. The 1926 Soviet census and Soviet literature both suggest that divorced career women found marriage, work, and political activity difficult to combine.

Anatole Glebov's play *Inga* and Valentin Kataev's comedy *Squaring the Circle* depict emancipated, career women in the late 1920s. Glebov depicts Inga as a shrewd factory director and diligent Party worker until she falls in love. Inga tells a friend that for years she had nothing of her own. Everything was for the Party, but now it's so different. Yet when her affair with a married factory worker interferes with production, she gives him up.[58]

Kataev's *Squaring the Circle* portrays the results of hasty marriages. His young couples blithely marry, discover their incompatibility, divorce, and marry each other's mate. His character Tonia is a serious Komsomolka, who marries a Communist with bourgeois tastes, while Ludmila desires coziness and comfort but is married to an austere Komsomol who finds curtains at the window bourgeois. Sharing the same room, the couples cease to respect each other, and fall in love with the spouses whose values resemble their own. They correct their situation by going to the registry office to divorce their current mates and marry their new loves. The play shows how difficult it was to remain married to a person with different social and political values. It also drew attention to Soviet family law, which made marriage and divorce simple matters of registration. Such cavalier behavior created social problems in the 1920s, when many divorced women were not psychologically or economically prepared to provide for themselves.

Zhenia, Inga, and Tonia exemplify the New Woman, showing educated women having problems balancing love, marriage, work, and political activity. They indicate how common marriage, divorce, and separation were among the female intelligentsia. Characters such as Tonia and Inga believed in romantic love and took their Party responsibilities seriously. They thought they should set good examples for others but had trouble reconciling romance with Party responsibilities.

One tragic character is Polia Mekhova in Gladkov's novel *Cement*. She represents an idealistic revolutionary who is unable to adjust to NEP. Powerless to mitigate Party purges or resist the rapist Badin, Polia falls apart. When she has a nervous breakdown, Dasha takes care of her. They represent camaraderie, caring, and community. Unlike them, male Party members in the novel remain isolated and do little to help purged friends. *Cement* shows that the revolution has not changed men's attitudes toward women: Serge remains a hopeless romantic, Gleb hangs on to the double standard, and Badin rapes women wherever and whenever he desires. But Dasha and Polia represent sexually emancipated women who have let go of old ways and have begun building community.

With the exception of *Cement*, few Soviet writings confront the problems of married female Party members. A recent work, *Kremlin Wives* (1992), reveals the havoc many couples experienced living in the Kremlin. Ekaterina Kalinina, wife of the president of the Soviet Union, had difficulties combining love, marriage, children, and career. She felt so restricted as first lady that she hired a household manager and left to organize women's trade unions and literacy programs in Central Asia. She explains to her husband, President Kalinin, that she doesn't feel like a real person in Moscow. Because she belongs to the top rank, she can't speak and think as she wants. She resents the loss of ideals when the Party divides up into ranks and classes. Although she returns to Moscow, she is not healthy or happy living in the Kremlin. She wants to work as an activist, not perform official duties. Since Stalin disliked such strong women, she was purged in 1937 and imprisoned until 1946.[59]

Orthodox nuns are one group of educated women who are rarely discussed. Fading away for their own safety during the purges, they sought shelter and employment wherever they could. Elena Bonner's family employed a former nun as housekeeper since her mother worked full-time for the Party.[60] Some of the 70,000 nuns reported in the 1897 census found havens as cooks, domestics, and nannies, and some were imprisoned. Their story remains untold.

English Career Women

Many well-to-do English women suffered the loss of a brother, husband, father, or fiancé in the war. While most still led traditional married lives, those unable to marry due to wartime losses and other causes sometimes found meaningful professional work to support themselves. Writers providing insight into upper- and middle-class family and social life in the 1920s include Vera Brittain, Winifred Holtby, Virginia Woolf, Vita Sackville-West, and Radclyffe Hall. While they may not be representative of educated upper-class women, they dealt with common issues: rebellion against parental control, self-definition in patriarchal society, economic independence, and the desire of lesbians to live openly with their lovers in hypocritical English society.

In her novels, Virginia Woolf often depicts women characters who "smooth the way" for their husbands. Their careers are tending to their husbands. Having grown up in Victorian society, Woolf internalized the nurturing role of "Angel in the House." In *To the Lighthouse*, however, her character Lily refuses to be drawn in by her host's demand for sympathy. Lily refuses to be bullied into assuaging his grief at the cost of her own work.[61]

In a speech to professional women, Woolf confessed that it was not easy for women of her generation to take their own work seriously and free themselves from nurturing roles. In writing book reviews, she constantly battled the phantom who slipped behind her and whispered: "You are writing about a book written by a man. Be sympathetic; . . . flatter; deceive . . . Never let anybody guess you have a mind of your own." Then she has to catch the phantom and kill it. Had she not done so, it would have plucked the heart out of her writing. It was hard to kill it because it lurked in her mind. Similar phantoms, prejudices, and conventions stifled other career women.[62]

Woolf sensitively describes women's psychic struggles. Her short stories often portray shy women who feel upset at being defined as sex objects by their clothing and class objects by their social standing.[63] In *Orlando* (1928), Woolf describes how women's clothing hinders their actions and conceals their true natures. Clothes change our view of the world and the world's view of us.[64] She wonders whether, if men and women wore the same clothes, they would become more androgynous. Although she had a contented marriage to Leonard Woolf, she was occasionally drawn into affairs with women. In *Orlando*, she depicts an androgynous character modeled on her friend Vita Sackville-West. In her bohemian Bloomsbury circle, married people commonly had lovers.

Vita Sackville-West lived a covert yet active lesbian life within marriage. Vita and Virginia's relationship was unusual, since both were married. Both had been traumatized in childhood and adolescence. Virginia's mother died when she was young, and she may have been raped by her half brother in adolescence. Vita's mother constantly belittled her, making her feel ugly. Initially, her parents had opposed her marriage to Harold Nicolson because his family lacked social standing and money — two important ingredients for an upper-class marriage. Eventually, her father relented, and she married in 1913. Although she had lesbian lovers during her marriage, and Harold had male lovers, they remained together for fifty years. An early novel of hers showed the cynicism of her class: "you must never marry the person you love, for fear of spoiling it; you must marry someone you don't love, for then there is nothing to spoil."[65]

Analyzing her "dual personality" in her autobiography in 1920, Vita explained how the feminine and masculine elements alternately dominated, and how she thought lesbians would become more common as the century progressed. At times, she found it difficult to keep her two personalities separate. One part included her house, garden, husband, purity, simplicity, and faith. The other contained her passionate female attractions and the scornful side of her personality. She believed the sexes were becoming more alike and that more of her type existed than hypocritical English society admitted. In a talk for the British Broadcasting Corporation in 1929, Vita and Harold agreed that a successful marriage should be a lifetime association based on love, intelligence, mutual esteem, and respect. She also favored candor as well as easier divorce. An aristocrat, she thought such advances must come from the more educated and liberal classes.[66] When Vita fell in love with Virginia, people worried lest Vita's passion unsettle Virginia's fragile psyche. Apparently, Virginia was sexually frigid in her marriage to Leonard and also limited in her physical responses to Vita. Virginia described Vita as voluptuous but unreflective. In her letters to Harold, Vita assured him that her love for Virginia did not threaten their relationship because her love for Virginia was a mental and spiritual thing. Wary of arousing physical feelings in Virginia because of her mental instability, Vita remained attracted to Virginia's brilliant mind, fragile body, and childlike nature.[67, 68]

The lesbian writer who created the greatest stir was Radclyffe Hall. Her seemingly autobiographical novel *The Well of Loneliness* disclosed the pain of lesbians who could not be themselves in English society. In the novel, the mother and neighbors do not understand the heroine, insisting that women are incomplete without marriage. A friend encourages the heroine to go to Paris where she will find more acceptance than in London. Hall's heroine finds a lover on ambulance duty during the war. They realize that the world would treat them cruelly, finding only corruption and vileness in them. The heroine warns her lover that she could not protect her from persecution and could only love her.[69] The Parisian lesbian subculture provided sanctuary for many literary English and American lesbians. Hall and Sackville-West's writings reveal some of the difficulties historians have in discussing the topic. Most lesbians had to mask their sexuality and, as Martha Vicinus remarks: "we rarely know precisely what women in the past did with each other in bed or out, and we are not able to reconstruct fully how and under what circumstances lesbian communities evolved."[70]

Male losses in the war rendered many English women spinsters. Graduating from Oxford in the early 1920s, Winifred Holtby and Vera Brittain devoted themselves to writing and gave their political support to feminism, pacifism, the Labour Party, and the League of Nations. Both were middle class and experienced a great deal of parental interference. In *Testament of Youth* (1933), Vera Brittain describes the psychological wounds she experienced growing up in a patriarchal, middle-class British home prior to the war: "no ambitious girl who has lived in a family which regards subservience of women as part of the natural order of creation ever completely recovers from the bitterness of her emotions." She was also wounded that society found female artists interesting but female intellectuals ridiculous.[71]

Her parents' double standard rankled her. Though her brother was a poor student, her parents planned university study for him, when she was the better pupil. Moreover, they expected Vera to always be at their disposal. When her mother fell ill during the war, her father demanded she leave her nursing post to return home to care for her mother. He made no such request of his son, who was serving in the army. Brittain observed similar behavior in Winifred Holtby's family. During their university holidays, Winifred often had to surrender her bedroom to visitors. Both suffered from the adage "Great women, unlike great men, can never get rid of their relatives." Vera knew from her brother's experience that male students had no social duties and could spend their vacations preparing for exams.[72]

Holtby's dilemma lay in putting others first. At college, she fell prey to students with problems, including the grief-stricken Brittain who had lost her fiancé, her brother, and her religion during the war. Winifred's high-spiritedness refreshed Vera, and it was their camaraderie that healed some of Vera's emotional pain. Unlike many middle-class women who desired power through a husband, Vera wanted a career for herself and refused to live vicariously through a husband. She believed that dignity in marriage meant economic independence. Although Winifred's friendship restored her to life, it was romance and marriage in 1924 that revitalized Vera.[73]

An independent woman, Winifred refused the dream role her beau formed for her. She insisted they prove themselves and their love before settling into a serious relationship. When he married another woman and reappeared years later, Winifred did not know how to respond to him. She wrote to Vera: "I decided that if I could not have what I wanted, I would want what I could have. . . . After all, it is loving, and not being loved, which is the vitalizing experience."[74] Always giving more than she received, Winifred was a woman of her time, class, and country.

Before Brittain's marriage, she and Holtby shared a flat in London, working on political projects. While both pursued literary careers, they also taught part time. To free themselves for intellectual work, they hired a housekeeper to do the shopping, cooking, and cleaning. Likewise, Ellen Wilkinson, a member of Parliament in the 1920s, disclosed her need for a "wife" to help her with her duties. She mockingly commented: "Oh! for a wife. If I had a wife, she might have collected these [letters], drafted answers and finally typed them. She would help with the women's section, give a hand with the bazaar, and when I get home fagged out, have a delicious meal ready for me."[75]

French Career Women

World War I disillusioned French women as well as men. Some destroyed themselves through sex, alcohol, or drugs. Victor Margueritte's novel *La Garçonne* (*The Bachelor Girl,* 1922) portrays adulterous wives, emancipated artists, seduced maids, and alienated bourgeois women. The heroine Monique declares "since the war we have all become bachelor girls." Her worldly-wise mother remarks that if every woman looked on marriage as her daughter did, hardly anyone would get as far as the banns, and there would be more divorces than the judges could handle. Marriage is the dream of every girl but is not necessarily connected with love. Monique rejects her parents' ideas of arranged marriage, insisting that love and marriage are not mere investments but a woman's whole life! Repudiating her parents' choice of husbands, she decides to work as an interior decorator to give her life meaning. She also bobs her hair to look like a bachelor girl. Her bohemian life eventually sickens her, and she finds redemption in loving a "worthy" man.[76]

Simone de Beauvoir entitles her early reminiscences *Memoirs of a Dutiful Daughter,* although they describe her rebellion against bourgeois life. Her father, like Virginia Woolf's, expresses negative attitudes toward educated women. He prefers demure, elegant women to intelligent bachelor girls. Simone longs for him to take an interest in her intellectual work, but he is indifferent. Simone rejects her parents' values and refuses to serve tea, smile, and make small talk because she is searching for absolute truth.[77]

Her father's shaky economic position makes him lash out at his family, and he thinks she would become too liberal if she became a teacher. Something of a prude, Simone feels ill at ease with students of loose morals. Homosexual and lesbian students horrify her, and bourgeois affairs and adultery disgust her. Having internalized her father's patriarchal ideas, she wonders whether men marry intellectual women like herself and thinks she is doomed to solitude. She finds her male friends too conventional, since she cares less about respectability than about love.[78] A liberal feminist, Simone thinks men and women are equal human beings with equal benefits and privileges. In her circle, she thinks that no struggle between the sexes exists, and that male students are her friends and comrades. An "honorary man," she has a woman's heart and a man's mind.[79]

Simone's friend Zaza comes from a very wealthy bourgeois family. Although Zaza rejects her mother's attempts to show her off and arrange a good marriage for her, she cannot openly rebel. When she tells her mother that she does not love any of the men introduced to her, her mother explains: "My dear, it's the man who loves, not the woman." Rejecting her mother's marriage plans, she dies of grief rather than submit to such machinations.[80]

German Career Women

World War I affected German women adversely, creating a shortage of men and a great deal of disillusionment. Like Vera Brittain in England, Edith Stein in Germany lost her faith as a result of her nursing experiences. Stein later embraced Catholicism, despite strong family opposition. As a Jew and a woman, Stein found no university post open to her when she graduated with a Ph.D. in philosophy, so she taught at a convent school in Speyer from 1923 to 1931.[81]

In Weimar Germany, educated women with talent and pluck could pursue artistic, theatrical, political, or academic careers. Although many obtained higher degrees, some forsook them for the title Hausfrau. Yet young women—Lilo Linke, Toni Sender, and Louise Schroder—put political work ahead of marriage and family life. Linke felt that all of her life lay in front of her, and she did not want the restrictions that marriage, a household, and children imposed.[82] Rebelling against bourgeois life, Toni Sender told her mother not to provide a dowry for her because she did not intend to marry. She craved a meaningful life, not status. Serving on Reichstag Foreign Affairs and Economics Committees, she only reluctantly agreed to edit the SPD women's magazine *Frauenwelt* (*Women's World*).[83]

Not all German women regarded professional work and marriage as incompatible. Some doctors, such as psychoanalyst Karen Horney, combined career and marriage, but her male colleagues did not take her work seriously. Dubbed *Doppelverdiener* (double earners), many married women lost their jobs in the civil service. Conservatives and some women insisted that they make way for unemployed men and single women to ease the labor market and strengthen the family. Indeed,Weimar society remained an uneasy mix of conservative, traditional, bohemian, and socialist elements. As a young student, Hannah Arendt fell in love with her philosophy professor and had an affair with him. Yet when she married later, she became the traditional helper, typing her husband's thesis.[84]

Artist Hanna Hoch discovered that while men in the Dada movement gave lip service to women's liberation, they still belittled female talent. Her lover Raoul Hausmann even beat her and fantasized killing her when she demanded that he leave his wife for her.[85] He was not unique. Klaus Theweleit's *Male Fantasies* shows many German veterans expressing hostile, violent attitudes toward women after the war.

Free love was an interesting part of German bohemian culture in the 1920s. Artists and writers such as Emmy Ball-Hennings and Rahel Sanzara lived unconventional lives, sometimes living with female and male lovers.

As sexually emancipated women, they shocked conservative society. Even more scandalous were lesbian novels and nightclubs. In *The Scorpion* (1919), Anna E. Weirauch describes the grand passion of lesbian women who have become fully alive. German criminal code #175 made homosexuality illegal, but lesbianism was not, and lesbian culture flourished in the 1920s. In German cities, middle- and working-class lesbians could talk and dance in public halls, and the paper *The Girlfriend* printed advertisements for them to meet each other.[86] Thus, German culture remained an uneasy mixture of traditional and radical elements in the 1920s.

Notes

1. Kollontai wrote extensively about marriage, sexual relations, and the family. See "The Social Basis of the Woman Question," "Sexual Relations and the Class Struggle," "Love and the New Morality," and "Theses of Communist Morality in the Sphere of Marital Relations," trans. in Holt, *Alexandra Kollontai, Selected Writings*; novellas *Love of Worker Bees* (1923), *A Great Love* (1927), and "The New Woman," in *Autobiography of a Sexually Emancipated Communist Woman*, ed. I. Fletcher, 98–99. (cited hereafter as *Autobiography*).

2. Regarding Akhmatova's work for Vladimir Sheleiko and Nikolai Punin, see Roberta Reeder, *Anna Akhmatova*, 122, 182.

3. Zetkin, *Selected Writings*, 72-83; Karen Honeycutt, "Clara Zetkin," *F.S.*, 135; Wilhelm Reich, "The Sexual Misery of the Working Masses and the Difficulties of Sexual Reform," *The New German Critique* 1: 98–100.

4. Anne-Marie Sohn, "Between the Wars in France and England," *A History of Women*, 112–13; Sian Reynolds, *France Between the Wars*, 34, 269.

5. "The Constitution of the German Reich of August 11, 1919," *The Government and Administration of Germany*, 642–79; Gisbert H. Flanz, *Comparative Women's Rights and Political Participation in Europe*, 79–83; Renate Pore, *A Conflict of Interest: Women in German Social Democracy, 1919–1933*, 82; Helen L. Boak, "Women in Weimar Germany: The 'Frauenfrage' and the Female Vote," 156–66, in *Social Change and Political Development in Weimar Germany*; *SDDR 1925, Band 370, Kriminalstatistik fur das Jahr 1927*, 46–47.

6. See Flanz, *Comparative Women's Rights and Political Participation in Europe*, 83–85. Rose Gamble describes her mother's unsuccessful struggle to obtain a separation. Seeking relief from her abusive working-class husband, her mother discovered male magistrates granted separations only when there were marks of violence. Although she had suffered repeated physical and verbal abuse, because there were no present marks, the magistrates refused her a judicial separation. Rose Gamble, *Chelsea Childhood*, 144, 195–96, 200–1.

7. *Istoriia Sovetskoi Konstitutsii v dokumentakh 1917–1956*, 52–54, 92–93, 154–55; *Materials for the Study of the Soviet System, State and Party Constitutions, Laws, Decrees, Decisions, and Official Statements of Leaders in Translation*, 39–41, 172–76; Rudolf Schlesinger, *The Family in the USSR*, 81–235.

8. *Istoriia Sovetskoi Konstitutsii 1917–1956*, 490–92; Meisel, *Materials for the Study of the Soviet System*, 172–76; Schlesinger, *The Family in the USSR*, 81–235; "Soviet Proposes New Family Law," *New York Times*, 27 December 1925, 9; "Soviet Retreats on Marriage Laws," *New York Times*, 5 December 1926, Sec. 9: 7; personal interview with Elena Scriabina, Iowa City, Iowa, April 1984. Dr. Scriabina indicated that when she was recuperating in the Crimea, another woman at the same resort received a postcard announcing her husband's divorce from her. Regarding peasant behavior, see David and Vera Mace, *The Soviet Family*, 208.

9. "Abort," *Bol'shaia Meditsinskaia Entsiklopediia* 1: 40–57, 74–75; Frank Lorimer, *Population of the Soviet Union*, 126–28; Theodore Dreiser, "How Russia Handles the Sex Question," *Current History*, January 1929, 537–38; Korber, *Factory Life in Soviet Russia*, 200ff; Frewert, *Women in German History*, 185–91; Wilhelm Reich, "The Sexual Misery of the Working Masses," in *New German Critique* 1 (1974): 98–100; "Survey of Abortion and Birth Control Methods, Germany, 1913" in *European Women*, 205–10; Atina Grossman, "Abortion and Economic Crisis: The 1931 Campaign Against 218 in Germany," *New German Critique* 14: 119–37; Grossman, "The New Woman and the Rationalization of Sexuality in Weimar Germany," *Powers of Desire*, 153–71; *SDDR 1925*, Band 370, *Kriminalstatistik fur das Jahr 1927*, 46–47; Vera Lebedeva, "Nashi Dostizheniia," *Kom.*, November 1927, 66. For unhygienic abortion among English and French working-class women, see Angus McLaren, "Abortion in France: Women and the Regulation of Family Size, 1800–1914," *French Historical Studies* 10 (Spring 1978): 461–85; McLaren, "Abortion in England, 1890–1914," *Victorian Studies*, vol. 20 (Summer 1977).

10. S. Ravich, "Borba c prostitutsiei v Petrograde," *Kom.*, June 1920, 21–22.

11. Bronner, *La Lutte contre la prostitution en URSS*; Maurice Hindus, *The Great Offensive*, 210–17; Alice Field, "Prostitution in the Soviet Union," *The Nation*, 25 March 1936, 373–74; Dr. Rochelle Yarros, "Observations," *Journal of Social Hygiene* 16 (1930): 455; 18 (1932): 360.

12. Elaine Feinstein, *Marina Tsvetayeva*, 80–81; Victoria Glendinning, *Rebecca West: A Life*, 125; A. Nukhrat, "Osnovnye voprosy soveshchaniia," *Kom.*, June 1928, 77–80; R. Kh. Aminova, *The October Revolution and Women's Liberation in Uzbekistan*, 112–37; Halle, *Women in the Soviet East*, 170–200; E. Bochkareva and S. Liubimova, *Women of a New World*, 120–22. There were 226 cases of kidnapping and murder involving Uzbek women who discarded their veils in 1928–1929. In Central Asia, more than 800 women were murdered for becoming emancipated in the late 1920s.

13. A male law student saw modern women as "These beings — without breasts, without hips, without 'underwear,' who smoke, work, argue and fight exactly like boys, . . . There aren't any more . . . women." Quoted by Mary Louise Roberts in "'This Civilization No Longer Has Sexes': La Garçonne and Cultural Crisis in France After World War I," *Gender and History* 4 (1): 54.

14. "Enough Is Enough! Against the Masculinization of Women," *The Weimar Republic SourceBook*, 659; Vicki Baum, "Leute von Heute" (1927), trans. as "People of Today," *The Weimar Republic SourceBook*, 665–67.

15. Bock, "Women in Weimar Germany," 166, in *Social Change and Political Development in Weimar Germany*; Marian Kaplan, *The Making of the Jewish Middle Class*, 233–34.

16. Frevert, *Women in German History,* 186-95; Willem Melching, "'A New Morality': Left-Wing Intellectuals on Sexuality in Weimar Germany," *Journal of Contemporary History* 25 (1990): 69–85.

17. Colette Yver, "Femmes D'Aujourd'Hui, Voyageuses de Commerce et Aviatrices," *Revue des Deux Mondes* 50 (March–April 1929): 929–32; "Femmes D'Aujourd'Hui, Enquete sur les Nouvelles Carrieres Feminines," *RDDM* 49 (January–February 1929): 84–89.

18. John R. Gillis, *For Better, For Worse: British Marriages, 1600 to the Present*, 233–54; Margery Spring Rice, *Working Class Wives*; Gamble, *Chelsea Child,* 129–30; Cookson, *Our Kate*; Scannell, *Mother Knew Best*; Robert Roberts, *Classic Slum*; Chinn, *They Worked All Their Lives*, 137–39; Carles, *A Life of Her Own,* 149, 164, 168–71.

19. In the Soviet Union, alimony referred to the money paid for the upkeep of children, not former spouses. Figures for the 400,000 unemployed, 530,000 divorced, and alimony recipients in *Perepisi 1926 g.* 51: 28; Table III, 34: 8–9.

20. *Perepisi 1926 g.* 51: 44.

21. Pearl S. Buck, *Talk About Russia with Masha Scott*, 25–26. Masha Scott was the daughter of a peasant woman from Kalinin Oblast who demanded better treatment from her husband. Having married an American engineer and emigrated to the United States, she was interviewed by Pearl S. Buck in 1945. For Orel province, see "Striking Wives Win Pledge for Kind Treatment," *New York Times*, 18 March 1926, Sec. 2: 1. Belorussian women quoted by Anna Strong in "New Women of Russia Test Lenin's Theories," *New York Times,* 20 March 1927, 14.

22. Zetkin, "In the Muslim Women's Club" (1926), *Selected Writings*, 161.

23. For the peasant women's situation, see *Perepisi 1926 g.* 51: 18–38; 34: 10–11; *RSDRP 1926*, Tome I, 4eme partie, 38-39; *SDDR 1925*, Band 402, II: 446–47.

24. William T. Shinn, "The Law of the Russian Peasant Household," *Slavic Review* 20: 612; Mark Harrison, "Resource Allocation and Agrarian Class Formation, The Problem of Social Mobility Among Russian Peasant Households, 1880–1930," *The Journal of Peasant Studies* 4 (1976–1977): 150; Nevierov, "Andron the Good-for-Nothing," in Fen, *Soviet Short Stories*, 135–46.

25. Isabel A. Tirado, "The Village Voice, Women's Views of Themselves and Their World in Russian *Chastushki* of the 1920s," in *The Carl Beck Papers in Russian and East European Studies,* no. 1008: 2–12, 23–33, 50–52. Tirado examines *chastushki* from the province of Riazan.

26. Tirado, "The Village Voice," 4–11, 13–14, 20–33.

27. *Socialist Construction in the USSR*, 401–3, 454–55.

28. *Perepisi 1926 g.* 51: 18–38; 34: 16–38; *RSDRP 1926*, Tome I, 4eme partie, 38–39; *Gt. Britain Census of 1921 for Eng. and Wales*, 64–84; *SDDR 1925* Band 402, 3: 446–47.

29. *Perepisi 1926 g.* 51: 46–55; *An. Stat.* 49 (1933): 12–13.

30. Chinn, *They Worked All Their Lives*, 23, 157–58, 165; Cookson, *Our Kate*, 133; Gamble, *Chelsea Child*, 41–42; Scannell, *Mother Knew Best*, 59.

31. Roberts, *The Classic Slum*, 201–3.

32. Chinn, *They Worked All Their Lives*, 84–93.

33. Chinn, *They Worked All Their Lives*, 90–94; Gamble, *Chelsea Child*, 129–30; Cookson, *Our Kate*.

34. Roberts, *The Classic Slum*, 38–39, 84–92, 203–34; Bessel, *Germany After the First World War*, 240.

35. Judy Giles, "A Home of One's Own, Women and Domesticity in England 1918–1950," *Women's Studies International Forum* 16 (3): 239–47; Gamble, *Chelsea Child*, 129–30; Cookson, *Our Kate*; Scannell, *Mother Knew Best*; Roberts, *Classic Slum*; Chinn, *They Worked All Their Lives*.

36. Cookson, *Our Kate*, 37.

37. For birth rates, see Gamble, *Chelsea Child*, 33; Scannell, *Mother Knew Best*, 5–6, 16, 297–98, 301–2. For infant and maternal mortality, see Chinn, *They Worked All Their Lives*, 135–40; Brittain, *Lady into Woman*.

38. Chinn, *They Worked All Their Lives*, 145, 148; Cookson, *Our Kate*, 15–17, 112–13, 147. Cookson also felt humiliated by her mother's drunkenness.

39. Scannell, *Mother Knew Best*, 108–14; Cookson, *Our Kate*, 15–17, 37, 93–94.

40. Gamble, *Chelsea Child*, 177–93.

41. Cookson, *Our Kate*, 114, 129, 132.

42. Roberts, *The Classic Slum*, 206, 218, 226; *SDDR 1925* Band 370, *Kriminalstatistik fur das Jarh 1927*, 39, 43–47; Bessell, *Germany*, 242.

43. de Beauvoir, *Memoirs of a Dutiful Daughter*, 224–25; Frevert, *Women in German History*, 176–82; Linke, *A German Girl's Autobiography*, 112; Bessel, *Germany After the First World War*, 229, 248; Atina Grossman, "German Women Doctors from Berlin to New York: Maternity and Modernity in Weimar and in Exile," *Feminist Studies* 19 (Spring 1993): 75.

44. Korber, *Factory Life in Soviet Russia*, 202; Grossman, "German Women Doctors from Berlin to New York," *Feminist Studies* 19 (1): 68–71; Reich, "The Sexual Misery of the Working Masses," *New German Critique* 1 (1974): 101.

45. Linke, *Autobiography*, 102. While a high school student, Linke delivered flyers to working-class families who had not paid their church taxes. She was surprised at the negative reception she met in poor areas of Berlin at the end of the war.

46. Strumilin, "Biudzhet vremeni russkogo rabochego," *Kom.* 6 (1923): 22–23.

47. Gorsuch, "Flappers and Foxtrotters, Soviet Youth in the 'Roaring Twenties,'" *The Carl Beck Papers* 1102: 3–18.

48. Fedor Gladkov, *Cement*, 292. This is a reprint of Arthur and Ashleigh's translation done in the 1930s, not a translation of a later "toned down" version that Gladkov made to please Stalinist censors.

49. Anatole Glebov, *Inga, Six Soviet Plays*, 375.

50. Anatole G. Glebov, *Inga, Sbornik P'es*, 342–43.

51. Gladkov, *Cement*, 155.

52. Margot Klages-Stange, "Prostitution," 1926, *The Weimar Republic SourceBook*, 728; Bronner, *La Lutte contre la prostitution*.

53. Cookson, *Our Kate*, 114, 129, 132; Gamble, *Chelsea Child*, 130–33, 186.

54. Frevert, *Women in German History*, 176–82; Klages-Stange, "Prostitution," *The Weimar Republic SourceBook*, 728–29.

55. Information about Margarethe Bockholt Haussleiter (1895–1986) from an oral interview with her daughter, Dr. Ilse Irwin, El Paso, Texas, 16 November 1995. Haussleiter worked in a halfway house for prostitutes and abused women in the 1920s and wrote her Ph.D. dissertation in 1927 at the University of Marburg on socially nonproductive women. She thought it was better for the state to provide for unproductive people in a communal setting than to have them wandering around aimlessly. In 1928, she happily abandoned her work to marry an economist. See also Victoria Glendinning, *Rebecca West: A Life*, 70.

56. Kollontai, *Autobiographie Einer Sexuell Emanzipierten Kommunistin*, 30; English translation *Autobiography of a Sexually Emancipated Communist Woman*, 22.

57. Kollontai, *Novaia Moral'*, 5–6, 9–10, 12, 18, 19–20, trans. as "The New Woman," in *Autobiography;* Kollontai, "Liubov' Trekh Pokolenii," *Liubov' Pchel Trudovykh*, 43–44, trans. as "Three Generations," *Love of Worker Bees*, 206–7.

58. Glebov, "Inga," 335, 384–87; Marcelline Hutton, "Voices of Struggle: Soviet Women in the 1920s: A Study of Gender, Class, and Literature," *Feminist Issues* 11 (2): 65–80.

59. As quoted by Larissa Vasilieva in *Kremlin Wives*, 120, 116–24.

60. Elena Bonner, *Mothers and Daughters*, 241ff. Bonner was writing about the 1930s, but it is feasible that nuns may have worked as domestics, cooks, and nannies in the 1920s also. See also V. Shapovalov, *Women's Barracks*, for information about the imprisonment of nuns in the 1920s ands 1930s.

61. Virginia Woolf, *The Voyage Out* (1915), *Mrs. Dalloway* (1925), and *To the Lighthouse* (1927), 151.

62. Virginia Woolf, "Professions for Women" (1931), *Collected Essays* 2: 285–89.

63. "The New Dress," "Lappin and Lapinova," and "A Summing Up," in Virginia Woolf, *A Haunted House and Other Short Stories*, 47–57, 68–78, 144–148.

64. Virginia Woolf, *Orlando*, 123.

65. Nigel Nicolson, *Portrait of a Marriage*, 3–46, 66, 88–89.

66. Vita Sackville-West, "Autobiography" in Nicolson, *Portrait of a Marriage*, 110, 137, 204–5.

67. Nicolson, *Portrait of a Marriage*, 221–23.

68. Quoted by Quentin Bell in *Virginia Woolf* 1: 117–18; and in Nicolson, *Portrait of a Marriage*, 219–20.

69. Radclyffe Hall, *The Well of Loneliness*, 122, 195, 233, 264, 344–45.

70. Martha Vicinus, "They Wonder to Which Sex I Belong: The Historical Roots of the Modern Lesbian Identity," *Feminist Studies* 18 (Fall 1992): 469–70, 487.

71. Vera Brittain, *Testament of Youth*, 59, 73.

72. Vera Brittain, *Testament of Friendship*, 88–89, 103, 303, 390.

73. Brittain, *Testament of Friendship*, 92, 181.

74. Brittain, *Testament of Friendship*, 105, 391.

75. As quoted by Melville E. Currell in *Political Woman*, 16.

76. Victor Margueritte, *The Bachelor Girl*, 43, 55, 81, 83, 88, 91, 99, 106–8, 121–22, 132–33, 141, 165; M. L. Roberts, "This Civilization No Longer Has Sexes," *Gender and History* 4 (Spring, 1992), 50–64.

77. de Beauvoir, *Memoirs*, 175–78.

78. de Beauvoir, *Memoirs*, 143–45, 179, 240, 325.

79. de Beauvoir, *Memoirs*, 190, 295–96.

80. de Beauvoir, *Memoirs*, 222, 322.

81. Edith Stein, *On the Problem of Empathy,* vii; Edith Stein, *Life in a Jewish Family 1891–1916*, 16–17.

82. Linke, *A German Girl's Autobiography*, 380. After Hitler came to power, Linke left Germany and wrote her autobiography in the United States.

83. Sender, *The Autobiography of a German Rebel*, 20–29, 262–64. Sender emigrated in 1933, came to the United States, and wrote her autobiography there.

84. Karen Horney, "Flucht aus der Weiblichkeit," trans. as "The Flight from Womanhood, The Masculinity-Complex in Women as Viewed by Men and by Women," in *Feminine Psychology*, 54–69; Frevert, *Women in German History*, 197-98; Ettinger, *Hannah Arendt/Martin Heidegger*, 16–19, 31, 38.

85. Dana Micucci, "A Cut Above," *Art and Antiques*, February 1997, 75–76. See also Theweuleit regarding German men's fantasies about women after World War I.

86. Diana Orendi-Hinze, *Rahel Sanzara Eine Biographie* (1981); Emmy Ball-Hennings, *Ruf und Echo, Mein Leben mit Hugo Ball*; *Lesbians in Germany: 1890s–1920s*, 99; Martha Vicinus, "They Wonder to Which Sex I Belong," *Feminist Studies* 18 (Fall 1992): 486.

Chapter 6

Education in the 1920s

During and after World War I, women gained greater access to all levels of education and career opportunities than they had in the nineteenth century. Education was a key factor in women's advancement, but access to it varied according to gender, class, and ethnic group. This chapter analyzes peasant, working-class, and middle- and upper-class women's educational experiences, contrasting the greater educational opportunities of Soviet women with those of European women in the 1920s.

In the late nineteenth century, governments made much less provision for girls' education than for boys'. While elementary education became compulsory in Europe after 1870, in the Russian Empire 90% of Slavic peasant women and 98% of indigenous women in Central Asia remained illiterate. While 30% of women in the meshchane (merchant) estate attended elementary school, most women in the clerical and noble estates attended secondary school and several thousand had taken higher education courses by 1897. Generally, women's educational situation had improved by 1925; 56,000 Soviet women were engaged in university level study, and roughly 10,000 in Germany, France, and England were so engaged. Likewise, the number of girls in secondary school in the 1920s increased to 640,000 in the Soviet Union; 292,000 in Germany; 173,000 in England; and 48,000 in France.[1]

World War I created extraordinary opportunities for French and Russian women at major universities. French women made inroads in the faculties of law, science, pharmacy, and the humanities, while Russian women did so in art, education, medicine, and agriculture. The loss of upper- and middle-class men in the war led to increased university enrollments for females in the 1920s. In France, many young middle-class women pursued higher education because there was a shortage of men to marry and inflation had eroded their dowries, making marriage impossible. Similar social and economic factors operated in Germany and England: increasing numbers of middle-class women were attending university. As a result of the war, the number of French female students in higher education expanded from 3,800 in 1910 to 16,000 in 1929. In Germany, they increased from 3,700 in 1910 to 17,000 in 1929, in England from a few hundred in the 1890s to more than 8,000 in the 1920s, and in Russia from 9,300 in 1910 to 56,000 in 1926.[2]

The displacement of huge populations during World War I, the Civil War (1918–1921), and the famine of 1919–1920 interrupted Russian children's schooling and produced hundreds of thousands of refugees and orphans with disjointed educations. Many young Soviet women, especially the *byvshie liudy* (formerly well-to-do), faced hardships pursuing education after the Civil War. At the same time, millions of peasant and working-class Soviet females gained access to all levels of education. Literacy among women aged nine to forty-nine rose from 16.6% in 1897 to 42.7% in 1926.[3] There were half a million students in higher education in the prerevolutionary period, but 1.5 million by 1928–1929.

Russian Peasant Women

Although the Soviet educational system was too poor and underdeveloped to absorb large numbers of peasants, it encouraged new educational attitudes toward girls. Whereas nineteenth-century families thought that girls did not need to attend school because their mothers taught them housekeeping skills at home, by the 1920s many had changed their minds regarding education, and their literacy rate increased from 9% in 1897 to 30% in 1926.[4]

In efforts to eliminate illiteracy, the Bolsheviks established special literacy programs for adults as well as *rabfaks* (*rabochie fakultety* or worker schools) at plants and factories so that workers could become literate through on-the-job education. About 1.5 million people (largely women) learned to read in "Down with Illiteracy" classes. As a result, 30% of peasant women, 52% of domestic servants, and 70% of female factory workers became literate.[5] Indeed, Bolshevik educational policy allowed peasant and working-class girls to replace their low educational expectations with new dreams of educational attainment.

Stories of peasant women learning to read abounded in the 1920s. The humorist Mikhail Zoschenko entitled one of his short stories "The Woman

Who Could Not Read." It tells of a woman who resisted learning to read until she found a perfumed note in her husband's jacket. Then jealousy drove her to learn to read. In other cases entire peasant families obtained higher education. Typical peasant women who took advantage of the new educational opportunities in the 1920s were Dunia Ermoshkina and Klavdia Bikova. Born into a peasant family in the 1880s, Ermoshkina took a job as a maid for a wealthy Moscow family at the time of the October Revolution. Working as a charwoman during the Civil War, she enrolled in a school for illiterates. At the age of forty, she learned to read and write and became active in the eradication of illiteracy. She also became superintendent of an adult school and deputy chief of the Workers Education Department of the Moscow Soviet. Klavidia Bikova, likewise, was born into a poor peasant family and immigrated to Moscow after the revolution. She worked as a nursemaid for three years, then took a job in a textile factory, joined the Komsomol, became secretary of the Komsomol, and was elected a delegate to the City Council from the Cotton Workers' Trade Union.[6]

By introducing more egalitarian coeducation, the Bolsheviks drew millions of lower-class students into all levels of study. Zhenotdel (the women's department of the Party) cooperated with the Department of Education in staffing reading rooms in urban and rural areas. It created 800 reading huts (or rooms) in the Caucasus and 500 in Uzbekistan. By 1926, 6% to 20% of indigenous women in Central Asia had become literate, a tremendous increase over their illiteracy in the nineteenth century.[7]

The lack of secondary schools in villages meant that only the most determined peasant women pursued secondary or higher education. Many of them emulated nineteenth-century female educational patterns by studying medicine and education. It is difficult to determine the class origin of workers and employees in the 1920s, since gentry and bourgeois youth sometimes disguised themselves as workers in order to enter institutes of higher education. Still, peasant women seem to have constituted a large proportion of the midwives and nurses, who increased from 15,000 in 1897 to 60,000 in 1926. In the 1920s, the Soviet government encouraged upward occupational mobility by inspiring orderlies to become nurses, nurses to become midwives, and feldshers to become doctors. Such mobility was possible because medical occupations required only technical training, not university education.

Although the Soviet government lacked funds to introduce secondary education in the countryside, it did establish favorable quotas for workers and peasants in urban institutions. Usually students from the intelligentsia had to pay fees to attend technicums (technical schools) and universities, while the government provided free tuition and small stipends to working-class and peasant students. Yet the stipends were so small that many students had to take menial jobs to earn money for clothing, books, and lodging. Some young peasant women migrated to nearby towns, took a job in a factory, and attended a rabfak. Often they worked during the day, taking courses at night, or worked the late shift and studied in the morning. Upon completion of rabfak schooling, they sometimes pursued higher education in secondary schools or technicums. Highly motivated ones willingly undertook such struggles while dreaming of upward social and economic mobility.

Higher education did not necessarily guarantee peasant women an easy life. The salaries for doctors and teachers were low and the work exhausting. Their pursuit of such careers suggests that they shared some of the dreams of the nineteenth-century intelligentsia who had also accepted the sacrifices of low pay and hard work in backward villages to help downtrodden peasants. Although in the 1920s doctors earned lower wages than factory workers, they enjoyed higher social status, which many peasants and workers craved.

Millions of peasant women in the Soviet Union found the 1920s a time when life improved, although it still involved struggle. After the famine of 1920 dissipated, more peasants established nuclear families, acquired education, and experienced greater longevity than ever before. Whereas prior to the revolution approximately 65% of the peasantry fell into the category of poor peasants, by 1928–1929 only 35% did so. Since Europeans had introduced free compulsory primary education in the 1870s, most of the rural populace were literate by the mid 1920s.

Working-Class Women

Working-class families usually needed the wages of their adolescent children. Few European families could afford to send their daughters to secondary school due to school fees, the cost of uniforms, and the need for their wages. While some of these conditions also existed in the Soviet Union, the Bolsheviks made tremendous strides in educating working-class women in the 1920s.

The Soviet Union

Having made the revolution in the name of the workers, Bolsheviks paid special attention to improving their educational situation in the 1920s. Hoping to win the allegiance of working-class women, they provided them educational, employment, and political opportunities. By 1921, trade unions had organized 12,500 schools to eliminate illiteracy, and female factory workers' literacy had increased. By promoting public nurseries and educational opportunity, the government improved workers' lives and helped many develop self-esteem. One woman maintained that before the revolution she hadn't been treated as a human being and couldn't read, but the Bolsheviks taught her.[8] The program to emancipate working women allowed some to achieve greater self-respect and attain more social, educational, and economic mobility than had been possible before the revolution.

Even low-level service workers became more literate and enjoyed more educational opportunities than before. By 1926, 52% of domestic servants had become literate, up from 36% in 1897. Since free, compulsory education existed in late nineteenth-century Europe, it is likely that servants in those countries already possessed high degrees of literacy by the 1920s.

The distribution of women in the Soviet economy in the 1920s shows that although most women remained in light industry, increasing numbers worked in heavy industry. In the non-Russian republics, large numbers engaged in handicrafts and cottage industry. Although little is known about their educational situation in the prerevolutionary period, the 1926 Soviet census shows urban female handicraft workers 71.9% literate and rural ones 43.2%.

In the 1920s, significant numbers of Soviet women workers became literate, pursued higher education and technical training, joined labor unions, and participated in politics. In analyzing working-class women's situation, it appears that Soviet programs yielded mixed results, providing more opportunity than equality, especially in the non-Russian republics. While the Bolsheviks expanded public education, their ban on religious schools cut women in priestly families off from seminary training and ended the preference for gentry-class Russian Orthodox women in higher education. In closing Hebrew schools, the Communists eradicated one of the institutions that passed on Jewish consciousness, traditions, and heritage. Some Orthodox Jews railed against this goyishness or Gentilism. Although the Bolsheviks allowed instruction in Yiddish, Jews realized that they needed to learn Russian to advance in the new system. The closing of Hebrew schools and the movement of many Jews into urban areas in the 1920s encouraged assimilation into secular Soviet culture.[9]

The Soviet Ministry of Education, trade unions, and Zhenotdel all worked to "liquidate" women's illiteracy. Whereas 21% of female factory workers were literate in 1897, 25% in 1908, and 37% in 1918, over 70% were literate by 1926. The government also reserved places for women in the workers' universities and other institutions of higher education. By 1929, these programs were bearing fruit: women constituted 16% of the students in the rabfaks, 37% in technicums, and 28% in universities. Workers who completed the factory courses were eligible to attend FUZ (worker universities), and by 1929 about 2,000 women were attending worker universities. Some factory workers even attended regular universities and technical schools. By 1929, the Soviets mandated quotas of 30% female students. Throughout the 1920s, Slavic working-class women in Russia, Ukraine, and Belorussia profited more from educational opportunities than did women in the non-Slavic republics. Russian women accounted for 74% of those attending factory schools in 1928; Ukrainian women constituted 11% of rabfak students.[10]

Certainly Slavic female workers had much greater access to higher education than didtheir counterparts in Europe, where higher education remained a male, upper-class preserve. English trade unions granted scholarships to male working-class students to attend Ruskin College, Oxford, but founded no similar institution for working-class women. Some middle-class women (Virginia Woolf in prewar England and Simone de Beauvoir in postwar France) lectured to working-class women in evening classes, but no regular program of study existed, aside from reading circles in the Women's Cooperative Guild in England or in Socialist societies in France and Germany. Although 75% of the places in the technicums and 30% of university places in the Soviet Union were reserved for workers and peasants, these rules did not mean that most students were working class, because former bourgeois sometimes worked briefly in factories to claim worker status and qualify for the proletarian quota. Workers made up half of rabfak students.

While it is difficult to assess the exact impact that Soviet educational programs had, they paved the way for working women's social, political, and economic mobility. The Soviet press proudly reported examples of women's upward mobility. Two examples are Anna Yevseevna, a worker who became assistant foreman in a mill in 1924, and Aleksandra I. Sidorenko, the daughter of an impoverished worker, who graduated as a mechanic from a technical school in Taganrog in 1924.

The new Soviet government provided technical education so that women could improve their job skills, become skilled workers, and earn higher wages. Their commitment to technical education was quite different from the situation in Europe, where factory owners expected women to drop out of the labor force at the time of marriage and had invested little in their technical education. In contrast, Soviet women who took advantage of education and job training often earned better wages and achieved higher levels of self-esteem than did uneducated women. Like peasant women, female factory workers preferred education and medicine to agriculture, industrial, or social-economic courses.

Fewer married than single women factory workers attended courses in higher education, since their daily struggles over low pay, inadequate child care, and crowded housing consumed much of their time and energy. It was mainly young, single women who profited most from training programs. Women factory workers generally spent more time reading newspapers, books, and journals; attending circles, schools, courses, and meetings; and participating in political organizations than did peasant and working-class housewives. Whereas peasant women considered the survival of the family their major goal, urban workers were exposed to educational possibilities and increased self-esteem through paid work. Certainly, the Bolsheviks hoped that paid work would enable women to become economically independent and provide greater equity in the family. Bolshevik feminists Inessa Armand and Aleksandra Kollontai espoused women's need for economic and personal independence. Kollontai expected single workers to take advantage of the regime's educational and job training programs, and some did. In 1921, Madeleine Pelletier, a visiting French socialist, observed startling differences between French and Soviet education. She met a young pastry cook who was working part-time while studying to become an engineer. Such opportunities did not exist in France, where engineering was dominated by bourgeois men at the Polytechnic. Pelletier thought that the revolution had ushered in a happier life for many people, and the masses had gained access to enlightenment.[11]

England, France, and Germany

In the 1920s, most working-class families needed their children to contribute to the family economy. Only 15% of the English population pursued education after the age of fourteen, and most working-class children took jobs as soon as they could. Bright young English working-class girls sometimes had access to secondary education if their elder siblings already had jobs and were contributing to the family income. Then younger siblings might stay in school and take advantage of grammar school scholarships. This happened in Rose Naylor Gamble's family: her older sisters Dodie and Lu quit school at fourteen to begin working. Their contributions to the family economy enabled Rose to accept a grammar school scholarship. Although it was a struggle for her parents to pay for her uniforms and books, they made the sacrifice. Several English working-class writers indicate that schools and libraries became their havens in the heartless world of slum life. Yet they often felt uneasy in bourgeois cultural domains. Rose experienced class conflict when she attended a predominantly middle-class school. Since she could no longer settle her differences with her fists, she had to learn more subtle behavior to deal with the snubs and slights of the middle-class girls.[12]

In France, secondary lycée education remained costly, and few working-class families could afford to invest in their daughters' education. Usually, working-class boys followed a course of apprenticeship, and girls began work at age fourteen. Some exceptional young women attended elementary teacher training in their respective départements.

In Germany, inflation and unemployment forced working-class families to skip secondary education for their daughters. Lilo Lenke indicates that it was mainly middle-class girls like herself who could afford gymnasium education. Her descriptions of Berlin working-class neighborhoods show destitute families filled with despair due to the inflation they could not understand.[13]

Middle- and Upper-Class Women

In the 1920s, Soviet women dominated some educational establishments. By 1926, 52% of medical students were women, and more women than men actively practiced medicine.[14] It was then that the feminization of medicine and education became pronounced in the Russian republic. Yet medicine remained male dominated in many of the non-Slavic republics and in Western Europe. The feminization in teaching had taken place in England and France, but not in Germany. English women constituted about 60% of pedagogical students and French women 50%. German women represented a much smaller proportion of students in higher education.

Table 6.1. Students in Universities, 1920s*

Country	Female	Male
Soviet Union	57,300	145,000
Germany	9,400	70,900
France	12,200	58,500
England	8,400	33,600

*Calculated from *An. Stat.*, 52: *276; *Perepisi 1926g.*, Table II, 51: 103.

Generally, higher educational opportunities were much more open to Soviet than to European women, as table 6.1 indicates. This table shows a more balanced gender ratio in Soviet than in European higher education.

Building upon Russian educational traditions, Soviet medicine and education became more female dominated. Although many Russian women had studied medicine and pedagogy, the Tsarist government (like most European regimes) adhered to a double standard regarding gender and education. It did not underwrite the cost of women's secondary or higher education, as it did men's. While it supplied scholarships to needy boys and male university students, it provided financial aid mainly to upper-class female students at expensive women's boarding schools. As a result, women secondary students usually came from well-to-do families, had wealthy benefactors, or lived in abject poverty during their student days. Most female students had to be highly motivated because of the expense and travel involved in studying. In nineteenth-century Europe and Russia, women's secondary education differed significantly from men's because there were fewer scholarships for girls than for boys, and far fewer places for women to pursue advanced study. Prior to World War I, the Tsarist government introduced a more scientific curriculum into women's secondary education than happened in the finishing schools of England or Europe.[15]

Of course, patterns in Soviet secondary education changed in the 1920s as education became more open to women and people of all classes and ethnic groups. Although increasing numbers of European women attended secondary schools in the 1920s, this generally remained a privilege of the well-to-do. Yet by 1926, relatively high numbers of Soviet youth had obtained secondary education; 960,000 men and 640,000 women were attending secondary schools. The gender discrepancy was greater in France, where 117,400 men but only 48,400 women gained secondary education, and in Germany, where 552,000 men but only 300,000 women obtained secondary education. England had the greatest gender equity in secondary education: 199,400 men and 178,200 women attended secondary schools. The English pattern varied from the French and German because middle-class women greatly outnumbered men, necessitating their education for careers since many could not hope to marry. Some middle- and upper-class English women did not wish to marry, and their efforts to reform and improve female education bore fruit even in the late nineteenth century, when almost half the students in secondary education were women. Class inequality still existed in English education, as few working-class families could afford the luxury of schooling their children beyond the age of fourteen.[16]

The Soviet Union

In the late nineteenth century, women were excluded from all Russian universities and could attend only "special higher education courses" in major cities. During World War I, the government opened higher education to women, but it was the Bolshevik government that made education freer of gender, class, ethnic, and linguistic restrictions. Nor did the regime severely discriminate against married career women, as the European civil service did. During World War I, the Tsarist regime, unlike European ones, allowed female doctors to treat soldiers at the front and permitted women to enroll in the major universities, resulting in the feminization of medicine and education.

The Soviets expanded women's educational opportunities by introducing coeducation, encouraging women's entrance into the professions, advocating married women's employment, adopting quotas of 30% for women in educational institutions, and encouraging peasant and working-class women to pursue higher education. Initially, it proved difficult for lower-class girls to take advantage of these educational opportunities because they lacked an academic background. Unlike gentry-class girls who had French governesses for years, lower-class girls were less well prepared for academic study. In her memoirs, Elena Scriabine describes tutoring a peasant girl in French at the secondary school in Lukoyanov in 1918. Providing equal educational opportunities produced large numbers of career women in the mid 1920s. Still, in both the 1890s and the 1920s, upper and middle-class Slavic and Jewish women dominated the female intelligentsia. Living in urban areas, they had greater access to higher education and consequently to most careers. Of 56,000 women university students in 1926,

Table 6.2. Distribution of Women in the Professions, 1920s*

Occupation	Soviet	English	German	French
Teachers	190,000	187,352	98,000	164,000
Doctors	20,000	1,253	2,572	921
Pharmacists	12,800	—	2,720	6,600
Midwives	27,000	5,507	2,700	11,057

*Calculated from *Perepisi 1926g.*, 34: 142-61; *An. Stat.*, 52: *35, 133-35; *RSDRP 1926*, Tome I, Troisième Partie, 156/166; *Gt. Br. 1921 Census*, 100-8; *SDDR 1925*, Band 401-18, Band 402, Teil 3, 801-11; Band 408, 302-3.

78% were Russian. Slavic and Jewish women also constituted half of the Kazakh female student body, three-quarters of the Turkic, and one-fifth of the Kirgiz. The 1926 Soviet census shows that Russian and Ukrainian women constituted 60% to 80% of teachers, doctors, and political workers in Central Asia. In Belorussia and Ukraine, Jewish women predominated in medicine, while Russian women dominated in teaching and political work.[17] Table 6.2 shows some of the gains Soviet women made in the 1920s, compared to European women.

Specific patterns in women's employment had already established themselves in the late nineteenth century, and these became more pronounced as the number of women in the helping professions skyrocketed in the 1920s. The only significant decline in Soviet women's occupations was in religion, a decline that occurred when convents were closed after the revolution. Thus, religion became more male dominated in the 1920s, and medicine more feminized. In Europe, both medicine and religion remained male-dominated. Secularization of education in Germany and France reduced the number of nuns in those two countries. Yet French bourgeois women enjoyed access to careers in law and engineering. In England, male domination of religion continued because the Anglican Church had few convents and excluded women from the priesthood until the 1990s.

The Soviet government was unique in allowing older, married students to matriculate. Older students more often took advantage of elementary and middle schooling, while younger ones enrolled in higher education. The 1926 Soviet census found that 40% of women students were less than twenty years old, another 40% were twenty to twenty-nine years old, and only 20% fell into the age group twenty-five to forty. These figures show higher education remaining a preserve of the young and presumably unencumbered. Among female university students, 42,000 (75%) were single,

8,000 (14%) married, and 1,500 (2%) widowed or divorced. Although the number of older, married students was small, they had opportunities that did not exist in Europe. In Germany, 119,828 or 99% of female students in higher education and seminaries were single. Less than 1% were married (313), widowed, or divorced (308).[18]

An unusual feature of Soviet education in the 1920s was the empowerment of students. In some schools, pupils decided on the curricula, and teachers simply taught. The idea of allowing pupil input into education came during the time of the Provisional Government and continued during the early Soviet period. One fifteen-year-old gentry-class Russian girl remembered the fun they had at her private school when the Provisional Government took it over in 1917 and made it coeducational. She loved having boys in her classes and school. She also enjoyed participating in the organization of the school. Students even invited artists from the Moscow theaters to give talks. They organized clubs and dancing and singing circles, and produced plays. Still, food shortages in 1917 meant students spent a lot of time searching for food. Since the state also gave students free tickets to the theater, cinema, and art exhibitions, many enjoyed themselves immensely.[19] When the Soviets came to power in November 1918, innovative educational ideas continued until 1929 because Nadezhda Krupskaia, Deputy Minister of Education, had been influenced by American educators Horace Mann and John Dewey.

England

English higher education remained a male upper-class bastion. Boys' public schools such as Eaton and Harrow possessed more status than did ordinary girls' grammar schools, although similar numbers of boys (199,376) and girls (178,164) attended them. The male network produced a small, self-conscious educated elite, from which most boys and all girls were excluded. Leading universities maintained restrictive quotas: one woman to six men at Oxford and one to ten at Cambridge. In 1920, there were 4,181 male but only 549 female undergraduates at Oxford. Still, this number represents a tremendous increase from the 1890s, when only 700 women attended all the universities combined. Well into the 1920s, however, antifeminist views among professors and male students continued to make it difficult for women to excel. In fact, university prizes for excellence, which had been closed to women in the nineteenth century, remained closed to them after the war. Interrupting her university studies to serve as a nurse in 1914, Vera Brittain discovered an unwelcome change in the postwar period. Prior to the war, women students had focused on intellectual attainment, but after the war sexual attractiveness became their hallmark.[20]

At Oxford and Cambridge, women were barred from earning degrees. Neither of the famous universities granted women degrees equal to men's, nor allowed women graduates to matriculate. By 1920, women college principals, through delicate negotiations, obtained degrees for women at Oxford on the same basis as men. Prior to this announcement, the principals insisted on circumspect behavior on the part of female students. Although an editor offered Vera Brittain a good salary for writing articles about the women's colleges, the female principals refused her permission to do so. Both Brittain and the editor were shocked at this decision, since male students regularly wrote human interest stories about their colleges. The principals' refusal shows the conservative policies they enforced. Brittain was allowed to contribute stories and poems to the paper, but not columns on the women's colleges.[21] The famous bookseller Basil Blackwell chose her as one of three editors for *Oxford Poetry* in 1920; fewer female than male poets were included in the volume.

Another problem was the poor economic situation and meager endowments of women's colleges compared to the men's. Indeed, their resources were so depleted after the war that the principals asked alumnae to participate in bazaars and book sales to earn money for their alma maters. Since most female graduates earned considerably less than their male counterparts, the endowments and scholarships of the women's colleges were always smaller than those of the men's.[22] Female students also encountered discrimination from male students and professors. Some male undergraduates thought it monstrous to have female students at Oxford.[23]

Low parental expectations for daughters continued well into the 1920s. Whereas sons could use their holidays to read and prepare for exams and papers, daughters were often burdened with domestic responsibilities. Both Vera Brittain and her friend Winifred Holtby remembered having their school holidays interrupted by family illness and other domestic crises. In 1921, Brittain had to nurse her mother through a bout of influenza and could only study from ten P.M. till one A.M. Similarly, Holtby's family expected her to spend her school holidays entertaining family relations and friends and ignoring her work. She pretended to enjoy parties to please her family. While their families supported them financially, if not psychologically, many other female students faced financial struggles as well as disapproving parents.

Both Brittain and Holtby experienced gender discrimination at the time of graduation. Both received second class instead of first class degrees.

However, they saw some benefit in this since they wanted to write more than teach, and receiving a second prevented their tutors from steering them into unwanted academic careers.[24]

France

World War I, like the Franco-Prussian War, changed French society. As a result of the war, secondary and higher education became more available and necessary for middle-class French women. War losses meant that many bourgeois women could not expect to marry and instead had to pursue higher education and careers. The war produced countless widows and orphaned daughters in dire need of earning a living. In addition, inflation undermined family savings, and many parents were unable to provide dowries for their daughters. Simone de Beauvoir's family suffered downward economic mobility after the war. They moved from a spacious apartment with a maid to a smaller flat without a servant. She recalled her father's warning that she and her sister would never marry because they had no dowry. They would have to work for a living. Although it pained him to say this, Simone rejoiced because she thought married life and housekeeping boring, and she found the prospect of studying and working infinitely preferable to marriage. She wanted to *do* things. Although her father was resigned to his daughters' need for education and work, some bourgeois friends thought it unseemly for young ladies to seek higher education. To train for a profession instead of marrying was a sign of defeat in bourgeois society. While Simone's father liked intelligent, witty women, he detested female intellectuals and teachers—the kind of woman Simone wanted to be.[25]

For a variety of economic and social reasons, then, French society was ready to change women's education. Even in the late nineteenth century, some French liberals had questioned the emphasis on moral education for young women, when a scientific orientation was needed to keep France abreast of industrial and technological modernization. Real change in women's education occurred in 1924, when baccalaureate studies were introduced into girls' secondary schools, and women were prepared to attend university on the same basis as men. Bourgeois society recognized only the baccalaureate degree and exam as the gateway to professional work and earning a living. During the Belle Epoque, separate educational tracks for girls and boys had been acceptable, but the grim reality of the postwar period forced increasing numbers of women to obtain university degrees to make careers for themselves. On a positive note, French society supported women teachers and separate girls' secondary schools with female teaching staffs. Separate schools and teaching staffs reduced male professional jealousy because the men did not fear losing their jobs to their female counterparts who did not compete with them. This attitude was contrary to the situation in England and Germany, where the professions were crowded and career women lost their jobs if they married. French society also tolerated married career women because of the traditional low birth rate and population deficits due to war. French women became journalists, doctors, dentists, pharmacists, aviators, and lawyers.[26]

Class still permeated French education, and less than 5% of lycée students came from the working class or peasantry. Whereas primary schooling had become free and compulsory in the nineteenth century, the lycées, which were the primary dispensers of the baccalaureate, charged tuition and required school uniforms that poor working-class or peasant children could not afford. So secondary and higher education remained largely a middle-class preserve. Twice as many boys as girls attended lycées, and three times as many boys as girls attended the colleges. All together, 121,000 boys but only 54,000 girls attended some form of secondary school. Still, these figures represent significant growth over the 16,000 women who had obtained secondary education in 1900. A significant difference at the university level also remained: 12,200 women compared to 58,500 men. Yet that number far surpassed the number of women—600—attending French universities in 1900.[27]

Although the introduction of the baccalaureate degree and exams for women was helpful, the underfunding of women's schools meant that separate did not mean equal. Male *professeurs* (teachers) had smaller classes, worked shorter hours, and earned considerably higher salaries than did their female equivalents. Moreover, boys' lycées, colleges, and secondary schools all possessed greater libraries, financial resources, and scholarships for poor students than girls' schools.[28] It became possible for women to train as professeurs for secondary education, but it remained almost impossible for them to teach at universities. Patriarchal structures yielded, but they did not collapse.

Germany

Like France and England, the Weimar Republic retained separate girls' schools with semiclassical education for girls. And teachers in girls' secondary schools held lower rank in the civil service than did those in boys' gymnasia. For administrative purposes, the higher girls' schools were lumped with elementary schools instead of with boys' secondary schools. While their grammar-school education was supposedly of equal value, it was not identical, since girls' schools offered less mathematics and science and no Greek. Like the situation in France and England, mainly middle- and upper-class girls availed themselves of secondary education. Girls' gymnasia charged tuition, which poor working-class families could not afford. University tuition and books were inexpensive, yet even minor costs excluded many lower middle-class as well as most working-class women. German families were often so hard up that they could not afford fancy dresses for school farewell dances, and daughters sometimes could not afford to attend such dances. Not all secondary school graduates desired university study. Some, such as Lilo Linke, found the idea of six more years of study repulsive. Indeed, 300,000 young German women attended secondary schools, but only 9,400 pursued university study.[29]

German women's education provided slightly different experiences for Protestants, Catholics, and Jews. Like Russian Jews, German Jews tended to be overrepresented in higher education and the professions. From 1897 to 1906, Jews accounted for 4% of the Berlin population, but 20% of those attending public and private secondary schools. In 1913–1914, Jewish women accounted for 13% of female students at German universities and 22% of those studying in Berlin. Although the proportion of German Jewish female students was high, their actual numbers were small. Most came from wealthy, bourgeois families who lived in university cities and respected learning. In the 1920s, many Jewish families had money for education and observed patterns of late marriage. Since most Jews were cosmopolitan, it was economical for their children to live at home or with relatives in other university cities where they could study. Edith Stein was an example of a middle-class Jewish student who lived at home and with relatives while attending university during and after the World War I.[30]

Jewish university students often suffered from the anti-Semitic and antifeminist attitudes of Gentile students and faculty. Some professors addressed female students as *Herren* (gentlemen), while others patronized them as *Kindschen* (child). Like their patriarchal English colleagues, German professors often refused women the prizes and titles they deserved. One female medical student deserved to graduate summa cum laude, but the dean of the medical school refused to bestow such an honor on a woman. Some professors ridiculed female students, and male students often belittled their achievements. Some Gentile female students harbored anti-Semitic views and excluded Jewish female students from the few university women's organizations. Yet there were so few female students at German universities that they usually had their pick of male friends.[31]

A recent book about Hannah Arendt and Martin Heidegger suggests that women sometimes encountered sexual advances from their professors. Apparently Heidegger was captivated by Arendt's cosmopolitan aura, while she was impressed with his status as a famous philosophy professor. Having lost her father and grandfather in childhood, Arendt found Heidegger a father figure as well as mentor and lover. She was flattered that he took an interest in her, and she became his willing lover. Praising the qualities of her mind and soul and sharing his work with her, Heidegger overwhelmed Arendt. Apparently Heidegger was an insecure man in constant need of worship and flattery, and Arendt offered him the adulation he desired. Their affair endangered his family and career during the years 1924 to 1928. Her idolatry pleased and excited him, and they shared a mutual love of German high culture and developed a spiritual and intellectual companionship that he and his wife lacked. Eventually, Arendt left Heidegger to study with Karl Jaspers in Heidelberg. After completing her Ph.D. on St. Augustine, she turned her interest to the eighteenth-century German Jewish woman Rahel Varnhagen.[32]

Some problems bedeviled both Jewish and Gentile female students. Patriarchal attitudes pervaded German universities. When a woman earned a Ph.D. in physics at the University of Berlin, the speaker announced that her scientific studies should not interfere with her being a high priestess of the domestic hearth. Like their English sisters, German women had to struggle against low parental educational expectations and the greater willingness of parents to sacrifice for their sons' than for their daughters' education. Even in the twentieth century, a dowry, not academic achievement, held greater importance in German society. Psychoanalyst Karen Horney complained in her diary that her father spent thousands of marks educating his stepson, but begrudged her higher education. Like many German fathers, he wanted her to stay home so he could dismiss the domestic servant and save the wages. Daughters also had to contend with the fear that educated women were unmarriageable. In many families, it was socially unacceptable for a girl to study for the abitur exam or to attend the university. Of 1,078 female students who had matriculated in Prussian universities from 1908 to 1912, only 346 or 32% had married by 1917.[33] These figures made bourgeois families shudder.

German men also perceived the professions as overcrowded, and they opposed women's competition. Jews were not allowed to teach in most

schools or hold civil service positions, but they could enter the free professions of law and medicine. It was primarily medicine that attracted Jewish
female students. While only 15% of German Gentile female students studied medicine in the 1920s, 34% of Jewish female students did so.[34] Most
German women students, including Arendt and Stein, clustered in the humanities—philosophy, history, and philology. A few exceptions, such as
Karen Horney, studied medicine and psychiatry. By 1929, German women
accounted for 20% of university students and, like their counterparts in
other countries, found the field of medicine more open to them than the
field of law.

Notes

1. *Obshchii Svod 1897 g.* 2: xxxvi,xxxvii, 4, 200–7; *Ezhegodnik 1915*, 118–19; *An. Stat.* 52: 274*, 276*; *Statesman's Year Book 1929*, 23, 851, 927.

2. *An. Stat.* 52: 276*; Charrier, *L'Evolution Intellectuelle Feminine*, 175–85; Ivan Kurganov, *Zhenshcheny i Kommunizm*, 26; *Statesman's Year Book 1929*, "The British Empire," 23.

3. *Perepisi 1959 g. SSSR,* svodnyi tom, 88.

4. *Village of Viriatino*, 122; L. D. Filippova, "Iz Istorii zhenskogo obrozovaniia v Rossi," *Voprosy Istory* 2 (1963): 209–18; *Perepisi 1926 g.* 34: 10.

5. Bochkaryova, *Women of a New World*, 164; *Perepisi 1926 g.*, table III, 34.

6. "Once Illiterate Charwoman Now Heads School," *MDN*, 3 June 1933, 4; "Topics of the Day," *MDN*, 16 November 1933, 2.

7. *Stat. Spravochnik SSSR za 1928,* 878–79; Serebrennikov, *Women in the USSR*, 236; *Sotsialisticheskoe Stroitel'stvo*, 411; "Illiteracy Is Being Eliminated: Now Nearly 22 Million Children in Soviet Schools," *MDN*, 28 July 1934, 2.

8. Madeleine Marx, "The New Russian Woman," *The Nation*, 7 November 1923, 509.

9. *Hindus, Humanity Uprooted*, 266–78; discussion by Professor Michael Stanislawski at NEH Seminar on Russia and the Nationality Question, Columbia University, July 1996.

10. *Stat. Spravochnik*, 879; *Zhenshchiny i deti v SSSR*, 53; *The USSR in Figures, 1935*, 258–59; *SSSR Strana Sotsializma*, 90; N. M. Katuntseva, *Rol' Rabochikh Fakul'tatov v Formirovanii Intelligentsii SSSR*, 20; Bochkaryova, *Women of a New World*, 173; Carr, *Foundations of a Planned Economy*, 10: 473.

11. Gordon, *The Integral Feminist*, 162–63.

12. Albisetti, *Secondary School Reform in Imperial Germany*, 33–35; Winifred Holtby, *Virginia Woolf*, 24; *Statesman's Year Book, 1900*, "United Kingdom," 33–39. See also English working-class autobiographies by Gamble, *Chelsea Child*, 177–93; Cookson, *Our Kate: An Autobiography*, 114, 129, 132. Cookson realized that she would have to leave school at fourteen, and the only sort of job she could get was in domestic service, which she detested.

13. Lenke, *A German Girl's Autobiography*, 102, 110.

14. *Perepisi 1926 g.* 34: 10, 20–28, 74; *Svod Perepisi 1897 g.* 2: 206–7; Buck, *Talk About Russia with Masha Scott*, 72ff. In the 1890s, only 9% of Russian peasant women and only 36% of domestic servants were literate.

15. Tatiana V. Toporkova, *Memories of Revolution, Russian Women Remember*, oral interview by Elena Snow and Frances Welch, 19–20. Her secondary education was interrupted by World War I, but she remembered having a laboratory for physics classes at the St. Catherine Institute in St. Petersburg, that half of the female students did not pay for their education, and that various government organizations paid for everything. Smolny was the elite gymnasium for gentry-class Russian girls.

16. Kurganov, *Zhenshchiny i Kommunizm*, 26; *The Statesman's Year Book 1926*, "British Empire," 23-23; "France," 848–49; "Germany," 922–23.

17. *Perepisi 1926 g.* 34: 86; *KSP 1926 g.* 25–33; *Perepisi 1939 g. Chast' III*, 13-164; Skrjabina, *Coming of Age in the Russian Revolution*, 40–41; *Zhenshchiny i Deti v SSSR*, 53; *The USSR in Figures, 1935*, 258–59. The increase in the number of Russian women having higher, secondary, and incomplete secondary education rose from 77 per 1,000 in 1939 to 295 in 1958. Similar increases occurred in other republics. *Perepisi 1959 g.* tom 8, 234.

18. *Perepisi 1926 g.* 34: 86; *SDDR 1925* Band 402, 794–95. Journalist Lily Korber noticed that students at Soviet universities were often older than their Austrian counterparts and that they often attended university after having worked in a factory or served in the Red Army. See Korber, *Life in a Soviet Factory*, 124–25.

19. Tidmarsh, *Memoires of Revolution*, 62–63.

20. Albisetti, *Secondary School Reform in Imperial Germany*, 33–35; Holtby, *Virginia Woolf*, 24; *Statesman's Year Book, 1900*, "United Kingdom," 33–39; Brittain, *Lady into Woman*, 87; Brittain, *Testament of Youth*, 498.

21. Brittain, *Testament of Youth*, 500–6.

22. Brittain, *Testament of Youth*, 543–44.

23. Brittain, *Testament of Youth*, 508–9.

24. Brittain, *Testament of Friendship*, 47, 514–18.

25. de Beauvoir, *Memoirs of a Dutiful Daughter*, 104, 175–78; Margadant, *Madame le Professeur*, 249–64; Persis Hunt, "Syndicalism and Feminism among Teachers in France, 1900–1920"; Karen Offen, "The Second Sex and the Baccalaureat in Republican France, 1880–1924," *French Historical Studies* 13 (1983): 252–96.

26. Colette Yver, "Femme D'Aujourd'Hui, Voyageuses de Commerce et Aviatrices," *RDDM* 50 (March–April 1929): 929–32; "Femmes D'Aujourd'Hui, Enquète sur les Nouvelles Carrières Feminines," *RDDM* 49 (January–February 1929): 84-89.

27. Talbott, *The Politics of Educational Reform in France, 1918–1940*, 173; *Statesman's Year Book, 1900 – 1929*, 1921: 517–20; 1929: 851–52; *An. Stat.* 52: *276.

28. Margadant, *Madame le Professeur*, 266–74.

29. *Statesman's Year Book* (1900), "Germany," 591–93; (1929), "Germany," 927–28; *An. Stat.* 52: *276; Frevert, *Women in German History*, 122; Albisetti, *Secondary School Reform in Imperial Germany*, 113, 252, 291; Linke, *A German Girl's Autobiography*, 113, 117.

30. Kaplan, *The Making of the Jewish Middle Class*, 137–38; *The Collected Works of Edith Stein, Life in a Jewish Family: Her Unfinished Autobiographical Account*, 185-222, 239-317, 397-414.

31. Kaplan, *Making of the Jewish Middle Class*, 138-40; interview with Frank Oppenheimer, 19 August 1994, El Paso, Texas. Oppenheimer studied law at German universities in Berlin, Freiburg, and Frankfort in the late 1920s and early 1930s. While he remembered Jews being excluded from Gentile university fraternities, he did not recall antifeminism. He thought female students had their pick of men since they were such a small minority of the student body.

32. Ettinger, *Hannah Arendt/Martin Heidegger*, 5, 16, 17, 19ff.

33. *The Adolescent Diaries of Karen Horney*, 25-26; Kaplan, *Making of the Jewish Middle Class*, 140-43, 149-50; Brittain, *Testament of Youth*.

34. Kaplan, *Making of the Jewish Middle Class*, 145.

Chapter 7

Employment in the 1920s

This chapter analyzes Soviet and European women's economic situation in the 1920s, focusing on peasant, working-class, service worker, and career women. It compares their economic situation with that of women in the nineteenth century. It shows both continuity and change in their struggle for economic equity and independence.

The Versailles Peace Treaty sanctioned "equal pay for equal work" in 1919, but signatory powers failed to honor it.[1] Only the new Soviet state, which was not invited to the peace conference, endorsed women's economic equality. Before and after the 1917 revolution, the Bolsheviks supported women's liberation, thinking that they could emancipate women and gain their support by providing political, economic, and educational opportunities. They encouraged married women's equality by establishing communal institutions and increasing their economic participation. European governments were less committed to women's liberation than were the Bolsheviks, and nowhere did women gain economic equality.

In 1918, the Bolsheviks passed innovative labor legislation. They provided the eight-hour day, paid vacations, and unemployment and accident insurance—benefits many European workers already enjoyed. However, Soviet labor law uniquely promoted women's interests by sanctioning a minimum wage, equal wages for equal work, maternity benefits, job security for pregnant and nursing women, child care at large enterprises, and educational and job-training programs. In addition, the Soviet government instructed trade union leaders and factory managers to treat women workers fairly, to provide them with job security in the event of pregnancy, and to establish daycare centers.

In terms of theoretical and legal support, Soviet women were among the best-protected workers. Yet their actual work lives were not so enviable. It was easier to sponsor programs of liberation than to reshape a poor, backward, male-dominated society. Definite limitations soon appeared in the Soviet ability to promote women's economic equality. It did not extend maternity benefits, child care, education, or job training to peasant women, who constituted the bulk of the female labor force. Instead, programs focused on urban women workers. Although some programs remained more theoretical than real, the aim was women's economic equality. In contrast, England and Germany inaugurated far fewer economic programs for women, while France made significant inroads in admitting educated women into the professions and in wage parity in some posts.

The Weimar Constitution of 1919 promised German women equality, but the deeply divided Reichstag failed to pass liberating legislation. Reichstag committees tabled bills designed to eradicate gender differences in the workplace. The only protective legislation the Reichstag passed was for women doing piecework at home. This failure had several causes. Female Reichstag delegates failed to act as a bloc, and instead closed ranks with male party members. Indeed, some female Reichstag delegates, such as Toni Sender, were more interested in foreign policy than in women's issues. Only the small Communist Party focused on women's conditions. Lack of male support in the dominant political parties and political divisiveness remained problems.[2] British politicians were equally insensitive to women's needs. It took twenty years for Parliament to pass a family allowance act that Eleanor Rathbone suggested in the mid 1920s. Although French legislators did not enfranchise women in the 1920s, they drafted some beneficial legislation, such as child care for working mothers. They also legislated equal pay for equal work among primary-school teachers, low-level hospital workers, and public utility employees.

Although Soviet women factory workers constituted a small proportion of the total labor force, they were important because they represented the government's and the Party's hope for the future. Moreover, time-budget studies of the early 1920s indicated that women factory workers spent more time than peasant women did in reading; in attending circles, schools, courses, and meetings; and in political organizations. Their world was more complex than that of housewives or peasant women. Most peasant women focused on their family, while urban workers realized the importance of paid work, economic independence, self-esteem, and equality in family life. The foremost exponent of women's economic and psychological independence was the Bolshevik feminist Aleksandra Kollontai.[3]

Despite good intentions, Bolshevik policy makers sometimes undermined women's economic interests. Family legislation of 1918 and New Economic Policy (NEP) legislation in 1921 weakened the economic position of many married women. The new family law granted men and women legal equality in marriage and divorce, but it did not take into account women's inability to provide for themselves in the event of divorce or high unemployment. The new law stipulated that spouses support each other for only one year after divorce. In times of high unemployment, which occurred during NEP (1921–1930), this policy made little sense, and it hurt women who could not find jobs to support themselves and their children. The 1926 Soviet census records 400,000 unemployed women and 530,000 divorced women, but only 12,000 women receiving alimony for their children.[4] Thus, the Soviet regime undermined some women's economic position by curtailing their economic dependence on men without making them self-supporting. Divorce, lack of alimony, and high unemployment created serious problems for several hundred thousand urban women.

During the 1920s, most Soviet and European women remained economically dependent housewives, working on family farms or in family enterprises. Yet significant numbers carried a double burden of housework and low-paid work outside the home. There were, however, some profound differences between Soviet and European women's patterns of economic participation. Since the Soviet economy was so undeveloped, the number and proportion of Soviet women engaged in agriculture far exceeded that of European women, while the number and proportion of European women engaged in the industrial sector surpassed Soviet women workers. In addition, European industrial women workers remained young, single, and literate, while Soviet factory workers were usually older, married, and often illiterate. While the majority of Soviet women worked in exceptionally large plants, many remained in handicraft production, as did French women. Finally, the Soviet and French patterns of combining marriage and career differed from those of England and Germany, where most women who married had to leave public professional posts.

Ideological disparities regarding women's work also undergirded Soviet and European societies. Bolsheviks thought that women had a duty to work outside the home and that they were entitled to educational and job training programs so they could compete in the job market with men. The prevailing European view was that work preceded marriage and motherhood, that the husband's wage should provide for the family, and that women did not require education or job training because their work was temporary.

Given their economy and ideology, Soviet women experienced a higher rate of economic participation than did European women. The 1926 Soviet census listed 48 million adult women, of whom 35 million were considered employed, while 13 million were designated inactive or dependent. Agriculture occupied 32 million (92% of the employed female labor force); manufacturing 1.2 million (3.4%); and services 1.5 million (4.2%). Since so many women were engaged in agriculture, the participation rate of Soviet women in the economy was very high—47%. The participation rates for French, German, and English women were 40%, 36%, and 30% respectively. Since few English women worked in agriculture, their participation rate was low. Table 7.1 shows agriculture employing 92% of the Soviet, 43% of the French and German, but only 2% of the English female labor force.

Peasant Women

One of the unintended effects of the Russian revolution was that the redistribution of land delayed industrialization and urbanization. More equitable land distribution increased the number of small-scale producers, retarded the flow of labor from the villages to the towns, reduced agricultural output by breaking up the large estates, and diminished the volume of agricultural marketing. By 1926, Bolshevik economic policies had not drawn significant numbers of peasants into urban life (table 7.2).

Migration, urbanization, and industrialization before and after the 1917 revolution were moderate. Moscow and Leningrad each had roughly 300,000 industrial workers in 1897 and in 1926. During the period 1897–1926, 20 million peasants engaged in long-distance rural-rural migration, but only 12 million in short-distance rural-urban migration.

Table 7.1. Distribution of Women in the Economy, 1920s*

Country	Agri-culture	Manufac-turing	Commerce & trans.	Service & dom.	Profes-sional
USSR	32,000,000	1,200,000	404,600	815,000	300,000
France	3,300,000	2,111,270	1,153,579	687,720	494,015
Germany	4,900,000	3,000,000	1,530,100	1,370,100	655,500
England	63,000	1,601,000	1,365,000	1,845,000	438,000

*Calculated from *Perepisi 1926 g.*, 51: 28–61; *An. Stat.*, 49 (1926): 10–13; *Stat. Jarbuch*, 49: 19–24; *Gt. Br. Census of Eng. and Wales 1921*, 54–106.

Table 7.2. Russian Population Changes, 1897–1926*

Date	Urban population	Rural population
1897	11.5 %	88.5 %
1914	15.0 %	85.0 %
1926	17.9 %	82.1 %

*Alexander Gershenkron, "The Rate of Industrial Growth in Russia," *Journal of Economic History* 7 (1947): 159; S. Sul'kevich, *Naselenie SSSR*, 13.

During World War I and the Civil War (1914–1921), life was difficult for peasant women because many had to farm alone. Grain requisitions and famine during the Civil War made life precarious. Famine forced some Ukrainian farmhands to work in coal mines. By the mid 1920s, most peasant women could marry, have a family, and help on the family plot. Most preferred traditional ways that offered security and respectability. Some had participated in land seizures from 1917 to 1921 and saw land redistribution offering an opportunity to establish their own homes. Several million new households emerged between 1918 and 1929. Many women were able to escape from domineering in-laws, and the number of extended families declined. About 28 million peasant women worked on family farms with a male head of household. Of 2.5 million female-headed households, almost 1 million had lost their husbands in the wars. Widows often managed their farms with a married child living at home who helped on the family plot. Only 200,000 female heads of household employed paid workers. Nearly 330,000 women worked on *sovkhozy,* or state farms, where life was primitive and harsh. Some worked as farm hands for wealthy kulak families, or as stable hands at a kolkhoz (table 7.3).[5]

The dominant pattern among Soviet peasant women, therefore, was that most women married and worked in family enterprises. Few farmers would survive without the help of spouses and children, and only 5.6 million adult peasant women were listed as economically inactive in 1926. Four and a half million of this number were married and presumably had children to help in their place or husbands sufficiently wealthy not to require their help. This pattern persisted because land redistribution provided plots for most families to till. Table 7.4 shows the marital status of women engaged in agriculture.

A high proportion of peasant women who worked alone were widows: 47% of Soviet, 51% of French, and 44% of English women. Among em-

Table 7.3. Women in Agricultural Work*

Women occupied in:	USSR	Germany	France	England
Family farms	**30,400,000	3,575,500	2,374,500	N/A
Alone	815,000	325,000	345,000	9,700
Employers	193,000	N/A	921	9,980
Employees	328,000	1,053,700	670,000	63,400
Unemployed	4,000	N/A	2,647	N/A
Total	31,740,000	4,954,000	3,393,068	83,080

*Calculated from *An. Stat.*, 49 (1933): 12; *Perepisi 1926 g.*, 34: 10; 51: 28, 38, 48–61; *Gt. Br. 1921 Census for Eng. and Wales*, 54; *SDDR 1925*, Band 401–18, Band 402, Teil 3, 801–11.

**27.9 million worked in families with a male head of household.

ployers, the proportion of widows was 64% for the Soviets, 72% for the English, but only 8% for the French. Among employees and workers, the proportion of single women was exceptionally high: 77% in France, 66% in England, and 54% in the Soviet Union.[6]

Soviet ethnographic and sociological studies indicate that traditional values and mores remained strong, and that most peasant women worked long hours on their family plots. In Voronezh province, they worked an average of 15 hours per day in the summer: 7.6 hours at agricultural labor and 7 hours at household work. In the winter, they worked 4 hours per day at farm labor and 9 hours at household work. Nor were their work patterns unique: German and French women also worked 14 to 16 hours in the summertime. On small, undermechanized holdings, German women often had large families, a heavy burden of backbreaking work, plus household chores. Day laborers earned only half the wages of German men.[7] French farm girls envied school friends who became factory workers, since they

Table 7.4. Married Women Working in Agriculture*

Married women	Soviet Union	France	England
Family farms	18,800,000—67%	2,221,000—94%	48,000—21%
Alone	223,000—27%	92,000—26%	1,000—18%
Employers	45,000—23%	200—21%	17,000—10%
Employees	72,000—22%	100,000—15%	1,000—28%

*Calculated from *An. Stat.*, 49 (1933): 12; *Perepisi 1926 g.*, 34: 10; 51: 28, 38, 44–61; *Gt. Br. 1921 Census for Eng. and Wales*, 54; *SDDR 1925*, Band 401-418, Band 402, Teil 3: 801–11.

had a day off, earned wages for their work, kept some of their pay, could buy new dresses, could attend films and dances, and had time to read magazines. Peasants lacked these advantages; they had to do backbreaking work in the fields and wash their clothes in frigid river water in the winter. Few English women worked in agriculture. Those who did earned half of men's wages even though they paid the same for board and lodging.[8]

In the 1920s, it was difficult for many Soviet peasant families to maintain themselves on their allotted land since livestock and implements were not well distributed, and many had to lease horses and plows to farm. By 1928, the Soviet peasantry fell into three groups: *bedniaks* (poor peasants) (35%), *seredniaks* (middle peasants) (60%), and *kulaks* (wealthy peasants) (5%). Only 1% worked on state or collective farms. Still, rural life meant more than work. Peasant women in Voronezh continued their traditions of resting on Sundays and holy days. In 1922–1923, women spent 199 hours a year in religious ceremonies, but only 10 hours in education. Age affected women's religious activity: 71% of those aged twenty-five to thirty-nine participated in religious rituals, while 100% of those aged forty to fifty-nine did so.[9]

Despite tradition, some peasant women demanded better treatment from their husbands. They became less afraid of their husbands and began to participate in local political life. One short story describes a peasant man who is confused by the change in women's position. He agreed that a man could sweep the floor if his wife is sick or pregnant, but he wondered if he should do so when his wife attended a political meeting. Husbands were used to ordering their wives about, not the other way around. Perhaps the position of ordinary peasant women is best summed up by one who remarked: "If God gives us enough grain to last through the year, it's all right—if not, how are these women's rights you talk about going to help us?"[10] Yet the lives of some peasant women improved, as the threat of divorce frightened some peasant men into better behavior.

In both the 1890s and 1920s, unmarried women could seldom survive in the village. Usually widows either married again, moved in with relatives, had grown children farm with them, or left the countryside. World War I and the Civil War produced a shortfall of 1.4 million men fifteen to twenty-four years of age. Hence, not all peasant women could marry. Agricultural work yielded low wages: eight rubles per month in money and eight rubles in food on private farms, and seven to twenty-seven rubles per month on state farms.[11]

Migration to the cities remained risky. While rural unemployment was low, urban unemployment was high. One typical pattern involved migrating to a large nearby city, working as a maid for relatives, and eventually finding a factory or low-level service job. Those who followed this pattern often experienced considerable upward mobility. As factory workers, they earned thirty to fifty rubles per month, considerably more than in agriculture.

Some peasant women who migrated to the cities and worked in factories retained land in their native villages. In Leningrad, 2% of women textile workers did so, in Moscow 4%, and in Moscow province 14% to 21%.[12] It is not clear whether these women textile workers were widows who possessed land, or whether they were farmers' daughters who migrated to the cities to augment their families' incomes.

NEP did not create enough jobs in the 1920s to absorb peasant migrants. They constituted 40% of prostitutes in the prophylactoria, which provided medical treatment, education, housing, and job training. Some migrants found husbands instead of jobs. In 1926, there were 1.2 million employed adult working-class women but 2.7 million dependent urban ones, 70% of whom were married.[13]

The regime encouraged upward mobility. It urged women to take low-level jobs as hospital orderlies, then study to become nurses, midwives, feldshers, or even doctors. This was possible because medical occupations required technical, not university, education. Doctors received lower salaries than did factory workers, but they enjoyed higher social status.[14]

After the famine and grain requisitions abated, peasant life improved for millions of women as land redistribution permitted the formation of more nuclear families. While the Soviets did not eradicate peasant poverty, they reduced it from 65% in 1897 to 35% in 1929. Poor peasants often earned only 264 rubles per year, whereas middle peasants made 400 rubles per year and had larger houses with more furniture. More peasant women and their children acquired education and experienced greater longevity than ever before. Whereas life expectancy for women in 1897 was thirty-three years, by 1926 it was forty-seven. High infant mortality of 133 in 1,000 for children up to age four in 1897 declined to seventy-nine in 1,000 by 1926.[15] Certainly the struggle for existence for most remained difficult, but many achieved more than ever before. One wonders how long independent farmers would have lasted, if collectivization had not ended traditional family farming in the 1930s.

Working-Class Women

Three important economic transformations occurred in the 1920s. The first occurred in France and Germany and included the rationalization of industry or, as the French called it, *l'organisation scientifique du travail* (OST). OST included the mechanization of manufacturing and the substitution of women for men since women could be paid less than men. The second involved the mechanization of clerical work and the substitution of women for men in white-collar jobs, and this took place in all four countries. The third transformation occurred in the Soviet Union, where factory production superseded domestic production in the Slavic republics. Yet the fact that the 1926 Soviet census listed only 5.4 million workers shows the low industrialization of the country. While the Soviet Union had a population of 147 million, England and France had populations of 40 million and industrial labor forces of 7 million in the mid 1920s. Germany had a population of 63 million and a labor force of 13.6 million.[16]

During the NEP (1921–1929), Soviet women workers often experienced unemployment. While Party leaders supported NEP as a way of rebuilding the war-torn economy, many workers were not so pleased, since NEP reintroduced some capitalist features, including unemployment. By 1926, light industry had regained prewar capacity, but heavy industry still lagged behind. Bolshevik ideology promised women emancipation through work, but there were not enough jobs, and women's participation in the labor force was not much higher than in 1897. Indeed, among those classified as *rabochie* (working-class), only 1.4 million were employed, while 4.7 million were not. Whereas 30% of women workers were married, 71% of working-class women were married. In France, women textile workers had increased 200,000 since the 1890s, but the number of English women engaged in manufacturing remained the same. Mechanization drew almost 2 million additional German women into manufacturing, as table 7.5 reveals.

Table 7.5 shows how underdeveloped the Soviet economy was; table 7.6 shows the higher employment of European women in specific areas such as metals, printing, leather (shoes), and chemicals—statistics that indicate the rationalization of labor and the substitution of women and machines for skilled male workers. As mentioned earlier, this process occurred prior to the war in England and during the 1920s in France and Germany.

While 700,000 Soviet women worked in factories and plants, 450,000 (40%) remained in domestic and handicraft production. Whereas the ma-

Table 7.5. Women in Manufacturing, 1890s and 1920s*

Country	1890s	1920s
Russia	1,000,000	1,200,000
Germany	1,500,000	3,300,000
France	1,900,000	2,100,000
England	1,600,000	1,600,000

*Calculated from *Svod Perepisi 1897 g.*, 2: 242–52; *Stat. Jarbuch*, 35: 16–17; *SDDR 1925*, Band 402, III: 446; *An. Stat.*, 20: 22; 49: 139; *P.P., Gt. Br. Census 1891*, 97: 180, *Gt. Br. Census 1921*, 56–92; *Perepisi 1926 g.*, vols. 25–33; *Abstract of British Historical Statistics*, 160–61.

jority of Russian women workers were employed in factory production, half of Ukrainian and Belorussian women and most Transcaucasian and Central Asian women remained in domestic production. Like European women, twice as many Soviet working-class women were unemployed housewives as were gainfully employed. Another similarity between Soviet and European women was their high participation rate in manufacturing during wartime and their replacement by returning veterans.[17]

After World War I

The economic position of Soviet women factory workers differed during wartime Communism (1918–1921) and NEP (1921–1929). During wartime Communism, food, fuel, and raw materials were so scarce that many factories closed and workers fled. In Petrograd, flour cost 700 rubles

Table 7.6. Women in Manufacturing by Area, 1920s*

Industry	USSR (1926)	France (1926)	Germany (1925)	England (1921)
Textiles	507,500	554,000	672,800	634,000
Clothing	194,000	921,000	870,200	544,000
Food	58,000	129,000	420,000	77,000
Metals	63,000	147,000	150,000	123,000
Printing	25,000	101,000	171,000	97,000
Leather	23,000	77,000	24,000	59,000
Chemicals	19,000	45,000	78,000	4,000

*Calculated from *Perepisi 1926g.*, vols. 25–33; *An. Stat.*, 49: 139; *Stat. Jahrbuch fur das Deutsche Reich*, 19-21; *Abstract of British Historical Statistics*, 60–61; *Gt. Br. 1921 Census*, 56–92.

per *pud* in 1919, but only 63 in rural provinces. While the Civil War raged, the Soviet regime tried to retain women workers who had joined the labor force during World War I. Its motto was, "Those who do not work shall not eat." During wartime Communism, this slogan applied to both men and women. Thus, women's factory participation rate, which was 30% in 1913, rose to 40% in 1917. It remained high until the end of the Civil War when it fell to 23%. This pattern was not uniquely Russian. European women's participation during wartime was even greater: in Germany the number of women factory workers rose from 3.4 million in 1914 to 4 million in 1917, in France from 470,000 to 600,000, and in England an additional 1.2 million women joined the industrial labor force.[18]

Another similarity between Russian and European women workers was their high participation rate in trade unions during the war. The number of English female trade union members increased from 433,000 in 1913 to 1,209,000 in 1918, but fell to 300,000 in 1922. The number of German women in the SPD unions rose from 210,000 in 1914 to 1,710,000 in 1920, declining to 660,000 in 1926. There were 81,000 French women trade union members in 1921, but 173,000 in 1926.[19]

Since the Tsarist government legalized trade unions only in 1905, the number of women in the trade unions was quite small during the war. However, women's membership in textile trade unions rose dramatically from 69,800 in 1917 to 437,800 in 1918. In contrast to Europe, where female union membership declined in the 1920s, 1 million (90%) Soviet women industrial workers belonged to unions by 1929. The increase in their union membership was partly due to the link between union membership and social insurance benefits. Union members received preferential access to sanatoria, holiday camps, childcare facilities, housing, education, pensions, maternity benefits, as well as unemployment, sickness, and accident insurance. Despite their high rate of trade union membership, their share of trade union administrative positions remained low. In fifteen Russian industrial provinces in 1920, women constituted 10% of union membership, but occupied only 1% of administrative positions.[20] Thus, they resembled European women workers in lacking female union leadership.

In wartime, Russian and European industrial workers experienced many of the same problems. During World War I, the English government promised not to dilute men's wages by hiring women and paying them less, but it did. In both England and the Soviet Union it proved easier to proclaim equal pay for equal work than to effect it. Wage discrimination persisted because women remained unskilled workers and worked in light industry (which paid lower wages than did heavy industry) and because society sanctioned lower wage rates for them. In 1924, both European and Soviet women earned roughly 64% of men's wages.[21]

In addition to receiving low wages, women workers also lacked child care. Postrevolutionary Soviet labor legislation promised working women public child care, but there were only twenty-seven nurseries in 1917 and 503 by 1923. European governments agreed to make child care available to women workers during World War I, but once again promises were more easily made than kept. A report of the French government during the war showed that of sixty-two plants employing large numbers of women, twenty provided child care, fourteen had provisional arrangements, fourteen had no projects, three utilized local nurseries, four made no arrangements, and seven did not reply to the government inquiry.[22] After this inquiry, the French government decided to provide municipal child care.

Child care was such a problem that Soviet novelists dealt with it. In *Vasilisa Malygina*, Kollontai depicts a worker who decides to form a child-care center at her factory. Judging from her problems organizing communal housing, one wonders how well her cooperative nursery would work. Gladkov's novel *Cement* (1925) also deals with the issue of child care. His heroine, Dasha Chumalova, sends her daughter to a communal nursery during the Civil War so that she will not starve. But without maternal love her daughter dies.[23]

Still the 1920s provided a few bright spots in women's lives. The government, Party, and trade unions officially endorsed their emancipation and tried to improve their lot. By 1921, trade unions had organized 12,500 schools to liquidate illiteracy, and women factory workers' literacy increased.[24] By promoting equal pay for equal work, public nurseries, and educational opportunity, the government improved the lives of some factory workers and helped many others develop self-esteem. The Bolshevik program to emancipate working women helped some achieve greater self-respect and obtain more social, educational, and economic mobility than had been possible in the Tsarist period.

1921–1929

With the exception of the labor aristocracy, most working-class women struggled to survive. Both men and women earned low wages, and had difficulty providing for their families. English and German men experienced severe unemployment and underemployment in the 1920s, and their wives and children often had to take jobs for their families to survive. Gendered attitudes that married women should not work outside the home did not match harsh economic reality. Mothers had to tend their children, cook, shop, cart coal for the fire, carry water for laundry, pawn the family linen and "best clothes," and then engage in odd jobs for the family to live. While husbands slumped in their chairs at the end of the day or went off to the pub, wives had to stay home minding the children. Keeping a family together during and after the war in Germany was also burdensome. Poverty kept many from paying the church tax. While female workers had household chores to do when they returned from work, their fathers and brothers could drink beer in the taverns.[25] Despite the notion that a married woman's place was in the home, many had to work for pay (table 7.7).

Marriage rates were low for young factory workers, but high for older ones: 93% of German factory workers sixteen to twenty-five years of age were single, but 46% of those thirty to forty years old were married. Only modest changes occurred in Russian women's industrial employment between 1897 and 1926. Except for garment makers, Russian women worked in basically the same occupations in both periods. Still, their proportion in domestic production fell while rising in factory production. In the 1920s, more of them than ever before became literate, pursued higher education or technical training, joined labor unions, and participated in politics. Soviet programs yielded mixed results, but their greatest success was in providing women opportunity, not equality. Factory workers did not obtain wage equity, but their wages rose from thirty rubles per month in 1924 to forty to fifty rubles in 1928, increasing to 67% of men's in 1928. This resembled the situation in England, France, and Germany, where women earned 50% to 70% as much as men.[26]

Wage disparities continued throughout the decade, with women in light industry receiving much lower wages than those of men in heavy industry. Of 600,000 Soviet women factory workers, 350,000 (53%) worked in tex-

Table 7.7. Marital Status of Women in Manufacturing, 1920s*

Country	# in Manufacturing	% Single	% Married	% Widowed/ Divorced
USSR	1,430,000	40	30	17 / 5
France	2,280,000	47	39	16
Germany	2,909,000	69	17	14
England	1,600,000	71	23	5

*Calculated from *SDDR 1925*, Band 402, III, Teil IV, 446–50; *An. Stat.*, 49: 13; *Perepisi 1926 g.*, 34: 8; *Gt. Br., P.P., 1921 Census of Eng. and Wales*, 62–92.

tiles. Two-thirds remained semi- or unskilled, a status that also depressed their wages. Even skilled women workers tended to work in low-paying light industry; for example, 175,000 of the 220,000 skilled Soviet women workers worked in textiles. Wage discrimination affected even qualified women workers, since male workers earned higher wages than women in the same rank. Initially, Bolsheviks thought that once women became skilled workers, they would command the same wages as men. Assuming a high correlation between employment, job training, and economic equality, they underestimated the persistence of gender discrimination. Women also continued to be plagued by unhealthy working conditions, such as poisonous fumes in tobacco and rubber plants. The Soviets reduced work hazards somewhat by shortening the work day to seven hours and improving ventilation and sanitation, but these reforms did not eliminate all toxins.[27]

European workers also suffered from wage exploitation and health problems due to speed-ups in production. German women working in heavy industry earned 20% to 50% less than men because of gender-based wage rates. Mechanization in German industry was also harmful. They worked more efficiently and productively than men but earned less. To earn higher wages they had to work faster and increase productivity. Job stress then undermined their physical and mental health.

Economist Judith Grunfeld observed that one man using a conical milling machine could turn out 600 articles a day. With mechanization, one woman with eight automatic machines turned out 6,000 a day. An enterprise that initially employed ninety-six workers in the assembly of bicycle chains soon used only five women with machines to do the work. The substitution of women for men in rationalized undertakings occurred because of women's greater efficiency and lower wages. They received less than men even when their output was higher! Their greater efficiency earned them 67% of men's wages. Wages in boot production were eighty-three pfennigs for adult male workers, sixty-two pfennigs for women over twenty-one, and forty-six pfennigs for girls eighteen to twenty-one years of age. Wage differences between adult men and young girls meant that the latter would force the former out of work while increasing industrial profits. In Germany and the Soviet Union, the rates for semiskilled women machine minders remained lower than those for unskilled men. The speed-up in production exhausted women, causing some to seek relief in dancing, movies, and flapper culture.[28]

Marriage, motherhood, and manufacturing imposed constraints on European and Soviet women's educational, economic, and political mobility.

Acknowledgment of this problem is found in the remarks of Soviet workers who declared that they were elected as delegates to the trade unions, soviets, or Party because they had someone at home to look after their children. Time budget studies by sociologist S. G. Strumilin showed that working women had less free time than men did because they spent much more time at housework and child care. Yet they also spent more time in educational courses and political activity than did housewives. Although some European and Soviet writers deplored the second-class status of women workers, few recognized that it was their double and triple burden that prevented them from becoming first-class citizens. Officially, the Soviet government refused to recognize that working women could not achieve as much as men while shouldering household and family responsibilities. Most Bolsheviks and European socialists accepted male dominance in their society.

Inadequate child care also blocked women's economic advancement in both Europe and the Soviet Union. After the Civil War, the Soviet government devoted little money to nurseries or kindergartens. NEP introduced cost accounting into industry, and plant managers were loath to provide childcare facilities, since it raised the cost of production. A. V. Artiukina, head of Zhenotdel, estimated that it cost a factory thirty rubles per month to maintain a child in a nursery, a cost many enterprises refused to bear. Child care was important for Soviet factory workers because they were older than their European counterparts: 42% were married, 20% were widowed or divorced, and many had children. Small proportions of German and English women workers were married, widowed, or divorced. Only 15% of Soviet women factory workers were under twenty years of age, but 49% of English factory workers were under twenty-five, and 78% were single.[29] In 1925, the Commissariat of Public Health estimated that 1,000 working women created a need for 180 places in nurseries, while industry supplied only 30 to 60 places. By 1928, the Commissariat of Public Health estimated that factory daycare centers admitted 37 children per 1,000 women workers. Trade unions were supposed to allocate 5% to 10% of their funds for nurseries, but only the textile unions did so. Childcare facilities improved throughout the decade but remained woefully inadequate. By 1929, there were 863,000 women in industrial unions with 22,500 children in crèches, mostly in Russia or Ukraine.[30]

Factory workers responded to the lack of communal child care in a variety of ways. Some families used older children to supervise younger ones, while others employed relatives from the countryside as nannies.

Some children remained unattended. Between 1923 and 1926, both Moscow and Leningrad reported a tremendous increase in the number of domestic servants. Since employers were supposed to pay social insurance premiums for servants, one suspects that the number listed in the city censuses was underreported. Foreign observers remarked on the presence of domestic servants in working-class families. Apparently workers took relatives into the household if they minded the children and helped with the shopping and cooking, whereas professionals were unwilling to allow a servant into their already crowded apartments.[31]

The lack of adequate childcare facilities created a vicious cycle. Without adequate child care, most Soviet women could not fully participate in educational and job-training programs to improve their job qualifications and wages. Nor could they participate in trade union, government, or Party organizations. While trade unionists and Party members called attention to women's problems, industry and government failed to allocate money to improve women's social and economic positions. Time-consuming household and childcare responsibilities meant few could engage in trade union work. Those few found it easier to participate in local than regional or national organizations. By the end of the decade, Soviet women represented 6.4% of the top union officials, 7% of union delegates, and 12.5% of paid union organizers.[32]

Various interpretations have been offered regarding Soviet women's low union participation. Some argued that women were not qualified due to illiteracy, cultural backwardness, and old-fashioned views. Some thought male discrimination was responsible. Most lacked Party membership, which was necessary for high positions.[33] Since women were also absent from high positions in European unions, other explanations seem plausible. Their low participation rate was probably due to lack of time, low self-confidence, and male exclusion. Given their family responsibilities, they may not have sought regional or national union positions. They may have preferred local study circles and mutual aid groups to administrative work. Many lacked the time and self-esteem to pursue such positions. When Mariia Suvorova's comrades elected her to the local soviet, she was frightened and did not think she could cope with the work because of her lack of education. Perhaps the wonder is not that working-class women were so poorly represented in trade union administration but that they were there at all, and that their presence at all levels slowly increased during the decade.

In addition to low wages and poor working conditions, Soviet and European women factory workers also coped with crowded housing, too-frequent pregnancies, unemployment, and even prostitution. After the war, European governments built more public housing and the Soviet government provided cheap rents, but housing shortages remained troublesome. Massive in-migration to Soviet and German cities worsened housing situations, and abject poverty kept many English working-class families in slums. Lack of birth control contributed to housing crises. Working-class women generally were less likely to use contraceptives and had more children than well-to-do women. Bolsheviks believed that motherhood was a useful service to society, but they realized that crowded housing and poverty increased women's need for birth control. They decriminalized abortion in 1920 because they found the death rate from it unacceptable. They established hygienic abortion clinics in the cities, granting working-class women access to free, legal, hygienic abortion and birth control information. In contrast, most European countries turned a blind eye to these issues, allowing wealthy women access to private illegal abortion and birth control information, while denying working class women similar services.

One may fault the Soviets for providing abortion as the main form of birth control, yet it removed the dangers of mutilation, punishment, and imprisonment that threatened European women. In matters of unemployment and prostitution, the Soviets also tried to help working women, by establishing unemployment insurance and refuges for prostitutes. Some German churches and cities also established shelters for unemployed women and prostitutes. During NEP, unemployment among Soviet women soared from 63,700 in 1923 to 415,000 in 1926. While only 58,000 women factory workers were unemployed in 1926, 48% were married women whose families needed their wages to survive. Nor were they unskilled. Among unemployed women textile workers, 2,500 were qualified workers, 2,500 were semiqualified, and only 450 were unskilled. These figures suggest that returning veterans deprived some qualified women of their jobs and that some Soviet employers dismissed married women because they did not want to pay for maternity leaves, childcare services, or equal wages for equal work. It was only during the Five-Year Plans in the 1930s that unemployment significantly declined. In France, slightly fewer working-class women suffered unemployment: 41,000 of a total of 1,800,000 workers, roughly 2%.[34]

The effects of unemployment for most working-class families were devastating. Unemployment benefits were inadequate, and unemployment bureaus proved ineffective in securing new jobs. The final nightmare for some unemployed workers was prostitution, and they constituted 14% of the known prostitutes. Unfortunately, the Soviet government was unable to change gendered job and family patterns that were impediments to women's emancipation. Many Party members believed that the political revolution included social, economic, and cultural transformations to liberate women. But they miscalculated. By 1929, Soviet women, like their European sisters, still suffered from job segregation, were clustered in light industry, experienced wage discrimination, and lacked adequate child care. Their triple burden of housework, child care, and paid work seemed untouched by communal resources. Time budgets show that men did little housework or child care.

While the Soviet government was not able to guarantee women economic equality, abolish unemployment, or draw men into household production, it provided new educational and job training opportunities. Unlike their Western counterparts, they did not propagate escapist literature, "sexploitation" in films, or alluring advertising in shop windows and amusement places. Newspapers did not print sex scandals or sensational sex tales. Yet Soviet women, like their European cohorts, still loved to read sentimental, escapist literature.

In the 1920s, Soviet writers introduced politically conscious and sexually emancipated Communist women workers, and Glebov's character Mera, a Zhenotdel leader in his play *Inga* (1928), shames and chastises a male chauvinist worker. Boris Pilniak depicts women workers ostracizing a man for driving his wife to suicide.[35] Prior to the revolution, few writers bothered describing working women. Though it is hard to know how accurately literature reflects life, a new type of working woman with a greater sense of dignity emerged in Soviet writing.

Domestic Production

One important economic transformation in the 1920s was the change from domestic to factory production in Russia. Yet the fact that 40% of the female industrial force remained in domestic production reveals the country's economic backwardness. Of 450,000 women engaged in handicraft production, 215,000 worked in urban areas and 238,300 in rural ones. Most lived in the Russian republic, although they were better distributed in other republics than were factory workers. Domestic production had also declined in Great Britain, Germany, and France by 1925.[36]

Soviet women handicraft workers worked in textiles, sewing, and food preparation. Like women factory workers, they fell into the age group twenty to forty-five and were generally married, widowed, or divorced. Among domestic producers, twice as many women were housewives as were employed (1,049,984 were inactive, while 446,800 were active). Although urban cottage workers were twice as literate as rural ones, little is known about their situation.[37] Since they experienced little unemployment, few in this stratum resorted to prostitution. Working at home, they presumably had less need of child care than did factory workers. Perhaps future historians will investigate the situation of Soviet and European female handicraft workers.

Service Employees

Aleksandra Kollontai thought that liberated women needed to regard work as more important than romance. Party workers and career women could believe this, but peasant women, factory workers, domestic servants, and clerks had a more difficult time valuing their paid work more than romance and family life. Few Soviet women regarded their employment as seriously as Kollontai did, since 85% of the female urban population remained peasants. Among women service employees, only a portion regarded their work as emotionally gratifying. Most worked to survive, not for self-realization. New educational opportunities allowed more women to experience upward economic mobility and to view their work as a means of fulfillment. Evening courses and factory schools offered both young and older married women opportunities to rise out of their low status and plan more interesting jobs than they had held prior to the revolution. Peasant women could dream of becoming more than domestic servants or factory workers. Some became nurses, others midwives and doctors. It is tantalizing to reflect on those who experienced upward economic mobility in that decade.

In the 1920s, slightly more Soviet and European women were engaged in service sectors than in manufacturing. Another similarity between Soviet and European women is that many in this socioeconomic group were housewives and remained economically dependent. Approximately 2,247,000 female employees in Soviet service categories were economically inactive, while 1,450,000 were employed.[38]

Domestic Servants

One of the greatest changes in women's employment was the decline in domestic service in the 1920s. During the war, women in all the belligerent countries left domestic service to take better-paying jobs in industry and clerical work. The number of domestic servants declined about 1.4

million in the Soviet Union, 600,000 in England, 200,000 in Germany, and 130,000 in France. Except in France, most servants remained young and single (table 7.8).

As in the nineteenth century, both France and the Soviet Union had significant proportions of widowed and divorced women in positions of service, while in England and Germany, single women predominated. Although servants earned higher wages in the 1920s than in the 1890s, their conditions of work did not improve much. In the Soviet Union, they earned 150 to 250 rubles per year, compared to 15 to 25 rubles in the 1890s. Those in England earned 30 to 50 pounds, almost double the wages of the 1890s. French cooks and chambermaids earned 3,600 and 2,2000 francs per year, which was significantly more than their prewar wages of 600 and 400 gold francs. Cooks usually earned considerably more than parlor or kitchen maids.[39]

Domestic servants earned low wages, but they received room and board that other low-level employees did not. Most domestics were young and single and, as in the nineteenth century, migrated from the country to the city. Sometimes, their naïveté, abusive working conditions, and low wages led them into prostitution. Soviet and German prostitutes often came from peasant backgrounds. Unlike other service workers, domestic servants were less likely to have children or need child care. Unencumbered by husbands or children, some Soviet domestics took advantage of educational and job-training programs that the new regime offered. By 1926, half of Soviet domestics were literate, a vast improvement over their 36% literacy rate in 1897. Since many domestics immigrated from the countryside, it is doubtful that they joined trade unions or made contracts with their employers, as Soviet law stipulated.[40]

The position of English domestic servants did not improve much after the war. They still suffered from low wages, excessive hours, inferior so-

Table 7.8. Marital Status of Domestic Servants, Mid 1920s*

Country	Number	% Single	% Married	% Widow/Divorced
USSR	450,000	75	6	22
France	660,000	58	23	18
England	1,149,000	87	6	3
Germany	1,400,022	95	1	3

*Calculated from *Perepisi 1926 g.*, 34: 58–72; *P.P., Gt. Br. Census of Eng. and Wales, 1921*, 104–5; *An. Stat.*, 49 (1933): 13; *SDDR 1925*, Band 402, III, 452.

cial status, and severe restrictions on their time. Advertisements in the *Times* of London in 1925 indicate that cooks earned the highest wages: forty-five to fifty pounds per year, parlor maids received thirty to forty-five, kitchen maids twenty-six, and scullery maids twenty-eight.[41] Despite four parliamentary investigations into their harsh living and working conditions, employers still allocated semifurnished attics and dark, airless basements for their living quarters. Better jobs and treatment during the war made girls less willing to accept live-in positions, so many who left school at fourteen worked as weekly chars in well-to-do households.

French girls also viewed domestic service more negatively in the 1920s than previously. A French peasant woman named Rose Allais resented her sister's becoming a schoolteacher, since she herself could only work as a maid. German women also loathed domestic service work after having had higher-paid factory and clerical jobs during the war. They hated the restrictions and low wages that service imposed. Inflation impoverished much of the German middle class, preventing them from keeping servants. When socialists in the Reichstag tried to improve the situation of servants, suggesting that they be given nine hours of rest per night and that pregnant servants receive four weeks' rest prior to their due date, other Reichstag members and the Housewives' Association rejected these provisions. Instead, bourgeois housewives proposed a year of mandatory domestic science training in their households for all working-class girls. Of course, middle-class girls learned proper housekeeping from their mothers and would be excused from the training. Later, Hitler earned the respect of German bourgeois women by endorsing their proposal.[42]

The revolution of 1917 and the Civil War decimated the Russian gentry and bourgeois classes, and few could afford servants. A similar decline in laundresses occurred during this period. Table 7.9 shows some of the changes among low-level service personnel. While the number of Soviet women occupied in domestic service positions fell drastically between 1897 and 1926, half remained in occupations that paid less than agriculture work.

Bath attendants, laundresses, and hospital orderlies also earned low wages. During the Civil War, the urban population declined and women were needed in industrial production. Thus, the number of service workers declined until returning veterans replaced female factory workers, relegating them to service jobs once more.

Table 7.9. Select Low-Level Service Positions, 1897–1926*

Occupation	1897	1926
Domestic servants	1,300,000	450,000
Other service employees	500,000	40,000
Laundresses	103,000	23,400
Office cleaners	22,000	111,000
Bath attendants	2,800	2,500
Janitors & guards	2,500	131,000
Messengers & couriers	41	28,700
Hospital orderlies	12,000	68,000
Total	1,942,341	854,600

*Calculated from *Svod Perepisi 1897 g.*, 2: 296–300; *Perepisi 1926 g.*, 34: 58–72.

Low-Level Service Personnel

Soviet women in low-level service work were evenly divided according to marital status. Thirty percent of low-ranking medical personnel were single, 35% were married, 27% widowed, and 7% divorced. Whereas 70% of domestics were twenty-five years old or younger, only 27% of hospital orderlies were so young.[43] The struggle to survive was extremely exhausting for older, married workers since they had to carry triple burdens of low-paid work, child care, and household work. Although Soviet law obliged both spouses to support and educate their children, society usually held mothers responsible. For them, paid work did not necessarily provide liberation, but rather the oppression of low wages, inadequate child care, and crowded housing.

Domestic service did offer job security. In France, only 12,000 of 660,000 (1%) domestic servants were unemployed in 1926. Indeed, unemployment hit higher-ranking employees harder than lower ones in France and Russia. Among unemployed Soviet service workers, 63% were senior personnel, 27% mid-level, only 10% low ranking.[44]

Mid-Level Service Employees

The mechanization of office work revolutionized economies in the 1920s. Adding machines and typewriters led to the substitution of women for men in clerical work. After the war, young women generally preferred jobs as shop assistants, bank clerks, and typists to domestic service. Such work was clean, possessed more status, and sometimes paid higher wages than domestic or factory work. The effects of this revolution were greatest in Germany and France, where 1 million more women were employed in commerce in the 1920s than in the 1890s. During the same period, 800,000 additional English women took jobs in the commercial sector. A less dramatic increase from 500,000 to 850,000 occurred among Soviet women. Yet wages in commerce remained low, often subsistence level. Table 7.10 shows the changes occurring in these positions.

Unlike their European counterparts, Soviet women in mid-level positions tended to be older, married women. Although their wages were not as abysmally low as those of domestic servants, they probably did not exceed those of factory workers. In France, some female clerks earned about 8,000 francs per year when they began their careers, but received only 9,800 francs after fifteen years of work. Few French employers provided child care, although some department stores did.[45]

Although Soviet women employees often possessed higher education, they still clustered in low-paying jobs. Like their European sisters, they also endured sex discrimination and stereotyping. Some 60,000 women worked as guards in various enterprises, but fewer than 50 were employed in police or fire protection, a field that presumably paid better wages. Likewise, the 1926 Soviet census reported 630,556 men but only 378 women in the military. Despite programs to liberate women and include them in all forms of employment, only the most persistent escaped gender segregation. Nadezhda Sumarokova tried to enlist in a military aviation school in Yegoryevsk in 1923, but the commander initially refused her application. Yet she persevered, completed the course of training, and became an instructor in the Military Aviation Academy in 1926. She believed that a woman could shoulder a man's job if she really wanted to. Since aviation was a new branch of the military, it was less rigid than others. Still, sex stereotyping persisted in the Soviet Union and Europe in the 1920s.[46]

Table 7.10. Employees in Commerce, Service, and Transport*

Country	1890s	1920s
USSR	500,000	850,000
Germany	600,000	1,600,000
France	700,000	1,700,000
England	240,000	1,000,000

*Calculated from *Svod Perepisi 1897 g.*, 2: 250–55; *Perepisi 1926 g.*, 34: 58–72; 52: 86–87; *Stat. Jarbuch*, 35: 16–17; *SDDR 1925*, Band 402, III, 446; *An. Stat.*, 20: 22–37; 49: 13; *Gt. Br. Census, 1891*, 97: 180; *Gt. Br. Census 1921*, 92–99, 105.

As a group, mid-level service workers experienced little upward mobility and little unemployment. Only 60,000 Soviet women in this category and 11,000 French women in commercial positions were unemployed. Many of the unemployed were young workers, who as the last hired were the first fired. Russian noblewoman Elena Skrjabina gained and lost jobs quickly in the 1920s. After she learned to type, she found it easier to get new jobs.[47]

Soviet literature suggests that it was economically vulnerable gentry and bourgeois women who sometimes resorted to prostitution. Whereas nineteenth-century writers Dostoevsky, Tolstoy, and Chekhov portrayed prostitutes as downtrodden and pitiful characters, writers in the 1920s and 1930s were less sympathetic. It was ironic that while the government decriminalized prostitution and social agencies were rescuing prostitutes, segments of public opinion hardened against them. Tarasov-Rodionov's novel *Chocolate* (1922) describes an attractive, unemployed ballerina who lapses into prostitution and betrays the trust of a Cheka agent who had befriended her. Valentin Kataev's novels *The Embezzlers* (1926) and *Time Forward* (1933) also depict prostitutes as unsavory characters. In "Sisters," Kollontai treats prostitutes sympathetically and describes two educated, unemployed women who may have belonged to the mid-level category of workers. One of the unemployed women is a prostitute and the other a housewife. When the husband brings the prostitute home, the wife is initially hurt and angry. In the morning, she realizes that if she were not married, she too might become a prostitute. Kollontai's stories show the harmful effects of NEP and unemployment on women.[48]

In postwar Germany, inflation and economic chaos led to widespread prostitution. Some prostituted not only themselves but also their daughters. Some housewives and widows rented rooms in their houses to augment the family income. To mitigate social problems, German churches and local governments sometimes provided shelters for homeless women. The English general strike of 1926 also impoverished many working-class families and may have led to increased prostitution, but little is written on this topic. Male unemployment and underemployment doomed many English wives and children to low-paid work in order for their family to survive.

Career Women

A woman could not have a wife to keep inviolate her hours of
... work. —Emily Ford, 1922

The censuses of the 1920s yield fascinating information about career women. Sixty-two percent of Soviet women in the category "state employees" were unemployed; 38% were employed. In the "free professions," the number of dependent women outnumbered economically independent ones five to one. Although two-thirds in this category remained house-wives, their labor participation was higher than European women's, because Soviet society encouraged married career women to work. Kollontai reportedly told the American novelist Theodore Dreiser in 1927 that Soviet women did not want to be parasites and rejected the stigma of housewife. While 38% of Soviet career women were married, only 24% of French, 12% of English, and 5% of German career women were. In education and medicine, the discrepancies were higher: 42% of Soviet women teachers, but only 12% of English and 5% of German women teachers, were married. Sixty percent of female doctors in Paris were married, as were 52% of Soviet female doctors, but only 23% of English and 15% of German were wed. In the 1920s, English and German government authorities dismissed many married women teachers and civil servants.[49]

In Paris, 25% of married women doctors practiced medicine with their husbands, yet marriage ended many women's medical careers. According to Colette Yver, only 243 of the 900 women who had completed medical training in the previous twenty years were practicing in Paris in 1929. It was not government dictates that forced French women out of their careers, but their husbands. Yver found that spouses of doctors, pharmacists, and dentists demanded their wives' presence at home. Married female dental surgeons in Paris also renounced their professions, so most practicing ones were single. The higher her class, the less likely that a French woman worked outside the home. Since medical education cost 600 francs per year, and it took five years to obtain a degree, it took a substantial sum to educate a doctor. Only well-to-do families could afford such education, and husbands in those classes often demanded their wives' complete attention.[50]

Significant national differences occurred in women's distribution in the professions: most Teutonic women remained in teaching and religious vocations, while more Soviet and French women became dentists, pharmacists, lawyers, and engineers (table 7.11). French female lawyers were generally well accepted, since they were less ambitious than their male counterparts, were content with modest salaries, and performed well.[51]

The 1926 Soviet census lists significant numbers of women occupied as "leading personnel," including high-ranking political officials. In the new government, Aleksandra Kollontai became Commissar of Welfare, while Nadezhda Krupskaia, Vera Lebedeva, and Vera Iakovleva held high-ranking positions in the Commissariats of Education, Health, and Economics. In Germany, Toni Sender served as an executive member of the Independent Socialist Party, as did Clara Zetkin in the Communist Party and Lilo Linke in the Democratic Party. While Susan Lawrence and others were Executive Committee members of the Labour Party in England, only Margaret Bondfield held high cabinet office (1929). Lacking the franchise, French women remained outside high political office.

Medicine and education became feminized in the Soviet Union because these fields had become open to women during the last years of the Tsarist regime, and because the Bolsheviks allowed women into all professions. Prior to the war, women accounted for 70% of all students in feldsher and feldsher-midwife training. Jewish women were particularly attracted to medical careers, because they offered a passport out of the pale of settlement (the western edge of the country where the Tsar required most Jews to live).[52] By the mid 1920s, the Soviets were producing large numbers of career women, and women from the lower classes could dream of professional life. In France, normal schools also recruited bright working-class and peasant girls into teaching. Such social mobility happened less in England or Germany.

Career women generally clustered in education and low-level medical professions while other fields remained male-dominated. Given the Communist Party's endorsement of women's liberation, it is surprising that only 5,000 women occupied paid political and administrative positions. In 1926, Russian and Ukrainian women dominated the paid political workers in

Table 7.11. Distribution of Women in Professions, 1920s*

Occupation	Soviet	English	German	French
Teachers	190,000	187,352	98,000	164,000
Doctors	20,000	1,253	2,572	921
Dentists	5,000	296	418	2,666
Pharmacists	12,800	N/A	2,720	6,600
Midwives	27,000	5,507	2,700	11,057
Religious	1,000	12,000	22,000	48,200
Lawyers & Jud. Per.	1,300	37	11	13,600
Engineers	400	43	174	1,127

*Calculated from *Perepisi 1926 g.*, 34: 142–61; *An. Stat.*, 52: *35, 133–35; *RSDRP 1926,* Tome I. Troisieme Partie, 156/166; *Gt. Br. 1921 Census*, 100–8; *SDDR 1925*, Band 401, 418, Band 402, Teil 3, 801–11, Band 408, 302–3.

Kazakhstan and Central Asia, while Jewish women predominated in Ukraine and Belorussia.[53] Table 7.12 shows a considerable increase in the number of women in administration, education, and medicine from 1897 to 1926. The table reveals continuity in women's employment, with the exception of religion. The closing of convents and monasteries, but not parish churches, meant that religion became more male dominated in the 1920s than it had been in the 1890s. Medicine and religion remained male dominated in Europe.

Medicine

In many respects, the situation of career women resembled that of other workers. Just as female factory workers crowded into low-paying light industry, career women coalesced in low-paying professions such as medicine and education. During the Russian Civil War, doctors' salaries were too small to live on, and private practice was unprofitable, since the population lacked the means of paying for these services. Even well-known professors and clinicians became destitute. A chief physician in Vologda earned only twelve rubles, or six dollars, per month.[54] By the mid 1920s, the situation of professionals had improved, and female teachers and doctors earned 200 to 500 rubles per year. Still, their wages lagged behind those of workers.

German female physicians earned less than male doctors, but they received enough at municipal clinics to be able to afford servants. Excluded from the higher ranks, they appreciated the limited hours of clinic work and served as directors of municipal counseling centers and in welfare offices, schools, and prenatal clinics. Like their Soviet cohorts, most German women were general practitioners, or specialized in gynecology, obstetrics, dermatology, sexual diseases, or psychiatry.[55]

Table 7.12. Russian and Soviet Career Women*

Occupation	1897	1926
Doctors	608	19,000
Feldshers and midwives	10,000	27,400
Teachers, governesses, etc.	66,000	191,651
Government administrators	1,500	5,200
Institutional personnel	8,000	16,000
Judicial personnel	0	1,300

*Calculated from *Svod Perepisi 1897 g.*, 2: 296–300; *Perepisi 1926 g.*, 34: 56–75.

European and Soviet physicians differed in several respects. There were 20,000 Soviet female doctors compared to 1,000 English and 2,500 German. Abortion was illegal in Weimar Germany, and doctors risked their reputation, fines, and even imprisonment if they performed too many abortions. Consequently, they used sterilization as a form of birth control. In contrast, abortion was legal in the Soviet Union and tended to be a major form of birth control. The marriage rates of German female physicians correlated with their form of employment: among the self-employed, 48% were single, 44% were married, and 8% widowed or divorced. In clinics, 85% were single, 11% married, and 3% widowed or divorced. Some German female physicians avoided marriage and the added work of a husband, opting for a nice apartment and a housekeeper instead. Some lived openly lesbian lives. Atina Grossman suggests that those who married and had children combined family, career, and social activism without guilt or exhaustion by employing servants and nannies. She found urban women doctors more radical and rural ones more conservative.[56]

As in Germany, provincial Soviet doctors worked under trying circumstances. They had a minimum of drugs, simple rooms for patients, and horses for transportation. Although they could engage in private practice, taxes were heavy and fees difficult to collect. Since it was almost impossible to support themselves outside state employment, most worked in clinics. While Soviet teachers earned 678 rubles per year, medical personnel earned 200 to 400 rubles per year, and workers 843 rubles. French female doctors received fairly high salaries in government agencies, and World War I ushered in greater acceptance and respect for women physicians and surgeons. Yet their applications for medical posts often failed, and it was state insurance, inaugurated in 1928, that facilitated their work with women and children.[57]

Teaching

Time budget studies of Soviet teachers indicate that women spent about twenty-five hours per week teaching, nine to thirteen hours in preparation, and five to seven hours in administrative work. Male teachers spent the same time teaching and preparing, but more time in administrative work and in second jobs. Women teachers spent ten more hours per week than men in unpaid household work and more time in child care. Men spent two to three hours more time in sociopolitical work than women. Both groups spent similar amounts of time in professional training, meetings, travel, and reading.

The double standard in employment persisted, and few English women obtained university positions. One exception was the medievalist Eileen Power, who taught history at Girton College, Cambridge, from 1913 to 1921 and then became lecturer and reader at the London School of Economics. Local authorities often imposed a marriage bar on female, but not male, teachers. The fall in public expenditures in the 1920s led to the dismissal of hundreds of older, married women teachers. Firing them helped local school boards balance their budgets. The number of married women teachers fell from 18,600 in 1921 to 14,400 in 1927.[58] Most earned considerably less than their male counterparts, except at the elementary level. In Manchester, uncertificated male teachers earned 240 pounds per annum, while females earned 167 to 200. Technical-school teachers showed a similar disparity: men received 240 to 500 pounds per year, while women earned 225 to 400. A secondary-school headmistress in Halifax received 500 to 700 pounds per annum while a headmaster in Lyme Regis County earned 600 to 675. Governesses still earned the least—50 to 100 pounds per year.[59]

After 1921, it became harder for English married female teachers to keep their posts. The National Union of Women Teachers opposed the dismissal of married women teachers, but the practice spread. Visiting French female teachers were told that few local authorities employed married women teachers. One remarked: "But why not? What have they done?" They could not fathom that marriage could be the basis for dismissal.[60]

French female secondary-school teachers earned good, but not equal, salaries and pensions. Some women earned high salaries as clerks and librarians (15,000 to 28,000 francs per year), a government pension, and one month's holiday each year. When first in Paris in 1918, Emilie Carles assisted at a private Catholic school where she earned 25 to 75 francs per month plus housing. By 1920, she was studying at the Sorbonne and coaching students for their exams, earning 400 francs per month. When she became a full-time teacher and civil servant, her salary increased several hundred francs per month. More important than salary was her satisfaction in living and teaching in the countryside. Still, she encountered many of the same problems that dogged rural Soviet schoolteachers: abysmal housing, remote teaching appointments, family obligations, gossip, insults, and sexual harassment. In the late 1920s, she married, had children, helped her husband run a hotel, and cared for several family members. Coming from peasant stock, she did the housework herself.[61]

Politics

Female politicians earned modest salaries. The German Democratic Party paid Lilo Linke well enough for her youth organization work to keep her own apartment. Likewise, Toni Sender, who was a member of the Executive Committee of the Independent Socialist Party and a Reichstag delegate, lived reasonably well. Yet when she fell ill and had to go to Switzerland for convalescence, she wondered if she would be able to pay her medical expenses. During her convalescence, she wrote for several European journals to pay for her care.[62]

Similar to German party women, most Russian Communist Party officials lived rather spartan lives, receiving wages equivalent to those of factory workers. They encountered a great deal of sexism and were often relegated to work on women's and children's issues. Few shaped economic or foreign policy. When Kollontai opposed NEP in 1921, Lenin accused her of sexual misbehavior. In Germany, Toni Sender discovered that a woman had to make more effort and show more efficiency than a man to be considered an equal. Some resented the condescension and threats of male Reichstag colleagues and left in disgust. If women on committees caused trouble and did not resign of their own free will, fewer women's names graced the next Party election list. The few on the list were mainly a concession to the feminine electorate.[63]

Problems

While career women enjoyed a social status that working-class women lacked, they did not necessarily escape the sexual stereotyping, harassment, low wages, inadequate child care, and household work that plagued other working women. In England, the double standard meant that women with university education often took demeaning jobs. After Cecil FitzGerald (Woodham-Smith) graduated from St. Hilda's College, Oxford, in 1917, she became a typist and copywriter with an advertising firm. Only decades later did she turn to serious biographical writing. Sexism also affected French women. Geneviève Tabouis felt that her editor behaved in a condescending manner and that a woman's opinion carried no weight in France. Still, professional opportunities varied. English writers Virginia Woolf, Rebecca West, Winifred Holtby, and Vera Brittain worked as paid columnists for a variety of British papers, and Lady Rhondda established a female-owned and -operated journal *Time and Tide* to propagate feminist views. It had women on the board of directors, hired women journalists, and made Holtby its director.[64]

Unlike Teutonic countries that discouraged married career women, many Soviet career women married and needed child care. Fifty-five percent of educational and cultural personnel were married, widowed, or divorced. In France, 24% of career women were married, and 18% were widows. In contrast, 10% of English career women were married and 5% were widowed. In Germany, only 6% of career women were married or divorced. Many German female physicians preferred clinical work to private practice, because of the shorter hours.[65]

French and Soviet career women, like their working-class sisters, often needed child care. Since such provision was inadequate, many had a difficult time juggling professional and household work. Yet the workday of Soviet professionals was about an hour less than that of factory workers. Soviet white-collar workers spent fewer hours than workers in child care and household chores, but they spent similar amounts of time in sociopolitical work. Most career women belonged to trade unions, but only a few participated in union administration. More than 1.5 million *sluzhashchie* belonged to trade unions, but they held only 2,300 (1.5%) of the paid union positions. In the Soviet Union, workers in a given field, e.g., medical workers from orderlies to surgeons, belonged to the same union.[66] In Europe, class distinctions remained strong, and career women joined professional organizations, not unions with workers.

Soviet career women shared other problems with working-class women, such as fear of unemployment and prostitution. Of 415,000 unemployed women, 138,000 were high-ranking service personnel, including a sizable number of career women. In the Russian republic, unemployment among service workers appeared in a variety of fields: 24,000 in trade and credit; 13,000 in accounting and bookkeeping, 15,000 in factory personnel, 8,000 in medicine, 13,000 in education, almost 2,000 in cultural positions. In such an underdeveloped country it seems odd to find high unemployment among technical and educational personnel. Yet during NEP the central government withdrew its support from many clinics and schools, and local Soviets refused to tax themselves to pay qualified personnel.

High unemployment may also have indicated educated people's reluctance to leave the cities to settle in the hinterland where jobs may have existed but working conditions, wages, and housing were wretched. Unemployment in this group may account for the high proportion of gentry-class and bourgeois prostitutes that Soviet sociologists report in the 1920s. In contrast, only 8,000 of 470,000 French women, or 1% of those in the liberal professions, were listed as unemployed in the 1920s.[67]

Notes

1. *Treaty of Peace with Germany Signed at Versailles, on the 28th of June, 1919*, Part XIII LABOUR, Section II, Article 427, General Principles, 596; Brittain, *Lady into Woman*, 139.

2. Koonz, *Mothers in the Fatherland*, 33–34.

3. Strumilin, "Biudzhet vremeni russkogo rabochego," *Kom.* 6 (1923): 17–21; "Svobodnyi trud v robochikh semiakh," *Kom.* 8 (1923): 22–23; A. Rashin, *Sostav fabrichno-zavodskogo proletariata* 152–53; Anne Bobroff, "Russian Working Women: Sexuality in Bonding Patterns and the Politics of Daily Life," *Powers of Desire*, 206–27; Kollontai, "Sexual Relations and the Class Struggle," "Communism and the Family," and "Love and the New Morality," *Selected Writings of Alexandra Kollontai*; Kollontai, *Autobiography*.

4. Alimony meant upkeep of children, not former spouses. Figures for unemployed, divorced, and those receiving alimony in *Perepisi 1926 g.* 51: 28.

5. Bennet, *Village of Viriatino*, 243; Pasha Angelina, *My Answer to an American Questionnaire*, 4. Angelina detested the kulak family she worked for from 1923 to 1927, but liked the Lenin kolkhoz where she worked from 1927 to 1929.

6. Bennet, *Village of Viriatino*, 243; Angelina, *My Answer*, 4.

7. Prof. Derlitzki, Director of the Pomeritz Institute, in "The Rationalization of the Work of Farm Women in Germany," *ILR* 23 (January–June 1931): 561; *ILR* 26 (1932): 707–9.

8. Brittain, *Lady into Woman*, 131-32; Georges Dupeaux, *French Society 1789–1970*, 164, 241–43; Clark, *Position of Women in France*, 26–31; Carles, *A Life of Her Own*, 119, 128. Carles did not mind washing clothes in a cold brook, and she rinsed one woman's clothes in exchange for meals.

9. *SSSR v Tsifrakh*, 173; *SSSR Strana Sotsializma Stat. sbornik*, 65.

10. Quoted by Jessica Smith in *Women in Soviet Russia*, 32.

11. *Perepisi 1926 g.* 5: 44–45; *Stat. spravochnik SSSR za 1928*, 559.

12. Rashin, *Sostav fabrichno-zavodskogo proletariata*, 33.

13. Yarros, "Social Hygiene Observations in Soviet Russia," *Journal of Social Hygiene* 16 (8): 449–64. Soviet sociologist Wolfson found 43% of prostitutes in Moscow in the 1920s had peasant backgrounds, as quoted by Stites in *Women's Liberation Movement*, 372–73. Soviet venereologist Dr. Bronner gives a class analysis for prostitutes in the 1890s, but not 1920s, in *La Lutte Contre Prostitution en URSS*. For marriage rates, see *Perepisi 1926 g.* 51: 28.

14. Halle, *Woman in Soviet Russia*, 286-300; Fitzpatrick, *Education and Social Mobility in the Soviet Union 1921–1934*, 105–10; *Village of the Viriatino*, 294; Scott, *Beyond the Urals*, 120-23; Ramer, "Childbirth and Culture: Midwifery in the Nineteenth Century Russian Countryside," *The Family in Imperial Russia*, 226. The number of hospital orderlies increased to 68,000 in 1926; midwives increased from 9,800 in 1897 to 27,000 in 1926; and the number of nurses rose from 5,000 to 29,000. *Svod Perepisi 1897* 2: 236–55; *Perepisi 1926 g.* 34: 96.

15. "Sotsialisticheskoe sel'koe khoziaistvo Soiuza SSR," *P Kh.* 7 (1939): 163; Ruth Kennell, *Theodore Dreiser and the Soviet Union*, 123-24; CSB, *Women in the USSR*, 97.

16. *An. Stat.* 49: 10–13; *Stat. Jarbuch* 49: 19–24; *Svod 1897 Perepisi* 2: 296; *Perepisi 1926 g.* 34: 8; Mitchell, *European Historical Statistics 1750–1900*, 19; Reynolds, *France Between the Wars*, 11, 101–2.

17. *KSP 1926 g.* Part VII, 13; Part IX, 13.

18. Milovidova, *Zhenskii vopros i zhenskoe dvishenie*, 148–50; *Russian Year Book* (1916), 477; Baron Alexander F. Meyendorff, "Social Cost of the War," *Cost of the War to Russia*, 198.

19. *An. Stat.*, 45 (1932): 99; 52: 99; Milovidova, *Zhenskii Vopros*, 471–74; Patrick Lavin, "Angliiskie zhenshchiny v professional'nykh organizatsiiakh," *Kom.* 1-2 (1923): 24-25; Lucy Middleton, *Women in the Labor Movement*, 206; Boone, *Women's Trade Union Leagues*, 38; Webb, *History of Trade Unions*, 495; Gertrude Hanna, "Women in the German Trade Union Movement," *ILR*, 1923: 26–29; Thonnessen, *The Emancipation of Women*, 144; G.D.H. Cole, *Trade Unionism and Munitions*, 183, 216–17; Clark, *Position of Women in France*, 78.

20. B. Kanatchikova, "Nasha Robota," *Kom.* 10–11 (1921): 39–43; Susan Kingsbury and Mildred Fairchild, *Factory, Family, and Woman in Soviet Union*, 85.

21. Beatrice Webb, "Minority Report. Part I: The Relation between Men's and Women's Wages; Part II: The War Pledges of the Government with Regard to the Wages of Women," War Cabinet, Committee on Women in Industry, *Women in Industry*, Cmd 135, 167 (1919) 1: 254–334; L. M. Kogan, *Starye i novye kadry proletariata*, 25; Rashin, *Formirovanie Robachego Klassa Rossi*, 603–5; A. Riazanova, "Professional'noe dvizhenie," *Kom.* 4 (1924): 19–23; B. Markus, "Rabotnitsa v proizvodstve," *Kom.* April 1925, 49; *ILR* 23 (January–June 1931): 560.

22. Vera Lebedeva, "Nashi dostizheniia," *Kom.* November 1926, 64; *Kom.* 1921, 10–11: 42; 12–13: 24–25. Milovidova, *Zhenskii Vopros*, 203; Marcel Frois, *La Santé et le travail des femmes pendant la guerre*, 136.

23. Kollontai, "Vasilisa Malygina," in *Liubov' pchel trudovykh*; Gladkov, *Sobranie Sochinenii. Tom vtoroi, Tsement.*

24. N. M. Katuntseva, *Rol' Rabochikh Fakult'tetov v Formirovanii intelligentsii SSSR*, 20; Kollontai, "The Woman Worker," *Selected Articles and Speeches*, 174.

25. Willmott, *Growing Up in a London Village*, 134; Linke, *A German Girl's Autobiography*, 112; Frevert, *Women in German History*, 183.

26. *Svod Perepisi 1897 g.* 2: 242–50, 296–301; *KSP 1926 g.*, vols. 25–33. In 1928, English men in chemicals and printing earned sixty-one to sixty-eight shillings per week to women's twenty-five to twenty-eight. In textiles, the discrepancy was less: forty-eight shillings for men, twenty-nine for women. French men earned twenty-eight francs per day in 1928, but women received only sixteen. German male factory workers earned thirty to forty-four marks per week, while women earned twenty to twenty-nine. "Wages of Male and Female Workers in Various Countries," *ILR* 23 (January–June 1931): 560–62; Judith Grunfeld, "Rationalisation and the Employment and Wages of Women in Germany," *ILR* 29 (May 1934): 630; Frevert, *Women in German History*, 184; Rashin, *Sostav fab.-zav. proletariata*, 36–38; Hyacinthe Dubreuil, *Employeurs et Salaries en France*, 148–49.

27. Regarding tobacco and rubber workers, see Kennell, *Theodore Dreiser and the Soviet Union, 1927–1945*, 153–54; regarding rubber workers, Veresaev, *Sestry*, 234–37, 303.

28. Grunfeld, "Wages of Women in Germany," *ILR* 29 (5): 621–28.

29. *Perepisi 1926 g.* 34: 16, 18: 38; 51: 18–38; *An. Stat.* 48 (1932): 12–13; *Gt. Britain Census of 1921 for Eng. and Wales*, 64–84.

30. Lebedeva, "Nashi dostizheniia," *Kom.* November 1926, 64; Kingsbury, *Factory, Family, and Woman in the Soviet Union*, 148–52; *Socialist Construction in the USSR, 1936*, 454–55.

31. Korber, *Life in a Soviet Factory*, 193.

32. G. Mal'nechanskii, "Profsoiuzy i 8 marta," *Kom.* February 1925, 14–15; Smith, *Women in Soviet Russia*, 19; Carr, *Foundations of a Planned Economy*, 2: 470–71.

33. Kingsbury, *Factory, Family, and Woman*, 96–98; Smith, *Women in Soviet Russia*, 19; Rashin, *Sostav fab.-zav. proletariata*, 147ff.

34. *Perepisi 1926 g.* 52: 46–55; *An. Stat.* 49 (1933): 13.

35. Conference of Chiefs of Women's Sections, RCP(b)" 24 January–2 February 1924, *Youth and the Party, Documents*, 61–62; Glebov, "Inga," *Sbornik P'es*, 327ff; Boris Pilniak, *The Volga Flows into the Caspian Sea*, 288–89.

36. *Perepisi 1926 g.* 51: 31, 39, 45; 34: 2–3; Stearns, *Lives of Labour*, 33.

37. *Perepisi 1926 g.* 51: 31, 39, 45; 34: 2–3.

38. *Perepisi 1926 g.* 51: 36-38.

39. Kollontai, *Iz Moei Zhizni i Raboty*, 18–19; Clarke, *Soviet Economic Facts, 1927–1970*, 26; *Times* (London), 4 May 1895, 6; 2–4 February 1925, 3–4; Stevenson, *British Society, 1914–1945*, 158, 131–32; *An. Stat.* 52: 248; Clark, *Position of Women in France*, 34; Kennell, *Theodore Dreiser and the Soviet Union*, 34. The ruble was worth fifty-two American cents in 1927, the same as in the 1890s.

40. The number of domestic servants in Leningrad rose from 3,057 in 1923 to 25,312 in 1926, and in Moscow from 14,335 to 42,217. *KSP 1926 g.*, Part IX (Leningrad), 89; Part VIII (Moscow), 88. Their age, marital status, and literacy, in *Perepisi 1926 g.* 34: 74. For unions and contracts, Kennell, *Theodore Dreiser and the Soviet Union*, 28.

41. *Times* (London), 2 February 1925, 3; 4 February 1925, 4.

42. Brittain, *Lady into Woman*, 132–33; Frevert, *Women in German History*, 195, 200, 218; Reagin, *A German Women's Movement*, 231–32; Carles, *A Life of Her Own*, 59.

43. *Perepisi 1926 g.* 52: 86–87.

44. *An. Stat.* 49 (1933): 13; *Perepisi 1926 g.* 52: 86–87.

45. *Perepisi 1926 g.* 34: 58–72; *An. Stat.* 49: 13; *Gt. Br. 1921 Census*, 92–108; *SSSR Strana Sotsializma Stat. Sbornik, 1936*, 26; Skriabina, *Coming of Age in the Russian Revolution*, 56–64; Roberta Reeder, *Anna Akhmatova*, 168–81; Clark, *Position of Women in France*, 20–26. The Soviet government paid poorly, as these intellectuals discovered.

46. "The First Woman Air Commander," *MDN*, 9 February 1933, 4; *Perepisi 1926 g.* 34: 12–13, 172–73. Sex stereotyping was also strong in Europe, and the 1921 British census revealed only 279 women in police work, and none in the military. *Gr. Br. 1921 Census*, 99.

47. *An. Stat.* 49 (1933): 13; *Perepisi 1926 g.* 51: 48; Skjiabina, *Coming of Age*, 56–64.

48. Kollontai, "Sisters," *Love of Worker Bees*, 291–321; Alexander Tarasov-Rodionov, *Chocolate*; Valentine Kataev, *The Embezzlers*; Kataev, *Time Forward*.

49. *Perepisi 1926 g.* 34: 70–71; 51: 48, 76–77; *An. Stat.* 49: 13; *Gt. Bt. Census 1921*, 101; *SDDR 1925* Band 402, Teil 3, 810–11; Brittain, *Lady into Woman*, 99, 104; Kennell, *Theodore Dreiser and the Soviet Union*, 36–37. Invited to the Soviet Union for the tenth anniversary of the revolution in 1927, Dreiser met Kollontai. He was more impressed by Kollontai's physical charms than her feminist ideas. (Kollontai had returned to Russia after a diplomatic stint in Mexico and briefly resumed her post at the Commissariat of Social Welfare in 1927.) Only 21 of 2,718 married women in the Reich Post Office in 1923 remained employed in 1924.

50. Yver, "Femmes D'Aujourd'Hui, Enquète sur les nouvelles carrières famines," *RDDM* 49 (January–February 1929): 84–85, 88–89; Yver, "Nos Grandes Ecoles, La Faculté de Médécine," *RDDM* 51 (May–June 1929): 786; Silver, "Salon, Foyer, Bureau: Women and the Professions in France," *Journal of Sociology* 78 (January 1973).

51. Yver, "Femmes D'Aujourd'Hui, Avocates et Doctoresses" *RDDM* 49 (January–February 1929): 73–89; "Ingénieurs," *RDDM* 49 (January–February, 1929): 352–71; "Phar-macienne," *RDDM* 50: 133–46; "Redactrices et Journalistes," *RDDM* 50 (March–April 1929): 592–603.

52. Ramer, "The Transformation of the Russian Feldsher, 1864–1914," *Imperial Russia 1700–1917, Essays in Honor of Marc Raeff*, 47–154.

53. *Perepisi 1926 g.* 34: 94; *KSP 1926 g.*, vols. 25–33.

54. W. Horsley Gantt, "The Soviet's Treatment of Scientists," *Current History* 31 (October–March 1929–1930): 1151–57; Gantt, *Russian Medicine*, 185.

55. Grossman, "German Women Doctors," *Feminist Studies* 19 (Spring 1993): 66–68, 77.

56. Grossman, "German Women Doctors," 71–79; *SDDR 1925*, Band 408, 302–3.

57. "The Provision of Work for the Unemployed in the U.S.S.R.," *ILR* 22 (1): 59; M. E. Walker, "How Russian Women Are Working," *Contemporary Review* 196 (August 1934): 214–15; Tuve, *First Russian Women Physicians*, 124; *SSSR Strana Sotsialisma Stat. Sbornik*, 51; Clarke, *Soviet Economic Facts*, 26; Clark, *Position of Women in France*, 44–45. Soviet teachers earned 389 rubles per year in 1924, workers 536 rubles, and leading personnel the highest wages.

58. See "Cecil Blanche Woodham-Smith," *DNB* 1971–1980: 924; R. H. Tawney, "Eileen Edna le Poer Postan," *DNB* 1931–1940: 718; Alison M. Oram, "Serving Two Masters? The Introduction of a Marriage Bar in Teaching in the 1920s," *Sexual Dynamics of History*, 134–47.

59. Teachers' time budgets for 1926–1927 are cited by Zuzanek in *Work and Leisure in the Soviet Union*, 202–4. For English teachers' and governesses' salaries, see *Times Educational Supplement*, 7 January 1922, 11; 14 January 1922, 23; 1 January 1927, 12; *Times* (London), 2 February 1925, 3; 4 February 1925, 4.

60. *Times Educational Supplement*, 8 January 1927, 15; "Primary School Notes, The Women's Conference," *Times Educational Supplement*, January 1927, 9. The NUWT also protested unequal salaries and the takeover of headmistresses' jobs by headmasters in junior schools.

61. Clark, *Position of Women in France*, 53–54; Carles, *A Life of Her Own*, 75–125.

62. Sender, *Autobiography of a German Rebel*, 179–84. A socialist and a Jew, Sender fled Germany in 1933.

63. Linke, *Restless Days*, 336; Sender, *Autobiography*, 245; *Literary Digest*, 17 May 1930, 105.

64. "Cecil Blanche Woodham-Smith," *DNB* 1971–1980; Geneviève Tabouis, "Newspaper Woman: French Style," *The Living Age*, August 1939, 563; Brittain, *Testament of Friendship*, 264–67.

65. *Perepisi 1926 g.* 34: 70; *An. Stat.* 49: 13; *Gt. Br. 1921 Census*, 100–9; *SDDR 1925*, Band 402, III, 442.

66. Strumilin, "Time-budget of clerical employees in 1923," *Work and Leisure in the Soviet Union*, 181–82; Tuve, *First Russian Women Physicians*, 124–29.

67. Stites, *Women's Liberation Movement*, 372–73; Bronner, *La Lutte contre la Prostitution en URSS*; Field, "Prostitution in the Soviet Union," *The Nation* 142 (25 March 1936): 373–74; *An. Stat.* 49 (1933): 13.

Chapter 8

Political Dreams in the 1920s

After the First World War, feminism seemed triumphant, but it had only modestly transformed society. The war had decimated the male population, and English and French politicians feared being swamped by the female vote if they granted women suffrage. Consequently, only English women over the age of thirty were enfranchised, and French senators refused women the vote. For a variety of reasons, pacifism eclipsed feminism in France and England. In Germany, women's political activity resembled a U-shaped curve. Scores were elected to the Constituent Assembly and Reichstag at the beginning of the decade; their number declined in the mid 1920s but increased at the end of the decade. Soviet women's political activity increased in an upward slope among most classes and nationalities but was limited to the lower ranks of one party.

The franchise produced less change than expected. In England, gentry-class, business, and professional men continued to wield political power, leaving women and poor men underrepresented. In the German Social Democratic Party (SPD), seniority prevailed, undermining female participation. In the Soviet Union, the militarization of the Party during the Civil War excluded women from high positions. European governments showed little interest in ending class and gender distinctions. They adopted piecemeal legislation, eradicated some of women's civil incapacities, but withheld full equality.

In 1919, Soviet economists Nikolai Bukharin and Evgeny Preobrazhensky believed communal resources would facilitate women's economic and political participation, but failed to co-opt men into housework. Stalin thought that women's participation in economic and political life was essential for the state because they constituted half of the population.[1] He

233

saw women as instruments and was uninterested in their personal emancipation.

Socialists often gave lip service to women's emancipation, arguing that political and economic concerns took precedence over social, sexual, and cultural ones. Interpreting sexual morality as a "private affair," not a political issue, the Bolsheviks distanced themselves from the sexual revolution. Lenin scolded Zetkin for concentrating on sex problems when the political instruction of working-class women needed attention. He urged sexual restraint, believing that the proletariat did not need the intoxication of alcohol or sexual excess. Three Russian Communist Party leaders committed to women's liberation were Inessa Armand, Aleksandra Kollontai, and Iakov Sverdlov. In 1919, they urged the Party to establish Zhenotdel, a women's department, to draw women into the Party and liberate them from their downtrodden position. Zhenotdel published eighteen journals for women of various classes and nationalities, discussing women's emancipation, education, employment, health, and hygiene.[2] Unfortunately, Sverdlov's and Armand's untimely deaths in 1920 left Kollontai to advocate for women's liberation. Bolsheviks Elena Stasova, Angelika Balabanova, and Varvara Iakovleva were personally liberated, disdained work with women, and preferred "more serious" assignments. Nadezhda Krupskaia, Paulina Vinogradskaia, and Sophia Smidovich rejected women's sexual liberation. They accused Kollontai of advocating sexual license, whereas she endorsed sexual fulfillment, not libertine sexuality.[3]

Unlike European regimes, the Soviet government sponsored a variety of programs to liberate women and create a more egalitarian society. They established legal equality in the family, encouraged lower-class women to pursue higher education, provided legal advisers to inform women of their new rights, decriminalized prostitution, created mother and child health clinics, and legalized abortion. Unable to completely change their society in one decade, they ushered in limited progress. While some analysts focus on the inadequacy of Bolshevik emancipation programs, this chapter shows that increasing numbers of Soviet women of various classes and ethnic groups experienced increasing political empowerment. It compares their behavior with that of European women, who also made modest advances.[4]

Gaining the Vote

One of the major goals of nineteenth-century feminists was suffrage. Another hope was that "morally superior" enfranchised women would raise the tone of public life and transform existing systems. None anticipated scenarios in which feminists would not be elected or that those elected would be co-opted into the system without radically changing it. This chapter focuses on women's political achievements and struggles as well as their unrealized dreams.

Russia, 1917

When the Provisional Government replaced the Tsarist regime in February 1917, Russian women demonstrated to gain the vote in municipal and national elections. Women twenty years of age and over also received the right to serve as jurors and attorneys and obtained equal rank and title in the civil service. Sofia Panina became Deputy Minister of Education in the Provisional Government, fulfilling many feminist dreams.

After the Provisional Government pardoned political prisoners, many female revolutionaries returned from exile to participate in political life. One of the most dramatic persons to return was Maria Spiridonova (1884–1941), a Socialist Revolutionary (SR). Elected mayor of Chita in May 1917, she ordered all the prisons blown up. In the fall of 1917, Spiridonova and other leftist SRs supported the new Soviet government headed by Lenin, but by 1918 she and her colleagues had become disenchanted with Bolshevik policies. When an SR shot and wounded Lenin, Spiridonova was arrested and spent the remainder of her life in and out of Soviet prisons. She and other female revolutionaries and feminists saw their hopes trounced by the Bolsheviks. Yet their sad stories are only part of women's political experience in the 1920s.

The Soviet Union, 1918–1929

The new Soviet government confirmed women's right to elect and be elected in July 1918. It extended the franchise to those eighteen years of age and older, but weighted the votes of workers more heavily than those of peasants. The regime also excluded *byvshie liudy* (formerly privileged people) from suffrage. This class-based legislation excluded well-to-do feminists such as Anna Miliukova, Countess Sofia Panina, and Ariadna Tyrkova-Williams, who had worked so hard for women's suffrage. They had tangled with the new government, criticized Kollontai, and left Russia without realizing their dreams of participatory democracy.[5] Yet other suffragists, including Dr. Anna Shabanova, stayed in Russia, but did not participate in politics as they had anticipated doing. While women active in the SR and SD parties initially participated in the new Soviet government, during the Civil War (1918–1921) the Bolsheviks became more militant, excluding all other parties from politics.

By 1922, the Russian Communist Party Bolshevik (RKPb) had triumphed in Ukraine, Belorussia, and the Caucasus, and the Party became more authoritarian and less friendly toward women. By 1925, it controlled the Kirgiz, Uzbek, Tadzhik and Turkmen republics. The adjective *Soviet* applies to Slavic and Caucasian women from 1922 to 1925, and to all women in the Union from 1925 to 1929. As a noun, *soviet* refers to an organ of government: village (*volost*), city (*gorod*), county (*uezd*), province (*gubernia*), district (*oblast*), republic, or all-Union.[6]

Throughout the 1920s Russians predominated among women holding office at the gubernia and oblast levels in the national republics. In Ukraine and Belorussia, Jewish women constituted nearly half the paid officials at *okrug* and uezd levels. Russian and Jewish women pervaded paid political positions, Party membership, Party congresses, Zhenotdel, and some local soviets. However, the ethnic composition of female Party members changed, as the 1922 and 1927 Party censuses reveal (table 8.1).[7]

The increase in Party membership in all ethnic groups suggests that the *hudjum,* or "onslaught," to unveil and liberate Muslim women was drawing indigenous women into the Party.

Germany, 1918–1919

Following the German revolution of 1918, women aged twenty and older were enfranchised. Major political parties placed their names on voting lists, and they obtained almost 10% of the Reichstag seats and 2% of local council seats. They could vote in municipal elections in several states

Table 8.1. Female Party Members

	1922	1927		1922	1927
Russian	20,000	58,000	Tatar & Turkic	170	540
Jewish	5,000	9,000	Armenian	200	542
Ukrainian	1,000	5,600	Uzbek	16	83
Georgian	180	7,000	Kirgiz	11	84
Belorussian	200	——			

since 1907–08, and they soon composed 3% to 9% of the membership of the bourgeois political parties, 12% of the German Communist Party (KPD), and 22% of the German Social Democratic Party (SPD). With 900,000 members in bourgeois feminist groups and over 200,000 members in the SPD, they seemed poised to change society. Legally and socially their situation was democratic, with sizable numbers of workers and educated women elected to the Constitutional Convention (1919) and the Reichstag. However, antifeminism remained strong, and a suffrage opponent ran for a seat in the 1919 Assembly and won. Still, their overall involvement in local (*Gemeinde* and *Bezirk*) and state (*Staat* or *Landtag*) politics remained weak.[8]

England, 1918–1929

Unlike the 1918 German revolution, which granted an extremely democratic franchise to women, the British government in 1918 enfranchised women over the age of thirty who were householders, wives of householders, occupiers of property of five pounds annual value, or university graduates. These restrictions excluded 70% of wage-earning women from suffrage.[9] English women of property had participated in municipal, school board, Poor Law, and some county council elections prior to 1900, but they sought the parliamentary franchise to improve women's situation.

While some have argued that the British government granted the franchise as a reward for women's support on the home front during the war, this conclusion is debatable since the franchise was limited to women over the age of thirty and excluded young workers who had contributed to the war effort. Some have suggested that in the wake of revolution in Russia and Germany, it behooved British politicians to quiet dissatisfied groups by enfranchising soldiers, male servants, sons living at home, and women over thirty years of age, broadening the parliamentary electoral base from 7.7 million in 1910 to 21.3 million in 1918. In 1928, the government extended the parliamentary franchise to women twenty-one to twenty-nine years of age, expanding the electorate to 28.8 million. Although the franchise became more democratic in 1929, university graduates and businessmen retained a second vote, so the English electoral system had a different class bias from the Soviet. While the British franchise became more open, political life remained elitist. Men still dominated politics, and it was difficult for women to find safe constituencies in which to run.[10]

France, 1919–1924

French suffragists expected to win the vote as a reward for their war work, but they underestimated the anticlericalism and social conservatism of French Radical politicians. They were unprepared for a backlash linking feminism with Bolshevism and the depopulation of the nation. French deputies voted to enfranchise them in 1919 and 1924, but senators of the Radical Party blocked these attempts, believing that women would support conservative politicians if given the vote. Nor did French Socialists help, since they subordinated women's issues to the struggle against capitalism. During the 1920s, only the French Communist Party consistently supported women's issues. The French government remained Janus-faced, denying women political and legal equality and drafting pro-natalist antiabortion laws yet providing increased educational opportunities and equal pay for equal work in some occupations.[11]

Women's Initial Political Activity

English women's political participation on the national level was weaker than that of German and Russian women. Only 11 women, less than 1%, took seats in the 600-member House of Commons from 1919 to 1929. In contrast, German women accounted for 7% to 10% of Reichstag delegates, and Soviet women represented 9% of the delegates of the thirteenth Congress of Soviets in 1924. Voters in the Russian republic elected more than 500 women to governmental bodies and 25 to the Moscow City Soviet in 1917. Older, educated women initially predominated among politically active English and Soviet women. Yet, by 1929, Soviet women from all classes and ethnic groups had become politically active. Still, their participation was modest, given an adult female population of 42 million.[12]

The Soviet Union

Although many high ranking Bolshevichki (prewar women Party members) did not seek positions of power, many held significant posts in the Party and government. Kollontai (1872–1951) was appointed Commissar of Social Welfare (1917–1918) and Commissar of Agitation and Propaganda in the Ukraine (1919), served on the Central Executive Committee of the Russian Congress of Soviets (1920–1921), headed Zhenotdel (1920–1922), and held the post of Soviet ambassador to various Scandinavian countries from 1922 to 1945. Krupskaia (1869–1939) served as deputy in the Commissariat of Enlightenment until 1929. Inessa Armand (1875–1921) played an active part in the Central Executive Committee (TsIK) of the Moscow Provincial Soviet and the All-Russian Congress of Soviets, and headed Zhenotdel (1919–1920). Another Bolshevichka, Liudmilla Stal' (1872–1939) simultaneously served in the presidium of the Kronstadt Party Committee and the Executive Committee of the Kronstadt Soviet in 1918. Elena Stasova (1873–1966), known as Comrade Absolute, discharged her duties in the Party Central Committee and Secretariat (1919–1920). Sofia Smidovich (1872–1934) worked in the Commissariat of Enlightenment (1917–1919) and Zhenotdel (1922–1924). Klavdia Nikolaeva (1893–1941) and Alexandra Artiukina (1889–1969) directed Zhenotdel from 1924 to 1930. Rozaliia Zemliachka (1876–1947) fit in with the confrontational style of the Party and served in the Central Control Commission (CCC).[13]

The Party and state sought women's support to stabilize the regime and to improve women's lives. By 1929, 40% of peasant women and 65% of urban women in the Slavic republics were voting. Whereas 500 women had been elected to Soviet offices in 1917, by 1929 they held 300,000 local, regional, and national government positions. About 280,000 women held posts in rural soviets and 29,000 in city soviets.[14]

In terms of power, women's representation was small in the policy-making bureaus of the Party, but stronger in local soviets dealing with the "feminine issues" of welfare and education. Marie Mullaney found that women revolutionaries differed from their male counterparts in disdaining the cult of leader, rejecting the conquest of power, and refusing to make a fetish of leadership. They emphasized love, thinking that socialism meant community and devotion to the poor. Few cultivated the sangfroid that leadership demanded. Mullaney suggests that the problem was not men excluding women from politics, but women themselves shunning policy-making positions, preferring to be policy facilitators and executors instead. Barbara Clements agrees that Bolshevichki preferred local Party positions where they could directly influence workers and women. A few exceptions helped make policy prior to 1921, but after the Civil War they occupied the lower levels. Soviet women were not unique. European women also remained outside Party executive committees. Still, women's membership in the RKPb increased from 10,000 (2%) in 1917 to 30,500 during the Civil War to 137,000 (13%) in 1929. In contrast to the SPD, most of whose female members were housewives married to Socialist men, the Russian Communist Party identified women according to occupation: 42% of female members were white-collar workers and professionals; 6% students; 30% workers; 16%: artisans, domestic servants, and housewives; only 6% were peasants.[15] The Komsomol (Communist youth organization) claimed more than 430,000 young female members by 1929.

Germany

During the Weimar Republic (1919–1932), German women voted in impressive numbers, electing eighty-five female Reichstag delegates. Their combined SPD and KPD membership of 270,000 far outdistanced English and Soviet women's Party affiliation. Yet they accounted for few Party executive committee members, Party congress delegates, or provincial or city councilors.[16] The SPD used the seniority system to assign members to executive committees. Since German women had been excluded from political parties before 1908, men possessed greater seniority in committees.

Like British female M.P.s, female Reichstag members closed ranks with male Party members instead of acting as a gender bloc. Only slowly did they realize the shallowness of male support. Their colleagues ignored their requests, tabling all bills for women's access to education and abortion, divorce reform, or protective labor legislation. Moreover, it was "womanly women," not radicals, who triumphed in German politics in the 1920s.[17]

Reichstag biographies show incredibly busy women. Like some Bolshevichki, German women held a combination of national, state, and local government posts simultaneously. SPD members Marie Kunert and Louise Schiffgens served in the Reichstag and Prussian Landtag, while Johanna Reitze was in the Reichstag and Hamburg Parliament. In the Center Party, Helene Weber and Hedwig Dransfeld served in both the Reichstag and Prussian Landtag. Dr. Doris Hartwig-Bunger of the conservative Deutsche Volkspartie participated in the Reichstag and Saxony Landtag. Maria Schott and Annagreta Lehman, members of the rightist Deutchenationale Volkspartie, served in the Reichstag and the Saxony and Prussian Landtags. The lone Bavarian Party member in the Reichstag, Thusnelda Lang-Brumann, also participated in the Munich *Stadtrat* (city council). Clara Zetkin (KPD) held office in both the Reichstag and a Landtag.[18] Hildegard Wegschneider and Gertrude Hanna participated in the Prussian Landtag, and Minna Schilling, Emmy Beckman, Marie Luders, Anna Blos, and Frieda Hauke on the municipal level.

Although their Reichstag representation of eighty-five was much greater than the eleven British female M.P.s, their voting and office holding represented a U-shaped curve, declining during the middle of the decade but rising again in 1928 as politics became more polarized. Unlike the Soviet situation, where women's political gains were greatest on the local level, only 400 to 500 German women were elected to state and local posts in the 1920s. Women workers' replacement by returning veterans in the postwar years and the dismissal of married women workers in the mid 1920s undermined their political and trade union activity. Their membership in the SPD fell from 200,000 in 1920 to 130,000 in 1923, while in the trade unions it declined two-thirds from 1920 to 1926. Female SPD municipal officials dropped from 413 in 1919–1920 to 197 in 1925.[19]

The BDF (Bund Deutscher Frauenvereine) had 900,000 women members, while Jewish German women accounted for 50,000 in the JFB (Judischer Frauenbund). They were socially conservative, adhering to the doctrine of separate spheres where women's maternal nature, mildness, and patience complemented men's initiative in the public sphere.[20] The Protestant Ladies Auxiliary possessed half a million members in 1925, and women also belonged to the nationalist, anti-Semitic Konigin Luise Bund.

Female Nazi sympathizers and Party members felt hostile to the liberal Weimar Republic and wanted to return Germany to its mythical volkish past. In 1927, they composed half the spectators at Hitler's rally in Heidelberg, and they initially enjoyed a degree of autonomy because Nazi men ignored them. Some formed nationalist and religious groups, while others organized sewing circles where they discussed Nazi ideology. Modernists and traditionalists coexisted, agreeing that women had lost status in the modern industrialized world. Traditionalists emphasized devotion to family. Modernists believed that women had been reduced to mere decorative objects and wanted to revitalize German life. While Nazi men would "clean up the streets," they would improve the quality of life by working in the spheres of health, education, and social work. Many resembled Elfride Heidegger, wife of the philosopher Martin Heidegger, who admired German nationalism, romanticism, and the superiority of the German race. Protestants often believed God was using Hitler to restore Germany to its greatness. Yet these early leaders were eclipsed by Gertrud Scholtz-Klink, who brought all women's organizations into the Frauenschaft in 1933.[21]

Most preferred social work to politics, and the 1925 German census listed more than 34,000 women in social welfare positions, but only 286 in high-ranking political office. The Katholischer Frauenbund, a charitable church organization, had 1,660,000 female members. While 2,000,000 young women belonged to sports clubs, only 20,000 participated in the Socialist Labor Youth.[22] Their more active participation in church, welfare, and sports groups than in political organizations resembled English women's participation in the Women's Cooperative Guild and Soviet women's quasi-political delegatki meetings.

England

While women age thirty and over gained the parliamentary franchise in 1918, a backlash against them and ideological splits among feminists hindered women's election to Parliament and local government after the war. A leading suffragette, Annie Kenney, retired from politics when she married in 1921, thinking that since women had gained the franchise, everything would run smoothly. However, further splits developed among women as they joined the Conservative, Liberal, and Labour parties. Eleanor Rathbone concentrated on the problems of mothers and widows more than those of career women, while many "old style" suffragists continued to work for gender equality, not family allowances. Rathbone analyzed the feminization of poverty and how to counteract it. After her election to Parliament in 1929, she discovered that most male M.P.s were indifferent to women's issues at home and in the colonies. Few male reformers supported the banning of child marriage and clitoridectomy, and the *Times* was silent on these subjects. Whereas the Soviet government legally opposed child marriage and oppression of women in the Central Asian republics in the 1920s, English male politicians defended African men's right to "control their women."[23]

Further splintering occurred when some became preoccupied with pacifism in the 1920s. Still others formed the Six Point Program to promote widows' pensions, equal rights of guardians, equal pay for teachers, and equal opportunities for women in the civil service.[24] This political fragmentation resulted in the election of few women to Parliament prior to 1929.

Nancy Astor, the first woman member of Parliament, was conservative and antisuffragist. Wife of a wealthy M.P., she was elected to fill her husband's seat for the Conservative Party when he was called to the House of Lords in 1919. Ardent suffragettes Emmeline and Christabel Pankhurst, Emmeline Pethick Lawrence, and Ray Strachy stood for election, but lost. Instead, titled women such as Lady Astor and the Duchess of Atholl won. In her maiden speech of February 1920, Lady Astor noted that she was speaking for hundreds of women and children who could not speak for themselves. Even so, male acquaintances shunned her in the House of Commons and laughed at "women's issues."[25]

Gradually, female membership in political parties increased. By 1929, about 7,000 women belonged to the Independent Labour Party, 600 to the

British Communist Party, and 300,000 to the Labour Party. Like their SPD sisters, Labour Party M.P.s often emerged from the ranks of the trade unions: Ellen Wilkinson from the Amalgamated Union of Co-operative Employees, and Margaret Bondfield and Agnes Hardie from the Shop Assistants' Union. Wilkinson had also worked with suffragists in 1913, and Hardie as women's organizer for the Labour Party in Scotland from 1918 to 1923.[26] In 1929, the Labour and Liberal parties presented three times as many female candidates for election as did the Conservative Party, and nine female Labourites were elected, but only three Conservatives. Like men, women tended to be elected when their Party won in a landslide and to leave office when their Party lost.

Middle-class English women were most successful in local elections. In the 1919–1920 local elections, 680 women were returned to school boards, 2,039 to Poor Law boards, 263 to rural district councils, and 320 to county councils. By 1929, they accounted for 2,000 of 23,000 unpaid magistrates. Some working-class women were elected, and the number of Women's Cooperative Guild magistrates rose from 12 in 1920 to 125 in 1928. The guild had 190 Poor Law guardians in 1920, but 283 in 1928. The Labour Party had more than 500 serving as Poor Law guardians. Few women were elected to municipal and county councils because the positions were unpaid, involved time and travel, and were dominated by affluent, elderly gentry-class and professional men. By 1928, only four well-to-do women had been elected to the Lancashire county council.[27]

As women became more politically active, they participated in the Women's Advisory Committees of the major parties and guilds. The Women's Cooperative Guild membership rose from 30,000 in 1918 to 83,000 in 1929. Like German women, English women preferred philanthropic to political work. The 1921 English census recorded 2,727 social welfare workers, but only 233 paid political association officials.[28] It did not list unpaid political helpers or charity workers.

France

French feminism also suffered from divisions. One feminist group, the Conseil National des Femmes (National Women's Council), had a membership of 150,000. Others such as La Ligue pour le Droit des Femmes (League for the Rights of Women) had 100,000 members, the Union Française pour les Suffrages des Femmes (French Union for Women's Suffrage) had more than 100,000 in 1928, and the church-approved L'Union

National pour le Vote des Femmes (National Union for the Vote for Women) had a substantial membership. The shock of not obtaining the franchise increased the membership of many groups. Socialists and Communists gave lip service to women's equality, but women accounted for only 2% of the French Socialist Party's membership and 1% of the Communist Party membership in the 1920s. While 9,000 subscribed to the Communist Party's journal *Ouvrière (Woman Worker)*, only 2,000 women belonged to the French Communist Party. The Radical Party endorsed women's suffrage in the mid 1920s and appointed ten women to its executive committee, but they constituted only 1% of its membership. Though women did not gain the vote, they helped shift attention to social problems such as housing, health, and equal pay for government employees.[29]

Trade Unions

French women were also better represented in the quasi-political trade unions than in electoral politics, and they constituted 172,700 members (nearly 10%) of syndicat members in 1926. In England, 300,000 women belonged to trade unions, and 227 served as paid union officials. Two million German women participated in trade unions in the early 1920s, but their membership fell drastically due to the declining economy. In contrast to the German situation, Soviet female trade union members increased from 1 million to 3 million in the 1920s. This growth occurred because Soviet trade unions provided services such as housing, child care, vacation resorts, and educational programs. While feminists generally lamented the discrepancy between women's trade union activity and their low political participation rate, party leaders seemed uninterested in this problem.[30]

Social and Ethnic Factors

Social and ethnic factors also shaped women's political activities. In England, France, and the Soviet Union, it was mainly older, middle- and upper-class women who held high political posts. While German and Russian working-class women constituted strong minorities in their socialist parties, they seldom held top positions. Unlike England and Germany, where rural women played little part in politics, Slavic peasant women composed a high number of elected Soviet officials and delegatki (table 8.2).

The Communist Party's youth organization Komsomol also made headway among some young peasant women. According to Isabel Tirado, some

Table 8.2. Peasant Women's Political Participation, 1929*

Delegatki members	700,000
Elected to rural soviets	273,000
Presidents of village soviets	4,951
Volost executive committees	13,000
Uezd executive committees	2,270
Gubernia executive committees (RSFSR)	222
Central executive committee (USSR)	137
Paid positions in party or government	1,347

*Smitten, "K voprosu o regulirovani i rosta zhenshchin v partii," *Kom.*, Nov. 1923, 24-30; Roiatov, "Zhenskoe Dvizhenia," *BSE*, 25: 245-48; Nurina, "Delegatki," *BSE*, 33: 142; "Statisticheskie svedeniia o VKPb," BSE, 11: 542; T. H. Rigby, *Communist Party Membership in the USSR, 1917-1967*, 359-63; Kingsbury, *Factory, Family and Woman*, 267; Clements, "Baba and Bolshevik Russian Women and Revolutionary Change," *Soviet Union* 12 (Part 2, 1985): 161-84.

peasant girls' *chastushki* (songs) described the new, emancipated Soviet woman. Despite parental opposition to the regime due to the harsh grain requisitions of the early 1920s, some young girls became attached to Party members and even joined the Komsomol. One song announced: "I loved a Komsomol, I kept it hidden, But now everyone knows. All the same I'll love him." Another declared: "I am now a Komsomolka, I no longer wear a cross, Without any shame, To a meeting I will go." By 1925, women constituted 16% of the Komsomol, partly because it offered educational and cultural activities. Some Komsomolki rejected expensive church marriages and baptisms because civil ceremonies and Party rituals were cheaper.[31]

Ethnicity

Little ethnic diversity occurred among English female elected officials in the 1920s. Only one female M.P., the Duchess of Atholl (Conservative), represented a Scottish constituency in the mid 1920s. In 1929, another Scots woman, Jenny Lee (Labour, daughter of a miner), was elected to the House of Commons from New Lanark, Scotland. No women appear to have been elected from Wales. In Germany, the Reichstag rosters of 1924 and 1928 reveal few recognizable Jewish, Polish, or Danish names, and only three delegates were born outside Germany. Since only German citizens could be elected to the Reichstag, even Hitler, who was Austrian, could not be elected to the Reichstag.

More ethnic diversity existed in the Soviet Union, but Russian and Jewish women predominated in political life. In 1927, Russian women constituted 71% of the female Party membership. Jewish women's proportion fell from 16% in 1922 to 8% in 1927, partly because many identified themselves as Russian. The 1926 Soviet census found Russian women constituting 73% of all high-ranking female administrative officials, 66% of all mid-level okrug and uezd administrators, and 80% of low-level *raion* and *volost* officials. In Kazakhstan, Russian women constituted 68% of the paid political officials, in Azerbaidzhan 47%, in the Kirgiz republic 64%, in Turkistan 54%, and in Uzbekistan 66%. Russian and Jewish women also dominated political and administrative positions in Ukraine and Belorussia. Living in urban areas, Russian and Jewish women had greater access to higher education than did peasant and indigenous women. Of 56,198 women university students in 1926, 78% were Russian.[32]

Party Elite: Upper- and Middle-Class Women

In terms of socioeconomic status, half of female members of the VKPb were educated white-collar workers and students (mainly old gentry and middle class), 30% were workers; 16% artisans, domestic servants, and housewives; a mere 6% peasants. These numbers are similar to those of England, where female M.P.s were mainly middle- and upper-class: Lady Astor and the Duchess of Atholl, Conservative; Lady Iveagh and Vicountess Runciman, Liberal. Labour Party leaders Susan Lawrence, Grace Colman, and Margaret L. Davies also came from middle-class families. While some Labour leaders were born into working-class families, they often became middle-class by dint of their work as trade union officials or their university education. German female politicians emerged from a mixture of professional, middle-class, and trade union backgrounds.[33]

In the Soviet Union, Russian and Jewish women predominated in political life because they were more urban and better educated and had more time for political activity. Time budget studies show that professional workers had shorter workdays, spent less time at housework than did factory workers or peasants, and spent more time at political work. Some female Party members devoted themselves more to work than to romance. Kollontai depicts such a character, who remarks: "I have read many novels, and I know just how much time and energy it takes to fall in love, and I just do not have the time. Presently, we have an enormous load of work on our hands in the district."[34]

An analysis of women in Communist Party congresses, the Reichstag, and Parliament shows little circulation into those political elites. Soviet records indicate a small female leadership, composed mainly of Bolshevichki, with relatively few new members. Only nineteen female Party members attended three or more Party congresses from 1918 to 1927, while 80% attended only one. This resembled the situation in Germany and England, where Party elites were select, the disparity between women's activity in the trade unions and political parties was great, women's representation at Party congresses was weak, and women served as facilitators of policy, not makers of it.[35]

Despite the election of German working-class women to the Constituent Assembly in 1919, few of them were chosen again as Reichstag delegates. The majority of SPD female Reichstag delegates listed their occupation as housewife, even though they had worked as political activists or teachers. Born in the 1870s and 1880s, most were middle-aged in the 1920s and were free of childcare concerns. Soviet female political leaders were also middle-aged, but many were single, divorced, or separated. The correlation of marital status and political participation of German and English women was inversely related: most leftist female M.P.s were single, while Liberal and Conservative ones were married. Leftist SPD female Reichstag delegates were married, while those in bourgeois parties were single.

Biographies of female Reichstag delegates indicate that bourgeois deputies tended to have a secondary, teacher's seminary, or even university education, while SPD members usually attended only primary, middle, trade union, Party, or commercial school. Again, the situation of the English was the reverse: Labour female M.P.s possessed university degrees, while well-to-do Conservative and Liberal female M.P.s lacked higher education. The Bolshevichki had usually completed gymnasium but had no higher education, since universities remained officially closed to them prior to the war. Some Russian women revolutionaries studied at European universities, but few graduated.

Politically active families often spawned like-minded daughters. Kollontai and Stasova shared the same Russian radical governess, and Lenin's sisters had brothers active in revolutionary parties. In England, Lady Astor, the Duchess of Atholl, and Lady Iveagh were all married to M.P.s who had taken seats in the House of Lords. Cynthia Mosley, Eleanor Rathbone, and Susan Lawrence also emerged from politically active families. Mosley and

Lawrence rejected their families' Conservative politics by joining the Labour Party in the 1920s, and Rathbone broke with her family's Liberal Party affiliation by running as an independent in 1929. Margaret Bondfield, Mary Hamilton, and Jennie Lee came from families active in trade unionism. German Reichstag delegates came from bourgeois feminist as well as trade union and Party backgrounds. Hedwig Drausfeld, Gertrude Baumer, Anna Gierke, and Else Hofs had been active in the feminist movement; while Margaret Behn, Gertrude Hanna, Wihelmine Kahler, Ernestine Lutze, Anna Simon, and Johanna Tesch emerged from the trade unions; and Clara Zetkin, Minna Bollmann, Marie Juchacz, Frieda Luhrs, Elizabeth Rohl, Elfriede Ryneck, and Louise Schroder came from SPD ranks.[36]

Among the women elected to Parliament from 1918 to 1929, six were elected to seats previously held by their husbands: Lady Astor, Mrs. Philipson, and Lady Iveagh, Conservatives; and Mrs. Wintringham, Lady Terrington, and Vicountess Runciman, Liberals. They were experienced in electioneering and had public personae as philanthropists. Party Executive Committee members tended to be older women: Lady Astor, the Duchess of Atholl, Lady Iveagh, Susan Lawrence, Mary Macarthur, Grace Mary Colman, and Dr. Marian Phillips.[37]

After the Labour gains in 1924, Ellen Wilkinson, Susan Lawrence and Margaret Bondfield gained Party sponsorship for Parliament seats. The Labour victory of 1929 returned several single female trade unionists and socialists such as Jennie Lee, Mary Hamilton, Dr. Marian Philips, E. Picton-Turbervill, Dr. Ethel Bentham, and Dorothy Jewson. Eleanor Rathbone, elected as an Independent, was also unmarried. The female political elite was well-to-do, and more working-class English women participated in the Women's Cooperative Movement than in the British Labour or Communist parties. Susan Lawrence, Mrs. B. Ayrton-Gould, and Mrs. J. L. Adamson represented women on the Labour Executive Committee for years, preventing the circulation of other women into that body.[38]

Working-Class Women's Politics

Working-class women were more active in trade unions than in political parties. By 1927, several hundred thousand Soviet women factory workers had joined trade unions, but only 40,000 had joined the Communist Party.[39] A fundamental difference between German and Soviet working-class women was that women in the SPD were more likely wives of workers, whereas Communist Party members were workers themselves as well as wives of workers. Working-class women also differed in their expectations. English and German women often left work at the time of marriage, whereas Soviet and French women tended to combine work and marriage. European culture promoted the notion that women's self-realization lay in married life and encouraged romantic escapism in novels and film, whereas Bolshevik culture prescribed economic and political emancipation and participation for married and single women. Inculcating this message into traditional society was not easy, and Bolshevik rhetoric appealed mainly to young women workers.

Although the Communist Party census of 1927 ignored the marital status of Party members, the 1926 census indicates that 49% of female textile workers were married. Therefore, a typical working-class female Party member was a young, married, Russian textile worker. This profile was widely accepted, and Soviet writers used it to depict Party activists. They differed greatly from European workers addicted to romantic escapism. German poet Bruno Schonlank found factory workers, sales girls, and seamstresses spinning golden fairy tales of true love. They went to the movies, swallowed the lies, and let themselves be led astray.[40]

Young English girls also went to the pictures to escape into a dream world for a while. Soviet workers also indulged in daydreams and escapist literature, but such behavior was not the prevailing message of Soviet art and propaganda. Romantic escapism undermined the discipline and time commitments that political participation required. Yet without adequate household help and child care, it was almost impossible for married workers to assume political duties. While Bolshevik literature advised women to become politically conscious, it was not easy because many husbands resented political work that took their wives away from them.[41]

Working-class women who were elected to city soviets showed a higher degree of Party affiliation (*partiinost'*) than did urban delegatki (delegates). They were more politically active than European women, constituting 25% of elected city officials, compared to German and English women's 5%. Like their Soviet sisters, working-class women in England found advancement in the Labour Party difficult unless they held important union positions or were married to a high-ranking trade unionist.[42]

Given the hostility to women's liberation and lingering patriarchal attitudes in European and Soviet society, it is amazing that some Soviet women workers developed the political consciousness they did. One Soviet woman appreciated that the Soviets taught her to read and explained things about politics. Many working-class Party members worked in textile production, but not all. The famous Bolshevichka Klavdiia Nikolaeva (1893–1944) was a printer who came from a poor family. She participated in the printers' union and was arrested and imprisoned. She became a Marxist and Kollontai's protégé. In 1925, Nikolaeva backed Zinoviev in the inter-Party struggles and subsequently lost her post as head of Zhenotdel.[43]

Soviet working-class heroines made incredible sacrifices in giving up marriage, children, even their old selves to follow their principles. Kollontai's heroine Vasilisa Malygina rejects marriage to a philandering NEP man. Leaving him, she says: "No more Vladimir now, just the Party. I feel as though I have been through a personal revolution."[44] Gladkov's heroine Dasha Chumalova sacrifices her daughter Nurka for her political work. Glebov's character Glafira gives up her old self in order to become a more resolute woman. She tells her wandering husband that she has her own road to travel, and she will not permit him to block her path. A river does not flow backwards, and she will not be as she was. The majority of ordinary working-class women in Europe and the Soviet Union seemed to feel comfortable with the old ways. They were seldom able to take advantage of the changes that were legally available since household and factory work prevented their "real" emancipation.[45]

Struggles for Empowerment

European and Soviet women occupying high political posts shared several common characteristics: they were well educated, middle-aged, had few or no children, and worked in deputy positions or in "feminine" fields such as education, public health, housing, unemployment, or social welfare. Soviet women also served in Zhenotdel and the investigative divisions of the government (RKI) and Party (CCC).[46] Few working-class or peasant women held high positions because they lacked the education and time such posts required.

The Soviet Union

Just as European women shunned private clubs and bars, where decisions and serious politics took place, Soviet women avoided policy-making bodies such as the politburo and Central Committee. Many were at odds with the Party elite. At the Tenth Party Congress in 1921, Kollontai and Balabanova objected to NEP's capitalist elements and to the suppression of the soldiers, sailors, and workers at Kronstadt. Kollontai rejected Lenin's view of the Party as the vanguard of society, insisting that communism cannot be created from above but develops from below. In retaliation, Lenin accused Kollontai of "syndicalist deviations" and scandalous personal behavior, that is, marriage to a revolutionary half her age. For punishment, the Party exiled her, making her ambassador to Scandinavia from 1923 to 1945. From abroad, she continued criticizing sleazy NEP men and women in her novellas. But her stories were published in small editions and reached mainly a female audience.

Horrified by Kronstadt and Lenin's vicious attacks on Kollontai, Balabanova wrote to Trotsky:

> You see, Lev Davidovich, I am on a razor's edge: another
> slight move . . . and I shall be a demagogue. I cannot speak
> today as I did before the new economic policy. Things have
> changed: I would not be able to speak the truth, therefore, I
> prefer to leave. I have given thousands of speeches, I may
> have been mistaken more than once, but never have I spo-
> ken a word which was not consistent with my convictions.[47]

She then resigned from the Party and left. In 1925, Bosh committed suicide in protest against Stalin's role in the Party and Trotsky's dismissal as head of the Red Army.[48]

Kollontai and Balabanova had been unprepared for the attacks against them for opposing NEP and the suppression of Kronstadt. Still, no class of Soviet women escaped male abuse. One factory worker complained that her husband was a good revolutionary but did not want her to be one. Another told of her husband's objections to her meetings and that he took a chair to hold her back by force. She picked up another chair and told him that he hadn't killed her under Nicholas, and now she was free to attend meetings. Peasant women were often harassed by their menfolk, who grumbled that they had not made the revolution so that their wives would be elected and they (the men) would sit at home.[49] Nor was it easy for women to combat the old-fashioned ideas of husbands and fathers who felt disgraced if their wives or daughters were elected to a local soviet. Although verbally and physically attacked for attending the quasi-political delegatki or Zhenotdel meetings or for being elected to village soviets, Slavic peasant women seemed to escape the maiming and killing their Muslim sisters sometimes encountered when they challenged established customs by participating in unveiling ceremonies in the late 1920s.[50]

Thus, the Party silenced insubordinate female members by demotion, disregard, exile, and suicide. It tolerated deferential ones, such as A. V.

Artiukina and E. G. Smitten, who accepted the Party line and only criticized the Party's failure to seriously recruit women.[51] Few Bolshevichki possessed or cultivated the behavior that Party leadership required. By 1929, few women remained in positions to object to collectivization, industrialization, the purges, or the closing of Zhenotdel and its journals *Kommunistka* and *Delegatka*.

Muslim Women in the Soviet Union

In the late 1920s, some Russian female Party activists and emancipated Muslim women in Central Asian republics experienced abuse, mutilation, even death. When they sought redress in local courts, Muslim male Party leaders often refused to protect them. Contrary to Party and government directives encouraging women's liberation, some Muslim Party members forbade their wives to unveil or to attend meetings. The Party's policy of *Korenizatsiia* (the promotion of national culture and cadres) usually meant the advancement of native men to positions of authority in the Party, government, and cooperatives, undermining women's liberation and lowering the proportion of indigenous women voting and being elected.[52] Although President Kalinin encouraged local Central Asian officials to inform women of their new rights and to emancipate them from the "old ways," most Muslim political leaders did little to facilitate women's emancipation. The real liberators of Muslim women proved to be Russian, Ukrainian, and Jewish Zhenotdel members. They directed Red propaganda trains, established reading rooms, health clinics, and legal aid bureaus, and organized unveiling ceremonies called *hudjum* (Turkish for *onslaught*).

These activities yielded mixed results. While Muslim men still oppressed women, some glimmers of hope appeared in newly established women's clubs and legal consultations. On a visit to Tiflis in 1924, Clara Zetkin heard some Muslim women tell of being sold into marriage when they were only ten or twelve years old, beaten with clubs or whips, treated like slaves, and rented out as mistresses. No official helped them until Zhenotdel provided legal advisers in the mid 1920s. In the midst of such subjection, the women's club in Tiflis grew from 40 members in 1923 to 1,400 in 1929. It was difficult for the Party to propagandize among these downtrodden women, because most of them were illiterate and they felt obliged to uphold the culture which oppressed them. As late as 1926, less than 1% of Turkic and Kirgiz women were literate. As transmitters of culture, many Muslim women probably did not want to be "liberated" from their cultural traditions. Another problem was the linguistic limitations of activists, who seldom understood indigenous languages and were unable to communicate with down-trodden Islamic women. As a result, much of their political work focused on Slavic women in the Central Asian cities. When Party activists understood the indigenous women's languages, their work proved successful. In the Sterlitamaksky canton of the Bashkir republic, Zhenotdel leaders drew 700 Bashkir women into cooperative organizations where they elected 75 women to district delegatki meetings.[53] Unveiling tens of thousands of women proved so socially disruptive that the Party abandoned this tactic on the eve of collectivization in 1929.

Muslim women were not all the same. Although most women in Baku still wore veils and shawls on the streets in the 1920s, agitation for the education and unveiling of women had occurred since 1900. The Ali Bayramov Club in Baku provided legal, educational, and social services for several thousand Turkic women. It provided a nursery and classes in sewing, embroidery, rug making, midwifery, music, dancing, and literacy. By 1929, Russians took control of the Azeri women's movement, its Zhenotdel, and its journal *Sharg Gadini*. Although some educated Azeri teachers contented themselves with running social and literacy clubs, others objected to their role as a "surrogate proletariat" within the male-dominated Party. One emancipated Azeri woman criticized Korenizatsiia because it promoted men, not women, to authoritative positions. She believed that women needed to assume more leadership roles and should not be confined to feminine occupations. Her complaints stopped when Russian editors took over *Sharg Gadini*. Russian and Azeri factions also developed over the wearing of the veil. Azeri who worked in the clubs often wore the veil, whereas Russian activists did not, and they criticized those who did. Still, the Azeri women's clubs increased literacy and participation in vocational, technical, and political education. By 1928, Azeri women constituted 26% of the female Party membership. Similarly, Turkmen women constituted 31% of their republic's Party membership in 1929.[54]

England

English women also experienced obstacles in exercising political power. Countess Markiewicz, an Irish rebel, was elected to Parliament in 1918. Imprisoned for her Irish political activity, she was unable to take her seat. So Lady Astor, who was the sole female M.P. from 1919 to 1922, asked Conservative Party members to nominate more women candidates because it was impossible for her to singlehandedly represent the women's point of view. Some Conservative chairmen endorsed women candidates, but others balked at promoting women in their constituencies. The Liberal and Labour parties also gave lip service to women's participation, failing to support female candidates, provide them safe districts in which to run, or raise campaign funds for them on an equal basis with men. In 1919, Emmeline Pankhurst ran as the Conservative candidate in Whitechapel, even though the poor, foreign-born population was unlikely to vote for a Conservative. For years, Eleanor Rathbone lacked a safe constituency. Defeated in 1922, she won in 1929 as an Independent for the Combined Universities, which appreciated her well-reasoned arguments and political independence.[55]

As a youth, Vera Brittain found the patronizing attitudes of men in the Liberal Party repulsive. When the men had finished their speeches, they invited the "ladies" to give their views. However, this was really the signal for refreshments, since no lady's views could possibly be worth hearing. She thought Liberal Party officials were terrified of change.[56]

No English party nominated women for uncontested seats in the 1924 general election. Of 41 female candidates standing for election, only 4 won: Miss Wilkinson (Labour) and Lady Astor, the Duchess of Atholl, and Mrs. Philipson (Conservative). In 1929, the Labour Party endorsed 68 women among 1,734 candidates, and a paltry 9 Labour women were elected, along with 3 Conservatives and 1 Liberal.[57]

During the 1920s, English female politicians discovered that issues such as widows' pensions were acceptable to address, whereas equality, equal pay for equal work, or the enfranchisement of women under thirty were resisted. In 1924, Susan Lawrence objected to the limited female franchise and was assured by other M.P.s that what she perceived as obstruction was "nothing like the real thing."[58] Mrs. Terrington was also stunned at the lack of political equality. After five years in Parliament, Lady Astor understood that men did not want women in the House of Commons and made it an uncongenial place. Women felt uncomfortable with the combative oratory, the late hours, and the drinking in bars and cloakrooms. Some lamented the lack of a helpmeet. Ellen Wilkinson complained:

> Oh! for a wife. If I had a wife, she might have collected these (letters), drafted answers and finally typed them. She would help with the women's section, give a hand with the bazaar, and when I get home fagged out, have a delicious meal ready for me.[59]

Nor did the 1919 Sex Disqualification (Removal) Act provide equity. Lady Rhondda asked the House of Lords if she might occupy her deceased father's seat, but they replied that the new law granted women opportunity, not rights. While a few women gained entry to the legal profession, and served as jury members, none gained a seat in the House of Lords, became a priest in the Church of England, or obtained high posts in the civil service. The Duchess of Atholl indicated that the Sex Disqualification (Removal) Act made women eligible for public functions but did not guarantee access to or employment in previously closed arenas.[60] Despite its title, it failed to restructure English society.

France

French women's energy also splintered into a variety of feminist and pacifist groups in the 1920s. Although they could not serve as delegates or permanent officials to the League of Nations, some found more political freedom in Geneva than in Paris. Some worked for the League as secretaries, clerks, translators, and typists, and a few as deputy heads of sections or in the International Labour Organization. Some French women went to Geneva to "have a good time," and their behavior tarnished the reputations of serious women who were subject to sarcasm and anecdotes in the French press.[61]

Germany

The fate of German female Reichstag delegates resembled that of English M.P.s. As long as they confined themselves to family issues, they found support among male politicians. When they discussed reforms such as pay equity or employment rights for married women, they found little encouragement, except among Communists. Like their English sisters, German women were unprepared for heckling on the Reichstag floor and felt uneasy in a system that declared: "If you want to be heard, you have to say everything three times and pound your fist on the table."[62]

Conclusion

Women in the Soviet Union and Europe had similar political dreams, struggles, and nightmares in the early twentieth century. Although Soviet women did not achieve political equality in the 1920s, significant changes increased their political consciousness, reducing the passivity, patriarchy, and semisavagery in their lives. Indeed, many Soviet peasant women and working-class women gained a new sense of dignity through their participation in the delegatki movement and work in local Soviets. As one peasant woman remarked in 1927:

> Yet I think it is a little better. Men are ashamed to beat their
> wives so often. Formerly after holidays one could not get
> up from the beating. . . . ʹI think also they are afraid. A
> Woman in the next village got a divorce.[63]

Just as many well-to-do Russian women had become self-conscious and strong-minded in the nineteenth century, increasing numbers of working-class and peasant women did so in the 1920s.

One of the saddest aspects of women's emancipation in the Soviet Union was its sacrifice to the Five-Year Plans in the 1930s. Just as women were beginning to participate in politics, the Party called a halt to their political emancipation so it could mobilize the energy of the country for industrialization and collectivization. Deciding that women's liberation was not too important, the Party abandoned the unveiling ceremonies for Muslim women and closed the Zhenotdel, its journal *Kommunistka,* and many delegatki organizations in 1930. Moreover, Azeri women's continued demands for political roles antagonized the center, and a Party secretary purged the leadership of the journal *Sharg Gadini* in 1933.[64]

In England, women's progress occurred more slowly than anticipated. From 1918 to 1928, only eleven women were elected to the House of Commons, but with the extension of the franchise in 1928, the number of female M.P.s doubled in the election of 1929. Yet society did not change overnight, because many English men and women opposed change. In turning from suffrage to social reform, many women encountered significant opposition.[65]

In Germany, women got off to a good start in the elections to the Constituent Assembly in 1919, but the female political elite declined in the mid 1920s. The decade that began by promising so much for women ended up with more modest participation than expected. However, in light of their total exclusion from power in the nineteenth century, modest inroads were made. By the late 1920s, female membership in the SPD, trade unions, local politics, and elections increased again. At the end of the decade, neither Soviet nor European women anticipated the effect that Stalin, Hitler, the Great Depression, and pronatalism would have on their lives in the next decade.

Notes

1. Clara Zetkin, "My Recollections of Lenin: An Interview on the Woman Question," *Feminism, The Essential Historical Writings*, 337–39; N. Bukharin and E. Preobrazhensky, *ABC of Communism*, 178–79, 399; Vladimir Lenin, *The Emancipation of Women*, 66–72; *Woman Question, Selections from the Writings of Marx, Engels, and Stalin*, 44.

2. The journal *Kommunistka* (*Woman Communist*) was for party members and leaders. *Delegatka* (*Woman Delegate*) was for newly active women, *Krest'ianka* for women peasants, *Rabotnitsa* for women workers, *Kummunarka Ukrainy* for Ukrainian women, *Krasnaia Sibiriachka* for Siberian Women, *Sharg Gadini* (*Women of the East*) for Azeri women in Azerbaidzhan, and *Ael Tendygi* (*Equality for Women*), Kazakhstan. There were others for domestic servants, and different ethnic groups.

3. Paulina Vinogradskaia, *Pamiatnye Vstrechi*, 53; Alix Holt, *Alexandra Kollontai, Selected Writings*, 201–4.

4. Historians discussing the social revolution for women include: Elizabeth Wood, *The Baba and the Comrade*; Wendy Goldman, *Women, the State, and Revolution*; Mary Buckley, *Women and Ideology in the Soviet Union*; Barbara Evans Clements, *Bolshevik Women* and "The Birth of the New Soviet Woman," in *Bolshevik Culture*; Helene Carrere d'Encause; *The Great Challenge: Nationalities and the Bolshevik State 1917–1930*; Wendy Z. Goldman, "Women, the Family, and the New Revolutionary Order in the Soviet Union," in *Promissory Notes: Women in the Transition to Socialism*, ed. S. Kruks; Gail Lapidus, *Women and Soviet Society*; Richard Stites, *The Women's Liberation Movement in Russia*.

5. Ariadna Tyrkova-Williams left Russia and recounted her displeasure with the new Soviet government in *From Liberty to Brest-Litovsk: The First Year of the Russian Revolution*, 78–79, 405–9. She criticized Aleksandra Kollontai for her pacifism during World War I and for making the Alexander Nevsky Monastery into a home for invalids. She described Kollontai as a "militant atheist, whose logical capacity is not so strong as her revolutionary ardour." She had trouble publishing her criticism because Kollontai was married to a Bolshevik sailor named Dubenko, whose friends would lead an armed response.

6. Meisal, *Materials for the Study of the Soviet System*, 49–50, 85–89; Barbara Clements, *Bolshevik Women*; NEH Seminar on Russian State Building and Imperialism, led by Mark von Hagen, Columbia University, Summer 1996.

7. *KSP 1926 goda*: "Russia" 26: 146, 162; "Ukraine" 28: 134, 205; 29: 66, 134; 30: 70, 270, 384; "Belorussia" 27: 116–17; "Armeniia" 31: 279; "Kazakh ASSR" 25: 70; "Azerbaidzhan SSR" 30: 182; "Kirgiz ASSR" 33: 243; "Turkman SSR" 33: 48; "Tadzhik ASSR" 32: 177–78; "Uzbek SSR" 32: 76; "Gruzii SSR" 31: 382–83; *Perepisi VKPb 1927 g.* 139; Institut istorii partii pri TsK KP Tadzhikistana, *Kommunisticheskaia Partiia Tadzhikistana v Tsifrakh za 50 let (1924–1974)*, 18; Institut istorii partii pri TsK KP Turkmenistana, *Kommunisticheskaia Partiia Turkmenistana v tsifrakh, 1924–1974*, 17, 26; P. "Dobrovol'noe obshchestvo 'Za novye byt'," *Kom.* July 1928, 84–85; G. N. Serebrennikov, *Zhenskii trud v SSSR*, 175ff Azade-Ayse Rorlich, "The 'Ali Bayramov' Club," 221–39. Census figures do

not always match other sources because there could be Russian, Jewish, and indigenous women in a republican party.

8. *Reichstags Handbuch, II and III Wahlperiode 1924 and IV Wahlperiode 1928*; Hans Beyer "Die Frau in der politishcen Entscheidung" (1932) as excerpted in Otto Busch, Monika Work, and Wolfgang Wolk, *Wahlerbewegungen in der deutschen Geschichte*, 302; Won Dr. R. Hartwig, "Das Frauenwahlrecht in der Statistik," *Allgemeines Statistisches Archiv* 1 (1931): 173–81; Marion Kaplan, "Sisterhood under Siege: Feminism and Anti-Semitism in Germany, 1904–1938," 174–93 in Renate Bridenthal, *When Biology Became Destiny*; Pore, *A Conflict of Interest: Women in German Social Democracy 1919–1933*, 56; Koonz, *Mothers in the Fatherland*, 30ff; Frevert, *Women in German History*, 168–74; Jean H. Quataert, *Reluctant Feminists in German Social Democracy, 1880–1917*; Oral interview with David Hackett History Department, UTEP, April 3, 1992.

9. Dorothy Jewson, *Times* (London), 1 March 1924, 4.

10. Ray Strachy, *The Cause*, 367–84; D. E. Butler, *The Electoral System in Britain Since 1918*, 172; Brian Harrison, "Women in a Men's House, The Women M.P.s, 1919–1945," *Historical Journal* 29: 3 (1986), 625; *The History of Lancashire County Council 1889–1974*, 50–75.

11. Steven C. House, "More Minerva than Mars: The French Women's Rights Campaign and the First World War," 99–113 in *Behind the Lines, Gender and the Two World Wars*; "Frenchwomen and the Vote," *Times* (London), 18 February 1929, 11; Reynolds, *France Between the Wars, Gender and Politics*; Steven House and Anne Kenney, *Women's Suffrage and Social Politics in the French Third Republic*; Charles Sowerine, "The Organization of French Socialist Women, 1880–1914: A European Perspective for Women's Movements," *Historical Reflections* 3 (2): 3–4; Marilyn Boxer, "French Socialism, Feminism, and the Family," *Third Republic/TR* (1977), no. 3–4: 164–67; Clark, *Position of Women in Contemporary France*, 83, 239.

12. *VPN 1926 g.*, Table II, 51: 27.

13. *Slavnye Bolshevichki*, 43–44, 86–87, 204–8; "Tri sud'by, zhenshchiny russkoi revoliutsii, S. Smidovich, L. Stal, and A. Kollontai," *Rabotnitsa* (1972), 3: 10–11; Clements, *Bolshevik Women*.

14. E. Smitten, "K voprosu o regulirovanii i rosta zhenshchin v partii," *Kom.*, November 1923, 24–30; F. Roiatov, "ZhenskoeDvizhenia," *BSE* 25: 245–48.

15. Mullaney, "Gender and the Socialist Revolutionary Role, 1871–1921," *Historical Reflections* 11 (1984): 124–32; Samokhvalova, "Sostav Kommunistok," *Kom.* 9 (1926): 26; *BSE* 11: 542; Clements, *Bolshevik Women*, 162.

16. *Reichstags-Handbuch II and III Wahlperiode 1924 and IV Wahlperiode 1928*; Koonz, "Conflicting Allegiances: Political Ideology and Women Legislators in Weimar Germany," *Signs* 1 (Spring 1976): 664ff.; Frevert, *Women in German History*, 171–74; Thonnessen, *The Emancipation of Women*, 16, 132–33, 144; Pore, *A Conflict of Interest*, 40, 56; Richard Hunt, *German Social Democracy 1918–1933*, 71–103. Comprising 8% of the Reichstag delegates, they constituted less than 4% of city council delegates.

17. Koonz, *Mothers in the Fatherland*, 32–34.

18. Other SPD Reichstag delegates serving in city and county offices included Elise Vicker Bartels, Marie Kunert, and Matilde Wurm (Berlin); Maria Arning

(Duisburg); Anna Nemitz (Charlottenburg); Louise Schiffgens (Aachen); Louise Schroeder (Altona); Berta Schulz (Herne); Tony Sender (Frankfurt); Anna Siemsen (Dusseldorf); and Anna M. Stegman (Dresden). *Reichstags Handbuch* II, III: 370–559; IV: 273–471; *Grosse Frauen der Weltgeschichte*, 49–56, 71, 135, 186, 208, 302, 422, 436–37, 453, 492, 509; *International Dictionary of Women's Biography*, 289, 419, 450, 490, 515.

19. Koonz, *Mothers in the Fatherland*, 30; Thonnessen, *The Emancipation of Women*, 144, 116, 132.

20. Marion Kaplan, "Sisterhood under Siege: Feminism and Anti-Semitism in Germay, 1904–1938," *When Biology Became Destiny*, 175–81.

21. Koonz, "Nazi Women before 1933: Rebels against Emancipation," 555–63; Ettinger, *Hanah Arendt/Martin Heidegger*, 33, 52–53; Michael Phayer, *Protestant and Catholic Women in Nazi Germany*, 26; Johnpeter Horst Grill, *The Nazi Movement in Baden, 1920–1945*, 223–24.

22. *SDDR 1925, Band 402, III*, 758, 794; Frevert, *Women in German History*, 173-77, 202-3; Thonnessen, *The Emancipation of Women*, 144.

23. *Times* (London), 12 December 1929, 9b; Susan Pedersen, "National Bodies, Unspeakable Acts: The Sexual Politics of Colonial Policy-Making," *Journal of Modern History* 63 (December 1991): 664–65.

24. Hilda Kean, "Searching for the Past in Present Defeat: The Construction of Historical and Political Identity in British Feminism in the 1920s and 1930s," *Women's History Review* 3 (1994): 57–80; Muriel Mellown, "Lady Rhondda and the Changing Faces of British Feminism," *Frontiers* 9 (1987): 7–13.

25. Brittain, *Lady into Woman*, 50, 73; House of Commons, *Women in the House of Commons*, Public Information Office: London, 3. Thanks to Laurie Tice for information about Eleanor Rathbone in her History Honors paper, University of Texas, El Paso, May 1994.

26. About 200,000 English women belonged to the Labour Party and 400 to the British Communist Party in the mid 1920s. *Times* (London), *The Labour Party Report of the 27th Annual Conference*, 20, 24; F. W. Craig, *British Electoral Facts 1885–1975*, 96–97; Strachey, *The Cause*, 350–86; Artiukhina, "8 marta v 1928 gody," *Kom.*, February 1928, 13; Pamela M. Graves, *Labour Women, Women in British Working-Class Politics 1918–1939*, 156, 231; oral interview with John Stack, 20 April 1992.

27. Appendices B and C in *Ladies Elect, Women in English Local Government 1865–1914* by Patricia Hollis; Brittain, *Lady into Woman*, 15–19, 42–49; Elsie M. Lang, *British Women in the Twentieth Century*, 24-25; Graves, *Labour Women*, 168–76ff; *A History of Lancashire County Council 1889–1974*, 58, 60–63, 405.

28. Gt. Br., *Census for Eng. and Wales 1921*, 19.

29. Artiukhina, "IV s'ezd VKP(b) i nashi zadachi," *Kom.*, January 1926, no. 1: 14; "8 marta v 1928 godu," *Kom.*, February 1928, 13; Clark, *The Position of Women in Contemporary France*, 83, 210–51; Reynolds, *France Between the Wars*, 170–71. Reynolds found 400 French women in the party in 1929, and Artiukhina 2,000 a few years earlier.

30. Associations et Syndicats," année 1926 in *Annuaire Statistique de la France* (1929) 45: 99; Clark, *Position of Women in France*, 78; Gt. Br., *Census of Eng. and Wales 1921*, 19; Gertrud Hanna, "Women in the German Trade Union

Movement," 8 (1923): 26–29; Thonnessen, *The Emancipation of Women*, 144; Y. D. Yemelyanova "The Social and Political Activity of Soviet Women," in *Soviet Women*, 53; "Zhenskoe Dvizhenie," *BSE* 25: 251; Artiukina, "XIV S'ezd VKPb i nashi zadachi," *Kom.*, 1926, no. 1: 10–15; E. Smitten, "K voprosu o regulirovanii rosta zhenshchin v partii 1927 g.," *Kom.*, 1927, no. 11: 25–30; *Labour Party, Report of the Annual Conference*, 160; Lucy Middleton, *Women in the Labour Movement*, 194; Pamela Brookes, *Women at Westminster*, 65–68; Eastman, *On Women and Revolution*, 141–42; McKenzie, *British Political Parties*, 277.

31. Isabel Tirado, "The Village Voice," *The Carl Beck Papers* 1008: 17–18, 35–47, 50–52.

32. *KSPN 1926 g.*, "Russia" 26: 146, 162; "Ukraine" 28: 134, 205; 29: 66; 30: 70, 270, 384; "Belorussia" 27: 116–17; "Armeniia" 31: 279; "Kazakh ASSR" 25: 70; "Azerbaidzhan SSR" 30: 182; "Kirgiz ASSR" 33: 243; "Turkmen SSR" 33: 48; "Tadzhik ASSR" 32: 177–78; "Uzbek SSR" 32: 76; "Gruzii SSR" 31: 382–83. Russian women held 47% of high-ranking positions in Ukraine, Jewish women 29%, and Ukrainian women 23%. In Belorussia, high-ranking female employees were 53% Jewish and 13% Russian. At lower levels, Jewish women predominated in both republics.

33. Samokhvalova, "Sostav Kommunistok," *Kom.* 9 (1926): 26; Hunt, *German Social Democracy*, 103. One survey found the female SPD membership to be 8% petty bourgeois, 18% workers, 67% housewives, 6% pensioners.

34. Strumilin, "Biudzhet vremeni russkogo rabochego, *Kom.* 6 (1923): 22–23; Kollontai, "Liubov' Triokh Pokolenii" in *Liubov' Pchel Trudovykh*, 43–44; Kollontai, "Three Generations," in *Love of Worker Bees*, 207.

35. VII S'ezd RKPb., *Stenograficheskii otchet*, 200–6 (hereafter abbreviated *S.O.*); VIII S'ezd RKPb, *S.O.*, 451–90; IX S'ezd RKPb., *S.O*, 573 ff; X S'ezd RKPb., *S.O.*, 716–59; XI S'ezd RKPb., *S.O.*, 583–604; XII S'ezd RKPb., *S.O.*, 729–59; XIII S'ezd RKPb., *S.O.*, 710–60; XIV S'ezd RKPb., *S.O.*, 1004–29; XV S'ezd RKPb., *S.O.*, 1479–1539; "Zhenskoe dvizhenie," *BSE* 25: 242; E. H. Carr, *Foundations of a Planned Economy* 2: 480; Hunt, *German Social Democracy*, 82–97.

36. *Reichstags-Handbuch; Grosse Frauen der Weltgeschichte*; Jean Quataert, *Reluctant Socialists*, Appendix: "SPD Women Elected to the Constituent National Assembly 1919: A Biographical Sketch."

37. Shturm, "Mezhdunarodnoe dvizhenie Rabotnits," *Kom.* 2 (February 1926): 13–22; Joyce M. Bellamy and John Saville, *Dictionary of Labour Biography*, "MacArthur" 2: 25–60; "Colman" 3: 34–38; "Lawrence" 3: 128–32; *Who's Who of British Members of Parliament, Vol. III 1919–1945*, 12, 35, 182, 204, 281, 352, 388.

38. Milovidova, *Zhenskii vopros i zhenskoe dvizhenie*, 453; Artiukhina, "IV s'ezd VKP(b) i nashi zadachi," *Kom.*, 1 (Jan. 1926): 14, "8 marta v 1928 godu," *Kom.*, February 1928, 13; McKensie, *British Political Parties*, 521.

39. Samokhvalova, "Sostav Kommunistok," *Kom.*, September 1926, 26.

40. *VPN 1926 g.* 34: 23–34; *KSPN 1926 g.* 26: 124; "Perepis' partii 1927 goda," *BSE* 11: 542; *BSE* 25: 63, 65, 144; poem in Brian Peterson in "The Politics of Working Class Women in the Weimar Republic," *Central European History* 10: 96–97.

41. Chinn, *They Worked All Their Lives*, 166; D. Jewson, *Times* (London), 24 January, 12; Schonlank's poem in Peterson, "The Politics of Working Class Women in the Weimar Republic," 98; "Sostav Kommunistok," *Kom.* 9 (1926): 26; T. D.

Ionkina, "Delegatki I Vsesoiuznogo S'ezda Sovetov," *Voprosy Istorii* 9 (1982): 179–80; V. Veresaev, *Sestry*, 249–51.

42. Pamela Brooks, *Women at Westminster*, 68; Harrison, "Women in a Men's House," 625–26.

43. Marx, "The New Russian Woman," *The Nation*, 7 November 1923, 509; "Perepis' partii 1927 goda," *BSE* 11: 542; 25: 63, 65, 144; Samokhvalova, "Sostav Kommunistok," *Kom.*, September 1926, 20–28; *VPN 1926 g.* 34: 23–34; 51: 28–30; Clements' *Bolshevik Women*, 28, 234–35; L. Karaseva, "Klavdiia I. Nikolaeva," *Slavnye Bolshevichki*, 229–44.

44. Kollontai, "Vasilisa Malygina," *Liubov' pchel trudovykh*, 301; *Love of Worker Bees*, 178.

45. Gladkov, *Sobranie Sochinenii, Tom vtoroi, Tsement*, 58-61; Glebov, *Inga, Sbornik P'es*, 297; Marcelline Hutton, "Voices of Struggle, Soviet Women in the 1920s: A Study of Gender, Class, and Literature," *Feminist Issues* 11 (Fall 1991): 65–80.

46. *Slavnye Bolshevichki; Literary Digest*, 17 January 1934, 13; *Asia*, May 1931; Harrison, "Women in a Men's House: The Women M.P.s, 1919–1945," 626–54.

47. Balabanoff, *Impressions of Lenin*, 121.

48. Clements, *Bolshevik Women*, 237–39.

49. Strong, "New Women of Russia Test Lenin's Theories," *New York Times*, 20 March 1927, 14; V. Veresaev, *Sestry*; E. H. Carr, *Foundations of a Planned Economy*, 2: 470.

50. "Slav Women Clamor for Public Life," *New York Times*, 15 August 1926, Sec. 8, 17; "New Women of Russia Test Lenin's Theories," *New York Times*, 20 March 1927, Sec. 9, 14–15; *New York Times*, 21 January 1924, 1; Glebov's play, *Inga*; and Gladkov's novel *Cement*, especially 62–64.

51. Artiukina, "XIV S'ezd VKPb i nashi zadachi," *Kom.* 1 (1926): 10–15; Smitten, "K voprosu o regulirovanii rosta zhenshchin v partii 1927 g.," *Kom.* 11 (1927): 25–30.

52. Nukhrat, "Osnovnye voprosy soveshchaniia," *Kom.*, June 1928, 77–80; Dobrovolnoe obshchestvo 'Za novyi byt,'" *Kom.*, July 1928, 84–85; Bochkareva, *Women of a New World*, 120–22; Aminova, *The October Revolution and Women's Liberation in Uzbekistan*, 102–7, 112–37; Azade-Ayse Rorlich, "The 'Ali Bayramov' Club," 232; Stephen Jones, "The Establishment of Soviet Power in Transcaucasia: The Case of Georgia 1921–1928," *Soviet Studies* 40 (October 1928): 616–28. More than 800 women were murdered for becoming emancipated in Central Asia in the late 1920s.

53. Zetkin, "In the Moslem Women's Club" (1926) in *Selected Writings*, 161; Azade-Ayse Rorlich, "The 'Ali Bayramov' Club," 229–30; Serebrennikov, *Position of Women in the USSR*, 234; 1926 Soviet census; Glebova, "V national'n respublikh v Bashkirii," *Kom.* 1 (January 1925): 69–70; "Rabota sredi zhenshchin po Gruzii," *Kom.* 1 (January 1925): 71–73. Glebova noted that activists in Bashkiria knew the Bashkir and Tatar languages so they could work well with the indigenous women; however, there was a lack of literature and propaganda in Georgian and in other languages.

54. In 1907, the Azeri secular intelligentsia called for instruction in the native language, improving educational facilities for girls, and abandonment of the veil. Yet Muslim city councilors wanted Azeri women to be good citizens and mothers, not emancipated women. Audre Altstadt-Mirhadi, "Baku, Transforation of a Muslim Town," in *The City in Late Imperial Russia*, 296–97, 303; Serebrennikov, 29; Azade-Ayse Rorlich, "The Ali Bayramov' Club," 221–32; Kennell, *Theodore Dreiser and the Soviet Union,* 167–68; *KPTurkmenistana v tsifrakh (1924–1974)*, 20–26.

55. Of 487 Labour Party parliamentary candidates, only 30, or 6%, were women. *Labour Party, Report of the Annual Conference*, 160; Middleton, *Women in the Labour Movement*, 194; Brookes, *Women at Westminster*, 65–68; Eastman, *On Women and Revolution*, 141–42; Craig, *British Electoral Facts 1885–1975*, 96-97; Harrison, "Women in a Men's House: The Women M.P.s, 1919–1945," 623–54; McKenzie, *British Political Parties*, 277; Sylvia Pankhurst, *The Life of Emmeline Pankhurst*, 172; Elizabeth Vallance, *Women in the House, A Study of Women Members of Parliament*, 59.

56. Brittain, *Testament of Youth*, 574–75.

57. "Results of the Election," *Times* (London), 3 October 1924, 6; 20 October 1924, 7. See also "The General Election," *Times* (London), 1 June 1929, 6, 12, viii.

58. Lady Atholl, "Parliament," *Times* (London), 1 November 1929, 8-9; Atholl, *Times* (London), 29 May 1924, 9; S. Lawrence, "Votes for Women of 21," *Times* (London), 30 May 1924, 10; *British Feminism in the Twentieth Century*, 52–63. Eleanor Rathbone worked for family allowances from 1922 until 1945 when the Labour government granted them.

59. "Women Liberals," *Times* (London), 29 May 1924, 9; "Parliament," *Times* (London), 28 March 1924, 11; Harrison, "Women in a Men's House," 629–30; Melville E. Currell, *Political Woman*, 16.

60. Duchess of Atholl (M.P.), *Women and Politics*, 98.

61. Reynolds, *France Between the Wars*, 185–88.

62. Koonz, "Conflicting Allegiances: Political Ideology and Women Legislators in Weimar Germany," *Signs* 1 (Spring: 1976): Part L, 666, 674.

63. Quoted by Anna Louise Strong, "New Women of Russia Test Lenin's Theories," *New York Times*, 20 March 1927, 14.

64. Azade-Ayse Rorlich, "The A. B. Club," 236.

65. Johanna Alberti, *Beyond Suffrage: Feminists in War and Peace, 1914–1938*, 126–29.

Chapter 9

Society in the 1930s

I would not be able today to determine which, the dream or the reality, failed more in living up to its promises. Men live in dreams and realities.

—Milovan Djilas

Djilas's words describe his disillusionment with Communism, but one may apply them to the social position of women in the 1930s. Women's idealization of marriage and motherhood in those hard times made it hard to know which to fault more—the dream or the reality. Their quest for honor as wives and mothers cut across class and national lines. Pronatalists in Europe and the Soviet Union all glorified motherhood. The French Family Allowance Act of 1932 provided bonuses and grants for children, medals for mothers of five children, and the celebration of Mother's Day. Unemployment and underemployment in England made motherhood difficult, and the backlash against career women hurt many middle-class English women.

Hitler and Stalin glorified motherhood to secure women's allegiance and exploited their self-sacrificing nature for the state's advantage. Soviet women were asked to participate in collectivization, industrialization, paramilitary training, and family life to make the country strong and prosperous for future generations. They received education and job training, paid vacations, pregnancy leave, free health care, medals if they had many children, pensions at retirement, child support in the event of divorce, and communal services such as laundries, nurseries, and public dining. Along with these benefits came low wages. Both the Nazis and the Soviets criminalized prostitution and limited abortion in the 1930s. The Nazis also required some women to be sterilized. They forced career women to make their jobs available to unemployed men, restricted women's university study, asked mothers to dedicate their children to Hitler Youth, and punished Jewish, pacifist, socialist and uncooperative women.

While the Nazi and Soviet regimes glorified motherhood, they also arrested, imprisoned, and killed their uncooperative menfolk. Fewer women than men suffered these punishments, but their indirect suffering is incalculable. In both countries, women were haunted by fear of losing their loved ones and waited in vain for their menfolk to return from labor camps and prisons. Those imprisoned endured long years of separation from their children.

Under Hitler, many German women lived in fear. Even children could be held incommunicado or be sent home in coffins. Mothers and wives were occasionally permitted to visit their loved ones in prison. The shadowy side of the glorification of motherhood was the abusive treatment of families who resisted the regime.

Many women's dreams died in the 1930s as emancipation was rejected and motherhood sanctified. Pronatalist policies were popular, and millions celebrated Mother's Day. While many women's desires for family life initially coincided with the aims of the state, circumstances sometimes made this difficult. Changes in France and England were not as drastic as in the Soviet Union and Germany, yet patriarchal power remained entrenched in all four countries. European men blamed women for unemployment. In England and Germany, married career women often lost their positions. To save money during the Depression, Parliament excluded married women from benefits they had paid for. French employers provided family allowances, but these dried up during unemployment. Without bonuses and grants for their children, French working-class families often fell into dire poverty. Only in 1939 did the French government make family allowances part of the Code de la Famille. Unemployment was less severe in France (about half a million) compared to England (3 million) and Germany (5 million to 9 million).[1]

Soviet women served the state through productive and reproductive work. The 1936 Constitution proclaimed women's equality, and scholars pronounced the "woman question" solved as full-time work and family life were declared compatible. When threats of war loomed, the Party expected women to also participate in civil defense. Just as it adopted a harsher line toward the nationality question in the 1930s, so too it changed views on women. Both the Germans and the Soviets scrapped the progressive social policies of the 1920s, incarcerating prostitutes in mental hospitals, prisons,

and camps and pretending to redeem them through forced labor. Both regimes outlawed abortion, but only the Nazis sterilized prostitutes as degen-
erates.[2]

Stalin's grandiose industrialization scheme drew millions of women into
the labor force, while Hitler initially took women's jobs for men. Many
German women factory workers agreed that employment and family life
were hard to manage, but many career women disagreed. Female doctors
who employed servants and nannies did not find work and family life mutually exclusive. Yet thousands of career women, particularly Jewish ones,
lost their jobs after Hitler came to power. When poor women sought abortion rather than motherhood, the Reich forbade it. They sterilized certain
categories of women, but denied others this option.

Social and Marital Life

Besides state policies, the influence of gender imbalance, urbanization,
crowded housing, economic depression, patriarchy, class, and nationality
also shaped women's lives. The preponderance of women to men was
greatest in England (1,088 to 1,000), less in France and Russia (1,076 and
1,070 to 1,000), but lowest in Germany (1,058 to 1,000). Still, aggregate
marriage rates for women thirty-five to forty years old were similar: 76%
of English, 77% of German, 78% of French, and 82% of Soviet women.[3]
The Soviets had the highest rate because marriage was almost universal
among its huge rural population. While large numbers of women married,
World War I produced record numbers of widowed women. Problems of
adjustment after the war and freer social attitudes increased the number of
divorced women, but negative social attitudes and expense kept the English
divorce rate lower than others. In 1931, there were 19,000 divorced English women, 198,000 French, 312,000 German, and 500,000 Soviet (1926).
Between 1925 and 1933, 200,000 more German women became widowed
and 130,000 more divorced, but it was the divorce figure that dismayed
people.[4] Conservatives blamed rising divorce on liberal Weimar legislation
and culture. Soviet divorce statistics were not included in the 1939 census,
probably because they were higher than authorities desired. Since the Soviets had a large population, the number of divorced women in 1926 distorts
their proportion.

Marriage and Birth Rates

The number of French marriages declined from 315,000 in 1932 to 258,000 in 1939, and officials worried more about declining marriage and birth rates than about divorce. The number of German marriages increased from 517,000 in the early 1930s to 774,000 at the end of the decade. In England, they rose from 307,000 to 439,000.[5] Soviet marriage figures are difficult to locate since frequent marriage, divorce, and remarriage may have skewed statistics. Crude marriage rates increased from 1897 to 1926, but then declined in the 1930s. Their marriage rates remained higher than in Europe, but declined where collectivization created starvation. Among Kazakh women aged twenty to twenty-nine, the rate fell from 928 per 1,000 in 1926 to 836 in 1939. In the Ukraine, it slipped from 746 to 690, and in Russia from 745 to 696. Marriage rates also fell in older age cohorts. While men in those age cohorts had died in World War I and the Civil War, many more perished from collectivization, industrialization, and the purges in the 1930s.[6]

Low birth rates also worried politicians and demographers. England's crude birth rate fell from 21.4 per 1,000 in 1921 to 14.8 in 1939. France's declined from 17.3 in 1932 to 14.6 in 1939, as death rates exceeded birth rates. Only Germany increased its birth rate from 15.1 in 1932 to 20.4 in 1939. The Soviet birth rate surpassed European ones but decreased from 43.6 in 1926 to 38.9 in 1939. In cities, it hovered around 30.1, with abortions exceeding live births in Moscow. These figures and fear of a two-front war with Japan and Germany spurred Stalin's adoption of a pronatalist policy and abortion ban in 1936.[7]

Abortion

The need for abortion varied according to class. Middle-class women had better access to birth control than did working-class women, and some English feminists thought the only difference between therapeutic and criminal abortions was the ability to pay a doctor's fee. The depression in Europe and low wages and crowded living conditions in the Soviet Union made abortion necessary to limit the size of families. Working-class women often felt ashamed of using birth control, were too poor to buy contraceptives, or lacked the knowledge and privacy to use them. Many working-class English parents lacked the vocabulary to discuss birth control with their children.[8]

England

English working-class women believed that the use of abortifacients to induce menstrual periods was different from abortion as a surgical procedure. Moreover, abortion could be performed legally only to save the life of the mother, and most doctors were loath to do it. Working-class women who could not afford more children relied upon gin, quinine, saltpeter, hot baths, soapy douches, teas, and falls to end a pregnancy. If these failed, they resorted to midwives. In 1934, the percentage of English maternal death due to septic abortion increased. The lack of legal, hygienic abortion spurred some English feminists to law reform efforts, but this move was thwarted by press censorship and male politicians who defined birth control and abortion as "personal problems." Although the Women's Cooperative Guild advocated legal abortion, no political party supported it. When Lady Astor requested the Ministry of Health to dispense birth control information, an M.P. retorted that the trilogy of birth control, abortion, and sterilization would turn the Ministry of Health into the Ministry of Death! In concert with the falling birth rate, reported illegitimate births also fell in the 1930s.[9]

France

Laws against birth control and abortion existed in France, but enforcement was lax. In 1923, abortion became an offense instead of a crime, and judicial statistics reveal few people accused or condemned of infanticide or abortion. Indeed, the number of offenders dropped from 519 in 1921 to 78 in 1934. Of the accused, 30 were simply acquitted, while 30 who had been condemned received suspended punishment. As in earlier periods, French judges and juries refused to convict women of these offenses, and abortion remained common. One pronatalist estimated that 400,000 births were lost due to abortion in 1939. Yet the government arrested Dr. Madeleine Pelletier, who advocated and performed abortions, and incarcerated her in a mental hospital, where she soon died.[10]

Germany

Kindermord (infanticide) and *abtreibung* (abortion) were linked in penal paragraph #218 in the German Legal Code. While 1 million abortions were performed each year in the late 1920s and early 1930s, few patients or doctors were arrested or incarcerated. In 1937, Heinrich Himmler estimated that almost 1 million secret abortions still occurred each year. Criminal statistics for 1932 and 1933 show a decrease in the number of women accused of criminal abortion in 1933. The decline was probably due to the harsh punishment of doctors and patients, who could receive five to seven years' penal servitude. Imprisonment was severe, and upon release prisoners might be taken to concentration camps for further punishment. Besides discouraging hygienic abortion, the Nazis forbade contraceptives and closed birth control centers. As male unemployment declined, and as marriage loans and financial benefits for large "Aryan" families ensued, the German birth rate rose while the reported illegitimacy rate fell from 140,000 in 1930 to 102,000 in 1936.[11]

The Soviet Union

While outlawed in Europe, abortion remained legal in the Soviet Union until 1936. Moscow had three times as many abortions as births in 1934. The 1920s showed high abortion rates among those in the free professions. During the abortion debate of 1935, one professor noted that a single child tied a career woman down, while two or more deprived her of social life and a career. He opposed the abortion ban because he thought birth control and better housing would make abortions obsolete.[12]

Initially, the regime invited public discussion of the ban. Many opposed it because of the lack of housing, nurseries, children's clothing, and furniture. Others complained that more children interfered with their careers and restricted their productivity. One married student indicated that she wanted to have children after she completed her medical studies, but she saw the abolition of abortion as premature because she lacked a room of her own. If she became pregnant, she would fall behind in her studies and have to leave Moscow.[13]

Soviet women usually sought abortion after the birth of one or two children, yet some foreigners thought Soviet society took a nonchalant attitude toward abortion. Still, its ban created difficulties for women of all classes. Coitus interruptus remained a standard form of birth control among the "old" intelligentsia.[14] In 1936, the regime mounted a campaign to raise the birth rate by banning abortion and venerating motherhood. Since women's political organizations had been disbanded in the early 1930s, they lacked a voice to collectively oppose the ban.

The Soviet Family Law of 1936 limited abortion access to those suffering from physical or mental disease. Unlike the Germans, the Soviets did not sterilize women for social deviancy or poor health.[15] Fear of war made the regime pronatalist. In pursuing industrialization and collectivization, the Communist Party had grown accustomed to issuing decrees "from above," and they did so in banning abortion.

Divorce

The Soviet law for the protection of motherhood in 1936 required divorce to be recorded in passports and introduced charges of 50 rubles for the first divorce and up to 300 rubles for the third and subsequent ones. It required divorced spouses to pay set amounts of their salary in child support payments and prosecuted those not making payments. Many women endorsed traditional attitudes towards marriage and divorce because they felt betrayed by the divorce laws of 1918 and 1926, which had not provided them financial protection. They supported stronger laws on child support and thought the cult of motherhood offered respect for their reproductive work. The new legislation increased layette allowances from 32 to 45 rubles, raised grants for nursing mothers from 5 to 10 rubles, expanded day care, provided job protection for pregnant women, granted maternity leave of 112 days for office and factory workers, and gave state aid to mothers of very large families. International Women's Day (March 8) began to be observed like Mother's Day. While the regime promised women adequate resources, it failed to provide them. In 1937, the number of pregnant women exceeded the number of maternity beds. While the regime planned 458 new maternity hospitals in Moscow, it built 251; it promised 1,489 nurseries but completed 641; it proposed 288 new kindergartens but finished 41.[16] Until 1936, infant and maternal mortality had steadily declined. Then women once again resorted to illegal abortion and infanticide to control the size of their families. Despite some negative features, the glorification of motherhood remained popular and had widespread support from below.

Contrary to the expectations of Marxists, the family and state became stronger in the 1930s instead of withering away. In 1936, *Pravda* (the official Party paper) launched a campaign against free love and "lightminded" attitudes toward marriage and divorce. Party members were sometimes purged for frivolous attitudes toward women or the frequent changing of wives. By 1939, marriage was described as a lifelong union in which spouses experienced the happiness of parenthood and properly brought up their children.[17]

Treatment of Social Deviants

In the 1930s, Germany and the Soviet Union made abortion, prostitution, and social deviance criminal offenses. The Soviets renounced their policy of noncustodial sentences and began sending offenders to labor camps for "rehabilitation." Initially, the Bolsheviks had not defined prostitution, abortion, bigamy, incest, adultery, homosexuality, or hooliganism as crimes, but in the 1930s they made abortion, prostitution, and homosexuality punishable offenses. Parents became responsible for their children's "hooligan" behavior and could be fined up to 200 rubles. The arbitrary manner of changing laws showed the harsh nature of Stalin's regime. Prostitutes, who had previously received treatment in refuges, could now be arrested, imprisoned, or sent to labor camps.[18]

Prostitution

In the early 1930s, unemployment and prostitution still plagued Soviet society. During times of full employment such as the Civil War and the second Five-Year Plan (FYP), prostitution was considered unnecessary and illegal. During NEP (1921–1929) and the first FYP (1929–1932), the regime provided refuges for prostitutes and unemployed women where they could find shelter, work, education, and medical care. Supposed full employment during the second plan (1933–1937) made prostitution unacceptable. Yet prostitution continued because men with money and women without money created flourishing conditions for it. While the number of professional prostitutes remained low, casual prostitution thrived. The suspension of unemployment benefits in the early 1930s was premature and may have pushed some women into casual prostitution. Like the Nazis, the Stalinist regime declared "hardened" prostitutes parasites and sent them to labor camps for rehabilitation or to mental hospitals for treatment. Although the number of prostitutes remained low, social attitudes toward them became more hostile.[19]

Nazi Sterilization Policies

The Third Reich also passed laws against deviants, called asocials, and encouraged the castration and sterilization of physically and mentally defective Germans to "cleanse" the race. Before marriage, couples had to obtain health certificates, and only the healthy could wed. Those suffering from disease had to wait until they were cured to marry. Child molesters, lesbians, and anti-Nazis were forbidden to marry. One million Germans were mental patients, unable to work and state supported. Doctors and demographers feared that criminals and asocials produced more children than healthy citizens did, so they advocated castration and sterilization of defectives, prostitutes, alcoholics, criminals, Gypsies, and eventually Jews. About 2,000 men were castrated between 1934 and 1939, but more than

375,000 women were sterilized—an indication of Nazi sexism. By 1936, 250 sterilization courts had been established, composed of a magistrate and local doctors. Doctors who neglected to supply information regarding people's health lost their right to practice medicine. Yet healthy Aryan women burdened with children were refused sterilization.[20]

Peasant Women

Despite political changes, peasant culture remained strong. While Soviets and Nazis tried to introduce new rituals into rural life, many traditions and conventions remained intact. A Soviet study of the village of Viriatino showed most women retaining old customs and religious conventions. One woman remarked: "I don't want people coming to visit and find no icons in our house." The percentage engaging in religious rites was higher among independent farmers than among collective farmers because religious activity was not permitted on the *kolkhozy* (collective farms). About 70% of young women living on independent farms carried out religious rites, whereas only 12% of young kolkhoznitsy did. Many women remained superstitious, scoffing at female tractor drivers, ridiculing the use of incubators, and condemning communal nurseries.[21] A huge generation gap existed in the countryside. Young peasants could go to the cities to work as domestics, opt for higher-paying jobs in factories or construction sites, or pursue higher education and careers,leaving older women behind.

Peasant girls still took a dowry with them into marriage. With the advent of collective farms, the dowry sometimes included their labor days earned on the kolkhoz. Both German and Soviet brides sang laments about leaving their parents' home when they married, and they kept old rituals of dancing, feasting, and singing happy songs after weddings.[22]

Germany

Like Soviet and French peasants, the life of German farm women remained hard. In some areas, they cared for the vineyards and did the family baking, cooking. cleaning, sewing, and laundry. They worked longer hours than the menfolk did, who rested when the grapes were ripening. They filled their cellars with baked goods, boiled hams, spiced sausages, roasted chickens, and meats. Poor Saxon farmers worked from four in the morning until sunset. Yet their hard work earned them only boiled potatoes and curds.[23] Hitler tried to win farmers' support by supplying young people to help with field work, housework, child care, gardening, and milking. In the summer, up to 50,000 girls helped peasant women with their work in fields, gardens, vineyards, houses, and kitchens. Since there were over 4 million peasant women, this program helped very few. How they reacted to this program is not well known.

France

French rural life reflected continuity and change. Peasant women still engaged in the traditional customs of dowry and arranged marriage. The English writer Cicely Hamilton observed that the English social unit was the individual, while French marriage involved extended families, not just two individuals. French marriages based on family affinity and partnership endured longer than English ones based on romantic love that might wane. In some villages, the medieval clan system survived, with married couples having private lodging but eating their meals and spending their leisure under the roof of the village head. Life continued in traditional ways, and farm work remained so arduous that girls often migrated to the cities to find easier work as maids or shopkeepers. Some areas lacked enough brides for farmers. Other areas lacked sufficient agricultural laborers, so they employed foreigners. Hitler tried to keep German farmers in the countryside, but France and the Soviet Union experienced an exodus of young people looking for better-paying jobs with more free time in the cities.[24]

Meme Santerre, A French Woman of the People illustrates the hard life of peasants. In the 1930s, Santerre's husband worked in sugar refineries on large farms while she worked as a maid for wealthy farmers. She describes both benevolent and harsh patriarchs. She and her husband were surprised at the strikes and demonstrations that occurred, but they were grateful for the holidays, social security, and agricultural contracts that Leon Blum's socialist government provided. Having worked twelve- to fourteen-hour days all her life, she was unaccustomed to having Sunday off. At one job, she could hardly believe she only had to work from eight A.M. to six P.M.[25]

A French peasant schoolteacher named Emilie Carles grew up in Val des Près in southeastern France after the turn of the century. Having seen much marital abuse among peasants, she postponed marriage. Her sister Marie Rose was so traumatized by her husband's beatings that she was hospitalized to recuperate. This same sister also suffered from French pronatalist policies. Her ne'er-do-well husband thought their fifth child entitled him to the government bonus of 25,000 francs that was paid for the birth of a fifth child. Since this baby later starved to death, they lost the bonus. He then set fire to the house, increasing their poverty.[26]

Celestine, Voices from a French Village also testifies to country women's hard work. It shows them doing their laundry in the river, even in the winter. Most women in Chassignolles married and prudently managed their households by having small families. Once married, they no longer attended village dances but devoted themselves to their families. World War I left many widows, but they did not always live alone. Some lived with relatives, remarried, or found a *bon ami* (lover). Some ended their days in a home run by nuns.[27]

The Soviet Union

In 1929, the Communist Party decided to collectivize agriculture because the peasants were not marketing enough grain to finance industrialization and feed the urban population. Keeping more of their grain had led to an increase in peasant life span and decreased infant mortality. Yet industrialization created an increase in imports and a growing urban population, and collectivization had to pay for these changes. When peasants reduced the amount of marketed grain in 1927–1928, the Party decided to eliminate *kulaks* (well-to-do farmers) and organize the peasants into efficient kolkhozy. Kulaks constituted about 1.1 million households, or about 4 million people. Though the elimination of the kulaks may have seemed a minor problem, it created havoc for peasant households. Having established viable households in the 1920s, millions had their dreams shattered when their households disappeared and their menfolk were exiled, arrested, imprisoned, or sent to labor camps during dekulakization and collectivization. Hundreds of thousands of peasants were exiled to Siberia, while several million ordinary peasants in Ukraine and Georgia, along the Volga, and in Kazakhstan perished during the famine that accompanied collectivization. While officials lamented women's low participation in the kolkhozy, many areas suffered from rural overpopulation, and men often lacked work. Collectivization and industrialization created massive population shifts. People often left the kolkhozy, migrating to cities and construction sites, thereby increasing the urban population by 30 million rural migrants in the 1930s.[28]

During the dekulakization drive of 1929, women were treated more leniently than men, and fewer women than men were arrested, imprisoned, or shot. Since it was their menfolk who were punished, the women's suffering was more indirect but not necessarily less intense. Entire families were subject to exile and resettlement, so the number of women uprooted probably equaled the number of men deported. In exile, men more often perished from harsh outside work building canals and factories, while women often had inside jobs as servants.

The rough treatment of kulaks in 1929 and 1930 struck terror into the hearts of other peasants. With the aid of 25,000 workers from the cities in February and March 1930, the number of households on collective farms increased from 8 to 14 million. Since each household had four or five members, huge numbers were involved in this transformation. Collectivization created such chaos that Stalin tried to rectify the situation by accusing local leaders of forcing, rather than leading, peasants into the kolkhozy. The disarray produced smaller grain yields than expected. Poor soil and equipment also reduced production. Through ignorance, many farmers ruined tractors that the government provided to increase production.

At first, a small proportion of peasant women participated in the kolkhozy. Yet life for some of the poorest improved, as they obtained beds, radios, and sewing machines. Hardworking peasants earned special awards and even political appointments. Young women usually adapted better to the changes than did older ones. Some young women became tractor drivers and earned high salaries. Before the kolkhoz started, one woman had been looked down upon by the village, because she was poor. Now, she had become an *udarnik*, an outstanding worker.[29]

Since the kolkhozy initially paid their members only 36 puds of grain and 100 rubles in cash per household each year, a family needed to augment its income by tilling its private plot and performing other traditional work for cash. Women earned money by selling fruits, vegetables, and eggs at local markets and even rented rooms to city dwellers who wanted to stay in the country in the summer or wanted to send their children there.[30]

Amid dekulakization and collectivization, some traditional ways continued while others changed. Girls who belonged to the Komsomol usually gave up their political activities after marriage. Suspicions about day care declined, and the number of children in rural nurseries rose from 200,000 in 1929 to 5 million in 1934; the number in kindergartens rose to 420,000 in 1933. Millions attended elementary school, and illiteracy declined.[31]

Working-Class Women

Economic depression in England and Germany threw millions out of work. France suffered modest unemployment, while Soviet industrialization created high employment. The Nazis put men back to work but ignored unemployed women. Wages were lower in 1937 than in 1932, the cost of living rose, and German families suffered. The average worker's wage was 25 marks per week ($6.50), not enough to support a family.[32] The Nazis, like the Soviets, exploited workers by paying them low wages.

Germany

Diaries of German working-class mothers reveal the strain that motherhood, housework, and low-paid factory work produced. One Bavarian woman wants to be a hausfrau. Instead, she rises at 4:45, works nine hours at her job, and mends some clothes during her lunch break. In the evening, she prepares the next day's lunch, does the laundry, and makes dinner. On Fridays and Saturdays she does the wash. Sundays she irons, bakes, and cooks. During her vacation, she does the spring cleaning even though her health is not very good and she needs to rest.[33]

Another woman rises at 4:30, washes, dresses, and makes food for the day. She takes her son to the babysitter, catches the 6:00 train, and begins work at 7:00. Controlling two looms when she is pregnant is hard. She leaves work at 4:00, picks up her son, and does housework. She cannot afford a cleaning lady, since part of her earnings are spent on child care and transportation. Factory and housework occupy her Saturdays, so on Sunday she bathes her son, mends, and does other chores. She knows nothing about the Sundays prescribed in church and wonders what she lives for.[34]

Hitler's glorification of motherhood and women's removal from the workplace probably sounded good to overworked married factory workers, although the reduced family wage made life difficult. Workers saw the idealization of motherhood as unrelated to their struggles. They recognized that florists and capitalists gained more from its commercialization than they did.

Socialists criticized Mother's Day:

> Mother's Day? A salvation you said?
> When we haven't got diapers, not to mention a bed.
> Neither mother nor child can celebrate
> When motherhood is a helpless fate . . .
> And pregnant women must be afraid
> Because there is no financial aid. . . .[35]

England

> A family might survive without its father, but not without
> its mother.[36]
>
> —Carl Chinn, *They Worked All Their Lives*

Women's unpaid household work and child rearing were essential for the family and society. Since husbands went out to work, they received the best food and the children the remainder. As in previous decades, housewives often subsisted on bread, butter, and tea. Social workers noticed the toll that cooking, cleaning, washing, and shopping took on poor housewives as they lost their looks and neglected their health. The National Health covered pregnancy care but none of women's minor ailments. While most women accepted their lot and liked their work, it often adversely affected their tempers, health, and happiness.[37]

Unemployment and underemployment wreaked havoc on respectable family life. In some places, half the men were permanently out of work. Others had not worked for three to five years. When women married, they were expected to leave work, because jobs were scarce and respectable women did not work outside the home. The burden of birth control also fell on them. Bearing children and keeping them alive wore women down. Infant mortality declined to 80 per 1,000 in 1930, but child mortality remained about 50% for infants less than one year old. Measles, pneumonia, and whooping cough killed large numbers of toddlers. Wives believed they had to make the best of what life offered. Among the respectable working class, marriage was a matter of survival, not romance and passion. In the midst of poverty and drink, husbands sometimes became physically and verbally abusive.[38]

Despite the Depression, respectable married women thought their lives were good. Most lacked vacuums and washing machines but found housework and child rearing satisfying and rewarding. Some attended church, but not all. Many found more comfort at the pub or among other housewives than in church. Generally, girls aspired to the economic security of marriage, not careers. To achieve their goal, they acted modestly with young men and "played hard to get." They avoided "rough" women at work and during their free time enjoyed girl's clubs, movies, dances, and strolls with young men.[39]

Historians distinguish between respectable, employed working-class families and the impoverished "rough." In both groups, marriage conferred adult status and dignity, and wives and mothers strove for cleanliness and modesty in their households. The respectable possessed greater prudence, thrift, sobriety, routine, and common sense than the rough did. While respectable working-class women suffered repeated pregnancies, they had smaller families than did slum dwellers. Wives in both groups often felt ashamed of using contraception, whereas their daughters seemed better informed and less embarrassed about sexual matters.[40] Their health was often so poor that it took several pregnancies to produce one live child.

While life was a struggle for the employed, it turned into a nightmare for the unemployed. Life in London's slums meant overcrowding, decayed streets, gloomy houses, damp basement flats, peeling wallpaper, foul odors, rats, mice, and bugs. Yet a variety of employed, underemployed, and unemployed people lived in the slums, some because of the proximity to their work. They earned enough to live there, but not enough to pay for transportation to the suburbs. Many suffered from episodic employment. A daughter in one family commented: "You can wear out your feet and your heart too, looking for work and never finding it."[41] Families became destitute when members fell sick and lost their jobs. Some entire families were unemployed. After they exhausted unemployment payments, a family had to apply for public relief. Wives sometimes had to sell or pawn their furniture, even their wedding rings, before receiving assistance. Since their wedding rings symbolized respectability, they felt ashamed without them and dreaded interviews with welfare officials.[42]

Higher infant mortality (102 per 1,000) was found in slums than in better areas such as South Kensington (75 per 1,000). Slum-dwelling families slept in the room with the fireplace, since the dampest rooms of the apartments ruined their clothes and turned the food moldy. A family of seven often shared one bed for lack of blankets. The housing was often dark, dank, foul-smelling, and below street level, without running water or baths. Some women lived on the verge of nervous breakdowns from coping with the squalor. One exhausted mother let herself be arrested and sent to prison for stealing so she could find peace, quiet, food, and sleep.[43]

One investigative journalist was amazed to find slum wives as cheerful, patient, clean, orderly, and energetic as they were. Most accepted pregnancy and birth with resignation, welcomed new babies, grieved over illness and death, and experienced isolation.[44]

France

The situation of French working-class women was better than what German and English women endured. Whereas several million German and English women were unemployed in the 1930s, only half a million French were. Unemployment worsened in 1935–1936, but it was not rampant. Moreover, French workers received family allowances from their employers. Large families had access to good housing, whereas in England families with more than three children were barred from public housing. French women also received benefits such as paid maternity leave one month before and one month after the birth of a child and a stipend of sixty francs per month while nursing their baby. Employers also provided bonuses to pay for the layette and furniture of a first child. French employers kept wages low, spreading bonuses and grants to families with children, reallocating wealth from childless couples to those with children. Some enterprises, for example the Michelin tire company, provided free nurseries and medical care for workers' children. The government also provided discounts on train fares to large families. When unemployment remained low, this system worked well. However, when it increased in 1935–1936, even benevolent employers could no longer provide benefits. Fortunately, unemployment was relatively low in France and of shorter duration than elsewhere. Unlike French workers, English trade unionists believed that a working man's wages should provide for the family and feared that family allowances would dilute their wages.[45]

The Soviet Union

Time budget studies of working-class housewives and factory workers in Moscow varied considerably. Women workers spent seven and one-half hours at work and four hours a day at housework compared to ten hours for housewives and one hour for male workers. They also spent more time in self education and social activity than housewives did, but less than male workers spent. They had less time for eating, resting, and sleeping than did male workers or housewives.[46] Perhaps diaries, instead of time budgets, would reveal the same exhaustion that German working women felt.

Soviet working-class women were plagued by patriarchal husbands, crowded housing, low wages, and inadequate communal services. They lacked pots and pans, heat, and food during the first plan, but their situation improved during the second FYP, when wages rose and food and consumer goods became more plentiful. Families of Stakhanovite workers (those who exceeded the norm) often obtained higher wages and better vacations, housing, and consumer goods. In the new industrial city of Magnitogorsk, couples who arrived with a suitcase in 1933 owned furniture, gramophones, motorcycles, clothing, and shoes by 1936. Yet the men there often married in order to have a wife take care of them—do their laundry, cooking, and cleaning. Since the men engaged in hard drinking, swearing, and wife beating, marriage and family life were difficult there and, one imagines, elsewhere.[47]

As health services became available in the cities, life improved. In 1935, urban women made 27 million visits to clinics, while rural women made only 4.6 million. Infant mortality declined more quickly in cities than in the country. Yet in some new cities it remained high—222 in 1,000 births. In addition to health services, women utilized abortion clinics to limit the size of their families because housing was so crowded.[48] The ban on abortion in 1936 produced higher rates of infanticide, while the new divorce law provided alimony for some children.

Germany

Marriage remained popular among German women in every class and kind of employment. An English reporter interviewed a young manicurist who hoped marriage would deliver her from her misery. She feared that family alcoholism would disqualify her from a government dowry, since her health report depended on information about relatives for three generations. Fearing disgrace if her request was rejected, she decided to remain at her job and live with her family to save money for her future home.[49]

Bourgeois Housewives

England

> The woman who washes dishes, knits woollies, and makes junkets when she might be leading a local education committee . . . is as much an example of national waste as a brilliant playwright condemned to darn stockings.[50]
> —Vera Brittain

While the glorification of motherhood became pronounced in Germany and the Soviet Union in the 1930s, it had begun back in the 1890s in England. Motherhood was linked to imperialism and the desire to increase the middle-class white population. Still, middle-class English women began limiting the size of their families in the 1870s and never increased them. The depression of the 1930s so impoverished many middle-class families that women ignored pronatalist rhetoric altogether.[51]

Even middle-class socialists such as Margaret Cole (1893–1980) espoused traditional views about marriage. She thought marriage was a satisfactory arrangement for children, companionship, and economic security. She advised educated women to marry because their salaries would not provide them a proper standard of living. Her criticisms of marriage resembled those of other feminists who also found housework senseless and distasteful. Cole found the Soviet solution of communalization attractive, but knew it did not strike a chord among the English middle class. She also accepted the impossibility of drawing husbands into housework and rejected the idea that husbands should pay their wives for doing housework. Although the Anglican marriage service included the words "with all my worldly goods I thee endow," this seldom occurred, and finances proved serious problems in marriage.[52]

Cole recognized that women's subordinate status undermined marriage, while conceding some truth to Havelock Ellis's idea that women desired subjection to a lover. Yet she also believed that once the bloom had worn off the romance, many women desired an equal partnership. In patriarchal English society, this status was difficult to achieve. Moreover, while men tended to settle into their ideas early in life, married women began to entertain new ideas and develop intellectually at midlife, a situation that produced strains in marriage.[53]

Nor was divorce an easy solution to marital problems, since it remained socially unacceptable. Those in teaching and other fields found monogamous fidelity strictly enforced. Violation resulted in loss of one's job. The Church so opposed divorce that it forced King Edward to abdicate in order to marry a divorcée. The legal bases for divorce included adultery, desertion, cruelty, or unsound mind. Women could also obtain divorce on grounds of rape, sodomy, or bestiality.[54] Economic and social sanctions kept the number of English divorces far lower than Soviet or European ones.

Vera Brittain also criticized marriage, motherhood, and society. While not typical of her class, she symbolized the politically active, married career woman. As a wife, mother, and writer, she understood the struggles women of her class faced. She thought that English society regarded women's careers as a hobby and accepted marriage as an excuse for terminating one's career or refusing public service.[55] Still, it was not easy to engage in them all at the same time. Few professional women had children. Vera's friend Winifred Holtby was a writer but a spinster, as were politicians Eleanor Rathbone and Ellen Wilkinson. The famous historian and economist Eileen Power married in middle age but had no children. Upper-class Conservative members of Parliament such as Lady Astor and the Countess Iveagh had only one or two children, tutors to raise them, and servants to run their households.[56] Exceptional women such as Cole and Brittain employed nannies and domestic servants to do the household work and child rearing so they could succeed in both their careers and family life.

Brittain suggested changes in conventional domestic arrangements so women could fill positions of leadership. She believed that women could make a significant contribution to national and international politics. She and Cole advocated some of the changes Lenin had recommended in the 1920s. They too denounced household work as stultifying. They proposed that women's public participation be eased by communal cooking, laundries, and child care. Brittain suggested communal sharing of cleaning women and vacuums. She felt entitled to a cleaning lady, but not her husband's help in household work. Just as Lenin excused Russian men as too backward and patriarchal to share in domestic work, Brittain and Cole did not imagine men helping at home so that wives could participate in public life. Domestic duties fell to low-paid domestic servants and cleaning women. Brittain never saw her right to maids' labor resembling a husband's privilege to his wife's service in providing him a cozy home at no inconvenience to himself.

While Brittain regarded a happy marriage and the rearing of healthy children as useful work, she objected to educated women's shouldering all the domestic responsibilities. She chided fathers for not taking a role in the care and upbringing of their children. While not all educated women would be drawn into public work, she thought present arrangements excluded many talented women. She saw wifehood as falsely identified with domestic economy, and domesticity as the enemy of monogamous marriage. She believed marriage changed an educated, emancipated woman into a subordinate being, while domesticity chained wives to trivial cares, making them resentful and destroying their allure to their husbands.

Brittain complained that most wives accepted the prevailing norm of cooking their family hundreds of separate meals and raising their children in a nuclear family. She believed that neither domestic concerns nor children should destroy women's social effectiveness. Parents should lead lives of their own and not neurotically concentrate on their children. To increase their participation in public life, she wanted to reconstruct married women's work, rationalize housework, eliminate wasted time and energy through cooperative efforts, emphasize women's education, stress their public responsibilities, and teach them that domestic work is not life, but merely a means to living.[57]

Brittain sadly noted that the government spent 176 million pounds on armaments but only 20 million pounds on national health. This policy produced high maternal mortality and poor medical care for unwed mothers and children.[58]

France

English writer Cicely Hamilton observed profound differences between British and French family life in the 1930s. The French seemed more careful and businesslike about marriage than the English, who made haphazard, individual choices. French bourgeois families did not insist upon uncongenial matches but steered their children to appropriate marriage partners. She thought French marriages were more enduring than English love matches because they were based on family alliances and economic considerations. Love might wane, but marriage alliances lasted. Still, parents sometimes demanded that a daughter sacrifice her beloved if he belonged to an inappropriate class or family. Bourgeois family life remained patriarchal, as husbands asked their wives to give up their professional lives to maintain the family. Rebelling against bourgeois life, Simone de Beauvoir (1908–1986) eschewed marriage with its affairs and double standards in favor of an intellectual alliance with Jean-Paul Sartre. Yet she replicated some of the worst features of her parents' relationship, since Sartre's affairs with other women hurt her as much as her father's liaisons had wounded her mother.[59]

Germany

Both the Soviet Union and Germany approved of women's philanthropic work, glorified motherhood, rewarded prolific mothers, and exploited women's altruistic nature. In both states, well-to-do women had historically participated in philanthropic work. The German Protestant Women's Aid organization performed social work during the 1920s and 1930s, and its membership grew from 600,000 in 1929 to 900,000 in 1936. It trained women as deaconesses, congregational helpers, and caregivers for new mothers, the sick, and the elderly. In 1936, it came under the control of the Deutsche Frauenwerk (German Women's Bureau).[60]

Hitler turned women's self-sacrificing nature into devotion to the state through elaborate Mother's Day celebrations. Mother's Day had become a national holiday and folk festival in the 1920s, with the honoring of mothers of four or more children. It became more extravagant in the 1930s as mothers (qualified by race, health, and demeanor) received a gold, silver, or iron cross on Mother's Day. It also became an occasion for denouncing birth control and abortion and praising women's sense of sacrifice. Imitating French pronatalist policies, the Nazis established marriage loans that were forgiven with the birth of children, imposed punitive taxes on unmarried workers, and provided benefits to large families.[61]

In the 1920s, hausfrauen had helped defeat Socialist legislation to regulate servants' working conditions. To counteract their declining fortunes and status, many housewives defined themselves as professionals who could train young girls as servants in their households. With free household labor, they could regain status lost during inflation. Their ideas fit perfectly with Hitler's notion of a year of youth service. They presented their plan to the government for the training of girls as servants, and Hitler endorsed it, since it cost the state nothing. The year of service was for lower-class girls, since middle-class daughters were properly raised and exempt from such training! Bertha Hindenburg-Delbruck, a leader of the housewives' organization and a member of the conservative German Nationalist People's Party in the late 1920s, joined the Nazi Party thinking that she would wield power in women's separate sphere. She became disillusioned when her organization was submerged into Deutsche Frauenwerk.[62]

The Reich developed training camps to teach girls domestic skills. In one camp, girls were groomed as wives for German farmers in Africa. By 1938, several women had arranged marriages by correspondence.[63] An unusual camp was the *lebensboon* (a camp where unmarried women mated with soldiers to produce children for the state). Some women frowned upon this policy and questioned these methods. However, those who criticized too much found themselves imprisoned.

The Soviet Union

> The mother instinct is noble, and we consider it a great force;
> but we do not want our women to devote their lives to rearing
> children only. We do not want . . . their married life to separate
> them from public work.
> —Nadezhda Krupskaia, 1935

Krupskaia's words epitomize the situation of Soviet women. Their regime asked women to perform both reproductive and productive labor. Whereas the Soviets ended the decade with the glorification of motherhood, they began it with some harsh measures aimed at housewives. In 1932, the government proposed the suspension of bread and sugar rations to unemployed housewives. Industrialization initially created a labor shortage, and the 1931 urban census showed 6 million wives, daughters, and mothers unemployed. The decision to suspend their bread ration and draw them into production was cruel, given the limited child care facilities. In 1931–1933, there were spaces for approximately 500,000 children in urban kindergartens and nurseries, but there were 4 to 5 million working women. With the number of nannies declining from 500,000 in 1929 to 200,000 in 1935, child care remained inadequate. The American welder John Scott was amazed when his Soviet schoolteacher wife informed him that she expected a nanny to care for their baby. Yet high-ranking Party members often hired servants to manage their households and governesses to supervise their children's education.[64]

Like the Nazis, the Soviets put state needs ahead of women's. During the Civil War, women had been drafted into economic production; consequently, when labor shortages arose in the early 1930s, the regime reasserted its claims. Socialist ideology asked citizens to put social service ahead of personal happiness. Housewives' rations were threatened and their employment sanctioned in 1932.

The Soviets used various methods to secure women's allegiance. They turned the celebration of International Women's Day (March 8) into a kind of Mother's Day. Until 1936, newspapers and journals had featured female workers wearing red scarves signifying emancipation. Then they began to portray women as well-dressed mothers surrounded by adoring children, and March 8 resembled the Mother's Day of capitalist countries. Before 1929, the media had encouraged women's emancipation, but in the 1930s the regime modified its values, praising women's participation in industrialization, collectivization, reproductive work, even civil defense operations.

The five-year plans required women's participation. Fearing war and a declining birth rate, the regime also asked women to bear children while working. Some protested that without adequate housing, nurseries, laundries, and public feeding programs, full-time work and child rearing were incompatible. Thus the law banning abortion promised more communal services. By 1935, social scientists were expressing the Party line that motherhood, work, and social activity existed in harmonious conjunction, mutually complementing one another.

The period 1929 to 1939 is often called Stalin's "revolution from above," and refers to collectivization, industrialization, and the terror that accompanied them. It also signaled a new direction in women's affairs. When the Party adopted the first plan, it closed Zhenotdel, suspended women's political journals, and ended campaigns to liberate Muslim women. These decisions drastically altered women's situation.

Soviet Philanthropists

> In taking their part in the great cultural work of the country, these women are also making their own lives more interesting.
> — *Moscow Daily News*, May 10, 1936

Like their German cohorts, many Soviet housewives found themselves under the direction of the state. Wage differentials allowed managers, engineers, military personnel, and some Party members to provide for their families, and the Party promoted their image as helpers for their husbands and society. Party leaders presented them awards for their "socially useful" work. At the 1936 Congress of Wives of Engineers in Heavy Industry, they were praised for organizing nurseries, canteens, and other communal services for workers, thus helping the state and their husbands to run enterprises more effectively. Engineers' wives in Magnitogorsk organized a cafe at the theater, and the local paper announced the opening with their photograph.[65]

In 1936, the Party established the journal *Obshchestvennitsa* (*Woman Social Worker*), which reflected middle-class views. This was possible because the second FYP (1933–1937) relied on wage differentials, and high-ranking personnel could support their wives. Traditional family behavior was reinforced because many Party leaders were uneducated and sexist. By 1932, half of the Old Bolsheviks had been purged, exiled, retired, or killed. Those who endorsed women's emancipation no longer occupied positions of power. In their place came boorish politicians—Stalin, Yagoda, Ezhov, and Khrushchev. They embodied lower-class values and patriarchal attitudes toward women. They gave lip service to women's economic and educational equality but accepted women's subordination in the family. They felt more comfortable with wives, mothers, and philanthropists than with liberated women. The media and literature replaced the image of the liberated woman with the glorification of mothers, wives, and Stakhanovite workers. By 1939, the media showed women as pilots, parachutists, and sharpshooters marching in parades to celebrate International Women's Day.

Career Women

England and France

English career women often found life precarious during the Depression. Government agencies dismissed married female teachers and civil servants, denying them unemployment benefits they had paid for. Some professional women felt the strains of competing in a male world. Some French intellectuals such as Simone de Beauvoir chose not to marry, living in consensual unions instead. Many left their positions upon marriage, and only 15% to 18% of employed French career women were married in 1931.[66]

Germany

Married German career women found their lives as well as their jobs in jeopardy. Hitler not only dismissed Jews from the civil service, but also women whose positions were not in women's or youth sectors. While many German women doctors were managing their careers with the help of nannies and servants, the Reich forced them out of public clinics. Dismissed Jewish career women had a hard time finding employment, and many Jewish families became impoverished. Even ordinary female teachers found survival difficult since the regime paid such meager salaries. Leftists and pacifists were vulnerable to arrest, imprisonment, torture, and murder by the Gestapo. Therefore, many fled the country.

The Soviet Union

Mexican writer José Mancisidor visited the Soviet Union in the 1930s and noticed that Soviet career women could talk about films, theater, politics, or science without fear of losing their femininity. They were not conspicuous consumers, but human beings who thought, acted, and worked for socialism.[67] The FYPs created an immense need for educated personnel, and those obtaining higher education and jobs found their dreams come true. Many felt immense gratification in serving their country as teachers, doctors, and scientific personnel. Yet little was said about how to combine family responsibilities and work. Unlike the 1920s, few studies show how they divided their time between paid employment and unpaid household work.

The 1930s proved a dangerous time for critically minded scholars and writers, who had difficulty getting their works published or obtaining employment. Byvshie liudy found work hard to get, and strong-minded Party members could lose their jobs, even their lives, in the purges. Yet those in teaching and medicine experienced low purge rates. Vertical job segregation, which hindered women's advancement, afforded protection, since it was high-ranking officials who were usually purged. Still, wives of generals, engineers, plant managers, and administrators could be given five- to eight-year sentences as the spouses of "wreckers" and "traitors."

Surrogate Prison Families

A new form of family life emerged in the 1930s. Soviet- and German-imprisoned women formed alliances and surrogate families that displayed nurturing characteristics and helped them survive inhumane conditions. They shared food, cared for weaker members, and usually bonded on the basis of common political, educational, or religious affiliation. Unlike the Nazis, who initially imprisoned only 3,000 women for political crimes, the Soviets had incarcerated several hundred thousand by 1937. Estimates of men and women sentenced to prison or forced labor camps vary from 2 million in 1932 to 10 million in 1939. The 1937 Soviet Census indicates that women constituted about 20% of those in prison or camps in the Russian republic. Nadezhda Joffe indicates that 1,700,000 people had been shot or imprisoned or were in camps by 1939.[68] At least 400,000 women were in custody.

Many Soviet prison camp memoirs were written by educated Party members; fewer by imprisoned nuns, peasant women, and criminals. The writings of non-Party women Marie Avinov and Natalia Sats differed considerably from those of Party members such as Maria and Nadezhda Joffe, Evgenia Ginzburg, and Anna Larina. While memoirs show common themes, they also reveal differences in personality, philosophy, social position, talent, attitude, resoluteness, creativity, and spirituality.

Treatment was unpredictable. Evgenia Ginzburg and others at Yaroslavl prison were able to buy notebooks for writing in 1936, and Natalia Sats received library books and notebooks while in Moscow prison in 1939. Physical torture was widespread, but it was not used against everyone. Anna Larina (Nikolai Bukharin's wife) suffered not physical torture but mental anguish while being interrogated by former friends. These women's lives bear investigation because many of them survived decades of demoralizing and debilitating punishment, yet they refused to be crushed or lose their humanity.

Family Life in Exile

In the early 1930s, arrest, exile, and imprisonment were not always crushing. As a young wife and mother, Nadezhda Joffe was able to keep her family intact during her first exile, and she was able to keep part of her family together during her second imprisonment. Prior to 1937, Soviet families were sometimes allowed to go into exile and labor camps together. During her first exile, Nadezhda worked, reported for interrogation every ten days and had a nanny to care for her infant daughter. Later, she joined her husband in the Far East. When her term ended, she and her husband returned to Moscow. There, her husband was arrested and lost his Party membership and job because of his wife's Trotskyite views. Pressured by family and friends, she recanted so that she could work while her husband was unemployed.[69]

Arrested again in 1936 at the age of thirty, Nadezhda and her husband initially lived together in Siberia. In Kolyma, she became pregnant and bore their fourth child. Their other three daughters lived with relatives during this imprisonment. When pregnant, she became part of an extended family. An imprisoned priest who received food parcels gave her butter, sugar, and dried fruit. A carpenter made a crib for her baby, and some criminals protected her belongings so she would not be robbed. Lenient treatment of prisoners and their families ended in late 1937, when her husband was shot and her child sent to a home run by convict prisoners.[70]

Maria Joffe

Nadezhda Joffe's stepmother, Maria Joffe, belonged to a variety of surrogate families. She experienced relatively lenient treatment in 1932, when her son visited her in exile. Later, she survived the horrors of solitary punishment due to the care of her cell mates and her strong mind and spirit.

Like German women political prisoners and Holocaust victims, Soviet female prisoners formed support groups on the basis of shared interests. Maria Joffe, an editor, became close friends with the philologist Olga Tolchanina, the dancer Zoya, and the teacher Zina Kozlova. They formed an inner circle in their cell and took care of each other. Maria Joffe also developed spiritual and mental kin. In solitary confinement, Joffe found unexpected spiritual comfort. A crack in the door let a tiny "ray of light" into her "kingdom of darkness." She felt this was a miracle. During this experience, she felt a small spark of happiness and peace. She no longer felt abandoned, and believed the miracle would strengthen her the rest of her life. To retain her sanity, she engaged in communication with an imaginary friend she called "the professor." She analyzed prison life and Soviet society. Her thoughts occupied her time and helped her survive. Dubbed Scheherazade for her storytelling skills, she entertained the commandant Kashketin to save her cellmates from interrogation and torture.[71]

Evgenia Ginzburg

Party member Evgenia Ginzburg also describes surrogate prison families and religious experiences in her memoirs. Her surrogate families partially replaced the children and spouse she left behind when she was arrested. In prison processing rooms, women got to know each other in only a few hours. A sisterhood developed among the women prisoners, as they shared soap and stockings. In Kolyma, friends bribed officials to allow Ginzburg to have life-sustaining inside work.[72]

Life, light, and human kindness kept breaking through the gloom that surrounded her. Her healthy body found miraculous ways of preserving the flicker of life from extinction. Ginzburg thought something intervened which was a manifestation of the Supreme Good that rules the world. She found that suffering lay bare the real nature of things and was the price paid for a deeper, more truthful insight into life.[73]

Anna Larina

In 1937, Anna Larina participated in the surrogate families of Bolsheviks and military officers in Astrakhan. Initially, they were allowed to have their children with them, but eventually their children were taken away and placed in orphanages. Even if family members wanted to care for them, the NKVD, like the Gestapo, seldom allowed it. Sentences for the wives of "traitors" varied and were often extended. Larina's sentence was extended to twenty years of prison and exile, and she only met her son again in 1956. Surrogate families, youth, and beauty helped her survive.[74] Whereas others were physically tortured, Larina became unhinged when interrogators turned out to be childhood friends.

Non-Party Surrogate Prison Families

Natalia Sats and Marie Avinov were not Party members, and the alliances and surrogate families they formed were unlike those described here. After her husband was arrested as a "traitor," Sats received a sentence of five years. On the way to Siberia, Liudmila Shaposhnikova befriended her, and Sats met many women whose husbands had also been slandered. The experienced ones showed her the ropes, sharing their food and blankets. In December 1937, Sats arrived at a Siberian camp. There she was taken care of by criminals, who formed another surrogate family. Unlike other political prisoners, Sats did not find women convicts disgusting. She decided that prostitutes, bandits, pickpockets, and thieves could teach her about the underworld and help her become a better theater director. Even Stanislavsky had visited Moscow flophouses before producing Gorky's *The Lower Depths*. As a director, she organized prisoners into theatrical groups, orchestras, and choruses. She thought her work redeemed talented criminals and helped the camp as well as society. Afraid of the cold, she prayed for deliverance and was sent to a milder camp.[75]

Sats's surrogate families and artistic work gave meaning to her life and helped her maintain her sanity and spirit. Her mother's visits allowed her to retain more contact with her children than most women had. Her mother's intervention with the authorities helped her return to prison in Moscow, where she was able to see her family and study theatrical history. She was given a special study where she wrote Marxist analyses of the roles of women and children in Shakespeare's and Molière's plays. The last years of her sentence she spent in a minimum security camp where her family visited and she organized musical productions.[76]

Marie Avinov's memoirs reveal the experiences of a gentry-class woman, and she allied with non-Party people. When first imprisoned, abbess Mother Tamara befriended her, while the prostitutes, thieves, and convicts taunted and rejected her. The abbess taught her that the criminals resented her offering them tea and sugar because she was not one of them. Only when Avinov suffered as they did would they accept her gifts. Mother Tamara told her to look for the memory of the Creator in everyone, and she would find it. Marie prayed continually to St. Seraphim and experienced various miracles during her imprisonment and exile. In another cell, Avinov formed a surrogate family with Theosophists. After four months in Butyrka, she was released.[77]

When her husband was imprisoned for the eighth time in 1937, Avinov was rearrested too. This time she experienced a moral and spiritual crisis. She interacted with gentry-class women, nuns, even disillusioned Communists and she kept her sanity by mentally translating poetry and praying. After being treated for malaria in the prison hospital, her cell "sisters" welcomed her back with a feast of cigarettes, sugar, and sausage.

Several weeks later, Avinov was exiled to a small Siberian village. Left to starve, she found an exiled Ukrainian peasant named Seraphima (her saint's namesake), who took her in. They formed a surrogate family, and when her Moscow friends sent her several thousand rubles, she bought meat at the village market to share with Seraphima.[78]

Regardless of class, Russian and German women formed surrogate families during their detention. In torturous circumstances, they revealed the marvels of the human spirit. They supported each other with acts of kindness. In or out of prison, women were not just victims, but often defined themselves and their existence. As in earlier times, they had to have grit to survive.

Notes

1. Gisela Bock, "Poverty and Mothers' Rights in the Emerging Welfare States," *A History of Women*, 427–28; Susan Pedersen, *Family Dependence, and the Origins of the Welfare State: Britain and France 1914–1945*, 268–88; Cicely Hamilton, *Modern France As Seen by an Englishwoman*, 57–58.

2. The thirty-three Soviet prophylactoria for prostitutes in 1930 declined to nineteen in 1934, and disappeared by 1939. Whereas women had been free to leave the refuges in the 1920s, guards appeared at the doors in the mid 1930s. By the mid 1930s, 70% of prostitutes were considered "hard-core" professionals. The decline in unemployment and the change in the social character of prostitutes led to their being sentenced to labor camps. Bronner, *La Lutte contre la prostitution*, 41–42, 49, 66; Rachelle Yarros, "Moscow Revisited," *Journal of Social Hygiene* 23 (1937): 204–6; Yagoda, "Heroes Who Were Saved from the Underworld by the OGPU," *MDN*, 22 June 1933; Nikolai Pogodin, "The Aristocrats," *Four Soviet Plays*; Red Goals, *A Woman's Experiences in Russian Prisons*.

3. *SDDR*, June 1933, Band 451.2, 2/46 and 2/61; TsSU, *Chislennost', Sostav, i Razmeshchenie Naseleniia SSSR: Kratkie Itogi Vsesoiuznoi perepisi naseleniia 1959 goda*, 24 (hereafter cited as *Itogi perepisi 1959 g.*)

4. *SDDR*, Band 451.2, 2/57.

5. *Demographic Yearbook 1948*, 32–34, 458, 460, 464; *Times* (London), 24 January 1930, 15; *An. Stat.* 54 (1938): 13*; B. R. Mitchell, *European Historical Statistics 1750–1970*, 27–32.

6. Upravlenie Statistiki Naseleniia Goskomstata, *Vsesoiuznaia Perepis' Naseleniia 1939 goda, Osnovnye Itogi*, 89 (hereafter cited as *Perepisi 1939g*).

7. *Statistical Yearbook*, 1948, 32–34; *Times* (London), 24 January 1930, 15; *An. Stat.* 54 (1938): 13*; Mitchell, *European Historical Statistics*, 21–25.

8. Duchess of Atholl, "Sex Education," *Times* (London), 6 February 1932, 9. She thought that parents lacked the language to discuss birth control, and that teachers should provide this information.

9. Barbara Brookes, "The Illegal Operation: Abortion, 1919–39," *The Sexual Dynamics of History*, 165–76; Mrs. Cecil Chesterton, *I Lived in a Slum*, 134–35; "Survey of Abortion and Birth Control Methods," *European Women, A Documentary History*, 205–9; *Statesman's Year Book, 1935 and 1940*, "Great Britain," 18, 19.

10. *An. Stat.* 54 (1938): 47*, 56; Gisela Bock, "Poverty and Mothers' Rights in the Emerging Welfare States," *A History of Women*, 5: 426; Susan Pedersen, *Family Dependence, and the Origins of the Welfare State: Britain and France, 1914–1945*, 407–8.

11. *Stat. Jahrbuch* (1933): 533–35; *Stat. Jahrbuch* (1935): 532; *Statistisches Jahrbuch fur den Freistaat Bayern, 1928*, 546–48; *1938*, 409–10; Bock, "Racism and Sexism in Nazi Germany," *When Biology Became Destiny: Women in Weimar and Nazi Germany*, 274–79, 292; Wallace R. Deuel, *People Under Hitler*, 243–52; *Statesman's Year Book, 1935* and *1940*, "Germany," 949, 959.

12. *SSSR Strana Sotsializma*, 90; Lorimer, *The Population of the Soviet Union*, 127; M. Gernet, "Povtornye i mnogokratnye aborty," *TSU, Statisticheskoe Obozrenie* (1938) 12: 110–14; Mitchell, *European Historical Statistics*, 31; Rudolph Schlesinger, *Changing Attitudes in Soviet Russia: The Family in the USSR*, 257–59, 265–66.

13. K. B. "I Object," Letter from a student on the banning of abortion, *Changing Attitudes in Soviet Russia*, 255–56.

14. Lili Korber, *Life in a Soviet Factory*, 194–202. A personal interview with Dr. Elena Skrjabina, in Iowa City, Iowa, Spring 1983, confirmed the use of coitus interuptus among the Russian middle classes. Regarding contraception in England, see Stevenson, *British Society 1914–1945*, 152–54.

15. Lorimer, *Population of the Soviet Union*, 128; interview with Dr. Elena Skrjabina, Iowa City, Iowa, Spring 1983, who indicated that TB remained a basis for abortion in the 1930s.

16. For widespread discussion on the law on abortion, see *MDN*, May–June 1936 and *Pravda* and *Izvestiia*, May–June 1936; Janet Evans, "The CPSU of the Soviet Union and the Woman Question: The Case of the 1936 Decree 'In Defense of Mother and Child,'" *Journal of Contemporary History* 16: 770; "Decree on the Prohibiting of Abortions," G. N. Serebrennikov, *Position of Women in the USSR*, 261–75; "Women in Soviet Industry, *New York Times*, 27 May 1933, 2; *New York Times*, 28 June 1937.

17. Vladimir Gsovskii, "Marriage and Divorce in Soviet Law," *Georgetown Law Journal* 34: 220.

18. In detention, Iadviga Verzhenskaia found herself in a prison where prostitutes occupied cells on the lower floor and political prisoners those upstairs. "Iadviga Verzhenskaia, "Episodes of My Life," *Women's Barracks*. At Solovki, there were initially 30,000 male and 400 female prisoners. About 60% of the women were prostitutes and criminals, and 40% were political prisoners, including nuns, wives of priests and professors, intellectuals, and peasants. Men lived in tents, but women lived in barracks that protected them from temperatures of -38 degrees. *Red Gaols*, 41–50, 61–65.

19. Bronner, *La Lutte contre la prostitution*, 41–42, 49, 66; Maxim Gorky, *The Baltic White Sea Canal*; Alice Field, "Prostitution in the Soviet Union," *The Nation*, March 1936, 373–74; Yarros, "Moscow Revisited" (1937), 204–6; Yarros, "Observations," 455; Peter Solomon, "Soviet Penal Policy, 1917–1934," *Slavic Review* 39 (2): 212–17. *The Baltic White Sea Canal* indicates that some prostitutes and criminals became "rehabilitated" through socially useful work on the canal.

20. Nora Waln, *Reaching for the Stars*, 174–75; Bock, "Racism and Sexism in Nazi Germany," *When Biology Became Destiny*, 280; Deuel, *People Under Hitler*, 220–36. Deuel estimated the numbers castrated and sterilized prior to the war.

21. *SSSR Strana Sotsializma*, 65; "Ustina of the Collective Farm," *MDN*, 11 March 1933, 2; *Village of Viriatino*, 271–72, 285; Furniss, "'Class War' Linked with Anti-Religion in Soviet Policy," *Current History* 31: 607.

22. Waln, *Reaching for the Stars*, 177–89.

23. Waln, *Reaching for the Stars*, 151–58; Madeleine Kent, *I Married a German*, 82–84.

24. Cicely Hamilton, *Modern France*, 6, 123–36.

25. *Meme Santerre, A French Woman of the People*, 100–17.

26. Emilie Carles, *A Life of Her Own*, 141–48, 164–65, 170–71.

27. Gillian Tindall, *Celestine, Voices from a French Village*, 233–51.

28. For the influx of peasants, see Lorimer, *Population in the Soviet Union*, 231–36; Medvedev, *Ibid.*; "Ob itogakh Vsesoiuznoi perepisi naseleniia SSSR 1939 g.," *Planovoe Khoziaistvo* 6 (1939): 12; Ellen Moore Watt, *Back Stage in Soviet Russia*, 17ff; Koerber, *Factory Life in the Soviet Union*. Lorimer found a discrepancy between the expected and reported population in the 1939 population of 4.8 million, and he assigned these excess deaths to collectivization, industrialization, and the purges. The Ukrainian population declined from 31.2 million in 1926 to 28.1 million in 1939.

29. "Now We Amount to Something," *MDN*, 8 March 1933, 3.

30. "Sotsialisticheskoe sel'skogo Khoziaistvo Soiuza SSSR," *PKh.* 7 (1939): 166, 180; *MDN*, 14 May 1932, 1.

31. *SSSR Strana Sotsializma*, 91; Clarke, *Soviet Facts 1917–1970,* 29.

32. Judith Grunfeld, "Conditions of Employment in Present Day Germany," *New York Times*, 26 September 1937, E8; Doris Kirkpatrick, "Role of Women in Germany," *New York Times*, 26 September 1937, D7.

33. "Textile Workers, My Workday, My Weekend," *The Weimar Republic Sourcebook*, 208–9.

34. *Weimar Republic Sourcebook*, 211–12.

35. SPD newspaper, *Vorwarts*, 19 May 1934, "Mother's Day in the Weimar Republic," *When Biology Became Destiny,* 146–47, 152.

36. Chinn, *They Worked All Their Lives*, 17.

37. Rice, *Working-Class Wives*, xv, 18.

38. S. K. Ratchliffe, "The Two Englands," *Survey Graphic*, May 1937, 258; Rice, *Working Class Wives*, xi; Anna Davin "Imperialism and Motherhood," *History Workshop* 5 (Spring 1978): 32; Wilmott, *Growing Up in a London Village*, 111, 134, 141–42.

39. Regarding courting, see Judy Giles, "Playing Hard to Get: Working-Class Women, Sexuality and Respectability in Britain, 1918–1940," *Women's History Review* 1 (1992): 242–47; Jephcott, *Girls Growing Up*, 56–61.

40. Judy Giles, "Playing Hard to Get," *Women's History Review* 1 (1992): 242–47; Margery Spring Rice, *Working-Class Wives, Their Health and Conditions*, iv–xi, 15–18.

41. As quoted by Mrs. Cecil Chesterton, *I Lived in a Slum*, 77.

42. Chesterton, *I Lived in a Slum,* 39–43, 88–89.

43. Chesterton, *I Lived in a Slum*, 77, 111, 261.

44. Chesterton, *I Lived in a Slum*, 111.

45. Pedersen, *Family, Dependence, and the Origins of the Welfare State: Britain and France 1914–1945*, 224–85, 357–413; Hamilton, *Modern France*, 34–56.

46. Vladimir Mikheev, *Biudzhet vremeni rabochikh i sluzhashchikh, Moscvy i moskovskoi oblasti*, 17, 77.

47. Stephen Kotkin, *Magnetic Mountain*, 173, 178, 181, 192, 478 fn.86, 481 fn.115, 487 fn.179. One case told of a woman so long abused by her husband that she killed him with an ax. Her trial so fascinated the public that it was moved to the sports stadium, where more than 1,000 people attended.

48. In 1931, Moscow was short of food and fuel. Henry Wales, "Visitor in Moscow Finds Life Rigorous," *New York Times*, 10 March 1931, 10. The ratio was 154,000 abortions to 57,000 live births. *SSSR Strana Sotsializma*, 90; Lorimer, *The Population of the Soviet Union*, 127. Regarding high infant mortality at Magnitogorsk, see Kotkin, *Magnetic Mountain*, 179, 481.

49. Chesterton, *Sickle or Swastika?*, 35–36, 42–43.

50. Vera Brittain, "I Denounce Domesticity" (1932), *Testimony of a Generation, The Journalism of Vera Brittain and Winifred Holtby*, 139–44.

51. For motherhood and imperialism, see Davin, "Imperialism and Motherhood," *History Workshop* 5: 9–23.

52. Cole, *Marriage Past and Present*, 153–54, 168, 289–91, 297–300.

53. Cole, *Marriage Past and Present*, 286–88.

54. Cole, *Marriage Past and Present*, 125–33.

55. Brittain, "The Professional Woman: Careers and Marriage" (1928), *Testimony of a Generation*, 123–26.

56. Regarding the family and marital status of these female politicians, see chapter 8.

57. Brittain, "I Denounce Domesticity," *Testimony of a Generation*, 139–44.

58. Brittain, "The Care of Motherhood" (1930), 130–34; "Nursery Schools" (1929), 136–39, in *Testament of a Generation*.

59. Hamilton, *Modern France*, 123, 127–28, 132–33, 169; Simone de Beauvoir, *Prime of Life* and *A Very Easy Death*, in which she describes her parents' marriage; and Colette Yver's interviews with women physicians who give up their careers so their husbands could have a bourgeois life. Colette Yver, "Femmes D'Aujourd'Hui, *RDDM* (1928/29): xx.

60. Hausen, "Mother's Day in the Weimar Republic," *When Biology Became Destiny*, 143.

61. From *When Biology Became Destiny*: Hausen, "Mother's Day," 137–48; Renate Bridenthal, "'Professional' Housewives: Stepsisters of the Women's Movement," 153–71; Nancy Reagin, *A German Women's Movement*, 221–48.

62. Reagin, *A German Women's Movement*, 226–47; Bridenthal, "'Professional' Housewives," *When Biology Become Destiny*, 153–71.

63. F. Winder, "Nazi Amazons," *The Living Age* 353 (January 1938): 452–53.

64. "Soviet Bars Food for Housewives under 56: All Must Work in Industry to Get Bread," *New York Times*, 30 December 1932, 1; "Would Recruit Women for Soviet Industries," *New York Times*, 30 December 1930, 9; "Soviet Considers Draft-

ing Housewives, State Caring for Babies while Mothers Work," *New York Times*, 9 February 1931, 1; Scott, *Behind the Urals*, 130-31; Svetlana Alliliueva, *Twenty Letters to a Friend*, 40–41; Nadezhda Joffe, *Back in Time*, 75; Evgenia Ginzburg, *Journey into the Whirlwind*, 55.

65. *Pravda, Izvestiia*, and *Moscow Daily News*, May 1936; *Magnitogorskii rabochii*, 15 December 1936 and 28 April 1937, in Kotkin, *Magnetic Mountain*, 186, 484.

66. Melville E. Currell, *Political Woman*, 16; Wesley Camp, *Marriage and the Family in France Since the Revolution*, 64; Silver, "Salon, Foyer, Bureau: Women and the Professions in France"; Yver, *Review de Deux Mondes*, 49: 84–85, 88–89, 352–71; 50: 133–46, 592–603; 51: 786.

67. Jose Mancisidor, *Ciento veinte dias*, 59, 121, as quoted by William Richardson in "'To the World of the Future': Mexican Visitors to the USSR, 1920–1940," *The Carl Beck Papers in Russian and East European Studies*, 1002: 32.

68. Judith Tydor Baumel, "Social Interaction among Jewish Women in Crisis during the Holocaust: A Case Study," *Gender and History* 7 (April 1995): 64–79; *Women in the German Resistance and in the Holocaust: The Voices of Eyewitnesses*, 150–54; Louise Mauer, *Women in the German Resistance*, 155–58; *Vsesoiuznaia Perepisb Naseleniia 1937g. Kratkie itogi*, 166–67; Nadezhda Joffe, *Back in Time, My Life, My Fate, My Epoch*, 210; Lorimer, *The Population of the Soviet Union*, 164; Pares, *Moscow Admits a Critic*, 72; Wheatcroft, "On Assessing the Size of Forced Concentration Camp Labour in the Soviet Union, 1929–1956," *Soviet Studies* 33 (2): 265–95; Alexander Solzhenitsyn, *Gulag Archipelago* (1974–1978). Lorimer, Pares, and Wheatcroft thought 2 million were in Soviet labor camps in 1932 and about 10 million by 1939. Solzhenitsyn believed there were 8 million to 16 million in the camps.

69. Joffe, *Back in Time, My Life, My Fate, My Epoch*, 67–71, 75–85.

70. Joffe, *Back in Time*, 89–115. For more information about Soviet political prisoners, see Marcelline Hutton, "Social and Religious Experiences of Female Soviet Prisoners in the 1930s," Festschrift in honor of Jaroslaw Pelenski.

71. Maria Joffe, *Odna Noch': Povest' o pravde*, 56–58; *One Long Night: A Tale of Truth*, 105–9.

72. Evgenia S. Ginzburg, *Journey into the Whirlwind*, 80–88, 131, 140, 145, 156, 264–65.

73. Ginzburg, *Journey into the Whirlwind*, 411.

74. Anna Larina, *This I Cannot Forget, The Memoirs of Nikolai Bukharin's Widow*, 172–78, 181–83, 185ff, 238–39; Natalia Sats, *Zhizn'-Iavlenie Polosatoe*, 295, 307–11; Larissa Vasilieva, *Kremlin Wives*, 161–82.

75. Sats, *Zhizn'-Iavlenie Polosatoe*, 314–26; Sats, *Sketches from My Life*, 263–69.

76. Sats, *Zhizn'-Iavlenie Polosatoe*, 271–81.

77. Marie Avinov, *Pilgrimage through Hell: An Autobiography told by Paul Chavchavadze*, 121–32.

78. Avinov, *Pilgrimage through Hell*, 143–81.

Chapter 10

Education in the 1930s

This chapter considers continuity and change in women's education during the 1930s. Some of the changes resulted from the impact of World War I, the Great Depression, and deliberate Nazi and Soviet policy. In postwar France, women made great strides in secondary and university education and continued this trend in the 1930s. In England, the Depression resulted in reduced government revenues, the firing of married women teachers, and cutbacks in the number of women accepted into university study and teacher-training programs. In Germany, low birth rates from the time of World War I and antifeminism reduced the number of women students. Considering womanliness and motherhood incompatible with intellectualism, the Nazis restricted women to 10% of university students. Antifeminists denounced higher education for weakening women physically and undermining their ability to produce children for the nation. The falling birth rate encouraged claims of women's primary role as wife and mother. The Mannerbund Mystique, unemployment, and the crowded liberal professions were excuses for excluding Jews and women from the universities in the mid 1930s. However, after the purge of Ernst Roehm and the Sturm Abteilungen (Storm Troopers, SA) in 1934, the Nazis toned down some of their most vitriolic antifeminist rhetoric.[1]

In contrast, the Soviets espoused the compatibility of intellectualism and motherhood. Industrialization created a great demand for technical personnel and favorable educational and employment situations for women. Hundreds of thousands of peasant and working-class women gained access to secondary and higher education, which had been restricted mainly to the middle and upper classes in the Tsarist era. Female quotas of 30% were mandated in higher education, and women constituted 70% of those in medicine and 50% in education.[2]

Each country discriminated against particular social groups. In France and England, peasant and working-class children were generally excluded from higher education. In contrast, the Soviets prevented upper-class children of the gentry and clerical estates, kulaks, and purge victims from attending prestigious universities. In Germany, Reich authorities withdrew scholarships from Communists and nonsupporters of the regime, prohibited Jews from studying in state schools, and restricted university study for all women.[3]

Despite all these problems, education remained a key factor in women's advancement. As in earlier periods, class and gender affected women's access to higher education, as European governments made less provision for female than for male education. Under the new Bolshevik government of the 1920s, education became freer of gender and ethnic restrictions than it had been. Yet Russification returned in the 1930s, and Russian became the predominant language of university instruction.

Educational Policies

The Soviet Union

The Soviets mandated female quotas at educational institutions. They sponsored literacy classes, developed factory education, and allowed married and older women to pursue higher education. Few other countries encouraged working-class, peasant, or married women's pursuit of higher education. Soviet policy encouraged peasant and working-class girls to adopt high educational expectations and attainment. Sometimes all the children in a peasant family obtained higher education. Soviet institutions were more open to the lower classes than were European ones. Suffering from tremendous illiteracy, the Soviets increased literacy among women aged nine to forty-nine from 17% in 1897 to 43% in 1926, and to 87% in 1939. The number of girls in primary school increased from 2.7 million in 1924 to 8.2 million in 1932.[4]

The Soviets rejected the "progressive" educational policies of the 1920s, particularly John Dewey's project and laboratory methods. They were disgusted at the low standards these methods yielded. Party members wanted well-trained, disciplined workers for industrialization. They curtailed student interference in teaching and administration that the cultural revolution had spawned (1928–1932). Teacher control returned, and children once again rose when the teacher entered the room. Traditional teaching methods and exams resurfaced. Authorities placed greater stress on reading, writing, grammar, and mathematics, as well as punishment of unruly children.[5]

While most Soviet educational policies were positive for women, several groups suffered discrimination. One group included children of peasants who resisted collectivization. They were barred from higher education from 1930 to 1936. Another group were the children of purge victims, who were often sent away to orphanages or had their education interrupted in a variety of other ways. A third group included non-Russian youth when Russian again became the language of university instruction in many republics. A fourth group comprised rural youth who had less access to secondary schools, institutes, technicums, and universities, which were located in big cities. This was also true of European countries, where rural female students lacked secondary and higher educational opportunities.

Europe

Compared to the egalitarian Soviet system, little change occurred in education in England or France. Oxford and Cambridge still limited women to 10% of the student body. Middle-class English and German families still invested less in their daughters' than in their sons' education. French reformers tried to make higher education available to the poor by abolishing tuition at the lycées, but most working-class girls still could not afford higher education. Class attitudes and culture shaped educational expectations and performance. Lower-class families did not cultivate the language or mores of academe, and less than 5% of working-class children enrolled in prestigious lycées.[6] However, some ambitious peasant and working-class young women did attend teacher-training colleges and schools.

Nazi rhetoric proclaimed the army and universities male preserves. To stem the falling birth rate, the Reich declared women's primary role as wife and mother. Unemployment and the notion that higher education undermined women's ability to produce children for the nation were used to justify the exclusion of Jews and women from the universities. In 1933, Nazi laws barred Jews entirely and restricted women to 10% of university students. In 1935, they quietly canceled the restrictions against women. Yet antifeminist and anti-intellectual policies, the Depression, and the low birth rate during World War I kept the number of female university students low.[7]

Jacques R. Pauwels argues that by 1935 the Nazi regime had realized its need of a German female intelligentsia to augment declining male enrollments due to low birth rates during World War I and to military conscription. While the Nazis used foreigners in agricultural and factory work, they kept them out of the liberal professions. Thus, they quietly sanctioned women's higher education to replenish posts vacated by conscripted men or Jews and Socialists who had emigrated or been incarcerated.[8] After the invasion of Poland in 1939, the Reich again redefined educational policy, proclaiming the compatibility of intellectualism and womanliness. Since military service funneled men away from university study and created shortages in the professions during World War II, women sometimes outnumbered men in certain fields of study.[9]

Elementary Education

The English, French, and German governments had introduced compulsory education in the nineteenth century, so elementary school enrollments remained fairly stable. Roughly 5 million English and French children and 8 million German children attended elementary school in the 1890s and the 1930s. However, class distinctions remained strong even at the primary level. Wealthy French families sent their children (about 900,000) to lycée primary schools, while public schools educated the children of workers and peasants (about 4,200,000). In England, the Depression intensified class issues. School medical officers thought the Depression was undermining the health and education of young children and feared malnutrition if the government discontinued school meals. Nazi educational policies eliminated church schools in the 1930s. While 65% of children attended church schools in 1935, only 5% did so in 1937, and by 1939 denominational schools had almost disappeared.[10]

While the Russians had provided elementary education for 7 million children in 1914, the Soviets educated 17 to 24 million children in 1933, and 22 to 30 million in 1937. Tremendous increases in literacy levels among peasants and indigenous peoples occurred.[11] At the same time the regime provided egalitarian education, some Communist Party members behaved like the European bourgeoisie by hiring tutors for their children or sending them to special schools.

Moreover, dekulakization, collectivization, and the purges dislocated millions of people, interfering with children's education. While some collective farms built new schools in the early 1930s, several million kulak children suffered disturbances in their education. During the second Five-Year

Plan (1933–1938), collectivization created a more positive experience, with more grain produced and allocated to farmers, less starvation, and fewer families arrested, deported, or exiled. From 1936–1938, the purges destroyed many high-ranking members of the intelligentsia and Party. The arrest, imprisonment, and sometimes death of parents provoked physical and emotional trauma in children's lives and education. Abandoned children were sent to orphanages or to live with less vulnerable relatives. On the positive side, the Soviets established literacy programs for adults and factory schools so workers could engage in on-the-job education. The number of people (largely women) who learned to read in the "Down with Illiteracy" classes increased from 1.5 million in the 1920s to 14 million by 1935. Moscow pioneers even visited domestic servants in their quarters to make sure that they were attending night school, doing their lessons, and becoming literate.[12]

Secondary-school students in Soviet villages often attended new schools and taught peasants to read. Masha Scott remembered the fine school her collective farm built. It had many windows and a lovely garden. She also recalled the informal instruction her mother had given her, teaching her to work in the fields, clean the house, supervise younger siblings, sew, embroider, and knit.[13]

Millions of peasant women migrated to cities during the 1930s, constituting 26% to 41% of new factory workers and large proportions of those studying at the rabfaks (factory schools). Women who took advantage of work site opportunities might be migrant peasants, girls entering the factory for the first time, or politically active women. Komsomol members constituted half of rabfak students.[14]

Unprecedented opportunities for workers existed in the 1930s. At the Krasni Proletari Diesel Plant, most of the new women workers became literate, and 10% began studying at the machine tool school. Upwardly mobile peasant women abounded. In 1931, the illiterate peasant Anna Berdysheva went to Sverdlov to work at the Ural machinery plant. She obtained a job as a scrubwoman and in two years became a skilled worker. Similarly, Olga Zakharova came to Moscow semiliterate, got a factory job, and attended school at night. She believed that unskilled workers could study four to five hours a day and become technical workers or engineers.[15] This was easier for single women, since married women with children usually did not have free time for studying.

Elena Bonner provides a fascinating glimpse of pampered Party children's education. Since Moscow was expanding so quickly, her classes kept moving to new buildings. Under the influence of John Dewey, her teachers used innovative teaching methods. She and her friends discovered that working in small groups meant that one answered for all, allowing most of them to loaf. She had little homework, found arithmetic "laughably easy," and learned memorization assignments during class time. Children of the intelligentsia often brought books from home to read since school was so simple. After school, they went sledding or gathered at each other's apartments for snacks.[16]

Secondary Education

French and Soviet secondary education expanded in the 1930s. Economic expansion in the Soviet Union created a tremendous need for technical experts, and trade unions funneled young people into technical education, especially the rabfaks and FZUs (*fabzavuch,* or factory universities). By the mid 1930s, 300,000 women were studying in technica, 89,000 in rabfaks, and 167,000 in FZU, constituting 42% of technical school and 30% of factory school enrollment. Countless peasant and working-class women became technicians, even career women, something only middle- and upper-class women could do during the old regime. Indeed, the number of female secondary education students rose from 78,000 in 1900 to 500,000 in the 1930s. Unlike Western Europeans, the Soviets adopted coeducation at all levels and trained girls in the same subjects as boys. In 1936, an American visitor saw girls as well as boys studying carpentry, performing in balalaika orchestras, and attending factory schools where they studied three hours per day and worked four hours.[17]

England

The number of English girls attending secondary and grammar schools more than doubled from 114,000 in the 1890s to 264,000 in 1937. Some working-class girls earned scholarships to grammar school, but few finished, since they often felt ill at ease in the bourgeois environment, lacked money for uniforms and books, or had to drop out to help their families economically. Surrounded by snobbish middle-class girls, scholarship students often masked their working-class origins. During the Depression, bright working-class lasses could seldom aspire to university study and 280,000 girls annually left school at the age of fourteen to work. Most lacked the stamina and determination to go to night school. Girls' schools also remained poorly endowed, offering fewer scholarships than famous boys' schools such as Eton and Harrow. English laws passed in the 1920s to democratize education were not enforced, and grants dwindled as fees increased during the Depression. Nor would the government raise the school-leaving age to fifteen. The situation was no better in the country-side, where three girls but forty-two boys received scholarships to the Kent Farm Institute in the late 1930s.[18]

France

The number of young French women in secondary education soared from 16,200 in 1900 to 93,000 in 1938. It is difficult to know if this increase was due to the elimination of fees in 1930, to changes in parental attitudes, to demographic factors, or to the increase in the school-leaving age. In 1936, the French Minister of Education raised the school-leaving age from thirteen to fourteen, and this change may have contributed to the number of students in secondary education. Still, boys outnumbered girls by a ratio of 2 to 1. While the gender disparity in secondary education decreased in all countries, the smaller numbers in secondary as opposed to elementary schools show how strong class distinctions were, since it was primarily the well-to-do who sent their daughters to secondary school. Despite the abolition of fees, only 3% of lycée students came from working-class families and a paltry 1.5% from the peasantry. Still, only France and the Soviet Union had growing student populations and expanding educational systems demanding more teachers. French officials anticipated a need for 2,000 more teachers in 1936 and 4,000 more in 1937. In contrast, the English and German educational systems shrank as the number of students enrolled in higher education declined due to the Depression and low birth rates during World War I.[19]

Germany

In Germany, the number of women attending secondary schools declined from 437,222 in 1926 to 205,000 in 1937. A condition of attending secondary school was membership in the Hitler youth movement, and most belonged to the BDM (Bund Deutscher Mädel, or German Girls' League). Only 213 girls, compared to 9,300 boys, graduated from technical schools. Likewise, few girls in rural areas could afford the books, tuition, fees, and transportation for secondary education.[20]

Between 1933 and 1935, Jews were excluded from secondary education and could make up only 1.5% of those enrolled in vocational schools. Before these restrictions, Jewish girls constituted about one-third of secondary-school pupils. Moreover, many Jewish girls were assimilated and had not defined themselves as Jews prior to the new laws. Excluded from future careers, many also faced profound psychological crises in confronting their Jewishness. Charlotte Salomon was allowed to study at the Berlin Art Academy because her reserved manner posed no threat to Aryan men and because 1% of the enrollees could be Jews. Still, she suffered existentially in defining herself as a Jew. Facing reduced employment possibilities, many Jewish women shifted their focus to jobs in tailoring, domestic service, or commerce. Having planned to follow in her father's footsteps and become a lawyer, Hedwig Oppenheimer realized that this was impossible and left the Victoria Schule in Frankfurt in 1935 without taking the abitur exam. She later took commercial courses in Switzerland and England.[21] Some families believed that their daughters would not need a career because they would marry, so Jewish welfare organizations gave preferential treatment to boys seeking career training.

Nazi policies also restricted education for Gentile women. Whereas the Weimar Republic had allowed girls to take classes at Hohere Lehranstalten for boys, the Reich limited these opportunities. By 1937, the regime had divided the girls' *Oberschule* into two kinds, one stressing language, the other domesticity. The latter prepared women to be good wives and mothers, providing instruction in cooking, gardening, handicrafts, health, nursing, and work in nurseries, kindergartens, or the family. The number of girls in private preparatory schools declined from 10,000 in 1928 to 3,000 in 1935. The Nazis also liquidated private and religious schools. Countless Gentile and Jewish women restricted their education, realizing they could never achieve their dreams. Independent girls who rebelled against Nazi rules were punished with bad grades. Without the help of caring teachers, some would not have graduated from secondary school.[22]

The Soviet Union

Although many more girls in the Soviet Union were able to attend secondary school, it was primarily urban, Slavic girls who did so. Most peasant children lacked adequate preparation and funds for secondary education. Still, many ambitious peasant children found the means to travel to nearby cities, obtain secondary education, and even pursue university study.

Peasants and Workers

A great Soviet success was providing elementary education in the countryside, and hosts of highly motivated peasants obtained secondary education in the 1930s. Masha Scott and her siblings obtained secondary education in Kalinin Oblast. Her village took over a brick Kulak house for the secondary school and employed gentry-class people and their governesses as teachers. In both the 1920s and 1930s, secondary-school students had to perform social duties in exchange for education. In the "Down with Illiteracy" program, they taught older, illiterate peasants. The local education committee examined the peasants to see if they could read and write. Students like Masha received no payment for their teaching, except the pride of a job well done or the gift of a book. At election time, they mobilized peasant women to vote, going from house to house and village to village. When her parents learned to read in the 1920s, her father became less envious of wealthy kulak peasants, and her mother became more liberated. Masha appreciated Soviet education, because she remembered how expensive it had been for her elder sisters and brothers prior to the revolution.[23]

The Smolensk Archive presents a more critical view of secondary education. Documents from the archive, which was captured during World War II by Germans and later by Americans, reveal poor living conditions for teachers and students in Smolensk Oblast factory schools and technicums. Secondary schools often lacked books, paper, technical equipment, and sufficient dormitories. To attract worker and peasant students to Smolensk University in the early 1930s, institutes established rabfaks to raise the educational level of poor students so they could undertake university study. Unfortunately, some peasant and worker students were so ill prepared that they performed poorly, dropped out, or even committed suicide.

Soviet educational expansion created a tremendous shortage of teachers. In fact, the Smolensk Ponezovyi Raion Department of Public Education in 1937 had to close its secondary school due to lack of teachers. There were no history, mathematics, or literature teachers. For the schools to function, they had to use members of the "old intelligentsia." One principal thought it better to work with them than to leave the schools with fewer teachers. The purges often decimated the teaching cadres in the countryside. Even the head of the Smolensk Department of Public Education, G. E. Khaikin, an old party member, came under attack because he had married a teacher who was the daughter of a clergyman.[24]

Throughout the 1930s, Slavic women in Russia, Ukraine, and Belorussia profited more from educational opportunities than did women in other republics. Russian women accounted for 66% of those attending factory schools in 1933, while Ukrainian women constituted 18%. The proportion of Ukrainian women in the rabfaks illustrates the growth in industrial development in that area during the first Five-Year Plan. Indeed, half the 4,200 female employees at the Stalin Electro Mechanical Plant in Kharkov, Ukraine, were studying in worker schools or technical colleges in 1936. All told, Slavic women represented 86% of rabfak and 73% of technicum female students in the mid 1930s.[25]

Party Members' Children

In *Twenty Letters to a Friend* (1967), Svetlana Alliliueva (Stalin's daughter) complains that her mother was always busy working and that she was raised by a governess and educated by a tutor. Svetlana recalls that although no one called them governesses, they had the complete responsibility of raising the children. She remembers her mother taking great care to choose a good tutor for her, but it was not common for a woman Party member to spend much time with her children. Her mother worked on the staff of a magazine, studied at the Industrial Academy, attended meetings, and spent her free time with Stalin, not with her daughter.[26] Elena Bonner, the daughter of high-ranking Party members, also had nannies but attended public schools.

Nina Kosterina's diary provides unusual insight into life in the 1930s. She remained a Komsomol member and "true believer" even after her own father was arrested and imprisoned. In the midst of the purges of Party members, she tells how young girls grew up, fell in love, went to New Year's parties, attended school, and studied for exams. She goes ice skating, skiing, and dancing. She engages in paramilitary activities at a stadium, even throwing grenades. She describes a close relationship with her teacher and Komsomol adviser Nina Andreyevna and reveals sexual harassment by her male political history teacher, whom she loathes but fears. One student pursues her, but only to "pluck the flower of innocence." She prefers the innocent love of her classmate Grisha.[27]

Nina complains about her exams in 1937 and realizes she must do better in German to get into the institute of her choice. She also describes her family's summer holidays in the countryside, where she swims, sews, and plays. In 1938, she analyzes her classmates, dividing the girls into three groups: the *bog*—poor students who gossip a lot; *baryshnii*—young ladies who curl their hair, wear nail polish, and flirt; and the *Komsomolki*, or good students, who are serious and have friendly relations with the boys.[28]

In 1939, Nina passes her exams and decides to attend an industrial institute in Moscow. When the director of the institute inquires about her family, she tells him about her father's arrest. Then she discovers that students whose fathers have been arrested are lepers. They cannot study at any of the prestigious institutions and have to accept situations at second-rate provincial universities.[29]

Higher Education

Class and gender continued to influence women's access to universities in the 1930s. Soviet egalitarian policies of the 1920s quadrupled the number of female university students from 57,000 in 1926 to 206,000 in 1938. French female university students increased from 12,000 in 1926 to 18,000 in 1936. Little change occurred in English women's situation, since Oxford and Cambridge limited their enrollments. The Reich reduced the number of female university students from 22,000 in 1931 to 6,000 by 1938. European higher education remained elitist, with French and German working-class female students accounting for less than 3% of enrollments. Despite the abolition of tuition, French schools prepared mostly middle- and upper-class students for the baccalaureate exam that was the prerequisite for university study. In England, few bright working-class young women allowed themselves to dream of university education. As the Depression deepened, English female university students declined to 22% of the total in 1938.[30]

Tables 10.1 and 10.2 show the tremendous increase in the numbers of French and Soviet women in higher education.

Table 10.1. Female University Students, 1920s*

Country	Number	Percent
USSR	57,300	28
France	12,000	17
Germany	9,400	12
England	8,400	23

*Calculated from *An. Stat.* (Paris, n.d.) 52: *276; *Perepisi 1926 g.*, Table II, 51: 103; Anderson, *Universities and Elites in Britain since 1800*, 15.

Table 10.2. Female Students in Higher Education*

Country	Number	Percent
USSR	206,242	43% of total student body in 1938
France	18,259	39% of university students in 1936
England	8,400	22% of university students in 1938
Germany	6,200	14% of university students in 1937

*Calculated from *Sotsialisticheskoe Stroitel'stvo Soiuza SSR (1933-38)*, 125; Winkler, *Frauenarbeit im Dritten Riech*, 196.

Germany

In 1932, there were 22,000 German women university students, but by 1937 only 6,200. Male students also declined due to low birth rates during the war and the required army and labor service. The number of women studying math, science, social science, and law declined more than those in medicine.[31] In both Germany and Russia, medicine remained a good field for women. In the Soviet Union, children of kulaks, clergy, and other "former people" were able to study medicine when they were excluded from other fields, partly because medicine was not a high-status or highly paid profession.

Nazi policies also reduced the number of women studying at technical universities to 213 in 1938. Teacher-training college enrollments rose by several thousand, but it is unclear how many of these students were women. Perhaps many like Hedwig Jakob (1915–1992) graduated from Catholic Teacher Training Colleges before the Nazis closed them in 1938. Jakob had completed the teacher's seminary of Magdalena Cloister in Speyer in the early 1930s.[32]

A rise in the birth rate in 1934 encouraged the German government to revise its attitude toward female students. In 1935, it lifted the restrictions against women, but many young women had already abandoned their studies. Moreover, it was mainly upper- and middle-class women who pursued higher education. In his study of German universities, Pauwels found that not as much changed from the 1920s as experts used to think. Even in the 1920s, women students received only 2% of state scholarships, and Nazi quotas in the 1930s were not the reason that women were now only 10% of the student population. The reduction in students was due more to the low birth rate during World War I and the Great Depression than to Nazi policy. The decline in lower-middle-class female students was a sign that parents still invested more in their sons' than their daughters' education.[33]

Nazi political and social groups drew women into their work in various ways. Professor Margaret Green knew a student who had passed her examinations but could not be admitted to state teachers' training because she had not completed her labor service to the Reich. Fortunately, the student obtained temporary work in a private school and devoted part of her free time to the BDM. Afterwards, she was admitted to state teachers' training. Another student commented: "Ah, yes, you can't get on nowadays without sacrifice and service." While the obligation to serve the Reich was strong, there were not enough programs to accommodate women students in the summer of 1934.

Nazi youth organizations at Greifswald University could exclude students from taking final examinations, and students studying abroad had to secure their consent before leaving. Professors and lecturers were asked to volunteer for the SA. Some accepted the decree cheerfully and obediently submitted, but many thought it interrupted their scientific and scholarly work. A university career depended not solely upon intellectual attainments, but upon willingness to cooperate with National Socialist approval.[34]

Pauwels's interpretation differs slightly from Green's. He found that most women still belonged to traditional Catholic and Protestant student organizations and that few joined Nazi student groups. He noticed that those who staffed the Nazi student organization were politically unreliable and opportunistic. Moreover, attempts to engage female students in athletics, charity, welfare, agricultural, or factory work bore little fruit. In 1937, only 20% of female students participated in summer agricultural service projects. In 1938, only a handful of women university students relieved women factory workers so they could have a holiday. Although the Nazis thought their policy of "fist and brain" showed the breaking down of class barriers, many female middle-class students retained their parents' views and remained insensitive to working-class women's needs. They disdained Hitler's social revolution, regimentation, indoctrination, or service to the "folk." Yet some helped farm wives in the household, milked cows, or established village child care centers. Some tried to disseminate Nazi propaganda, but found that farmers resisted their message. Students were supposed to encourage folk culture, not degenerate jazz, in the villages.[35]

One of the most successful Nazi programs was *Frauendienst,* or compulsory civil defense training for women. In future wars, even the civilian population would have to help defend the homeland. Most of the courses took only a few hours per week and lasted only a month. They could choose first aid, air protection, signaling, gas mask use, or Morse code. Like other groups in the German population, female students conformed outwardly with compulsory policies but refused to identify with the regime by participating in "voluntary" labor service, since there was no penalty or punishment imposed for noncompliance. One student confided to Professor Green that the Nazis had not developed programs for women parallel to men's and that they didn't know what to do with women. Initially, female students mended the men's SA uniforms, but after the assassination of Roehm that ceased. They attended classes in folk-singing, dancing, and racial theory.[36]

While Frauendienst trained young girls in political ideology and first aid, it did not train them in the use of weapons. Only one camp, which trained young women for marriage to farmers in former German colonies in Africa, provided rifle instruction. One hundred twenty women learned horseback riding, shooting, languages, and first aid for tropical diseases. These activities instilled confidence in the girls, and male instructors were surprised that women learned shooting more quickly than men did.[37]

England

Like the German situation, English women's university study resembled a bell-shaped curve, rising in the early 1930s, then declining later in the decade. English female university students totaled 25% in 1930, but 22% in 1938. In *Three Guineas*, Virginia Woolf lamented women's limited access to higher education and professional employment. While Oxford granted women degrees in 1920, Cambridge still gave them only titular degrees, excluding them from a share in the government of the university and hiring no women as literature professors. It also restricted the number of women receiving instruction or working in the laboratories and museums to 500. Few notable English women historians held university chairs or served as mentors to female students. While Francis Clarke and Ivy Pinchbeck pioneered women's labor history, no prestigious university employed them. Only Elaine Power served as a lecturer at the London School of Economics in the 1920s and 1930s and as lecturer in English history at Oxford in 1938.[38]

English universities remained bastions of the upper and middle classes. Working-class students at Ruskin College made up less than 5% of Oxford's enrollment and were co-opted into middle-class manners and mores, eschewing the class struggle.[39] However, teacher-training colleges offered higher education to girls from the lower-middle and working classes. Catholic teacher's colleges such as La Sainte Union in Southampton offered upward educational, economic, and social mobility to Catholic women. Louie

Rollin (1914–1979), the elder daughter of a Yorkshire train engineer, gradu-ated from La Sainte Union in the early 1930s and returned to Sheffield to teach in elementary school. Her friends Eileen Mallender and Cecilia Backhouse Jackson graduated from Catholic training schools in Liverpool and taught at Sheffield elementary and Scarborough grammar schools, re-spectively.[40]

France

In contrast to Germany and England, the number of female university students in France steadily increased from 12,200 (17%) in 1925 to 18,260 (39%) in 1936. Yet class origin changed little. Peasant and working-class girls were usually limited to teacher-training programs, since each département provided scholarships, and such study did not entail the cost of moving to a large city.[41]

The Soviet Union

In contrast to the handful of German and English women obtaining higher education, huge numbers of Soviet women did so in the 1930s. Women were needed at all levels to carry out the FYPs. Mandated quotas of 30% women in educational institutions were soon met and surpassed. By 1934, women constituted 36% of university students, 44% of those attending technicums, 23% of students in the Ministry of Heavy Industry, 28% in Light Industry, 47% in Education, and 45% in Health. By 1939, 378,000 women had completed university education, and 6,600,000 some form of technical or secondary education.[42]

To engage working-class and peasant students in higher education, collective farms, factories, and institutes offered them scholarships. In Kalinin Oblast, members of the Red Banner Collective Farm jointly decided who would receive scholarships for study. Some students joined the Komsomol or the Party to gain a scholarship. Unlike diffident German university stu-dents, Soviet Komsomol members had a host of duties to perform. They taught in "Down with Illiteracy" classes, helped with collectivization, par-ticipated in the League of Militant Godless, and took part in the military training of Osoaviakhim (Soviet civil defense). Paramilitary organizations were attached to educational institutions, to factories, and even to collec-tive farms. Many thought war was inevitable, and college students prac-ticed battles in the snow. Unlike German civil defense, Osoaviakhim trained women in sharpshooting, flying, parachuting, and other military skills. These activities could be time consuming, but they also offered camaraderie. One Soviet university student of the 1930s described sharpshooting and camping as great fun. Women sometimes studied engineering, construction, interpreting, and even aviation at military educational institutions. A company of women usually marched in the military parades on Red Square in the 1930s. They wore uniform coats, calf-length skirts, and high boots. While female interpreters often served in the armed forces in Central Asia, others served in army intelligence or the medical corps.[43]

Komsomol students sometimes focused on political work, missed lectures and laboratories, and therefore performed poorly in the classroom. Scholarship students also experienced problems in obtaining funds from Oblast or Republican education institutions. The Medical Institute of Smolensk University sought financial resources from the Ministry of Health, and 60% to 70% of its students received scholarships in 1932. Ordinary grants paid twenty-seven rubles per month, but Party ones sixty to seventy-five rubles—an inducement to join the Komsomol or Party. Like German students in Nazi youth organizations, Soviet students joined the Komsomol for opportunistic as well as altruistic reasons. According to Masha Scott's recollections, study was very important. Outstanding students got higher stipends, and those who failed their exams lost their grants. Good students usually helped poorer ones. Although stipends were small, Masha Scott and her siblings found theirs adequate to cover room and board, books, and entertainment. Though the Smolensk Archive describes crowded dormitories and meatless cafeterias, Masha describes their food rations as tea for breakfast, and borscht, meat, potatoes, and fruit compote for lunch and supper. The best food, even for students, was often in Moscow, not the provinces.[44]

While Masha and her sister and brothers found dormitories crowded, their conditions were not as bad as those at the Smolensk Medical Institute, where 200 students lacked rooms and places to sleep in 1931. After Masha complained about the crowded conditions at a Party cleansing, she and her sister received better accommodations. Many students lacked clothing, books, and other necessities. To avoid the harsh working conditions of the countryside, some students at Smolensk University transferred to Moscow so they would not have to remain in the countryside as poorly paid medical workers or teachers. Rural doctors sometimes lived 200 miles from the closest town, lacked medical and pharmaceutical supplies, and lived in substandard housing. Still, Smolensk University offered upward social and economic mobility to poor peasants and workers, and their quota of 50% female students in the medical and pedagogical faculties enabled more women than ever before to obtain higher education. Masha's engineering college was evenly split between male and female students, but the medical faculty where her sister studied had 75% female enrollment.[45]

Peasant Women

Some peasant women took advantage of favorable quotas to pursue higher education. Large numbers became teachers, doctors, dentists, engineers, and agronomists. In Masha Scott's peasant family, one sister became a physician, another an economist, and Masha a teacher. Indeed, peasants made up 11% of medical students in Moscow in 1932. By January 1933, they represented 20% of those in higher education. To achieve these goals, Party chiefs sometimes ordered villages to send their youth to regional cities to train as teachers, and the number of peasant women studying agronomy increased from 4,000 in 1928 to 19,000 in 1933.[46] Students often received subsidized theater and opera tickets. The student union organized excursions, vacations, and volunteer work in factories and farms. Voluntary work included teaching, forming dramatic groups, and helping workers make their own newspapers. Masha's class had a newspaper in which they published students' poetry. In addition to studying chemical engineering, she worked in a chemical factory and laboratory. Her sister, who was a medical student, interned in a hospital. They all went skiing and skating and participated in the paramilitary activities of Osoaviakhim. In their free time, college students volunteered at factories, farms, or schools. In contrast to the flapper look of the 1920s, Soviet students in the 1930s did not wear lipstick or makeup or dress stylishly. It was better to be modest than chic, so they dressed simply, cut their hair short, or wore it in braids. However, they still loved the foxtrot.[47]

Unfortunately, not all peasant women were good students. Tractor driver Pasha Angelina had difficulties keeping up at the Timiryazev Academy of Agriculture. Only semiliterate, she had studied grammar and arithmetic at the secondary school in Staro-Byeshevo and found her courses at the academy extremely taxing. She succeeded, but not everyone did. In Magnitogorsk, the American welder John Scott had unpleasant experiences with a peasant woman dentist named Galia. She had attended elementary school, worked as a maid, and then taken a crash course in dentistry before coming to Magnitogorsk. Galia meant well, but she lacked training as well as the necessary mechanical and pharmaceutical supplies to effectively treat the 250,000 workers at Magnitogorsk. The shortage of dentists meant that she and others had to work two shifts a day. In the mid 1930s, medical care at Magnitogorsk was primitive: hospitals consisted of twenty barracks without running water, heat, or sewage facilities, yet as the decade progressed, the medical situation improved.[48]

Masha Scott's life in Magnitogorsk differed from her husband, John's. Coming from an impoverished peasant family, she had low expectations. Masha had abandoned study at the engineering college in Moscow to go to Magnitogorsk to help industrialize her country. There, she decided to pursue mathematics at the educational institute. She studied during the day and taught workers at night. Workers came directly to the school from their jobs, and it was there that she met Scott, who was studying mathematics. For Masha, Magnitogorsk represented the excitement of a new city. Whereas Moscow was old and dark, Magnitogorsk was new and sunny. While Scott lamented the lack of running water, Masha did not notice its absence. She appreciated the new parks, children's choirs, and other features.[49]

Women's education in the 1930s shows that the Soviet regime was not as monolithic as previous scholars have presented it. One Soviet physician who emigrated to the United States after World War II indicated that medicine was a field in which one's social origin mattered less than it did in engineering or economics. The daughter of an exiled kulak, she studied medicine without any hindrance. Elena Bonner remembered her grandmother hiring Zinka, the daughter of a clergyman, to work in her family's communist household. Zinka took a job at a factory and attended rabfak courses. Since her factory job and courses were easy, she attended the theater nightly, using the tickets that high-ranking Party members like Elena's mother received. Zinka also joined the factory Komsomol to legitimize her status as a qualified worker. In 1935, she studied medicine in Leningrad. Despite obstacles, women in excluded groups often found ways to secure higher education.[50]

Working-Class Women

Soviet policies helped countless working women obtain higher education. In the 1930s, the Party wanted to educate its own technical experts so that the regime would not have to rely upon Tsarist-trained engineers and managers during industrialization. Many factories offered courses to workers during the day and evening. About half of new medical students in 1932 attended evening courses, and a large proportion of them were workers. Some factories and unions provided scholarships for workers: the Krasni Proletari Diesel Plant sent ten women workers to study engineering in

1934. Most new engineers came from the working-class and formed a new Soviet "Red" intelligentsia.[51] Throughout the decade, the Komsomol, Party, and trade unions recruited working-class women for higher education. In the new industrial city of Kuznetsk, there were 8,000 Party members, 12,000 Komsomol members, and 40,000 trade union members in 1932. Between 10% and 20% of the students at the Ministry of Heavy and Light Industry belonged to the Party and 5% to the Komsomol. Of the 17,000 students in the various ministerial institutes, only 11% came from the working class.[52]

Case histories of upwardly mobile women who benefited from Soviet policies in the 1930s are legion. Four examples are Christina Sverdlova, Vera Orekhova, Aleksandra Sidorenko, and Ekaterina Furtseva. A Party committee chose Sverdlova, a shy textile worker, to work on the journal *Rabotnitsa (Woman Worker)*. By 1932, Sverdlova had become a member of the journal's editorial board and was attending classes at the Communist Institute. Likewise, Orekhova, a worker at the Red Rose Textile Factory in Moscow, was elected to the district soviet. To efficiently perform her work for the soviet, she obtained secondary education. Sidorenko belonged to the Komsomol and attended engineering school in the Ukraine. The rector of the university asked her to become an example to others by studying in the blast furnace department. After her graduation, the Party supported her when technicians opposed her employment in Nazhezdenski. Eventually, the Party sent her to Kuznetstroi, where new blast furnaces had just been built and where she developed new processes for casting machines. These stories illustrate the importance of Party and government promotion in working-class women's higher education and professional employment.[53]

Perhaps the best-known example of educational and political advancement of a working-class woman is that of Ekaterina Furtseva, who became Khrushchev's Minister of Culture in the 1960s. Born to a textile worker's family in 1910, she joined the Komsomol and made a career for herself in that organization. In 1935–1936, she served as the assistant head of the political department of Aeroflot Aviation Technicum, and from 1936 to 1937 taught at the All Union Komsomol. In many ways, her educational and political advancement resembled that of Khrushchev and Brezhnev, who also rose in Party channels rather than in their field of training.[54]

It is difficult to know what proportion of working-class women actually attended courses, since Soviet sources seldom separate students by gender and class. Aggregate figures indicate that working-class students composed 38% of students in 1928 and 64% in 1931. From 1930 to 1936, children of kulaks, purge victims, and white-collar workers sometimes worked in factories to disguise themselves so that they could enter institutions of higher education with working-class status. However, a safe estimate is that women workers constituted a sizable proportion of the female student population during the Five-Year Plans.[55] This was quite different from the situation of women in Western Europe.

Intelligentsia

Some Soviet women participated in the highest levels of university life. The expansion of the university system in the 1930s created a great need for academicians, and the number of female professors, academicians, and top administrators in educational institutions increased from 2,600 in 1926 to 35,000 in 1939. Although Soviet educational and scientific institutions remained male dominated, women penetrated the highest levels. Anna M. Pankratova served as head of the history department at Moscow University from 1934 to 1937 and edited important periodicals. Likewise, philologist Olga Freidenberg organized a department of philology at Leningrad Institute of Philosophy, Language, Literature, and History in the early 1930s. She hired eminent Classics scholars who had fallen on hard times, including women such as E. E. Pipshits and Professor Malozemova.[56] Thus, some students had female mentors in the 1930s.

While there were half a million students in higher education in the pre-revolutionary period, there were 3.5 million by 1932–1933. A large number, if not a high proportion, of Slavic women were pursuing higher education and were reaping the benefits of upward economic, social, and political mobility. Equal educational opportunities increased the number of women in technical and scientific work, but also resulted in the continued feminization of the helping professions.

By 1939, Soviet education had created an immense female intelligentsia. In terms of class, peasant and working-class women were penetrating higher education. In terms of nationality, Russian and Jewish women still predominated in the professions, while Ukrainian and Belorussian women made inroads into the teaching and medical professions. By 1939, Georgian and Armenian women constituted two-thirds of those in the helping professions in their republics. In Central Asian republics, a small native female intelligentsia emerged, although Russian women still predominated.[57] A negative aspect of women's education during the Stalinist period was that the purges of family members restricted children's access to higher education. Strangely enough, some of the children remained idealistic and continued their Komsomol work. They often worked with pioneers, young children eight to fourteen years old, in activities similar to the Boy and Girl Scouts in the United States. Memoirs of Nina Kosterina show how confusing it was to continue believing in the Party as the purges intensified. Her own father was arrested in 1938, and Nina could no longer fathom what was happening. When some of her friends left or were drummed out of the Komsomol, she remained devoted to it. She found little fault in the Party or Komsomol and worked even more intensely with the pioneers. After her father's arrest, her aunts encouraged her to "accommodate" the situation, but she refused to compromise her Komsomol honor in order to "get on" in life. Nina and many others found it hard to reconcile their idealistic beliefs with the purges.[58]

Conclusion

In some ways, educational policies changed less in the 1930s than was previously supposed. In secondary and higher education, class and gender remained important factors in European women's education. In Europe, working-class and peasant women experienced little of the upward educational and employment mobility of women in the Soviet Union. Moreover, neither the Nazi nor the Soviet regime was able to carry out its educational policies as completely as scholars used to think. Just as German university rectors turned a blind eye toward female students who did not participate in agricultural and factory labor service, so some Soviet educators refused to purge students of questionable class origin. Olga Freidenberg refused Party requests to lower the marks of children of white-collar workers and raise those of children of blue-collar workers.[59] Her refusal indicates that Party control, though threatening and unpleasant, was not as total as formerly thought. During the early 1930s, restrictions against children of kulaks and capitalists were never completely enforced and finally disappeared in 1936. Finally, the different civil defense training of European and Soviet women reveals ingrained attitudes. In Germany, women were trained in first aid and Morse code, befitting German notions of women as nurturers and caregivers. In contrast, the egalitarian paramilitary training that Soviet women received reflected ideas that women were strong and capable, not mere decorative objects.

Notes

1. Jacques R. Pauwels, *Women, Nazis, and Universities: Female University Students in the Third Reich, 1933-1945*, 3-94; Geoffrey J. Giles, "Higher Education Policy in World War II," *Central European History* 17 (4, 1984): 343; Jill Stephenson, "Girls' Higher Education in Germany in the 1930s," *Journal of Contemporary History* 10 (1975): 46–64.

2. *Sotsialisticheskoe Stroitel'stvo SSSR, Stat. ezhegodnik*, 593; *MDN*, 8 March 1934, 2.

3. Green, *Eyes Right!*, 222 and Hiltgunt Zassenhaus, *Walls*, 21–22. Disenchanted with the British Labour Party, Green went to Germany and taught at Greifswald University from 1930 to 1934. She wrote about the Nazi revolution in *Eyes Right!* Zassenhaus learned that avoiding Nazi activities meant loss of university scholarships. Her entire family tutored to earn money for the children's higher education.

4. *Itogi perepisi 1959 g.*(svodnyi tom), 88; *Sotsialisticheskoe Stroitel'stvo, SSSR, Stat.Ezhogodnik 1934*, 410–11; "Illiteracy Is Being Eliminated," *MDN*, 28 July 1934, 2; Ella Winter, *Red Virtue*, 318.

5. "Teaching Methods in the Soviet Schools," *School and Society* 39 (24 March 1934): 361–62; Walter Duranty, "The Reorganization of Higher Education in Soviet Russia," *School and Society* 36 (15 October 1932): 505–6.

6. Talbott, *Politics of Educational Reform in France*, 172–73, 247–50.

7. Pauwels, *Women, Nazis, and Universities*, 3-94; Giles, "Higher Education Policy in World War II," *Central European History* 17 (4): 343; Stephenson, "Girls' Higher Education in Germany in the 1930s," *Journal of Contemporary History* 10: 46–64.

8. Pauwels, *Women, Nazis, and Universities*, 3–91.

9. Stephenson, "Girls' Higher Education," *J. Contemporary History* 10: 57–64.

10. Talbott, *Politics of Educational Reform in France*, 29–33; "Health of the English School Child," *School and Society*, 37 (17 June 1933); Martyn Housden, *Resistance & Conformity in the Third Reich*, 55.

11. *Narodnoe khoziaistvo SSSR za 60 let*, 575; Clarke, *Soviet Facts 1917–1970*, 29; *Statesman's Year Book, 1900*, 33–39, 517–30, 591–93, 933–37; *Statesman's Year Book, 1935*, 22–24, 873–75, 1266–67.

12. Bochkaryova, *Women of a New World*, 164; Leo Lania, "A Pair of Street Scenes: A Moscow Tomboy," *The Living Age*, December 1932, 357.

13. Pearl Buck, *Talk About Russian With Masha Scott*, 25, 31.

14. *SSSR Strana Sotsializma, Stat. Sbornik, 1936*, 98; *The USSR in Figures*, 260–63; and "Can the Russian Peasant Become Machine Conscious?" *MDN* 12 June 1932, 2.

15. "Krasni Proletri to Reward 25 Women," *MDN*, 8 March 1934, 2; "A Peasant Girl's Chance to Become an Engineer,' *MDN*, 1 May 1934, 2; "Women of the Urals Issue Appeal," *MDN*, 10 March 1933, 4.

16. Bonner, *Mothers and Daughters*, 111, 117–19.

17. *Izvestiia*, 8 March 1932, 3; *The USSR in Figures, 1935*, 258–59; *SSSR Strana Sotsializma* (1936), 81, 90; N. M. Katuntseva, *Rol' Rabochikh Fakult'tatov v Formirovanii Intelligentsii SSSR*, 20; Bochkaryova, *Women of a New World*, 173; *USSR in Figures*, 1935, 239; Adams, "Economic and Social Status of Women

in Russia Since 1917," 92; S. W. Downs, "School Changes in Russia," *School and Society*, 43 (27 June 1936): 881. Impressed by some things, Downs was dismayed at the shabbiness in fairly new school buildings.

18. *Statesman's Year Book* (1900), "United Kingdom," 33–39; *School and Society* 44 (4 July 1936): 6; "A Survey of British Education," *School and Society* 44 (28 November 1936): 714–15; "English Training Colleges," *School and Society* 37 (28 February 1933): 258–59; "Education and Unemployment in England," *School and Society* 39 (19 May 1934): 637–38; "The English Labor Party and Education,"*School and Society* 40 (17 November 1934): 652; Jephcott, *Girls Growing Up*, 35, 50–52; "English Country Children," *School and Society* 49: 382–84.

19. Talbott, *Politics of Educational Reform in France*, 172–73; *Statesman's Year Book* (1900), 517–20; *Album Graphique, RSDRP* (1901), 236; *Statesman's Year Book* (1935–1940), 875, 882; "Education under the New French Government," *School and Society* 36 (24 September 1932): 411; Reynolds, *France Between the Wars*, 47.

20. *Statesman's Year Book* (1900), 591–93; (1935), 952; (1940), 962; "The German Secondary School Census," *School and Society* 36 (24 September 1932): 411; Angela Rodaway, *A London Childhood*, 65–85.

21. "Exclusion of Jewish Children from the Public Schools in Germany," *School and Society* 41 (25 May 1935): 697; Mary L. Felsteiner, *To Paint Her Life, Charlotte Salomon in the Nazi Era*, 30–39; Marion A. Kaplan, "Jewish Women in Nazi Germany: Daily Life, Daily Struggles, 1933–1939," *Feminist Studies* 16 (Fall 1990): 588; Melita Maschmann, *Account Rendered*, 38-39; interview with Hedwig Oppenheimer Apt, 5 August 1995. When her father died, Hedwig realized that as a Jew there was no point in her taking the abitur, so she left Germany and took clerical courses in Geneva and London in 1936–1937.

22. William T. Meyer, "Reorganization of Secondary Schools of Germany," *School Review* 47 (January 1939): 37–43; Hans Nabholz, "Elimination of Private Preparatory Schools in Germany," *School and Society* 44 (12 September 1936): 346; Zassenhaus, *Walls*, 21.

23. Buck, *Talk About Russia with Masha Scott,* 17, 28–29, 56.

24. Merle Fainsod, *Smolensk Under Soviet Rule*, 395–96, 418.

25. *Zhenshchiny i deti v SSSR*, 53; *The USSR in Figures, 1935*, 258–59; *SSSR Strana Sotsializma* (1936), 90; *Katuntseva, Rol' Rabochikh Fakul'tatov v Formirovanii Intelligentsii SSSR*, 20; "Country Prepares for International Woman's Day," *MDN*, 3 March 1936, 1; Bochkaryova, *Women of a New World*, 163–64; Pearl Buck, *Talk About Russia With Masha Scott*, 71–83.

26. Alliliueva, *Twenty Letters to a Friend*, 40–41.

27. "Dnevnik Niny Kosterinoi," *Novy Mir*, Tom 38 (12 December 1962): 40–42, 60–64; *The Diary of Nina Kosterina*, 30–37, 92, 163 (hereafter cited as *Dnevnik N.K.* and *Diary of N.K.*)

28. *Dnevnik N.K.*, 40–43, 67; *Diary of N.K.*, 37–38, 99–100.

29. *Dnevnik N.K.*, 78-82; *Diary of N.K.*, 130–41.

30. *An. Stat.*, 52: *276; *Perepisi 1926 g.*, Table II, 51: 103; R. D. Anderson, *Universities and Elites in Britain since 1800*, 15; *Sotsialisticheskoe Stroitel'stvo Soiuza SSR (1933–1938)*, 125; Winkler, *Frauenarbeit im Dritten Riech*, 196; Green, *Eyes Right!*, 191; Pauwels, *Women, Nazis, and Universities*, 151; "RSFSR Cultural

Plan," *MDN*, 17 January 1933, 1; Rueschemeyer, *Professional Work and Marriage, An East-West Comparison*, 19; Talbott, *Politics of Educational Reform in France*, 172–73, 248–50.

31. Pauwels, *Women, Nazis, and Universities*, 147; Giles, "German Students and Higher Education Policy in the Second World War," *Central European History* 17 (1984): 335; "Enseignement supérieur,"*An. Stat.* 52: 276*. Giles shows 19,900 students, *An. Stat.* 21,800. Those studying chemistry declined from 500 to 200; in law, from 1,000 in 1932 to 59 in 1937–1938; in economics from 1,000 in 1931 to 194 in 1937–1938. *Stat. Jahrbuch* (1933): 522–23, (1934): 534–35, (1937): 580–81; Stephenson, "Girls' Higher Education in Germany in the 1930s," *Journal of Contemporary History* 10 (1975): 54–56.

32. *Statesman's Year Book, 1935 and 1940*, 952, 962; Stephenson, "Girls' Higher Education in Germany in the 1930s," *Journal of Contemporary History* 10 (1975): 55–57; interview with Helmi Mays, niece of Hedwig Jakob, 8 August 1995; interview with Helmtrud Schaaf, sister of Hedwig Jakob, 19 September 1995.

33. Green, *Eyes Right!*, 191; Pauwels, *Women, Nazis, and Universities*, 36–39, 151; "RSFSR Cultural Plan," *MDN*, 17 January 1933, 1; Rueschemeyer, *Professional Work and Marriage*, 19.

34. Green, *Eyes Right!*, 124, 222–26.

35. Pauwels, *Women, Nazis, and Universities*, 73–86.

36. Pauwels, *Women, Nazis, and Universities*, 80–91; Green, *Eyes Right!*, 55–56, 185–95.

37. Winder, "Nazi Amazons," *The Living Age*, 353: 452–53.

38. "Enseignement supérieur," *An. Stat.* 52: 276*; Virginia Woolf, *Three Guineas*, 26, 132–35, 234; Eileen Postan, "Elaine Power," *Dictionary of National Biography, Supplement 5*, 1931–40.

39. "Oxford University Discusses Communism—Theoretically," *MDN*, 8 August 1932, 4.

40. Personal communiques with my mother-in-law, Louie Rollin Stack, in Iowa City, Iowa, and Kansas City, Missouri, 1970–1974; and interview with Frieda Stack, London, 10 March 2001.

41. *An. Stat.* 52:46, *276.

42. *Sotsialisticheskoe Stroitel'stvo SSSR* (1936), 593; *The USSR in Figures 1935*, 260; *Zhenshchiny i Deti* (1969), 53.

43. Oral interview, El Paso, Texas, 6 April 1996. Source wishes to remain anonymous. See also Nikolaus Basseches, *The Unknown Army*, 168; Ellen Jones, *Red Army and Society*, 99.

44. Buck, *Talk About Russia with Masha Scott*, 71-74. Meat shortages arose in the early 1930s when peasants slaughtered their animals and consumed the meat instead of delivering it to the market.

45. Fainsod, *Smolensk Under Soviet Rule*, 355–63; *USSR in Figures 1935*, 260–63; *SSSR Strana Sotsializma*, 98; Buck, *Talk About Russia with Masha Scott*, 44, 76–80.

46. "A Peasant Girl's Chance to Become an Engineer," *MDN*, 1 May 1934, 2; "The Old Women Speak," *MDN*, 12 May 1933, 1; *MDN*, 14 July 1932, 3; *MDN*, 17 January 1933, 1; "The Progress of Women's Employment in the U.S.S.R.," *ILR* 31

(Feb. 1935): 237; *MDN,* 14 July 1932, 3; Field, *Doctor and Patient in Soviet Russia,* 66–69.

47. Buck, *Talk About Russia with Masha Scott,* 74–82.

48. Angelina, *My Answer to an American Questionnaire,* 60–62; Scott, *Behind the Urals,* 128–30, 219ff.

49. Buck, *Talk About Russia with Masha Scott,* 91–97.

50. Field, *Doctor and Patient in Soviet Russia,* 60–69; Bonner, *Mothers and Daughters,* 142–43.

51. *MDN,* 14 July 1932, 3; Field, *Doctor and Patient in Soviet Russia,* 66–69; "Krasni Proletarii to Reward 25 Women," *MDN,* 8 March 1934, 2; Pamelia Pearl Jones, "Adult Education in Other Lands: Russia," *School and Society* 46: 634; Shelia Fitzpatrick, *Cultural Revolution in Russia, 1928–1931*; Fitzpatrick, *Education and Social Mobility in the Soviet Union 1921–1934*; Fitzpatrick, "Stalin and the Making of a New Elite, 1928–1939," *Slavic Review* 38 (1979): 377–402.

52. *SSSR Strana Sotsializma, Stat. Sbornik,* 98; *The USSR in Figures, 1935,* 260–63; *Sotsialisticheskoe Stroitel'stvo SSSR* (1936), 593; "Can the Russian Peasant Become Machine Conscious?" *MDN,* 12 June 1932, 2.

53. "Engineer, Mother, Student — The New Woman," *MDN,* 6 November 1933.

54. K. N. Ciboski, "A Woman in Soviet Leadership: The Political Career of Madame Furtseva," *Canadian Slavonic Papers* 14: 2–3; Henry Lane Hull, "E. A. Furtseva," *Modern Encyclopedia of Russian and Soviet History* 12: 47–49.

55. On the children of *byvshie liudy* posing as workers to obtain entrance to the universities during the years 1928 to 1932, see Shelia Fitzpatrick, *Cultural Revolution in Russia, 1928–1931* and *Education and Social Mobility in the Soviet Union 1921–1934*.

56. *Perepisi 1926 g.,* tom. 34, 56–75; *Itogi perepisi 1959 g.,* tom 16, 161–70; "A. M. Pankratova," Larry Holmes, *Modern Encyclopedia of Russian and Soviet History* 26: 224–29; *Correspondence of Boris Pasternak and Olga Freidenberg,* 147–48.

57. *Vsesoiuznaia perepis' naseleniia 1939 goda, Osnovnye itogi, Chast' III,* 13–164; Ts.SU, *Zhenshchiny i Deti v SSSR* (1969), 53; *The USSR in Figures, 1935,* 258–59. The number of Russian women per 1,000 having higher, secondary, and incomplete secondary education rose to 77 in 1939. The number in Georgia was 121; Armenia, 92; Ukraine, 68; Belorussia, 56; Uzbekistan and Kazakhstan, 6; Azerbaidzhan, 21; Tadzhikstan, 4; Turkmenistan, 3. *Itogi Perepisi 1959 g.,* tom 8, 234.

58. *Diary of N.K.,* 32–37, 42–46, 56–99, 128–63.

59. *Correspondence of Pasternak and Freidenberg 1910–1954,* 153–54.

Chapter 11

Employment in the 1930s

It was the best of times, it was the worst of times.
— Charles Dickens

The Depression created economic havoc and unemployment for millions of European women. One to three million English and German women were unemployed, and 250,00 French women were unemployed. French women in manufacturing were more adversely affected than those in government service. Unlike French women, English and German career women, especially married ones, were laid off early in the decade. German career women who had established themselves during the Weimar Republic lost their prestigious positions when Hitler came to power. However, some young factory workers took advantage of special dowries that allowed them to leave low-paid jobs, marry, and create a household. Both English and German girls trained for domestic service in labor camps, to reduce the ranks of the unemployed. However, German girls who wanted to serve their country by becoming lawyers or professionals found their dreams dashed.[1]

The 1930s also produced substantial changes in Soviet women's economic participation. Just as unemployment affected European women differently, so too collectivization and industrialization produced different effects. Industrialization created new jobs in the 1930s, and educational quotas drew women into technical education and job-training programs. It reduced the number of unemployed and provided the state with more technical, industrial, and agrarian experts as well as more teachers and doctors. Thus, hundreds of thousands became career women in the 1930s. Still, millions of peasant and working-class women experienced the early 1930s as a time of food shortages and struggle for survival. Collectivization reduced several million peasants to starvation and exile. Education and job training helped many working-class women achieve higher status and wages.

By the end of the second plan, about 1 million skilled women were earning fairly good wages. The remaining 2 million unskilled women received low wages, but higher ones than in agriculture or domestic service.

Soviet programs encouraged assertive factory workers to become foremen, supervisors, even heads of factories. Although those who experienced upward economic mobility represented a minority, they became models to emulate. One of the surprises of the period was that only a small proportion of urban women became factory workers. In the nonagrarian labor force of 14 million, only 3 million were engaged in manufacturing, mining, and construction. Like European women, they became full-time housewives if their husbands could support them, and many preferred low-level service jobs to factory work.

Between 1929 and 1930, the Soviet nonagrarian female labor force rose by 500,000. This surge was a mixed blessing, since half the new jobs entailed harsh living and working conditions in construction and heavy industry. During the first plan (1928–1932), wages were low and living conditions harsh. Food, clothing, housing, medical service, and child care facilities were inadequate, and family life was difficult to maintain. However, peasant women may not have perceived urban conditions as harsh, since they were accustomed to hard farm labor and primitive dwellings. Many young female construction workers were idealistic Komsomol members who saw themselves building socialism.

Soviet women in the service sector may also have regarded their work with mixed feelings. Low-paid jobs in food service increased from 34,000 in 1929 to 279,000 in 1939. The number of women in low-paid educational and medical employment rose to 1,134,000 in 1937. Yet teachers and doctors may have resented the regime's greater investment in heavy industry than in social welfare.

Since collectivization resulted in unprecedented rural–urban migration, it seems unlikely that new jobs and technical education and training absorbed all unemployed women. Yet the government announced in October 1930 that unemployment had ended and it was suspending benefits to 500,000 women. Although industrialization created a great demand for labor, not all unemployed women were willing or able to locate at construction sites, new cities, or factories or as low-level service employees. Low wages, difficult living conditions, and lack of child care facilities probably discouraged many from taking "available" jobs. During the first Five-Year Plan (FYP), the government introduced more stringent regulations for maternity benefits. Only women who had worked uninterrupted in their jobs for three years qualified for full maternity benefits. Moreover, the amount spent on layette allowance and nursing bonuses declined from 81 million rubles in 1926–1927 to 54 million rubles in 1936.[2]

The situation of working-class women resembled that of peasants. During the first FYP, life was harsh in urban areas due to crowded housing, food rationing, and lack of consumer goods. However, during the second FYP, food and consumer goods became more plentiful, wages increased, and housing improved. In both periods, there were particular burdens and blessings that made Soviet working-class life unique. Indeed, their destitution often resembled that of unemployed and underemployed European workers.

The 1930s changed Soviet women's employment pattern more than European women's. Whereas 32 million members (92%) of the female labor force in 1926 were engaged in agriculture, by 1939 this figure had dropped to 20 million (59%). Likewise, the number of female factory workers increased from 1.2 to 3.4 million; and the number of women in service jobs rose from 1.4 to 7.2 million. Since peasant women constituted the majority of the population in both Russia and Europe, let us analyze their situation first.

Agriculture

Agriculture required hard physical labor in all countries. Well into the decade, Soviet peasants used wooden plows, sowed crops by hand, harvested with sickles and scythes, and threshed grain by hand. European women tended livestock, worked long hours in the fields, washed clothes in cold streams, and baked bread in communal ovens. Millions of women did this work. In Germany and France, the farm population declined gradually, but in the Soviet Union precipitously. In Germany, women's rural employment resembled a U-shaped curve, declining early in the decade but rising at the end as men went into military service.

As table 11.1 shows, the greatest decline occurred in the Soviet Union, which had long suffered from rural overpopulation. The harshness of collectivization pushed millions out of rural areas, while Soviet educational policies and industrial development pulled millions into schooling, manufacturing, commercial, and even professional work. It was a time of dreams come true for those advancing politically and economically. Some achieved high social status by becoming doctors, dentists, and teachers, while others earned good wages as agronomists, tractor drivers, or udarniks (productive

Table 11.1. Women Engaged in Agriculture, 1920s and 1930s*

Country	1920s	1930s	
England	83,000 (1921)	56,000 (1931)	
France	3,400,000 (1926)	3,100,000 (1931)	2,900,000 (1936)
Germany	4,970,000 (1925)	4,650,000 (1933)	4,900,000 (1939)
USSR	32,000,000 (1926)		20,000,000 (1939)

*Calculated from *Stat. Handbuch, 1928-1944; An. Stat.*, 52:133; *SYB League of Nations* (Geneva, 1935), 44–46.

workers). Yet some groups of peasant women experienced terrible disaster during dekulakization (1929–1930) and collectivization (1930–1933).

A kulak was a peasant who employed others in farming operations. According to the 1926 occupational census, there were roughly 650,000 male and 200,000 female heads of household who farmed with paid help. With family dependents, they totaled 2.4 million. Other statistics indicate that kulaks constituted about 1.1 million households, or about 4 million in 1929.[3] Though dekulakization was easily adopted as a policy, it proved difficult to redistribute so many people. Kulak households could be exiled, arrested, imprisoned, shot, or sent to forced-labor camps. Women usually were treated more leniently than men. Since entire families were subject to exile and resettlement, the number of women probably equaled the number of men sent away. Construction of the Baltic–White Sea Canal and Magnitogorsk used male kulak labor, while women often worked inside as servants.[4]

Some women vigorously resisted dekulakization and collectivization. When Pasha Angelina and her female tractor brigade went to plow the fields of their kolkhoz in the spring of 1933, they were met by a crowd of angry women barring the road and shouting: "Turn back! We'll allow no female machines on our fields. You'll spoil the crops! . . . We'll pull your hair out and kick you out of here!" Angelina knew they meant what they said, so she sought out the local political boss to clear the way for her brigade. Soviet writers have attributed such behavior to the influence of kulaks and priests and have described peasant women as petty bourgeois in spirit but not counterrevolutionary.[5]

Collectivization

In the 1920s, Soviet planners did not expect collectivization to produce famine instead of plenty. They did not foresee peasants slaughtering their horses and cattle, creating a sudden need for tractors, oil, and meat. Nor did they anticipate the worldwide depression that reduced their ability to acquire foreign machinery for industrial development. In July 1929, only a few hundred thousand peasants lived on collective farms (kolkhozy), but by March 1930, 14 million households had been squeezed onto 111,000 kolkhozy. Since each household had four to five members, collectivization involved millions.[6] Such radical change provoked chaos, and Stalin tried to deflect criticism by blaming local leaders for excesses. In his speech "Dizzy with Success" (March 2, 1930), he did not reject collectivization but suggested that Party members should lead, not frighten, the peasants into kolkhozy. As the regime let up, the kolkhoz population declined from 14 million to 6 million.

Vikenty Veresaev's novel *Sisters* (1933) describes activists facilitating collectivization. He depicts overzealous figures prowling about the villages, denouncing, arresting, and dispatching peasants to exile.[7] He portrays one sister, Lelka, as doctrinaire, punishing all those who did not cooperate in forming the kolkhozy. In contrast, her sister Ninka suggests that Party members think for themselves and be guided by their hearts. She wonders if the regional committee is right. After Stalin's speech, Ninka is vindicated as someone persuading the peasants to accept collectivization rather than forcing them into kolkhozy.[8] Veresaev's appraisal of Party members during collectivization was noted, and he published nothing for many years.

Another view of Soviet peasants appears in the memoirs of English journalist Mrs. Cecil Chesterton. At the Lenin Commune near Moscow, Chesterton met a well-educated Komsomolka named Natasha, who went to the countryside to shepherd the peasants into collective farms. While she drew many into the kolkhoz, she was unable to persuade her parents to join and take advantage of the modern conveniences. Her parents remained independent farmers, even though they could barely produce enough to pay the high taxes levied on them. Children of such parents often migrated to the cities or joined a collective farm. Chesterton thought Stalin had miscalculated the peasantry, since 20% resisted collectivization and preferred to retain their holdings despite high taxes. She also observed a generation gap in religion: older peasants tended to keep religious observances while young ones did not. Despite campaigns to eliminate religion, churches remained open, particularly in Belorussia and Ukraine.[9]

Comparing her trips of 1930 and 1934, Chesterton noticed a tremendous improvement in diet and standard of living. By 1934, the communal dining room of the kolkhoz had heat, electricity, and a radio. For their midday meal, farmers had soup, vegetables, and apples to eat and cider or tea to drink. The women's dormitories were airy with whitewashed walls, iron bedsteads, brightly colored quilts, rugs, pictures, and flowers.[10] In many ways, they resembled the barracks of German girls who performed rural labor service in the 1930s.

Officials denounced women's lack of participation in the kolkhozy, but rural overpopulation meant lack of work for men, depressed rural wages, and the migration of 9 million peasants from rural to urban areas (1930–1932). Some fled looking for higher-paid factory work in the cities; others left to disguise their kulak background. Another migration pattern involved part-time factory and construction workers who returned to their villages to share in the redistribution of land during collectivization.[11]

Contrary to expectations, kolkhozy were inefficient. Lack of machinery and low wages and morale produced poor grain yields. Seeing little correlation between their work and pay, peasants planted less grain in 1931–1932, thinking that they could change government policy by refusing to produce set quotas. Some kolkhoz managers were embezzlers, some illiterate and untrained. Poor kolkhoz management contributed to low productivity. When the government decided to pay farmworkers according to *trudodni* (number of days worked), many managers could not tally the labor days.[12] Farmers felt cheated by poor bookkeeping and administration. Thus, it is difficult to tell if peasants' low productivity was due to deliberate sabotage, slovenliness on a grand scale, or a combination of factors.

Farm managers often misled local, regional, and provincial Party bosses in their reports. Some feared admitting actual crop production and inflated figures to please their superiors. Thus, a combination of factors (low yields, misrepresentation of productivity, slovenliness, and ruthless grain requisitions in 1931–1932) produced the famine of 1932–1933. Peasants had produced a good harvest in 1930, which allowed for government requisitions and adequate supplies for themselves. But the harvests of 1931 and 1932 were smaller and didn't provide enough for the urban population. Consequently, the regime reacted harshly. Instead of importing grain from abroad, they increased grain procurements. Farms that had already fulfilled their quotas had to meet additional levies. In Ukraine, Belorussia, North Caucasus, and along the Volga, officials took grain saved for fodder, spring planting, and wages. These actions produced famine.[13]

In the areas of intense grain requisitions, people often died from famine. Even those who escaped dekulakization and famine found life difficult. Women earned the lowest wages on the kolkhozy, and they worked hard on their family plots to augment family income. Officials mounted a campaign to involve older women in kolkhoz production to shame young people into working more efficiently. Newspapers praised grandmothers as good workers who fulfilled their quotas while younger ones did not. Yet young people who left could obtain better jobs than domestic service when they migrated to the cities. The regime offered them two possibilities: education and job opportunity for those who cooperated, or hard times for those who resisted.[14]

Soviet Peasants and the Second Five-Year Plan

Tell them we're going from the dark into the light.
— Tatiana I. Pankratova, 1934

During the second FYP (1934–1937), grain production increased, and peasant families received more grain and wages for their labor. Whereas kolkhoz households had received only 36 puds of grain and 108 rubles in cash for their work in 1932, they received 106 puds of grain per household and 376 rubles in cash by 1937. On productive farms like the Lenin vegetable farm, collective farmers earned 3,000 rubles a year. Located near Moscow, it was able to market its vegetables, mushrooms, flowers, and fruits at good prices for its members. Family income generally increased from 2,000 rubles in 1932 to 6,000 rubles in 1937. The number of tractors in the Soviet Union increased fourfold in the late 1930s, and mechanization increased production.[15] Collectivization was Janus-faced: those who resisted paid dearly, but those who cooperated found new avenues of social, economic, and political advancement open to them.

During the mid thirties, most peasant girls received an elementary education, and literacy increased in the Central Asian and Caucasian republics.[16] Some pursued technical and higher education, becoming teachers, doctors, dentists, agronomists, administrators, and even politicians. Propaganda depicted women tractor drivers rolling over the *staryi byt* (old ways), forging new paths. By 1934, several thousand women headed collective farms, managed dairy farms, and drove tractors. By 1937, tens of thousands of women earned high wages as tractor drivers (40,000), combine operators (13,000), and machine operators (30,000).[17]

On her 1934 trip, Mrs. Chesterton interviewed a sixty-year-old woman farm manager. Illiterate before the revolution, she was elected manager for three years, decorated three times, and praised in the papers. Under her direction, crop and animal productivity increased. Before the revolution, she worked like a horse, was always hungry, and had no clothes; her children went barefoot. But now they lived in fine rooms and had good clothes.[18] Women of all ages achieved outstanding levels of production and were honored as *udarnik* and *stakhanovite* workers (those who fulfilled and overfulfilled their work quotas). Middle-aged women such as Tatiana I. Pankratova and Maria T. Senatskaya became udarniks and heads of collective farms. In the 1920s, Pankratova had been a poor brick worker, but in 1934 the District Party Committee invited her to manage a hog farm, and she made it flourish. In a discussion with Moscow reporters, she explained her life since the revolution. Who would ever have thought that she, a poor illiterate woman, would walk into the Moscow Soviet? Prior to the revolution, she would not have been allowed to loiter near the building, let alone enter it. Now she was invited to meetings and dinners there. She told reporters to tell her story to others and to say, "We're going from the dark into the light."[19]

Another heartwarming story is that of Liubov Semenets. Prior to the revolution, she earned 35 rubles a year as a nanny and field hand in a kulak household. In 1929, she and her mother joined a collective farm and took adult literacy courses. In 1934, Liubov became a tractor driver and joined the Komsomol. As a tractor driver, she earned 573 labor days per year, a carload of wheat, and 1,500 rubles. She was able to buy iron beds with mattresses, wool and silk dresses, shoes, and books.[20]

During the second FYP, the government awarded Maria Demchenko and Pasha Angelina the Order of Lenin for their outstanding work in sugar beet production and tractor driving. Village men harassed Angelina for driving a tractor, but she persevered and organized several women's tractor brigades. By 1936, she had trained female teams in Russia, Ukraine, and Uzbekistan. Both Demchenko and Angelina were elected to the Supreme Soviet and served as models of peasant women's possibilities.[21]

Peasant women could also improve their economic situation by becoming construction and factory workers. Unlike in Tsarist times, they did not have to become maids or remain servants very long. They constituted 26% to 41% of new factory workers and were able to take advantage of rabfak educational opportunities. Olga Zakharova left her village when she was nineteen years old. Semiliterate, she studied in the factory school for six years, becoming a technical worker and udarnik. Her story of upward mobility was not unique, and she urged others to do as she had done. Although most young girls found employment in the cities and at construction sites, not all were lucky. Some found not jobs but prostitution. Visiting Moscow prophylactoria in 1930, an American doctor noticed that most of the residents were peasants eighteen to twenty-three years old who lacked education and vocational training.[22]

Patriarchal Patterns in the Countryside

While hundreds of thousands of Soviet peasant women experienced new forms of upward mobility, life for millions of others remained subject to patriarchy, as men dominated family life, collective farm management, local soviets, and Party organizations. Another aspect of traditional life was the dowry, which consisted of the labor days (trudodni) a woman earned on the kolkhoz. The collective farm chairman transferred a woman's trudodni from her father's household to that of her father-in-law or husband. Despite Soviet contentions that kolkhoz work offered women economic independence, wages in-kind were not paid to individuals but to households. The division of labor remained the same, with women performing 42% of the productive work on the kolkhoz, 76% of the unproductive work, and 95% of the household work. They earned only 34% of wages paid because their work was "less valuable" and earned fewer labor days. Household work left women less time than men had for reading, rest, or sleep. E. M. Delafield, an English woman who stayed on a state farm near Rostov in 1936, noticed women engaged in heavy work from 5:15 A.M. to 9:30 P.M. during the summer.[23]

Rural life in the Soviet Union included a mixture of triumph, struggle, and destruction. For millions, it was a time of dreams come true, with new educational, job, and management opportunities. Many obtained a better standard of living, acquiring dishes, sewing machines, beds (instead of straw to sleep on), overcoats and shoes (instead of shawls and bast sandals), new schools, motorcycles, and trips to health resorts.[24] Yet dekulakization and collectivization also brought pain and destruction to several million others.

German and French Peasant Women

German and French peasant women escaped the famine and persecution that many Soviet peasants experienced in the 1930s, yet their lives in the patriarchal rural culture remained arduous. Their subordinate status and harsh work had scarcely changed from the nineteenth century. The American Quaker Nora Waln thought German peasant women worked incredibly hard in family vineyards, baking bread in the communal ovens, washing laundry in the river, and sewing their family's clothing. Like Soviet women, German farm wives worked longer hours than men. In the late summer, the men rested, while farm wives scrubbed, cleaned, cooked, and baked, filling their storerooms and cellars with food and meats. On a holiday to Saxony in 1931, another foreigner observed farm families working from four in the morning until sunset. It was painful to see the farmers creeping along the roads, baskets taut on their thin shoulders, their gnarled hands folded meekly over their breasts.[25]

German farm women did increasing amounts of farm labor as men were siphoned off for military service in the late 1930s. Whereas there were 4.6 million women in agriculture in 1933, there were 4.9 million by 1939. Their duty was to produce children, grow food for the Reich, and maintain the family farm as a center of racial purity and German culture. A typical sixteen-hour day included field work, tending livestock and the garden, supervising farmworkers, caring for children, cleaning house, sewing, and preparing meals. A wife slept only five hours a night during harvest season. Such hard work wore women out, and daughters left the countryside as soon as they could find jobs in the city. By 1936, some German farmers could not find brides to share this harsh life that caused miscarriages and health problems. So, in the late 1930s, the Reich required young girls to assist farm families for a few months before they could take a job in commerce or manufacturing. Since only 30,000 girls helped on farms in 1938, they did little to alleviate the workload of 4 million farm wives. Nor did conservative farmers initially welcome city girls, who might be too weak for farm work or too critical of country ways and superstitions. Once the war began, prisoners were used to help on the farms.[26]

Farm life in France was also demanding, and half a million women left agriculture between 1926 and 1936. Perhaps because of this decline, there was little unemployment among them—only 5,000 in 1936, less than 1%. Female agricultural workers worked long hours for little or no pay. Patriarchal work contracts between farmers and agricultural workers stipulated that men receive two bottles of wine in addition to their wages, and women one bottle.[27] When socialist labor organizers came to rural areas, they found female workers deserting the country for easier city jobs where they had at least one day off during the week. Like their German cohorts, French farm wives washed their clothes in streams, and ironed and mended them. One well-to-do farm wife in 1935 prepared breakfast at four A.M., lit the fires, milked the cows, fed the chickens and farmhands at six A.M., cleaned the house, prepared the noonday meal, drew water from the well, watered and fed the animals, prepared dinner, washed the dishes, took care of the garden, and went to bed late.[28] Farm life was solitary and monotonous. To stop emigration, French départements organized fifty-five schools to train young girls in household management and technical agricultural tasks. The Catholic Church organized farm unions, study circles, consumer cooperatives, and a special newspaper, *La Femme a la Compagne,* which gave practical social advice. Countess Keranflech-Kernezne also reached out to women farmers, publishing a monthly paper, *La Fermière,* which stressed domestic science courses. In 1930, about 45,000 belonged to farm unions, and 10,000 subscribed to women's farm journals.[29]

Manufacturing

> To slacken the tempo would mean falling behind. And those
> who fall behind get beaten. But we do not want to be beaten.
> —Stalin, 1931

While Europe was devastated by the depression of the 1930s, the Soviet Union plunged into industrialization to avoid being beaten by capitalists. It developed heavy industry during the first FYP (1929–1933) and second FYP (1933–1937). However, fears of war with Germany and Japan in the mid 1930s limited the development of light industry. The regime also stressed building socialism more than workers' welfare or women's liberation. As an editor of *Rabotnitsa* noted, it was "not a question of men versus women, but the problem of the whole working-class in the building of socialism."[30]

Soviet citizens believed in sacrificing for the good of their country. Just as collectivization forced peasants to make painful adjustments, so too rapid industrialization brought suffering and pain to workers. The costs of modernization were high. The FYPs were drawn up before the world-wide depression, and Soviet economists had not anticipated a situation in which the price of Soviet raw materials plummeted while the cost of imported machinery remained high. They had not foreseen international bankers replacing long-term loans with more costly short-term ones, nor reckoned on German cartels charging them more for manufactured goods. They had not expected collectivization to reduce the amount of grain and oil available for export and had not planned "capital accumulation" to come from squeezing the peasants and workers. This happened partly because the world-wide depression dried up foreign investment.[31]

Regulations Affecting Women Workers

One significant difference between Soviet and European women workers in the 1930s was the development of heavy industry in the Soviet Union, which created hundreds of thousands of new jobs, while the Depression produced economic stagnation, unemployment, and declining wages for European workers. Legal differences also distinguished the German and Soviet situations from the British and French laissez-faire labor policies. A 1934 German law provided for the exclusion of single women under the age of twenty-five from the industrial labor force and their replacement with male heads of families. Some of the dismissed women received a government dowry or marriage loan on the condition that they let married men take their places at work. The marriage loan depended on a woman's ability to trace her family's good health and Aryan blood for three generations; without this document, she did not receive it. A portion of the loan was rescinded with the birth of a child. A 1938 German law stipulated that single women under twenty-five years of age who were seeking employment in factory or commercial work had to first engage in farm service (*Landdeinst*) or household training with the BDM. These laws were hard to implement because the regime did not build enough facilities to train girls for service. In 1939, there were 10,000 girls but 200,000 boys in labor camps. As the economy recovered in the late 1930s, it desperately needed female workers, so policy changed again. Female industrial workers who had received marriage loans and withdrawn from the labor force were permitted to take paid jobs if their husbands were on compulsory military or labor service. However, wages declined throughout the period.[32]

The Soviets also passed decrees affecting women. One law required factories to provide training programs for women to upgrade their skills. However, the surge in female workers meant that many remained unskilled despite official policy. The announcement that unemployed housewives would no longer receive ration cards after January 1932 drew more housewives into employment, yet it also increased demand for child care and public feeding programs. Bolsheviks had not intended that nursery school attendants, canteen cooks, and waitresses be poorly paid while factory workers and career women earned higher wages. Yet this was a cost of industrialization. Other costs included shortages in food, consumer goods, and housing. Of course, many French and English workers experienced similar problems and lived in slums. Accommodation was cheapest in Germany due to housing construction during the Weimar period.

Employment and Unemployment

Unemployment among women workers was highest in Germany (1 to 3 million in 1931–1932), moderately high in England (about 700,000 in 1931 and 500,000 in 1932), low in France (89,000 in 1931 and 148,000 in 1936), and unrecorded in the Soviet Union. Of course, census data understated the problem, and many part-time workers and married women knew it was useless to apply for unemployment compensation.[33] Table 11.2 shows that the number of French women engaged in manufacturing remained stable in the early 1930s, while the number of English and Soviet women increased, and the number in Germany resembled a U-shaped curve, declining in the early 1930s while expanding at the end of the decade. Although the census recorded low rates of unemployment among French workers, they suffered from short hours and temporary jobs that paid low wages. Since many women did not work full time, they were ineligible for the two-week paid holiday the Blum government introduced in 1936. Since factory work was gender segregated, men could not always replace women during unemployment.

By 1936, 600,000 more German women were employed in manufacturing than in 1933. Rearmament, military service, and Four-Year Plans for recovery drew women back into manufacturing. Gender-specific occupations such as spinning, weaving, and the production of artificial yarn demanded female labor, and German capitalists appreciated women's dexterity, patience, and cheaper labor in textile work.[34]

Although the Soviet female labor force expanded 200%, it remained proportionately smaller than European ones due to its larger population. By 1930, the Soviet Union had a population of 150 million, Germany 65 million,

Table 11.2. Women's Employment and Unemployment, 1930s*

Country	1920s Employment	1931–1933 Employment	1931–1933 Unemployment	1936–1939 Employment
France	2,111,000	2,057,000	89,000	2,058,000
Germany	3,000,000	2,758,000	1,000,000	3,310,000
England	1,600,000	2,100,000	700,000	2,480,000
USSR	1,200,000	2,644,000	N/A	3,786,000

*Calculated from *An. Stat.*, 49: 10–1; 52: 128, 188; *Stat. Jarbuch*, 49: 19–24; 236–43; *Gt. Br. 1921 Census*, 54–106; *Gt. Br. P.P. Accounts and Papers, 1933–34*, 26: 4–10; *Perepisi 1926 g.*, 51: 28–61; *Itogi perepisi 1959 g.*, 16: 67–68; *PKh.* (1939), 16 (10): 107–20; *Problemy Ekonomiki*, 12 (7): 106–122. Regarding working conditions, see Reynolds, *France Between the Wars*, 86–87, 112, 114, 118, 127.

and France and England 42 million each. Although 3 million Soviet women were in the industrial labor force, out of the total female labor force of 34 million, the percentage was small—about 9%.[35]

Heavy Industry

The Soviet female labor force was also distributed differently. Whereas textiles, clothing, and food occupied the bulk of the European female labor force, many Soviet women worked in heavy industry, mining, and construction (table 11.3).

Construction, mining, and heavy industry were difficult, but most peasants were accustomed to hard work, and they found compensation in the higher wages and paid vacations manufacturing offered. Udarniks who fulfilled their quotas received special privileges. Generally, peasant migrants found urban amenities such as medical clinics, running water, electricity, gas stoves, and indoor plumbing to be improvements over rural life. However, the in-migration of 9 million people to the cities strained housing and municipal services.[36]

Everyday Lives of Working-Class Women

Foreign observers often commented on the harsh lives of Soviet working women, as well as their stoicism and willingness to sacrifice for their

Table 11.3. Women in Manufacturing, 1930s*

Industry	USSR (1939)	Germany (1939)	France (1936)	England (1939)
Textiles	805,000	757,000	404,000	732,000
Clothing	555,000	689,000	746,000	500,000
Food	274,000	581,000	194,000	283,000
Metals	522,000	443,000	138,000	420,000
Printing**	104,000	210,000	95,000	201,000
Chemicals	95,000	121,000	44,000	77,000
Building***	488,000	64,000	12,000	16,000
Mining****	178,000	10,000	11,000	10,000

*Calculated from *An. Stat.*, 49: 10–11; 52: 128,188; *Stat. Jarbuch*, 49: 19–24, 236–43; *Gt. Br. 1921 Census*, 54–106; *Gt. Br. P.P. Accounts and Papers*, 26: 4–10; *Perepisi 1926 g.*, 51: 28–61; *Itogi perepisi 1959 g.*, 16: 67–68; *PKh.*, 16 (10, 1939): 107–20; *Problemy Ekonomiki*, 12 (7): 106–22.

**Includes paper making.   ***Figures for 1937.   ****Figures for 1933.

country. Mexican writer Jesus Silva Herzog was surprised at their patience in waiting one to three hours in breadlines. He thought some waited out of fear, some because they were accustomed to suffering, and others out of a spirit of conscious sacrifice, so that future generations would have a life less wretched than theirs. He believed that their capacity for suffering was limitless.[37] Another observer noted that the nerves of the Germans gave way after four years of privation during World War I, while Russians endured the sufferings of that war, the Civil War, and the Five-Year Plans as well.[38] Long suffering and patience aided the development of the Soviet state in the 1930s.

Soviet and European women were plagued by poor housing, low wages, unhealthy working conditions, inattentive trade unions, and sexual harassment. Vast differences in pay and standards of living existed between skilled and unskilled workers. Unskilled workers in Moscow often lived in crowded, dilapidated housing. Their apartments sometimes had oil lamps, bare floors, and curtainless windows. To collect overdue rents, apartment entrances posted the names of rent defaulters, and the courts forced employees to pay or be evicted. Workers guilty of slackness or alcoholism could lose their trade union card and right to work in Moscow. Then they might have to take jobs at construction projects where labor was so scarce that union cards were unnecessary. As in the previous century, factory workers were sometimes overcome with sulfur fumes. But in the Soviet period, they could go to a first aid office to inhale oxygen.[39]

Of course, London workers also suffered from intense overcrowding, high rents, and low wages. English women continued to earn significantly less than men regardless of occupation. In 1935, the average weekly earnings of adult male textile workers were 49/9 (49 shillings 9 pence) and those of women 28/8; in tobacco 79/7 and 39/7; in leather 61/9 and 29/6. No wonder English women retired from factory work upon marriage. Girls earned even lower wages. Most young working-class girls gave their wage packet to their mothers, who bought their food and clothing until they were twenty years old. In York, half the children in working-class families lived in poverty for ten or more years of their lives. When they became adolescents with jobs, they indulged in cigarettes, cocoa, chocolate cakes, and dancing.[40]

While Soviet women worked under harsh conditions, European women often experienced alienation and underemployment. One young English girl found her work as a seamstress frustrating since she was never given a whole garment to sew. Nor could she and her coworkers talk or giggle, because a foreman was watching them all the time. She worked a short shift and made only four shillings a week. Initially, she was afraid to face her mother with such a meager wage packet, because she knew it cost that much for her mother to feed her each day.[41]

French working-class women also experienced falling wages and rising unemployment: 90,000 without jobs in 1931 and 120,000 in 1936. Hardest hit were those in textiles and clothing. French women in heavy industry suffered less unemployment. The 1931 census shows that over 60% of unemployed female industrial workers were married, widowed, or divorced, suggesting that those with children suffered especially from unemployment. The census also listed 41% of unemployed female workers as born outside the département where they worked and 9% born outside the country. A shortage of workers in the 1920s attracted many foreign workers to France, and many of them were sent home to save jobs for French citizens. Like other working women, married French women suffered from low pay, irregular work, and lack of time and energy for their double burden of household and factory work.[42]

Trade Unions

Soviet and European women often received short shrift from the trade unions. In Germany, Hitler neutralized the unions, leaving workers without the protection they had previously enjoyed. Soviet trade unions were subordinate to the Communist Party and lacked authority. Although male dominated, they provided some important benefits for women: the eight-hour day; literacy classes; elementary and secondary school classes at the factory; study circles; paramilitary training; subsidized tickets to the theater, opera, and ballet; access to cooperative housing; vacations; rest homes; maternity coverage if one stayed on the job three years; on-site child care; and nursing breaks for their babies. Because social welfare benefits were linked to union membership, almost all Soviet workers belonged to a union.

In contrast, French and English women's union membership fell off following their rout from industry after World War I. In France, women accounted for only 150,000 members (12%) of industrial and commercial unions in 1930, a decline from their previous high of 240,000 in 1920. The French Communist Party was not very successful in organizing women. Apparently female campaigners found it difficult to leave their domestic duties to organize. By 1932, the French Communist Party had organized 32,000 women in the Red trade unions in textiles, hospitals, railways, transport, postal, telegraph, and telephone services. The failure of the Communists to organize more widely was due to male indifference and women's difficulties in leaving their household duties for organizational work. Catholic trade unions organized about 40,000 women by 1935. They provided benefits in cases of sickness, old age, or unemployment. They also offered employment bureaus, clothing clubs, rest homes for members, courses for apprenticeship, general and technical instruction, and study circles and lectures on social and trade union questions. French women constituted only 8% of union members in the 1930s because their double burden at home and factory left little time or energy for union participation. Yet the national strike of 1936 increased textile workers' unionization from 6,000 to 100,000.[43]

Sexual Stereotyping and Harassment

Sexual stereotyping and harassment pervaded European and Soviet workplaces in the 1930s. European society identified factory work and apprenticeship with men and failed to provide women skills and advancement. Despite their greater efficiency, fewer unjustified absences from work, more productive use of work time, lower labor turnover, and less time wasted smoking than men, women still earned lower wages. Soviet newspapers and novels sometimes dealt with these problems. In *The Volga Flows into the Caspian Sea* (1931), a woman reminds her comrades that they do not have to suffer indignities from male supervisors and workers, and they walk off their jobs to participate in a friend's funeral. At the internment, they condemn a man for his wife's suicide and try to throw him into her grave. This incident shows working women who have stopped being victims and who have developed political consciousness and solidarity. By marching together at Maria's funeral, they showed their supervisors that they would no longer tolerate harassment. Komsomolki at construction sites often changed the atmosphere. At Kuznets, 2,200 Komsomolki worked on construction. They came from urban areas and helped older women value themselves as good workers and worthy human beings. They helped women resist sexual harassment.[44]

Although many Soviet women resisted sexual harassment at work, some feared losing their jobs. During the early 1930s, wages were so low that a household needed both spouses' incomes for the family to survive. In times of economic hardship, women endured sexual overtures unless they had trade union or Party officials to back them up. In Europe, the Depression weakened women's right to employment and decreased their ability to resist sexual harassment.[45]

Service Workers

Cleaning women, hospital attendants, nursery school teachers, canteen cooks, and waitresses suffered from low wages and low social status in Europe and the Soviet Union. Yet some women in these ranks experienced the 1930s as a time of upward mobility. But it was not an easy time for critically minded women in any country. Simone de Beauvoir, who refused to teach pronatalist doctrines, was denounced to her supervisors. Virginia Woolf's *Three Guineas* (1938), which attacked patriarchy in England, was not much appreciated. Soviet writers Olga Friedenberg and Anna Akhmatova found it difficult to publish their works. German socialists and strong-minded Communist Party members in the Soviet Union were jobless, exiled, or imprisoned. For Soviets who accepted the status quo, there was ample educational and economic opportunity. Those who opposed the regime, however, suffered accordingly. The Party generally found less sabotage among mid-level female doctors, teachers, administrators, and technical personnel than among high-level male engineers and managers. Consequently, career women often suffered a lower rate of arrest, imprisonment, and death than did male professionals.[46]

Domestic Servants

The 1930s witnessed some reversals in women's employment. The sharp decline among Russian and European servants from 1890 to 1925 leveled off in the 1930s (table 11.4).

Table 11.4. Women in Domestic Service, 1920s and 1930s*

Country	1920s	1930s
Germany	1,300,000	1,200,000
England	1,150,000	1,364,000
France	661,000	666,000
USSR	475,000	511,853

*Calculated from *An. Stat.*, 49 (1933): 13; 52 (1936): 13, 243*; 56 (1940–45): 144; P.P., *Census of England and Wales, 1921*, 104; *Gt. Br. P.P. Accounts & Papers,* 26 (1933–34), cmd. 4625; *21st Abstract of Labour Statistics of the United Kingdom*, 13; *Stat. Handbuch*, 29; *SYB League of Nations*, 44. The 1937 Soviet census listed 511,853 women as *domrabotnitsy. Vsesoiuznaia perepis naseleniia 1937 g: Kratkie itogi*, Section 29, 129. The 1939 Soviet census hid domestic servants by listing them with other categories. Economist E. Orlikova estimated that they constituted 1.8% of the nonagrarian labor force, or 170,000. Orlikova, "Zhenskii Trud v SSSR," *PKh*, (1939) 16 (10): 113.

As the Depression spread, the number of unemployed domestics grew to 35,000 in France, to 107,000 in England, and to 180,000 in Germany by 1933. Hard times forced many households to dispense with servants. After the Nazis gained power, significant differences arose between English and German domestics. The English phased out training camps for young people when employment picked up, but by 1938 working-class German girls had to participate in a summer camp or contribute a year of labor service. Some worked as servants in rural areas, helping farmer's wives with child care, cooking, housework, milking, or gardening. In 1938, the Reich required job-seeking spinsters less than twenty-five years old to first work as a servant for one year at minimal pay.[47] After the Nuremberg Laws of September 1935, German female servants less than thirty-five years old could not work in Jewish households. Of course, some loyal servants ignored the law. When they did, Brownshirts sometimes forcibly took them away. Jewish households had difficulty replacing servants because of the poisonous propaganda against them. Yet the pluck of some servants was amazing. When Madeleine Kent's husband lost his job due to his socialist views, their cleaning lady, Frau Zetzschke, remained with them. She was proud to work for them and stood up for them against informers.[48]

In England and France, domestic service changed little. Rural English girls continued migrating to town to become servants as they had in earlier decades. Their wages remained stagnant: salaries for cooks were 55 to 60 pounds per annum; those for parlor maids, kitchen maids, and nannies, 35 to 50 pounds; and housekeepers, 150 pounds.[49] As in the 1920s, English girls entered service as a last resort. One was shocked to learn that she had ten pairs of shoes to polish in the morning and dishes to wash for eleven people! At home her father had always polished her shoes, and there were only four people to wash up after. She quit when the milkman told her that her employer hired a new maid every week. Moreover, she earned only 6 shillings a week, or 15 pounds a year.[50]

In France, the wages of domestic servants rose from 1926 to 1930, then declined in the mid 1930s. Cooks earning 4,800 francs a year in 1930 received only 4,500 in 1935. Likewise, wages of chambermaids fell from 3,700 francs in 1930 to 3,500 in 1935. Female cooks earned half the wages of their male counterparts, while valets and chambermaids earned about the same. Still, they suffered little unemployment, 3% in 1931 and 5% in 1936. Higher proportions of the unemployed came from those born outside the département where they worked and among the foreign born; for example, Russian women employed as domestics in France experienced 8% unemployment in 1931.[51]

Although some girls disdained domestic service, desperate ones took such jobs. In the early 1930s, the British Ministry of Labour established training centers for the unemployed. Most of the girls who completed domestic service training and older women who became cooks found employment. British centers were voluntary, not politically doctrinaire, nor as extensive as German camps that also trained unemployed youth. Generally, the labor camps reduced the number of people looking for work and kept young people physically fit, mentally alert, and off the streets. As English unemployment abated in 1933, training centers closed.[52]

What English society did voluntarily, Germany did through legislation. In 1933, German families who employed servants received special tax reductions and benefits. The Nazis developed urban and rural training centers for young women. In 1934–1935, one Berlin bureau trained 45,000 girls in household and child care work. In the Berlin–Brandenburg district, there were 100 retraining centers. On farms, four to five girls trained at a time, with courses in housework and light farm work lasting three to four months. They received room and board, while the farmer received one mark from the state for the girl's lodging and eight pfennigs per hour for instructing them.

Visiting Germany in 1934, Mrs. Chesterton compared English and German training camps. German dormitories were "airy, beautifully clean, and nicely furnished." Family photographs and flowers decorated the walls and tables. The greatest difference was that German camps were designed to bring women of all classes and locales together and to break down class and regional differences, while English training centers were not. Other visitors noticed that the German girls enjoyed themselves, despite the discipline. Those working as milkmaids rose at four A.M., the others at five in the summer and six in the winter. Their work included cooking, washing, fetching firewood from the forest, chopping wood, sewing, making furniture, and gardening. Those helping local farm wives did so from nine A.M. until three P.M. In the afternoon, they rested, wrote letters, sewed, or read. In the evening, they had singing, folk dancing, political talks, and good times.[53]

The 1939 Soviet census did not list domestic service as a category. However, the 1937 census (which was suppressed for fifty years) listed about 500,000 in domestic service. Girls could easily find jobs in manufacturing during the FYP, and about one-third left service each year. Career women and high-ranking Party members often employed nannies to rear their children while they worked. The Bonner household even hired daughters of village priests and former nuns as nannies. Denied access to higher education, some daughters of priestly families came to Moscow, worked for a family, and took evening courses at a factory so they could be classified as workers and pursue higher education. Wives of army officers and factory executives also kept servants. In Magnitogorsk, the American welder John Scott was amazed when his wife, who was a teacher, hired a kulak to care for their child. They paid her 50 rubles a month. Apparently, 800 rubles a year was the average wage. The wife of the president of the village soviet also employed servants.[54]

Low-Level Employees

Service workers have been hidden from history. Little is known about office cleaners, laundresses, bath attendants, canteen workers, hospital orderlies, or hairdressers. The 1926 Soviet census listed these categories separately, but the 1939 census did not. Aggregate numbers skyrocketed from 300,000 in 1926 to 2.2 million in 1939, but it is unclear which categories changed most. The Institute of Public Feeding provided 20,000 meals a day in Moscow in 1930, but 2.3 million in 1934, so the number of food service workers exploded. Institutional child care occupied 8,000 women in 1926, but 241,000 in 1939. Domestic servants earned even less than canteen workers, who received 1,060 rubles per year. European and Soviet women preferred low-level service occupations to manufacturing. In Germany, the proportion in factory work increased 6% from 1925 to 1939, while the percentage in low-level public service rose 148%.[55]

Unemployment was low among French servants but higher among hairdressers and manicurists. The 1931 census listed 29,000 female hairdressers, but 5,000 (19%) unemployed. English statistics showed about 8% unemployment in domestic service and 5% in hairdressing, manicure, and chiropody.[56] It is difficult to say how many German beauticians were unemployed, but manicurists often worked long hours for little pay. One earned fifteen shillings a week for ten-hour days. She thought of taking a position as a maid, but that paid even less and entailed longer hours of work, so she kept her job. Before 1933, there had been talk of a trade union for manicurists and beauticians, but it ended after Hitler took power. Luckily, low rents offset the low wages.[57]

Well-dressed, coiffured, and manicured Soviet *devushki* (girls) sold cigarettes, postcards, and periodicals at hotels. Like European workers, they lived at home, contributed to their family income, and went to dances and enjoyed the cinema. Working an eight-hour day, they sometimes attended evening lectures on literature, economics, and history.[58]

Life could be severe for German service workers. When a fishmonger at a Berlin market called out: "Herring—he-e-ring, thick and fat as Goering," storm troopers took her to a concentration camp. After two weeks of punishment, she promised not to insult Nazi honor. Returning to her market stall, she sang: "Herring, herring. Thick and fat as—week before last." Punishment in nearby camps could turn people's hair white overnight.[59]

Some English girls preferred laundry work to domestic service despite the possibility of layoff. Laundresses earned six to ten shillings a week—enough to contribute to the family income. English lasses often spent their evenings at girls' clubs. Mentors there helped them complete their school-leaving certificate so they could escape dead-end jobs and train for other occupations.[60]

Mid-Level Employees

Huge numbers of women worked in commerce and banking (table 11.5). Such work was clean but paid low wages. In England, girls worked ten to twelve hours a day as shop assistants but earned only 12 pounds a year, about what servants received. One girl thought her employer never trusted her. Shopkeeping jobs were easily gained and lost, and 52,000 commercial workers suffered unemployment in 1931.[61] Wage differentials based on age and gender existed, with men in commerce earning sixty-five shillings per week, while women received forty. In banking, insurance, and public services the gap was ninety to fifty.[62]

Gradually, commerce became mechanized and feminized. Between 1926 and 1931, 160,000 more French women took jobs in commerce and

Table 11.5. Women in Commerce and Banking, 1920s and 1930s*

Country	1920s	1930s
England	793,000 (1921)	870,600 (1931)
France	970,000 (1926)	1,130,000 (1931)
Germany	1,600,000 (1925)	1,964,000 (1933)
USSR	261,000 (1926)	1,970,000 (1939)

*Calculated from *An. Stat.*, 52: 243*; *SYB League of Nations*, 44, 46.

banking. They took such work because men shunned it; their education enabled them to staff such posts; and employers believed they were content with low wages, would not join unions, or seek promotions. Thus, they filled lower positions while men got the higher ones. They experienced little unemployment: only 17,000 (1.5%) in commerce and banking were unemployed in 1931, and 28,000 (2%) in 1936. French typists and bookkeepers registered higher levels of unemployment (64% and 46% in 1931). The Soviet census listed 21,000 female telephonists and telegraphers in 1926, but 180,000 communications workers in 1939. About 100,000 worked as clerks, secretaries, and typists in 1926, but 380,000 a decade later. Similarly, 80,000 women were listed as accountants and bookkeepers in 1926, but over 600,000 in 1939. Mechanization of office work occurred in Europe in the 1920s, but in the 1930s in the Soviet Union. Both European and Soviet mid-level employees received low wages. Soviet trade and communication workers earned about 1,300 rubles per year. However, typists who worked for foreign firms earned more. Clerks earned so little that some studied to become career women. Countless nurses became midwives, feldshers, and even doctors, and some mid-level employees became engineers, factory directors, and directors of city soviets.[63]

Professional Workers

> While the gospel of Fascism is proclaiming that woman should revert to her original status of domestic drudge . . . dependent on the man, the Soviet woman is absolutely free to develop her own individuality and work out her own destiny . . . to master culture, science, the arts, public administration, and industrial production.
>
> —Olga Leonova, *The Soviet Comes of Age* (1938)

Olga Leonova's words illustrate German and Soviet attitudes toward women. An expanding economy and favorable educational policies produced a Soviet female intelligentsia of 1.3 million, which far surpassed its European cohort.

Although French patriarchal attitudes remained strong, several thousand women entered the professions and found protected posts in lower civil service ranks; for example, more became barristers and notaries than judges or magistrates and many female doctors worked in clinics. The number of women in religious life increased to 55,000. Like German women, French female doctors mainly worked in clinics. Significant numbers became elementary and secondary teachers, but only five held university posts in 1934. Still, their situation was vastly superior to the position of German women, who were restricted to so-called women's spheres and limited in their access to higher education. In 1933, many German career women were unemployed. Those in high-ranking positions declined from 89,000 in 1933 to 87,900 in 1939. Self-identified Jewish women constituted about 5,000 in the liberal professions in the 1933 census and figured among those fired. Other German women were surprised to find themselves defined as Jews since they had never thought of themselves as Jewish, having come from mixed marriages or converted Jewish families and considering themselves "cosmopolitan" Germans. English career women also faced male resentment, and many married career women lost their posts in the Depression. A few made inroads at the London School of Economics.[64]

Nightmares in Germany

On a visit to Germany in 1934, Mrs. Chesterton found female lawyers who had been ruthlessly dismissed and a Berlin lawyer who had become a telephone operator on a starvation wage. Unemployment hit middle-aged female civil servants the hardest. Their menfolk had often been killed in World War I, and they had spent years of work obtaining modest posts. The Nazis ignored all laws of contract and reduced them to typists and translators. In government departments, women beyond marriageable age could only be employed as typists or stenographers—positions wielding no responsibility or power. They also had to prove Aryan descent for three generations. One distressed woman had mislaid her paternal great-grandmother's papers. If she could not find them, she might lose her job! Fortunately, her fair hair and blue eyes were accepted as proof of Aryan blood. The regime also policed teachers, and nonconformists lost their jobs. Under these pressures, 97% of teachers joined the Nazi Teachers Organization by 1936. The regime stopped subsidizing women's lodging, leaving many career women dependent upon relatives for housing. Yet despite their precarious situation, Chesterton saw no unemployed women as pathetic as those haunting English cities.[65]

The Nazis dismissed Jewish female doctors, leftists, and *Doppelverdiener* (married women workers). Some Jewish career women emigrated abroad, taking menial jobs in foreign countries to escape persecution. Jewish teachers and professors had to resign since they could not teach in the "true German spirit." Elisabeth Blochmann, a convert to Christianity, lost her job as professor at the Pedagogic Academy at Halle/Saale.

Table 11.6. Women in Select Professions, 1930s*

	USSR (1939)	France (1931)	Germany (1933)	England (1931)
Doctors	75,000	900	5,500	2,800
Dentists	12,000	2,800	6,200	390
Teachers	707,000	187,000	85,000	300,000
Engineers	33,000	1,200	618	209
Judges	2,746	1,500	36	79
Lawyers, notaries, etc.	8,300	13,700	252	116
Religious vocations	——	50,000	76,000	18,000

*Calculated from *Perepisi 1926 goda*, 34: 56–75; *Itogi perepisi 1959 g*, 16: 161–70; *Gt. Br. Accounts & Papers, 1933/4*, 26 (cmd 4625): 12; "Staffs Employed in Government Departs," *Gt. Br. Parl. Papers Accounts & Papers*, 20: 1937–38; *Census Eng. and Wales 1951*, Occupational Tables, 662; *RSDR, 1931*, Tome I, Troisième Partie, 162–68; *Stat. Handbuch*, 1928–1944, 32–33.

She emigrated to England in 1937, where she taught German at Oxford University. Fledgling Jewish scholars Edith Stein and Hannah Arendt had no academic future. The Reich dismissed Kathe Kollwitz, a socialist and a feminist, from her position in a government art school and forced artist Hanna Hoch to tone down the social parody in her work. It blacklisted both as "cultural Bolshevists." They survived only in seclusion. Those who protested flirted with danger.[66]

England

In 1931, 20,000 English career women were unemployed, and those with jobs experienced discrimination and resentment. English attitudes toward career women were more patriarchal than Soviet or French ones. For example, when the London Library Committee approached Virginia Woolf about serving on its board, the tacit understanding was that she would say no. While English women had gained the right to vote and to enter most professions, their situation in the civil service remained precarious. One writer suggested that men replace women in government offices and that career women be redirected into domestic service. Another complained that women had gained too much liberty in the war and that they had been praised and petted out of all proportion to their performance.[67]

At the London School of Economics (LSE), a male graduate student complained about female fanatics. Yet women constituted only half the student body and usually took two-year certificates in social work and the social sciences, not higher degrees as men did. Still, a small network of scholarly women flourished there. Eileen Power taught at the LSE from 1921 to 1938 and became a lecturer in English history at Oxford in 1938. A specialist in medieval economic history, Power founded and edited the *Economic History Review*. Other female historians and economists—such as Ivy Pinchbeck, Mabel Buer, Julia Mann, and M. G. Jones—obtained higher degrees at the LSE and became readers and tutors at university colleges. Some graduates became businesswomen, political activists, or even secretaries. A survey of English university posts in 1931 found only 13 female professors compared to 829 males, and 583 women lecturers compared to 3,103 men. Women held 13% of university posts, clustered in the lower grades, and earned less than 300 pounds per year.[68]

They also suffered from gender and wage discrimination in the civil service. A committee on sex differentiation in pay reported in June 1937 that while it adhered to the principle of equal pay, men could earn up to 20% more than women for the same work. Only the junior grades paid the same salaries.[69] The Women's Primary School Teachers Association fought the dismissal of married women teachers, lobbied against unequal salaries, and asserted their right to serve as head of mixed schools of girls and boys. Teachers generally earned 300 pounds per annum, while male administrators earned 500 to 600 and women 400 to 500. Women teachers often helped in girls' clubs and coached working-class girls to qualify for better jobs.[70]

In 1934, Princess Helena Victoria sponsored the Women's Employment Federation. It drew together eighty affiliated societies for women engineers, pharmacists, journalists and so forth. Despite the patronage of aristocratic and middle-class women, the society lacked funds to provide job training, and the government refused to support it.[71]

France

French career women were considerably better off than their Teutonic sisters. Having gained professional positions after the war, by 1931 they accounted for 228,000 of those in public administration and 325,000 in the liberal professions. By 1936, those in public administration had increased by another 10,000, while falling by 12,000 in the professions. Their unemployment was only 4%, but higher for those born outside of the département where they worked and among the foreign born. Russian-born women working in French administration experienced no unemployment in 1931, but 10% of those in the professions did. About 11% of translators and 20%

of industrial designers were unemployed. One-third of unemployed career women were married.[72]

French female primary-school teachers earned the same wages as men and did not lose their jobs upon marriage. In 1936, the peasant teacher Emilie Carles earned 700 francs per month, which provided for her extended family. Still, women secondary-school teachers earned less than men and received smaller pensions on retirement. Only teachers who became unwed mothers lost their posts. In the civil service, women earned adequate wages and felt secure in their jobs.[73]

While the French government did not punish or dismiss married women workers as the Germans and English did, patriarchal attitudes remained strong. Geneviève Tabouis (1892–1985) encountered sexist attitudes among editors when she wanted to become a correspondent for the League of Nations in 1934. The editor of *Petite Girone* told her she would have to sign her articles G. R. Tabouis and write in the masculine form to disguise her gender. When she worked for *Oeuvre*, government ministers failed to explain foreign affairs as thoroughly to her as they did to men. In publishing her book *Tout Ank Amon—The Pharaoh*, one editor said: "Madame, how *can* you expect me to publish such a serious book by a woman! A novel with a love story—yes, or possibly a travel book, but a historical work—impossible!" Another suggested she sign it G. for George or Gaston. Readers would not know it was written by a woman, and it would be a great success.[74]

The Soviet Union

Soviet career women numbered 1.3 million in 1939. Although educational and scientific institutions remained male dominated, new opportunities allowed women to follow their dreams in deciding upon a career. According to the 1939 Soviet census, women filled 44% (91,688) of all leading educational, scientific, and artistic higher education posts; 42% (60,900) of special educational institution positions; 55% (657,556) of elementary and secondary school situations; and 34% (32,907) of positions as professors and lecturers at universities.[75]

They held five times more university posts than English women did and were free to pursue the career of their choice due to state-subsidized education and an expanding economy. Whereas a Soviet girl could train as an airplane designer, English families of limited means could not afford such training, and an English girl would not be hired for such work. Careers were also open in the theater. Natalia Sats became the director of the

Children's Theater in Moscow when she was a teenager. No one paid attention to her during the revolution and Civil War. When she directed the Berlin Opera's production of *Falstaff* in 1931, she caused a sensation because Europeans were not accustomed to women opera directors. German papers praised her for bringing a breath of fresh air to opera, and tickets sold out quickly. Yet fascist papers denounced her as a Russian Jew whose production succeeded in only a few "temperamental scenes."[76]

Despite widespread opportunity, Soviet women still had to contend with patriarchal ideas. The regime continued to endorse women's educational and economic equality but deemphasized their liberation in the 1930s. While the Depression undermined European career women's employment, the expanding Soviet economy encouraged it. The English census listed more than 400,000 women employed in the liberal professions, the French census more than 500,000, the German census more than 800,000, but the Soviet census recorded over 1 million.[77] Since the Soviet population was much larger than the English, French, or German, the proportion of Soviet career women was not as great as the numbers suggest, but their continued gains in the 1930s were impressive. Women progressed partly because the professions they chose were not crowded, did not threaten Soviet men's economic or political power, and met the needs of the FYPs. Table 11.7 shows women's significant presence in education and medicine, but their smaller role in factory management and politics.

Soviet media touted women's achievements. Women of all classes and ethnic groups enjoyed access to higher education. Although Slavic women predominated, non-Slavic women pursued higher education and careers in greater numbers than in the Tsarist era. In 1932, 52% of Muscovite medical students were working class in origin and 11% were peasant. This situation differed from that of Europe, where higher education remained a middle-class preserve. Another unique feature of Soviet education was night school. Half of the new female medical students in 1932 attended evening courses. Night schools allowed working women to achieve educational, economic, and social mobility.[78]

Politics also affected women's pursuit of higher education. In 1937, *Moscow Daily News* featured thirty-two-year-old Klavdia Varfolomeeva, who combined the duties of wife, mother, and white-collar worker while serving in various city councils. As a reward for her work in the Saratov soviet, the All Russian Central Executive Committee sent her to study construction in Moscow. Komsomol and Party organizations encouraged both married and single women to pursue higher education and become part of

Table 11.7. Soviet Women in Select Professions, 1926–1939*

	1926	1939
Doctors	19,000	75,000
Dentists	5,400	12,000
Feldshers & midwives	27,400	110,000
Teachers	192,000	707,000
Cultural & scientific	16,000	158,000
Engineers	400	33,000
Agronomists	1,500	32,000
Political administrators	5,200	54,000
Factory managers	2,300	46,000
Totals	269,200	1,227,000

*Calculated from *Perepisi 1926 goda*, 34: 56–75;

the new Soviet intelligentsia. While some men opposed women's employment as engineers, the Party upheld their rights.[79] One of the most famous examples of political recruitment is that of Ekaterina A. Furtseva. She joined the Komsomol at fourteen, served as secretary of the Chemistry Institute's Party organization in Moscow in 1937, and continued to advance. Whereas European women lacked supportive networks, the FYP made career women both needed and common.

One flaw in the political system was the lack of quotas for drawing women into the Komsomol and Party. While women constituted over one-third of those attending institutions of higher education and large proportions of those in the helping professions, they composed only one-fifth of Party members. (Of course, the majority of men also lacked political influence during the 1930s!) In government work, women constituted 33% of those on the local level in 1939. Yet the number of paid women political administrators (54,000) remained small compared to the number of men (445,000) or the number of women in other professions. Still, women in all ethnic groups increased their visibility. The percentage of Kazakh women in the Raion district of the CEC increased from 13.7% in 1929 to 23% in 1933. Some headed soviets and state farms. Rose Magamayeva declared, "It is more than a dream to us to see Kazakh women, downtrodden yesterday, driving tractors and speaking at meetings. This is what socialism has done for us Kazakh women."[80]

Their Party activity revealed two persistent problems: their clustering in the helping professions and male political dominance. Professional women predominated in low-paid areas such as medicine and education, not in engineering or management, which paid more. Women usually became factory directors in female-dominated light industry, not in heavy industry. A few thousand women became engineers, architects, factory managers, or political workers, but several hundred thousand became cultural, medical, and educational workers.[81]

Discrimination in the Professions

Clustering in the helping professions at low levels also occurred in Germany, France, and England, where authorities also thought it more appropriate to hire women as elementary-school than secondary-school teachers. English school boards paid women teachers less than men even though they performed similar work. Male teachers with degrees earned 276 to 528 pounds per annum, while women received 264 to 420. Likewise, male teachers without degrees earned 204 to 432 pounds per year, and women 192 to 342. One headmistress felt humiliated giving a check to a male teacher that was larger than her own. Male teachers received pensions worth 199 pounds in 1935–1936, while the average woman's was 126 pounds. Death gratuities for men teachers amounted to 420 pounds, but were only 257 for women.[82]

While female elementary teachers predominated, the number of female secondary teachers expanded in the 1930s. Separate schools for girls and boys resulted in large numbers of female secondary teachers in England and France. Even before 1933, German women seldom became secondary teachers because such posts were part of the civil service, which was crowded and male dominated.

In the 1930s, Soviet women predominated in elementary education and made significant inroads into secondary teaching. Although the feminization of teaching took place in most republics (50% to 90% women), it did not occur in higher education. Fewer women held high university positions, constituting only 3–7% of professors, 11% to 19% of docents, and 22% to 34% of assistants and lecturers. They represented about 30% of technicum lecturers and 46% of those in rabfaks. Outstanding successes were Anna M. Pankratova, head of the history department at Moscow University (1934–1937), and Olga Freidenberg, Director of Philology at Leningrad Institute of Philosophy, Language, Literature, and History (1932–1939).[83] Although the highest levels of the professions remained male-dominated, Soviet women penetrated these bastions further than their European sisters did.

Despite their generally positive situation, Soviet women encountered some peculiar forms of discrimination. In the 1930s, *byvshie liudy* (intellectuals educated in the Tsarist period and those born into the gentry and clerical classes) found it extremely difficult to obtain employment. Gentry-class women such as Marie Avinov had problems obtaining work, espcially after her husband was arrested. Government publishing agencies refused to hire her because of her aristocratic past. Only her friends' intercession helped her obtain translating and typing jobs. As the wife of "an enemy of the people," she had trouble keeping her room in Moscow. Assessors levied 10,000 rubles in taxes on her, but her friends helped her refute the appraisal.[84] Both German career women and Soviet byvshie liudy took low-status, low-paying jobs as translators and typists in order to survive.

Struggles

Women's employment in the 1930s included obstacles as well as accomplishments. While they attained a great deal, they also paid for success. Soviet writers have often eulogized rather than analyzed the lives of career women, and Western scholars have often emphasized Soviet problems, while ignoring the struggles that plagued European career women. Tabouis's story of breaking into journalism and publishing shows patriarchal problems French women had to deal with. Condescending male attitudes also predominated in the Church of England, when some women tried to become lay readers.[85]

Soviet apologists argued that women could work, develop their personality and interests, and improve their own and their families' health. Article 22 of the 1936 Soviet Constitution proclaimed women's equality, indicating that nothing further needed to be done. These views marked a change in official attitude toward women. In the 1920s, Party members had drawn attention to unequal wages, inadequate child care, and the need for legal abortion and prophylactoria. In the 1930s, such criticism disappeared, and Stalin's motto "Life is better, life is more joyous" appeared. While they deserved to congratulate themselves on providing women greater access to education and professional work than existed in Tsarist Russia or in contemporary Europe, the Party's glorification of women's achievements obscured low pay, inadequate child care, crowded housing, sexual harassment, and insufficient training.

Women often clustered in the middle and low ranks of the professions because family and household obligations hindered their professional advancement. Many English career women never married or married very late in life and remained childless. Running her country house, hiring domestic servants, tallying household accounts, coping with bank managers, arranging family holidays, hiring tutors for her children, and juggling social obligations all drew E. M. Delafield away from her writing.[86]

Many Soviet professors and students realized that children usually slowed women's educational and professional advancement. They thought the ban on abortion was premature in 1936 because the housing situation did not allow for children, and nurseries and baby equipment were in short supply. Time budget studies of the 1930s do not reveal how women divided their time between paid work and unpaid household work, since this was one of the "sensitive" subjects that Soviet scholars ignored. In the 1920s, women clerical workers spent twenty more hours each week in household obligations than their male counterparts, and one suspects the situation remained similar in the 1930s. A job satisfaction study of blue- and white-collar workers revealed that female white-collar workers expressed more dissatisfaction with their time budgets than others.[87]

Low Pay in the Professions

Educated women generally received lower pay than men. Virginia Woolf drew attention to the situation in England by comparing salaries of office-holders in the Church of England. In 1938, an archbishop earned 15,000 pounds, a bishop 10,000, a dean 3,000, and a deaconess—the only position a woman could hold—a paltry 150 pounds. Margaret Cole noted that only Oxford or Cambridge men were chosen for posts carrying a stipend of 1,000 pounds or more. If the salary were 500 pounds, a nonuniversity man could take the position. If the remuneration were 250 pounds, a competent woman or a man half-time could be hired. Women's salaries, raises, and pensions were so much lower than men's that Cole advised educated English women to marry a man of similar talent to live decently.[88]

The wages of Soviet workers rose in the 1930s, while those of medical personnel remained low. At the end of the first plan, the yearly wage of medical personnel was 1,248 rubles a year, which slightly exceeded that of agricultural workers. By the mid 1930s, physicians earned 200 to 400 rubles a month, while feldshers received 180 to 225 rubles a month in town and 160 to 200 rubles in the country.[89] Women clustered at the lower end of the professions. Of 550,000 medical workers in 1939, only 6,500 leading personnel in medical institutions were women. Of 830,000 female educational personnel, only 35,000 held posts as university professors or heads of scientific research institutes. Most female educational personnel worked as teachers (660,000), earning 240 to 300 rubles a month in rural areas, while some held even lower-paying jobs as nursery-school teachers. Still, the wages and living standards of career women rose during the second FYP (1933–1937). More food, hot water, and better clothing became available. Soviet journalists earned good salaries of 650 rubles per month—two to three times what physicians earned. Since most Soviet women worked, families in which both spouses were employed might live well.[90]

Poor Working Conditions

Career women also coped with inadequate resources. The restaurants for Soviet writers and professional workers were considerably better than those for workers, but child care remained inadequate. Whereas trade unions encouraged factories to provide child care for working women, government institutions, which also employed large numbers of professional women, balked at doing so. Consequently, many career women hired nannies.[91] As domestic service declined in the late 1930s, career women enjoyed even less support with family responsibilities. Nor did crash medical courses properly train women for their work. Many lacked training, equipment, and supplies to do their work well. At Magnitogorsk, dentists were in such short supply that they often had to work two shifts a day. They earned high wages for their double shifts, 800 to 1,200 rubles per month when the average wage for medical personnel was only 2,249 rubles per year. Abortion clinics were also primitive and overcrowded. While Soviet medicine was passably hygienic, it could be psychologically deplorable.[92]

Rural doctors sometimes lived 200 miles from town, had a horse and springless cart for transportation, possessed the barest necessities of life, treated patients with a minimum of drugs, and received their pay two to three months late. After seeing patients during the day, a doctor might lecture to villagers in the evenings on hygiene, first aid, and sanitation. Still, most served the regime willingly and selflessly.[93]

Conditions for French and German teachers in the 1930s were also harsh. They usually received positions in remote villages and put up with inferior school buildings and inadequate housing. Hedwig Jacob, an elementary-school teacher in rural Germany in the 1930s, had to share a room over the school with another teacher. Rural teachers were often poorly paid and sometimes had to room with a village family in partial payment of their salary.[94] Teachers in Sheffield had large classes of forty or more and had to teach standard English to children who spoke Yorkshire on the playground.

Conclusion

Working women shared many of the same aspirations, struggles, and problems. In low-level service jobs and manufacturing, European women suffered from layoffs. The Nazis forced many women to give their jobs to male heads of household. Working-class women lacked protection because the socialist party in Germany was driven underground, while in France and England their interests were subordinated to men's. In Germany, trade unions were outlawed, and in the Soviet Union they were subjected to the Party and state. Mechanization of factory work and the speed-up of production undermined women's health everywhere.

French women in civil service posts suffered little unemployment, while English and German married career women lost their civil service positions. Soviet career women who were byvshie liudy or wives of enemies of the people faced unemployment or even imprisonment. Yet the expanding Soviet economy created a need for huge numbers of career women. Still, low wages, inadequate child care, crowded housing, discrimination, and sexual harassment bedeviled domestic servants, factory workers, and even career women in the 1930s.

Notes

1. *An. Stat.*, 56: 144; 49: 10–11; 52: 128, 188; *Stat. Jarbuch*, 49: 19–24, 236–43; *Gt. Br. 1921 Census*, 54–106; *Gt. Br. P.P. Accounts and Papers*, 1933–34, 26: 4–10; *Statistical Year Book of League of Nations*, 1934/5, 44 (hereafter cited as *SYB League of Nations*).

2. "The Working of Social Insurance in the USSR," *ILR* 28 (October 1933): 539–48; Michael Florinsky, "Social Insurance," *Encyclopedia of Russia and the S.U.*, 519–22, 614.

3. *Perepisi 1926 g.*, 34: 10–11; *SSSR v Tsifrakh*, 9; *PKh.*, 1938, 7: 133; 1939, 8: 142; *Narodnoe Knoziaistvo SSSR za 60 let*, 8.

4. Initially, 30,000 men and 400 women worked on the Baltic White Sea Canal in 1931. Men lived in tents and women in barracks, and more than 300,000 men died during construction of the canal. See *Red Gaols, A Woman's Experiences in Russian Prisons*, 41–50, 61–65; John Scott, *Behind the Urals*, 130–33; Nikolai Pogodin, "The Aristocrats," *Four Soviet Plays*, 179–303; *The White Sea Canal*; GPU Chief

Yagoda, "Heroes who were Saved from the Underworld by the OGPU," *MDN*, 22 June 1933; John Littlepage, *In Search of Soviet Gold*, quoted in Thomas Riha, *Readings in Russian Civilization Vol. III*, 599. Littlepage, who worked in the Siberian gold fields from 1928 to 1937, noticed that kulak men were required to work in the mines, while women were not.

5. Angelina, *My Answer to an American Questionnaire*, 25–26; Vladimir Kirshon, "Bread," (1930), *Four Soviet Plays*; F. Nurina, *Women of the Soviet Union*, 56; Martha Brill Olcott, "The Collectivization Drive in Kazakhstan," *Russian Review* (1980), 40: 122–42; David Lane, "Ethnic and Class Stratification in Soviet Kazakhstan, 1917–1939," *Comparative Studies in Society and History* (April 1975), 17 (2): 165–89; "Party Cleaning Under Way in No. Caucasus," *MDN*, 11 January 1933, 3.

6. "Sotsialisticheskoe sel'skoe khoziaistvo Soiuza SSSR," *PKh.* 7 (1939): 142; "Sotsialisticheskoe stroitel'stvo Soiuza SSSR," *PKh.* 8 (1939): 187; R. Abramovitch, *The Soviet Revolution 1917–1939*, 335–470; "The Collectivization of Agriculture in the Soviet Union," *ILR* 26 (September 1932): 389–90.

7. Veresaev, *Sisters*, 262.

8. Veresaev, *Sisters*, 263–85.

9. Mrs. Cecil Chesterton, *Sickle or Swastika?*, 247–49, 257–59, 263–64.

10. See Chesterton, *Sickle or Swastika?*, 247–49; E. M. Delafield, *I Visit the Soviets, The Provincial Lady in Russia*, 1–79 (originally published in 1937). Delafield spent considerable time visiting a state farm, and her impression was more austere, although the farm near Rostov in 1936 had 13,000 hectares, 530 workers, tractors, electricity, a bathhouse, five brick buildings, horses, pigs, chickens, vineyards, a bakery, a barracks for young girls, and one for boys.

11. *Kollektivist* shows kolkhozy could employ only 38% of the men and 23% of the women from April to June and 77% of the men and 71% of the women during harvest time, July to September. "The Collectivisation of Agriculture in the U.S.S.R.," *ILR* 26 (September 1932): 408; Zuzanek, *Work and Leisure in the Soviet Union*, 12; *The Village of the Viriatino*, 178; "New Life in the Village," *MDN*, 15 December 1933, 2; Moshe Lewin, "Rural Society in Twentieth Century Russia," *Social History* 9 (2): 177–79.

12. See Scott, *Behind the Urals*, 95–98, 126; Rosenberg, *Socialism in a Single Land, 1927–1932*, 255; V. Kuibishev, "Report," *MDN*, 17 January 1933; "Sotsialisticheskoe sel'skoe Khoziaistvo Soiuza SSSR," *PKh* 7 (1939): 135; E. J. Stirniman, "No Stranger to Trouble," *Cedar Rapids Gazette*, 1962. Stirniman was an engineer from Iowa who help teach collective farmers how to use tractors and other farm equipment.

13. "Ob itogakh ... perepisi 1939 goda," *PKh* 6 (1939):12; Frank Lorimer, *The Population of the Soviet Union*, 161–62; Olcott, "The Collectivization Drive in Kazakhstan," *Russian Review* 40: 122–42. Out-migration to urban areas reduced the rural population, but the tremendous loss in Kazakhstan and Ukraine indicates that famine and grain requisitions were especially severe there in the 1930s. Lorimer found shortages in rural populations of 20% in Kazakhstan, 20% Lower Volga and Don areas, 17% Central Volga area; 16% Ukraine, 10% Central Black Soil areas, and 6% Urals.

14. "Women Farmers of the North Caucasus Issue Appeal to Grandmothers," *MDN*, 9 May 1933, 1; "Veteran Zakharova Says," *MDN*, 6 March 1933, 3.

15. One pud equals thirty-six pounds. See "Sotsialisticheskoe sel'skoe khoziaistvo Soiuza SSR," *PKh* 7 (1939): 166; "The Collectivization of Agriculture," *The Modern Encyclopedia of Russian and Soviet History* 7: 160; Chesterton, *Sickle or Swastika?*, 135, 246-49; Lorimer, *Population in the Soviet Union*, 103; R. A. Clarke, *Soviet Facts, 1917–1970*, 74–75.

16. TSU, *Zhenchiny i Deti*, 47; "Sotsialistcheskoe sel'skoe khoziaistvo," *PKh* 7 (1939): 169; *Village of Viriatino*, 288–90; "New Life in the Village," *MDN*, 15 December 1933, 2; *SSSR Strana Sotsializma, Statisticheskii Sbornik*, 114–15.

17. *Izvestiia*, 8 March 1930, 1; "The New Soviet Woman," *MDN*, 8 March 1934, 2; E. Orlikova, "Sovetskaia zhenshchina v obshchestvennom proizvodstve," *Problemy Ekonomiki* (1940) 12, 7:119; 1939 census.

18. Chesterton, *Sickle or Swastika?*, 255–56.

19. "A Farm Woman Speaks, *MDN*, 18 February 1934, 2.

20. "We Live Well—The Story of a Woman Tractorist by Liubov Semenets," *MDN*, February–March 1935.

21. Angelina, *My Answer to an American Questionnaire*, 11, 22–36. Her comrades at the MTS laughed at her, saying, "She's a woman, what else can you expect of her?"

22. See Olga Zakharova, "A Peasant Girl's Chance to Become an Engineer," *MDN*, 1 May 1934, 2. Regarding prostitution, see Dr. Rachelle Yarros, "Observations in Soviet Russia," *Journal of Social Hygiene* (1930), 16: 455; "Moscow Revisited," *Journal of Social Hygiene* (1937), 25: 201; Alice Field, "Prostitution in the Soviet Union," *The Nation* 142 (25 March 1936): 373–74; Valentin Kataev, *Time Forward!*; Victor Serge, *From Lenin to Stalin*, 135–38.

23. *Village of Viriatino*, 254-56; *SSSR Strana Sotsializma*, 74, 88, 117; *Izvestiia*, 22 December 1936, 1; Zuzanak, *Time Budget Studies*, 183–86, 219–20; Delafield, *I Visit the Soviets*, 53, 79.

24. "Kul'turnyi inventar' u kolkhoznikov (v 1934)," *SSSR Strana Sotsializma*, 57; *Village of Viriatino*; "Now I Have a Cupboard Full of Books," *MDN*, 3 March 1933, 3; "Now We Amount to Something," *MDN*, 8 March 1933, 3; *My Answer to an American Questionnaire*, 55. Discussing changes in rural life, Angelina mentions that one villager built a brick house, one bought a motorcycle, one went to a health resort, and one sent his daughter to music college.

25. Nora Waln, *Reaching for the Stars*, 151–58; Madeleine Kent, *I Married a German*, 82–84. Waln was an American writer married to an English musician; they traveled in Germany from 1934 to 1938. Kent was an English woman married to a German.

26. Clifford R. Lovin, "Farm Women in the Third Reich," *Agricultural History* 60 (Summer 1986): 109, 116–20; Melita Maschmann, *Account Rendered*, 32–33. Maschmann was an organizer for German youth and worked in farms in East Prussia. She found the hours of work long — fifteen hours a day in the summer — and the farmers resistant to help from city girls.

27. For contracts, see Hyacinthe Dubreuil, *Employeurs et Salaries en France*, 142. For unemployment, see *An. Stat.* 56 (1940–1945), 143; 52: 133.

28. As quoted by Sian Reynolds, *France Between the Wars, Gender and Politics*, 91.

29. Clark, *Position of Women in Contemporary France*, 101–4.

30. "Women of USSR Are Responding Well to Their New Opportunities," *MDN*, 6 August 1932, 3.

31. Clarke, *Soviet Economic Facts 1917–1970*, 46; Michael Dohan, "The Economic Origins of Soviet Autarky, 1927/28–1934," *Slavic Review* 35: 603–35.

32. Frieda Wunderlich, "Deutsch-mann uber Alles," *American Scholar* 1: 99; "Women in Industry: Promotion of Domestic Service in Germany," *Monthly Labor Review* 41 (August 1935): 362–63 (hereafter cited as *MLR*); "Obligatory Domestic Service for Single Women in Germany," *MLR* 46 (May 1938): 1176; "Movements in the General Level of Wages," *ILR* 26 (5): 716–27; Marguerite Thibert, "The Economic Depression and the Employment of Women," *ILR* 27 (April 1933): 454; Dorte Winkler, *Frauenarbeit im "Dritten Reich,"* 193–203.

33. *An. Stat.* 56: 144; Marguerite Thibert, "The Economic Depression and the Employment of Women," *ILR* 24 (April 1933): 454–55; Stevenson, *British Society 1914–1945*, 176–77; Stephenson, *Women in Nazi Society*, 101.

34. "Increase in Woman Workers in Germany," *MLR* 46 (April 1938): 902–3.

35. See Table VIII, *An. Stat.* 52:*248–49; *Statesman's Year Book* (1939), 12; *Itogi perepisi 1959 g.* 16: 161–70.

36. Regarding women's efficiency, see "The Soviet Woman Enters Industry," *MDN*, 14 November 1932, 2; "Women's Efficiency in Industry Found Often Superior to Men's," *MDN*, 8 March 1933, 4. For living conditions of peasant migrants, see Kingsbury and Fairchild, *Factory, Family, and Women in the Soviet Union*, 211.

37. Jesus Silva Herzog, *Aspectos economicos de la Union sovietica*, 48–49, quoted by William Richardson in "'To the World of the Future,' Mexican Visitors to the USSR, 1920–1940," *The Carl Beck Papers in Russian and East European Studies*, no. 1002.

38. Klaus Mehnert, *Youth in Soviet Russia*, 35.

39. Chesterton, *Sickle or Swastika?* 183, 218–21; Delafield, *I Visit the Soviets*, 280–81.

40. See Chesterton, *Sickle or Swastika?* 183, 218–21; Jephcott, *Girls Growing Up*, 36–37; Margaret Cole, *Marriage Past and Present*, 150.

41. Mary Smith, "One Girl's Story," in Jephcott, *Girls Growing Up*, 21.

42. See *An. Stat.* 52: 168*–69*; 56: 143–44; Sian Reynolds, *France Between the Wars*, 112, 119.

43. See Clark, *Position of Women in Contemporary France*, 88-104; Reynolds, *France Between the Wars*, 124–25.

44. Boris Pilniak, *The Volga Falls to the Caspian Sea*, trans. Charles Malamuth, 240–41, 288–89, 292; "On the Siberian Industrial Front: Youth on One of the World's Biggest Jobs, Five Year Plan at Kuznetsk," *MDN*, 4 June 1932, 2; Reynolds, *France Between the Wars*, 104–8.

45. Reynolds, *France Between the Wars*, 114. To get hired at Renault in 1935, Simone Weil had to dress up and wear make-up.

46. For Soviet female physicians' low rate of *partiinost'* (degree of party membership or party-mindedness) and low purge rate in the 1930s, see Mark Field, *Doctor and Patient in Soviet Russia*, 60–69.

47. See *An. Stat.* 49 (1933): 13; 52 (1936): 13; 56 (1940-45): 144; *P.P., Census of Eng. and Wales, 1921*, 104; *Gt. Br. P.P. Accounts & Papers*, 26 (1933–34), cmd. 4625; *21st Abstract of Labour Statistics of the UK*, 13; *SYB League of Nations*, 44, 46; Chesterton, *Sickle or Swastika?*, 20–24.

48. Kent, *I Married a German*, 98–99, 307–8; Wunderlich, "Deutsch-mann uber Alles," *American Scholar* 1: 101.

49. *Times Educational Supplement*, 1 February 1936, 3; 3 February 1936, 3; 9 January 1937, 15; "English Country Children," *School and Society* 49: 383, 25 March 1939, showing that of 20,000 school leavers of country schools, 70% of girls entered domestic service.

50. "One Girl's Story," in Jephcott, *Girls Growing Up*, 22–23.

51. *An. Stat.* 52: 13, 248; 56: 144; *RSDR, 1931*, Tome I. Troisième Partie, 164–65.

52. For domestics in the 1930s, see *SYB League of Nations*, 46. For English training camps, see "Transfer System for Training Insured Unemployed Workers in Great Britain," *MLR* 39 (August 1934): 381–82; Chesterton, *Sickle or Swastika?*, 20–24.

53. Margaret M. Green, *Eyes Right!*, 131–34. Like some other former members of the Labour Party, Green was fascinated by National Socialism and its ability to rally German citizens and provide them hope during a difficult time.

54. Regarding servants, see *Perepis naseleniia 1937 g: Kratkie itogi*, Section 29, 129; "The Busy Moscow House worker Trains Herself for Other Jobs," *MDN*, 20 November 1932, 4; "The Progress of Women's Employment in the U.S.S.R.," *ILR* 31 (2): 235; Serebrennikov, *Zhenskii trud v SSSR*; Bonner, *Mothers and Daughters*, 97, 104–5, 125, 140; Scott, *Behind the Urals*, 133; *Sotsialisticheskoe stroitel'stvo SSSR*, 316–17; Clarke, *Soviet Economic Facts*, 26; W. P. Coates and Z. K. Coates, *The Second Five Year Plan of Development of the USSR*, 120–21; "Red Servant Problem," *Literary Digest* 125 (1 January 1938): 28.

55. *Sotsialisticheskoe stroitel'stvo SSSR*, 316–17, 410–11; Serebrennikov, *Zhenskii trud v SSSR*, 228; L. Gek, "Women in Socialist Construction," *MDN*, 8 March 1934, 2; *MDN*, 5 February 1933, 1; *BSE* 25: 169–70; Gantt, *Russian Medicine*, 170; Clarke, *Soviet Economic Facts*, 26; Coates, *The Second Five Year Plan*, 120–21; Winkler, *Frauenarbeit im "Dritten Riech,"* 194–95; *Stat. Handbuch 1928–1944*.

56. *RSDR*, 1931, 164–65; *Census of Eng. and Wales, 1931*, Industry Tables, 10–11.

57. Chesterton, *Sickle or Swastika?*, 35–36, 42–43.

58. Chesterton, *Sickle or Swastika?*, 196–97.

59. For the Berlin market, see Doris Kirkpatrick, *The Commonweal* 31 (8 December 1939): 149. Regarding Brownshirts in the mid 1930s, see Kent, *I Married a German*.

60. "One Girl's Story," in Jephcott, *Girls Growing Up*, 23–29.

61. Jephcott, *Girls Growing Up*, 20; *SYB League of Nations*, 46.

62. Cole, *Marriage Past and Present*, 152.

63. Reynolds, *France Between the Wars: Gender and Politics*, 93; *RSDR*, 1931, 160-63; *An. Stat.* 52 (1936): 135; *Sotsialisticheskoe Stroitel'stvo SSSR*, 316–17; Chesterton, *Sickle or Swastika?*, 230; *Perepisi 1926 g.* 34: 58–72; *Itogi perepisi 1959 g.* 16: 161–70.

64. Reynolds, *France Between the Wars*, 95–95; *RSDR, 1931*, Tome I, Troisième Partie, 162–68; *RSDR*, 1931, Tome I, Cinquième partie, 82; *An. Stat.* 36: 144; 52: 133. The 1933 German census identified 37 Jewish women engineers, 3 judges, 587 doctors, 283 dentists, 99 pharmacists, 826 nurses, and more than 700 teachers. *SDDR, Band 451, Heft 5, Die Glaubensjuden im Deutschen Reich*, 5/94–5/96; *Stat. Jarbuch 1928–1944*; Winkler, *Frauenarbeit im "Dritten Reich,"* 194–95; *SYB League of Nations, 1934/5*, 44.

65. *SYB League of Nations*, 44; Chesterton, *Sickle or Swastika?*, 13–19; Martyn Housden, *Resistance and Conformity in the Third Reich*, 75–76.

66. Alice Hamilton, "Below the Surface," *Survey Graphic* (1933), 22: 452; Atina Grossman, "German Women Doctors from Berlin to New York: Maternity and Modernity in Weimar and in Exile," *Feminist Studies* 19 (Spring 1993): 80–86; Ettinger, *Hannah Arendt/Martin Heidegger*: 4, 58; Wunderlich, "Deutsch-mann uber Alles," *American Scholar* 1: 104. Hamilton observed a female Jewish teacher still teaching arithmetic and indoor gymnastics in 1933, but not field gymnastics since no Jew could teach a defense sport in the "true German spirit." After 1935, Jews were excluded from all professions. For Hoch, see Dana Micucci, "A Cut Above," *Art and Antiques* 20 (February 1997): 79. For the persecution and murder of politically active German women, see Hanna Elling, *Frauen im deutschen Widerstand 1933–1945*, 172–207; Sender, *The Autobiography of a German Rebel*; Linke, *A German Girl's Autobiography;* Martha Kearns, *Kathe Kollwitz: Woman and Artist*, 206–7.

67. See Virginia Woolf, *Three Guineas*, 17, 26, 77, 81, 132–35, 156, 234; *The Virginia Woolf Reader*, 326, diary entry for 9 April 1935.

68. Berg, "The First Women Economic Historians," *Economic History Review* 45 (1992): 308–9, 318; Tawney, "Eileen Edna le Poer Postan," *DNB*, 1931–1940: 718; Dyhouse, "The British Federation of University Women and the Status of Women in Universities, 1907–1939," *Women's History Review* 4 (4): 478.

69. "Salary Differentials of Women in British Civil Service," *MLR* 45 (September 1937): 631–32.

70. *Times Educational Supplement*, 3 February 1934, 37; 10 March 1934, 78; 19 May 1934, 155; 17 November 1934, 387; 9 January 1937, 15; Jephcott, *Girls Growing Up*, 30, 56–65. Principals commanded higher salaries of 550 to 750 pounds per year.

71. *SYB League of Nations*, 46; *Times Educational Supplement*, 17 November 1934, 387.

72. *RSDR*, 1931, Tome I, Cinquième partie, 82, 162–65; *An. Stat.* 36: 144; 52: 133.

73. *RSDR*, 166–69; Carles, *A Life of Her Own*, 158, 173. Emilie's husband turned her father's house into a hotel, offering cut-rate holidays to workers. Since they charged low prices, they never made money on the hotel and lived on her wages. Moreover, the laundry fell to Emilie to do after teaching, caring for her family, and working in the fields in the summer.

74. Geneviève Tabouis, "Newspaper Woman: French Style," *The Living Age* 356: 563–65.

75. TsU, *Perepisi Naseleniia 1939g.*, Osnovnye Itogi, Chast' II: 11 and 18; *Perepisi 1959 g.* 16: 169–70.

76. Chesterton, *Sickle or Swastika?*, 212; Natalia Sats, *Sketches From My Life*, 156–65.

77. *SYB League of Nations* (1935), 46; *An. Stat.* 52: 244*; *Itogi perepisi 1959 g.* 16:161–70.

78. "Oxford University Discusses Communism—Theoretically," *MDN*, 8 August 1932, 4; "RSFSR Cultural Plan," *MDN*, 17 January 1933, 1; Reuschemeyer, *Professional Work and Marriage, An East-West Comparison*, 19.

79. "Woman's Energetic Work Brought Her the Opportunity for Greater Things," *MDN*, 8 March 1937, 3; account of Aleksandra Sidorenko, "Engineer, Mother, Student —The New Woman," *MDN*, 6 November 1933.

80. See Bette D. Stavrakis, "Women and the Communist Party in the Soviet Union, 1918–1935," Ph.D. dissertation, Case Western Reserve University, 1961, 84–94. Stavrakis argues that the party more actively recruited workers and soldiers than women. For Kazakh women, see "From Slave Block to Real Emancipation," *MDN*, 28 August 1932, 2–4; "Rose Magamayeva, A Woman Commisar Tells Life Story," *MDN*, 1935.

81. *MDN*, 8 March 1934, 2.

82. W. C. Ruediger, "English Secondary Education," *School Review*, June 1933, 436; "English Teachers," *Times* (London), 1 January 1932, 12c; Fletcher Harper Swift, "England's State Systems of Teachers' Pensions," *School and Society* 49 (April 22, 1939): 521; *Times Educational Supplement*, 9 January 1937, 15.

83. For women teachers, see I. A. Kraval, *Zhenshchina v SSSR*,108–9; "A. M. Pankratova," by Larry E. Holmes, *Modern Encyclopedia of Russian and Soviet History* 26: 224–29; *The Correspondence of Boris Pasternak and Olga Freidenberg 1910–1954*, 147–48.

84. *Marie Avinov, Pilgrimage Through Hell*, An Autobiography told by Paul Chavchavadze, 75, 96–98, 133–34, 142.

85. "Women and the Church," *Times* (London), 23 January 1932, 6. Women became ordained priests in the Anglican Church only in the 1990s.

86. Berg, "The First Women Economic Historians," 324; Delafield, *The Provincial Lady in London*, 48–50, 258, 263, 265–67, 288, 292.

87. Zuzanek, *Work and Leisure in the Soviet Union*, 182, 212–14.

88. Woolf, *Three Guineas*, originally published 1938, 124; Cole, *Marriage Past and Present*, 152–53.

89. "Sredengodovaia zarobotnaia plata rabochikh i sluzhashchikh," *Pkh* 5 (1939):170; *SSSR Strana Sotsializma*, 51; Coates, *The Second Five Year Plan*, 120–21; Clarke, *Soviet Economic Facts*, 26; Gantt, *Russian Medicine*, 185; Mark Field, *Doctor and Patient in Soviet Russia,* 104–5.

90. See *Itogi perepisi 1959 g.* 16: 169–70. (The 1939 census became available in comparative tables in the 1959 census.) See also Chesterton, *Sickle or Swastika?*, 183.

91. Memoirs of the 1930s show female Party members employing nannies and tutors so that they could continue their professional work. Svetlana Alliluieva,

Twenty Letters to a Friend, 40-41; Bonner, *Mothers and Daughters*, 97, 104–5, 125, 140; Joffe, *Back in Time: My Life, My Fate, My Epoch*, 67–85; personal interview with Vladimir Kostelovsky, whose mother was a Party worker in Moscow and employed a peasant servant to raise him while she worked. Interview, November 1984, Iowa City, Iowa.

92. Scott, *Behind the Urals*, 128–30; Clarke, *Soviet Economic Facts*, 26; Korber, *Life in a Soviet Factory*, 194–202.

93. M. E. Walker, "How Modern Russian Women Are Working," *The Contemporary Review*, August 1934, 212–20; Roberta T. Manning, "Government in the Soviet Countryside in the Stalinist Thirties, The Case of Belyi Raion in 1937," 20.

94. Hedwig Jacob's teaching experiences in the 1930s discussed by her sister, Helmtrud Schaaf, interview, El Paso, Texas, 19 September 1995.

Chapter 12

Political Participation in the 1930s

Lavish celebrations of Mother's Day made millions of Russian and European women feel appreciated. Yet they were squeezed back into to the role of flatterer and follower as feminist critiques of society waned and nationalism, militarism, and pronatalism became more pronounced. Pacifist and antifascist movements attracted English, French and Soviet women, as feminism ebbed and the backlash against their liberation intensified. German women risked imprisonment for expressing pacifist or antifascist sentiments. Soviet intellectuals feared the purges, and countless numbers were arrested, imprisoned, or killed.

Female Reichstag delegates were ousted in 1933. While many German women dreamed of being of service to the Reich, some found their role minimized and somewhat pagan, because of Nazi-extolled rituals they were expected to follow. By the mid 1930s, women's organizations were completely subordinated to the Nationalsozialistische Frauenschaft (National Socialist Woman's Organization).[1]

Politically active English women had great expectations following their full enfranchisement in 1929, but they were soon disappointed. They were not imprisoned as German and Soviet dissidents were, but patriarchy restricted their influence. Few were elected to Parliament, and little legislation improved their lot or that of colonial women. Women teachers had their salaries cut, and married career women lost their jobs.

Like the Nazis, the Soviets asked women to serve the state. Collectivization required peasants to work in agriculture, and industrialization drew several million women into manufacturing, construction, and white collar and professional work. Performing both productive and reproductive work, many Soviet women experienced upward social, economic, and political mobility. Yet countless peasants, intellectuals, and Party members found the state requisitioning not only the samovar but life itself.

France

French women's political activity fragmented into pacifist, antifascist, maternal, and feminist sectors. The League of Mothers and Educators for the Country recruited among peasant women and rural primary-school teachers, whereas the League for International Peace and Freedom attracted intellectuals. Women constituted only 3% of the French Socialist Party and 1% of the French Communist Party. The militant feminist Madeleine Pelletier became an ardent pacifist and risked punishment because she advocated women's emancipation, denounced pronatalist policies, and performed abortions. During the socialist era of Leon Blum (1936–1938), she was safe; but Daladier's nationalist government arrested her and sent her to a mental hospital, where she soon died. Before her death, she described the torture of being a sane person in an insane asylum. Her incarceration was a political act against a defenseless woman.[2]

Antifascist and pacifist work attracted many French women. Feminist groups within the teachers' union dissolved, thinking it more important to resist fascism than fight for equality. Many joined the World Wide Committee of Women Against War and Fascism. In 1932, Marthe Bray denounced war as feminists' worst enemy. As givers of life, women refused to produce cannon fodder. Outraged at the conscription bill of 1935, some became more conciliatory when Hitler threatened Europe.[3]

Many women were apolitical. Campaigning for municipal office, the journalist Louise Weiss (1893–1983) found most women indifferent. Peasant women were dumbfounded when she spoke to them about the vote. Working women laughed. Shop women shrugged their shoulders. Upperclass ladies turned away in horror. Even Simone de Beauvoir (1908–1986) was blasé, noting that if she had possessed the franchise she would not have voted! Some of her colleagues demonstrated and joined the Trotskyite faction of the Communist Party, but she remained an "armchair" socialist. She rejected political discussions with Fascists and refused to tout the government's pronatal line at school. Like many leftists, she initially thought that Hitler could not revive the German economy and would not last. Traveling with Sartre in Germany in 1934, she changed her mind when she realized how intimidating the Brownshirts could be.[4]

Pronatalists dominated French politics, blaming women for declining birth rates, unemployment, and a France too weak to withstand Hitler's attack. Feminist Arria Ly committed suicide in 1934 to protest pronatalist masculine culture, but few noticed. Instead, the Catholic Feminist Civic and Social Union launched campaigns to return mothers to the home. Even feminists and Communists adapted pronatalist platforms. Cecile Brunschvicg (1877–1946), president of the French Union for Women's Suffrage, declared that feminists were well aware of their maternal duties. The French Communist Party stopped supporting birth control and extolled motherhood. Only a few protested women's return to domestic drudgery and the sale of a woman's body, either to one man by marriage or to many by prostitution.[5]

Pronatalists, feminists, mothers, industrialists, and government officials all approved of family allowances. The Family Allowance Act of 1932 obliged employers to contribute to family allowances, and a substantial portion of national income was redistributed. Pronatalists supported marriage loans and tax rebates. While the government banned abortion and the distribution of birth control, it did not rigorously enforce these policies. Discreet doctors and patients were seldom punished for violating the antiabortion law.

A few French women wielded political influence. Cecile Brunschvicg, Suzanne Lacore (1876–1976), and Irene Joliot-Curie served as undersecretaries of Health and Welfare in Blum's government. Brunschvicg and Suzanne Schreiber also exerted influence through their salons, while Geneviève Tabouis (1892–1985) and Louise Weiss did so in journalism. Marquisse de Crussol (mistress of Prime Minister Edouard Daladier) and Comtesse de Portes (mistress of Prime Minister Paul Reynaud) used their liaisons to affect politics.[6]

England

Patriarchy stymied gender equity in England. Politicians decided that the Sex Disqualification (Removal) Bill of 1919 had done enough for women and that female teachers and civil servants deserved 80% of men's wages. In that atmosphere, feminists switched their focus from equal rights to the needs of mothers and children.

Parliament

Women's political participation increased on the local level, but their parliamentary presence remained negligible. Fifteen female M.P.s were elected in 1931 and thirteen in 1935. Since parliamentary agendas were set by political parties, which ignored women's issues, female M.P.s could not promote feminist causes. Ellen Wilkinson (Labour M.P.) introduced a bill for equal pay for equal work, but the Conservative government maneuvered around it. Women did not receive equal allowances in the civil service, military pensions, or compensation for war injuries. Women also lost their citizenship if they married a foreigner.[7] Like German Reichstag delegates, English female M.P.s usually divided along party lines, although social welfare, antifascism, and women's needs sometimes united them. Several fought the exclusion of married women from the civil service and from the receipt of benefits to which they had contributed. However, unemployment undermined women's chances of obtaining their due.

In 1933, English women's groups met to discuss the plight of German women. Dismayed at German women's dismissal from government posts, they felt that an injury done to the women of one nation affected them all. They sent their resolution to the German ambassador and to the *Times* of London.[8] In 1934, female M.P.s pushed for women's suffrage in India and the banning of child marriage and clitorectomy in the colonies. Male M.P.s torpedoed those bills because they thought the loyalty of African men more important than women's health.

The Conservative landslide of 1931 ousted most female Labour M.P.s. Four Conservative female M.P.s were elected in the 1920s, but thirteen in 1931 and 1935. Feminists were amazed that titled women—Lady Astor, Duchess Atholl, and Viscountess Iveagh—continued in office throughout these decades. Nine additional Conservative M.P.s also served in the 1930s. Others elected to Parliament included Eleanor Rathbone, an Independent, Lady Megan Lloyd George (1929–1951), a Liberal, and four Labour M.P.s: Ellen Wilkinson (1924–1945), Agnes Hardie (1937–1945), Dr. Edith Summerskill (1938–1955), and Janet Adamson (1922–1931, 1935–1945).[9] Mary Agnes Hamilton came in with the Labour landslide of 1929 but was ousted in 1931.

Municipal Councils

The number of female municipal council members increased to 111 in 1930. Local positions often served as stepping-stones to Parliament, and those losing parliamentary seats sometimes sought local ones.[10] Like Soviet women, English women found it easier to participate in local than national politics.

Issues and Ideology

English activists focused on feminism, pacifism, and social welfare. Not all feminists nor all mothers were pacifists, but they often shared a belief in democracy, peace, equality, and social justice.[11] Having lost family and friends in World War I, many feminists became pacifists after the war. Two journalists who linked feminism and pacifism were Vera Brittain and Winifred Holtby. Equal rights feminism had preoccupied Brittain before the war, but she portrayed her generation's disillusionment with war in *Testament of Youth* (1933).

She found hope in pacifism and recommended it to others. She despised militarism for reducing funds for housing and health care and thought mothers should not send their sons to schools with officer training corps. A League of Nations enthusiast, she believed women could stop war if they were less absorbed in private life and more interested in international events.[12]

Brittain believed that a powerful peace movement needed gifted leaders, militant tactics, and advertising experts to thwart fascism. She accepted the Munich settlement because she thought war would lead to the annihilation of Czechoslovakia, the massacre of Jews in fascist countries, the fascization of the democracies, and the death of civilization. Her friend Winifred Holtby also attacked fascism.[13]

Labour Party Delegates

Labour lost the parliamentary election of 1931, but women aired their political views at annual Party conferences, where they discussed international, national, local, and personal issues. Many supported pacifism and the League of Nations. Dorothy Woodman condemned Hitler for his treatment of socialist prisoners. Ivy Condon objected to the Party's support of rearmament and requested a new peace conference in 1939. She believed war was a product of the capitalist system, and that the Labour Party should endorse peaceful solutions to international problems. Others criticized the economy, the dole, and unemployment. Mrs. B. Ayrton Gould demanded shorter working hours and higher salaries since new machinery made workers more productive. She denounced British capitalists for employing fewer workers and paying them starvation wages. She thought poorly paid men could not buy consumer goods, and the government's reductions in unemployment pay further crippled the economy. Only a socialist government could prevent low wages and unemployment, as well as produce and distribute goods for the benefit of the masses.[14]

Labour women demanded more respect and money for educational programs and political campaigns. In 1935, they ran four summer schools for workers, wives, and unemployed men. Some complained about the lack of trade union backing and party funds for elections. Leah Manning criticized Parliament's reduction of secondary-school scholarships and teachers' salaries. As a teacher she saw her dreams for working-class children dashed by these cuts.[15]

Little change occurred among the female elite of the Labour Party. Susan Lawrence, Ellen Wilkinson, Jennie Adamson, Mary Carlin, Barbara Ayrton Gould, and Mabel Smith dominated the Party Executive Committee and the Women's Advisory Council. About sixty-five Labour Women's Advisory Councils existed, and seventy-eight federations organized county divisions. The Annual Conference of Scottish Women drew about 200 delegates yearly, and Women's Month attracted new members through rallies and conferences.[16]

Germany

Millions initially supported Hitler, believing that God was using him to save Germany from the Depression. Many dreamed of serving the fatherland under the Führer. Yet some support eroded as women's organizations came under male domination. As ordinary German women began to fear the Gestapo, some conformed and acquiesced, some denounced their neighbors, and some resisted by secretly helping Jews. Jewish women struggled against economic and social restrictions. Expelled from their jobs and denied civil service pensions, many led precarious lives and some fled. Socialist women who hoped to improve the economy and defeat the Nazis had their hopes dashed when Hitler turned the Gestapo against the leftist parties in 1933. Even before taking power, the Nazis had bullied Socialist politicians and turned their campaigns into nightmares.

Some female politicians resisted Nazi intimidation. In July 1932, twenty-seven women were elected to the Reichstag on a variety of party slates. Most were leftists belonging to the SPD (twelve) and the KPD (eight). A few came from the German National Popular Party, the Bavarian Popular Party, the German Popular Party, and Catholic Center Party. Yet their election came to naught when Chancellor Bruning failed to form a coalition, ruled mainly by decree, and called new elections in November. When Hitler became chancellor in January 1933, he disbanded the Reichstag, outlawing all parties but his own. While many had initially thanked God for sending Hitler to restore the Reich, leftists and pacifists were persecuted, arrested, and tortured, died in detention, committed suicide, languished in camps, or fled to save their lives.[17]

Hitler Supporters

Millions of Germans shared some Nazi values, such as full employment, marriage loans, holidays for workers, honor for country, state benefits for mothers, day care centers for children, a year of service for girls, and the glorification of motherhood. Many upper-class Protestant women had despised the Weimar Republic and its liberal ideas. They felt it unfair to push women into the man's world where they were not wanted and could not compete. They saw capitalism making wage slaves of women, and yearned for the restoration of feminine values, which they believed Hitler would revive. Some subscribed to Aryan and Volkish ideas. Many worked as honorary officials, and a few experienced upward mobility. Gertrud Scholtz-Klink headed Frauenwerk's 8 million members, while Melita Maschmann and Trude Mohr led the BDM (League of German Girls), which grew from 600,000 in 1933 to 2.8 million in 1937.[18] Hitler's policies also appealed to women employed in dead-end, low-wage jobs.

Some Catholics perceived the glorification of motherhood as neopaganism. Most Catholics married and had children, but they venerated the Virgin Mary and esteemed virginity more than motherhood. They rejected the right-wing Protestant view that blood shed by Aryan mothers was as efficacious as that of Christ.[19]

At first, women continued their welfare work. Protestant and Catholic groups each had a million members engaged in social work. They supported scores of mother care and rest homes, hospitals, orphanages, kindergartens, homes for the aged, soup kitchens, and health clinics. In 1935–1936, the Reich dissolved these Christian organizations and developed its own. It disgraced Agnes von Grone, the president of the Protestant Ladies Auxiliary, and dragged her through several trials (1936–1939).[20]

In 1935, those who joined church organizations instead of the Frauenschaft could be accused of disloyalty and their husbands could lose their jobs. By 1936, the Nazis controlled Protestant youth groups and kindergartens and infused children with their doctrines. To cleanse the race,

Nazis refused welfare to the infirm and to Jews. However, they allowed Catholics to tend the ill. Some theological differences divided Christians: Protestants accepted divorce of Jewish spouses and sterilization of the unfit, while Catholics believed marriage was a sacrament, opposed sterilization, and rejected the glorification of racism. Those suspected of helping Jews came under Gestapo surveillance and punishment, so few helped, and sympathizers had to be careful.[21]

Some foreigners observed great enthusiasm for Nazism. Margaret Green, a visiting professor from England, thought that Germans appreciated the benefits and order Hitler brought. He subsidized trips and holidays for workers and provided unemployed people with free tickets to concerts and the theater. Thus, Germans were willing to put up with a lot to be rid of "Communist and Jewish influence." Most English people were ignorant of the constructive aspects of National Socialism, especially Hitler's employment program. The American Quaker and pacifist Nora Waln encountered mixed support for Hitler. She saw intellectuals and pacifists victimized by storm troopers and ordinary Germans intimidated by the Gestapo as their neighbors were denounced, arrested, and returned in coffins. Yet she also met a hotel maid who worshiped Hitler and thought God had sent him to protect the Germans.[22]

Some German girls found excitement and pageantry in Nazi parades and satisfied their desire to belong to something great by joining the BDM. Melita Maschmann was attracted to the "socialist" aspect of National Socialism and devoted herself to the youth movement. She rejected her parents' conservative, bourgeois attitudes and appreciated the community and commitment she found among Nazi youth. She wanted to serve her people, and willingly worked fifteen hours a day on farms in East Prussia. Blinded by German nationalism and Nazi devotion, she learned to ignore unpleasant aspects of the regime. She thought the Nazi Party was not made up of gangsters and roughnecks but decent, intelligent, and moral people.[23]

Some loyal Germans denounced relatives to the Gestapo, and family division over politics occurred. Madeleine Kent's husband was denounced by his sister, and he lost his job. Many Germans closed their eyes to the arrest and torture of workers, pacifists, leftists, aristocrats, and intellectuals. They insisted that no "true" German was in any danger. Some got mystical satisfaction out of "serving" the state by "sacrificing" their friends.[24]

Hausfrauen such as Elfride Heidegger endorsed Hitler's rise to power and believed in the superiority of the Aryan race. She was not unusual. Millions of housewives belonged to clubs with nationalistic views and felt their status enhanced by Nazi ideology. The most extreme group in the late 1920s was the Louise League, which affiliated with the male paramilitary Stahelm organization.[25]

Bourgeois hausfrauen opposed emancipated women, population decline, divorce reform, abortion, Doppelverdiener (married woman workers), and the title Frau for all adult women. The head of the Hanover Housewives Association, Bertha Hindenberg-Delbruck, articulated the differences between career women who belonged to the liberal BDF (Union of German Women) and her group. The BDF concentrated on women—their importance and their rights—while the housewives' movement focused on the family, the Volk, and the nation. Even so, the party took control of her group in 1935.[26]

Opposition and Resistance

Nazi terror made the Reichstag campaigns of 1930 and 1932 dangerous. Jewish socialist Toni Sender had to cope with both Communists and Nazis drowning her out with their chants of "Red Front" and "Heil Hitler." Ashamed of the Communists and harassed by the Nazis, she used the Iron Front (SPD militia) for protection. Nazi student sympathizers disrupted her speeches and meetings. Emboldened by their electoral gains in July 1932, Nazis smashed windows and destroyed Jewish shops, cafes, and department stores. Warned not to speak in the Reichstag, Sender presented the Finance Committee report and was interrupted by catcalls and laughter from the Nazi delegates. However, when she confronted them, they stopped.[27]

In 1932, campaigning became increasingly unsafe, as Nazis dynamited and firebombed the homes of political opponents and shot opposition politicians. Yet the courts treated the Nazis leniently. In Saxony, Nazis threw a stench bomb into one of Sender's meetings, slashed the tires of her car, and threatened to ambush her. In Berlin, they threw stones through her windows, tapped her telephone, and slandered her in their papers. Yet judges refused to convict them. Undaunted, Sender resisted Nazi gangsters and bureaucrats. In February 1933, she spoke to a crowd of 65,000 Dresden citizens who had assembled in the snow. After her speech, the police warned her to be careful because a Dresden Nazi paper carried a death threat against her. As a socialist she expected to die in battle, not be murdered. When storm troopers plotted to arrest her, she fled across the border to Czechoslovakia and eventually to the United States, where she worked in leftist causes and wrote her autobiography.[28]

After the Nazis outlawed leftist parties in 1933, socialist women continued their meetings. They met at sports events, coffees, or birthday celebrations. By the mid 1930s, some people condemned the regime for sentencing women to death. One maid exclaimed: "It is against Nature. No good can come of such ways."[29]

Politics often divided families. Lilo Linke joined the liberal Democratic Party in the 1920s, while her parents and brother supported the Nazis. In 1931, she saw pacifism melt like snow in the blazing sun. Since the Nazis did not flinch from using force, she joined the SPD to fight the Nazis. In 1933, she had to flee.[30]

Although Hiltgunt Zassenhaus feared the Gestapo vehicles passing her house at night, she did not let them deter her from teaching Jews a second language to use upon emigration. When the Gestapo questioned her neighbors about her "pupils," she decided to tutor them at their apartments instead. Her family helped Jews, but they did not tell each other about their good deeds, lest they implicate one another under torture.[31]

Women of all classes participated in Resistance movements. Opposition arose in political and religious groups. Some assisted those targeted by the Nazis, while others distributed Resistance literature or smuggled eyewitness accounts of torture out of the country. Initially a supporter of Hitler, Guida Diehl deplored violence against Jews and detested Nazi honor bestowed on unwed mothers. Although a Nazi Party member and head of the Protestant Women's Federation, Agnes von Grone was accused of treason for aiding Protestants of Jewish ancestry. Only her advanced age saved her from execution. Grone thought the Nazi Party would respect her independent leadership, but it did not; and she spent the remainder of the decade clearing her reputation. Dr. Gertrud Luckner, head of Catholic Charities, was arrested and incarcerated in Ravensbruck for helping Jews. It was so dangerous to oppose the regime that most helped Jews secretly. The most tragic stories were of those who left but were arrested later in France or the Soviet Union.[32]

Tens of thousands of Jewish women and scores of politically active women left in 1933. Both SPD and KPD Reichstag deputies fled to save their lives. After eluding Nazi storm troopers, Toni Sender had a physical and mental breakdown in Czechoslovakia. Staying near the border, she retained contact with her SPD constituents in Berlin. When she realized that the party would not call a general strike to fight fascism, she became disillusioned. Slowly, she realized that the workers had been silenced but were keeping the faith. Since so many refugees had crowded into Czechoslovakia, she went to Belgium and wrote for a Socialist paper there. Later, she emigrated to the United States.[33] Although the Nazis crushed women's opportunities, they could not annihilate their spirits.

Violence in the Reich

> The tears ran down upon her aged cheeks.
> "May I see Him? Or will he soon be free?"
> A man behind a table to her speaks:
> "Sorry, he's dead! And not so nice to see."
> —"A German Mother," by Erich Weinert (1935)

Nazis even tortured young children, who returned to their parents in coffins. Thus, German women suffered when their husbands, sons, and brothers were arrested, tortured, and killed. When a family member was imprisoned, mothers lost unemployment relief payments and could not support their children.[34]

The arrest of pacifists shocked the American Quaker Nora Waln, who lived in Germany in the mid 1930s. She could not believe that armed Brownshirts could enter homes and take people away. Families, churches, and university clubs could not protect their own. Those arrested lacked hope of legal recourse. They had all heard of people taken away and returned crazed in mind, starved in body, or in closed coffins. People thought: "This terrible time will pass. It can't last." Or "Herr Hitler does not know what is done in his name. He is a good man. He will straighten it out . . ."[35]

Slowly, the bloom of the regime faded. A grocer explained that if she failed to say "Heil Hitler" to her customers, she might be denounced and taken to a camp. What would happen to her children? Having received an anonymous clipping about shopkeepers who failed to give the proper greeting, she recognized the possibility of arrest. If the Gestapo arrested her, there was no court of appeal. Relatives seldom discovered the whereabouts of their kin, and more persons went into concentration camps than came out. Interrogation by the Gestapo and torture in local concentration camps turned people's hair white overnight. Punishment of a few deterred others from joking or complaining about the regime and its policies or officials.[36]

Politically active Germans experienced some of the same problems that Soviet women had. They were harassed, humiliated, arrested, interrogated, detained, imprisoned, and tortured. Some committed suicide. Many fled. One could be arrested for her own religious and political activity or used as a hostage to control her menfolk. Both pacifists and leftists were imprisoned. Elise Augustat, Franziska Kessel, and Helene Kirsch (KPD, German Communist Party) were arrested in 1933. Augustat was released in 1939 but died as a result of torture. Accused of high treason, Kessel was killed in 1934 and Kirsch sentenced to three years in jail. KPD Olga Korner, Helene Overlack, and Lisa Ullrich were repeatedly arrested and sent to concentration camps.[37]

While many Communists were killed, some survived. Louise Mauer was arrested in March 1933, released six months later, and then spent the next two years smuggling antifascist literature into Germany from Switzerland. Arrested again in August 1935, she spent a year in prison awaiting trial and was eventually sentenced to four years in Waldheim penitentiary. After solitary confinement, she entered a cell block where friends took care of her. On Sundays, when most of the prisoners went to church, the communists discussed politics. Political prisoners formed surrogate families based on solidarity and mutual aid, which helped them survive prison and camp.[38]

Many SPD Reichstag deputies were arrested and imprisoned. Minna Cammens was arrested in March 1933 for distributing anti-Nazi leaflets and was murdered during detention. Toni Pfulf, Minna Bollman, and Mathilde Wurm died or committed suicide as a result of their incarceration (1933–1935). For protesting against the arrest and beating of a friend, Clara Bohm-Schuch was arrested in 1933 and died as a result of her detention. Between 1933 and 1939, about 3,000 women became political prisoners.[39]

The Nazis also arrested Landtag deputies. Leni Rosenthal was murdered by the Gestapo in October 1936, and Marie Jankowski was arrested and severely beaten by the SA in Berlin in March 1933. Some were arrested, sent to camps, or tortured as hostages because their husbands had escaped Nazi control.[40] The arrest, torture, and killing of some served as a warning to others not to oppose the regime. Ordinary Germans often shrugged off the arrest of leftists, not realizing that their liberties were also jeopardized.

By 1935, the Reich reigned supreme. It disbanded the Hanover Housewives Association and absorbed its membership into the male-dominated Deutsche Frauenwerk. Its officers were purged or relegated to obscurity. Pacifists and gypsies were arrested. While Jewish women were not imprisoned in 1933, they were subject to insults, slander, and unemployment. Deprived of work and status, many Jewish career women experienced existential crises. Professor Elisabeth Blochmann wrote to Martin Heidegger that she could not imagine losing her job. As a baptized Protestant and half

Jew, she thought her job and pension were safe. But she had to emigrate, and Heidegger helped her gain a fellowship at Oxford. While a few Jewish women languished in prisons and concentration camps in the 1930s, none imagined the Holocaust lurking in the future.[41]

Like Soviet women, German political prisoners loathed being incarcerated with prostitutes and common criminals. In both countries, imprisoned women lost their children and were punished by having their children placed in state orphanages, where they were indoctrinated. Deprived of mail and packages, women found that their isolation sometimes led to nervous breakdowns. They were punished by food deprivation and solitary confinement. In both countries, survival depended on luck, work skills, physical strength, membership in support groups, and even sexual favors.[42]

Lenient camp guards could be punished and imprisoned. Johanna Langefeld, who had been trained in reformist penal policy in the Weimar period, tried to mitigate some of the worst abuses at the concentration camps. She was subsequently arrested for dereliction of duty and tried by an SS tribunal in 1943. Few German women volunteered for camp duty, although some were attracted by the high salaries and promises of advancement.[43]

The Soviet Union

Just as English men believed that the Sex Disqualification (Removal) Act of 1919 solved woman's situation, so the Soviets declared the "woman question" settled when the 1936 Constitution proclaimed women's equality. Yet statistical and literary evidence reveal women's continued class and ethnic inequality. They advanced in uneven ways, achieved some of their dreams, struggled to improve their society, but were haunted, thwarted, and destroyed by the purges.

The Soviets created laws and programs to liberate women, but underlying patriarchal social structures changed less than feminist revolutionaries had hoped. Laws modified gender relations in education and work but sexism remained in politics and family life. Zhenotdel's closing in 1929 narrowed women's political base. Instead of touting women's liberation in the 1930s, the Party praised them for motherhood, building socialism, and paramilitary activity. Exemplary women workers received political as well as financial rewards. Agrarian Stakhanovite workers Pasha Angelina and Maria Demchenko became members of the Supreme Soviet (national government) and delegates to Party congresses. They symbolized peasant women's achievement.[44]

Political Participation

Women's political activity increased in all levels and republics, even though the FYPs deflected their energy away from women's liberation. Countless women experienced upward political, social, and economic mobility in the 1930s. However, the cost was high, since Party policy resulted more in women's mobilization than in their empowerment. Since the woman question had been "solved," nothing further needed to be done for them. Their participation in government and Party posts increased, but the purges undermined their political sway and hopes for transforming society.

Their presence in the soviets increased from 380,000 in 1934 to 460,000 in 1939. Although their participation was greatest at the local level, the number of female deputies to the All-Union Congress of Deputies rose from 58 (3.7%) in 1924 to 419 (21%) in 1936. Two and a half million participated in the quasi-political women's delegate groups, and the Komsomol claimed 1,600,000 girls in 1932. Female Party membership fell from 500,000 in 1932 to 294,000 in 1937 as a result of the purges, then rose to 335,000 in 1939 when the terror abated. The ethnicity of female Party members changed, with fewer Jews and more Muslims reported, suggesting that the *hudjum,* or unveiling of Muslim women, was drawing them into the Party in the late 1920s and early 1930s.[45]

Gender and Politics

Women were affected by the Stalinization of the Party, family obligations, locale, ethnicity, and social status. Peasant women participated in village soviets because they could combine local political activity with their household and child care duties. By 1939, indigenous women composed 80% of the presidents and vice presidents of local village soviets, but only 49% at the district and 29% at the republic level. In Belyi Raion in the Western Oblast, women made up only 14% of Party members in the mid 1930s. Administrative work required education, which rural and Muslim women usually lacked but Slavic and Jewish urban female Party members possessed, so they often held higher Party positions. Working-class women could combine city soviet work with their jobs and family life, but few reached higher positions.[46]

Female Party Elite

Soviet women in mid-level political positions shared some characteristics with English and German Socialists. Many were well educated, middle-aged, and childless, or had grown children or nannies to care for their offspring. They worked in "feminine" or deputy positions. In the RKPb, women served in the Agitation and Propaganda or the Central Control commissions. They also held government positions in education, health, housing, social welfare, the Workers and Peasants Inspection (RKI), or the trade unions.[47]

The Soviet female political elite, like their British counterparts, experienced little growth in the 1930s. Stenographic Party records show Bolshevichki (Party members prior to 1917) dominating female Party leadership. They occupied mid- and low-level positions but seldom carved out political enclaves to guarantee reelection to Party congresses. About 400 women attended Party congresses held in the 1930s. Only 29 attended more than one, and 25 of the 29 were Bolshevichki, who worked as facilitators, not makers, of Party policy. About 100 of the female congress delegates joined the Party in the late 1920s and early 1930s. Yet few imitated Ekaterina Furtseva and studied at the Party school in Moscow as preparation for upward political mobility. A Party member since 1930, Furtseva worked in the Komsomol and survived the purges.[48]

The female elite remained small, but some change occurred. Several unmarried Bolshevichki, including Lenin's sisters, retired in 1932, while married women, such as Nadezhda Alliliueva, Ruth Bonner, Ekaterina Kalinina, and Evgenia Ginzburg, became more common. Some token working women—Ekaterina Furtseva, Pasha Angelina, and Maria Demchenko—rose in the political hierarchy. It is unclear if women shunned political power and policy making, but they held more eminent posts in the government than in the Party. As in the 1920s, they worked as facilitators of policy rather than creators of it. By the early 1930s, some had retired from Party and government service, some were exiled, some went along with the Party line despite the personal cost, and many were purged. Mid-level Party members Evgenia Ginzburg, Sophia Prokofieva, Ekaterina Kalinina (wife of President Kalinin), Olga Davidovna (Lev Kamenev's wife and Trotsky's sister), Liudmila Shaposhnikova (wife of second secretary of the Leningrad District Party Committee), and Anna Larina (Bukharin's wife) were arrested, imprisoned, or shot.

Following Lenin's death in 1924, Party members allegedly took a pledge "to preserve the Soviet regime, whatever the cost." The cost in the 1920s was exile, demotion, and reassignment. In the 1930s, the cost increased. Stalin's wife committed suicide. Some suffered arrest and imprisonment on trumped-up charges. Some Party members were forced to contribute to the cult of Stalin, while others served as judges in trials, sat on purge commissions, denounced colleagues, or preserved the regime though silence. Today, it seems strange that strong-minded women remained so loyal to a party that treated them so shabbily. Having sacrificed so much for the Party, they apparently could not imagine themselves outside the Party, nor the country without Stalin.[49]

Reflecting on this period, Suzanne Rosenberg realized that an atmosphere arose in which silence and acquiescence crippled the psyche of the nation, and millions of loyal supporters went to their death. Many turned into apologists and executors of Stalin's politics. People behaved shamefully: publicly approving the denunciations of colleagues, while privately knowing of their innocence.[50]

Nightmares and Purges

> I . . . had never belonged to the opposition, nor had I ever had
> the slightest doubt as to the rightness of the party line.
> —Evgenia Ginzburg[51]

When the FYPs were adopted in 1929, they were considered necessary for building socialism. Yet Klavida Nikolaeva warned that the Party would have to use "iron discipline" against NEP men, kulaks, and Party members opposed to the new line. Until recently, many historians have demonized Stalin for terrorizing Soviet society. They focused on the totalitarian aspects of his regime, treating it as something supernatural and inexplicable, similar to their treatment of Hitler and Nazism. A more careful investigation of the purges reveals more intra-Party conflict and denunciation than has hitherto been acknowledged. Zealots accepted the terror accompanying collectivization.[52]

One may distinguish different periods of the purges. The first period (1929–1930) was a time when some Party stalwarts attacked kulaks for sabotaging collectivization and engineers for undermining the FYP. People were arrested, imprisoned, or exiled, but not necessarily killed. Newspapers, memoirs, and Stalin's famous "Dizzy with Success" speech document this period. During the second period, 1931–1932, thousands of Party members were ousted for opposing the Party line or for personal failings. Oppositionists could still recant, keeping their lives and jobs. During these periods, kulaks could also be arrested and sent to work in labour camps.

The third period, 1933–1935, included a general cleansing of several hundred thousand cadres who had joined during the collectivization campaign. They lost their Party cards and jobs, but not their lives. Cleansings did not always entail arrest, imprisonment, or death. The fourth period (1936–1938) was when Ezhov (head of the NKVD) purged ordinary citizens as well as high-ranking Party, military, government, and trade union leaders and their relatives. Countless numbers were shot, exiled, imprisoned, or sent to labor camps. In 1939, the purges abated, and Party membership increased as war approached.

Purges, 1929–1930

In 1929–1930, Stalin adopted a merciless attitude toward kulaks and members of the opposition. He manipulated Party elections and allowed others to behave savagely during collectivization. Soviet literature depicts some of this unsavory behavior. Vladimir Kirshon, a Party member who participated in collectivization, in his play *Bread* (1930) portrays an over-zealous Komsomolka who obediently enforces grain requisitions. In one scene she says: "Let's take all of it from the kulaks. Half of the peasants in this village are kulaks, and the rest follow like sheep."[53] Her hyperbole typifies many activists at this time.

Veresaev's novel *Sisters* (1932) portrays a similar Komsomolka named Lelka. She was one of 25,000 workers who went to the countryside to organize the peasants. Harshly enforcing the Party line, she raves: "They've destroyed all the cattle! There will be no milk, no meat . . . Shooting isn't good enough for them." When a comrade questions her vehemence, she warns him against deviating to the right out of pity for the peasants. She orders the confiscation of property, including the peasants' felt boots. She epitomizes fanatics later denounced by Stalin in 1932. Lekla's sister Ninka wonders if the best Party members are those who unquestionably obey orders. She believes in standing up for humane beliefs and not giving in to hard-liners. Her way is later vindicated by Stalin.[54]

In Vasily Grossman's *Forever Flowing*, a "true believer" named Anna Sergeevna regards kulaks as less than human. She sees GPU agents arrest and shoot peasants during the winter of 1929 and spring of 1930 and remains unperturbed. She drives kulak families from their homes, exiles them from their villages, and purges the "kulak spirit" from recalcitrant peasants in the Ukraine and North Caucasus. But the process of terrorizing the peasants degrades her.

After dekulakization, the amount of cultivated land fell and crop yields dropped. Officials concealed those facts, demanding the standard amount of grain when less had been planted. Requisitions resulted in the starvation of several million peasants. Anna exonerates herself by believing that the peasants would be fed from the state grain fund. Troops guarded train stations and blockaded highways to keep peasants from fleeing to the cities to get food. Teachers and farm administrators left when entire villages died of starvation. Later, soldiers harvested the winter wheat that remained. Peasant women died of starvation or were criticized for refusing to participate in the collective farms, but they were not arrested, exiled, or shot as frequently as their menfolk.[55]

Third Period of Purges

Then came the purges against oppositionists and parasites. Between 1932 and 1934, female Party membership fell 20%. While cleansings led to loss of Party cards and privileges, they did not necessarily involve loss of life. In Moscow province, members were purged for violation of Party discipline, inactivity, nonfulfillment of duties, bureaucratism, political double dealing, and moral degeneracy. In 1933, Comrade Levchina was accused of concealing her bourgeois background, worming her way into the RKI, demoralizing a village soviet, and creating difficulties in the Kuban region.[56] Women were probably more often charged with inactivity, since their household duties and child care conflicted with their Party duties.

Terror and Survival, 1936–1938

While terror provoked conflict, suffering, and fear in the Party and society, it also produced solidarity, helpfulness, and even love affairs. Prison survivors' memoirs contain stories of mutual support and the development of surrogate families, as well as rape and torture. Terror brought out the best and worst in the population.[57]

Nadezhda Joffe belonged to the Trotskyite opposition and was arrested in 1929. She received lenient treatment because she was pregnant and finishing her studies. In Krasnoyarsk, she worked and reported for interrogation at the GPU every ten days. Her investigator was restrained because he never knew when people would recant and return as his boss! After her exile, she joined her husband in Khabaravsk. Later, they returned to Moscow, where she recanted her views so that she could get a job to support their family.[58]

Arrested again in 1936, she and her husband were exiled to Siberia, where their fourth child was born. In some instances, married couples and their children lived together in exile. In 1937, her husband was killed and her daughter taken away. She saw criminal prisoners eat the food intended for the children. Although her daughter survived, a friend's did not. She also describes the gang rape and dismemberment of a young female prisoner by criminals at Kolyma. While she never reports being raped or tortured, she records cases of those who were. Like many educated Party members, she considered the criminal prisoners despicable.[59]

Nadezhda's stepmother, Maria Joffe, was also arrested for her Trotskyite beliefs in 1929 and survived imprisonment and hard labor until 1957. In the early 1930s, her punishment was not so harsh, and in 1932 her son visited her in exile. During the height of the purges (1936–1938), conditions became harsher as inmates were shot, worked to death, tortured, or became shadows of themselves. A good raconteur, Maria often distracted Vorkuta camp commandant Kashketin from torturing and interrogating other prisoners by telling him stories. Her memoirs show women bonding together in surrogate families to survive the labor camps.[60]

Unlike the Joffes, Evgenia Ginzburg never belonged to the opposition and never questioned the Party line. She was stupefied when the regional Party commission reprimanded her for not denouncing a colleague. In 1935, failure to denounce someone resulted in the loss of one's teaching license and a severe reprimand, although later it meant arrest, imprisonment, or death. In 1935, the Party enforced harsh but not always brutal treatment. Jails and prisons were so crowded that sometimes people were charged but not immediately arrested and imprisoned. Prior to her imprisonment, friends and family urged her to admit her guilt and repent or to disguise herself and live in obscurity until the scandal blew over. She refused to run away or recant. Her honor impugned, she fought the denunciation, thinking she would easily vindicate herself. Later, she learned that some people escaped punishment by hiding in remote areas. Her hubris cost her twenty years' imprisonment, yet helped her survive. Arrested in the spring of 1937, she escaped physical torture during interrogation. Her pain came from punishment cells and the gruelling outdoor work in subzero weather. Those who worked outside soon died. Ginzburg survived because she became a medical assistant, working in hospitals where food was better and living conditions easier. Yet the unpredictability of camp life was frightening. After she obtained a good job, a commandant sent her to a punishment camp. Friends bribed officials to return her to indoor work.[61]

Like Ginzburg, Valentina Ievleva-Pavlenko thought she would soon clear up the misunderstanding of her arrest, and she took only her coat with her when she was arrested. Warned by an NKVD officer and family friend to leave Moscow, Iadviga Verzhenskaia fell sick and was arrested before she could flee.[62] Ruth Bonner's mother advised her to hide, but she too refused. She and her husband had seen many of their friends disappear and wondered when their turn would come. Her daughter was astonished at the radiance on her face when she was taken away. Sentenced to eight years, she was eventually allowed to write letters and receive food parcels. A true believer, she instructed her daughter to continue her Komsomol work! She survived due to her inner strength, family, and prison friends.[63]

As the purges intensified, many realized that they were doomed. Wives of famous Party leaders such as Olga Kameneva knew they would be arrested. Exiled to Gorky for three years, Kameneva died in 1941.[64] The terror horrified the Party intelligentsia, but it did not crush everyone. Theater director Natalia Sats remained undaunted. She found purpose in camp life by training prisoners for theatrical and musical productions. She believed in the redeeming value of cultural activities, and her ability to find good in the midst of evil kept her sane. Upon her release in 1941, she went to Central Asia, where she directed opera and a children's theater.[65]

The years 1936 to 1938 were the most terrifying. Party members often lost their Party cards and their lives. Many were expelled, exiled, arrested, shot, imprisoned, or sentenced to hard labor. The wives of Generals Tukachevsky, Iakir, Gamarnik, and Uborevich were killed. Even Kalinina, the wife of the president of the Russian republic, was arrested and sent to prison.

From 1932 to 1937, female Party membership fell by 200,000. In Moscow province, the purge rate of Bolshevichki was 23%, compared with 56% of male Old Bolsheviks. Several factors account for this difference. Stalin apparently did not take women seriously or see them as a threat. By 1932, many Bolshevichki had retired or been pensioned off and were out of harm's way. Since few held high posts in the Party, government, or industry, they were not among the targeted groups, and their chance of being denounced as wreckers was less than men's.[66]

Anna Larina was typical of purged female Party wives. She was imprisoned in Astrakhan, Moscow, and Siberia. The wife of a leading Party member who had been denounced as a traitor, she received an eight-year sentence, which was later extended to twenty years in prison and exile. During interrogation, Beria warned her not to betray herself to spies and to quit exonerating Bukharin or she would be shot. Although he tried to spare her, she resented him.[67]

Rebuilding the Party, 1939

Female Party membership plummeted in the mid 1930s but rebounded to 335,000 in 1939. The purges decimated the educated female Party elite, but new cadres of working-class, peasant, and indigenous women became politically active. In Kazakhstan, women's Party membership fell from 9,900 in 1932 to 6,000 in 1936, but rose to 17,464 in 1941. Likewise, 5,000 women belonged to the Uzbek Communist Party in 1938, but 5,500 by 1939. Having lived through the purges in Magnitogorsk, the American John Scott thought the Soviet Union could recover, and the Party did.[68]

Resistance to Terror

Like German women, Soviet women resisted the terror in many ways. When organizing a new department of philology, Olga Freidenburg hired scholars who had been victimized by the regime and the academic community. She refused to obey Party directives by raising the grades of working-class students and lowering those of middle-class ones. Yet her opposition provoked denunciation of her book *Poetics of Plot and Genre* (1936) and shunning by her colleagues. After an appeal to Stalin, her work was published. Then her colleagues acted as though nothing had happened and congratulated her on her new book, an example of how frightened intellectuals turned against friends and how they colluded with the system.[69]

The regime did not have to arrest the entire intelligentsia to terrorize it. Punishing a few kept others submissive and compliant. When production and construction did not proceed according to plan, inspectors often accused plant managers and economic planners of "wrecking." In adopting a rational plan for industrialization, the regime did not allow for human error. When work was not completed on time, engineers, administrators, managers, and scientists were arrested and charged with wrecking. Their imprisonment struck fear into the hearts of wives who realized they too were doomed when their husbands were imprisoned for wrecking.

Terror also silenced writers and artists. Osip Mandelstam (1892–1938) remarked, "Poetry is respected only in this country. . . . There's no place where more people are killed for it." His wife, Nadezhda Mandelstam, overtly complied by leaving Moscow after Osip's second arrest and imprisonment, but she covertly disobeyed by memorizing his poetry and saving it for posterity. The regime killed her husband and refused to publish his work, but she preserved it and in the 1970s clandestinely circulated it along with her memoirs describing the torment of intellectuals. She helped his poetry become famous in the West and in Russia after glasnost.[70]

Some writers criticized the regime but hid their work for future publication. Fame spared famous women such as Anna Akhmatova and Aleksandra Kollontai, but their sons were arrested as hostages. In "Requiem" (1935–1940), Akhmatova describes her ordeal of standing in line to send packages to her son. She observed how suffering turned women's hair white overnight:

> I have learned how faces fall to bone . . .
> how glossy black or ash-fair locks
> turn overnight to tarnished silver . . .
> And I pray not for myself alone . . .
> for all who stood outside the jail . . .[71]

Komsomol Members

Young people aged eighteen to twenty-five joined the Komsomol, ignoring the purges in their idealism. The memoirs of Nina Kosterina, Suzanne Rosenberg, and Elena Bonner show their efforts to reconcile the purges with their Komsomol beliefs. Rosenberg told a beau that a romantic entanglement was the last thing she wanted because she was joining the Komsomol and building socialism. When the purges intensified, these young women were perplexed at adult criticism of the Party. Rosenberg refused to accept a book by Trotsky when a friend offered it, because she knew it was dangerous and thought it wrong for a loyal Communist to read things maligning Soviet policies. In the mid 1930s, she fell in love with a Party member but could not share her thoughts with him for fear of betraying him under torture.[72]

Nina Kosterina was puzzled at the arrests of her uncle, cousins, and friends, but stunned at her father's arrest in 1938. Some of her friends were expelled from the Komsomol when their relatives were arrested, but she remained devoted to it. Her aunts encouraged her to "accommodate" herself to the situation, but she refused to compromise her Komsomol honor to "get on" in life. Yet she found it increasingly difficult to justify Party loyalty and the purges. Slowly, she realized that her father's arrest had separated her from her friends and found life boring without them. Celebrating the New Year in 1940 was funereal. When her favorite teacher left Moscow because of a relative's arrest, Kosterina lost hope. She felt melancholy until joining the partisans. The war offered escape from disillusionment. Unfortunately, she died one month after enlistment in December 1941.[73]

During the purges, Elena Bonner also felt confused. She sent her imprisoned parents money and food parcels, but she refused to denounce them as traitors or to renounce her Komsomol card as her Komsomol organizer encouraged her to do. Her loyalty to the Komsomol, like Kosterina's, was absolute. Denied entrance to Leningrad University, Elena studied at a pedagogical institute in the evening while working days.[74]

Ethnicity and Political Participation

Russian and Jewish women predominated in Party membership and at Party congresses because they were often urban, educated, and from politically active families. Many were career women who had shorter workdays, spent less time on housework than factory workers or peasants did, and consequently had more time for political work. In Central Asia, Russian and Ukrainian women participated in Party and soviet politics. At Magnitogorsk, a Ukrainian woman named Rudenko was active in the city soviet, organizing block and environmental committees, selling subscriptions to the journal *Woman Worker*, checking on housing, and managing a Ukrainian chorus.[75] While more non-Russians in 1939 than in 1926 were listed as paid political and administrative officials at the republic level, Russians still predominated (table 12.1).

Non-Russian women were better represented in low-level positions. Armenian women constituted 93% of those in village and factory administrative posts, Georgian women 68%, Ukrainian 56%, and Belorussian 50%. Yet in Central Asia, indigenous women composed only 20% to 30% of low-ranking officials.

By 1939, more non-Russian women had obtained higher education. In social status, most paid political officials were *sluzhashchie*, not workers or peasants. Although the number of women administrators increased in the republics, they tended to be educated, and by Western standards probably middle-class. Yet some lower-class women served in government positions.[76]

In the 1930s, it still remained dangerous for Muslim women to take political posts. In the unveiling campaigns of the late 1920s, Muslim and Russian women activists experienced verbal and physical assaults, mutilation, even death. Still, progress occurred among Uzbek women in the 1930s. Tens of thousands became active in delegatki meetings and, in 1931, 200 indigenous Uzbeks attended the Komsomol Congress in Tashkent. By 1938–1939, more than 7,000 had been elected to government posts, and 5,000 belonged to the Uzbek Communist Party. In Kazakhstan, the number of

Table 12.1. Paid Female Officials, 1920s and 1930s*

Republic	Date	# of officials	# of indigenous women
RSFSR	1926	4,000	4,000 Russian and Jewish
	1939	39,000	39,000 Russian and Jewish
Ukraine	1926	732	275 Ukrainian
	1939	5,000	3,000 Ukrainian
Belorussia	1926	159	43 Belorussian
	1939	1,000	500 Belorussian
Uzbekistan	1926	118	34 Uzbek
	1939	1,100	400 Uzbek
Tadzhikistan	1926	18	2 Tadzhik
	1939	450	154 Tadzhik
Turkmenistan	1926	13	2 Turkic
	1939	404	93 Turkic
Kirgizistan	1926	5	0 Kirgiz
	1939	433	148 Kirgiz
Azerbaidzhan	1926	75	9 Azeri
	1939	571	213 Azeri
Armenia	1926	24	23 Armenian
	1939	228	250 Armenian
Georgia	1926	92	44 Georgian
	1939	606	400 Georgian
Kazakhstan	1926	100	0 Kazakh
	1939	1,500	500 Kazakh
Abhazia ASSR	1939	88	4 Abhazian
Bashkir	1939	521	88 Bashkir
Dagestan	1939	251	121 Dagestani

*In 1939, 39,000 Russian and Jewish women occupied administrative posts in the RSFSR, 427 Russian and Jewish women were in paid positions in Ukraine, 106 in Belorussia, 118 in Georgia, 95 in Armenia, 30 in Azerbaidzhan, 46 in Uzbekistan, 56 in Kazakhstan, 10 in Turkmenistan, 13 in the Tadzhik SSSR, and 12 in the Dagestani ASSR. *Chislennost' naseleniia SSSR na 17 ianvaria 1939 g.*, Chast' III: 1–164; Chast' IV Vypusk I: 18–22. Russian women also predominated among university students in the 1920s and 1930s. *Kratkie Svodki, Perepisi 1926 g.*

delegatki increased to 45,870 (18,507 Kazakh), and Party membership increased to 9,923 in 1932, dropping to 5,946 during the purges but rising later. Voting also changed: 22% of Kazakh women voted in soviet elections in 1927, but 99% did so a decade later. Of the 60 women elected to the Kazakh Supreme Soviet in 1939, 27 were Kazakh.[77]

Although Russian women predominated in politics, Central Asian women became more active. By 1931, 44% of the 5,700 female Party members in the Tatar republic were indigenous. During collectivization, female membership in the Turkmen and Tadzhik parties surged to 2,155 and 1,378 respectively, but the reregistration campaign of 1935 reduced their ranks to 875 and 695. In 1936–1938, personnel fell off another 150 members.[78] Without memoirs, it is hard to know if the reregistration of Party cards and loss of Party membership resulted in minor or grave punishments.

Working-Class Women

Komsomol, Party, and trade union officials recruited young working-class women for higher education and political activity. Among worker students in Kuznetsk in 1932 were 8,000 Party members, 12,000 Komsomolki, and 40,000 trade union members.[79] While the purges decimated the Party intelligentsia, new cadres of working-class women replenished the ranks in the late 1930s. Like Europeans, more Soviet working-class women participated in trade union than in Party activity. Most joined trade unions because they provided housing, child care, vacation resorts, and educational programs. Few had time for Party work.

Countless workers experienced educational, economic, and political upward mobility. Famous ones included G. S. Sagautdinova and K. S. Ukolova, who began as workers in the 1920s but became heads of factories in the 1930s. Praskovia Pichugina left the countryside, worked in a Moscow factory, became a foreman in 1932, served in the Moscow district soviet in 1937, then the Supreme Soviet. As chair of the district soviet, she controlled a budget of 137 million rubles and was responsible for parks, streets, public baths, laundries, public works, and local industries. Advancement followed a common pattern among textile workers and Komsomolki. Party and government sponsorship helped workers advance educationally, professionally, and politically.[80] Although it was extremely difficult for working-class women to combine family and political life, the purges were not as costly for them as for the intelligentsia. Workers often reacted to Party cleansings differently from intellectuals. When confronted with poor performance, workers usually admitted their faults, accepted reprimands, and that was the end of the matter. Officials reprimanded them for incompetence or slovenliness, but charged engineers and managers with "wrecking" or "sabotage." Confused about this double standard, a visiting Austrian journalist asked whether the factory's leaky roof was the result of "wrecking" or "slovenliness on a grand scale." Of course, those who criticized the system risked job loss and punishment.[81]

Working-class women may have suffered less from the purges than intellectuals because they held fewer Party, government, or managerial posts and could not be accused of sabotaging the FYP. Their toughness also helped them survive. In Gladkov's novel *Cement*, a working-class heroine chides her intellectual friend for being high-strung. She reminds her that Communists must have hearts of stone to carry out their political tasks, do their work, and care for their families.[82] Some, like Furtseva, possessed the political savvy to flourish.

Peasant Women

Soviet institutions provided peasant women scholarships for higher education and co-opted them into administrative and Party positions. Their political participation was much greater in village soviets and delegatki organizations than in the Party. By 1932, more than 10 million women were participating in delegatki programs, and 400,000 peasant women were elected to local Soviets by 1939. Three-quarters of the female members of village soviets came from the ranks of the delegatki. Few belonged to the Party. Like workers, their participation was greatest at the local level, where they could combine their household, child care, and political duties. They constituted 32% of female delegates to the Thirteenth Congress of Soviets.[83] Their representation in high levels remained weak, but non-Russian women's participation increased, as table 12.2 shows.

Committed Party members experienced career advancement. In the 1920s, M. P. Smirnova became first a delegatka, then a Party member, and then Volost Executive Committee member. Likewise, Rose Magomayeva, a Dagestani woman, entered a Party school and upon graduation worked for the Party District Executive where she drew 1,347 Dagestani women into social and political work. In 1931, she became People's Commissar of Social Welfare of the Dagestan Autonomous Republic. By 1939, Dagestani women made up 48% of the paid female administrators in their republic.[84]

Some peasant women came from politically active families. Pasha Angelina and her sister Lyolya joined the Komsomol in the late 1920s and

Table 12.2. Women as Presidents of Village Soviets, 1939*

Republic	# elected	# indigenous
Armenia	28	24
Georgia	27	22
Ukraine	668	556
Turkmenistan	22	20
Azerbaidzhan	37	22
Kazakhstan	236	160
Belorussia	78	62
Uzbekistan	155	117
Dagestan ASSR	31	29

*Chislennost' naseleniia SSSR na 17 ianvaria 1939 g., Chast' III: 1–164 and Chast' IV Vypusk I: 18–22.

the Party in the 1930s. Pasha received the Order of Lenin for her productive agricultural work and her organization of female tractor brigades. She was also elected to the Supreme Soviet in 1939. Although she met Stalin in 1935 at the Second All-Union Congress of Collective Farm Shockbrigaders, she also aroused opposition. In 1929, some kulaks shot at her and her sister; in 1933, kulaks ran her over with a cart.[85]

Maria Demchenko (a field worker) and Pasha Angelina (a tractor driver) represent peasant women who gained rewards through hard work. They exemplify strong-willed, politically active peasant women who endured ridicule and believed in the FYPs. Their service in the Party and the Supreme Soviet did not influence policy, but highlighted peasant women's political involvement, a change from the olden days when peasant women were called *baba,* or hag. Still, liberated peasant women often separated from husbands who objected to their social and political work.[86] Yet the adulation some won in building socialism and serving in the Supreme Soviet may have enhanced the dignity of others. Some working-class and peasant women developed and followed their own dreams within the confines of the Party line.

Notes

1. *Reichstags Handbuch, VI Wahlperiode 1932*, 8–12, and Gisbert H. Flanz, *Comparative Women's Rights and Political Participation in Europe*, 79–83.

2. Reynolds, *France between the Wars*, 192, 170–71; Pedersen, *Family, Dependence, and the Origins of the Welfare State*, 224–88, 357–411; Felicia Gordon, *The Integral Feminist: Madeleine Pelletier*, 175–77, 214–230; Bonnie Smith, *Changing Lives*, 347, 357. In 1932, Pelletier attended the World Congress against Imperialist Wars in Amsterdam and joined the pacifist group Mundia.

3. Anne-Marie Sohn, "Between the Wars in France, 119; Smith, *Changing Lives*, 487; Gordon, *Integral Feminist*, 175–77; Sandi E. Cooper, "Pacifism, Feminism, and Fascism in France," *International History Review* 19 (February 1997): 110.

4. De Beauvoir, *Prime of Life*, 132–33, 156–59, 161–62.

5. Pedersen, *Family, Dependence*, 405; Gordon, *The Integral Feminist*, 214–15.

6. Reynolds, *France Between the Wars*, 210–11, 156–64, 170–71; G. Flanz, *Comparative Women's Rights*, 78; Smith, *Changing Lives*, 439–42; Sohn, "Between the Wars in France and England," *A History of Women in the West*, 5: 116–19; de Beauvoir, *Prime of Life*, 45, 93, 111, 132, 172–75; Pedersen, *Family, Dependence*, 404–5.

7. Olive Banks, *The Politics of British Feminism, 1918-1970*, 45-54, 67; Penny Summerfield, "Women and War in the Twentieth Century," *Women's History: Britain, 1850–1945*, 318.

8. "Nazi Treatment of Women," *Times*(London), June 2, 1933, 9.

9. "Mary Ada Pickford," *Who's Who of British Members of Parliament*, 3: 282 (hereafter cited as *Who's Who of Parliament*); "Frances Davidson," *Who's Who of Parliament*, 4: 83. Other Conservative M.P.s included: Dame Florence Horsbrugh, Mrs. Thelma Cazalet Keir, Mrs. Mavis Tate, Dame Irene Ward, and Mrs. Sarah A. Ward (1931–1939); Mrs Frances Graves, Mrs. Norah Runge, and Mrs. Helen Shaw (1931–1935); and Mrs. Mary Ada Pickford (1931–1934). Baroness Frances Davidson assumed her husband's seat upon his death in 1937.

10. Patricia Hollis, *Ladies Elect, Women in English Local Government 1865–1914*, 487; Mrs. Frances Graves, "Mrs. Norah Runge," and "Mrs. Helen Shaw," *Who's Who of Parliament*, 3: 134, 312, 324; "Janet Adamson," *Who's Who of Parliament*, 4: 1; "Mary Agnes Hamilton," and "Dorothy Jewson," *Who's Who of Parliament* 3: 148, 186. Graves served in Holborn Borough Council (1928–1934), in Parliament (1931–1935), and then in the Dorset County Council. Runge held office in Parliament (1931–1935) and in the London County Council (1937–1961). Shaw served as Conservative M.P. (1931–1935) and was then elected to Lanarkshire County Council. Labour Party member Adamson served in the London County Council (1928–1931) and was elected to Parliament in 1938. Summerskill served in the Middlesex County Council (1934–1941) before being returned to Parliament in 1938. Hamilton became an alderman of the London County Council in 1937. Dorothy Jewson served as an M.P. (1923) and then in the Norwich City Council (1927–1936).

11. Judith Wishnia, "Pacifism and Feminism in Historical Perspective," *Genes and Gender VI On Peace, War, and Gender*, 85, 90.

12. Brittain, "Can the Women of the World Stop War?" in *Testament of a Generation, The Journalism of Vera Brittain and Winifred Holtby*, 216–20.

13. Brittain, "The Lighter Side of Peacemaking," and "No Compromise with War," *Testament of a Generation*, 222–31; Winifred Holtby, "Shall I Order a Black Blouse? and "The Man Colleague," *Testament of a Generation*, 60–63, 170–73.

14. Miss Ivy Condon (Bermondsey, West, D.L.P.), Resolution on peace, *The Labour Party Report of 38th Annual Conference*, May 29–June 2, 1939, 246 (hereafter cited as *LPR*); Dorothy Woodman, "Leipzig Trial," *LPR*, October 2–6, 1933: 139–40; *LPR*, September 30–October 4, 1935: 3, 15, 17; Mrs. B. Ayrton Gould, Northwich D.L.P., "Working Hours," *LPR*, 1932: 246; Mrs. C. D. Rackham (Cambridge T.C. and L.P.), "Children and Young Persons Bill," *LPR* 1932: 172.

15. Mrs. Betty Fraser (London University L.P.), "Organisation of Women: Week-end Schools," *LPR*, September 30–October 4, 1935: 144; Mrs. B. Jones, "Organisation of Women," *LPR*, 1935: 144; Mrs. M. MacIves (Leeds Central D.L.P.) and Mrs. Jennie L. Adamson (Vice-Chairman), *LPR*, 1935: 145; Leah Manning, "Education," *LPR*, 1932: 248.

16. Dr. Marion Phillips, *Who's Who of Parliament*, 3: 281; *LPR*, 1933: 43–45; "Organisation of Women," *LPR*, 1935: 40–41.

17. *Reichstags Handbuch, VI Wahlperiode 1932*, 6–12; Hanna Elling, *Frauen im deutschen Widerstand 1933–45*, 173–207. Elling indicates it was female Communists and Socialists, students and Jehovah's Witnesses who were murdered in prison or died in camp for their resistance to fascism. During the war, many other resistance groups arose, and women were killed for belonging to them.

18. Claudia Koonz, "Nazi Women Before 1933: Rebels Against Emancipation," *Social Science Quarterly* 56 (March 1976): 535–60; "The Fascist Solution to the Woman Question in Italy and Germany," *Becoming Visible*, 513–28; Michael Phayer, *Protestant and Catholic Women in Nazi Germany*, 49, 52, 77–78, 98–99; Frevert, *Women in German History*, 240–52; Reagin, *A German Women's Movement*, 211–57, Smith, *Changing Lives*, 464–57; Doris Godl, "Women's Contributions to the Political Policies of National Socialism," *Feminist Issues*, 35–36; Susan Groag Bell, *Women, the Family, and Freedom, Vol. Two, 1880–1950*, 254, 262–63.

19. Phayer, *Protestant and Catholic Women*, 59–61, 67, 145, 235.

20. Phayer, *Protestant and Catholic Women*, 27–28, 50–51, 150–59, 250.

21. Phayer, *Protestant and Catholic Women*, 199, 121, 118, 222–29.

22. Green, *Eyes Right!*, 54, 127, 230; Zassenhaus, *Walls*, 22–35; Waln, *Reaching for the Stars*, 26–28.

23. Melita Maschmann, *Account Rendered*, 10–24, 32, 40–46, 83–86, 221.

24. Martyn Housden, *Resistance and Conformity in the Third Reich*, 70–71; Kent, *I Married a German*, 97–98, 211–33, 248.

25. Ettiger, *Hannah Arendt/Martin Heidegger*, 58; Reagin, *A German Women's Movement*, 221–57; Godl, "Women's Contributions to the Political Policies of National Socialism," 34–37.

26. Reagin, *A German Women's Movement*, 245–46.

27. Sender, *Autobiography*, 274–79, 282–86. Initially, many leftists thought Hitler would not last and did not take him seriously. The SPD invited the KPD to join together to defeat the Nazis in November 1931, but they refused.

28. Sender, *Autobiography,* 294–310.

29. Housden, *Resistance & Conformity in the Third Reich*, 32; Kent, *I Married a German*, 248.

30. Lenke, *A German Girl's Autobiography*, 264–401.

31. Zassenhaus, *Walls,* 22–29ff.

32. Koonz, "The Fascist Solution to the Woman Question in Italy and Germany," *Becoming Visible*, 524–25; Milton, "Women and the Holocaust," 232–35.

33. SPD Deputies Toni Sender, Anna Siemsen, Marie Kunert, Luise Schiffgens, Adele Schreiber Kriezer, Anna Stegman, Marie Arning, Margarethe Starrman, and Marie Juchatz fled in 1933. Reichstag KPD delegates Lote Zinke, Clara Zetkin, Maria Reese, Hanna Sandter, Maria Blum, Elfrieda Golke, and Roberta Grapper also left. Grapper and Reese went to the Soviet Union, but were imprisoned there. Zinke and Golke returned to work in Resistance groups and were rearrested. *M.d.R. Die Reichstagsabgeordneten der Weimarer Republik in der Zeit des Nationalsozialismus*; Sender, *Autobiography*, 310–14, 319.

34. *Women and Children under the Swastika*, compiled by Theodore Deak and Rae Einhorn, 5–11.

35. Waln, *Reaching for the Stars,* 78–80, 109–14.

36. Waln, *Reaching for the Stars,* 77–78, 112–15; Kirkpatrick, *The Commonweal* (December 8, 1939) 31: 149; Kent, *I Married a German*, 208–23; Zassenhaus, *Walls*, 22–23, 35.

37. Thanks to Fred Schmidt for information about female Reichstag officials after 1933: Kommission fur Geschichte des Parlamentarismus, *M.d.R. Die Reichstagsabgeordneten der Weimarer Republik in der Zeit des Nationalsozialismus, Politische Verfolgung, Emigration und Ausburgerung 1933–1945, Eine biographische Dokumentation Mit einem Forschungsbericht zur Verfolgung deutscher und auslandischer Parlamentarier im nationalsozialistischen Herrschaftsberich*; Sybil Milton, "Women and the Holocaust: The Case of German and German-Jewish Women"; Carol Ritter; John Roth, *Different Voices, Women and the Holocaust*, 215–16.

38. *Women in the Resistance and in the Holocaust, The Voices of Eyewitnesses,* 150–58.

39. *M.d.R. Die Reichstagsabgeordneten der Weimarer Republik in der Zeit des Nationalsozialismus*; Milton, "Women and the Holocaust," 215–16.

40. Milton, "Women and the Holocaust," 216.

41. Reagin, *A German Women's Movement*, 242; Milton, "Women and the Holocaust," 216–18; Joachim W. Storck, "Martin Heidegger and Elisabeth Blockmann, The Rector and the Emigrant: A Correspondence between Friends," *Martin Heidegger: Politics, Art, and Technology*, 44, 52–53.

42. Milton, "Women and the Holocaust," 219–20, 227.

43. Milton, "Women and the Holocaust," 225; Frevert, *Women in German History*, 249.

44. Bochkaryova, *Women of a New World*, 150–53; Roberta Manning, "Government in the Soviet Countryside in the Stalinist Thirties," *The Carl Beck Papers*, 301: 30. Manning indicates that the Party regarded rural Stakhanovites as a Party reserve from which Party members and future leaders should be drawn.

45. Kraval, *Zhenshchina v SSSR*, 155; *Stat. spravochnik SSSR za 1928*, 54; *Women Today*, 47; Winter, *Red Virtue*, 318; *Perepisi VKPb 1927 g.*, 139; "Dobrovol'noe obshchestvo 'Za novye byt'," *Kom.*, July 1928, 84–85; Serebrennikov, *Zhenskii trud v SSSR*, 175ff; Azade-Ayse Rorlich, "The 'Ali Bayramov' Club," *Central Asian Survey* 5 (3/4): 221–39; Institut istorii partii pri TsK KP Tadzhikistana, *Kom. Partiia Tadzhikistana v Tsifrakh za 50 let (1924–1974)*, 18; Istittut istorii partii pri TsK KP Turmenistana, *Kom. Partiia Turkkmenistana v tsifrakh, 1924–1974*, 17, 26 (hereafter cited as *KPTad, 1924–74* and *KPTurk, 1924–27.*)

46. For rural officials, see Manning, "Government in the Soviet Countryside in the Stalinist Thirties," 18–19, 31; *Chislennost' naseleniia SSSR na 17 ianvaria 1939 g.*, Osnovnye Itogi, Chast' III: 1–164 and Chast' IV Vypusk I: 18–22.

47. *Perepisi naseleniia 1926 g.*, Table III-a, 34: 95; *Slavnye Bolshevichki*; *Literary Digest*, 17 January 1934, 13.

48. For women in the party congresses, partiinost', and positions held, see VII S'ezd RKPb., *Stenograficheskiiotchet*, 200–6 (cited hereafter as *S.O.*); VIII S'ezd RKPb, *S.O.*, 451–90; IX S'ezd RKPb., *S.O.*, 573 ff; X S'ezd RKPb., *S.O.*, 716–59; XI S'ezd RKPb., *S.O.*, 583–604; XII S'ezd RKPb., *S.O.*, 729–59; XIII S'ezd RKPb., *S.O.*, 710–60; XIV S'ezd RKPb., *S.O.*, 1004–29; XV S'ezd RKPb., *S.O*, 1479-1539; "Zhenskoe dvizhenie," *BSE* 25: 242; E. H. Carr, *Foundations of a Planned Economy* 2: 480; Hunt, *German Social Democracy*, 82–97.

49. E. D. Stasova, *Vospominaniia*, 176–77, 190–210; "Greet E. D. Stasova on 60th Birthday, *MDN*, Oct. 15, 1933, 1; Vinogradskaia, *Pamiatnye Vstrechi*; Nadezhda Krupskaia, *The Emancipation of Women; Slavnye Bolshevichki*, 27-29, 98–03, 130–32, 135–56, 168–72, 213–38; Stavrakis, "Women and the CPSU, 1918–1935," Ph.D dissertation., Case Western Reserve University, 1961, 224; McNeal, *Bride of the Revolution*, 230, 274-75; *Khrushchev Remembers*, 45–47; oral interview with Vladimir Kostelovsky regarding his grandmother M. I. Kostelovskaia, March 27, 1986, Iowa City, Iowa.

50. Suzanne Rosenberg, *A Soviet Odyssey*, 50–69.

51. Ginzburg, *Journey into the Whirlwind*, 31.

52. Klavdia Nikolaeva, XVI Konferentsiia VKPb, Aprel' 1929 g., *S.O.*, 193–94; A. G. Rabinach, "Towards a Marxist Theory of Fascism and National Socialism," *New German Critique* 3 (1974): 127–53; J. Arch Getty and Roberta Manning, *Stalinist Terror*; Iuri Daniel, *This Is Moscow Speaking*, which suggested that Soviet society was guilty of the purges.

53. Vladimir Kirshon, "Bread," in Lyons, *Six Soviet Plays*, 251.

54. Vikenty V. Veresaev, *Sestry*, 351–52; English translation, *Sisters*, 262-64, 283; Joseph Stalin, "Dizzy from Success," *Works*, 12 , 197–205.

55. Grossman, *Forever Flowing*, 142–61; F. Nurina, *Women of the Soviet Union, The Role of Women in Socialist Construction*, 56; Andrew Smith, *I Was a Soviet Worker*, 156–59.

56. J. A. Getty, "Party and Purge in Smolensk, 1933–1937," *Slavic Review*, Spring 1983: 70; "Party Cleaning Under Way in Northern Caucasus," *MDN*, 11 January 1933, 3.

57. Kotkin, *Magnetic Mountain*, 328–29, 347–48, 589 fn.; Veronica Shapovalov, ed., *Remembering the Darkness: Women in Soviet Prisons* (forthcoming). In a personal interview, Shapovalov indicated that few memoirs describe rape scenes, and most women hesitated to write about it. Interview at Slavic Section, Western Social Sciences Conference, Albuquerque, New Mexico, April 24, 1997.

58. Joffe, *Back in Time: My Life, My Fate, My Epoch*, 67–71.

59. Joffe, *Back in Time*, 75–85, 112–30. For other descriptions of families being exiled together, see Shapovalov, Kovach-Astafeva, "Letters," in *Remembering the Darkness*.

60. Maria Joffe, *Odna Noch': Povest' o pravde*.

61. Ginzburg, *Journey into the Whirlwind*, 10–22, and *Within the Whirlwind*, 34, 98–107. For crowded prisons at Magnitogorsk and the house arrest instead of imprisonment of women charged with political crimes, see Kotkin, *Magnetic Mountain*, 333, 578. For examples of other women who had done nothing wrong and thought they could clear up the "misunderstanding" of their arrest, see Shapovalov, Valentina Ievleva-Pavlenko, "Unedited Life," in *Remembering the Darkness*.

62. Valentina Ievleva-Pavlenko, "Unedited Life" and Iadviga Verzhenskaia, "Episodes of My Life" in Shapovalov, *Remembering the Darkness*.

63. Bonner, *Mothers and Daughters*, 229–30, 320–25.

64. Larissa Vasilieva, *Kremlin Wives*, 47–55; Sats, *Zhizn'-Iavlenie Polosatoe*, 295.

65. Sats, *Zhizn'-Iavlenie Polosatoe*, 315–26, 333–48; Sats, *Sketches From My Life*, 263–69, 271–81; Victor Karasin,"Natalya Satz, Grande Dame of Children's Theater," *Soviet Life*, July 1991, 36–38; Ginzburg, *Journey into the Whirlwind*, 204–11. In 1965, Sats organized a children's music theater in Moscow and worked there until 1991, when she was eighty-eight years old.

66. Vasilieva, *Kremlin Wives*, 123, 137; *Sotsialisticheskoe Stroitel'stvo SSSR, 1936*, 593; J. A. Getty and William Chase, "The Moscow Party Elite of 1917 in the Great Purges," *Russian History* 5 (Part I): 108; Barbara Katz, "Purges and Production: Soviet Economic Growth, 1928–1940," *Journal of Economic History* 35 (3–4): 567–90; Roy Medvedev, "New Pages from the Political Biography of Stalin," in Tucker, *Stalinism, Essays In Historical Interpretation*, 212-23.

67. Larina, *This I Cannot Forget*, 172–88, 181–83, 185–89; Sats, *Zhizn'-Iavlenie Polosatoe*, 295, 307, 311.

68. Kraval, *Zhenshchina v SSSR*, 155; *Women Today*, 47; *Kom. partiia uzbekistana i rabota sredi zhenshchin respubliki (1938-1959)*, 32, 70, 112; G. Nurbekova, *Zhenshchiny Kazakhstana—fronty*, 27; Scott, *Behind the Urals*, 205.

69. *Correspondence of Boris Pasternak and Olga Freidenberg*, 147–48, 153–54. Her brother's arrest and death showed how dangerous it was to question or oppose the regime.

70. Nadezhda Mandelstam, *Hope Against Hope*, 159; *Hope Abandoned*, trans. Hayward.

71. Anna Akhmatova, *Poems of Anna Akhmatova*, xx.

72. Rosenberg, *A Soviet Odyssey*, 41–42, 53.

73. "Dnevnik N.K.," 40–43, 61–62, 78–83, 93, 103–5; in English, *The Diary of N.K.*, 32–37, 42–46, 56–99, 128–63.

74. Bonner, *Mothers and Daughters*, 320–25.

75. Strumilin found that industrial workers spent more time than white-collar workers in productive and household work and consequently less time in political work. "Biudzhet vremeni russkogo rabochego, *Kom.*, 6 (1923): 22-23. For the lack of Kazakh teachers at Magnitogorsk in the 1930s, see Kotkin, *Magnetic Mountain*, 504, 543.

76. Shelia Fitzpatrick argues in *Stalin's Peasants* that these gains did not last until the end of the decade. My data regarding women elected to local soviets and listed in paid political positions suggests that considerable gains continued relative to women's low political participation of the 1920s. Fitzpatrick, *Stalin's Peasants*, 181–83.

77. Aminova, *Oktiabr' i reshenie zhenskogo voprosa v Uzbekistane*, 168–84; *KPUz. 1938–59*, 32, 70, 112; G. Nurbekova, *Zhenshchiny Kazakhstana Frontu*, 26–27.

78. In 1927, 125 of 592 female party members in the Turkmen Communist Party in 1927 were Turkic; by 1929, 207 of 667 female party members were Turkic. *KPTurk., 1924–74*: 21, 26, 15–52; Busygin, *Sel'skaia zhenshchina v semeinoi i obshchestvennoi zhizni* (Kazan University, 1986), 45; *KPTad., 1924–1974*, 18–33.

79. *SSSR Strana Sotsializma, Stat. Sbornik, 1936*, 98; *The USSR in Figures*, 260–63; "Can the Russian Peasant Become Machine Conscious?" *MDN*, 12 June 1932, 2.

80. Serebrennikov, *Zhenskii trud v SSSR*, 180; Pichugina, "Women in the USSR," 29–31; "Engineer, Mother, Student — The New Woman," *MDN*, 6 November 1933; K. N. Ciboski, "A Woman in Soviet Leadership: The Political Career of Madame Furtseva," *Canadian Slavonic Papers*, 14: 2–3; Henry Lane Hull," E. A. Furtseva," in *Modern Encyclopedia of Russian and Soviet History*, 12: 47–49.

81. Korber, *Factory Life in the Soviet Union*, 46-47, 252–54; Andrew Smith, *I Was a Soviet Worker*, 77.

82. Gladkov, *SS, Tom vtoroi, Tsement*, 238, 264.

83. Members of the Red Banner Collective Farm in Kalinin Oblast decided which workers would receive scholarships for higher education, and some joined the Party for opportunistic reasons. Fainsod, *Smolensk Under Soviet Rule*, 355–63; *USSR in Figures*, 260–63; *SSSR Strana Sotsializma*, 98; Buck, *Talk About Russia with Masha Scott*, 44, 76–80; Stavrakis, "Women and the CPSU, 1918–1935," 227; Serebrennikov, *The Position of Women in the Soviet Union*, 210; Nurina, *Women in the Soviet Union*, 76, 90.

84. *Perepisi partii 1927 goda*, 85; "VKPb," *BSE*, 11: 542; "Rose Magomayeva, A Woman Commissar Tells Life Story," *MDN*, 1935; *Chislennost' naseleniia SSSR na 17 ianvaria 1939 g.*, Chast' III: 13–158 and Chast' IV, Vypusk I: 18–22.

85. Angelina, *My Answer to an American Questionnaire*, 12–13, 16, 42–43.

86. Clements, "Baba and Bolshevik Russian Women and Revolutionary Change," *Soviet Union* 12 (Part 2, 1985): 161–84; "Kaganovich Speaks at Moscow Kolkhoz Women's Conference," *MDN*, 18 October 1933, Nurinan, *Women in the Soviet Union*, 66–67.

Conclusion

Gender, class, and nationality have been central themes in this study. Gender shaped women's lives, yet class also influenced their situations. Peasant women, factory workers, white-collar workers, career women, and housewives often lived quite separate lives. Conditions within these groups also varied. Wealthy peasant women differed greatly from poorer ones. Likewise, upper-class women who pursued higher education and careers differed considerably from well-to-do women who married and had families. In the nineteenth century, class more than nationality defined women.

During the 1920s, nationality became more important. Perhaps it was the shared experience in World War I that united women in the various nation states. The Bolshevik Revolution opened up higher education to women of all classes in the Soviet Union, whereas secondary and university education remained prerogatives of the middle classes in Europe. The expansion of white-collar work in Europe blurred class distinctions, and the franchise distinguished English, German, and Soviet women from French.

Profound economic depression in England and Germany affected women adversely in the 1930s. In the Soviet Union, collectivization and the purges negatively affected women, whereas industrialization created jobs at all levels of the economy. Accompanying these economic impacts was the glorification of motherhood and cruel pronatal demands for more children in hard times. Yet women developed a variety of strategies to weather the difficulties that accompanied each epoch.

Women's Social Situation

In the late nineteenth and early twentieth centuries, European and Russian society generally encouraged women to marry, and most did so. Yet women received different messages regarding their social status in different periods. In the mid-nineteenth century, the English critic Francis Cobbe warned educated women against marriage since it often led to genteel poverty and even spouse abuse. In the 1930s, the socialist Margaret Cole advised educated middle-class English women to marry, since she thought they would be unable to support themselves well on their own earnings and would need a husband to provide them the style of life in which they had been raised. In the 1920s, feminists Virginia Woolf and Aleksandra Kollontai encouraged educated women to develop their own talents and not make love and romance the sole basis of their lives. Soviet and German women received mixed messages regarding education and marriage in the 1930s. Soviet society encouraged women to combine work and marriage, since their participation was needed to fulfill the Five-Year Plans for industrialization and collectivization. In contrast, the Nazis encouraged career women to marry and quit their jobs, since they regarded education and womanliness as incompatible and wanted jobs for men, not women, in the mid 1930s.

Education

Education remained a key factor in women's advancement from 1860 to 1939. Yet educational policies varied according to class and country. Unlike Western European governments, the Tsarist government had not made elementary education free or compulsory in the late nineteenth century. Consequently, 90% of Slavic peasant women and 99% of Central Asian women were illiterate in 1897. About 30% of women in the middle classes attended elementary school, and some attended secondary school. In contrast, most middle-class European women completed primary school, and tens of thousands attended secondary school. Russian women in the clerical and noble estates attended secondary school, and some even obtained higher education at special courses for women, a situation similar to the European pattern where well-to-do women attended secondary school and a few score enrolled in university study prior to World War I. During the war, increasing numbers of European and Russian women attended university and became career women. Indeed, Russian female students dominated medicine and education during World War I.

After seizing power in 1917, the Bolsheviks introduced egalitarian, coeducational legislation and drew peasants and workers into elementary and higher education. Whereas 7 million students attended primary school in 1914–1915, 9 million did so in 1920–1921, and 18 million in 1932–1933. In Europe, primary school had become compulsory in the 1870s, and the number of pupils remained almost the same: 5 million English and French and 8 million German children attended primary school in the 1890s, 1920s, and 1930s. Bolshevik educational policy produced tremendous increases in literacy, especially among peasants and indigenous peoples. By 1939, 60% to 80% of peasant and indigenous women age nine to forty-nine had become literate.

In their efforts to eliminate illiteracy, the Bolsheviks established special programs for adults: they introduced worker faculties at factories so that workers could complete elementary and secondary education. They also introduced evening classes that made it easier for working people to attend technicums and institutes of higher education. By 1929, the Soviets had introduced quotas of 30% women for educational institutions. This policy produced 200,000 female university students, 300,000 in technicums, 89,000 in rabfaks, and 167,000 in workers' universities in the mid 1930s. Equal educational opportunities increased the number of women in technical and scientific work and resulted in the feminization of professions such as education and medicine in the 1930s. By the end of the 1930s, these educational opportunities had created a new, largely Slavic and Jewish female intelligentsia.

German women made great strides in secondary and university education during the Weimar Republic, but the Nazis discouraged higher education for women, and the number of female university students fell from 23,000 in 1931 to 13,000 in 1934. In England, the Depression cut grammar-school scholarships for poor students and reduced the number of university grants for teachers. In France, the socialist government of Leon Blum increased the school-leaving age from thirteen to fourteen years, and a steadily increasing number of women obtained secondary and university education. While 1,000 French women were enrolled in university study in 1900, 12,000 did so in 1926, and 23,000 in 1935.

Women's Distribution in the Economy, 1897–1939

A surprising discovery of this investigation is the enduring employment patterns among women. During the late nineteenth and early twentieth centuries, an overwhelming proportion of European and Russian women worked in agriculture. German women in agriculture declined slightly from 43% of the female labor force in 1895 to 38% in 1939, and French women from 43% to 40%. In the Soviet Union, the percentage declined from 92% in 1926 to 60% in 1939. Most women agricultural workers remained fairly traditional, working on family farms, while collectivization in the Soviet Union brought them into artels and kolkhozy in the 1930s. Collectivization was Janus-faced, producing famine, death, and exile for many in the early 1930s, but offering high status and wages to women tractor drivers and machine operators. Still, most continued as wives, mothers, and unskilled agricultural laborers, while some took advantage of new educational and economic opportunities.

Except in England, manufacturing employed fewer women than did agriculture. In Germany, 24% of the female labor force worked in manufacturing in 1895 and in 1933. In France, the percentage declined from 30% in 1896 to 27% in 1931. In Russia, about 1 million worked in manufacturing in 1897 and 1926. Real change came in the 1930s, when the FYPs drew 2 million more women into manufacturing and construction. In terms of nationality, only a few hundred Central Asian and Caucasian women were occupied in factory production in 1897, a few thousand in 1926, but tens of thousands in 1939.

Another surprising discovery about Russian and Soviet women's participation in manufacturing was the similarity of patterns. In 1914, Russian women constituted 25% of the industrial labor force. During the Civil War they constituted 35%, but fell back to 26% during NEP. Russian women workers in 1897 and 1926 were older and more likely to be married than their European counterparts. In 1897, 40% of Russian women workers were married, and in 1926 45%. High marriage rates distinguished Slavic women workers from Teutonic women, who tended to work in factories prior to but not after marriage. Only the French had similar high marriage and employment rates among women engaged in manufacturing. During the late nineteenth and early twentieth centuries, both Soviet and European women predominated in light industry. Yet differences arose in the 1930s as the FYP drew several hundred thousand Soviet women into construction work, heavy industry, and mining.

Prior to World War I in England, in the 1920s in Germany, and in the 1930s in the Soviet Union, plant managers substituted women and automated machines for skilled male workers. Managers preferred female workers because they produced more and accepted lower wages than men. Some German industrialists publicly remarked that it cost 50% less to employ women than men, and women took less time to produce finished products than men did.[1] Soviet employers seldom publicly made such sexist comments because the regime was officially committed to equal wages for equal work. Yet most Soviet women industrial workers earned lower wages than men because they were less skilled, and they found factory wages higher than those in agriculture or domestic service. One of the major changes that accompanied industrialization in the Soviet Union was the lowering of the age of women factory workers. According to 1897 and 1926 census data, most women workers were twenty to thirty years old. Although the 1939 census did not correlate age and employment, trade union censuses show the average age of women working in metallurgy, machine building, and industrial construction as twenty-four. In transport, over half the women workers were less than twenty-three years old. European and Russian women suffered from low wages, crowded housing, inadequate child care, and sexual harassment. The Soviets tried to improve housing and child care but were unable to keep pace with the urbanization that accompanied industrialization and worsened urban living conditions. Although the Nazis in 1934 forced women out of manufacturing in order to lower male unemployment, by 1938–1939 they were recruiting women into manufacturing, increasing their numbers from 2.7 million in 1933 to 3.4 million in 1939. Official Soviet policy forbade sexual harassment, but the government was less interested in eradicating sexism than in speeding up industrial production, and women's needs did not receive priority.

The period 1890 to 1939 also witnessed substantial changes among women in service occupations. In the 1890s, domestic service employed the largest number of women outside agriculture. Russia and England had 1.8 million, Germany 1.6 million, and France almost 1 million. Whereas the number of French and German domestic servants declined slightly in the 1920s, the number of English and Soviet servants plummeted several hundred thousand. Little change occurred in the 1930s except in England and Germany, where 200,000 more women joined those ranks. While the number of domestic servants sharply declined in the Soviet Union, hundreds of thousands worked as low-paid service employees in public institutions—cooks, waitresses, and nursery-school teachers. They increased thirtyfold in public child care, and sixty times in public feeding, between 1926 and 1939. The number of janitors, guards, office cleaners, laundresses, and couriers increased from 500,000 in 1926 to 2 million in 1939.

The mechanization of office work had drawn hundreds of thousands of European women into commerce by the 1920s. This happened a decade later in the Soviet Union, when the FYPs quadrupled the number of clerical and communications workers. These changes reflect the bureaucratization that accompanied industrialization, but which economic planners had not forecast. While the number of career women mushroomed, career choices remained similar in the nineteenth and twentieth centuries. In the 1890s, women's chief occupation was teaching, and many still chose religion as their vocation. Few practiced law, medicine, or engineering. In the 1920s and 1930s, the rank orders of careers remained similar. Several hundred thousand European and Soviet women became teachers, and a few thousand worked in medicine, engineering, and law. The only significant change was in religion, where the number of French and German women increased in the 1930s, perhaps due to the economic depression, while this category disappeared from the Soviet census.

The numerical increase in career women was much greater in the Soviet Union than in Europe, but the Soviet population was two to three times larger than that of Germany, England, or France. By 1939, teaching and medicine had become feminized: there were 707,000 women in teaching, 224,000 in medical careers, 158,000 in cultural and scientific work, 11,000 in law, and 33,000 in engineering. The number of women teachers increased slowly in England, France, and Germany between the 1890s and 1930s, but women in other professions and administrative personnel increased exponentially from a few thousand to several hundred thousand by the 1920s. While the number of European women in the professions declined slightly during the Depression, the number in public administration increased substantially in Europe. In contrast, Soviet women in the professions grew from 300,000 in 1926 to about 1.3 million in 1939, and those in public administration increased from 400,000 to 2 million.

Nationality remained a dominant feature in Soviet women's progress. The 1926 Soviet census, which cross-referenced occupation, gender, and ethnicity, showed Russian women constituting 60% to 80% of the women teachers, doctors, and political workers in the Central Asian republics. In Belorussia and the Ukraine, Jewish women dominated medicine, while Russian women were overrepresented in teaching and political work. These disparities continued in the Central Asian republics until after World War II. Both European and Soviet women clustered in the helping professions. While engineering was one of the best-paid professions in the 1930s, there were only 33,000 women engineers compared to 700,000 teachers. Unfortunately, both the Tsarist and Soviet regimes paid teachers and doctors low salaries. In both periods, only the highest administrators in education and medicine earned good salaries, and in both times women clustered in the low and middle levels. One advantage of this vertical occupational stratification was that relatively few women occupied high posts in government agencies or Party organizations, so fewer career women than men perished in the purges.

Despite low pay, women teachers found their jobs rewarding, and many single women experienced "spiritual motherhood" as teachers. In the nineteenth century some Russian career women became disillusioned when their work failed to improve society, and some abandoned their careers to engage in revolutionary work. Disenchantment seemed to occur less often in the 1930s among the new Soviet intelligentsia than among the "old." In theory, the new intelligentsia could combine paid professional work with participation in the Party, Komsomol, or government agencies to build socialism. Certainly, many Soviet women worked diligently in government and Party organizations to achieve the goals of the Five-Year Plans.

Soviet career women seemed to have had modest expectations for improving society and seemed content to simply do their jobs. There were exceptions, of course. Evgenia Ginzburg, who was a teacher and Party member, had high expectations about vindicating herself during the purges of the mid 1930s. She was shocked to discover that justifying herself, even against trumped-up charges, was no easy matter. Eventually, she discovered that she had been living in a dream world and found herself in prison and labor camps. The diaries of Nina Kosterina and Suzanne Rosenberg indicate that idealism flourished among the young students in the 1930s. Participation in partisan activities in World War II offered Kosterina and many others an escape from the disenchantment with Soviet reality that the purges had produced. Indeed, the war offered many young people the opportunity to sacrifice themselves to avoid coming to grips with the terror of the purges.

Women's Political Activity

The study shows that middle- and upper-class Russian and European women were usually the most politically conscious and active in the late nineteenth and early twentieth centuries. It was they who belonged to "bourgeois" suffrage organizations and revolutionary parties. Yet Russian and Ukrainian peasant and working-class women became increasingly politically conscious and active during the revolutions of 1905 and 1917–1918. While few peasant women joined the Party or Komsomol in the 1920s, there were more than 700,000 peasant women delegatki, and about 270,000 had been elected to local soviets by 1929. During the 1930s, some peasant women demonstrated against collectivization, and their demonstrations may have influenced the Party to switch to a form of agricultural production whereby land and implements were collectivized but peasant households were allowed to keep a few animals and a small plot of land for their personal use. Party-mindedness remained low among peasant women in the 1930s, and most participated in village soviets rather than in Party organizations.

Working-class women's political activity resembled that of peasant women in several respects. Few of them participated in organized political parties or trade unions in the nineteenth century because such activity was illegal in Germany and Russia and because most working-class women did not have the time or inclination to do so. After World War I, however, increasing numbers of working-class women joined trade unions and political parties. In England, they participated in the Labour Party, in Germany and France the socialist parties, and in Russia the city soviets more than the Communist Party. Although relatively few working-class Soviet women held high positions in the unions, Party, or government, their election to local soviets or even the Supreme Soviet reminded people of their new political and social status. Some were even elected to city soviets in the Central Asian republics, and in 1934 Deshakhan Abidova was elected city manager of Tashkent. While Slavic women initiated political action in Central Asia in the 1920s, increasing numbers of indigenous women became involved in politics. Unveiling was a political action for Central Asian women, and female Party members supported these personal political acts. Although women did not achieve equality in the 1920s, they gained more political power than they had ever had before. Certainly Soviet women's political activity compared well with European women's. French women did not have the right to vote or to be elected in the 1920s or 1930s. Under Hitler, women could not be elected to public office. English political parties placed women on party slates but were loath to support women candidates, especially poor working-class women. One woman remarked in 1934:

> Although the women in Britain enjoy a measure of political rights, these are of no use to working-class woman. She is too oppressed by low paid labor, domestic slavery, unemployment, and laws and traditions which make her dependent on man.[2]

Of course, most Soviet working-class women also suffered from low wages and patriarchal family life, but their government had adopted laws and policies to improve their social, educational, economic, and political position. In the 1920s and 1930s, Soviet working-class women constituted strong proportions of the female Party and Komsomol memberships and represented impressive numbers of delegates elected to city soviets. Few, however, held important positions at the highest levels where Party and government policy was decided. Yet their interests seemed better represented than in Tsarist Russia or contemporary Europe.

One group of women whose political power declined during the Soviet period, however, was educated, gentry-class women. In the nineteenth century, gentry-class women had constituted 10% to 25% of the various revolutionary parties. They also represented the overwhelming majority of women in the Russian suffrage movement prior to 1917. After the revolution, some upper-class women emigrated, but those who had earlier joined the Bolshevik Party in the late nineteenth and early twentieth centuries continued to hold moderately high positions in the government and Party. However, the exodus of "Old Bolsheviks" such as Kollontai and Balabanova in the early 1920s and the purges of others reduced their number and proportion in political bodies. Although many Bolshevichki survived the purges, they did so at the cost of any further influence in the Party or government. Indeed, many well-born women Party members were pensioned off in the early 1930s, and many others simply faded away from political life.

With few women in high-ranking Party and government offices, women's interests were not well protected in the 1930s. Indeed, the passage of the 1936 Constitution—especially Article 122, which indicated that women had gained political, economic, cultural, educational, and social equality—made it appear as though the woman question had been solved. Lenin's warning that the country needed to make a cultural revolution in order to eradicate patriarchial attitudes fell on deaf ears, and patriarchal attitudes, especially in the home, went unchallenged. Although the Soviets officially encouraged women's equality and drafted laws and policies to help them, not enough was done to provide municipal services or to co-opt men into the domestic sphere to genuinely free women for the opportunities society provided. Municipalization schemes remained inadequate for women's complete liberation, and Soviet politicians and administrators remained preoccupied with fundamental economic and political problems and failed to perceive how women's domestic duties often prevented them from achieving the public political, economic, educational, and social equality that the revolution had promised them.

In comparing middle- and upper-class Soviet women's political situation with that of English and German women in the 1920s and 1930s, similarities and differences abound. In England, it was primarily upper-class women such as Lady Astor, the Duchess of Iveagh, and the Duchess of

Atholl who were regularly elected. In Germany, it was mainly educated, leftist women identified with worker interests who were elected. Both Conservative and Labour female M.P.s were surprised at the cavalier attitudes male M.P.s displayed toward "women's issues." One suspects that English party executives, like their German counterparts, often put women on their party ballots to attract the female vote, not because they were interested in women's issues. Like Soviet men who felt that the "woman question" had been solved by Article 122 in the Soviet Constitution, English men felt that enough had been done for women when the Sex Disqualification (Removal) Act was passed. Men generally were more concerned about economic issues than feminist ones.

So what does the history of Russian and European women teach us? First, it suggests that women had made inroads in government and politics. Second, access to higher education led to careers and to limited political and economic power and place, especially at the lower levels in England and the Soviet Union. Third, while large numbers of lower-class women remained in domestic service and manufacturing, huge numbers entered white-collar work and service industries in the 1920s and 1930s. Fourth, greater educational and economic opportunities created more leverage in marriage. Fifth, the greater availability of divorce allowed increasing numbers to escape abusive marriages and gave women more dignity within marriage. Finally, women proved incredibly resourceful in surviving difficult social, educational, economic, and political situations in both centuries. They revealed the strength of the weak in surviving, even flourishing, in unfair circumstances. They proved they were not the fragile flowers many thought they were, but hardy, nurturing women who lived respectable lives, survived hard times, and employed a variety of social, economic, and political strategies to obtain the lives they cherished.

Notes

1. Judith Grunfeld, "Rationalization and the Employment and Wages of Women in Germany," *ILR* 29 (5): 623.
2. "Stirring Report by British Women," *MDN*, May 1, 1934.

Bibliography

Government and Public Documents

Album Graphique de la Statistique Générale de la France, *Resultats Statistiques de recensement de 1901*. Paris, 1907.

British Parliamentary Papers, Industrial Revolution, Factories No. 28, "Reports and Correspondence on Factory Hours and Regulations, Industrial Health Hazards and the Berlin Labour Conference, 1872–1891," Shannon, Ireland: Reprint Series.

Central Statistical Board of the USSR Council of Ministers. *Cultural Progress in the USSR. Statistical Returns*. Moscow, 1958.

————. *National Economy of the USSR. Statistical Returns*. Moscow, 1957.

————. *Women and Children in the USSR: Brief Statistical Returns*. Moscow, 1963.

Great Britain. Parliament. *Parliamentary Papers. Accounts and Papers, 1933/34. Vol. 26 (1931 Census). Cmnd. 4625.* "Twenty-First Abstract of Labour Statistics of the United Kingdom."

Great Britain. War Cabinet, Committee on Women in Industry. *Women in Industry*, 2 vols. cmnd. 135 (1919).

House of Commons. *Women in the House of Commons*. London: Public Information Office, 3–9.

Institut istorii partii pri TsK KP Tadzhikistana. *Kommunisticheskaia Partiia Tadzhikistana za 50 let, 1924–1974*. Dushambe, 1977.

Institut istorii partii pri TsK KP Turkmenistana, *Kommunisticheskaia Partiia Turkmenistana v tsifrakh, 1924–1974*. Ashkhabad, 1975.

Istoriia Sovetskoi Konstitutsii v dokumentakh 1917–1965. Moscow, 1957.

Jahrbuch fur die Amtliche Statistik des Preussischen Staates. Berlin: Statistiches Bureau, 1883.

Kommision fur Geschichte des Parlamentarismus. *M.d.R. Die Reichstagsabgeordneten der Weimarer Republik in der Zeit des Nationalsozialismus, Politische Verfolgung, Emigration und Ausburgerung 1933-1945, Eine biographische Dokumentation Mit einem Forschungsbericht zur Verfolgung deutscher und auslandischer Parlamentarier im nationalsozialistischen Herrschaftsberich*. Dusseldorf: Droste, 1993.

409

Kommunisticheskaia partiia uzbekistana i rabota sredi zhenshchin respubliki 1938–1959. Tashkent, 1982.

KPSS. *VII S'—XVII ezd VKPb. Stenograficheskii otchet.* Moscow, 1926–1968.

Labour Party Report of the 27th Annual Conference. London, 1927–1939.

League of Nations Statistical Year-Book. Geneva, 1935.

Ministère du Commerce de l'industrie, *Resultats Statistiques du recensement des industries et professions.* Tome IV. Paris, 1901.

Parliamentary Papers. Vols. 23 and 97. Great Britain, *Census of England and Wales, 1891.* Session 1893–94. C.7058. London: Her Majesty's Stationery Office, 1893.

Parliamentary Papers. Vol. 108. Great Britain, *Census of England and Wales.* London: His/Her Majesty's Stationery Office, 1901.

Parliamentary Papers. Vol. 10. Great Britain, *Census of England and Wales.* London: His/Her Majesty's Stationery Office, 1911.

Registrar General. *Census of England and Wales, 1921. Occupations.* London, 1924.

Reichstags Handbuch. II Wahlperiode 1924, III 1928, and VI Wahlperiode 1932. Berlin: Bureaus des Reichstages, 1925, 1928, 1932.

Resolutions and Decisions of the Communist Party of the Soviet Union. Vol. 2, The Early Soviet Period: 1917–1929. ed. Richard Gregor. Toronto, 1974.

Rossiiiskaia Akademiia Nauk. Upravlenie statistiki naseleniia goskomstata. Vsesliuznaia perepis' naseleniia 1939 goda, osnovnye itogi. Moscow: Nauka, 1992. (Reprint of original census).

Russian Year Book, 1912, 1916. Ed. H. P. Kennard. London, 1912.

Sotsialisticheskoe Stroitelstvo, SSSR, Statisticheskii Ezhegodnik 1934. Moscow, 1934.

SSSR Strana Sotsializma, Statisticheskii Sbornik. Moscow, 1936.

Statistical Yearbook 1948. Lake Success, New York, 1949.

Statistik des Deutchen Reichs. Band 102. Religionsbekenntnik und Beruf der ermerkshatige, Bevolkerung des Reich am 14 Juni 1895. Berlin: Putt, Kamer, and Muhlbrecht, 1895.

Statistik des Deutchen Reichs. Band 203. Berufs und Betriebszaehlung vom 12 June 1907. Berufsstatistik. Berlin: Puttkammer and Muhlbrecht, 1910.

Statistik des Deutchen Reichs, Band 370. Kriminalstatistik fur das Jahr 1927. Berlin: Putt, Kamer, and Muhlbrecht, 1930.

Statistik des Deutchen Reichs, Band 402. Berufs und Betriebszaehlung vom 16 June 1925. Berlin: Putt, Kamer, and Muhlbrecht, 1927–1931.

Statistisches Handbuch von Deutschland, 1928–1944. Munich: Ehrenwirth, 1949.

Statistisches Jarbuch fur das deutsche Reich. Berlin: Reimar Hobbing, vol. 35, 1914; vol. 49, 1930; vol. 52, 1933.

Statistisches Jarbuch fur den Freistaat Bayern, 1928, 1938. Munich: J. Lindauer, 1928, and Bavaria, 1938.

Statisticheskii Spravochnik SSSR za 1928 g. Moscow, 1929.

Statistique Générale de la France. *Annuaire Statistique. Vols. 20, 30, 49, 52, 54.* Paris: Imprimerie Nationale, 1929, 1934, 1937, 1938.

Statistique Générale de la France. *Resultats Statistiques de dénombrement de 1896.* Paris: Imprimerie Nationale, 1899.

————. *Resultats Statistiques de recensement général de la population 1906.* Paris: Imprimerie Nationale, 1910.

————. *Resultats Statistiques de recensement général de la population effectué le 7 mars 1926. Tome I. Troisième Partie. Population Active, Etablissements.* Paris: Imprimerie Nationale, 1931.

Treaty of Peace with Germany Signed at Versailles, on the 28th of June, 1919, Part XIII LABOUR, Section II, General Principles. Ed. Gaston Griolet et al. Paris, 1920.

Tsentral'noe Statisticheskoe Upravlenie pri Sovete Ministrov SSSR. *Itogi vsesoiuznoi perepisi naselenie 1959 goda.* Moscow, 1963. Vols. 1–16, reprint edition.

————. *Narodnoe Khoziaistvo SSSR za 60 let.* Moscow, 1956, 1970, 1977.

————. *Sotsialisticheskoe Stroitel'stvo Soiuza SSR (1933–38).* Moscow, 1939.

————. *Vsesoiuznaia perepis naseleniia 1926 goda.* Kratkie svodki. Moscow: Izd. TsSU, 1930. vols. 26, 34, and 51.

Tsentral'nyi statisticheskii komitet. *Chislennost' i sostav rabochikh v Rossii na osnovanii danykh pervoi vseobshchei perepisi naseleniia Rossiisko imperii 1897 g.* St. Petersburg, 1906. 2 vols.

————. *Ezhegodnik' Rossii.* 4th, 5th, and 12th years. St. Petersburg: MVD (Ministry of the Interior), 1907, 1908, 1916.

————. *Obshchii svod po Imperii rezul'tatov razrabotki dannykh pervoi vseobshchei perepisi naseleniia Rossiisko imperii 1897 g.* St. Petersburg, 1905. 2 vols.

————. *Pervaia vseobshchaia perepis' naseleniia Rosiiskoi Imperii 1897 goda.* St. Petersburg, 1899–1905. 89 vols.

————. *Raspredelenie rabochikh i prislugi pogruppam zaniatii i po meistu rozhdeniia. . .* St. Petersburg, 1905.

Ts.U NUG pri SNK SSSR. *Zhenshchiny i Deti v SSSR. Statisticheskii sbornik.* Moscow, 1969.

TSU. *Vsesoiuznaia perepis naseleniia 1926 goda. Kratkie svodki.* Vols. 26, 34, 51. Moscow: Statistika, 1928.

Who's Who of British Members of Parliament, vols. 3 and 4. Sussex, 1979.

Newspapers and Journals

Annals of the Association of American Geographers
Canadian American Slavic Studies
Canadian Slavonic Papers
Central Asian Survey
Comparative Studies in Society and History
Contemporary Review
Current History
Economic History Review
Englishwomen's Review of Social and Industrial Questions, 1870–1910
Feminist Studies
French Historical Studies

Gender and History
Georgetown Law Journal
The Historical Journal
Historical Reflections
History of Education Quarterly
History Workshop Journal
International Labour Review: 1920s, 1930s
International Review of Social History
Izvestiia: 1921–1939
Journal of Central European History
Journal of Economic History
Journal of Peasant Studies
Journal of Social History
Journal of Social Hygiene: 1930–1937
Journal of the Royal Statistical Society: 1890–1910
Journal of Ukrainian Studies: Politics and Society
Kommunistka: 1920–1929
Krestianka
Labour Woman: 1925–1933
Literary Digest
Living Age
London Daily News: 8 September 1853
Monthly Labor Review
Moscow Daily News: 1932–1937
Nation
New German Critique
New Left Review
New York Times: 1924–1937
North American Review
Novy Mir
Obshchestvenitsa: 1937–1939
Pharmacy in History
Planovoe Khoziaistvo
Pravda: 1920–1939
Rabotnitsa
Radical America
Revue des Deux Mondes: 1890–1930
Revue des Etudes Slavs
Russian Literature Triquarterly
Russian Review
School and Society: 1932–1939
School Review
Signs
Slavic and European Educational Review
Slavic Review
Slavonic and East European Review
Social Research

Social Science History
Soviet Sociology
Survey Graphic
Third Republic/Troisieme Republic
Time and Tide
Times (London): 1895–1939
Times Educational Supplement: 1922–1937
Victorian Studies
Voprosy istory
Westminster Review
Women's Art Journal
Women's History Review
Women's Studies International Forum
Yale Law Review

Primary and Secondary Sources

"Abort." in *Bol'shaia Sovetskaia Entsiklopediia*, ed. N.I. Bukharin and O.E. Schmidt. Moscow: Sov. Ents., 1926-47. 1: 76 and in *Bol'shaia Meditsinskaia Entsiklopediia*, 1: 40–57.

Adams, Carole. *Women Clerks in Wilhelmine Germany*. New York: Cambridge University Press, 1988.

Afinogenov, Alexander. "Fear," trans. Charles Malamuth. In *Six Soviet Plays*, ed. E. Lyons. New York: Houghton Mifflin, 1934.

Akhmatova, Anna. *Poems of Anna Akhmatova*. Trans. Stanley Kunitz and Max Hayward. Boston: Little Brown, 1973.

Albisetti, James. *Schooling German Girls and Women*. Princeton: Princeton University Press, 1988.

———. *Secondary School Reform in Imperial Germany*. Princeton: Princeton University Press, 1983.

Alexander, Sally, Anna Davin, and Eric Hostettler. "Laboring Women, A Reply to Eric Hobsbawn." *History Workshop*, No. 7–8, 1979.

Alliliueva, Svetlana. *Twenty Letters to a Friend*. Trans. P. J. McMillan. New York: Harper & Row, 1967.

Alston, Patrick. *Education and the State in Tsarist Russia*. Stanford: Stanford University Press, 1969.

Altstadt, Audrey L. *The Azerbaijani Turks*. Stanford: Stanford University Press, 1992.

Altstadt-Mirhadi, Audrey. "Baku, Transformation of a Muslim Town." In *The City in Late Imperial Russia*, ed. M. Hamm. Bloomington: Indiana University Press, 1986.

Aminova, R. Kh. *The October Revolution and Women's Liberation in Uzbekistan*. Moscow: Nauka Publishers, Central Department of Oriental Literature, 1985.

———. *Oktiabr' i reshenie zhenskogo voprosa v Uzbekistane*. Tashkent: "Fan" UzSSSR, 1975.

Anderson, Barbara, and Brian Silver. "Demographic Analysis and Population Catastrophes in the USSR." *Slavic Review* 44, no. 3 (Fall 1985): 517–36.

Anderson, Bonnie S., and Judith P. Zinsser. *A History of Their Own: Women in Europe*, vol. 2. Cambridge, Mass.: Harper & Row, 1988.

Anderson, R. D. *Universities and Elites in Britain since 1900*. Cambridge: Cambridge University Press, 1995.

Andrews, Irene, and Margaret A. Hobbs. *Economic Effects of the World War upon Women and Children in Great Britain*. New York: Oxford University Press, 1921.

Angelina, Praskovya. *My Answer to an American Questionnaire*. Moscow: Foreign Language Publishing House, 1949.

Anikst, Olga. "Voprosy truda i byta." *Kommunistka*, March 1925.

Anthony, Katharine. "Alexandra Kollontai." *The North American Review* 230 (Sept. 1930): 277–82.

———. *Feminism in Germany and Scandinavia*. New York, 1915.

"Arctic Island Women Want Nurseries." *Moscow Daily News*, 6 June 1936, 2.

Artiukina, A. V. "XIV S'ezd VKPb i nashi zadachi." *Kommunistka* 1 (Jan. 1926): 10–15.

———. "8 marta v 1928 gody," *Kommunistka*, February 1928.

Atholl, Lady. "Parliament." *Times* (London), 29 May 1924; 1 November 1929.

Atkinson, Dorothy. *The End of the Russian Land Commune 1905–1930*. Stanford: Stanford University Press, 1983.

Atkinson, Dorothy, Alexander Dalli, and Gail Warshofsky Lapidus, eds. *Women in Russia*. Stanford: Stanford University Press, 1977.

Atkinson, J. Beavington. *An Art Tour to Russia*. London: Hippocrene Books, 1996. First pub. 1873.

Augustine, Dolores L. "Arriving in the Upper Class: The Wealthy Business Elite of Wilhelmine Germany." In *The German Bourgeoisie*, ed. David Blackbourn and Richard J. Evans. New York: Routledge, 1991.

Avdeeva, Ekaterina. *Karmanaia povarennaia kniga*. St. Petersburg, 1846.

———. *Rukovodstvo dlia khoziaek, kliuchnits', ekonomok' i kukharok'*. St. Petersburg, 1846.

Avinov, Marie. *Pilgrimage Through Hell, An Autobiography*. Told by Paul Chavchavadze. Englewood Cliffs, N.J.: Prentice Hall, 1968.

Balabanoff, Angelica. *Impressions of Lenin*. Ann Arbor: University of Michigan Press, 1964.

———. *My Life As a Rebel*. New York: Harper, 1938.

Ball-Hennings, Emmy. *Ruf und Echo, Mein Leben mit Hugo Ball*. Zurich: Benziger, 1933.

Banks, Olive. *The Politics of British Feminism, 1918-1970*. Brookfield, Vt.: E. Elgar, 1993.

Barry, Joseph, ed. *George Sand in Her Own Words*. London: Quartet Books, 1979.

Bashkirtseff, Marie. *Journal de Marie Bashkirtseff*. Tome Seconde. Paris: G. Charpentier, 1890.

———. *The Journal of a Young Artist 1860–1884*. Trans. Mary J. Serrano. New York, 1919.

Bater, James H. *St. Petersburg Industrialization and Change*. Montreal: McGill, Queen's University Press, 1976.

Baumel, Judith Tydor. "Social Interaction among Jewish Women in Crisis during the Holocaust: A Case Study." *Gender and History* 7, April 1995.

Baykov, Alexander. *The Development of the Soviet Economic System*. New York: Macmillan, 1948.

Bayley, John, ed. *The Portable Tolstoy*. New York: Viking, 1978.

Becker, Paula Modersohn. *The Letters and Journals*. Ed. Gunter Busch and Liselotte von Reinken. Ed. and trans. A. S. Wensinger & C. C. Hoey. New York, 1983.

Belinsky, Vissarion I. *Selected Philosophical Works*. Moscow: Foreign Language Publishing House, 1948.

Bell, Susan Groag, and Karen M. Offen. *Women, the Family and Freedom: The Debate in Documents*. Vol. 1, 1750–1880; Vol. 2, 1880–1950. Stanford: Stanford University Press, 1983.

Bellamy, Joyce, and John Saville, eds. *Dictionary of Labour Biography, Vols. I–III*. Clifton, N.J.: Augustus M. Kelley, 1974.

Benet, Sula, ed. and trans. *Village of Viriatino*. New York: Anchor Books, 1970.

Berberova, Nina. *The Italics Are Mine*. Trans. Philippe Radley. New York: Vintage, Inc., 1993.

"Berech' edinstvo partii, ukrepliat' partiinuiu distsiplinu, Rech' tov. Em. Iaroslavskogo." *Pravda*, 3 February 1934, 5.

Berg, Maxine. "The First Women Economic Historians." *Economic History Review* 45 (1992): 2.

Berman, Harold. "Principles of Soviet Criminal Law." *Yale Law Journal* 56 (1946–1947): 803–36.

———. "The Restoration of Law in Soviet Russia." *Russian Review* 6 (1): 3–10.

———. "Soviet Family Law in the Light of Russian History and Marxist Theory." *Yale Law Journal* 56: 26–57.

Berry, Paul, and Allen Bishop, eds. *Testament of a Generation: The Journalism of Vera Brittain and Winifred Holtby*. London: Virago Press, 1985.

Bessel, Richard. *Germany After the First World War*. Oxford: Clarendon Press, 1993.

Beyer, Hans. "Die Frau in der politishcen Entscheidung" (1932) as excerpted in *Wahlerbewegungen in der deutschen Geschichte*, ed. Otto Buesch, Monika Wolk, and Wolfgang Wolk. Berlin: Colloquium, 1978.

Bill, Valentine. *The Forgotten Class, The Russian Bourgeoisie from the Earliest Beginnings to 1900*. New York: Praeger, 1959.

Bisson, Cynthia Story. "Entre lui et sa femme: Domestic Violence in Nineteenth Century Provincial France." Paper given at the 110th Annual Meeting of the American Historical Association, Atlanta, Georgia, 7 January 1996.

Black, Clementina. *Married Women's Work*. London: Garland, 1980.

Blackburn, Robert. *Union Character and Social Class*. London: Batsford, 1967.

Blanchly, Frederich F., and Miriam E. Oatman, eds. *The Government and Administration of Germany*. Baltimore: Johns Hopkins University Press, 1928.

Boak, Helen L., "Women in Weimar Germany: The 'Frauenfrage' and the Female Vote." In *Social Change and Political Development in Weimar Germany*, ed. R. Bessel and E. J. Feuchtwanger. London: Croomhelm, 1981.

Bobroff, Anne. "The Bolsheviks and Working Women, 1905–1920." *Soviet Studies* 26 (1974): 545–67.

———. "Russian Working Women: Sexuality in Bonding Patterns and the Politics of Daily Life." In *Powers of Desire*, ed. Ann Snitow, Christine Stansell, and Sharon Thompson. New York: Monthly Review Press, 1983.

Bochkareva, Ekaterina I., and Serafima Liubimova. *Women of a New World*. Moscow: Progress Publishers, 1967.

Bock, Gisela. "Racism and Sexism in Nazi Germany: Motherhood, Compulsory Sterilization, and the State." In *When Biology Became Destiny: Women in Weimar and Nazi Germany*, ed. Renate Bridenthal et al. New York: Monthly Review Press, 1984.

———. "Poverty and Mothers' Rights in the Emerging Welfare State." In *A History of Women*, vol. 5, ed. F. Thebaud. Cambridge, Mass.: Belknap Press of Harvard University Press, 1995.

Bohachevsky-Chomiak, Martha. *Feminists Despite Themselves, Women in Ukrainian Community Life, 1884–1939*. Edmonton: Canadian Institute of Ukrainian Studies, University of Alberta, 1988.

———. "Feminism in Ukrainian History." *Journal of Ukrainian Studies* 12 (Spring 1982).

Bonnell, Victoria. *Roots of Rebellion*. Berkeley: University of California Press, 1983.

———. *The Russian Worker*. Berkeley: University of California Press, 1983.

———. "Trade Unions, Parties and the State in Tsarist Russia: A Study of Labor Politics in St. Petersburg and Moscow." *Politics and Society* 9 (1980): 299–322.

Bonner, Elena. *Mothers and Daughters*. Trans. Antonina W. Bouis. New York: Vintage Books, 1993.

Boone, Gladys. *Women's Trade Union Leagues*. New York: AMS Press, 1968.

Borland, Harriat. *Soviet Literary Theory and Practice during the First Five Year Plan*. New York: Kings Crown Press, 1950.

Bornat, Joanna. "Home and Work: A New Context for Trade Union History." *Radical America* 12 (Sept.–Oct. 1978).

Botchkareva, Maria. *Yashka, My Life as Peasant, Officer and Exile*. As Set Down by Isaac Don Levine. New York: Frederick A. Stokes, 1919.

Bowlt, John E., ed. and trans. *Russian Art of the Avant Garde: Theory and Criticism, 1902–1934*. New York: Thames and Hudson, 1988.

Boxer, Marilyn. "French Socialism, Feminism, and the Family." *Third Republic/ Troisième Republic* 3–4: 164–67.

———. "The Extraordinary Failure of Madeleine Pelletier." In *European Women on the Left*, ed. Jane Slaughter and Robert Kern. Westport, Conn.: Greenwood Press, 1981.

———. "Women in Industrial Homework: The Flowermakers of Paris in the Belle Epoque." *French Historical Studies*, 12 (3): 401–23.

Boxer, Marilyn, and Jean Quataert, eds. *Socialist Women European Socialist Feminism in the Nineteenth and Early Twentieth Centuries*. New York: Elsevier, 1978.

———. *Connecting Spheres, Women in the Western World, 1500 to the Present.* New York: Oxford University Press, 1987.

Branca, Patricia. *Women in Europe Since 1750.* London: St. Martin's Press, 1978.

Braun, Lily. *Selected Writings on Feminism and Socialism.* Trans. and ed. Alfred G. Meyer. Bloomington: Indiana University Press, 1987.

Breshkovskaia, Katherine. *Hidden Springs of the Russian Revolution.* Stanford: Stanford University Press, 1931.

———. *Little Grandmother of the Russian Revolution, Reminiscences and Letters of Catherine Breshkovsky,* ed. Alice Stone Blackwell. New York and Boston: Little, Brown, 1917.

Bridenthal, Renate. "'Professional' Housewives: Stepsisters of the Women's Movement." In *When Biology Became Destiny: Women in Weimar and Nazi Germany,* ed. Renate Bridenthal, Atina Grossman, and Marion Kaplan. New York: Monthly Review Press, 1984.

Bridenthal, Renate, and Claudia Koonz. "Beyond Kinder, Kuche, and Kirche: Weimar Women in Politics and Work." In *Liberating Women's History,* ed. Bernice A. Carroll. Urbana: University of Illinois Press, 1976.

Bridenthal, Renate, Susan Mosher Stuard, and Merry E. Wiesner. *Becoming Visible: Women in European History,* 3rd ed. Boston: Houghton Mifflin, 1998.

Briggs, Anthony D. "Twofold Life: A Mirror of K. Pavlova's Shortcomings and Achievement." *Slavonic and East European Review* 49 (114): 8.

Brittain, Vera. *Lady into Woman.* New York: A. Dakers, 1953.

———. *Testament of Friendship.* New York: Wideview Books, 1981. First pub. 1940.

———. *Testament of Youth.* New York: Penguin Books, 1993. First pub. 1933.

———. "The Care of Motherhood," "Nursery Schools," "I Denounce Domesticity," "Fellowship," "The Lighter Side of Peacemaking," "No Compromise with War." Reprinted in *Testament of a Generation,* ed. Paul Berry and Alan Bishop. London: Virago, 1985.

Bronner, V. *La lutte contre la prostitution.* Moscow, 1936.

Brookes, Pamela. *Women at Westminster.* London: P. Davies, 1967.

Brooks, Barbara. "The Illegal Operation: Abortion, 1919–1939." In *The Sexual Dynamics of History,* ed: London Feminist History Group. London: Pluto Press, 1983.

Brower, Daniel R. "Collectivized Agriculture in Smolensk: The Party, the Peasantry, and the Crisis of 1932." *Russian Review* 36 (April 1977): 151–66.

Buck, Pearl. *Talk About Russia with Masha Scott.* New York: John Day, 1945.

Buckley, Mary. *Women and Ideology in the Soviet Union.* Ann Arbor: University of Michigan Press, 1989.

Bukharin, Nikolai, and Evgenii Preobrazhenskii. *The ABC of Communism.* London, 1921.

Busygin, E. P., N. V. Zorin, and Z. Z. Mukhina. *Sel'skaia zhenshchina v semeinoi i obshchestvennoi zhizni.* Kazan: Izd-vo Kazanskogo universiteta, 1986.

Butler, D. E. *The Electoral System in Britain Since 1918.* Oxford: Oxford University Press, 1963.

Cadbury, Edward, M. Cecile Matheson, and George Shann. *Women's Work and Wages.* Chicago: University of Chicago Press, 1907.

Caine, Barbara. "Beatrice Webb and the 'Woman Question.'" *History Workshop Journal* 13, Autumn 1982.

Camp, Wesley D. *Marriage and the Family in France Since the Revolution.* New York: Bookman Associates, 1961.

"Can the Russian Peasant Become Machine Conscious?" *Moscow Daily News*, 12 June 1932, 2.

Carles, Emilie. *A Life of Her Own, A Countrywoman in Twentieth-Century France,* as told to Robert Destanque. Trans. A. H. Goldberger. New Brunswick, N.J.: Rutgers University Press, 1991.

Carr, E. H. *Foundations of a Planned Economy,* 2 vols. New York: Macmillan, 1971.

———. "The Revolution from Above." *New Left Review* 45 (Sept.–Oct. 1967): 17–27.

Chamberlain, William Henry. "Daughters of the Russian Revolution." *Yale Review* 18 (June 1929): 733–48.

Charrier, Edmée. *L'Evolution Intellectuelle Feminine.* Paris, 1931.

Chekhov, Anton. *Selected Stories.* Ttrans. Ann Dunnigan. New York, 1963.

Chernyshevskii, Nikolai G. *Selected Philosophical Essays.* Moscow: Foreign Language Publishing House, 1953.

———. *What Is to Be Done?* Trans. Benjamin Tucker. Revised and abridged by Ludmilla B. Turkevich. New York: Vintage, 1961.

Chesterton, Mrs. Cecil. *I Lived in a Slum.* London: Gollancz, 1936.

———. *Sickle or Swastika?* London: S. Paul & Co., 1934.

Chew, Ada Nield. "Assault and Battery." In *The Life and Writings of Ada Nield Chew.* London: Virago, 1982.

Chinn, Carl. *They Worked All Their Lives: Women of the Urban Poor in England, 1880–1939.* New York: Manchester University Press, 1988.

"Chistka ukrepila bol'shevistskie riady i vysoko podniala zvanie chlena partii." *Pravda*, 4 February 1934, 5.

Ciboski, Kenneth N. "A Woman in Soviet Leadership: The Political Career of Madame Furtseva." *Canadian Slavonic Papers*, 14 (Spring 1972): 1–14.

Clark, Linda. "A Battle of the Sexes in a Professional Setting: The Introduction of Inspectrices Primaires, 1899–1914." *French Historical Studies* 16 (Spring 1989), 31.

Clarke, Frances. *The Position of Women in Contemporary France.* London: P. S. King, 1937.

Clarke, Roger A. *Soviet Economic Facts, 1917–1970.* New York: John Wiley, 1972.

"The Cleaning of Tatiana Tikhonova." *Moscow Daily News*, 24 July 1933, 3.

Clements, Barbara. "Birth of the New Soviet Woman." In *Bolshevik Culture,* ed. Abbott Gleason, Peter Kenez, and Richard Stites. Bloomington: Indiana University Press, 1985.

———. *Bolshevik Feminist, The Life of Aleksandra Kollontai.* Bloomington: Indiana University Press, 1979.

———. "Emancipation Through Communism: The Ideology of A. M. Kollontai." *Slavic Review* 32 (1973): 323–38.

———. "Working Class and Peasant Women in the Russian Revolution, 1919–1923." *Signs* 8 (1982): 215–35.

Clements, Barbara Evans. *Bolshevik Women*. Cambridge: Cambridge University Press, 1997.

Clements, Barbara Evans, Barbara Alpern Engel, and Christine D. Worobec, eds. *Russia's Women: Accommodation, Resistance, Transformation*. Berkeley: University of California Press, 1991.

Clowes, Edith W., Samuel Kassow, and James L. West, eds. *Between Tsar and People: Educated Society and the Quest for Public Identity in Late Imperial Russia*. Princeton: Princeton University Press, 1991.

Clyman, Toby. "Women in Chekhov's Prose Works," Ph.D. dissertation, New York University, 1971.

Clyman, Toby, and Diana Greene, eds. *Women Writers in Russian Literature*. Westport, Conn.: Praeger, 1994.

Clyman, Toby W., and Judith Vowles. *Russia through Women's Eyes*. New Haven: Yale University Press, 1996.

Coates, W. P., and Z. K. Coates. *The Second Five Year Plan of Development of the USSR*. London: Methuen, 1934.

Cobbe, Frances Power. "Celibacy vs. Marriage." *Fraser's Magazine* 65 (Feb. 1862): 228–35.

———. "Wife-Torture in England." *Contemporary Review* 32 (April–July 1878).

Cocks, Geoffrey. *German Professions, 1800–1950*. New York: Oxford University Press, 1990

Cohen, Stephen F. *Bukharin and the Bolshevik Revolution: A Political Biography 1888–1938*. New York: Oxford University Press, 1973.

Cole, G.D.H. *Trade Unionism and Munitions*. Oxford: Clarendon Press, 1923.

Cole, Margaret. *Marriage Past and Present*. London: J. M. Dent, 1939.

The Colette Omnibus. Introduction by Erica John. Garden City, N.Y.: International Collectors Library, 1974.

"The Collectivisation of Agriculture in the U.S.S.R." *International Labour Review* 26 (1932): 408.

Collet, Clara. "Changes in Wages of Domestic Servants." *Journal of the Royal Statistical Society*, September 1908, 518.

———. "The Social Status of Women Occupiers." *Journal of the Royal Statistical Society*, September 1908, 513–15.

———. "Statistics of Employment of Women and Girls." *Journal of the Royal Statistical Society*, September 1895, 522–25.

Conroy, Mary Schaeffer. "Pharmacy in Pre-Soviet Russia." *Pharmacy in History* 27 (1985): 115–37.

Cook, Bernard A. "Agricultural Laborers," *Victorian Britain, An Encyclopedia*, ed. Sally Mitchell. New York: Garland, 1988.

Cook, Chris, and John Patton. *European Political Facts 1848–1918*. New York: Macmillan, 1978.

Cookson, Catherine. *Our Kate, An Autobiography*. New York, London, 1969.

Copelman, Dina M. *London's Women Teachers: Gender, Class, and Feminism, 1870–1930*. London: Routledge, 1996.

Coquart, Armand. *D. I. Pisarev et l'ideologie du nihilism Russe*. Paris: Institut d'études slaves de l'université de Paris, 1946.

Corbet, Charles. "Dobroljubov et Herzen." *Revue des Etudes Slaves* 27 (1951): 70–77.

Correspondence of Boris Pasternak and Olga Freidenberg, 1910–1954. Trans. and ed. Elliott Mossman. New York: Harcourt Brace Jovanovich, 1982.

Craig, F. W. *British Electoral Facts 1885–1975.* London: Macmillan, 1976.

Crossick, Geoffrey, and Heinz-Gerhard Haupt. *The Petite Bourgeoisie in Europe 1780–1914.* New York: Routledge, 1995.

Crossman, Richard, ed. *The God That Failed.* New York: Bantam, 1965.

Crowell, Phyllis. "Studies in Contradictions: The Effects of Gender Ideology on Middle Class Women in Late 19th Century England." M.A. thesis, University of Texas, El Paso, July 1996.

Currell, Melville E. *Political Woman.* London: Croom Helm, 1974.

Czap, Peter. "Marriage and the Peasant Joint Family in the Era of Serfdom." In *The Family in Imperial Russia,* ed. David Ransel. Urbana: University of Illinois Press, 1978.

Dalby, Louise E. *Leon Blum: Evolution of a Socialist.* New York: T. Yoseloff, 1963.

Daniel, Iuri. *This Is Moscow Speaking.* Trans. Stuart Hood. New York: Dutton, 1968.

Davidis, Frau. *The Housewife: A Present for Future Housewives*

Davidoff, Leonore. *The Best Circles: Women and Society in Victorian England.* Totowa, N.J.: Rowman and Littlefield, 1973.

Davies, Margaret L., ed. *Maternity: Letters from Working Women.* New York: Norton, 1978.

Dayus, Kathleen. *Her People.* London: Virago, 1982.

de Beauvoir, Simone. *Memoirs of a Dutiful Daughter.* Trans. James Kirkup. New York: Harper & Row, 1974.

———. *Prime of Life.* Trans. Peter Green. Cleveland: World, 1962.

Delafield, E. M. *The Provincial Lady in London.* Reprint of 1933 edition. Chicago: Academy Chicago Publishers, 1983.

———. *The Provincial Lady in Russia.* Reprint of 1937 edition. Chicago: Academy Chicago Publishers, 1985.

d'Encause, Helene Carrère. *The Great Challenge, Nationalities and the Bolshevik State 1917–1930.* Trans. Nancy Festinger. New York, 1992.

Derlitzki, Professor. "The Rationalization of the Work of Farm Women in Germany." *International Labour Review* 26 (1932): 707–9.

Deuel, Wallace R. *People Under Hitler.* New York: Harcourt, Brace & Co., 1942.

Dictionary of National Biography. "Eileen Edna le Poer Postan," 1931–40; "Cecil Woodham-Smith," 1971–80. London: Oxford University Press, 1975.

Djilas, Milovan. *Conversations with Stalin.* Trans. Michael Petrovich. New York: Harcourt, Brace & World, 1962.

Dobroliubov, Nikolai A. *Selected Philosophical Essays.* Moscow: Foreign Language Publishing House, 1948.

———. *Sobranie Sochinenii v deviati tomakh.* Moscow: Gosudarstvennoe izdatel'stvo khudozhestvennoi literatury, 1964.

———. *Sobranie Sochinenii v trekh tomakh.* Moscow: Gosudarstvennoe izdatel'stvo khudozhestvennoi literatury, 1962.

Dodge, Norton T. *Women in the Soviet Union, Their Role in Economic, Scientific, and Technical Development*. Baltimore: Johns Hopkins University Press, 1966.

Dohan, Michael. "The Economic Origins of Soviet Autarky, 1927/28–1934." *Slavic Review* 35: 603–35.

Donskov, Andrew. "The Peasant in Tolstoy's Thought and Writings." *Canadian Slavonic Papers* 21 (2): 183–96.

Dostoevsky, Fedor. *Crime and Punishment*. Trans. Constance Garnett. New York: Modern Library, 1951.

Dovnar-Zapol'skii, M. V. "Marriage and Family Relations Among the Collective Farm Peasantry," *Soviet Sociology* 16 (3): 20–22.

Downs, S. W. "School Changes in Russia," *School and Society* 43 (June 27, 1936).

Dreiser, Theodore. "How Russia Handles the Sex Question." *Current History*, January 1929.

Dubreuil, Hyacinthe. *Employeurs et Salaries en France*. Paris: F. Alcan, 1934.

Dudgeon, Ruth. "The Forgotten Minority: Women Students in Imperial Russia, 1872–1917." *Russian History*, 9 Pt. 1, 1982.

Dupeux, Georges. *French Society 1789–1970*. London: Methuen, 1976.

Durova, Nadezhda. *The Cavalry Maiden, Journals of a Russian Officer in the Napoleonic Wars*. Trans. Mary Zirin. Bloomington: Indiana University Press, 1988.

Eastman, Crystal. *On Women and Revolution*. New York: Oxford University Press, 1978.

Eastman, Max. *Artists in Uniform: A Study of Literature and Bureaucratism*. New York: Knopf, 1934.

Edmondson, Linda. *Feminism in Russia, 1900–1917*. London: Heinemann, 1984.

"Education and Unemployment in England," *School and Society* 39 (May 19, 1934).

Ehrenburg, Ilia. *Out of Chaos*. Trans. Alexander Bakshy. New York: Holt, 1934.

Eklof, Ben. "The Village and the Outsider, The Rural Teacher in Russia, 1864–1914." *Slavic and European Educational Review* 1 (1979): 1–20.

Elling, Hanna. *Frauen im deutschen Widerstand 1933-45*. Frankfurt am Main: Roederberg, 1978.

Elnett, Elaine. *Historic Origin and Social Development of Family Life in Russia*. New York: Columbia University Press, 1926.

Elshtain, Jean Bethke. *Women and War*. New York: Basic Books, 1987.

Engel, Barbara. *Mothers and Daughters*. New York: Cambridge University Press, 1983.

————. "Women Medical Students in Russia, 1872–1882: Reformers or Rebels?" *Journal of Social History* 12 (1979): 394–415.

Engel, Barbara Alpern. *Between the Fields and the City: Women, Work, and Family in Russia, 1861–1914*. Cambridge: Cambridge University Press, 1996.

Engel, Barbara A., and Clifford N. Rosenthal, ed. and trans. *Five Sisters: Women Against the Tsar: The Memoirs of Five Young Anarchist Women of the 1870s*. New York: Schocken Books, 1977.

Engelgardt, Aleksandr N. *Letters from the Country, 1872–1887*. Trans. and ed. Cathy A. Frierson. New York: Oxford University Press, 1993.

Engelstein, Laura. "Gender and the Juridical Subject: Prostitution and Rape in 19th Century Russian Criminal Codes." *Journal of Modern History* 60 (September 1988).

―――. *The Keys to Happiness: Sex and the Search for Modernity in Fin de Siècle Russia.* Ithaca: Cornell University Press, 1992.

―――. *Moscow, 1905: Working Class Organization and Political Conflict.* Stanford: Stanford University Press, 1982.

"Engineer, Mother, Student—The New Woman." *Moscow Daily News*, 6 November 1933, 3.

"English Country Children." *School and Society* 49 (March 25, 1939).

"English Labour Party and Education." *School and Society* 40 (November 17, 1934).

"English Training Colleges." *School and Society* 37 (February 28, 1933).

Englishwoman's Review, 6 September 1875; 15 March 1878.

Ettinger, Elzbieta. *Hannah Arendt/Martin Heidegger.* New Haven: Yale University Press, 1995.

Evans, Janet. "The CPSU and the Woman Question: The Case of the 1936 Decree, In Defense of Mother and Child." *Journal of Contemporary History* 16 (1981): 770.

Evans, Richard. "Feminism and Female Emancipation in Germany, 1870–1945: *Sources, Methods, and Problems of Research.*" *Journal of Central European History* 9 (1976): 323–51.

―――. *The Feminist Movement in Germany, 1894–1933.* London: Sage, 1976.

―――. *The German Bourgeoisie.* New York: Routledge, 1991.

―――. "Prostitution, State and Society in Imperial Germany." *Past and Present* 70 (February 1976): 106–29.

"Exclusion of Jewish Children from the Public Schools in Germany." *School and Society* 41 (May 25, 1935).

Faderman, L., and B. Eriksson. *Lesbians in Germany: 1890s–1920s.* Tallahassee: Naiad Press, 1990.

Fainsod, Merle. *Smolensk Under Soviet Rule.* Cambridge, Mass.: Harvard University Press, 1958.

Farnsworth, Beatrice. *Aleksandra Kollontai, Socialism, Feminism, and the Bolshevik Revolution.* Stanford: Stanford University Press, 1980.

―――. "Bolshevism, the Woman Question, and Aleksandra Kollontai." *American Historical Review* 81 (April 1976): 292–316.

―――. "The Litigious Daughter-in-Law: Family Relations in Rural Russia in the Second Half of the Nineteenth Century." In *Russian Peasant Women*, ed. Beatrice Farnsworth and Lynne Viola. New York: Oxford University Press, 1992.

Farnsworth, Beatrice, and Lynne Viola, eds. *Russian Peasant Women.* New York: Oxford University Press, 1992.

Felstiner, Mary L. *To Paint Her Life: Charlotte Salomon in the Nazi Era.* New York: Harper Collins, 1994.

Fen, Elisaveta. *Modern Russian Stories.* London: Methuen, 1943.

Field, Alice W. "Prostitution in the Soviet Union." *The Nation*, 25 March 1936, 373-74.

―――. *Protection of Women and Children in Soviet Russia.* New York: Dutton, 1932.

Field, Mark. *Doctor and Patient in Soviet Russia*. Cambridge, Mass.: Harvard University Press, 1957.

Figes, Eva. *Patriarchal Attitudes*. Greenwich, Conn.: Fawcett, 1971.

Figner, Vera. *Memoirs of a Revolutionist*. Trans. Camilla Chapin Daniels et al. New York: International Publishers, 1927.

———. *Memoirs of a Revolutionist*. Trans. Camilla Chapin Daniels et al. Intro. Richard Stites. DeKalb: Northern Illinois University Press, 1991.

Filippova, L. D. "Iz istorii zhenskogo obrazovaniia v Rossi." *Voprosy istory* 38 (1963): 209–18.

"The First Woman Air Commander." *Moscow Daily News,* 9 February 1933.

Fischer, Louis. "Moscow Frowns on Abortions." *The Nation* 141 (21 August 1935): 212–13.

Fisher, Ralph T. *Pattern for Soviet Youth, A Study of the Congresses of the Komsomol 1918–1954*. New York: Columbia University Press, 1959.

Fitzpatrick, Shelia. "Culture and Politics Under Stalin: A Reappraisal." *Slavic Review* 35 (1976): 211–31.

———. "Cultural Revolution in Russia, 1928–32." *Journal of Contemporary History* 9 (1974): 33–52.

———. *Education and Social Mobility in the Soviet Union 1921–1934*. New York: Cambridge University Press, 1979.

———. "The Foreign Threat during the First FYP." *Soviet Union* 5 (Pt. 1): 26–35.

———. "Sex and Revolution: An Examination of Literary and Statistical Data on the Mores of Soviet Students in the 1920s." *Journal of Modern History* 50 (June 1978): 252–78.

———. "Stalin and the Making of a New Elite, 1928–1939." *Slavic Review* 38 (Sept. 1979): 377–402.

———. *Stalin's Peasants: Resistance and Survival in the Russian Village after Collectivization*. New York: Oxford University Press, 1994.

Flanz, Gisbert H. *Comparative Women's Rights and Political Participation in Europe*. New York: Transnational Publ., 1983.

Florinsky, Michael, "Social Insurance." *Encyclopedia of Russia and the Soviet Union*. New York: McGraw Hill, 1961.

Fout, John, and Eleanor Riemer, eds. *European Women: A Documentary History*. New York: Schocken Books, 1980.

Fraisse, Genevieve, and Michelle Perrot, eds. *A History of Women in the West, IV. Emerging Feminism from Revoluton to World War*. Cambridge, Mass.: Belknap Press of Harvard University Press, 1993.

Franz, Nellie Alden. *English Women Enter the Professions*. Cincinnati: Privately printed, 1965.

Freeze, Gregory. "Caste and Emancipation: The Changing Status of Clerical Families in the Great Reforms." In *The Family in Imperial Russia*, ed. David Ransel. Urbana: University of Illinois Press, 1978.

"Frenchwomen and the Vote." *Times* (London), 18 February 1929.

Frevert, Ute. *Women in German History from Bourgeois Emancipation to Sexual Liberation*. Trans. Stuart McKinnon Evans, Terry Bond, and Barbara Norden. Oxford: Berg, 1988.

Frierson, Cathy A. *Peasant Icons: Representations of Rural People in Late Nineteenth Century Russia.* New York: Oxford University Press, 1993.

———. "Razdel: The Peasant Family Divided." In *Russian Peasant Women*, ed. B. Farnsworth and L. Viola. New York: Oxford University Press, 1992.

Frois, Marcel. *La Santé et le Travail des Femmes pendant la Guerre.* New Haven: Yale University Press, 1927.

Fuchs, Rachel G. *Poor and Pregnant in Paris, Strategies for Survival in the 19th Century.* New Brunswick, N.J.: Rutgers University Press, 1992.

Furniss, Edgar. "Class War Linked with Anti-Religion in Soviet Policy." *Current History* 31 (Oct. 1929–Mar. 1930): 606–8.

———. "The Soviet Union." *Current History* 31 (Oct. 1929–Mar. 1930): 1229–31.

Fuss, Henry. "Unemployment and Employment among Women." *International Labour Review* 31 (1935): 463–97.

Gamble, Rose. *Chelsea Child.* London: British Broadcasting Company, 1979.

Gantt, W. Horsley. *Russian Medicine.* New York: P. B. Hoeber, 1937.

———. "The Soviet's Treatment of Scientists." *Current History* 31 (March 1930): 1151–57.

Gasiorowska, Xenia. "The Career Woman in the Soviet Novel." *Russian Review* 15 (April 1956): 100–9.

"General Election." *Times* (London), 1 June 1929.

"German Secondary School Census." *School and Society* 36 (24 September 1932).

Gernet, M. "Povtornye i mnogokratnye aborty." Tsentralnoe Statisticheskoe Upravlenie, *Statisticheskoe Obozrenie* 12 (1928): 110–14.

Gershenkron, Alexander. "The Rate of Industrial Growth in Russia." *Journal of Economic History* 12 (1947): 163.

Getty, J. A. "Party and Purge in Smolensk, 1933–37." *Slavic Review* 42 (Spring 1983): 60–79.

Getty, J. A., and William Chase. "The Moscow Party Elite of 1917 in the Great Purges." *Russian History* 5 (Pt. I): 106–15.

Gheith, Jehanne. "Evgeniia Tur and Avdoti'ia Panaeva—The Precursors?" Paper presented at the American Association for the Advancement of Slavic Studies, November 1992.

Giddens, Anthony. *The Class Structure of the Advanced Societies.* London: Hutchinson, 1973.

Giles, Geoffrey J. "Higher Education Policy in World War II." *Central European History* 17 (4), 1984.

Giles, Judy. "A Home of One's Own: Women and Domesticity in England 1918–1950." *Women's Studies International Forum* 16 (3).

———. "Playing Hard to Get: Working-Class Women, Sexuality and Respectability in Britain, 1918–40." *Women's History Review* 1, no. 2 (1992).

Gillis, John R. *For Better, For Worse: British Marriages, 1600 to the Present.* New York: Oxford University Press, 1985.

Ginzburg, Eugenia. *Journey into the Whirlwind.* Trans. Paul Stevenson and Max Hayward. New York: Harcourt, Brace, Jovanovich, 1967.

———. *Within the Whirlwind.* Trans. Ian Boland. New York: Harcourt Brace Jovanovich, 1981.

Gladkov, Fedor. *Cement, A Novel.* Trans. A. S. Arthur and C. Ashleigh. New York: Frederick Ungar, 1980.

———. *Sobranie Sochinenii. Tom vtoroi, Tsement.* Moscow: God. izd. khudozh. litry, 1958.

Glasse, Antonia. "The Formidable Woman: Portrait and Original." *Russian Literature Triquarterly* 9 (Spring 1974).

Glebov, Anatole. "Inga." Trans. Charles Malamuth. In *Six Soviet Plays*, ed. Eugene Lyons. Boston: Houghton Mifflin, 1934.

———. "Inga." In *Sbornik P'es.* Moscow: Iskusstvo, 1967.

Glebova. "V national'n respublikh v Bashkirii " and "Rabota sredi zhenshchin po Gruzii." *Kommunistka* 1 (January 1925).

Glendinning, Victoria. *Rebecca West, A Life.* New York: Fawcett Columbine, 1987.

Glickman, Rose. *Russian Factory Women: Workplace and Society, 1880–1914.* Berkeley: University of California Press, 1984.

———. "The Russian Factory Woman, 1880–1914." In *Women in Russia*, ed. D. Atkinson, A. Dallin, and G. Lapidus. Stanford: Stanford University Press, 1977.

Goldberg, Lois Rochelle. "The Russian Women's Movement, 1859–1917." Ph.D. dissertation, Rutgers University, 1976.

Goldman, Wendy Z. "Women, the Family, and the New Revolutionary Order in the Soviet Union." In *Promissory Notes: Women in the Transition to Socialism*, ed. S. Kruks, R. Rapp, and M. Young. New York: Monthly Review Press, 1989.

———. *Women, the State, and Revolution: Soviet Family Policy and Social Life, 1917–1936.* New York: Cambridge University Press, 1993.

Golitsyn, N. N. *Bibliograficheskii Slovar Russkikh' Pisatelnits'.* St. Petersburg, 1889. Vol. 1.

Gordon, Felicia. *The Integral Feminist: Madeleine Pelletier, 1874–1939.* Oxford: Polity, 1990.

Gordon, Lyndall. *Virginia Woolf, A Writer's Life.* New York: Oxford University Press, 1984.

Gorky, Maxim. "Lower Depths." Trans. Jenny Covan. In *Great Russian Plays*, ed. Norris Houghton. New York: Dell, 1960.

———. *My Childhood.* Trans. Ronald Wilks. Baltimore: Penguin Books, 1966.

———. "On the Russian Peasantry." *Journal of Peasant Studies*, 4 (1), October 1976.

———, ed. *The White Sea Canal, Being an Account of the Construction of the New Canal between the White Sea and the Baltic Sea.* Trans. Amabel Williams Ellis. London: John Lane, 1935.

Gorsuch, Anne E. "Flapper and Foxtrotters, Soviet Youth in the 'Roaring Twenties.'" *The Carl Beck Papers in Russian and East European Studies* 1102 (March 1994).

Goscilo, Helena, ed. *Russian and Polish Women's Fiction.* Knoxville: University of Tennessee Press, 1984.

Gove, Antonia F. "The Feminine Stereotype and Beyond: Role Conflict and Resolution in the Poetics of Marina Tsvetaeva." *Slavic Review* 36 (June 1977): 231–55.

Graves, Pamela M. *Labour Women: Women in British Working-Class Politics, 1918–1939.* Cambridge: Cambridge University Press, 1994.

Gray, Camilla. *The Russian Experiment in Art: 1863–1922*. New York: Harry Abrams, 1962.

Green, Diana. "Karolina Pavlova's 'At the Tea Table' and the Politics of Class and Gender." *The Russian Review* 53 (April 1994).

Green, Margaret. *Eyes Right! A Left-Wing Glance at the New Germany*. London: Christophers, 1935.

"Greet E.D. Stasova on 60th Birthday." *Moscow Daily News*, 15 October 1933, 1.

Grill, Johnpeter Horst. *The Nazi Movement in Baden, 1920–1945*. Chapel Hill: University of North Carolina Press, 1983.

Grosse Frauen des Weltgeschichte. Wiesbaden: Loewit, 1975.

Grossman, Atina. "Abortion and Economic Crisis: The 1931 Campaign against #218 in Germany." *New German Critique*, Spring 1978.

———. "German Women Doctors from Berlin to New York: Maternity and Modernity in Weimar and in Exile." *Feminist Studies* 19 (1), Spring 1993.

———. "The New Woman and the Rationalization of Sexuality in Weimar Germany." In *Powers of Desire, The Politics of Sexuality*, ed. Ann Snitow. New York: Monthly Review Press, 1983.

Grossman, Vasily. *Forever Flowing*. Trans. Thomas P. Whitney. New York: Harper & Row, 1972.

Grunfeld, Judith. "Rationalization and Employment of Wages of Women in Germany." *International Labour Review* 29 (May 1934): 605–32.

———. "Wage Trends in Germany." *International Labor Review* 26 (November 1932).

———. "Women's Work in Russia's Planned Economy." *Social Research* 9 (2): 22–45.

Gsovski, Vladimir. "Marriage and Divorce in Soviet Law." *Georgetown Law Journal* 35: 209–23.

Gudvan, A. M. "Essays on the History of the Movement of Sales-Clerical Workers in Russia." In *The Russian Worker*, ed. Victoria Bonnell. Berkeley: University of California Press, 1983.

Guilbert, Madeleine. *Les Fonctions des Femmes*. Paris: Mouton, 1966.

Guillebaud, C. W. *The Social Policy of Nazi Germany*. Cambridge: H. Fertig, 1971.

Hall, Radclyffe. *The Well of Loneliness*. New York: Blue Ribbon Books, 1937.

Halle, Fannina. *Women in Soviet Russia*. Trans. Margaret Green. New York: Viking Press, 1934.

———. *Women in the Soviet East*. Trans. Margaret Green. New York: Dutton, 1938.

Halsey, A. H. *Trends in British Society Since 1900*. London: St. Martin's Press, 1972.

Hamilton, Alice. "Below the Surface." *Survey Graphic* 22 (1933).

Hamilton, Cicely. *Modern France*. London: J. M. Dent & Sons, 1937.

Hamilton, Mary Agnes. *Margaret Bondfield*. London, 1924.

Hamm, M. F. *The City in Late Imperial Russia*. Bloomington: Indiana University Press, 1986.

Handcock, W. D., ed. *English Historical Documents, 1874-1914*. New York: Oxford University Press, 1977.

Hanna, Gertrude. "Women in the German Trade Union Movement." *Internatinal Labor Review* 8 (1923): 24–5.

Harrison, Brian. *Prudent Revolutionaries: Portraits of British Feminists between the Wars.* Oxford: Clarendon Press, 1987.

———. "Women in a Men's House, The Women M.P.s, 1919–1945." *Historical Journal* 29, no. 3 (1986).

Harrison, Mark. "Resource Allocation and Agrarian Class Formation, The Problem of Social Mobility Among Russian Peasant Households, 1880–1930." *Journal of Peasant Studies* 4, no. 1–2 (1976–1977).

Harshin, Jill. "Syphilis, Wives, and Physicians: Medical Ethics and the Family in Late 19th Century France." *French Historical Studies* 16 (Spring 1989).

Hartwig, Dr. R. von. "Das Frauenwahlrect in der Statistik." *Allgemeines Statistisches Archiv* 1 (1931).

Hause, Steven, and Anne Kenny. *Women's Suffrage and Social Politics in the French Third Republic.* Princeton: Princeton University Press, 1984.

Hausen, Karin. "Mother's Day in the Weimar Republic." In *When Biology Became Destiny*, ed. Renate Bridenthal. New York: Monthly Review Press, 1984.

Hawthorne, Melanie, and Richard J. Golsan, eds. *Gender and Fascism in Modern France.* Hanover, N.H.: University Press of New England, 1997.

Hayden, Carole Eubanks. "The Zhenotdel and the Bolshevik Party." *Russian History* 3, Part 2 (1976): 150–73.

Heitlinger, Alena. *Women and State Socialism.* London: Macmillan, 1979.

Heldt, Barbara. *Terrible Perfection: Women and Russian Literature.* Bloomington: Indiana University Press: Garland, 1987.

Helsinger, Elizabeth K., Robin L. Sheets, and William Veeder, *The Woman Question, Social Issues, 1837–1883*, Vol. 2: *Society and Literature in Britain and America.* New York: Garland, 1983.

Herzog, Jesus Silva. *Aspectos economicos de la Union sovietica.* (Mexico City, 1930). As quoted by William Richardson in "'To The World of the Future,' Mexican Visitors to the USSR, 1920–1940." *The Carl Beck Papers in Russian and East European Studies*, No. 1002.

Higginbotham, Ann R. "'Since of the Age:' Infanticide and Illegitimacy in Victorian London." *Victorian Studies*, Spring 1989.

Higonet, Anne. "Images—Appearances, Leisure, and Subsistence." In *A History of Women in the West IV. Emerging Feminism from Revolution to World War*, ed. Genevieve Fraisse and Michelle Perrot. Cambridge, Mass.: Cambridge University Press, 1993.

Higonnet, Margaret R. et al., eds. *Behind the Lines: Gender and the Two World Wars.* New Haven: Yale University Press, 1987.

Hindus, Maurice. *Humanity Uprooted.* New York: Blue Ribbon Books, 1934.

———. *Mother Russia.* Garden City, N.Y.: Doubleday, 1943.

Hollis, Patricia. *Ladies Elect, Women in English Local Government 1865–1914.* New York: Oxford University Press, 1987.

Holtby, Winifred. *Virginia Woolf.* Chicago, 1978.

———. "The Man Colleague." Reprinted in *Testament of a Generation*, ed. Paul Berry and Alan Bishop. London, 1985.

Honeycutt, Karen. "Clara Zetkin A Socialist Approach to the Problem of Women's Oppression." *F.S.* (1976): 131–44.

Horney, Karen. *The Adolescent Diaries of Karen Horney*. New York: Basic Books, 1980.

———. *Feminine Psychology*, ed. Harold Kelman. New York: Norton, 1973.

Horsbrugh-Porter, Anna, ed. *Memories of Revoluton: Russian Women Remember. Interviews by Frances Welch and Elena Snow*. London: Routledge, 1993.

Housden, Martyn. *Resistance & Conformity in the Third Reich*. New York: Routledge, 1997.

Hunt, Persis. "Revolutionary Syndicalism and Feminism among Teachers in France, 1900–1921." Ph.D. dissertation, Tufts University, 1975.

Hunter, Anne E., ed. *Genes and Gender VI. On Peace, War, and Gender*. New York: Feminist Press at the City University of New York, 1991.

Hutchins, B. L. "A Note on the Distribution of Women in Occupations." *Journal of the Royal Statistical Society,* September 1904.

Hutton, Marcelline. "Voices of Struggle: Soviet Women in the 1920s: A Study of Gender, Class, and Literature." *Feminist Issues*, Fall 1991.

———. "Women in Russian Society from the Tsars to Yeltsin." In *Russian Women in Politics and Society*, ed. Wilma Rule and Norma C. Noonan. Westport, Conn.: Greenwood Press, 1996.

Iakir, Peter. *A Childhood in Prison*, ed. Robert Conquest. New York: Coward, McCann & Geoghagen, 1973.

Il'in (Osorgin), Mikhail Andreevich. *My Sister's Story*. Trans. Nadia Helstein and Gwen Harris. London: L. Martin Secker, 1932.

"Increase in Woman Workers in Germany." *Monthly Labor Review*, April 1939.

"Industry Must Put Out More Articles for Children." *Moscow Daily News*, May–June 1936.

Ingemanson, Birgitta M. "Under Cover: The Paradox of Victorian Women's Travel Costume." In *Women and the Journey*, ed. Bonnie Frederick and Susan H. McLeod. Pullman: Washington State University Press, 1993.

Institut istorii partii pri TsKP Uzbekistana. *KP usbekistana i rabota sredi zhenshchin respubliki (1938–1958)*. Tashkent, Uzbekistan: Glavnoe arkhivnoe upravlenie, 1982.

International Dictionary of Women's Biography, ed. J. S. Uglow. New York: Continuum, 1989.

"International Women's Day Celebrations in USSR." *Moscow Daily News*, March 9, 1936, 2–3.

Ivanov, A. E. "Facty, sobytiia, liudi." *Voprosy Istorii* 1 (1973): 208–10.

Jephcott, J. *Girls Growing Up*. London: Farber & Farber, 1942.

Jewson, Dorothy. *Times* (London), 1 March 1924.

Joffe, Maria. *One Long Night: A Tale of Truth.*Trans. Vera Dixon. London: New Park Publications, 1978.

———. *Odna Noch': Povest' o pravde*. New York, 1978.

Joffe, Nadezhda. *Back in Time, My Life, My Fate, My Epoch, The Memoirs of Nadezhda A. Joffe*. Trans. Frederick S. Choate. Oak Park, Mich.: Labor Publications, 1995.

Johanson, Christine. "Autocratic Politics, Public Opinion, and Women's Medical Education During the Reign of Alexander II, 1855–1881." *Slavic Review* 38: 426–43.

———. *Women's Struggle for Higher Education in Russia, 1855–1900.* Montreal: McGill–Queen's University Press, 1987.

Johnson, Eric. "The Roots of Crime in Imperial Germany." *Central European History* 15 (4).

Johnson, Robert E. "Mothers and Daughters in Urban Russia: A Research Note." *Canadian Slavonic Papers*, September 1988, 374–77.

———. *Peasant and Proletarian: The Working Class of Moscow in the Late Nineteenth Century.* New Brunswick, N.J.: Rutgers University Press, 1979.

Jones, Pamela P. "Adult Education in Other Lands: Russia." *School and Society* 46.

Kadelka-Hanisch, Karin. "The Titled Businessman: Prussian Commercial Councillors in the Rhineland and Westphalia during the 19th Century." In *The German Bourgeoisie*, ed. Richard Evans. New York: Routledge, 1991.

Kaes, Anton, et al. *The Weimar Republic SourceBook.* Berkeley: University of California Press, 1994.

"Kaganovich Speaks at Moscow Kolkhoz Women's Conference." *Moscow Daily News*, 18 October 1933, 1.

Kanatchikova, B. "Nasha Robota." *Kommunistka* 10–11 (1921): 39–43.

Kaplan, Marian. "Jewish Women in Nazi Germany: Daily Life, Daily Struggles, 1933–1939." *Feminist Studies.* 16 (Fall 1990).

———. *The Making of the Jewish Middle Class: Women, Family, and Identity in Imperial Germany.* New York: Oxford University Press, 1991.

———. "Sisterhood under Siege: Feminism and Anti-Semitism in Germany, 1904–1938." In *When Biology Became Destiny*, ed. Renate Bridenthal et al. New York: Monthly Review Press, 1984.

Kataev, Valentin. "Squaring the Circle." Trans. Charles Malamuth. In *Six Soviet Plays*, ed. E. Lyons. New York: Houghton Mifflin, 1934.

———. *Time Forward!* Trans. Charles Malamuth. New York: Farrar & Rinehart, 1933.

———. *The Embezzlers.* New York, 1930.

Katasheva, L. *Natasha, A Bolshevik Woman Organizer.* New York: Workers' Library Publishers, 1934.

Katuntseva, N. M. *Rol' Rabochikh Fakul'tetov v Formirovanii Intelligentsii SSSR.* Moscow: Izd. Nauka, 1966.

Katz, Barbara G. "Purges and Production: Soviet Economic Growth, 1928–40." *Journal of Economic History* 35 (Summer 1975): 567–90.

Kean, Hilda. "Searching for the Past in Present Defeat: The Construction of Historical and Political Identity in British Feminism in the 1920s and 1930s." *Women's History Review* 3, no. 1 (1994).

Kearns, Martha. *Kathe Kollwitz: Woman and Artist.* Old Westbury, N.Y.: Feminist Press, 1976.

Kelly, Alfred, trans. and ed. *The German Worker: Working Class Autobiographies from the Age of Industrialization.* Berkeley: University of California Press, 1987.

Kelly, Mary. "Goddess Embroideries of Russia and the Ukraine." *Woman's Art Journal*, Fall/Winter 1983:10–13.

———. "Goddess Embroideries: Women's Heritage Rediscovered." *Bulletin of International Studies,* State University of New York at Albany, Fall 1983: 2–5.

Kennan, George F. "Some Thoughts on Stalin's Foreign Policy." *Slavic Review* 36 (Dec. 1977): 590–91.

Kent, Madeleine. *I Married A German.* New York: Harper & Brothers, 1939.

Khrushchev, Nikita. *Khrushchev Remembers*, ed. Edward Crankshaw. New York: Bantam , 1971.

Kingsbury, Susan, and Mildred Fairchild. *Employment and Unemployment in Prewar and Soviet Russia.* The Hague: International Industrial Relations Association, 1931.

———. *Factory, Family, and Woman in the Soviet Union.* New York: Putnam, 1935.

Kirkpatrick, Doris. *The Commonweal,* 8 December 1939.

Kirshon, Vladimir. "Bread." Trans. Sonia Volochova. In *Six Soviet Plays*, ed. E. Lyons. New York: Houghton Mifflin, 1934.

Knight, Amy. "The Fritschi: A Study of Russian Female Radicals in the Russian Populist Movement." *Canadian-American Slavic Studies* 9 (1975): 1–17.

———. "Female Terrorists in the Russian Social Revolutionary Party." *Russian Review* (1979): 146.

Knight, Patricia. "Women and Abortion in Victorian and Edwardian England." *History Workshop* no. 4 (Autumn 1977): 57–68.

Knodel, John, and Maynes, Mary Jo. "Urban and Rural Marriage Patterns in Imperial Germany." *Journal of the Family* 1 (Winter 1976): 129–68.

———. "Town and Country in 19th Century Germany: A Review of Urban–Rural Differentials in Ethnographic Behavior." *Social Science History* 1 (Spring 1977): 356–82.

Koblitz, Ann Hibner. *A Convergence of Lives, Sofia Kovalevskaia: Scientist, Writer, Revolutionary.* Boston: Birkhauser, 1983.

Kochina, Pelageya. *Love and Mathematics: Sofya Kovalevskaya*, ed. A. Yu. Ishlinsky and Z. K. Sokolovskaya. Trans. Michael Burov. Moscow: Mir Publishers, 1985.

Koenker, Diane. *Moscow Workers and the 1917 Revolution.* Princeton: Princeton University Press, 1981.

———. "The Evolution of Party Consciousness in 1917:·The Case of the Moscow Workers." *Soviet Studies* 30 (Jan. 1978): 38–62.

Koestler, Arthur. *The God That Failed.* New York: Harper, 1945.

Kogan, L. M. *Starye i novye kadry proletariata.* Moscow, 1934.

Kohler, Siegfried. *Die Russiche Industriearbeitershaft an 1905–1917.* Berlin: Teubner, 1921.

Kollman, Wolfgang. "The Process of Urbanization in Germany at the Height of the Industrialization Period." *Journal of Contemporary History* 4, no. 3 (1969).

Kollontai, Aleksandra. *Autobiographie Einer Sexuell Emanzipierten Kommunistin.* Muchen: Rogner u Bernard, 1970.

———. *The Autobiography of a Sexually Emancipated Communist Woman.* Trans.

Salvatore Attanasio, ed. Irving Fletcher. Forward by Germaine Greer. New York: Schocken, 1975.

————. *Izbrannye stati i rechi*. Moscow: Gos. izd., 1972.

————. *Iz moei zhiani i raboty gody i liudi*. Moscow, 1974.

————. "Liubov' Trekh Pokolenii," *Liubov' Pchel Trudovykh*. Moscow, 1927.

————. *Love of Worker Bees*.Trans. Cathy Porter. Chicago: Academy Press, 1978.

————. *Novaia Moral'*. Moscow, 1919.

————. *Selected Articles and Speeches*. Trans. Cynthia Carlile. New York: International Publishers, 1984

————. *Selected Writings*, ed. Alex Holt. Westport, Conn.: Greenwood Press, 1977.

Kolokol'nikov, V. T. "Marital and Family Relations among the Collective Farm Peasantry." *Soviet Sociology* 16 (1977–1978): 20–21

Koonz, Claudia. "Conflicting Allegiances: Political Ideology and Women Legislators in Weimar Germany." *Signs* 1 (Spring 1976).

————. "The Fascist Solution to the Woman Question in Italy and Germany." In *Becoming Visible*, ed. R. Bridenthal, C. Koonz, and S. Stuard. 2nd ed. Boston: Houghton Mifflin, 1987.

————."Nazi Women Before 1933: Rebels Against Emancipation." *Social Science Quarterly* 56 (March 1976).

Korber, Lili. *Life in a Soviet Factory*. Trans. Claud W. Sykes. London: John Lane, 1933.

Kossak, Sophia. *The Blaze, Reminiscences of Volhynia 1917–1919*. London, 1927.

Kosterina, Nina. *Diary of Nina Kosterina*. Trans. Mirra Ginsburg. New York: Crown Publishers, 1968.

————. "Dnevnik Niny Kosterinoi." *Novy Mir* 38, no. 12 (Dec. 1962).

Kovalevskaia, Sofia. *Recollections of Childhood*. New York: Century, 1895.

————. *Vospominaniia detstva*. Moscow: God. izd. khudozh. litry, 1960.

Kovalsky, N. A., and Y. P. Blinova, eds. *Women Today*. Moscow: Progress Publishers, 1975.

Kraval, A. *Zhenshchina v SSSR, Statisticheskii Sbornik*. Moscow: Pedaktsionno izd. uprav., 1937.

Kropotkin, Peter. *Memoirs of a Revolutionist*. New York: Houghton Mifflin, 1899.

Kurganov, Ivan A. *Zhenshchiny i Kommunizm*. New York, 1968.

Labour Policy in the USSR, 1917–1928. New York, 1956.

The Labour Who's Who 1924. London, 1924.

Lamberti, Marjorie. "State, Church, and the Politics of School Reform during the Kulturkampf." *Central European History* 19: 1.

————. "Elementary School Teachers and the Struggle against Social Democracy in Wilhelmine Germany." *History of Education Quarterly* 32 (Spring 1992).

Lane, David. "Ethnic and Class Stratification in Soviet Kazakhstan, 1917–1939." *Comparative Studies in Society and History* 17 (April 1975): 165–89.

————. *The Roots of Russian Communism*. Assen, The Netherlands: Van Gorcum, 1969.

Lang, Elsie M. *British Women in the Twentieth Century*. London: T. W. Laurie, 1929.

Lania, Leo. "A Pair of Street Scenes: A Moscow Tomboy." Trans. from *Das Tage Buch* in *The Living Age*, Dec. 1932.

Lapidus, Gail Warshofsky. *Women in Soviet Society: Equality, Development, and Social Change*. Berkeley: University California Press, 1979.

Larina, Anna. *This I Cannot Forget: The Memoirs of Nikolai Bukharin's Widow*. Trans. Gary Kern. New York: Norton, 1994.

Laska, Vera. *Women in the German Resistance and in the Holocaust: The Voices of Eyewitnesses*, ed. V. Laska. Westport, Conn.: Greenwood Press, 1983.

Lavin, Patrick. "Angliiskie zhenshchiny v professional'nykh organizatsiiakh." *Kommunistka* 1–2 (1923): 24–25.

Lawrence, Susan. "Votes for Women of 21." *Times* (London), 30 May 1924.

Layton, Mrs. "Memories of Seventy Years." In *Life as We Have Known It*, ed. Margaret L. Davies. London: Norton, 1975. Reprint of 1931 edition.

Layton, W. T. "Changes in Wages of Domestic Servants during Fifty Years." *Journal of the Royal Statistical Society*, Sept. 1908.

Leaming, Barbara. "Engineers of Human Souls—The Transition to Socialist Realism in the Soviet Cinema of the 1930s." Ph.D. dissertation, New York University, 1976.

Ledkovsky, Marina. "Avdotya Panaeva: Her Salon and Her Life." *Russian Literature Triquarterly* 9: 423–31.

Lee, J. J. "Aspects of Urbanization in Germany, 1815-1914." In *Towns and Societies*, ed. Philip Abrams and E. A. Wrigley. New York: Cambridge University Press, 1978.

Leffler, Anna Carlotta, Duchess of Cajanello. *Biography of Sofia Kovalevskaia*. Trans. A. M. Clive Bayley. New York: Century, 1895.

Lenin, V. I. *The Development of Capitalism in Russia*. Moscow, 1974.

——. *Razvitie Kapitalisma v Rossii*. Moscow, 1936.

——. *The Emancipation of Women*. New York: International Publishers, 1972. Reprint of 1934 ed.

Leonard, Jacques. *La France Medicale: Médécins et malades au XIXe Siècle*. Paris: Gallimard, Julliard, 1978.

Leonov, Leonid. *Sot*, trans. Ivor Montagu and Sergei Nolbandov. New York: Putnam, 1931.

Leonova, Olga. "The Position of Women." In *The Soviet Comes of Age by 28 of the Foremost Citizens of the USSR*. Forward by Sidney and Beatrice Webb. New York, 1938.

Lepedeva, Vera. "Nashi dostizheniia." *Kommunistka* 12–13 (Nov. 1926).

Levin, Alfred. *The Second Duma*. Appendix D "Strikes." New Haven: Yale University Press, 1940.

Lewin, Moshe. *Lenin's Last Struggle*. Trans. N. Sheridan Smith. New York: Pantheon, 1968.

——. "Rural Society in 20th Century Russia: An Introduction." *Social History* 9 (May 1984): 171–80.

——. "Society and the Stalinist State in the Period of the Five Year Plans." *Social History* 2 (May 1976): 139–75.

——. "Stalinism Appraised and Reappraised." *History* 60 (February 1975): 71–76.

Lewis, Robert, and Richard H. Rowland. "Urbanization in Russia and the USSR, 1897–1966." *Annals of the Association of American Geographers* 59 (December 1969).

Lewis, Robert A., Richard H. Rowland, and Ralph S. Clem. *Nationality and Population Change in Russia and the USSR: An Evaluation of Census Data, 1897–1970.* New York: Praeger, 1976.

Lewytzkyj, Borys. *Stalinist Terror in the 1930s.* Stanford: Stanford University Press, 1974.

Lincoln, W. Bruce. *In War's Dark Shadows.* New York: Dial, 1983.

Linke, Lilo. *Restless Days. A German Girl's Autobiography.* New York: Knopf, 1935.

Lipinska, Melina. *Les Femmes et le Progrès des Sciences Médicales.* Paris: Masson, 1930.

Littlepage, John. "In Search of Soviet Gold." In Riha, *Readings in Russian Civilization,* vol. 3.

Litvinov, Maksim. *Notes for a Journal.* London: A. Deutsch, 1955.

Litvinova, G. I., and N. V. Popova. "Istoricheskii opyt resheniia zhenskogo voprosa v SSSR." *Voprosy Istorii.* 11 (1975): 7–17.

Lorimer, Frank. *The Population of the Soviet Union: History and Prospects.* Geneva: League of Nations, 1946.

Luders, Elsie. "The Effects of German Labour Legislation on Employment Possibilities for Women." *International Labour Review* 20 (Sept. 1929).

Luke, Louise. "Marxian Woman, Soviet Variants." In *Through the Glass of Soviet Literature,* ed. E. J. Simmons. New York: Columbia University Press, 1953.

Lunacharsky, A. V. *Revolutionary Silhouettes.* Trans. Michael Glenny. New York: Hill & Wang, 1967.

Luxemburg, Rosa. *The Russian Revolution.* Ed. Betram Wolfe. Ann Arbor: University of Michigan Press, 1961.

Lyons, Eugene, ed. *Six Soviet Plays.* Trans. Elmer Rice. Boston: Houghton Mifflin, 1934.

Maegd-Soep, Carolina de. *The Emancipation of Women in Russian Literature and Society.* Ghent: Ghent State University, 1968.

Magamayeva, Rose. "A Woman Commissar Tells Life Story." *Moscow Daily News,* 1935.

Malia, Martin. *Alexander Hertsen and the Birth of Russian Socialism.* Cambridge, Mass.: Harvard University Press, 1961.

Mal'nechanskii, G. "Profsoiuzy i 8 marta." *Kommunistka,* February 1925: 14–15.

Malony, Philip. "Anarchism and Bolshevism in the Works of Boris Pilniak." *Russian Review* 32 (Jan. 1973): 43–53.

Mandel, Ernest. "The Nature of the Soviet State." *New Left Review* 108 (Mar.–April 1978): 23–46.

Mandel, William M. *Soviet Women.* Garden City, N. Y.: Anchor Books, 1975.

Mandelstam, Nadezhda. *Hope Abandoned.* Trans. Max Hayward. New York: Atheneum, 1970.

————. *Hope Against Hope, A Memoir.* Trans. Max Hayward. New York: Atheneum, 1970.

————. *Mozart and Salieri.* Trans. Robert A. McLean. Ann Arbor: University of Michigan Press, 1973.

Margadant, Jo Burr. *Madame le Professeur.* Princeton: Princeton University Press, 1990.

Margueritte, Victor. *The Bachelor Girl.* Trans. Hugh Burnaby. New York: Macaulay, 1923.

"Marriage Makes No Careers in USSR." *Literary Digest,* 30 April 1932: 36–37.

Marsh, Rosalind, ed. *Women in Russia and Ukraine.* New York: Cambridge University Press, 1996.

Marshall, J. D., ed. *The History of Lancashire County Council, 1889–1974.* London: Martin Robinson, 1977.

Marx, Eleanor, and Edward Aveling. "The Woman Question." *Westminster Review* 125 (Jan. 1886): 211.

Marx, Madeleine. "New Russian Women." *The Nation* 117 (7 Nov. 1923): 508–10; (21 Nov. 1923): 549–51.

Mason, Tim. "Women in Nazi Germany." *History Workshop* 1 (Spring 1976): 74–113; (Autumn 1976): 5–32.

Massell, Gregory. *The Surrogate Proletariat.* Princeton: Princeton University Press, 1974.

Matossian, Mary. "The Peasant Way of Life." In *Russian Peasant Women,* ed. Beatrice Farnsworth and Lynne Viola. New York: Oxford University Press, 1992.

Mauer, Louise. *Women in the German Resistance,* ed. Vera Laska. Westport, Conn.: Greenwood Press, 1983.

Maynes, Mary Jo. *Schooling in Western Europe, A Social History.* Albany: State University of New York Press, 1985.

McAuley, Alastair. *Women's Work and Wages in the Soviet Union.* London: Allen & Unwin, 1981.

McBride, Theresa. "A Woman's World: Department Stores and the Evolution of Women's Employment, 1870–1920." *French Historical Studies* 10 (Fall 1978): 664–83.

———. "Social Mobility for the Lower Class: Domestic Servants in France." *Journal of Social History,* 8 (Fall 1974): 63–78.

McDougall, Mary Lynn. "Protecting Infants: The French Campaign for Maternity Leaves, 1890s–1913." *French Historical Studies* 13 (Spring 1983).

McGregor, O. R. *Divorce in England.* Melbourne: Heinemann, 1957.

McIntyre, Jill. "Women and the Professions in Germany 1930–1940." In *German Democracy and the Triumph of Hitler,* ed. A. J. Nichols and E. Mathias. New York: St. Martin's Press, 1972.

McKibbin, Ross. *The Evolution of the Labour Party, 1910–1924.* Oxford: Clarendon Press, 1974.

McKinsey, P. S. "An Uneasy Friendship: Conflicts Between Radicals and Workers." Paper given at the American Historical Association, December 1985.

McLaren, Angus. "Abortion in France: Women and the Regulation of Family Size." *French Historical Studies* 10 (Spring 1978): 461–85.

———. "Abortion in England, 1890–1914." *Victorian Studies* 20 (Summer 1977).

———. Women's Work and Regulation of Family Size." *History Workshop* 4 (Autumn 1977): 70–81.

McNeal, Robert. *Bride of the Revolution*. Ann Arbor: University of Michigan Press, 1972.

————. "Women in the Russian Radical Movement." *Journal of Social History* 5 (1971/72): 143–63.

Medvedev, Roy. "Bukharin's Last Years." *New Left Review* 109 (May–June 1978): 49–74.

————. "New Pages from the Political Biography of Stalin." In *Stalinism: Essays in Historical Interpretation*, ed. Robert Tucker. New York: Norton, 1977.

————. *On Stalin and Stalinism*. Trans. Ellen de Kadt. Oxford: Oxford University Press, 1979.

Medynskii, E. "Zhenskoe obrazovanie." *Bol'shaia Sovetskaia Entsiklopediia* 25: 258–66.

Mehnert, Klaus. *Youth in Soviet Russia*. Trans. Michael Davidson. London: Allen & Unwin, 1933.

Meisal, James, and E. S. Kozera. *Materials for the Study of the Soviet System*. 2nd ed. Ann Arbor: University of Michigan Press, 1953.

Meissner, Boris. ed. *Social Change in the Soviet Union: Russia's Path Toward an Industrial Society*. Trans. Donald P. Kommers. South Bend: University of Notre Dame Press, 1972.

Melching, Wilhelm. "'A New Morality': Left-Wing Intellectuals on Sexuality in Weimar Germany." *Journal of Contemporary History* 25 (1990).

Mellown, Muriel. "Lady Rhondda and the Changing Faces of British Feminism." *Frontiers* 9 (2): 1987.

Meyendorff, Baron Alexander. *The Cost of the War to Russia*. New Haven: Yale University Press, 1932.

Meyer, Alfred G. *The Feminism and Socialism of Lily Braun*. Bloomington: Indiana University Press, 1985.

Meyer, William T. "Reorganization of Secondary Schools of Germany." *School Review* 47 (Jan. 1939).

Meyers, Peter V. "Professionalization and Societal Change: Rural Teachers in Nineteenth Century France." *Journal of Social History* 9 (Summer): 542–58.

Mickiewicz, Ellen. *Handbook of Soviet Social Science Data*. New York: Free Press, 1973.

"Middle Volga Kolkhoz Farmers tell Stalin Troubles, Triumphs." *Moscow Daily News*, 30 January 1933, 1.

Middleton, Lucy. *Women in the Labour Movement*. London: Croom Helm, 1977.

Mill, John Stuart. "The Enfranchisement of Women." *Westminster and Foreign Quarterly Review* 55 (1851): 299–311.

————. *The Subjection of Women*. Introduction by Wendell R. Carr. London, 1984.

Millar, James R. "Mass Collectivization and the Contribution of Soviet Agriculture to the First F.Y. P." *Slavic Review* 33: 750–66.

Miller, Alice. *For Your Own Good, Hidden Cruelty in Child Rearing and the Roots of Violence*. Trans. H. and H. Hannum. New York: Farrar, Straus & Giroux, 1983.

Miller, F. "A. Y. Panaeva." in *Encyclopedia of Modern Russian and Soviet History* 26: 207–10.

Milligan, Sandra. "The Petrograd Bolsheviks and Social Insurance, 1914–1917." *Soviet Studies* 20: 373.

Milovidova, E. *Zhenskii vopros i zhenskoe dvizhenie*, ed. Clara Zetkin. Moscow, 1929.

Milton, Sybil. "Women and the Holocaust: The Case of German and German-Jewish Women." In *Different Voices, Women and the Holocaust*, ed. Carol Ritter and John Roth. New York: Paragon, 1993.

Mitchell, Brian R. *Abstract of British Historical Statistics*. Cambridge: Cambridge University Press, 1962.

———. *European Historical Statistics 1750–1970*. New York: Columbia University Press, 1975.

Moch, Leslie Page. "Government Policy and Women's Experience: The Case of Teachers in France." *Feminist Studies* 14 (Summer 1988).

Mommsen, W. J., ed. *The Emergence of the Welfare State in Britain and Germany 1850–1950*. London: Croom Helm, 1981.

Monter, Barbara. "Karolina Palova's A Double Life." *Russian Literature Triquarterly* 9: 343.

Moore, Barrington. *Social Origins of Dictatorship and Democracy: Land and Peasant in the Making of the Modern World*. Boston: Beacon Press, 1966.

Morozova, Vera. *Red Carnation*. Moscow, n.d.

"Moscow Enhances Position of Women." *New York Times,* 16 October 1927, Sec. 8, p. 3.

Moses, Claire. *French Feminism in the Nineteenth Century*. Albany: State University of New York Press, 1984.

Mossman, Elliott, ed. *The Correspondence of Olga Freidenberg and Boris Pasternak, 1910–1954*. New York: Harcourt Brace Jovanovich, 1982.

"Mother Sees Ban on Abortions as Backward." *Moscow Daily News*, May–June 1936.

Mowat, C. L. *Britain Between the Wars, 1918–1940*. Chicago: University of Chicago Press, 1958.

Mrs. Beeton's Cookery and Household Management. London: Wordlock, 1961.

Mulhall, Michael. *The Dictionary of Statistics*. London: Routledge & Paul, 1899.

Mullaney, Marie Marmo. "Gender and the Socialist Revolutionary Rose, 1871–1921: A General Theory of the Female Revolutionary Personality." *Historical Reflections* 11 (2): 1984.

Nabholz, Hans. "Elimination of Private Preparatory Schools in Germany." *School and Society* 44 (12 September 1936).

Naimark, Norman M. *The History of the "Proletariat": The Emergence of Marxism in the Kingdom of Poland, 1870–1887*. Boulder: East European Quarterly, 1979.

Nasonkina, L. L., and L. V. Filimonova. "Women's Education in Prerevolutionary Russia." In *Modern Encyclopedia of Russian and Soviet History*, ed. J. L. Wieczynski. vol. 44. Gulf Breeze, Fla.: Academic International Press, 1979.

"Nazi Treatment of Women," *Times* (London), 2 June 1933.

Neale, R. S. *Class and Ideology in the Nineteenth Century*. London: Routledge & Paul, 1972.

Neff, Wanda. *Victorian Working Women.* New York: Columbia University Press, 1919.

Negretov, P. I. "How Vorkuta Began." *Soviet Studies* 29 (October 1977): 565–75.

Neuman, Robert P. "The Sexual Question and Social Democracy in Imperial Germany." *Journal of Social History* 7 (3): 271–86.

Nicholson, Nigel. *Portrait of a Marriage.* New York: Atheneum, 1973.

Nightingale, Florence. "Cassandra." In Ray Strachey. *The Cause, A Short History of the Women's Movement in Great Britain.* Port Washington, N.Y.: Kennikat Press, 1928.

"Now I Have a Cupboard Full of Books." *Moscow Daily News,* 3 March 1933, 3.

Nukhrat, A. "Osnovnye voprosy soveshchaniia." *Kommunistka,* June 1928.

Nurbekova, G. *Zhenshchiny Kazakhstana Frontu.* Alma-Ata. 1968.

Nurina, F. 'Delegatki." In *Bol'shaia Sovetskaia Entsiklopediia* 33: 142.

———. *Women in the Soviet Union, The Role of Women in Socialist Construction.* New York: International Publishers, 1934.

"Ob itogakh Vsesoiuznoi perepisi naseleniia SSSR 1939 g." *Planovoe Khoziaistvo* 6 (1939): 12.

"Obligatory Domestic Service for Single Women in Germany." *Monthly Labor Review,* May 1939.

Odinetz, Dmitry M. *Russian Schools and Universities in the World War.* New Haven: Yale University Press, 1929.

Offen, Karen. "On the French Origin of the Words Feminism and Feminist." *Feminist Issues,* Fall 1988, 45–51.

———. "The Second Sex and the Baccalaureat in Republican France, 1880–1924." *French Historical Studies* 13 (Fall 1983): 252–86.

Olcott, Martha Brill. "The Collectivization Drive in Kazakhstan." *Russian Review* 40 (1981): 122–42.

"The Old Women Speak. . . ." *Moscow Daily News,* 12 May 1933, 1.

Olesha, Iurii. "Speech to the First Congress of Soviet Writers." In *Envy and Other Works,* trans. Andrew R. MacAndrew. New York: Anchor Books, 1967.

"On the Siberian Industrial Front: Youth on One of the World's Biggest Jobs, Five Year Plan at Kuznetsk." *Moscow Daily News,* 4 June 1932, 2.

"Once Illiterate Charwoman Now Heads School." *Moscow Daily News,* 3 June 1933, 4.

"125,000 Party Members From Moscow Province Are Cleaned." *Moscow Daily News,* 24 September 1933 1.

"Opinions for Modifying Draft." *Moscow Daily News,* 3 June 1936, 2.

Orendi-Hinze, Diana. *Rahel Sanzara Eine Biographie.* Berlin: Fischer & Taschenbuch, 1981.

Orlikova, E. "Sovetskaia zhenshchina v obshchestvennom proizvodstve." *Problemy Ekonomiky* 12 (1940): 106–22.

———. "Zhenskii trud v SSSR." *Planovoe Khoziaistvo* 16 (1939): 107–20.

Orlow, Damon. *Red Wedding.* Chicago: H. Regnery Co.., 1952.

"Osnovnye pokazateli itogov vtoroi piatiletki." *Planovoe Khoziaistvo* 5 (1939): 170.

Ostroumova-Levedeva, Anna P. *Avtobiograficheskie zapiski,* t. 1–2. Moscow: Izdatel'stvo Vizvrazitel'noe Iskusstvo, 1974.

Ostrovsky, Alexander. "The Storm" and "Poor Bride." In *Five Plays of Alexander Ostrovsky*, ed. and trans. Eugene K. Bristow. New York: Pegasus, 1969.

"Oxford University Discusses Communism—Theoretically." *Moscow Daily News*, 8 August 1932.

Pachmuss, Temira, ed. and trans. *Between Paris and St. Petersburg: Selected Diaries of Zinaida Hippius*. Urbana: University of Illinois Press, 1975.

———. *Women Writers in Russian Modernism: An Anthology*. Urbana: University of Illinois Press, 1978.

Pak, B. I. "Savva Timofeevich Morozov." *Soviet Studies in History* 20: 74–95.

Pankhurst, Sylvia. *The Life of Emmeline Pankhurst*. Boston: T. Werner Laurie, 1936.

Pares, Bernard. *Moscow Admits a Critic*. London: T. Nelson & Sons, 1936.

"Party Cleansing Reveals Rotten Elements." *Moscow Daily News*, 22 December 1932, 3.

"Party Cleansing Now Under Way in No. Caucasus." *Moscow Daily News*, 11 January 1933, 3.

Pauwels, Jacques R. *Women, Nazis, and Universities: Female University Students in the Third Reich, 1933–1945*. Westport, Conn.: Greenwood Press, 1984.

Pavlova, Karolina. "Dvoinaia Zhizn." In *Polnoe Sobranie Stikhotvorenii*. Moscow: Sovetskii pisatel', 1964.

———. *A Double Life*. Trans. B. H. Monter. Ann Arbor: University of Michigan Press, 1978.

Peacock, N., ed. *The Russian Almanac*. London: Eyre and Spottiswoode, 1919.

"A Peasant Girl's Chance to Become an Engineer." *Moscow Daily News*, 1 May 1934, 3.

Pedersen, Joyce Sanders. "The Reform of Women's Secondary and Higher Education." *History of Education Quarterly*, Spring 1979.

Pedersen, Susan. *Family Dependence and the Origins of the Welfare State, Britain and France, 1914–1945*. Cambridge: Cambridge University Press, 1995.

———. "National Bodies, Unspeakable Acts: The Sexual Politics of Colonial Policy-Making." *Journal of Modern History* 63 (4), December 1991.

Pelletier, Madeleine. *L'education feministe des filles*. Paris, 1914. Reprinted by Syros: Claude Maignien, 1978.

Perkin, H. J. "Condescension of Posterity." *Social Science History* 3 (1): 100

———. "Social Causes of the British Industrial Revolution." *Transactions of the Royal Historical Society* 5th Series, London, 1968: 123–44.

Perrie, Maureen. "The Russian Peasant Movement of 1905–1907: Its Social Composition and Revolutionary Significance." *Past and Present*, No. 57: 123–55.

———. "The Russian Peasantry in 1907–1908: A Survey by the SR Party." *History Workshop* 3–4 (Autumn 1977): 171–91.

———. "The Social Composition and Structure of the Social Revolutionary Party Before 1917." *Soviet Studies* 24 (2): 223–40.

Peterson, Brian. "The Politics of Working-Class Women in the Weimar Republic." *Central European History* 10 (1977): 87–111.

Pethick Lawrence, Emmeline. *My Part in a Changing World*. London: Victor Gollanz, 1938.

Phayer, Michael. *Protestant and Catholic Women in Nazi Germany*. Detroit: Wayne State University Press, 1990.

Phelps, Robert. *Colette: Earthly Paradise, An Autobiography Drawn from Her Lifetime Writings*. Trans. Herma Briffault, Derek Coltman, et al. New York: Farrar, Straus, and Giroux, 1996.

Pichugina, Praskovia. *Women in the USSR*.Moscow: Foreign Languages Publishing House, 1939.

Pilniak, Boris. *The Volga Falls to the Caspian Sea*. Trans. Charles Malamuth. New York: Cosmopolitan Book Corp., 1931.

Pinchbeck, Ivy. *Women Workers and the Industrial Revolution, 1750–1850*. London: Routledge, 1930.

Pisarev, D.I. *Selected Philosophical, Social, and Political Essays*. Moscow: Foreign Language Publishing House, 1958.

Pisarev, Dmitry. *Sochineniia D. I. Pisareva Polnoe Sobranie v shesti tomakh*. Tom pervyi. St. Petersburg: F. Pavlenkov, 1894.

———. *Sochineniia v chetyrekh tomakh*. Moscow: Foreign Language Publishing House, 1955.

Pisarev, I. "K itogam perepisi naseleniia SSSR 1939 g." *Problemy Ekonomiky* 7 (1940): 120.

Plekhanov, G. *Selected Philosophical Works*, vol. 1. Moscow: Foreign Language Publishing House, 1960.

Pogodin, Nikolai. "Tempo." Trans. Irving Talmadg. In *Six Soviet Plays*, ed. E. Lyons. New York: Houghton Mifflin, 1934.

———. "The Aristocrats." Trans. Anthony Wixley and Robert Carr. In *Four Soviet Plays*. New York: International Publishers, 1937.

Pokzovskaia, M. I. "A Woman Doctor's Report on Working Conditions for Women in Russian Factories." In *European Women: A Documentary History*, ed. John Fout and Eleanor Riemer. New York: Schocken, 1980.

Pope, Barbara Corrado. "Maternal Education in France, 1815–1848." *Proceedings of the Third Annual Meeting of the Western Society for French History*, 4–6 December 1975, 358–89.

Popp, Adelheid. *The Autobiography of a Working Woman*. London: Unwin, 1912.

Pore, Renate. *A Conflict of Interest: Women in German Social Democracy 1919–1933*. Westport, Conn.: Greenwood, 1981.

Power, Eileen. *Medieval Women*. New York: Cambridge University Press, 1975.

Priestley, Philip. *Victorian Prison Lives, English Prison Biography, 1830–1914*. New York: Methuen, 1985.

Quataert, Jean H. *Reluctant Feminists in German Social Democracy, 1885–1917*. Princeton: Princeton University Press, 1979.

Quinn, Susan. *A Mind of Her Own, The Life of Karen Horney*. Reading, Mass.: Addison-Wesley, 1988.

Rabinbach, A. G. "Toward a Marxist Theory of Fascism and National Socialism." *New German Critique* 3 (1974): 127–53.

Radziejowski, Janusz. "Collectivization in Ukraine in Light of Soviet Historiography." *Journal of Ukrainian Studies* 9 (Fall 1980): 3–17.

Rakovsky, Alexandra. "Modern Woman in Soviet Russia." *The Nation* 125 (9 November 1927): 509–10.

Ramer, Samuel. "Childbirth and Culture: Midwifery in the Nineteenth Century Russian Countryside." In *The Family in Imperial Russia*, ed. David Ransel. Urbana: University of Illinois Press, 1978.

———. The Transformation of the Russian Feldsher, 1864–1914." In *Imperial Russia 1700–1917 Essays in Honor of Marc Raeff*, ed. E. Mendelsohn and M. S. Shatz. DeKalb: Northern Illinois University Press, 1988.

Ransel, David, ed. *The Family in Imperial Russia*. Urbana: University of Illinois Press, 1978.

———. *Mothers of Misery*. Princeton: Princeton University Press, 1988.

Rappoport, A. S. *Home Life in Russia*. New York: Macmillan, 1913.

Rashin, A. G. *Formirovanie rabochego klassa rossi*. Moscow: Izd. sotsialno-ekon. litt-ry, 1958.

———. *Sostav fabrichno-zavodskogo proletariata*. Moscow, 1930.

Rassweiler, Anne D. "Soviet Labor Policy in the First Five-Year Plan: The Dneprostroi Experience." *Slavic Review* 42 (Summer 1983): 230–46.

Ratchliffe, S. K. "The Two Englands." *Survey Graphic* May 1937.

Ravich, S. "Borba c prostitutsiei v Petrograde." *Kommunistka*, June 1920, 21–22.

Reagin, Nancy. *A German Women's Movement*. Chapel Hill: University of North Carolina Press, 1995.

Red Goals, A Woman's Experiences in Russian Prisons. Trans. O. B. London. 1932/5?.

"Red Servant Problem," from *Novoye Russkoye Slovo*, New York. In *Literary Digest*, 1 January 1938.

Reeder, Roberta. *Anna Akhmatova: Poet and Prophet*. New York: St. Martin's Press, 1994.

Reich, Wilhelm. "The Sexual Misery of the Working Masses and the Difficulties of Sexual Reform." Trans. Kay Goodman. *The New German Critique* 1 (1974): 98–100.

"Results of the Election." *Times* (London), 3 October 1924; 20 October 1924.

Reynolds, Sian. *France Between the Wars, Gender and Politics*. New York: Routledge, 1996.

Riazanova, A. "Professional'noe dvizhenie, zarabotnaia plata promyshlennykh rabotnits." *Kommunistka* 4 (1924): 19–23.

———. Professional'noe dvishenie i rabotnitsa." *Kommunistka* 8–9 (April 1921): 18–21.

Rice, Margery Spring. *Working Class Wives*, 2nd ed. London: Virago, 1981. First pub. 1939.

Richards, Eric. "Women in the British Economy Since About 1700: An Interpretation." *History* 59 (October 1974): 343.

Rigby, Thomas H. *Communist Party Membership in the USSR, 1917–1967*. Princeton: Princeton University Press, 1968.

Riha, Thomas, ed. *Readings in Russian Civilization*, vols. 2 and 3. Chicago: University of Chicago Press, 1969.

Rimlinger, Gaston. "The Management of Labor Protest in Tsarist Russia." *International Review of Social History* 5 (Part 2): 226–48.

Rittner, Carol, and John K. Roth, eds. *Women and the Holocaust: Different Voices*. New York: Paragon House, 1993.

Rizel', F. "Delegatkskie sobranie 1925-26 g. v tsifrakh." *Kommunistka* 7 (July 1926): 32–47.

Roberts, Mary Louise. "'This Civilization No Longer Has Sexes': La Garçonne and Cultural Crisis in France After World War I." *Gender and History* 4, Spring 1992.

Roberts, Robert. *The Classic Slum*. New York: Penguin Books, 1983.

Robinson, Geroid T. *Rural Russia under the Old Regime*. Berkeley: University of California Press, 1972.

Rodaway, Angela. *A London Childhood*. London: Batsford, 1960.

Roitov, F. "Zhenskie Dvizhenie." *Bol'shaia Sovetskaia Entskilopediia* (Moscow, 1932) 25: 179–258.

Rorlich, Azade-Ayse. "The 'Ali Bayramov' Club, The Journal *Sharg Gadini* and the Socialization of Azeri women, 1920–1930." *Central Asian Survey* 5 (3/4).

Rosen, Andrew. *Rise Up, Women! The Militant Campaign of the Women's Social and Political Union*. London: Routledge & Kegan Paul, 1974.

Rosenberg, Suzanne. *A Soviet Odyssey*. Toronto: Penguin Press, 1991.

Rosenthal, Charlotte. "Zinaida Vengerova: Modernism and Women's Liberation." *Irish Slavonic Studies*, No. 8, 1987.

Ross, E. A. "Russian Women and Their Outlook." *Century* 96 (June 1918): 249–57.

Rostopchina, Evdokiia. "Pesnia Vozvrata." In *Stati o russkoi poezii*, ed. V. F. Khodasevich. Petrograd: Epokha, 1922.

Ruane, Christine. "The Vestal Virgins of St. Petersburg: Schoolteachers and the 1897 Marriage Bann." *Russian Review* 50, April 1991.

Ruckman, Jo Ann. *The Moscow Business Elite: A Social and Cultural Portrait of Two Generations, 1840–1905*. DeKalb: Northern Illinois University Press, 1984.

Ruediger, W. C. "English Secondary Education." *School Review*, June 1933.

Rueschemeyer, Marilyn. *Professional Work and Marriage, An East-West Comparison*. New York: St. Martin's Press, 1981.

Ruthchild, Rochelle G. "The Changing Nature of Women's Public Activity: The Russian Women's Mutual Philanthropic Society, 1895–1917." Paper presented at the 25th National Convention of the AAASS, Honolulu, Hawaii, Nov. 20, 1993.

Rynin, Seema. "A Farm Woman Speaks." *Moscow Daily News,* 18 February 1934, 2.

Sacks, Michael Paul. *Women's Work in Soviet Russia*. New York: Praeger, 1976.

———. *Work and Equality in Soviet Society: The Division of Labor by Age, Gender, and Nationality*. New York: Praeger, 1982.

Sackville-West, Vita. *The Edwardians*. London: Literary Guild of America, 1930.

Sagara, Eda. *A Social History of Germany 1648–1914*. New York: Holmes & Meier, 1977.

"Salary Differentials of Women in British Civil Service." *Monthly Labor Review* 45, September 1937.

Samokhvalova, G. "Sostav Kommunistok." *Kommunistka*, September 1926, 20–28.

Sand, Georges. "Letter to Hippolyte Chatiron, Feb. 1843" and "Letter to Abbe Lamennais, Feb. 28, 1837." Quoted and trans. Joseph Barry in *George Sand In Her Own Words*. New York: Quartet Books, 1979.

Santerre. *Meme Santerre, A French Woman of the People*. Compiled by Serge Grafteaux. Trans. and ed. Louise A. Tilly and Kathryn L. Tilly. New York: Schocken Books, 1985.

Sarabianov, D. V., and N. L. Adashina. *Popova*. New York: Harry N. Abrams, 1989.

Satina, Sophie. *Education of Women in Pre-Revolutionary Russia*. New York: n. publ., 1966.

Sats, Natalia. *Sketches from My Life*. Moscow: Raduga, 1985.

———. *Zhizn'-Iavlenie polosatoe*. Moscow: Novosti, 1991.

Scannell, Dorothy. *Mother Knew Best*. Bath: Chivers Press, 1981.

Schapiro, Leonard. *The Communist Party of the Soviet Union*. New York: Random House, 1960.

Schirmacher, Kaethe. *The Modern Woman's Right Movement, A Historical Survey*. New York: MacMillan, 1912.

Schlesinger, Rudolf. *The Family in the USSR*. London: Routledge, 1949.

Schneider, Joanne, "Volksschullehererinnen: Bavarian Women Defining themselves Through Their Profession." In *The German Family*, ed. R. J. Evans and W. R. Lee. Totowa, N.J.: Barnes & Noble, 1981.

Schomerus, Heilwig. "The Family Life-Cycle A Study of Factory Workers in Nineteenth Century Wurttemberg." In *The German Family*, ed. R. J. Evans and W. R. Lee. Totowa, N.J.: Barnes & Noble, 1981.

Schreiner, Olive. *Woman and Labour*. London: Virago, 1978. First pub. 1911.

Scott, Joan. "Gender: A Useful Category of Historical Analysis." *American Historical Review* 91 (Dec. 1986): 1053–75.

Scott, Joan, and Louise Tilly. *Women, Work, and Family*. New York: Holt, Rinehart & Winston, 1978.

Scott, John. *Behind the Urals*. Bloomington: Indiana University Press, 1962.

Sender, Toni. *The Autobiography of a German Rebel*. New York: Vanguard Press, 1939.

Sendich, Munir. "Karolina Pavlova: A Survey of Her Poetry." *Russian Literature Triquarterly* 3 (1972): 229–47.

Serebrennikov, G. I. *Position of Women in the USSR*. London: Victor Gollancz, 1937.

———. *Zhenskii trud SSSR*. Moscow: Sotsekgiz., 1934.

Serge, Victor. *From Lenin to Stalin*. Trans. Ralph Manheim. New York: Monad Press, 1973.

Shaffer, John. "Occupational Expectations of Young Women in 19th Century Paris." *Journal of Family History* 3 (1): 62–77.

Shapiro, Ann-Louise. "Housing Reform in Paris: Social Space and Social Control." *French Historical Studies* 12 (4), Fall 1982.

Shapovalov, Veronica, ed. *Remembering the Darkness: Women in Soviet Prisons*. Boulder: Rowman & Littlefield, forthcoming.

Shinn, William T. Jr. "The Law of the Russian Peasant Household." *Slavic Review* 20 (1961): 605–30.

Shkandrij, Myroslav. "Fiction by Formula: The Worker in Early Soviet Ukrainian Prose." *Journal of Ukrainian Studies* 7 (Fall 1982): 47–60.

Shtepa, K. F. "In Stalin's Prisons, Reminiscences, II." *Russian Review* 2 (April 1962):165–83.

Shturm, G. "Mezhdunarodnoe dvishenie Rabotnits, God mezhdunarodnoi Kommunisticheskoi raboty sredi zhenshchin." *Kommunistka*, February 1926.

Silver, Catherine. "Salon, Foyer, Bureau: Women and the Professions in France." *Journal of Sociology* 78 (January 1973): 838

Skrjabina, Elena. *Coming of Age in the Russian Revolution.* Trans. and ed. Norman Luxemburg. New Brunswick, N.J.: Transaction Books, 1988.

"Slav Women Clamor for Public Life." *New York Times* 15 August 1926, Sec. 8, 17.

Slavnye Bolshevichki, ed. V. Ignateva. Moscow: Gos. izdat. polit litry, 1957–1958.

Slonim, Marc. *Soviet Russian Literature.* New York: Oxford University Press, 1977.

Smith, Bonnie G. *Changing Lives, Women in European History Since 1700.* Lexington, Mass.: D.C. Heath, 1989.

Smith, Harold. *British Feminism in the Twentieth Century.* Amherst: University of Massachusetts Press, 1990.

Smith, Jessica. *Woman in Soviet Russia.* New York: Vanguard, 1928.

Smitten, E. "K voprosu o regulirovanii rosta zhenshchin v partii." *Kommunistka*, November 1923, 24–30.

———."Zhenshchina v partii." *Kommunistka*, November 1927, 26–27.

———. "Zhenshchina v R.K.P." *Kommunistka* 1–2 (January 1923): 30–32.

Snitow, Ann, Christine Stansell, and Sharon Thompson, eds. *Power of Desire: The Politics of Sexuality.* New York: Monthly Review Press, 1983.

Socialist Construction in the USSR. Moscow, 1936.

Sohn, Anne-Marie. "Between the Wars in France and England." In *A History of Women V. Toward a Cultural Identity in the Twentieth Century*, ed. Françoise Thebaud. Cambridge, Mass.: Harvard University Press, 1994.

Soldon, Norbet C. *Women in the British Trade Unions 1874–1976.* Totowa, N.J.: Rowen & Littlefield, 1978.

Solomon, Peter. "Soviet Penal Policy, 1917–1934: A Reinterpretation." *Slavic Review* 39 (June 1980): 195–217.

"Sotsialisticheskoe sel'skoe khoziaistvo Soiuza SSR." *Planovoe Khoiaistvo* 7 (1939): 160–165.

"Soviet Bars Food for Housewives under 56: All Must Work in Industry to Get Bread." *New York Times* 30 December 1932, 1.

"Soviet Considers Drafting Housewives, State Caring for Babies while Mothers Work." *New York Times*, 9 February 1931, 1.

"Soviet Proposes New Family Law." *New York Times*, 27 December 1925, 9.

"Soviet Retreats on Marriage Laws." *New York Times*, 5 December 1926, Sec. 9, 7.

"A Soviet Woman." *Moscow Daily News*, May 27, 1932, 2.

Soviet Women. Moscow: Progress Publishers, 1975.

Sowerwine, Charles. "The Organization of French Socialist Women, 1880–1914: A European Perspective for Women's Movements." *Historical Reflections* 3 (Winter 1976): 3–24.

Spies, Gerty. *My Years in Thresienstadt: How One Woman Survived the Holocaust.* Trans Jutta R. Tragnitz Amherst. New York: Prometheus Books, 1997.

Stalin, Joseph. *Works.* Moscow, 1955. Vols. 1-13.

Stasova, Elena. *Vospominaniia.* Moscow, 1969.

Statesman's Year Book. London: Macmillan, 1888–1939.

"Statisticheskie svedeniia o VKPb." *Bol'shaia Sovetskaia Entsiklopediia* 11: 542.

"Statistics: Workers' Family Budget Enquiries in Soviet Russia." *International Labour Review* 20 (October 1929): 568–79.

Stavrakis, Bette. "Women and the CPSU, 1918–1935." Ph.D. dissertation, Western Reserve University, 1961.

Stein, Edith. *Life in a Jewish Family 1891–1916*. Washington, D.C.: ICS Pub., 1986.

———. *On the Problem of Empathy*. Trans. W. Stein. The Hague: M. Nijhoff, 1964.

Stephenson, Jill. "Girls' Higher Education in Germany in the 1930s." *Journal of Contemporary History* 10 (1975).

——— *Women in Nazi Society*. New York: Barnes & Noble, 1975.

Stevenson, John. *British Society, 1914–1945*. London: A. Lane, 1984.

Stewart, Mary Lynn. *Women, Work, and the French State*. Montreal: McGill–Queen's University Press, 1989.

Stillman, Beatrice. "Sofia Kovalevskaia: Growing-up in the Sixties." *Russian Literary Triquarterly* 9 (1974).

Stirniman, E. J. "No Stranger to Trouble." *Cedar Rapids Gazette,* 1962.

Stites, Richard. "Kollontai, Inessa, and Krupskaia: A Review of Recent Literature." *Canadian-American Slavic Studies* 9 (1975): 84–92.

———. "A. M. Mikhailov and the Emergence of the Woman Question in Russia." *Canadian Slavic Studies* 3 (Summer 1969): 189–91.

———. *The Women's Liberation Movement in Russia: Feminism, Nihilism, and Bolshevism, 1860–1930*. Princeton: Princeton University Press, 1978.

———. "Zhenotdel: Bolshevism and Russian Women, 1917–1930." *Russian History* 3 (1976): 174–93.

Storck, Joachim W. "Martin Heidegger and Elisabeth Blockmann, The Rector and the Emigrant: A Correspondence between Friends." In *Martin Heidegger: Politics, Art, and Technology*, ed. Karsten Harries and Christoph Jamme. New York: Holmes & Meier, 1994.

Strachey, Ray. *The Cause, A Short History of the Women's Movement in Great Britain*. Port Washington, N.Y.: Kennikat Press, 1928.

Strong, Anna Louise. "New Women of Russia Test Lenin's Theories." *New York Times*, 20 March 1927, 15.

———. "Personal Glimpses." *Literary Digest*, 7 April 1928, 34.

Strumilin, S. "Biudzet vremeni russkogo rabochego." *Kommunistka* 6 (1923): 17–21.

———. "Svobodnyi trud v rabochikh sem'iakh." *Kommunistka* 8 (1923): 22–23.

Strumingher, Laura S. *Women and the Making of the Working Class of Lyons 1830–1870*. Montreal: McGill Queen's University Press, 1979.

Sul'kevich, S. *Naselenie SSSR*. Moscow: Gos. izd. polit litry, 1939.

Swift, Fletcher Harper. "England's State Systems of Teachers' Pensions." *School and Society* 49 (22 April 1939).

T. S. "Contemporary Life and Thought in Russia." *Contemporary Review* 32 (1878): 599–624.

Tabouis, Geneviève. "Newspaper Woman: French Style." *The Listener*, BBC; reprinted in *The Living Age*, August 1939.

Talbot, John. *The Politics of Educational Reform in France, 1918–1940*. Princeton: Princeton University Press, 1969.

Tarasov-Rodionov, Alexander. *Chocolate*. Trans. Charles Malamuth. New York: Doubleday, Doran, & Co., 1932.

Taylor, Barbara. *Eve and the New Jerusalem, Socialism and Feminism in the Nineteenth Century*. New York: Pantheon Books, 1983.

———. "Lords of Creation." *New Statesman*, 7 March 1980, 362–63.

Tchernavin, Tatiana. *We Soviet Women*. Trans. N. Alexander. New York: Dutton, 1936.

Tchernavin, Vladimir. *I Speak for the Silent Prisoners of the Soviets*. Trans. N. M. Oushakoff. New York: Hale, Cushman & Flint, 1935.

Tchernoff, Olga E. *New Horizons: Reminiscences of the Russian Revolution*. Trans. Crystal Herbert. Westport, Conn.: Greenwood Press, 1975.

"Teaching Methods in the Soviet Schools." *School and Society* 39, March 1934.

"Textile Worker Is Deputy to Moscow Soviet." *Moscow Daily News*, 8 March 1937, 3.

Thebaud, Françoise, ed. *A History of Women in the West, V: Toward a Cultural Identity in the Twentieth Century*. Cambridge, Mass.: Harvard University Press, 1994.

Thibert, Marguerite. "The Economic Depression and the Employment of Women." *International Labour Review* 27 (April 1933): 443–69.

Thonnessen, Werner. *The Emancipation of Women: The Rise and Decline of the Women's Movement in German Social Democracy 1863–1933*. Trans. Joris de Bres. Bristol, England: Pluto Press, 1973.

Thurston, Robert. "Developing Education in Late Imperial Russia: The Concerns of State, 'Society,' and People in Moscow, 1906–1914," *Russian History* 11, Spring 1984.

Tian-Shanskaia, Olga Semyonova. *Village Life in Late Tsarist Russia*. Ed. and trans. David Ransel. Bloomington: Indiana University Press, 1993.

Tickner, Frederick W. *Women in English Economic History*. New York: J. M. Dent & Sons, 1923.

Tilly, Louise A., and Joan W. Scott. *Women, Work, and Family*. New York: Holt, Rinehart, and Winston, 1978.

Tindall, Gillian. *Celestine, Voices from a French Village*. New York: Holt, 1996.

Tirado, Isabel A. "The Village Voice, Women's Views of Themselves and Their World in Russian *Chastushki* of the 1920s." In *The Carl Beck Papers in Russian and East European Studies*, No. 1008.

Tolstoy, Countess Alexandra. *I Worked for the Soviet*. New Haven: Yale University Press, 1934.

Tolstoy, Alexey. "The Viper." In *Modern Russian Short Stories*, ed. George Reavy. New York, 1961.

Tolstoy, Count Leo. *Anna Karenina*. New York: Modern Library, 1953.

———. *Resurrection*. New York, 1963.

Toporkova, Tatiana V. *Memories of Revolution, Russian Women Remember*, ed. Anna Horsbrugh-Porter. London and New York: Routledge, 1993.

Tovrov, Jessica. "Mother-Child Relationships among the Russian Nobility." In *The Family in Imperial Russia*. Urbana: University of Illinois Press, 1978.

"Transfer System for Training Insured Unemployed Workers in Great Britain." *Monthly Labor Review*, August 1934.

Treble, J. H. "The Seasonal Demand for Adult Labor in Glasgow, 1890–1914." *Social History* 3 (1).

"Tri sud'by, zhenshchiny russkoi revoliutsii, S. Smidovich, L. Stal, and A. Kollontai." *Rabotnitsa* 3 (1972).

Tristan, Flora. *Promenades dans Londres: ou L'aristocratie et les proletaires anglais.* Paris: F.Maspero, 1978.

Trotsky, Leon. *History of the Russian Revolution, Vol. I.* New York: Simon & Schuster, 1936.

———. *Portraits, Political and Personal.* New York: Pathfinder, 1977.

———. *The Real Situation in Russia,* trans. Max Eastman. New York: Harcourt Brace, 1928.

Troyat, Henri. *Daily Life in Russia under the Last Tsar.* Stanford: Stanford University Press, 1982.

Vasilieva, Larissa. *Kremlin Wives,* trans. Cathy Porter. New York: Arcade Publishing, 1994.

Watt, Ellen Moore. *Back Stage in Soviet Russia.* Chicago: n. publ., 1932.

Webb, Augustus. *The New Dictionary of Statistics.* London: E.P. Dutton & Co., 1911.

Webb, Beatrice. *The Diary of Beatrice Webb, Vol. I, 1873–1892,* ed. Nora and Jeanne MacKenzie. Cambridge, Mass.: Harvard University Press, 1982.

———. "Minority Report. Part I: The Relation between Men's and Women's Wages; Part II: The War Pledges of the Government with Regard to the Wages of Women Taking the Place of Men." In Great Britain, *War Cabinet, Committee on Women in Industry, Women in Industry.* 2 vols. Cmnd 135, 167 (1919) vol. i: 254–334.

Weber, Eugene. *Peasants into Frenchmen.* Stanford: Stanford University Press, 1976.

Wheatcroft, S. G. "On Assessing the Size of Forced Concentration Camp Labour in the Soviet Union 1929–1956." *Soviet Studies* 33 (April 1981): 265–95.

Wheeler, Robert. "German Women and the Communist International: The Case of the Independent Social Democrats." *Central European History* 8 (June 1975): 113–39.

Who's Who of British Members of Parliament. Sussex: Harvester Press, 1979.

"Widespread Discussion of Law on Abortion." *Moscow Daily News,* May–June 1936.

Wikander, Ulla, Alice Kessler-Harris, and Jane Lewis, eds. *Protecting Women Labor Legislation in Europe, the United States, and Australia, 1880–1920.* Urbana: University of Illinois Press, 1995.

Wilmott, Phyllis. *Growing Up in a London Village.* London: Owen, 1979.

Winder, F. "Nazi Amazons." *Living Age,* January 1938.

Winkler, Dorte. *Frauenarbeit im "Dritten Reich."* Hamburg: Hoffman & Campe, 1977.

Wishnia, Judith. "Pacifism and Feminism in Historical Perspective." In *Genes and Gender VI on Peace, War, and Gender.* Ed. Anne E. Hunter. New York: Feminist Press, 1991.

"Women Drawn into Ural Industry." *Moscow Daily News,* 12 June 1932, 2.

"Women Farmers of the North Caucasus Issue Appeal to Grandmothers." *Moscow Daily News*, 9 May 1933, 1.

"Women in Industry: Promotion of Domestic Service in Germany." *Monthly Labor Review*, August 1935.

"Women in Soviet Industry." *New York Times,* 27 May 1933, 2.

"Women of USSR Are Responding Well to Their New Opportunities." *Moscow Daily News*, 6 August 1932, 3.

"Women Play Important Role at AMO." *Moscow Daily News*, 30 May 1932, 3.

Wood, Elizabeth A. *The Baba and the Comrade Gender and Politics in Revolutionary Russia*. Bloomington: Indiana University Press, 1997.

Woodham-Smith, Cecil. *Florence Nightingale*. New York: McGraw-Hill, 1951.

Woodward, Kathleen. *Jipping Street*. London, 1983.

Woolf, Virginia. *Contemporary Writers*. New York: Harcourt Brace Jovanovich, 1965.

———. *The Diary of Virginia Woolf*, ed. A. O. Bell. vol. 5, 1936–1941. New York: Harcourt Brace Jovanovich, 1984.

———. *Mrs. Dalloway*. New York: Harcourt Brace and World, 1953. First pub. 1925.

———. *Orlando*. New York: New American Library, 1960. First pub. 1928.

———. "Professions for Women" (1931) in *Collected Essays*, vol. 2. London: Chatto & Windus, 1966.

———. *A Room of One's Own*. New York: Harcourt Brace Jovanovich, 1981. First pub. 1929.

———. *To The Lighthouse*. New York: Harcourt Brace Jovanovich, 1981. First pub. 1927.

———. *Three Guineas*. New York: Harcourt Brace Jovanovich, 1966. First pub. 1938.

———. *A Writer's Diary*, ed. Leonard Woolf. New York: Harcourt Brace Jovanovich, 1954.

"Working Conditions of a Female Textile Worker in Germany, 1880s and 1890s." In *Discovering the Western Past*, vol. 2, ed. Wiesner, Ruff, and Wheeler. Boston: Houghton Mifflin, 1989.

"The Working of Social Insurance in the USSR." *International Labour Review* 28 (October 1933): 539–48.

Worobec, Christine. "Customary Law and Property Devolution among Russia Peasants in the 1870s." *Canadian Slavonic Papers* 26 (June–September 1984): 220–34.

———. *Peasant Russian Family and Community in the Post-Emancipation Period*. Princeton: Princeton University Press, 1991.

"Would Recruit Women for Soviet Industries." *New York Times*, 30 December 1930, 9.

Wunderlich, Frieda. "Women's Work in Germany." *Social Research* 2 (August 1935): 310–36.

Yagoda, G. G. "Heroes Who Were Saved from the Underworld by the OGPU." *Moscow Daily News,* 22 June 1933, 2.

Yarros, Rachelle. "Moscow Revisited." *Journal of Social Hygiene* 23 (1937): 204–6.

————. "Social Hygiene Observations in Soviet Russia." *Journal of Social Hygiene* 16 (November 1930): 449–64; 18 (1932): 360.

Yates, Gayle Graham, ed. *Harriet Martineau on Women*. New Brunswick, N.J.: Rutgers University Press, 1984.

Yemelyanova, Y. D. "The Social and Political Activity of Soviet Women." In *Soviet Women*, ed. Y. Z. Danilova. Moscow: Progress Publ., 1975.

Young, T. "From Slave Block to Real Emancipation." *Moscow Daily News,* 28 August 1932, 2, 4.

Yver, Colette. "Femmes D'Aujourd'Hui, Avocates et Doctoresses," and "Ingénieurs." *Revue des Deux Mondes* 49, January–February 1929.

————. "Femmes D'Aujourd'Hui, Enquète sur les Nouvelles Carrières Feminines." *Revue des Deux Mondes* 49, January–February 1929.

————. "Femmes D'Aujourd'Hui, Pharmacienne," and "Redactrices et Journalistes." *Revue des deux Mondes* 50, March–April 1929.

————. "Femmes D'Aujourd'Hui, Voyageuses de Commerce et Aviatrices." *Revue des Deux Mondes* 50, March–April 1929.

Zaionchkovskii, P. A. "Officialdom." *Soviet Studies in History*, Fall 1979: 64-80.

Zavalishin, Vyacheslav. *Early Soviet Writers*. Freeport, N.Y.: Books for Libraries, 1958.

Zeldin, Theodore. *Conflicts in French Society: Anti-Clericalism, Education and Morals in the 19th Century*. London, 1970.

————. *France.*, vol. 1 Oxford: Clarendon Press, 1976.

Zelnik, Reginald. *Labor and Society in Tsarist Russia*. Stanford: Stanford University Press, 1971.

Zetkin, Clara. "My Recollections of Lenin: An Interview on the Woman Question." In *Feminism, The Essential Historical Writings,* ed. Miriam Schneir. New York: Vintage, 1972, pp. 335–43.

————. *Selected Writings*, ed. Philip S. Foner. Foreword by Angela Y. Davis. New York: International Publishers, 1984.

Zhenskaia Sud'ba v Rossii, ed. B. S. Ilizarova. Moscow: Rossiia Molodaia, 1994.

"Zhenskoe Obrazovanie." *Bolshaia Sovetskaia Entsiklopediia*, ed. N.I. Bukharin and O.E. Schmidt. Moscow: Sov. Ents., 1926-47. 25: 266.

Zoshchenko, Mikhail. *The Woman Who Could Not Read*. Trans. E. Fen. London, 1940.

Zuzanek, Jiri. *Work and Leisure in the Soviet Union, A Time-Budget Analysis*. New York: Praeger, 1980.

Index

Abidova, Deshakhan, 406
Abortion, 141, 143, 155, 156, 157, 171 (n.9), 213, 224, 263, 265, 266–68, 269–70, 279, 284, 354, 367; clinics, 213; legal issues, 141; rates, 156
Abtreibung, 267–68
Academicians, need for, 316
Adamson, Janet L. (Jennie), 248, 368, 370
Ael Tendygi, 257 (n. 2)
Aeroflot Aviation Technicum, 315
Agricultural workers, 74–76, 202–4, 325–33, 402, 406; peasant women, 74–76, 149–50, 200–4; Russian women, 18
Akhmatova, Anna, 140, 340, 386
Alarachinsky and Bestuzhev Courses, 65
Alexander I, 32
Alexander II, 55, 57, 65, 129, 132
Alexander III, 65
Alexander Nevsky Monastery, 257 (n. 5)
Ali Bayramov Club, 253
Alimony, Soviet, 148, 228 (n. 4)
All Russian Congress of Soviets, 239
All Russian Union for Women's Equality, 119, 133
All Union Communist Party Bolshevik, 246
All Union Komsomol, 315
Allais, Rose, 217
Alliance for Women's Suffrage, 124
Alliliueva, Nadezhda, 379
Alliliueva, Svetlana, 306
Amalgamated Union of Co-operative Employees, 243
Anderson, Elizabeth Garrett, 35

Andreyevna, Nina, 306
Angel: avenging, 128; "in the House," 24, 27, 146, 164; ministering, 12, 128
Angelina, Lyolya, 390
Angelina, Pasha, 313, 326, 330, 377, 379, 390-91
Anna Karenina, 30
Annual Conference of Scottish Women, 370
Annual Conference of the Labour Party, 10
Antifascist, 366
Antifeminism, 188, 297
Apt, Hedwig Oppenheimer, 319 (n. 21)
Arendt, Hannah, 169, 193, 194, 347
Armand, Inessa, 94, 128, 130, 133, 183, 234, 239
Army Surgical Academy, 61, 64
Arning, Maria, 258 (n. 18)
Arranged marriages, 151
Artiukina, Alexandra, 116, 239
Artiukina, A.V., 211, 251–52
Asocials, 270
Asquith, English Prime Minister, 122
Astor, Lady Nancy, 133, 242, 246, 247, 248, 253, 254, 267, 280, 368, 408
Atholl, Duchess of, 133, 242, 245, 246, 247, 248, 254, 255, 368, 408
Auclert, Hubertine, 123, 129, 131
Augustat, Elise, 376
Austen, Jane, 25
Avenging angel, 128
Avinov, Marie, 287, 289–91, 353
Ayrton-Gould, Mrs. B., 248
Azeri women's movement, 253, 256, 262 (n. 54)

449

Baader, Ottilie, 52
Balabanova, Angelika, 130, 131, 234, 250–51, 407
Ball-Hennings, Emmy, 169–70
Baltic White Sea Canal, 356 (n. 4)
Bardeneeva, E., 128
Bar maids, 86
Bartels, Elise Vicker, 258 (n. 18)
Bashkirtseva, Mariia (Marie), 36, 58, 97
Baumer, Gertrude, 248
Bavarian Popular Party, 370
BDF, see Bund Deutscher Frauenvereine
BDM, see Bund Deutscher Mädel
Bebel, August, 115, 116
Becker, Carl Woldemar, 27
Becker, Paula, 27, 91, 94
Beckman, Emmy, 240
Behn, Margaret, 48
Bell, Vanessa, 147
Bennett, Arnold, 144
Bentham, Dr. Ethel, 248
Berdysheva, Anna, 301
Beria, 384
Berlin Art Academy, 304
Bertaux, Madame, 98
Besant, Annie, 121, 129, 130
Bikova, Klavdia, 179
Birth control, 141, 153, 156, 157, 213, 224, 266–68, 367; rates, 153, 154, 266, 297, 299
Black Hundreds, 110, 133 (n. 2)
Blackwell, Basil, 189
Blavatsky, Madame, 130
Blochmann, Elisabeth, 346, 376
Bloody Sunday, 82
Blos, Anna, 240
Blum, Leon, 272, 335, 366, 367, 401
Bohemian culture, see "Flapper" culture
Bohm-Schuch, Clara, 376
Bokova, Mariia, 91
Bollman, Minna, 248, 376
Bolsheviks, 8, 140
Bondfield, Margaret, 86, 114, 133, 222, 243, 248
Bonner, Elena, 164, 301–2, 306, 314, 343, 379, 386, 387
Bonner, Ruth, 384

Bosh, 251
Botchkareva, Maria, 87
Braun, Lily, 52, 116, 129, 131
Bray, Marthe, 366
Bread, 381
Breshko-Breshkovskaia, Ekaterina (Katherine), 37, 58, 61, 94, 126, 127, 128, 129, 131
Breshkovskaia, Armand, 129, 133
Brezhnev, 315
Brion, Helene, 129
British Communist Party, 243
Brittain, Vera, 27, 55, 64, 146, 147, 164, 166–67, 169, 188–90, 226, 254, 279, 280–82, 369
Bronner, V. M., venereologist, 143
Brownshirts, 366
Bruning, Chancellor, 371
Brunschwicg, Cecile, 123, 367
Bryusov, Valery, 144
Bubikopf hair cuts, 3
Buck, Pearl S., 172 (n. 21)
Buer, Mabel, 348
Bukharin, Nikolai, 233, 287, 379
Bulgakov, Mikhail, 144
Bund Deutscher Frauenvereine (BDF), (liberal), 241, 373
Bund Deutscher Mädel (BDM), 303, 309, 371, 372
Busolt, German historian, 63
Butler, Josephine, 125, 130

Cammens, Minna, 376
Career: employment statistics, 221–25; expectations, 6; in medicine, 221, 223–24; in politics, 226; religious, 221; teaching, 221, 224.
Career women, 6–7, 12–13, 34–37, 87–98, 220–27, 323, 404; English, 34–35, 164–67, 286; French, 35–36, 167–68, 221, 286; German, 35, 169–70, 286; Russian, 35–36, 37; Soviet Union, 286–87
Career and family, marriage, see Family; Marriage
Carles, Emilie, 15, 50–51, 225, 272, 349, 361 (n. 73)

Carles, Maria Rose, 272–73
Carlin, Mary, 370
Castration (Nazi policy), 270–71
Catherine II, 58–59
Catholic Center Party (German), 370
Catholic Charties, 374
Catholic Church, effect on education, 57;
    Teacher Training Colleges, 308
Catholic Feminist Civic and Social Union,
    367
CCC, see Central Control Commission
Celestine, Voices from a French Village,
    273
Cement, 157, 158, 163, 208, 390
Center Party (German Catholic), 141
Central Asian population, 14
Central Control Commission, Soviet, 239,
    250
Central Executive Committee of the
    Moscow Provincial Soviet (TsIK), 239
Chagall, Bella Rosenfeld, 57–58
Chamberlin, Joseph, 34
Charity Organization Society, 130
Charwoman, 159
Chastushki, 245
Chauvin, Jeanne, 67
Chekhov, Anton, 14, 111, 144, 220
Chemistry Institute's Party, 351
Chernyshevsky, Nikolai G., 23, 33, 59,
    61, 65, 126, 127
Chesterton, Mrs. Cecil, 327, 329, 342,
    346
Chew, Ada Nield, 114, 123
Child care, 81, 84, 151, 198, 208, 211,
    212, 227, 284, 355; support for, 142,
    269
Chinn, Carl, 145, 151, 152, 276
Chocolate, 220
Church schools, see Education, religious
Civil Code (German), 141
Civil defense training, Soviet, 311; training
    (Frauendienst), 309–10
Clarke, Francis, 310
Class conflict, 184; distinctions, 24, 184;
    inequality, 186; statistics, 24
Claudel, Camille, 98
Clements, Barbara, 239
Clerical estate (religious), 28–29

Clerical work, 5–6, 85–86, 103–4 (n. 36),
    218–20, 344–45, 404
Cobbe, Frances Power, 22, 400
Code de la Famille, 264
Coeducation, 179, 186, 188, 302, 401
Cole, Margaret, 279–80, 281, 354, 400
Colette, Sidonie, 26, 36
Collective farms, 271
Collectivization, 273–74, 300–1, 323,
    324, 325, 326–29, 365, 399, 402
Colman, Grace, 246, 248
Commerce occupations, 85–87, 160, 218–
    20
Commissariat of Agitation and
    Propaganda, 238
Commissariat of Enlightenment, 239
Commissariat of Health, 143
Commissariat of Social Welfare, 157, 238
Communalization programs, 140, 280
Communist Party, 273; British, 243;
    French, 238, 244, 338; German, 222,
    237, 370; Russian, 239; Soviet, 248,
    249, 268, 338, 340; Stenographic
    Reports, 10
Compulsory education, see Education,
    compulsory
Condon, Ivy, 369
Congress of Wives of Engineers in Heavy
    Industry (Soviet), 285
Conseil National des Femmes Francaises,
    97, 243
Conservative Party, England, 242, 243,
    245, 246, 247, 253–54, 392 (n. 9, 10)
Contagious Diseases Acts, 125
Contraception, 143, 156
Cookson, Katherine, 154–55, 159, 194 (n.
    12)
Cooperatives, Soviet, 151
Courtship, 150–51, 153
Creighton, Canon, 63, 96
Crime, 155
Culture, Minister of, 315
Curie, Marie, 12, 88

Dada movement, 169
Daladier, Edouard, 366, 367
Davidovna, Olga, 379

Davies, Emily, 56, 63, 121
Davies, Margaret Llewelyn, 29, 246
de Beauvoir, Simone, 11, 144, 145, 146, 147, 168, 182, 190, 282, 286, 340, 366
de Crussol, Marquisse, 367
Dekulakization, 273–74, 300–1, 326
Delafield, E.M., 331, 354, 357 (n.10)
Delegatka, 252, 257 (n. 2)
de Maupassant, Guy, 15, 22
Demchenko, Maria, 330, 377, 379, 391
Democratic Party, Germany, 222, 226, 374
de Portes, Comtesse, 367
Depression, Great, 256, 264, 274–75, 285–86, 297, 300, 302, 307, 308, 323, 401
Deraismes, Marie, 129
Deutsche Frauenwerk, 282–83, 376
Deviance, treatment of, 166, 269–71
Dewey, John, 188, 298, 302
Diderot, 126
Diehl, Guida, 374
Discrimination, 61, 192, 219, 233, 265, 298, 299, 356–57 (n. 4), 402–3; in education, 70–71 (n.46), 188, 189, 191, 303, 304, 307, 310
Distribution of workers, 200
Divorce, 147, 148, 170 (n.6), 269, 280; legislation (Soviet), 142, 269; peasant, 148 ; postcard, 142; rates, 29–30, 146–49, 265; working class, 152
"Dizzy with Success," 327, 380
Djilas, Milovan, 263
Dmitrieva, Elizaveta, 128
Dobroliubov, Nikolai A., 24, 28, 59, 127
Domestic production, 16, 81–82, 152, 209; science studies, 48; wages, 216
Domestic servants, service, 5, 76–79, 99–100 (n. 8–11), 159, 212, 215–20, 230 (n. 40), 340–43; marital status of, 159, 216; responsibilities, 281; social status of, 158-59;
Doppelvendiener, 169
Dostoevsky, Fyodor, 24, 80, 144, 220
Double Life, A, 32–33
Double standard, 26, 27, 30, 47–48, 53, 163, 23, 166, 185, 188–90, 193, 225, 226

"Down with Illiteracy," 178, 301, 305, 311
Dowry, 5, 16, 23, 151, 271, 323, 331, 333
Dransfeld, Hedwig, 240, 248
Dreiser, Theodore, 221, 231 (n. 49)
Dubenko, 257 (n. 5)
Durova, Nadezhda, 32

Ecole Normale Supèrieure, 87
Economic dependence, 147, 151, 199; depression, 399; double standard, 62; independence, 198; participation, 200; situation, 5-7, 401–5
Economic History Review, 348
Education, 19–21, 47–71, 154–58, 177–94, 297–322, 400–1, 407; access to, 51, 62, 177, 186, 298, 350; affected by class, 54, 191, 300, 307; apprenticeship, 52; compulsory, 49, 93, 177, 180, 181, 300, 400; costs, 192; discrimination in, 61, 62, 70–71 (n.46), 189; double standard in, see Double standard; elementary, 48, 91, 177, 300–2, 305, 401; in England, see England; in France, see France; funding for, 189, 191; gender imbalance in, 63; in Germany, see Germany; higher, see Higher education; lycée, 184, 191; middle-class, 52–58, 184–94; noblewomen, 59, 60; party-workers' children, 306–7; peasant, 49–51, 178–80, 305–6, 313–14; religious, 56–57, 187, 300; scientific, 183, 190, 302, 311; secondary, 58, 91, 179–80, 185, 192, 302–17; secularization of, 187; semi-classical, 191–92; social constraints, 63; Soviet Union, see Soviet Union, education; "Special Courses," 61; statistics, 48, 60, 71 (n. 52, 55), 177, 185, 187, 192, 194, 303, 306, 307, 311, 321 (n.57), 401; technical, 183, 190, 302; underfunding of, 191; university, 29, 60–63, 65, 177–78, 188–90; upper-class, 52–58, 61, 184–94, 316–17; working-class, 51–52, 180–84, 305–6, 314–16
Educational achievements, 58–59; double standard, see Double standard;

expectations, 48, 51, 52, 63, 193, 298, 299, 314; financial inequalities, 54, 191; higher, 178, 183, 186–88, 307–17; nightmares, 61–63, 66–67; opportunities, 4, 177–78, 182, 214, 306, 401; policies, 298–99, 299–300; quotas, 65, 179, 297, 299, 323; rights, 60; situation, 4–5, 47–67, 177–94; 297–317; teacher-training schools, 48; village schools, 49; vocational schools, 48

Edward, King (England), 280

Edwardians, The, 30, 58

Elementary-school education, 48, 91, 177, 300–2, 305, 401; teaching, 88, 92

Eliot, George (Mary Ann Evans), 9, 30

Ellis, Havelock, 280

Emancipation, 234; legislation, 141–44, 146; negative attitude toward, 173 (n. 45), 252; of Labor Party (Marxist), 131; of Muslim women, 171 (n.12); of the serfs, 12; settlements, 111; Soviet Union, 256

Employment, 73–98, 142, 197–227, 340–56; agriculture, 74–76, 149, 200–4, 325–33; career women, 97–98, 220, 223–27; clerical, 85–86, 218–20; commerce, 85–87, 200, 219, 344; discrimination in, 352–56; domestic production, 18, 81–82, 200, 205, 214–15; domestic service, 76–79, 86–87, 200, 215–20, 340–43; factory, see manufacturing; low-level, 343–44; manufacturing, 79–81, 82–83, 84, 200, 206, 209, 333–39; married women, 145–46; mid-level, 344–45; peasant women, 200–5; professional, 87–94, 187, 200, 222, 345–52; regulations, 334; statistics, 17, 200, 205–7, 329, 335, 343, 345, 346, 402, 403; trade, see commerce; undervalue of, 140; working-class women, 205–15

Empowerment of students, 188

Encyclopaedia Britannica, 74

Endogamy, 23

Enfranchisement, see "Gaining the Vote"

Engelgardt, Aleksandr, 14, 16

England: abortion, 267; birth control, 267; education, 50, 51, 52, 53–56, 183–84, 188–90, 299–300, 302–3, 310–11; employment, 92–93, 102 (n.22), 103 (n. 36), 225, 337, 341, 342, 347–48, 356; legal situation, 22, 124; marital status of educated women, 164–67; marital status of working women, 154–55, 276–77; middle class women, 22; political activity, participation, 237, 242–43, 253–55, 367–70; political situation, 120–23, 125, 237, 242–43, 253–55, 256, 367–70; social situation, 101 (n.15), 154–55, 164–67, 267, 276–77, 279–82, 285–86; wage statistics, 337, 354; working-class women, 276

English Shop Assistants' Union, 86

"Equal pay for equal work," 197, 198, 207, 254, 368, 403

Equality, 254, 377; economic, 197–98, 353; legal, 199, 234

Ermoshkina, Dunia, 179

Escapism, romantic, 153

Ethnicity, 245–46, 298–99, 387

Exclusion of Jews and women, 297, 299

Exile (Soviet prison), 287–91

Exploitation, economic, 147

Ezhov, 285, 381

Fabian Socialism, 34

Fabian Socialist Women's Group, 130

Fabzavuch (factory universities) (FZU), 302

Factory: child day care, 211; production, 205, 206, 209, 214; work, 6, 19, 207; workers, 206

Family, extended, 111; farms, 145; legislation (Soviet), 142, 199, 268, 269; Muslim, 60; nuclear, 201, 281; peasant, 17; plus career, 163; surrogate, 287–91; traditional, 272

Family Allowance Act of 1932, French, 263, 278, 367

Family life, 20, 23, 26, 31, 32–33, 156, 199, 209, 251, 271–77, 281; prison, 287–91; working class, 20, 152; see also Social situation by country

Famine of 1932–1933, 328

Farm life, 16–18, 75, 111–12, 150–51, 179–80, 201–5, 271–74, 326–33

Fashions, boyish, 145

Fawcett, Millicent Garret, 121, 122

Federation Feministes Universitaire, 97

Federation for the Protection of Mothers (Germany), 146

Feldsher, 29, 88, 222

"feminism," feminist, 7, 8, 233, 369; liberal, 128; radical, 128

Feminization of education, medicine, 184, 352, 401, 404

Fictitious marriage, 33, 128

Figner, Vera, 58, 65, 132

Figner sisters, 61, 128

Filosofova, Anna, 128

Fines, 84

First Provisional Government, 118, 120

Fitzgerald, Cecil, see Woodham-Smith, Cecil

Five-Year Plan(s), 270, 284, 286, 301, 306, 316, 329

"Flapper" culture, 140, 145–46, 150, 153, 157, 160, 169

Flower making, 82

Food shortages, 357 (n. 13)

Forever Flowing, 381

France: abortion, 267; birth control, 267; education, 19–21, 50–51, 53–54, 56–57, 156, 183–84, 190–91, 299–300, 303, 311; emancipatory legislation, 141; employment, 93, 94, 217, 225, 331–33, 341–42, 348-49, 355; legal situation, 124–25; marital status of educated women, 167–68; marital status of working women, 156, 277–78; middle-class women, 22; political activity, participation, 238, 243–44, 255, 366–67; political situation, 123–24, 238, 243–44, 255, 366–67; rural life, 272–73; social situation, 156, 167–68, 267, 272–73, 277–78, 282, 285–86; working-class women, 277–78

Franchise, 233; England, 237; France, 238; Germany, 236–37; Russia, 235; Soviet Union, 235–36

Frauendienst, 309, 310

Frauenschaft, 241, 371

Frauenwelt, 169

Frauenwerk, 371

Free love, 169

Freidenberg, Olga, 316, 317, 340, 352, 385

French Communist party, 238, 244, 366, 367

French Radical party, 34, 238, 244

French Socialist party, 238, 244, 366

French Union for Women's Suffrage, 367

Furtseva, Ekaterina, 315, 351, 379, 390

FUZ, see Soviet worker universities

FYP, see Five-Year Plan(s)

FZU, see *Fabzavuch* (factory universities)

"Gaining the Vote," 234–38; England, 237, 254, 365; France, 238; Germany, 236–37; Russia, 235; Soviet Union, 235–36; see also Suffrage and Franchise

Galia, peasant woman dentist, 313

Gamarnik, General, wife of, 384

Gamble, Dodie, 159, 184

Gamble, Lu, 159, 184

Gamble, Rose Naylor, 154, 155, 170 (n.6), 184

Garrett, Elizabeth, 61, 64, 121

Gautier, Judith, 26, 87, 96

Gender discrimination, 348, 354, 367; equity, 367; imbalance, 2, 12, 13–14, 38 (n. 9), 53–54, 60, 99 (n.5), 101 (n.17), 177, 265, 303; in education, 185, 193, 303; segregation, 219

Generational differences, 153

Gentry-class women, 59, 88, 407; see also "Upper-class women"

George, Lady Megan Lloyd, 368

German Center Party, 141

German Civil Service, 27, 96

German Communist Party (KPD), 222, 237, 370, 376

German Democratic Party, 222, 226, 374

German Girls' League (Bund Deutscher Mädel), 303

German National Popular Party, 370

German Nationalist People's Party, 283

German Popular Party, 370

German Protestant Women's Aid, 282
German Reichstag Handbuchs, 8
German Social Democratic Party, 115, 140, 237
German Women's Suffrage League, 124
German Women's Teachers' Association, 97
Germany: abortion, 267–68; birth control, 267–68; education, 19–21, 49, 51, 69 (n.28), 156, 183–84, 191–94, 299–300, 303–4, 308–10; emancipatory legislation, 141; employment, 93, 106 (n.66), 198, 217, 220, 331–33, 341, 342, 344, 346–47, 355, 356; legal situation, 124–25; marital status of educated women, 169–70; marital status of working women, 156, 275, 279; middle-class women, 22; Nazi, see Nazi Party; political activity, participation, 83, 236–37, 240–42, 255, 370–77; political situation, 124, 236–37, 240–42, 255, 256, 370–77; rural (peasant) life, 271–72; social situation, 156, 169–70, 271–72, 275, 279, 282–83, 286; working-class women, 275, 279
Gierke, Anna, 248
Ginzburg, Evgenia, 287, 289, 379, 380, 383, 405
Gippius, Zinaida, 130
Girlfriend, The, 170
Girton College, Cambridge, 29, 64, 89
Gladkov, 157, 163, 208, 250, 390
Glebov, Anatole, 157, 162, 214, 250
Golubev, V. S., 129
Golubeva, Iasneva, 129
Golubeva, Maria, 37
Goncharova, Natalia, 98
Gore-Both, Eva, 114
Gorky, Maxim, 24, 80, 290
Gould, Barbara Ayrton, 369–70
Governesses, 53, 88
Grand Duchess Elena, 55, 59
Grazhdane, 14, 23, 24
Great Reforms in Russia, 88
Green, Margaret M., 309–10, 318 (n. 3), 360 (n. 53), 372
Greifswald University, 309

Gromova, Konkordia, 29, 64
Gromozova, Ludmilla, 132
Grossman, Atina, 224
Grossman, Vasily, 381
Grunfeld, Helene, 114
Grunfeld, Judith, 210
Guardianship Act (British), 142

Hall, Radclyffe, 164, 166
Hamilton, Cicely, 272, 282
Hamilton, Mary (Agnes), 248, 368
Handicraft workers, 18, 214
Hanna, Gertrude, 117, 240, 248
Hanover Housewives Association, 373, 376
Harassment, see Sexual deviant behavior
Hardie, Agnes, 243, 368
Hartwig-Bunger, Doris, 240
Hauke, Frieda, 240
Hause, Steven, 124
Hausmann, Raoul, 169
Haussleiter, Margarethe Bockholt, 161, 174 (n. 55)
Haute bourgeoisie, 14
Health services, Soviet, 279
Heavy Industry, Ministry of, 315
Heidegger, Elfride, 241, 372
Heidegger, Martin, 193, 241, 376-77
Helping professions, 7, 12, 58, 59, 60, 61, 66, 88, 89, 91, 128, 180, 316, 352, 404
Herzen, Alexander, 126
Herzog, Jesus Silva, 337
Higher education, 87–89, 307–13, 316–17; access to, 62, 177–78; England, 188–90, 310–11; France, 190–91, 311; Germany, 308–10; quota system, 65; Russia, 59; social support, 65; Soviet Union, 178–80, 186–88, 311–13; statistics, 177–78, 308, 350, 352; travel for, 61, 65
High infant mortality rates, 81
Hindenburg-Delbruck, Bertha, 283, 373
Hitler, 217, 241, 246, 256, 263–65, 271, 272, 283, 286, 303, 309, 323, 343, 366, 370–77, 405
Hitler Youth, 264
Hoch, Hanna, 169, 347

Hofs, Else, 248
Hohere Lehranstalten school for boys,
    304
Holtby, Winifred, 146, 147, 164, 166–67,
    189–90, 226, 280, 369
Holy Synod, The, 28
"Homes Fit for Heroes," England, 154
Homosexuality, 170, 270
Horney, Karen, 169, 193, 194
Household duties, 17, 20–21, 22, 31, 150,
    152, 271–73, 274, 275, 276, 281;
    manuals, 38 (n. 6)
Housing conditions, 80–81, 101–2 (n. 18,
    19), 154, 212
Housewives' Association, 217
Hudjum (unveiling, Muslim), 252, 378

Iakir, General, wife of, 384
Iakovleva, Varvara, 234
Iakovleva, Vera, 221
Ievleva-Pavlenko, Valentina, 383
Il'in, Mikhaill A., 25
Illegitimacy, 17, 78, 154–55; births, 77,
    154–55; in Great Britain, 154–55, 267;
    rates, 40 (n. 29), 77
Illiteracy, 75, 178–79, 181, 182, 298, 400
ILP, see Independent Labour Party
Imperial Free Economic Society, 111
Imperial Russian census, 13, 14, 49, 74
Imprisonment, 78
Independent Labour Party (ILP), England,
    114, 118, 122, 131, 242
Independent Socialist Party, Germany,
    226
Industrial Academy (Soviet), 306
Industrial: hygienists, French, 20, 21;
    production, 152, 217; workers, 200
Industrialization, 6, 200, 323, 324, 365, 399;
    effects of rapid, 333
Industry, Ministry of Heavy, 205, 311,
    315, 336
Industry, Ministry of Light, 205, 315
Infant mortality, 151, 276, 277
Infanticide, 17, 78–79, 143, 155, 267–68,
    279
Inflation, 184

Inga, 157, 162
Insurance factory boards (English), 118;
    lack of, 84
Intellectual inferiority, 58, 62
Intelligentsia, 23, 316–17
International Labour Organization, France,
    255
International Women's Day, 3, 118, 269,
    284, 285
Iron Front (German SPD militia), 373
Ivanovskaia, Praskovaia, 28–29, 64
Iveagh, Countess, 246, 247, 248, 280,
    368, 408
Izmailova, Katerina, 25

Jackson, Cecilia Backhouse, 311
Jaclard, Victor, 128
Jakob, Hedwig, 308, 355
Jankowski, Marie, 376
Jaspers, Karl, 193
Jewish customs, 145; experience, 57, 169,
    181, 192–93, 194, 196 (n. 31), 222,
    223, 236, 241, 246, 260 (n.32), 263–
    64, 286, 304, 319 (n.21), 341, 346, 361
    (n. 66), 370, 372, 374, 376, 387, 388,
    404; schooling, 181–82, 192
Jewson, Dorothy, 248
Jex-Blake, Sophia, 73
JFB, see Judischer Frauenbund
Job segregation, 286
Joffe, Maria, 287, 288–89, 383
Joffe, Nadezhda, 288, 382
Joliot-Curie, Irene, 367
Jones, M. G., 348
Journal des Femmes Artistes, 98
Juchacz, Marie, 117, 248
Judischer Frauenbund (JFB), 241

Kahler, Wihelmine, 248
Kalinin, President, 163, 379
Kalinina, Ekaterina, 163, 379, 384
Kalym (Muslim), 142
Kamenev, Lev, 379
Kameneva, Olga, 384
Kaplan, Marian, 145
Karanin, 30

Kashevarova-Rudneva, Varvara A., 91
Kashketin, 288, 383
Kataev, Valentin, 162, 220
Katholischer Frauenbund, 241
Kelly, Catriona, 23
Kennard, H. P., 12
Kenney, Annie, 242
Kent, Madeleine, 341, 372
Kent Farm Institute, 303
Keranflech-Kernezne, Countess, 333
Kessel, Franziska, 376
Khaikin, G. E., 305
Khrushchev, 285, 315
Kindermord, 79, 267
"Kingdom of Darkness," 24, 28
Kingsley, Mary, 12, 35, 56, 63-64, 67
Kirsch, Helene, 376
Kirshon, Vladimir, 381
Klein, German professor, 63
Koenker, Diane, 119
Kolkhozy, 5, 273–74, 328
Kollontai, Aleksandra, 37, 53, 58, 61, 94,
    114, 117, 118, 123, 128, 129, 131, 133,
    140, 142, 144, 146, 147, 158, 162, 183,
    198, 208, 215, 220, 221, 226, 231 (n.
    49), 234, 235, 238, 246, 247, 250–51, 257
    (n.5), 386, 400, 407
Komministka, 143, 252, 256, 257 (n.2)
Komsomol, 150, 157, 240, 244–45, 274,
    301, 306, 311–12, 314, 315, 317, 324,
    330, 339, 350, 376, 379, 384, 386–89
Komsomol Congress, 387
Konigin Luise Bund, 241
Kontrollmadchen, 78
Korber, Lily, 195 (n. 18)
Korenizatsiia, 252
Korner, Olga, 376
Korvin-Krukovskaia (Krukovsky), Aniuta
    (Anna), 55, 73, 128
Korvin-Krukovskaia, General, 73
Kostelovskaia, Maria, 37, 88
Kosterina, Nina, 306–7, 317, 386, 387,
    405
Kovalevskaia, Sofia (Sophia), 12, 29, 36,
    58, 60, 61, 63, 89, 128
Kovalevsky family, 23
Kovalskaia, Elizaveta, 128
Kozlova, Zina, 288

KPD, see German Communist Party
Krasnaia Sibiriachka, 257 (n. 2)
Krasni Proletari Diesel Plant, 301, 314–15
Krest'ianka, 151, 257 (n.2)
Kronstadt Party Committee, Soviet, 239,
    251
Kropotkin, Prince Peter, 61
Krupskaia, Nadezhda, 37, 88, 116, 128,
    129, 133, 142, 161, 188, 221, 234,
    238–39, 283
Kudelli, Praskovia, 117
Kulturkampf (Bismark), 93
Kummunarka Ukrainy, 257 (n. 2)
Kunert, Marie, 240, 258 (n.18)
Kupechskie (merchant), 23, 24–25
Kuskova, Ekaterina, 130
Kuzminskaya, Sonia (Tolstaya), 31
Kuzminskaya, Tatyana, 14, 31

Labor legislation, 197
Labour Party, England, 8, 10, 122, 222,
    242, 243, 245, 246, 247, 254, 368–70
Lacore, Suzanne, 367
"Lady MacBeth of the Mtsensk District,"
    25
Land distribution, Russia, 110, 150, 200,
    201
Land enclosure, England, 75
Land ownership, 5, 204
Lang-Brumann, Thusnelda, 240
Langefeld, Johanna, 377
Language barriers to education, 50
Language instruction, 53
Larina, Anna, 287, 289, 379, 384
Lavrov, 65
Lawrence, Emmeline Pethick, 26–27, 35,
    121, 122, 129, 242
Lawrence, Fred, 27
Lawrence, Susan, 133, 222, 246, 247–48,
    254, 370
League for International Peace and
    Freedom, 366
League of Militant Godless, 311
League of Mothers and Educators for the
    Country, 366
League of Nations, 255
Lebedeva, Vera, 221

Lebensboon (camps), 283
Lee, Jenny, 245, 248
Legal aid, clinics, 157
Legal situation, 141–44
Legislation: emancipatory, 140–44, 377; labor (Soviet), 197, 377; protective, 198
Lehman, Annagreta, 240
Lenin, 19, 118, 129, 226, 234, 235, 250–51, 281, 407
Lenin Commune, 327
Lenin, Order of, 330, 391
Lenin, sisters of, 379
Leningrad Institute of Philosophy, Language, Literature, and History, 316
Lenin's school, 65
Lenke, Lilo, 184
Leonova, Olga, 345
Lermontova, Iulia, 61, 62
Lesbian(s), 165–67, 169, 170, 270
Leskov, Nikolai, 25
Levchina, Comrade, 382
Liberal Party, England, 242, 243, 246, 247, 254
Life: expectancy, 204; farm (Germany), 271, 331–32; French family, 277–78, 332–33; middle-class, 11; slum (London), 277; Soviet working class, 278–79; style of housewives, 275, 328, 331–32, 337, 357 (n. 10); youth, Soviet Party, 306–7, 311–13
"Life is better; life is more joyous," 353
Light industry, Soviet Ministry of, 82-83, 311, 315
Ligue Francaise pour les Droits des Femmes, 123
Ligue pour la Regeneration Humaine, 123
Linke, Lilo, 146, 147, 169, 173 (n.45), 184, 192, 222, 226, 374
Linton, Eliza Lynn, 25, 35, 67
Lister Institute, 64
Literacy, 48–49, 208, 401; programs (Soviet), 178–79, 181–82, 298, 301; rates, 49, 62, 67 (n. 4), 178–79, 181–82, 208, 216, 300
Liudvinskaia, Tatiana, 37
Liverpool Women Citizens Association, 121
Lokhvitskaia, Mirra, 130

London Foundling Hospital, 77
London School Board, 35
London School of Economics and Political Science, 64, 310
London School of Medicine for Women, 66
Louise League (German), 373
Luckner, Gertrud Dr., 374
Luders, Marie, 240
Luhrs, Frieda, 248
Lutze, Ernestine, 248
Luxemburg, Rosa, 130, 131
Ly, Arria, 367

Mabille, Zaza, 145
MacArthur, Mary, 248
Magdalena Cloister, 308
Magomayeva, Rose, 351, 390
Maitland, Emma, 121
Mallender, Eileen, 311
Malozemova, Professor, 316
Mancisidor, José, 286
Mandelstam, Nadezhda, 385
Mandelstam, Osip, 385
Mann, Horace, 188
Mann, Julia, 348
Manning, Leah, 370
Manufacturing, 79–84, 151, 205, 209, 336, 402; economic position in, 206; marital status in, 209; mechanization of, 205, 210; textiles, 209–10
Margueritte, Victor, 3, 144, 161, 167–68
Marital status of: career women, 34–37, 161, 164, 285–86; domestic servants, 158–59; educated women, 161–70; employed women, 146; middle-class women, 22–28, 279–85; occupied women, 146; peasant women, 14–18, 149–51, 271–74; statistics, 29–30, 265; upper-class women, 29–34; women in commerce, 160; working-class women, 18–22, 151–58, 274–79
Markiewicz, Countess, 253
Marriage: arranged, 151; as career, 12, 26; attitude toward, 2–3, 12, 13–14, 15, 18–19, 33–34, 165, 168, 199, 279, 281; fictitious (for education), 61; laws, 19;

loan, see Dowry; peasant, 201; plus career, 3, 12, 13, 23, 35, 88, 94, 147, 160, 161, 163, 191, 210–11, 249; rates of, 13, 18, 149–50, 161, 209, 221, 224, 227, 265, 266, 402; statistics, 13–14, 15, 201–2, 266; working-class, 20–21
Married life, 17, 20, 147, 152; women in agriculture, 17, 149, 150, 202
Married Women's Property Act(s), 22, 124–25
Marshall, Alfred, 87
Martineau, Harriet, 27, 34
Marx, Eleanor, 116
Maschmann, Melita, 358 (n. 26), 371, 372
Maternity: Letters from Working Women, 29
Matriarchy, 16, 24–25, 145, 152
Matrimonial Causes Act (British), 141, 142
Mauer, Louise, 376
Medical care, England, 154; Soviet Union, 157, 279, 313–14
Medical career(s), professions, 91, 93, 221, 223–24, 308, 312–13; education for, 179, 185, 308, 312, 313–14; employment statistics, 228 (n. 14); upward mobility, 179
Medical secrecy, discriminatory, 28
Meme Santerre, A French Woman of the People, 272
Memoirs of a Dutiful Daughter, 168
Mendes, Catulle, 26
Meshchanstvo, 23–25
Meyer, German professor, 63
Michelin tire company, 278
Middle-class women, 22–28
Middlemarch, 30
Migration, 17–18, 19; patterns, 79, 201, 204, 324, 357 (n.13); peasant, 159, 200, 301, 328
Mikhail II, 96
Mikhailov, M. A., 59, 127
Military Aviation Acadamy, 219
Miliukova, Anna, 133, 235
Miliutin, Dmitri A.., 59, 88
Mill, John Stuart, 12, 21
Miller, Florence Fenwich, 35, 121
Mill on the Floss, 1860, 9

Minck, Paula, 129
Minister of Education: Soviet, 182; Tsarist, 61
"Ministering angels," 12
Ministry of Culture, Khrushechev's, 315
Ministry of Education, Soviet, 311
Ministry of Health, England, 267; Soviet, 311
Ministry of Heavy Industry, Soviet, 311, 315
Ministry of Light Industry, Soviet, 311, 315
Misme, Jane, 123
Mobility, 5, 48, 179, 180, 182, 204, 215, 220, 222, 316, 324, 330, 331, 340, 350, 366, 377, 379, 389
Modersohn, Otto, 4
Modersohn, Paula, see Becker, Paula
Mohr, Trude, 371
Morozov, Savva, 24
Morton, Honor, 121
Moscow Daily News, 350
Moscow Party Committee, 120
Moscow University, 33, 316
Moscow, Workers' Soviet, 119
Mosley, Cynthia, 247–48
Motherhood, glorification of, 263, 269, 275, 279, 282, 283, 371, 377, 399
Mother's Day, 3, 145, 263, 264, 269, 275, 282–83, 284, 365
Mullaney, Marie, 239
Municipal councils, England, 368–69
Muslim, 252–53, 262 (n.54), 387; divorce, 148–49; families, 60; marriage customs, 142; unveiling (hudjum), 144, 236, 252–53, 378
Mutual Philanthropic Society, 130
My Sister's Story, 25, 96

National Federation of Women Teachers (English), 97
National Health (England), 276
National Health Insurance Act of 1911, 21
National Socialism (German), 372
National Socialist Woman's Organization, 365

National Union for Shop Assistants and Clerks, 114
National Union of Women Teachers, England, 225
National Union of Women's Suffrage Societies (NUWSS), 21, 122
Nationalist People's Party, German, 283
Nationalsozialistische Frauenschaft, 365
Nazi Party, 283; educational policies, 299–300, 304, 308, 309, 346; intimidation, 370; policies, 267, 270–71; resistance to, 373–75; rituals, 365; social structure, 373–77, 400, 403
Nazi Teachers Organization, 346
Nekrasov, Nikolai, 17
Nemitz, Anna, 259 (n.18)
NEP, see New Economic Policy (Soviet)
"Nest of Gentlefolk," 24
New Economic Policy (NEP) (Soviet), 143, 152, 199, 205, 270
New Woman (Soviet), 146, 162, 163
Nicholas I, 126
Nicholas II, 57, 65
Nicolson, Harold, 34, 165-66
Nightingale, Florence, 27, 33, 73, 87, 130
Nikolaeva, Klavdiia, 116, 239, 249–50, 380
NKVD, 381
North of England Weavers' Association, 113
Nuclear family, 110, 111, 112
Nuns, 164, 174 (n. 60)
Nuremberg Laws, Germany, 341
Nurturing role, 164
NUWSS, see National Union of Women's Suffrage Societies

Obshchestvennitsa, 285
Occupational mobility, 179
October Manifesto, 120
October Revolution, 133
Office work, see Clerical work
Oppenheimer, Frank, 196 (n. 31)
Oppenheimer, Hedwig, 304
Orekhova, Vera, 315
Organization of German Women, 124
Orlikova, E., 340 (note, Table 11.4)

Orthodox church, 49; nuns, 164
Osoaviakhim (Soviet civil defense), 311, 313
OST, see Rationalization of industry
Ostroumova-Lebedeva, Anna, 23, 60, 73
Ostrovsky, Alexander, 9
Ostrovsky, Nikolai, 24, 25
Ouspensky, P. D., 127
Ouvrière (Woman Worker), 244
Overlack, Helene, 376
Oxford University, 27, 310

Pacifism, 8, 365, 369
Pale of Settlement, 57
Panaeva, Avdotia, 33, 59, 88, 126
Panina, Countess Sofia, 133, 235
Pankhurst, Christable, 67, 114, 122, 123, 131, 133, 242
Pankhurst, Emmeline, 26, 56, 120, 122, 123, 129, 133, 242, 254
Pankratova, Anna M., 316, 352
Pankratova, Tatiana I., 329, 330
Parental power, in marriage, 15
Paris Commune, 113, 132
Parliament (British), 141, 368, 392 (n. 9, 10)
Party membership statistics, 237, 246, 378, 384, 389; participation, 235–56, 379–80
Passport, internal system, 31
Patmore, Coventry, 24, 27
Patriarchal attitudes, 9, 19–20, 23, 75, 140, 168, 193, 285, 331, 345, 347, 349, 350, 407; authority, power, 19, 24, 141, 145, 191, 264; culture, society, 157, 161, 166, 280, 331; family life, 140, 278, 282, 331–33; legislation, 125; social views, 139–40, 144, 193, 203; work contracts, 331, 332
Patriarchy, 16, 20, 365, 367
Pauwels, Jacques R., 299, 308–9
Pavlovna, Karolina, 32, 59, 88, 126
Pay scales, 74, 83–84; agricultural work, 74–75; clerical work, 85–86; domestic production, 81–82; domestic service, 76–77; dressmakers, 82; manufacturing, 80; teachers, 87

Peasant education, 49–51, 178–80, 304–6; life, 16, 150, 200–4, 271–74, 390–91; political activity, 110, 245; songs (*chastushki*), 150; statistics, 203; women, 14–18, 49–51, 149–51; unpaid labor, 16, 74, 202

"Peasants, The," 111

Peasant Union, 111

Pelletier, Madeleine, 26, 34, 48, 129, 131, 183, 267, 366

People's Will, 65, 129, 132

Perovskaia, 129

Pethick, Emmeline, 55, 73, 89

Pfulf, Toni, 376

Philanthropic sphere, role, 130, 243, 282; Soviet, 285

Philips, Dr. Marian, 248

Philipson, Mrs., 248, 254

Physicians, Women, 89–90

Pichugina, Praskovia, 389

Picton-Turbervill, E., 248

Pilniak, Boris, 214

Pinchbeck, Ivy, 310, 348

Pirogov, N. I., 59

Pisarev, D. I., 59, 127

Pokrovskaia, Maria (Mariia), 77, 98, 128, 130

Political activity, participation: 10, 109–133, 235–56, 365–91, 397 (n.76), 405–8; ethnic factors of, 244–50; leadership, 379; marital status factors, 247; middle class, 119–24, 246–48; of Muslim women, 252–53; of party elite, 246–48, 379–80; of peasant women, 109–12, 245; of working-class women, 248–50; political party membership, 131–32, 243, 351; situation, 7-8, 109–33, 233–56; social factors of, 244–50; statistics, 238, 243, 387-89; upper class, 124–33; working class, 112–19, 248–50

Poor Law Guardians, 20, 118, 120, 122

Popova, Liubov, 23, 53, 98

Popova, Vera, 146

Posidelki, 150

"Postcard divorce," 142

Potter, Beatrice, see Webb, Beatrice Potter

Poverty, 11, 41 (n. 59), 75, 152, 154; among religious families, 28, 29; of working-class women, 152

Power, Eileen, 12, 64, 89, 139, 141, 225, 280, 310, 348

Pravda, 269

Preobrazhensky, Evgeny, 233

Primary school, see Education, elementary

Prison: family life, 287–91, 377; memoirs, 287–91; statistics, 287; surrogate families, 287–91

Production, see Domestic production; Handicraft workers; Industrial production

Profession(s): distribution in, 90, 222, 351; helping, 58, 59, 60, 61, 66, 88, 89, 91

Professional women, 87–98, 345–56; England, 63–64, 66–67, 95, 96, 347–48; France, 348–49; Germany, 346–47; Russia, 59; Soviet Union, 349–51

Prokofieva, Sophia, 379

Pronatalism, 3, 35, 256, 263, 264, 266, 268, 272–73, 283, 365, 367, 399; policy, France, 156, 238

Prophylactoria, 143, 291 (n.2)

Prostitutes, 59, 77–78, 85, 100 (n.12), 143–44, 213–14, 216, 220, 227, 228 (n.13), 263, 264, 270, 291 (n.2), 330; refuges for, 213, 331

Protective legislation, 83

Protestant Ladies Auxiliary (German), 241, 371

Protestant Women's Aid (German), 282

Protestant Women's Association, 124

Protestant Women's Federation, 374

Proudhon, Pierre, 116

Provisional Government (Soviet), 8, 119, 127, 133, 142

Pupil teachers, 52

Purges, 300, 380–84, 386, 389, 399, 405, 407

"Putting out" system, 81

Quotas, for workers, 179, 351; in education, 179, 188, 297–98, 308, 311, 313, 323, 401; Soviet Union, 298, 323, 351

Rabfaks (rabochie fakultety), 178–80, 301
Rabotnitsa, 257 (n. 2), 315, 333
Radical Party, French, 238, 244
Rape, 84, 165
Rathbone, Eleanor, 121, 143, 198, 242,
    247, 248, 254, 262 (n. 58), 280, 368
Rationalization of industry, 205, 210
Raznochintsy, 23
Reading rooms (huts), 179
Red Banner Collective Farm, 311, 397
    (n.83)
Red Rose Textile Factory, 315
Rehabilitation Center, 143
Reich, Wilhelm, 140, 156
Reichstag Economics committee, 169
Reichstag Foreign Affairs committee, 169
Reichstag Handbuchs, 8, 10
Reitze, Johanna, 240
Religion, -ious, 156; activities, 271, 327;
    effects on education, 56–57, 187, 309;
    effects on politics, 371–72;
    employment in, 105 (n.59), 345, 404
Religious schools, Soviet ban on, 181
Representation of People Act (British),
    141
Resistance, 374, 385, 393 (n. 17)
Revised Family Law of 1926 (Soviet),
    142
Revolution, 65–66
"Revolution from above," 284
Revolutionary, 128–29
Reynaud, Paul, 367
"Rhetoric of service," 37
Rhondda, Lady, 226, 255
Riazan Foundling Home, 77
Ritual shaming, 16
RKI, see Workers and Peasants'
    Inspection Bureau
RKPb, see Russian Communist Party,
    Bolshevik
Roberts, Robert, 152–53
Roehm, Ernst, 297, 310
Rohl, Elizabeth, 248
Rollin, Louie, 310–11
Romantic escapism, 153, 160, 162, 214,
    249
Roper, Esther, 114
Rosenberg, Suzanne, 380, 386, 405

Rosenthal, Leni, 376
Rostopchina, Evdokiia, 32, 126
"Rough" social groups, 276
Rousseau, 26, 126
Roussel, Nelly, 123
Royal School for Officers' Daughters, 64
Royal Schools Inquiry Commission, 47
RSDLP, see Russian Social Democratic
    Labor Party
Rudenko, 387
Rudneva, Varvara, 64
Runciman, Viscountess, 246, 248
Rural life, 150
Ruskin College, Oxford, 182, 310
Russia: education, 64–66, 93;
    employment, 74–77, 93, 94, 99 (n. 5,
    8), 100 (n. 12), 104 (n.48); "Gaining
    the Vote," 235; middle-class women,
    22–23; political situation, 119–20,
    126–27, 235–36; social situation, 101
    (n.18)
Russian Academy of Art, 60
Russian Communist Party Bolshevik
    (RKPb), 234, 236, 239, 379
Russian folk songs, 15
Russian Imperial census, 13, 14
Russian Social Democratic Labor Party
    (RSDLP), 116, 120
Russian Social Democratic Party, 37, 65
Russification, 49, 50, 54, 298
Ryneck, Elfriede, 248

SA, see Sturm Abteilungen (Storm
    Troopers)
Sacerdotal mission, 66, 91
Sackville-West, Vita, 30, 34, 58, 147,
    164–66
"Sacred Sacrament of Dinner," 33
Sagaiudinova, G. S., 389
Sainte Union, La, (England), 310, 311
Salomon, Charlotte, 304
Samodur, 23-24
Samoilova, Konkordia, 37, 88
Sand, George (Aurora Dudevant), 30
Santerre, Meme, 15
Sanzara, Rahel, 169–70
Sartre, Jean-Paul, 282, 366

Sats, Natalia, 287, 289, 349–50, 384, 396 (n. 65)

Scannell, Dorothy, 154, 155

Schiffgens, Louise, 240, 259 (n.18)

Schilling, Minna, 240

Schmahl, Jeanne, 123

Scholarship(s), 302, 312, 314, 390, 397 (n. 83)

Scholtz-Klink, Gertrud, 241, 371

Schonlank, Bruno, 249

Schott, Maria, 240

Schreiber, Suzanne, 367

Schroder (Schroeder), Louise Reichstag, 169, 248, 259 (n.18)

School-leaving age, 303

Schools: girls', 55; religious, ban on, 181 secondary, 55

Schulz, Berta, 259 (n. 18)

Scorpion, The, 170

Scott, John, 284, 313–14, 343, 385

Scott, Masha, 172 (n. 21), 305, 312, 313–14

Scriabina, Elena, 171 (n.8), 186, 220

SD, see Social Democratic Labor Party Russian

Second All-Union Congress of Collective Farm Shockbrigaders, 391

Secondary schools, 55, 60

Second Sex, The, 11

Secret Police of Tsar Nicholas I, 33

Self-realization, 89

Semenets, Liubov, 330

Senatskaya, Maria T., 330

Sender, Toni, 23, 57, 146, 147, 169, 198, 222, 226, 259 (n.18), 373, 374

Seraphima, peasant exile, 290–91

Serfs, emancipation of, 12

Service, domestic, 159, 215–17

Service ethic, 66, 73; occupations, 85–87, 215–20, 403

Seryozha, 30

Sex Disqualification (Removal) Act, 67, 141, 255, 367, 377

Sexist: attitudes, 91; behavior, 144

Sexual: deviant behavior, 166, 167; harassment, 84, 96–97, 155, 193, 226, 339, 403; liberation, 140, 144–45; morality, 234; mores of Soviet peasants, 16; reformers, 146; stereotyping, 226, 339

Shabanova, Anna, 98, 121, 128, 130, 235

Shaposhnikova, Liudmila, 289, 379

Sharg Gadini, 253, 256, 257 (n.2)

Siberia, 37

Sidorenko, Aleksandra I., 182–83, 315

Siemsen, Anna, 259 (n.18)

Simon, Anna, 248

Single women, 17–18, 25, 29, 34–37, 40 (n. 25), 150, 153, 166, 169, 203–4, 334, 405

Six Point Program, England, 242

Slave labor camps, statistics, 295 (n. 68)

Slum life, London, 277

Slutskaia, Vera, 117

Smedley, Ida, 64

Smidovich, Sophia (Sofia), 234, 239

Smirnova, M.P., 390

Smith, Mabel, 370

Smith, Mary Bentinck, 66

Smitten, E. G., 252

Smolensk Archive, 305, 312

Smolensk Ponezovyi Raion Department of Public Education, 305

Smolensk province, 16

Smolensk University, 305, 312; Medical Institute of, 312

Smolny Insrtitute, 55, 58

Snokhachestvo, 15

Social Democratic Labor Party Russian, 37, 65, 116, 131

Social Democratic Party (SPD): German, 233, 237, 239, 247, 248, 256, 258 (n.18), 260 (n.33), 370, 374, 394 (n. 33)

Social deviants, 269–71; passports (Russia), 125; situation, status, 2–3, 14–22, 123, 139–70, 228, 271–85; 400; welfare, 241, 369

Socialist Labor Youth, 241

Socialist Party, French, 244

Socialist Revolutionary Party (SR), 110, 127, 235

Society for Struggle for the Rights of Women, 128

"Song of Return," 32

Soviet, defined, 236

Soviet Union: abortion, 200–4, 268; birth control, 268; Constitution, 1936, 8; education, 20–21, 151, 156–58, 181–83, 186–88, 304–7, 311–17, 407; employment, 198–200, 216–18, 323–25, 354–55, 357 (n. 11); family legislation, 142, 163, 268; labor legislation, 197, 377; marital status of educated women, 161–64; marital status of working women, 156–58, 278–79; Ministry of Education, 182; peasant life, 271, 273–74; political activity, 83, 110, 235–36, 238–40, 250–53, 260 (n.32), 351, 377–91; political situation, 235–36, 238–40, 250–53, 256; prostitution, 270; social situation, 156–58, 273–74, 278–79, 283–85, 286; statistics, 315, 325; working-class women, 278–79
Soviet worker universities (FUZ), 182
Spiridonova, Maria, 128, 235
Spiritual motherhood, 66, 91
SPD, see Social Democratic Party, Germany
Spousal abuse, 15, 16, 20, 21, 147–48, 149
Squaring the Circle, 162–63
SR, see Socialist Revolutionary Party, Russia
St. Hilda's College, Oxford, 64
St. Petersburg, 50
St. Petersburg Workers' Soviet, 117
Stahelm (German paramilitary), 373
Stakhanovites, 394 (n. 44)
Stal', Liudmilla, 239
Stalin, 163, 251, 256, 263, 265, 285, 333, 353, 385, 391
Stalin, wife of, 380
Stalin Electro Mechanical Plant, 306
Stanislavsky, 290
Stasova, 133, 247
Stasova, Elena, 128, 129, 130, 131, 161, 234, 239
Stasova, Nedezhda, 128
Stegman, Anna M., 259 (n.18)
Stein, Edith, 169, 192, 194, 347
Stenographic Reports, Communist Party, 10

Sterilization, 156, 224, 263, 270–71; Nazi policies, 270–71
Stewart, Mary Lynn, 20
"Storm, The," 24
Strachy, Ray, 242
Strada (suffering), 74
Stroganov Art School, 60
Strumilin, S. G., 211
Student empowerment, 188
Sturm Abteilungen (SA), 297, 309, 310
Subjugation to husbands, 30–31
Suffrage (female), 109, 129, 142, 235–38, 368, 407
Suffrage des Femmes, 123
Suffragette, suffragist, 7, 233
Sukhanov, Nikolai, 118
Sumarokova, Nadezhda, 219
"Summer bride," 142
Summerskill, 368
Superstition, 16
Surrogate prison families, 8, 287–91, 376, 382
Suslova, Nadezhda, 50
Suvorova, Mariia,
Sverdlov, Iakov, 234
Sverdlova, Christina, 315
Syndicat, 83

Tabouis, Geneviève, 226, 349, 353, 367
Tamara, Mother, 290–91
Tarasov-Rodionov, 220
Tatlina, Praskovia, 12, 30, 55
Taylor, Helen, 121
Teachers' Unions, 97, 225
Teaching, 60, 87–88, 91, 224–25, 302, 404; traditional methods, 298; training for, 48–49; wages, 225
Technical education, 302, 314–15, 334
Terrington, Lady, 248, 254
Tesch, Johanna, 248
Testament of Youth, 166, 369
Textile production, 82; workers, marital status, 19
Theosophist, 130, 290
Theweleit, Klaus, 169
They Worked All Their Lives, 151
Third Section, 33

Thirteenth Congress of Soviets, 390
Three Guineas, 63, 310, 340
Tian-Shanskaia, Olga Semyonova, 14
Time and Tide, 226
Time Forward, 220
Timiryazev Academy of Agriculture, 313
Tirado, Isabel, 150, 244
Tkachev, 65
To the People Movement, 127
Tolchanina, Olga, 288
Tolstaya, Sonia, 31
Tolstoy, Leo, 14, 30, 31, 144, 220
Toporkova, Tatiana V., 195 (n. 15)
Trade unionism, 22, 83, 156–57, 244
Trade union(s) 113, 179, 181, 244, 338–
    39, 389; child care by, 211;
    membership, 227; participation in,
    227; schools (Soviet), 181, 208; Shop
    Assistants' Union, England, 243; see
    also Union
Trade Union Congress, 114
Tradition, 16, 156, 285; female roles, 94,
    202–4; teaching methods, 298–99
Training camps, 283, 342
Transport occupations, 219
Treitschke, German Historian, 63
Trepov, General, 132
Tretiakov, Pavel M., 134 (n.3)
Tristan, Flora, 25
Trotsky, Leo Davidovich, 118, 251, 386
Trubnikova, Maria, 128
Tsar Alexander I, 31, 32
Tsar Alexander II, 55, 57, 65, 129, 132
Tsar Alexander III, 65
Tsar Nicholas II, 57, 65
Tsarist budget, 28
TsIK, see Central Executive Committee of
    the Moscow Provincial Soviet
Tsvetaeva, Anastasiia, 53
Tsvetaeva, Marina. 53, 144
Tuition, free (Soviet), 180
Tukachevsky, General, wife of, 384
Tula, 15, 28–29
Turgenev, Ivan, 24, 76
Tyrkova-Williams, Ariadna, 133, 235,
    257 (n.5)

Uborevich, General, wife of, 384
Ukolova, K.S., 389
Ulianova, Anna, 161
Ulianova, Elizaveta, 161
Ullrich, Lisa, 376
Undercounted, 75
Underemployment, 208, 276–77
Unemployment, 78, 152, 184, 205, 208,
    213, 218, 220, 227, 264, 270, 276–77,
    285, 297, 323, 335–36, 346; insurance,
    213; postwar loss of jobs, 143, 335;
    statistics, 213, 227, 335, 338, 341, 402;
    training centers for, 342
Union(s), 114, 156–57; activity, age
    factor, 112; industrial, 211; male-
    dominated, 113, 115; membership,
    113, 207, 212, 244, 297, 338–39, 389;
    textile, 211; trade, 244, 338–39
Union des Femmes Peintres et Sculpteurs,
    98
Union Francaise Pour le Suffrage des
    Femmes, 123, 243
Union National pour le Vote des Femmes,
    243–44
University education, 307–17; women's
    access to, 307
University, Cambridge, 310
University of Edinburgh, 66
University of Paris, 64
University of Stockholm, 89
University of Zurich, 50
Unveiling (hudjum, Muslim), 252, 378,
    406
Upper-class women, 29–34; see also
    Gentry-class women
Urbanization, 200
Ushinsky, K. D., 59
Uzbek Communist Party, 385, 387

Vagabond, The, 36
Varfolomeeva, Klavdia, 350
Varnhagen, Rahel, 193
Vengerova, Zinaida A., 36, 129
Verbitskaia, Anna, 36
Veresaev, Vikenty, 327, 381
Veretennikova, A.I., 95, 106 (n. 67),

Vernadskaia, Mariia, 59, 88
Versailles Peace Treaty, 197
Verzhenskaia, Iadviga, 292 (n. 18), 384
Vicinus, Martha, 166
Victoria, Princess Helena, 348
Victoria Schule, Frankfurt, 304
Victoria Women's Settlement, 121
Vidal, Marie, 116
Village soviets, 391
Villars, Henri Gauthier, 36
Vinogradskaia, Paulina, 161, 234
Vitebsk, 29; Gymnasium for Girls, 58
VKPb, see All Union Communist Party
    Bolshevik
Vocational schools, 48
Volga Flows into the Caspian Sea, The,
    339
Voltaire, 126
Von Grone, Agnes, 371, 374
Vote: gaining of the, 235–38; loss of, 8;
    see also Franchise; Suffrage
Votes for Women, 27, 122
Votes for Women and Chastity for Men, 28

Wage(s), 41 (n. 39), 77, 83–84, 94–96,
    208, 209–10, 219, 224, 229 (n.26), 231
    (n. 57), 341, 345, 354–55;
    discrimination, 5, 95, 207, 210, 214,
    344, 348, 354; equity, 209, 210;
    medical, 224; teaching, 225, 352; rates,
    210, 216, 223, 229 (n. 26), 337, 345
Waln, Nora, 331, 358 (n. 25), 372, 375
Wardens in women's residence halls, 67
Webb, Beatrice Potter, 27, 34, 56, 67, 96,
    129, 130
Webb, Sidney, 34
Weber, Helene, 240
Wedding laments, 15
Wegschneider, Hildegard, 240
Weil, Simone, 359 (n. 45)
Weimar: Constitution, 8, 141, 198;
    Republic, 141; society, 169
Weinert, Erich, 375
Weirauch, Anna E., 170
Weiss, Louise, 366, 367
Welfare, social, 338, 371
Wells, H. G., 144, 161

West, Rebecca, 144, 161, 226
West, Vita Sackville, see Sackville-West,
    Vita
What Is to be Done?, 33, 61, 65, 127
White-collar work, 160
Wife beating, see Spousal abuse
Wilkinson, Ellen, 16, 147, 167, 243, 248,
    254, 280, 368, 370
Wintringham, Mrs., 248
Woman and Socialism, 115
"woman question," 7
Woman Social Worker, 285
Woman Worker, 116, 315, 387
Women Teachers' Association, Germany,
    96
Women Teachers' Franchise Union, 97
Women's Advisory Committees, England,
    243
Women's Bureau, Germany, 282
Women's Cooperative Guild, England,
    29, 118, 130, 182, 241, 243, 267
Women's Cooperative Movement, 248
Women's Employment Federation, 348
Women's Fate, 33
Women's Medical Courses, 4
Women's Medical Institute, 65
Women's Month, 370
Women's Politics, 120
Women's Primary School Teachers
    Association, 348
Women's Progressive Party, 119, 131
Women's Reform Association, 97
Women's Rights, 128
Women's Section, Annual Conference of
    Labour Party, 10
Women's Social and Political Union
    (WSPU), 122, 131
Woodham-Smith, Cecil, 64, 226
Woodman, Dorothy, 369
Woodword, Kathleen, 114
Woolf, Leonard, 165
Woolf, Virginia, 53, 56, 63, 118, 146,
    147, 164–166, 168, 182, 226, 310, 340,
    347, 354, 400
Worker schools (rabfaks), 178;
    universities, 182
Workers and Peasants' Inspection Bureau
    (RKI), 250, 379, 382

Workers' Compensation, 117
Workers' Education Department (Soviet), 179
Workhouse, England, 155
Working conditions, 210, 355–56; hours, teaching, 224
Working-class women, 10, 18–22, 151–58, 274–79, 336–38, 389–90, 406, 407; age of, 152; education of, 19–21, 51–52, 154–58, 180–84, 314–16, 407; life style of, 337–38
World Wide Committee of Women Against War and Fascism, 366
"wrecking," 287, 385, 390
WSPU, see Women's Social and Political Union
Wurm, Matilde, 258 (n.18), 376

Yagoda, 285
Yaroslavl prison, 287
Yevseevna, Anna, 182
Youth movement (Hitler), 303; service (Nazi), 283

Yver, Colette, 147, 221

Z, Count and Countess, 61
Zakharova, Olga, 301, 330
Zassenhaus, Hiltgunt, 318 (n.3), 374
Zasulich, Vera, 128, 132
Zaza (friend of Simone de Beauvoir), 168
Zeitz, Luise, 115
Zemliachka, Rozalia Zalkind, 120, 239
Zetkin, Clara, 109, 114, 116, 117, 129, 131, 140, 148–49, 234, 240, 248, 252
Zetzschke, Frau, 341
Zhadovskaia, Iuliia, 32, 126
Zhenotdel, 144, 149, 151, 158, 179, 182, 211, 234, 238, 239, 250, 252, 256, 284, 285, 377
Zinka, hired help, 314
Zinoviev, 250
Zoschenko, Mikhail, 178–79
Zoya (dancer), 288
Zurich, University of, 50

About the Author

Marcelline J. Hutton received her doctorate from the University of Iowa. She has taught Russian and Soviet history, European women's history, Western civilization, and world history at the University of Iowa, Hamilton College, University of Texas–El Paso, and Radford University. She currently teaches at Lithuania Christian College, Klaipeda, Lithuania, and is intent on a new research project: Soviet women in civil defense in the 1930s.